The Schillebeeckx Reader

Edward Schillebeeckx

The Schillebeeckx Reader

Edited by
Robert Schreiter

CROSSROAD • NEW YORK

1987

The Crossroad Publishing Company
370 Lexington Avenue, New York, NY 10017

Printed in the United States of America

Library of Congress Cataloging in Publication Data

Schillebeeckx, Edward, 1914–
    The Schillebeeckx reader.
    Bibliography: p. 297.
    Includes index.
    1. Theology, Doctrinal—Addresses, essays, lectures.
    2. Catholic Church—Doctrines—Addresses, essays,
lectures.   I. Schreiter, Robert J.   II. Title.
    BX891.S356   1984   230'.2   84-17568
        ISBN 0-8245-0663-4

        0-8245-0828-9 (pbk)

Contents

Foreword

From all the originally photographed footage, which had been worked on for years, a film of only a few hours is created. Choices are made, focusing is done, editing takes place.

Something similar to this happens in the compiling of a Reader. It differs from a film, however, in that it is ultimately not the product of the author about whom it is really concerned. *Someone else* makes his own film out of the reels of original footage, albeit with complete and integral preservation of the original material. In that sense he himself becomes an "author," who presents another author, introduces him, shows the way that he has taken, explains or tells why he went this way or that, why he took detours in order to arrive at the destination he had in mind (and moreover, he must reconnoitre that destination himself). And there is still so much more: he has above all to think along with that author in order to make clear, or even clearer what that author had to say. He is a kind of "guru" who initiates others into a certain "tradition." Constructing a Reader is, therefore, a hermeneutical process, that is, an interpretation event for which the compiler of the anthology is responsible, with the realization, however, that he intends to remain faithful to what he thinks he has heard in the work of the author he has studied.

A Reader has a many-sided function, therefore:

1. For those who, because of time, circumstances, or whatever, cannot read the entire oeuvre of a given author in whom they are for whatever reason interested, a Reader brings them directly, and not via someone else's commentary, into contact with their chosen author.

2. By choosing certain texts, a Reader tries to map out, as it were, the key junctures in an author's thought in a graphic manner.

3. A Reader takes into account the literary genres of an author. Is the author telling a story? Preaching? Reasoning or analyzing? Carrying out a historical investigation?

4. A Reader has to get at what really motivates an author. Why does the author write all those things? What does the author want to achieve with this?

5. The compiler of a Reader, in this case an anthology of my theological work, familiarizes my readers and others who have not read my works with the basic lines of my thought worked out in greater detail in my books, but in such a way as not to lose the forest for the trees. A Reader, in contrast with my individual books, gives the results of the research, while at the same time retracing the pathway of the investigation. This gives something special, something original to the Reader, even though it is an anthology from the work of the author's works.

6. This Reader is also very valuable for those who know my works. Within a shorter scope they are reminded of the wide variety of themes treated in my books and scattered articles. Their own use of my publications is facilitated in all kinds of ways by this Reader. The looking up of all kinds of texts is expedited.

The editor of this anthology, or Schillebeeckx reader, is Robert J. Schreiter, C.PP.S., presently Dean of the Catholic Theological Union in Chicago and Professor of Systematic Theology there. After his studies in psychology and philosophy at St. Joseph's College in Indiana, he came to Nijmegen to study theology. I was the director of his doctoral dissertation, which had to do with a study in eschatological language. This dissertation not only won the Nijmegen University Research Prize, but it was also deemed by an interuniversity jury to have been the best dissertation in the Netherlands in a ten-year period (1964–74). In recent years Schreiter has been concerned especially with "contextual theology," about which a book by him will soon appear.

The compilation of this Reader was, therefore, in good hands. I congratulate Schreiter not only for the competent selection he has made from my works but also for the short commentaries with which he introduces each new section. In his general introduction he gives a faithful and original picture of the development of my thought, a picture in which I fully recognize myself. I am also grateful to him that this Reader does not degenerate into a kind of apotheosis. Rather, he has tried to present objectively an author whose books are spread out over a long period, and to present them to a wider audience than those who already know my work. And he has done this in a way that does not betray or distort the meaning of my literary products, but even clarifies them.

Finally, I am thankful to him for spontaneously taking the initiative to compile this reader—even though it might seem somewhat premature in view of the fact that it brings together the work of a theologian who, thanks be to God, is still very much alive and hopes still to have something to say and to be able to say it in the future, but one who will gladly be *silent* when he has nothing more to say.

Nijmegen   *Edward Schillebeeckx*
July 5, 1984

Editor's Preface

Edward Schillebeeckx can be counted among the most important Roman Catholic theologians of the twentieth century. Over a period of forty years, in some four hundred publications, he has addressed a wide range of theological questions with astonishing breadth and depth. In his work with the bishops at the Second Vatican Council, he came to the world's attention as an original thinker deeply concerned with the problems facing Christians today. In the 1970s, his two magisterial volumes on Jesus attracted the attention of Catholics and Protestants alike. And in the 1980s, his bold contributions to questions about the future of ministry aroused considerable discussion. Although he is now retired from his professorial chair at the Catholic University of Nijmegen in the Netherlands, he continues to lecture and write at a steady pace.

Unlike many other theologians of similar stature, he has a large popular following as well. In the Netherlands, he is a public figure, appearing with some regularity on television, and writing in newspapers and weekly magazines. This is not because he seeks after publicity; rather it comes from his own sense of urgency in communicating with those most affected by the problems with which he grapples.

And people appreciate this. While his writing remains difficult for the nontheologian to follow, people sense that he is truly interested in their problems with belief and Christian action in the contemporary world. For that reason they try to read him, seeking out some illumination for the problems and challenges facing Christians today.

But even theologians admit that Schillebeeckx can be difficult to follow. There are two main reasons for this.

The first has to do with his writing style. Schillebeeckx is given to long, meandering sentences, which are regularly interspersed with parenthetical remarks, allusive references to other authors or periods of history, and a liberal use of qualifiers and emphases. These sometimes unwieldy sentences are then piled one on the other. And then, when it seems a conclusion is about to be reached, another element or issue is brought in, which prompts a lengthy excursus. Sentences and paragraphs are packed with qualifying adverbs, as though Schillebeeckx wants to be as specific as possible and not to exclude anything, all at the same time. Whether he is using the writing process to think or giving us the transcript of an imaginary lecture, as some close observers have suggested,[1] is hard to say. But it is true that a particularly involved sentence is often best understood when it is read aloud.

The second reason has to do with the content of his work. There is an immense erudition packed into Schillebeeckx's texts which often reveals itself only in shorthand form. Besides being intimately acquainted with the history of theology and much New Testament exegesis, he has appropriated several different philosophical approaches during his career and incorporates parts of them into his work. A single work can reveal his knowledge of Thomism, existential phenomenology, post-Heideggerian hermeneutics, Anglo-American philosophies of language, critical theory, structuralism and semiotics, and other forms of contemporary linguistics. In addition, ideas and concepts from other contemporary theologians mark his work. This can make his work difficult to follow for those who are not as widely read as he is—which would be most of his readership. The denseness of some of his texts, with names and concepts tumbling out together, can dishearten many.

The purpose of *The Schillebeeckx Reader* is to make his thought more accessible both to the general reader and to the theologian. Since Schillebeeckx has not worked with any single philosophical or interpretive frame of reference throughout his career, some orientation to his thought is necessary, particularly the pattern of its

---

[1]For the former opinion, see A. Van De Walle, "Theologie over de werkelijkheid: Een Betekenis van het Werk van Edward Schillebeeckx," *Tijdschrift voor Theologie* 14 (1974) 463–90. For the latter, see T. M. Schoof, "'. . . een bijna koortsachtige aandrang . . . ,'" in *Meedenken met Edward Schillebeeckx*, ed. H. Häring, T. Schoof, and A. Willems (Baarn: H. Nelissen, 1983) 11-34.

development. The *Reader* opens, then, with such an orientation, speaking about the relation between his career and his intellectual development, before moving on to the recurring themes in his work. At the end of the orientation, there is also a short section on the major philosophical frameworks from which he draws.

Then follow the eighty selections from his work. They are divided into six parts. The first part deals especially with the various dimensions of the anthropology and theory of society which inform his work. The second part takes up his theology of revelation, his understanding of theology itself, and his uses of interpretation theory or hermeneutics. The third part is devoted to Christology. The fourth part covers his understandings of church and life in the church. The fifth part takes up questions of the relation of church and world, and the final part looks at his work on spirituality.

Even with eighty selections, not every topic that Schillebeeckx has addressed receives coverage. Preference was given to those selections that best characterize his creative thought, offer some of his special insights, or address topics that have been of great interest to many people. Nearly a quarter of the material presented here is appearing in English for the first time. Many of these selections were considered clearer statements of his thought than others that might have already been familiar to the English readers.

In the case of this material, the translations are my own. In other cases, the published translation has been used. This leads to some unevenness at times (e.g., *basileia tou theou* is translated as "kingdom of God," "rule of God," and "reign of God"), but not to such an extent as to really confuse the readers, I think. More problematic is the issue of use of inclusive language. Inclusive language is used in the new translations. It seemed anachronistic, however, to correct older translations. They must stand with their time.

With the readings in each section is a brief commentary. The purpose of the commentary is to help situate the reading by providing some of its original context and, where necessary, to give background on the intellectual framework and supply definitions or references to certain allusions. The commentary is not intended to be a full account of Schillebeeckx's thought; that is best left to the readings themselves. The commentary is meant to continue the orientation section, to aid in appreciating and understanding Schillebeeckx's work.

At the end of each reading the date of the original publication is given. This is intended to help the reader appreciate both how Schillebeeckx's thought has developed and also how much certain themes recur. The selections cover most of his published work from the early 1950s to the mid-1980s.

Finally, Schillebeeckx's complete bibliography through 1983 appears here, both as a general tool for scholars and also for those readers who wish to pursue certain themes further.

Many people deserve thanks for helping bring the *Reader* about. The editors of Crossroad Publishing Company pursued me in a gentle but persistent way to undertake the project, one which turned out to be more of an intellectual joy than a chore; thanks certainly to them. Appreciation is due also to the Catholic Theological Union in Chicago, which granted me the sabbatical and some of the support that made it possible to work on this project. Kenneth O'Malley, C.P., Director of the CTU Library, prepared the index for this work. Warm thanks go to the Dominican community at the Albertinum in Nijmegen, under whose roof most of the selections in the *Reader* were originally written and where I found hospitality and good companionship while designing and putting together the *Reader*. Two persons there need to be singled out. Ted Schoof, O.P., for many years Schillebeeckx's secretary and the individual who is probably the most knowledgeable about the development of Schillebeeckx's thought, was invaluable in suggesting appropriate texts, answering questions, and helping search out references. He is also the compiler of the complete bibliography here. And finally, thanks to Edward Schillebeeckx himself, who reviewed the selections made here, offered suggestions about what to include and excise, and agreed to write the foreword. It is no doubt not easy to see one's work dismembered and reassembled in this fashion, but he showed good humor and help throughout. Needless to say, however, he is not responsible for the final choice or the commentary. That responsibility lies with myself.

15 March 1984   *Robert J. Schreiter, C.PP.S.*

Edward Schillebeeckx
An Orientation to His Thought

The lives of theologians are ordinarily without great external drama; it is their interior life that is of greater importance for understanding their theology. The case of Edward Schillebeeckx is no exception to that. Yet some account of his life is helpful in setting the stage for discussing his thought, since contact with certain people and participation in certain events have helped shape his theology.

Edward Cornelis Florentius Alfons Schillebeeckx was born into a middle-class Flemish family in Antwerp, Belgium, on 12 November 1914, the sixth of fourteen children. His family had moved there from Kortenbeek because of the outbreak of the war. After the war they returned to their home, where young Edward attended primary school. His secondary school education was at the Jesuit boarding school at Turnhout. Upon completing there in 1934, he entered the Flemish Province of the Dominican Order at Ghent. In an interview given a few years ago, he said that he chose the Dominicans over the Jesuits (he has an older brother who is a Jesuit) because, at the time, they seemed to him to combine a deeper sense of humanity with the intellectual life.

He pursued the usual course of philosophical and theological study at the Dominican house in Louvain and was ordained a priest in 1941. During his philosophical study, he was a student of D. De Petter, who was to be one of the great intellectual influences on his life. De Petter allowed him to read Kant, Hegel, Freud, and the phenomenologists, all of whom would have been forbidden for a priesthood candidate at that time. But more important, De Petter introduced him to a perspective on Thomas Aquinas quite different from the rather abstract and cerebral

1

scholasticism more commonly taught at that time. De Petter's approach combined the phenomenologist's concern for the ultimate inadequacy of human conceptuality to grasp experience with a Thomist theory of knowing. His concern for things like intuition was fresh and exciting. De Petter drew also on what was going on in contemporary psychology and sociology for shaping his theory of knowledge. De Petter remained very much a Thomist, however, both in mode of argument and in his approach to problems; but his approach to matters of truth, knowledge, and grace were to shape Schillebeeckx's own theology markedly down to the early 1960s. Even after he left De Petter's framework behind, Schillebeeckx continued to shape some basic insights of De Petter into fundamental theological issues: with De Petter, he continued to stress the absolute priority of God's grace over human endeavor, the ultimate inability of any conceptual system to express completely the richness of human experience, and God's infinite love for creation.

When Schillebeeckx completed his theological study in Louvain in 1943, he was assigned immediately to teach theology in the Dominican House. Personally, he was more interested in philosophy than in theology (theology still being far less creative in Catholic circles than was philosophy at the time), but he followed the wishes of his Order. At the end of the war, he went to Le Saulchoir, the Dominican faculty in Paris, to pursue doctoral work.

The two years in Paris provided the second major intellectual influence on his theology. Le Saulchoir was very much at the center of the *Nouvelle Théologie* movement. This movement promoted a *ressourcement*, or return to the patristic and medieval sources, as the way to engage in theological reflection, rather than continuing to rely on later commentators and manuals of theology. The movement embraced methods of historical-critical research as the way to rediscover the great Christian thinkers. This emphasis on doing historical research has clearly marked Schillebeeckx's own theology, most notably his work on the sacraments, marriage, eucharist, and ministry. In the 1970s he was to extend this "back-to-the-sources" approach to include a study of the exegetical research on the scriptures in preparation for his books on Jesus.

Schillebeeckx immersed himself not only in historical research but also in the intellectual currents alive in Paris in those postwar years. He met the existentialist philosopher Albert Camus and had several discussions with him. He attended lectures at the Sorbonne and the Collège de France. But the two figures who influenced him the most were his teachers in Le Saulchoir, Yves Congar and M. D. Chenu. Both of these men combined a commitment to scholarship with an extraordinary level of engagement in the contemporary world. Schillebeeckx worked especially closely with Chenu, whom he considers to be the single greatest influence on him as a theologian. Chenu's commitment to solid historical research on the one hand and to justice and the real problems facing the church on the other continues to be mirrored in Schillebeeckx's own work.

He returned to his teaching in Louvain in 1947 and began preparing his doctoral dissertation. He had hoped to write on the relation of religion and the world (his first published articles are on this theme), but he was going to have to lecture on the sacraments, so he chose sacraments as the theme of his dissertation. He completed his doctorate under the guidance of Chenu in 1951 and published a revised version of the first part of the dissertation the following year as *De Sacramentele Heilseconomie* (*The Sacramental Economy of Salvation*). The work is a masterful *ressourcement* of traditional sacramental theology in the patristic and medieval authors, giving fresh perspective on sacramental theory. He projected a second volume, building on the first, which was to develop a contemporary sacramental theology. This was published in abbreviated form in 1958 and was later translated into English as *Christ the Sacrament of the Encounter with God*. In this volume he combined the results of his historical research with an existentialist phenomenology of encounter, all within a renewed Thomism.

He continued to teach dogmatic theology in the Dominican House of Studies until 1958. During this time, he became editor of *Tijdschrift voor Geestelijk Leven*, a journal of spirituality. He also served as Master of the Dominican students, which meant that he was responsible for their spiritual formation. Many of the conferences he gave were published in the *Tijdschrift*. He also published a number of other papers, some of them originally given at meetings of the Flemish Theological Society, on topics of theology and revelation, truth, the nature of theology, and problems of theories of knowledge.

In 1956 he was appointed professor in the Institute of Higher Religious Studies in Louvain, but a year later he was called to the Chair of Dogmatics and the History of Theology at the Catholic University of Nijmegen in the Netherlands. He took up the post in 1958 and was to remain in that position until his retirement in 1983.

His lectures in Nijmegen have all been documented by T. M. Schoof.[1] Schillebeeckx was free to choose his own topics (he lectured only to post-ordination research students) and chose marriage in the early years. Recurring topics were Christology and eschatology. From the late 1960s he gave lectures on hermeneutics every term. In the early years, he also conducted seminars on historical topics.

Schillebeeckx's position in the university and his popularity as a lecturer throughout the Netherlands put him in a position to become an advisor to the Dutch bishops, and they soon availed themselves of his services. He was a principal influence on their joint pastoral letter at Christmas 1960, which achieved international attention for its outline of a liberal agenda for the planned Vatican Council. Schillebeeckx went to the Council as an advisor to the Dutch bishops. It was there that he first gained international recognition. Although he was never to become an official *peritus,* or expert, to the Council (he was considered far too progressive by the conservative curial elements), he lectured to large gatherings of bishops, commenting on the proposed schemas and providing the equivalent of continuing education as a background for their work on the Council floor. As a result of this, he had a significant influence on the development of the constitutions on the church, and the church in the modern world, although he worked directly only on the marriage section in the latter constitution. During this period, he was also writing his historical study on marriage, which was to be published in 1963. A projected second volume was

[1]T. M. Schoof, "'. . . een bijna koortsachtige aandrang . . . ,'" *Meedenken met Edward Schillebeeckx,* ed. H. Häring, T. Schoof, and A. Willems (Baarn: H. Nelissen, 1983) 11–39.

never published. During this same period he wrote many shorter pieces relating to issues being discussed at the Council, such as the emerging role of the laity, the renewal of religious life, and the role of the church in the world. He also wrote accounts of events taking place at the Council and revealed a journalistic talent alongside his theological ability.

The contact with other theologians and the world episcopate broadened his horizons in those Council years. They were expanded even further by his first trip to the United States in the mid-1960s, where he came into contact with secularization and the "God is dead" theology of radical theologians. In 1965, he helped found the international journal *Concilium.*

It was around this period that his theology underwent a marked change. Many of the basic issues remained the same, but there were significant shifts in approach and use of interpretive frameworks. Two things were especially evident.

First, the explicit Thomistic framework, developed and used since his contacts with De Petter in the 1930s, was set aside. After this period, Schillebeeckx's theology no longer shows a reliance on a single, unitary metaphysical framework. Rather, his thought shows evidence of a variety of different interpretive frameworks. It was also during this period that he undertook an intensive study of different systems of interpretation: the "new hermeneutics" of the neo-Heideggerians, Anglo-American analytic philosophy, and the critical theory of the Frankfurt school of social criticism. All of these theories, plus a few others, were to play a role in his subsequent thought, although critical theory was to have the principal part. His studies from this period (1966–71) have been collected in *The Understanding of Faith* and *God the Future of Man.*

Second, there was a marked shift in perspective. The effect of renewal within the church and the forces of secularization outside it meant that the more churchly assumptions and tone of his earlier theology were less feasible to maintain. The theological language that Schillebeeckx now began to employ was more accessible for a wider, non-Catholic, and even non-church audience. It also revealed more of the personality of the author, the intensity of his own search, the struggle with problems and ideas. One has only to compare his work on the sacraments from the 1950s with two incidental works, also on churchly subjects, from the 1960s: *Celibacy* (1966), and *The Eucharist* (1967). While both still exhibit the strong historical background, they are more forcefully and passionately argued. The difference is even more noticeable if one compares the Christology of *Christ the Sacrament* with the Jesus books of the 1970s. In the former work, the hypostatic union is the point of departure, reminiscent of the work of Karl Adam in the 1920s and 30s (another author to whom Schillebeeckx was introduced by De Petter). The Jesus books, on the other hand, are addressed to those who are trying to believe so as to eventually arrive at the point of confessing the divinity of Jesus. The majority of the selections in this reader come from this second period in Schillebeeckx's thought, since this has been the period that has been most influential on Christian life.

The late 1960s and the early 1970s were a period of intense study. During this period, as was already mentioned, Schillebeeckx developed his thought on interpretation or hermeneutics. With this he became more and more convinced of the limited and perspectival character of any attempt to capture human experience, a theme he had begun to explore with De Petter three decades earlier. He also developed his eschatology during this period, in dialogue with the works of theologians Wolfhart Pannenberg, Jürgen Moltmann, Johannes Metz, and philosopher Ernst Bloch.

It was around the turn of the decade that he embarked on a project to rethink Christology. Christology had always been an important theme for him, and he had written a number of shorter studies on it. But now two things helped shape his approach: the conviction that all the exegetical work on the New Testament had to be studied and that a new understanding of soteriology, or theology of salvation, had to be articulated. He envisioned a step-by-step approach, which would lead the inquiring person to the confession of Jesus as the salvation of God. The first volume of this study appeared as *Jesus* in 1974. It tries to reconstruct the process of growth in faith among the disciples from the beginning of Jesus' ministry up to the time of the formation of the books of the New Testament. A second volume, entitled *Christ* in English, appeared in 1977, taking up the Christology of the books of the New Testament along with a number of topics surrounding the meaning of salvation. A third volume has been projected.

If Schillebeeckx had not been known before, the *Jesus* book brought him to the attention of a vast audience. Here was an attempt to make the Jesus story intelligible to contemporary men and women without first insisting on all kinds of dogmatic definitions. Schillebeeckx was most certainly not opposed to those definitions but knew that for most people, they would have to represent an end point rather than a point of departure.

The two Jesus books aroused widespread praise and criticism. This led him to write a short response in 1978, entitled *Interim Report*, which clarified a number of controversial points.

Along with Christology, Schillebeeckx had always had an interest in issues relating to ministry. The growing shortage of priests and shifts in forms of ministry lead to his involvement in seminars and in the giving of lectures. Some of these he collected together in a little book entitled *Ministry*, which was published in 1980. It, too, has caused a great deal of discussion, since it argues that there are distinctive differences between forms of ministry in the first millennium of Christianity and the second and that we would be well advised to return to the patterns of the first as a way out of the current crisis. The book helped consolidate many of the feelings present among Roman Catholics and has been the subject of much discussion.

In 1982, Schillebeeckx announced his retirement from his professorship. He gave his farewell lecture in February 1983. The lecture was on hermeneutics and its impact on theology, a fitting way to conclude a period of fifteen years in which new ways of understanding had so influenced his own theology. But the lecture was by no means a conclusion. The only retirement has been from the formal responsibilities of a professor in a university. He intends to write the third volume of his Christology and to follow that with a major study in hermeneutics, "of about five or six hundred pages," as he says. The newest interest to emerge in that farewell lecture was in the problems Christians face in a world church: the problems of an intercultural theology. And so the farewell lecture had something in it of an agenda for the next stage in the theological career of Edward Schillebeeckx.

Any theologian who addresses directly the problems vexing the church as it confronts modernity is bound to evoke a wide range of responses. Schillebeeckx has been no different in that regard.

On the one hand, he has been widely honored. In 1969 he won the Quinquennial Prize of the Cultural Council in Flanders for his contribution to promoting Flemish language and culture. And it is without a doubt that Schillebeeckx has given Low Countries theology a prominence it has not enjoyed for several centuries. And especially because of him Dutch is now a language that the world theological community takes seriously. In 1982 he was awarded the prestigious Erasmus Prize by the Dutch Government for his contribution to the development of European culture. And he has received half a dozen honorary doctorates.

But, on the other hand, he has suffered at the hands of church authorities. Three times—in 1968, in 1976, and in 1982—the Vatican Congregation of the Doctrine of the Faith has initiated a formal examination of his work. In the first two instances he was exonerated; the last case is still pending. Schillebeeckx's handling of these conflicts reveals something of his own faith and his personality. He has cooperated with these investigations quietly, even when the procedure imposed would seem shocking and unjust in any contemporary court of law. His loyalty to the church, even when its authorities have treated him less than civilly, has remained. He has also remained a loyal member of the Dominican Order (its authorities have reciprocated that loyalty), and through all the tension, a kind, affable, and unassuming man despite his position in the world theology and church community.

Having sketched something of Schillebeeckx's career thus far, we can now turn more directly to aspects of his thought. The first reaction of many has been that there is no consistent thread running through his theology. He has written on so many diverse topics through the years; and some of his writings seem very much bound up with the times in which they appeared, as in the case of his writings on spirituality from the 1950s. Those writings seem to throw little light on the contemporary Schillebeeckx at all. Moreover, he has not worked from any one philosophical framework throughout his career as other theologians have. This contributes to giving a body of writing at least a surface sense of coherence. He has certainly not produced a systematic theology, moving from topic to traditional topic. Is there any comprehensive way of understanding his theology?

Toward the end of *Jesus,* Schillebeeckx discusses the issue of historical change with the image of a phonograph record on its turntable.[2] The periphery of the record seems to be moving very fast, similar to our experience of the day-to-day movement of time. But the closer one comes to the center, the slower the real movement seems to be. He goes on to explain that while surface events often seem to change quite rapidly, the deeper, fundamental changes move at a slower pace and are transformed much more gradually. This same image might be helpful for understanding the development of Schillebeeckx's own thought. One could envision the totality of his work as three concentric bands on a record.

The outermost band represents the topics on which he chooses to write at any given time. Like a record in movement, there is a good deal of recurrence; he has written on Christology, ministry, and church and world issues on several occasions. The middle band represents the different philosophical frameworks he has used to express his ideas: Thomism, existential phenomenology, critical theory, and so on. Again, like a record, they tend to recur. Thus, one can find the phenomenological language of encounter in his writings in the 1950s and also in the 1980s. And the innermost band (he calls it the "conjunctural" in *Jesus*) represents some deep convictions which have not really changed much over the years, and which direct the options chosen within the philosophical frameworks and give a distinctive stamp to the suggestions offered in his writings.

The rest of this orientation will explore the innermost and middle bands, that is, his "conjunctural" ideas and the philosophical frameworks he has employed. The selections of readings with the commentary are the outermost band and constitute the bulk of this reader.

[2]Edward Schillebeeckx, *Jesus: An Experiment in Christology* (New York: Crossroad, 1979) 554.

Some Conjunctural Elements

Different attempts have been made to give an overall characterization of Schillebeeckx's work[3] and to try to describe the basic elements in his thought. This present attempt will describe his thought in two ways: first through a general statement and then through a description of four fundamental theological options he has taken.

Put in terms of a general statement, Schillebeeckx's work could be seen as the results of trying to *understand concrete, contemporary Christian experience.* Or, put in more traditional theological terms, his basic concern has been the church-world question: What does it mean to be a Christian, a Christian community, in the contemporary world?

All of the words in the proposal—understand concrete, contemporary Christian experience—are important. Let us look at them one by one.

Understand

Schillebeeckx has had a continuing concern for simply making sense out of things. It explains partially the often concentric, exploratory character of his own language. Schillebeeckx does not usually give just the results of his quest for understanding; he makes the reader a partner in the search. His concern for how language affects our understanding, how time and place give us perspective and focus but at the same time limit our vision, what goes on in the act of knowing, how change affects our ability to understand a formulation—all of these are recurring themes in his writing. Even in his more philosophical writings on Thomism in the 1950s and early 1960s, he seems to have had more of a predilection for epistemology (or the theory of how we know) than for metaphysics (or the theory of who we are). Metaphysics is of course a concern, but it is viewed more as an endpoint arrived at in understanding, rather than as a beginning point from which things are surveyed. His writings on revelation are concerned

---

[3]A. Van De Walle calls his work a theology of reality ("Theologie over de Werkelijkheid: Een Betekenis van het Werk van Edward Schillebeeckx," *Tijdschrift voor Theologie* 14 [1974] 463–90); Tadahiko Iwashima calls it a soteriology systematically reflected upon (*Menschheitsgeschichte und Heilserfahrung* [Düsseldorf: Patmos, 1982]).

with how God is revealed as the pathway to understanding who God is—not the other way around. His massive explorations in Christology can be read as trying to come to understand how the first followers of Jesus came to recognize and confess him as Lord, in order that we might be able to do the same. His relative ease in borrowing concepts from other authors represents that same quest for understanding. And his willingness to engage a variety of hermeneutical frameworks rather than settling for just one exemplifies this in another way. In the Foreword to *Jesus*, Schillebeeckx points out that the book is written for a wider audience than theologians alone. Many who are not theologians may suspect that he has not succeeded in his purpose, but the intention is what is important here: to understand is of paramount importance. Thus, the latter parts of *Christ*, the second part of the Jesus trilogy, seem to wander far from the stated intention as Schillebeeckx takes up theories of history, models of anthropology, and problems of politics. But the need for system and order is always subordinate to the process of understanding. And this relentless quest for understanding in a pluralist and often confused world is one of the things that has made his work so attractive to so many readers.

Concrete

"Concrete" is one of Schillebeeckx's favorite words, as some of the selections below will attest. While principles and ideas are very important for him, he constantly is focusing his attention on the precise point where the action is taking place. He wants to discover what leads to the principles and ideas; this is more significant than what can be derived from them. Thus, one of his contributions to sacramental theory is his study of the concrete encounter with and in Christ in sacramental activity. He does not only want to know what the first disciples of Jesus thought about the resurrection; he wants to know how they arrived at their understandings. He is interested in examining the diversity that makes up the concrete, as his patient reconstruction of the pre-Christologies of the New Testament attest in *Jesus*. He feels that only by such an exploration of the concrete contours of history— as in his works on the sacraments, on marriage, on Jesus, and on

ministry—can one come to the realization of all the things that
feed into our current situation. Again, this can make the results
less tidy than a more logically argued case, but it makes them also
more immediate.

The concern for the concrete may also explain his concern for
praxis. This word came into his vocabulary in the late 1960s. It
means a combination of thought and action but usually stresses
the action part. His use of the term "orthopraxis" rather than the
more common "orthodoxy" is one example of this preference.
Perhaps his preference for the term praxis also has to do with his
emphasis on the concrete, on action.

Contemporary

Even in his historical research, the concern for the present situation is never far away in Schillebeeckx's writings. His very first
published writings in 1945 deal with the situation he was then
experiencing in France, and the challenge of humanism there.[4]
Indeed, much of his earlier published writings appeared in journals
and weeklies aimed at a wider audience, such as *Kultuurleven* and
Tijdschrift voor Geestelijk Leven in Belgium, and *De Bazuin* in the
Netherlands. And some of his best known works have been incidental ones, addressed to current and urgent problems: *The Eucharist, Celibacy,* and *Ministry* all fall into this category. But this has
also meant that as the contemporary situation changes, those
earlier writings can lose their immediacy and seem dated. One sees
more difference between the Schillebeeckx of the 1950s and 1980s
than one might see in a theologian like Karl Rahner. Perhaps that
is part of the price one pays for being, and trying to be, more
immediate. But at the same time one could not accuse him of chas-
ing after fashion. Many of his earlier pieces remain current, as can
be seen in the choice of readings below.

Christian

As a theologian, and a Christian theologian, Schillebeeckx is of
course interested in what it means to be a Christian. There is
nothing particularly unusual about that. But his special interest
has been how being Christian focuses or specifies the human. How

---

[4]"Christelijke Situatie," *Kultuurleven* 12 (1945) 82–95, 229–42, 585–611.

does being Christian relate to being human? Through the years, he has come more and more to emphasize the similarities rather than the differences in this particular question. From his early discussions about humanism in the 1940s and 1950s, through the secularization writings of the 1960s, to questions of emancipative freedom in the 1970s, one sees a progression in which the Christian approach remains integral but is less distinctive in the process of becoming human. The readings in Part V give evidence of that especially.

Seen from a collective point of view, Schillebeeckx's concern here lies at the heart of the church–world issue. Schillebeeckx's positive valuation of creation and God's activitiy within the world is what has made this approach possible. A constant concern has been: How does a Christian respond to this situation? How can one be truly Christian and truly human in this situation, since the two cannot ultimately be in contradiction? Schillebeeckx has also shown a strong interest in those who either cannot become Christian or find it hard to remain so. The struggle for faith in a secularized society and the struggle for justice within a sometimes oppressive and alienating church have colored how he tries to approach questions. Thus, *Jesus* is written to help those struggling to come to faith; it does not assume faith as its point of departure. In recent years, this concern for those who find themselves on the edges of the Church (either tempted to leave or hesitant to enter) has been more marked in his writing.

Experience

Schillebeeckx had learned from De Petter in the 1930s to begin with experience rather than the framework that might be used to interpret it. And it seems that the suspicion that many frameworks (such as forms of scholasticism) were not only not helpful, but were downright alienating, has reinforced his convictions about the importance of beginning with experience. In the late 1970s, with *Christ*, Schillebeeckx begins to speak concretely about what experience is and how it comes about. He insists that Christianity did not begin with doctrine but with an experience of Jesus which then, over a period of time, took on certain forms. This is no doubt one of the reasons why people will continue to struggle to understand Schillebeeckx, even when he is difficult to follow: there is always a sense that he is trying to take their experience seriously. Perhaps, too, this is why Schillebeeckx has felt so free to change interpretive frameworks as he has gone on his own quest and to modify them when necessary. The experience itself is quite simply always more important than the framework interpreting it. This has been at times the source of his trouble with the Vatican Curia, who have read his emphasis on experience as undermining the magisterium as the norm of truth. But Schillebeeckx has struggled to be faithful to both, since a magisterium without the experience of grace and the Holy Spirit is a dead letter indeed. And his own historical sense is too keen to permit him to lapse into a rootless enthusiasm.

Understanding the concrete, contemporary Christian experience—this is one way of finding a perspective on the thousands of pages this theologian has written. But to summarize Schillebeeckx's thought only in this way still seems a little too broad, indeed so broad that it could seem almost tautologous. For what Christian theologian does *not* try to understand the concrete, contemporary Christian experience?

For this reason, it would be helpful to take this examination of the conjunctural elements of his thought a step further. In this second step, four basic theological positions are set forth which represent options Schillebeeckx has taken. As a result of having followed out these options, his theology has one kind of contour. These options point to a specific way of working out basic theological insights. Keeping them in mind can help the reader find a path through the complexities of Schillebeeckx's argument in different circumstances.

1. *Mystery and the Ultimate Inadequacy of Concepts*

Schillebeeckx has always maintained a deep reverence for the fact that that which most interests us and draws us onward is always somehow beyond our grasp. Already in his early work on the sacraments he refers to this something as "mystery," a term that still appears in his most recent writings. Perhaps under the influence of Henri de Lubac on this subject, and certainly influenced by the concept of *mystērion* in the sacramental theology of the Greek Fathers, Schillebeeckx uses this term to point to the reality of God as it is presented to us. For despite all the human-centered concerns in his theology, the ultimate purpose of his investigations is to lead people into mystery where God dwells. This prompts Schillebeeckx to note on several occasions, as he does at the end of *Jesus,* that all theology must end in silence before the mystery. This is certainly not a new thought in Christian theology, but it is one often forgotten.

This reverence for the mystery at the heart of the theological enterprise carries over into the investigation of human experience. There is a kind of sacred character to human experience which can never be fully grasped by human concepts. Schillebeeckx is at his most eloquent on this when he speaks of human suffering.

This reverence for human experience follows, once again, De Petter. De Petter believed that our language and concepts can indeed grasp experience, but he believed also that this happens not because there is a natural relationship between our language and concepts on the one hand and experience (or mystery) on the other. At least such a relationship could not be proven. Rather, the belief that the two go together grows out of an intuition, not a proof, of the commensurability of the two. It is an act of faith, so to speak, that the two can go together. What this means is that our linguistic and conceptual grasp of reality is indeed real, but is only one perspective. There is no normative language or conceptual system, only a plurality of approaches with some being more adequate than others.

De Petter's point was not so much one of advocating pluralism as it was of emphasizing the nature of the bond between our interpretive frameworks and the experience. The bond is intuitive in nature; it is not demonstrable. It is an act of faith, not an act of logic. But from our perspective in time, it is easier to see how this approach could lay the foundation for plural approaches to language and understanding, while not at the same time leading to an indifferent approach to their relative values. Schillebeeckx was later to set aside De Petter's frameworks in his own theology, principally because the rational categories of this form of Thomisr became too constraining for the phenomena to be studied. B' something of the basic insight remains: the deep respect for experience, a belief that we can come to understanding, and the need to explore more than one way to understand. This philosophical point leads to a more clearly theological one.

2. *The Utter Graciousness of God and Our Need to Trust in God*

What assures us that the kind of act of faith which De Petter urges is in any way a responsible thing to do? The answer is: a belief in the utter goodness and graciousness of God. The consequence of this belief is a trust in God. While Schillebeeckx has noted that De Petter impressed this belief upon him, he also recounts that his own experience of God has always been like this, even as a child. This understanding of God can be found already in his writings on the sacraments, but especially in his description of the reign of God and Jesus' relationship to God as Abba in *Jesus.* The "God mindful of humanity," a phrase borrowed from J. Jüngel, becomes a favorite way of expressing this experience of God, from 1973 onward. This message of God's utter graciousness underlies his theology of grace in the 1950s, his understanding of revelation, and his later Christology of the 1970s. It gives an unmistakably optimistic tone to his theology. In the late 1960s he works out this theme in another way, through eschatology or looking at the future. Over against Jürgen Moltmann, he gave stronger emphasis to how much our salvation is already completed in God's gracious act in Christ. At the same time, he looks to the future completion, given now in promise. (In this particular period, "promise" as something surely given but not understood becomes a kind of equivalent of "mystery"—but mystery from the perspective of the future.) It is this unshakable conviction that feeds our sense of trust in God. And the fact that God could be this gracious to *us* makes a statement about the world and human life within it. While not deserving, humanity is somehow nonetheless able to receive such graciousness. As God's creation, as created in God's image, God not only "sees that it was good" but works concretely through this goodness.

3. *God Acts Concretely in and through Our History*

Schillebeeckx consistently affirms how much God's action in our world is through the concrete realities of our existence and history. It was this emphasis on the concrete that made his theology of revelation so attractive. Revelation does not drop out of the sky as a series of truths; it comes to us in experience in concrete, existential encounter. Later he is to talk of this in terms of experiences of contrast, in disclosure experiences. And, finally, he speaks of it in his Christology as the experience of the encounter with Christ. Few theologians have insisted as seriously as has Schillebeeckx upon how concretely God acts in history. At points he seems to take the human and human history so seriously that the divine seems to disappear. This is especially the case in some of his later writings. But one can misunderstand this as an uncritical view of human nature and human society if one fails to remember that this is a consequence of taking God's graciousness so seriously. Indeed, for Schillebeeckx, it is the human that is the royal road to God.

His theology, therefore, is very human-centered or anthropocentric, and has become increasingly so through the years. But his theology does not devolve into merely an anthropology, in spite of the empathy he can summon up for those who believe otherwise or not at all. This human-centered approach is and remains a path to the mystery, to the dwelling place of God. And people must tread this path to reach the fulfillment of the human for which they yearn. The human, or the "humanum" as he comes to call it, is not something given beforehand from which we and our history are then derived. It is something toward which and for which we strive. This is why it is so important to take human life and history seriously. They are constitutive parts of that struggle toward full humanity. The mention of that struggle for full humanity brings us to the fourth basic theological position.

4. *The Perspectival Character of Human Action in History*

In this human-centered approach, the quest for the humanum is not only not yet complete; it often goes awry along the way.

Although Schillebeeckx could be called an optimist about the human condition, he is keenly aware that human life and history are rife with suffering, oppression, and sin. It was especially contact with the Frankfurt school of social criticism and the work of Max Horkheimer that helped him formulate this in the late 1960s. Many of the keenest insights into human nature come in moments of suffering, when the reality of the present contradicts the fullness promised. These are experiences of contrast, a favorite phrase of his. It is those contrast experiences which make hope real, since hope then becomes so necessary. They reveal to us the fragility of the humanum and how incapable we are of saving ourselves. Our history of suffering becomes a powerful reminder of how the humanum can be threatened. It also becomes a "dangerous memory" (a phrase coined by J. B. Metz) which subverts any uncritical trust in the current state of things. It urges us forward to struggle for a world of greater justice. It inculcates within us a "critical negativity," a constant questioning character toward everything that promises to be the fulfillment hoped for. For a Christian, this means that our salvation comes from God alone and our struggle against oppression and injustice is part of our becoming more human—yet always short of the reality hoped for. Christians avoid falling into nihilism or fatalism in this struggle for a better humanity by their faith in the God of promise, who is calling us into that better future. It is that call which is the basis of our hope and the motivation to continue the struggle against suffering and evil.

Thus, the perspectival character of human existence is not only a conceptual one, as we saw in the first basic theological position. It has to do with human finitude as such. The critical theory of Jürgen Habermas, a student of Horkheimer, helped Schillebeeckx carry this idea forward. Theory is closely tied to action, since it always implies a way of acting and from that should lead to action itself. But action and theory are really co-constituting. Schillebeeckx's concern about human action attracted him to Habermas's theory, which tries to work out how action and theory come together for the transformation of society. Schillebeeckx captured this in the concept "orthopraxis." Orthodoxy, or right thinking, can only occur in orthopraxis, that is, in situations where right theory and right action both occur and mutually inform each other. Thus the struggle for justice is not just a possible consequence of reading the gospel; it is a necessary consequence of it.

To attempt to explain anyone's basic elements of thought is always difficult and hazardous, but these four basic theological options provide a way of seeing how Schillebeeckx approaches the same problems over and over again. Deeply trusting in God and affirming concrete human life and history, Schillebeeckx realizes at the same time that human finitude and suffering open up a chasm between the present reality and the promise to be fulfilled. The path to that fulfillment is not only an intellectual one but also one of action and struggle against the situations causing suffering in the world. But the struggle in itself will not be successful; it must be sustained by the firm faith in the overwhelming power of God's graciousness. God reserves the right (eschatological proviso) ultimately to save the world.

Philosophical Frameworks

The image given above has Schillebeeckx's basic theological insights being mediated through a series of philosophical or interpretive frameworks. Schillebeeckx's broad erudition has led him to explore a wide variety of such frameworks and to borrow concepts and approaches from a number of them. To those not familiar with these approaches some of his points can remain elusive.

There are five such frameworks that need to be singled out. The purpose of discussing them here is not to give an exhaustive description of any one of them. This introductory section remains an orientation, not a complete account. Rather, each will be treated briefly to note in what way it has contributed to Schillebeeckx's thought and to give some of the important concepts that Schillebeeckx has derived from these frameworks and has kept as part of his own conceptual apparatus. Where more information on the framework is needed, it is given in the commentary sections. Most of that information will be found in the commentary sections in Part II, where his interpretive theory is treated.

1. *Thomism*

The philosophy of Thomas Aquinas (1225–1274) lies at the beginning of Schillebeeckx's theological quest. Based on the work of Aristotle, it might be called a moderate realism, that is, it takes the empirical work seriously in all its individuality but also looks beyond it to grasp the full meaning. The most important aspect of Thomas's thought for understanding Schillebeeckx's work is Thomas's relative optimism about the knowability of God by humans. Thomas believes that the finite human can communicate with the infinite divine because of an analogy in being: the finite human participates in the being (*esse*) of God through a proportionate analogy—that is, in some way there is sufficient commonality to allow communication. In Schillebeeckx's own reading of this, this communication happens precisely through that analogy, the fact that the created share something of the creator. Thus God communicates with us through the medium of the created world and not through some other channel. That relative optimism means that, sinful and broken though the world may be, it remains a medium for this divine–human communication.

Thomism is most evident in Schillebeeckx's writing from the 1950s into the mid-1960s. This framework about the knowability of God shapes his theology of revelation (how God speaks to us) and how God communicates with us sacramentally in grace. It continues to be in some evidence in his later work in his theology of grace and his continued optimism about our ability to communicate with God.

Thomism is a very broad tradition. Schillebeeckx has studed Thomas not only directly but also under the influence of his teacher De Petter, who presents a twentieth-century refinement of Thomas's theory of knowledge. This was discussed in some detail above and will be taken up again in selection 2 below.

2. *Existentialist Phenomenology*

Schillebeeckx would have first come into contact with phenomenology in his student days in Louvain, where the archives of the founder of phenomenology, Edmund Husserl (1859–1938) are maintained. It influenced his teacher De Petter, as we have seen. Phenomenology concerned itself principally with the contents of consciousness. An accurate description of those contents had to be the way to the reality which consciousness had perceived.

In Paris, Schillebeeckx was exposed to existentialism, with its concern for the irreducibility of the individual and its emphasis on discovery of the other through dialogue. Existentialism and phenomenology, always closely related, flowed into each other in the Parisian environment.

The two thinkers perhaps most directly influential upon Schillebeeckx in this framework have been Maurice Merleau-Ponty (1908-1961) and Paul Ricoeur (1908—). Merleau-Ponty's phenomenology of subjectivity and the body lies behind Schillebeeckx's use of the term "bodiliness" in his sacramental theology. Being embodied is not secondary to consciousness; it is part of the experience of being human.

Ricoeur's early work on experience was influential on Schillebeeckx's own thought, and Ricoeur's later work on metaphor and narrative is much in evidence in Schillebeeckx's writings from the mid-1970s onward.

Schillebeeckx has retained a good deal of conceptual apparatus from existentialism and phenomenology. "Encounter," "dialogue," God as "the Other," the sense of "gift" in his treatment of the presence of Christ in the eucharist—all of these are derived from existentialist and phenomenological traditions. The principal contribution of these frameworks has been to give him a vocabulary for speaking about concrete and individual experience.

3. *Neo-Heideggerian Hermeneutics*

The thought of Martin Heidegger (1889-1976) could be seen as another variant on existentialist phenomenology, but it deserves to be singled out here. Heidegger tried to create a new philosophy of being by an existentialist analysis of the experience of being. Of more importance here is Heidegger's later work (from the 1930s on), which emphasizes language as the way to being, that being itself is linguistic (in the broad sense of linguisticality). This formed the basis for appropriating a tradition of interpretation theory of the nineteenth century within a firmer metaphysical framework. One no longer works just with the language of texts, language itself is the road to meaning. These insights are explored further in the commentary on selections 26-31.

The hermeneutics worked out by Heidegger's followers (notably Rudolf Bultmann, Gerhard Ebeling, Ernst Fuchs, and Hans-Georg Gadamer) gave Schillebeeckx his first major interpretive alternative to Thomism in terms of a formal interpretation theory. The language of "hermeneutical circle," "horizon of understanding," "preunderstanding," and "historicity of being" all come out of this framework.

The principal contribution to Schillebeeckx's thought from this kind of hermeneutics has been that it gave him a way to talk about the conditioned, historical character of all human activity in a more coherent manner.

4. *Anglo-American Philosophies of Language*

In the second half of the 1960s, Schillebeeckx read broadly in the analytic philosophies of language coming out of the United States and Great Britain. These philosophies share with the later Heidegger the insight that language is the key to reality, but they emphasize the empirical dimension of language—how what language says measures up to empirical reality. It is an a-metaphysical, and often anti-metaphysical, approach. Schillebeeckx has borrowed a number of things from the different authors he read. Among the authors, perhaps Ludwig Wittgenstein (1889-1951) has been the most influential, particularly through his posthumously published notes known as *Philosophical Investigations*. A key concept from this work for Schillebeeckx has been that of "language games," that is, that language is shaped by sets of rules that set up the scope of the range of meanings. Later Schillebeeckx is to talk in terms of models, which capture something of the same tenor as language games. Thus, religious language may be playing by a different set of rules for meaning than would the language of physics.

"Disclosure" is another term Schillebeeckx continues to use, drawn from the work of the religious philosopher of language, Ian Ramsey (1915-1972). Disclosure has to do with those situations in which an insight suddenly comes to us. Schillebeeckx uses this concept to talk of the revelatory activity of God and also of the apprehension of meaning.

One also comes across references to "verification" and "falsification," which reach back into the analytic philosophy of the

1930s (the latter phrase from Sir Karl Popper). They have to do with ascertaining in what ways our experience corroborates our concepts (verification) or what would constitute a negation of our hypothesis (falsification). These concepts are utilized especially in discussion about discerning the activity of God.

The principal contribution of these frameworks to Schillebeeckx's thought has been to give him a greater sensitivity to how theological language is used, the limits of its range of meaning, and attunement to the empirical referents of language.

5. *Critical Theory*

Critical theory is perhaps the most prominent interpretive framework in Schillebeeckx's theology in the 1970s and 1980s. It derives from the Frankfurt school of social criticism, a sociological approach begun in the 1930s. The group around this approach migrated to the United States during the Hitler period, and many of them returned to Germany after the war.

Theodor Adorno's (1903-1969) notion of negative dialectics has played an important role in Schillebeeckx's thought. It is explained in the commentary on selection 9 below. Basically it is the idea that we do not begin with an explicit idea of humanity but move away from the suffering and oppression of the present toward an implied future concept, called the "humanum."

The work of Jürgen Habermas (1929—) plays the most important role for Schillebeeckx. Habermas's major influences on Schillebeeckx are set forth in the commentary on selections 32–37 below. Habermas's work, which is a kind of Marxist sociology, addresses particularly the oppressed in society. It is particularly acute in analyzing how societies are kept stable to preserve the governing interests. Through Johannes Metz, the work of Habermas has been influential on Latin American liberation theologians. The use of the word "critical" in Schillebeeckx's work is usually in Habermas's sense, that is, of being aware of the forces that bring about equilibrium in society, often at the expense of one or more groups in that society.

The principal contribution of critical theory to Schillebeeckx's thought has been to provide a framework for developing a social concept of salvation and to offer a way of explaining the relation of human liberating activity to the salvation process of God in Jesus Christ. Schillebeeckx's concepts of "ideology," "ideology critique," "praxis," and "orthopraxis" are rooted in critical theory.

Other interpretive frameworks play some role in Schillebeeckx's thought as well. Work in linguistics, structuralism, and semiotics is influencing his hermeneutics. But these approaches are of less significance than the five areas outlined here.

With this, we are now ready to turn to the outermost band on Schillebeeckx's oeuvre, his actual works.

Part One

Experience and Human Liberation

1

Structures of Human Experience

COMMENTARY

Selections 1–4 deal with Schillebeeckx's basic understanding of the human condition and the nature of human experience.

In the first selection, Schillebeeckx summarizes what he calls "coordinates for an anthropology," that is, those things which have to be taken into consideration in any attempt to get a picture of the human condition. Humanity is at the center of Schillebeeckx's theology, and this selection represents the coming together of many years of reflection on this matter. It emphasizes how the fullness of humanity is yet to be realized and how we will not be able to understand what salvation is if we do not understand who is being saved. This sketch of the basics for an anthropology is also important for understanding his ethics (selection 74).

Selections 2 and 3 are statements on the relation of experience and knowledge. Experience has always been a key concept in Schillebeeckx's theology. In selection 2, he acknowledges his debt to De Petter and contrasts De Petter's thought with that of Maréchal, the figure who was to be the most influential in Karl Rahner's understanding experience. The selection emphasizes the relation of experience to the formation of concepts and represents the theories of knowledge coming out of the renewed Thomism of the time. Selection 3 appeared thirty-five years later. The expression of experience is still the concern, but now the emphasis is on the social context of knowledge and on the role of shifting interpretive frameworks. Schillebeeckx's concern with interpretation is much in evidence.

Selection 4 deals with how experience becomes meaningful and directs human life. It is basic for understanding his notion of revelation. He wants to situate the meaning-making process within the structures that shape and misshape society; hence the emphasis on the critical nature of this process. There is also a brief reflection on symbols (part f). The reference to "experiential competence" comes from critical social theory and refers to a free and unencumbered ability to experience, without the repressive structures of society.

1/ *Coordinates for an Anthropology*

What is it to be a true and good, happy and free man, in the light of the awareness of the problem which mankind has so far developed, while it looks for a better future, the problem with which man has been confronted since his origins? What is a livable humanity?

Today we have become more modest in our positive definitions of what humanity is. Ernst Bloch writes: "Man does not yet know what he is, but can know through alienation from himself what he certainly is not and therefore does not want to, or at least should not want to, remain false." We do not have a pre-existing definition of humanity—indeed for Christians it is not only a future, but an eschatological reality. However, there are people who give the impression that they have a blueprint for humanity. They have a fully drawn picture of man and a specific image of coming society, an "entire doctrine of salvation," a dogmatic system which, paradoxically enough, seems to be more important than the people with whom it is really concerned. This totalitarian conception intrinsically issues in a totalitarian action, which is simply a question of application, of technology and strategy. Moreover, in that case those who neither accept nor apply this concept of true humanity are obviously regarded as the enemies of true humanity. Even Christians sometimes think in this way.

Our time has become more modest here. Nature, "ordinances of creation" and Evolution (with a capital E) cannot give us any criteria for what is livable and true, good and happy humanity, and thus for what makes up the meaningful, ethically responsible action which furthers this true humanity. That cannot be either a so-called "universal human nature" which, like plant or animal, is governed from within and is by nature oriented towards a pre-destined goal, nor can it be any of the modern versions of this: i.e., so-called natural law. Furthermore, no reflection on oneself can arrive at a crystallization of a kind of general substratum of rationality among all men, independently of time and space. . . .

Thus what we have at our disposal is no more than a set of *anthropological constants*, rather than a positivistic outline, or a pre-existing definition of "human nature" in philosophical terms (e.g., in Aristotelian and Thomistic or Spinozan and Wolffian terms) or, finally, a product which is provided in itself through the profoundly rational course of history in necessary historical terms (which would then be the Marxist definition of true and free humanity). These may present us with human *values*, but we must make a creative contribution to their specific *norms* in the changing process of history. In other words, in very general terms these anthropological constants point to *permanent* human impulses and orientations, values and spheres of value, but at the same time do not provide us with *directly* specific norms or ethical imperatives in accordance with which true and livable humanity would have to be called into existence here and now. Granted, they present us with constitutive conditions (given the analysis and interpretation of any particular contemporary situation) which must always be presupposed in any human action, if man, his culture and his society are not to be vitiated and made unlivable. Taking into account the particular socio-historical forms of a particular society, and in the light of these spheres of values recognized as constant (in our time-conditioned awareness of the problem), it is in fact possible to establish specific norms for human action over a middle or longer term.

I want to analyse seven of these anthropological constants. I see them as a kind of system of coordinates, the focal point of which is *personal identity* within *social culture*. I am concerned with views of man and his culture, with constitutive aspects which we must take into account in the creative establishment of specific norms for a better assessment of human worth and thus for human *salvation*.

I. Relationship to Human Corporeality, Nature and the Ecological Environment

The relationship of the human being to his own corporeality—man *is* a body but also *has* one—and by means of his own corporeality to the wider sphere of nature and his own ecological environment, is constitutive of our humanity. So human salvation is also concerned with this.

If we take no account of this human reference in our action, then in the long term we shall dominate nature or condition men in so one-sided a way that in fact we shall destroy the fundamental principles of our own natural world and thus make our own humanity impossible by attacking our natural household or our ecological basis. Our relationship with nature and our own corporeality come up against *boundaries* which we have to respect if we are to live a truly human life and, in an extreme instance, if we are even to survive. Therefore what is technically possible has not by a long way been an ethical possibility for men, which makes sense for them and to which they can respond. This also applies to the physical and psychological limitation of our human strength. Although we may not be able (or perhaps may not yet be able) to establish by an empirical scientific method precisely where the *limits* of the mutability, conditioning and capability of humanity lies, we may be sure that such inescapable limits do exist. This certainty, which is *cognitive*, though it goes beyond the bounds of science, can also be seen manifested spontaneously in the individual and collective protests which emerge at the point where men feel that excessive demands are being made on them. The elementary needs of man (e.g., hunger and sex), their drives (e.g., aggression) and their corporeality cannot be manipulated at will without the realization that there is an attack on human goodness, happiness and true humanity (which will express itself in spontaneous resistance).

This first anthropological constant already opens up a whole sphere of human values, the norms needed for a relationship between our own corporeality and the natural environment of man worthy of our true humanity—norms, however, which we ourselves must establish in the context of the particular circumstances in which we now live. This already opens up the perspective of the relationships of mankind to nature, which are not exclusively provided by the human value of domination of nature, but are also provided by the equally human value of aesthetic and enjoyable converse with nature. The limitations which nature itself imposes on the way in which it can be manipulated by man to man's advantage open up for us a dimension of our humanity which is not exhausted in the purely technocratic domination of nature.

On the other hand, the same constants warn us against the danger of an anti-technological or anti-industrial culture. Scientists who reflect on what they are doing emphatically point to the anthropological relevance of instrumental reason. Cultural philosophers have worked out that man is not really capable of remaining alive in a *purely natural* world. In nature man must create an appropriate human *environment* if he is in fact to survive without the refined instincts and the strengths which animals possess. A rational alteration in nature is therefore necessary. A "meta-cosmos" (F. Dessauer) thus appears, which rescues man from his animal limitations and offers an opening for new possibilities. In times when this "meta-cosmos" was hardly different from nature, only a small stratum of the population shared in the advantages of culture, and the mass of mankind had to work slavishly for the liberation of a few from material cares. (However, we can ask whether things are very different in a highly industrial "meta-cosmos." It emerges from this that the first, fundamental "anthropological constant" is not enough in itself.) The meta-cosmos therefore offers man a better abode and a better home than the natural cosmos. So technology is not dehumanizing in itself, but is rather a service towards livable humanity; it is an expression of humanizing and at the same time a condition for the humanizing of man. Indeed, it is a fact that the establishment of a "meta-cosmos" has been the historical presupposition for reflection on questions about the meaning of life. Furthermore, this humanization of nature has yet to be completed, though that might easily be assumed, given the advance in technology. However, man can have an influence on his ecological position in nature, though he depends on it, as becomes clear above all when he destroys the conditions under which he lives. Now the concern on the one hand to emancipate man from nature without on the other hand destroying his own ecological basis is an eminently human task, which cannot be accomplished without "instrumental reason."

Moreover, it is evident that the outlining of meaning and of particular pictures of the world and mankind is also communicated through instrumental and technological reason, and is not just an immanent development of ideas. Ideas about marriage, love and sexuality have shifted in our time (e.g., from biblical conceptions), for the most part solely because science and technology have been able to provide means which were not at the disposal of people of former times. With technological possibilities available, intervention in *nature* in fact looks different from those times when any intervention was felt to be an irresponsible and therefore evil attack on the divine ordinances of creation. However, at the same time there arises the human danger that simply because of the availability of technological possibilities and capabilities, people believe that they can and may provide a *purely technological* solution for all their physical and psychological, social and general problems of life. However, the technocratic *interpretation* of the ideal of a livable life worthy of human beings is not the same thing as the anthropological relevance of science and technology. What is in reality often the dehumanizing character of technology does not come from technology itself, but from the question of meaning associated with it, which has *already* been solved in *positivist* terms. It is not science and technology, with their potentialities for improving man's condition, but their implicit presuppositions which are criticized.

Thus this first anthropological constant shows a whole series of partial constants—for example, that man is not only reason, but also temperament; not only reason, but also imagination; not only freedom, but also instinct; not only reason, but also love; and so on. Thus it is a matter not only of the active dimension of man and his control of the world, but also of his other dimensions, in contemplation, play and in love.

If Christian *salvation* is in fact the *salvation of men*, it will also have essential connections with this first "anthropological constant." To cite only one aspect from the past: Christian salvation is also connected with ecology and with the conditions and burdens which particular life (here and now) lays on men. To say that all this is alien to the meaning of "Christian salvation" is perhaps to dream of a salvation for *angels*, but not for *men*.

II. Being a Man Involves Fellow Men

Human personal identity at the same time includes relationships with other people. This, too, is an anthropological constant which opens up a sphere of human value in which people have to look for norms which will provide them with salvation here and now.

The element of being together, of contact with our fellow men, through which we can share ourselves with others and even be confirmed in our existence and personhood by others, is part of the structure of personal identity: authorization by others and by society that we, that I, may be, in my own name, in my own identity, a personal and responsible self, however distorted this may be. A society which out of so-called self-protection (sometime euphemistically called "the building up of society") leaves no room for the disabled person is not worth a fig.

This personal identity is only possible if I may be allowed by other fellow men, to be myself in my own inalienability, but at the same time in my essential limitation (*divisum ab alio*, as earlier philosophy put it), and if on my side I confirm the other. In this limited individuality the person is essentially related to other, to fellow persons. The human face in particular—a man never sees his *own* face—already indicates that man is *directed towards* others, is *destined for* others and not for himself. The face is an image of ourselves *for others*. Thus, already through his quite specific manifestation, man is destined for encounter with his fellow men in the world. This lays on him the task of accepting, in intersubjectivity, the other in his otherness and in his freedom. It is precisely through this mutual relationship to others that the limitation of man's own individuality is transcended in free, loving affirmation of the other, and the person himself arrives at personal identity. The co-humanity with which we encounter one another as people, i.e., as an aim and an end and not as a means for something or other, is an anthropological constant which looks for norms without which whole and livable humanity is impossible here and now. This also implies that well being and wholeness, complete and undamaged humanity, must be universal, must apply to each and every individual, and not only a few privileged ones—though it emerges from what has gone before that this wholeness will embrace more than inter-human relations on the *personal* level. No one can enter into a relationship of real encounter with everyone. Besides, there is more than the I–thou relationship. The presence of a *third*, a "he," is the basis for the origin of *society*, which cannot be derived from an "I–thou" and "we" relationship. This has been clearly seen above all by E. Lévinas, and the insight brings us to a third essential dimension of humanity.

III. The Connection with Social and Institutional Structures

There is, thirdly, the relationship of the human person to social and institutional structures. While we men bring these structures to life in the course of our history, they become independent and then develop into an objective form of society in which we live our particular lives and which again also deeply influence our inwardness, our personhood. The social dimension is not something additional to our personal identity; it is a *dimension* of this identity itself. When they become independent, these structures and institutions give the impression of being unchangeable natural regularities, whereas we ourselves can change them and therefore also their regularity. Independently of what men do, and independently of human reason and human will to preserve these structures, such highly praised sociological and economic regularities do not exist; in fact they are essentially subject to the *historical hypothesis* of the objectively given social and economic system. They are contingent, changeable and thus changeable by men (although sociologists and cultural anthropologists will perhaps be able to discover a deeper, almost immutable level and therefore structural constants in some perhaps even fundamental social changes). The empirical sciences often do not take into account that this appearance of regularity depends on the hypothesis of our given (changeable) objective form of society: given the hypothesis, they rightly discover these sociological or socio-psychological regularities, but sometimes treat them as though they were a natural law or a metaphysical datum.

This constant, too, shows us a sphere of values, above all the value of institutional and structural elements for a truly human life. This is once again a sphere of values which needs concrete norms. On the one hand there can be no permanent life worthy of men without a degree of institutionalizing; personal identity also needs social consensus, needs to be supported by structures and institutions which make possible human freedom and the realization of values. On the other hand, actual structures and institutions which have grown up in history do not have *general validity;* they are changeable. This gives rise to the specific ethical demand to change them where, as a result of changed circumstances, they enslave and debase men rather than liberate them and give them protection.

IV. The Conditioning of People and Culture by Time and Space

Time and space, the historical and geographical situation of peoples and cultures, are also an anthropological constant from which no man can detach himself.

Here, first of all, we are confronted with a dialectical tension between nature and history which cannot ever be removed, even by the best possible social structure. Nature and history come together in particular human cultures. Their dialectic is a given one, which is an element of our transitory human existence and of which death is only an extreme exponent, a boundary situation. That of itself means that apart from some forms of suffering which can for the most part be removed by man, there are forms of suffering and threats to life on which man can have no influence through technology and social intervention. This is where the question of the *meaning* of humanity emerges. The historicity and thus the finality of man, which he does not know how to escape so that he can adopt a standpoint outside time, makes him understand his humanity also as a *hermeneutical* undertaking, i.e., as a task of *understanding* his own situation and unmasking critically the meaninglessness that man brings about in history. Of course man can be helped in this attempt to understand himself, which also involves the question of truth and falsehood, by a variety of empirical, analytical and theoretical sciences, but at the same time he is conscious of the experience that the truth for man is only possible as *remembered* truth which at the same time is to be *realized.* If understanding is the original way in which men *experience,* this understanding is generally the same as history itself. That means that the presumption of adopting a standpoint outside *historical* action and thought is a danger to true humanity.

Numerous other problems are given with this constant. I shall only point to some of them. There can be historical and even geographically conditioned attainments which, although they appear late in human history and in particular places, and thus cannot be called necessary or universal *a priori* presuppositions, cannot be regarded *here and now* as random or arbitrary. Here values have grown up requiring norms which apply, for example, to highly industrialized and advanced cultural conditions in which Western men live, and which need not apply directly in other cultures.

Some examples may be enough. Because of their general prosperity, Western men have a duty to international solidarity, above all towards poor countries (regardless of the historical question of how far they themselves are the historical cause of the poverty of these poor countries). (This obligation also arises from the duties resulting from the second and third anthropological constants.) It also follows on the basis of these same constants, which produce the historical and geographical limitations of any culture, that taking into account the limited potential of the imagination of men in a particular culture, critical remembrance of the great traditions of mankind, including its great religious traditions, will be a necessary stimulus in the search for norms for action which here and now further healthy and realizable humanity (this critical remembrance is an element in man's hermeneutical enterprise, in which he seeks illumination for his coming action).

Finally, this fourth anthropological constant also reminds us of the fact that the explicit discovery of these *constitutive constants* has only come about in a historical process: their coming to consciousness is already a fruit of human hermeneutical practice.

V. Mutual Relationship of Theory and Practice

The essential relationship between theory and practice is likewise an anthropological constant. It is a constant insofar as through this relationship human culture, as a hermeneutical undertaking or an understanding of meaning, and as an undertaking of changing meaning and improving the world, needs *permanence*. On a sub-human level, i.e., in the animal world, permanence and the possibility of the survival of the species and the individual are ensured by instinct and the elasticity with which it can adapt itself to changed or changing conditions, and, finally, by the law of the survival of the fittest in the struggle for life. Now unless men want to make their own history into a kind of spiritual Darwinism, a history in which only will and thought, the power of the strongest and the victor, dictate to us what is good and true for our humanity, then on the human level a combination of theory and practice will be the only humanly responsible guarantee of a permanent culture which is increasingly worthy of man—of what brings man *salvation*.

VI. The Religious and "Para-Religious" Consciousness of Man

The "utopian" element in human consciousness also seems to me to be an anthropological constant, and a fundamental one at that.

Here we are concerned with man's future (see above). What kind of future does he want? Under this utopian element I would place a variety of different conservative or progressive totalitarian conceptions which make it possible for man in society in some way to make sense of contingency or finitude, impermanence and the problems of suffering, fiasco, failure and death which it presents, or to overcome them. In other words, I am talking about the way in which a particular society has given specific form to the hermeneutical process in everyday life (see the fourth constant) or looks for another social system and another future in protest against the existing attribution of "meaning." These are totalitarian approaches which teach us to experience human life and society, now or in the future, as a good, meaningful and happy totality for man—a vision and a way of life which seek to give meaning and context to human existence in this world (even if only in a distant future).

Here we find "totalitarian views" of both a religious and a non-religious kind—views of life, views of society, world-views and general theories of life in which men express what ultimately inspires them, what humanity they choose in the last resort, what they really live for and what makes life worth living. All these can also be called *cognitive models of reality*, which interpret the whole of nature and history in theory and practice, and now or later allow it to be experienced as a "meaningful whole" (yet to be realized).

In most, though not all, of these "utopias" man is understood as an active *subject* who furthers humanity, interpreted as being good and true, and the establishment of a good human world, though on the other hand individuals are not personally responsible for the whole of history and its outcome. For some, this all-controlling principle is fate or *fatum*, for others evolution, for yet others humanity, the "genre man" as the universal subject of the whole of history, or, less definitely, nature. For religious men this is the living God, the Lord of history. But no matter what form such a totalitarian view may take—unless one glorifies nihilism and professes the absurdity of human life—it is always a *form of faith*, in the sense of a "utopia" which cannot be scientifically demonstrated, or at least can never be completely rationalized. And so in fact "Without faith you're as good as dead." In this sense "faith," the ground for hope is an anthropological constant throughout human history, a constant without which human life and action worthy of men and capable of realization become impossible: man loses his identity and either ends up in a neurotic state or irrationally takes refuge in horoscopes and all kinds of *mirabilia*. Furthermore, faith and hope are strengthened as necessary human constants by the nihilistic claim which calls livable humanity an absurdity and thus has no faith and no hope. That implies that faith and hope—whatever their content—are part of the health and integrity, the worthwhileness and "wholeness" of our humanity. For those who believe in God, this implies that *religion* is an anthropological constant without which human salvation, redemption and true liberation are impossible. In other words, that any liberation which by-passes a *religious redemption* is only a partial liberation, and furthermore, if it claims to be the *total* liberation of man by nature, destroys a real dimension of humanity and in the last resort uproots man instead of liberating him.

VII. Irreducible Synthesis of These Six Dimensions

Insofar as the six anthropological constants which we have discussed form a *synthesis*, human culture is in fact an *irreducible autonomous reality* (which cannot be reduced either idealistically or materialistically). The reality which heals men and brings them salvation lies in this synthesis (and therefore the synthesis itself must be called an anthropological constant). The six constants influence one another and go over into one another. They delineate man's basic form and hold one another in equipoise. It may sound fine and even right to talk of the priority of "spiritual values," but such talk can in reality at the same time destroy the material presuppositions and implications of "the spiritual," *to the detriment of* these spiritual values. Failure to recognize one of these profoundly human constants uproots the whole, including its "spiritual" component. It damages man and his society and distorts the whole of human culture. Whether consciously or not—even under the flag of the "primacy of the spiritual"—this represents an attack on true and good, happy and free humanity.

On the other hand, it may have become clear from what has already been said that these anthropological constants, which open up a perspective on the fundamental values of "humanity," in no way provide us with specific *norms* which must apply here and now, taking into account our objective form of society and given culture, in order to arrive at conditions more worthy of man. As I said, these constants simply outline, as it were, the system of coordinates in which specific norms must be sought through general considerations and after an analysis and interpretation of the position of the person in it. The minimum requirement for starting—and perhaps this too is an important factor in considering what is specifically "worthy of man"—is that we should be at the *level of awareness of the problem which has already been achieved.* From that point we can then carry out an analysis of the gulf between ideal and reality, on the basis of negative experiences or experiences of contrast, and also on the basis of experiences which we have already had, in the light of what is seen to be "utopia." This differential analysis will show the *direction* which we must take (always in the form of different possibilities), a direction which we have to agree in defining and for which we have to make urgent specific norms which are valid here and now.

I said that there would always be different possibilities. For men have very different views both of the details of this utopian element in our human consciousness and of the analysis and above all the interpretation of the result of this analysis (for a utopian consciousness with a particular direction is always involved *in* the manner of this analysis). This gives rise, even in scientific analysis (which takes place in conscious or unconscious framework of interpretation), to *pluralism* even in the sphere of specific norms—even when people recognize the same *basic values* to which the "anthropological constants" draw our attention. However, the proposed norms which we ourselves adopt at our own risk must also be tested for inner logic and discussed in dialogue if we are also to challenge others with them. Even if their fundamental *inspiration* comes, say, from a religious belief in God, *ethical* norms, i.e., norms which make life more worthy of men, must be capable of being given a rational foundation in valid inter-subjective discussion, i.e., discussion which is accessible to all rational men. None of the conversation partners can hide behind a threadbare "I can see something that you can't" and nevertheless compel others simply to accept this norm. All too often in discussions the initial situation can be of this kind: that one of the conversation partners sees something that others do not. But in that case the others must also be enlightened in a free and rational process of communication. No one can appeal here to a "zone of tranquillity" (even if other conversation partners cannot *per se* arrive at a consensus on the basis of the arguments presented). One of the tasks of a livable modern humanity will be that of learning to live with different conceptions of specific norms for a worthwhile human life which is called for here and now. The pain of this pluralism is part of our *condition humaine,* above all in modern times; we must cope with it, and not by means of the dictatorial rejection of other conceptions. This art is also an element of true, good and happy humanity within the limitations of our historicity and transitoriness— that is, unless we want to become "megalomaniacs" who have got it in their heads that they can step out of their human finitude. However, the concern for the salvation of each and every individual cannot on the other hand simply begin from "politics" as the so-called art of the possible, what can be done or achieved. Politics, rather, is the difficult art of making possible what is *necessary* for human salvation.

Thus *Christian salvation,* in the centuries-old biblical tradition called redemption, and meant as salvation from God *for men,* is concerned with the whole system of coordinates in which man can really be man. This salvation—the wholeness of man—cannot just be sought in one or other of these constants, say exclusively in "ecological appeals," in an exclusive "be nice to one another," in the exclusive overthrow of an economic system (whether Marxist or capitalist), or in exclusively mystical experiences: "Alleluia, he is risen!" On the other hand, the *synthesis* of all this is clearly an "already now" and a "not yet." The way in which human failure and human shortcomings are coped with must be termed a form of "liberation" (and perhaps its most important form). In that case that might then be the all-embracing "anthropological constant" in which Jesus the Christ wanted to go before us. [1977]

2/ The Growth of Experience into Knowledge: I

The school of De Petter is in accord with that of Maréchal in affirming that concepts as such cannot reach reality or truth, and therefore that they can do so only as elements of a greater whole. In addition, this trend of thought also affirms that a non-conceptual aspect is the basis of the validity of our conceptual knowledge. Maréchal did not, however, situate this non-conceptual aspect formally in a real intellectual element, but in an extra-intellectual element—that is, in the dynamism of the human spirit. De Petter and his followers, on the other hand, speak of a non-conceptual dimension of knowledge itself, and thus of an "objective dynamism"—that is, of an objective dynamic element in the contents themselves of our knowledge, which themselves refer to the infinite.

According to De Petter, the concept is ". . . a limited expression of an awareness of reality that is in itself unexpressed, implicit, and pre-conceptual." This pre-conceptual awareness of reality is in itself not open to appropriate expression. Our concepts refer to this non-conceptual awareness essentially as to something that they aim to express, but to which they can only give inadequate and limited expression. It is therefore not an extra-intellectual dimension—the dynamism of the human spirit—that enables us to reach reality in our concepts, but a non-conceptual consciousness through which we become aware of the inadequacy of our concepts, and thus transcend our conceptual knowledge and approach reality, although in a manner that is no longer open to expression. According to this view, the concept, or the "conceived," has a value of a definite *reference* to the reality, which is, however, not grasped or possessed by it. By virtue of the inexpressible and non-conceptual consciousness which is implied in our explicit or conceptual knowledge, or in which this conceptual knowledge is included, the concept indicates the objective direction in which reality is to be found, and—what is more—indicates a *definite* direction— the direction which is inwardly pointed out by the abstract conceptual content. Therefore, although concepts are insufficient and even do not reach reality in themselves—that is, seen in their exclusive abstract character—they have a certainly inadequate but nonetheless real truth and validity as included in the non-conceptual consciousness, because they—and they alone—impart a direction and meaning to the transcending beyond the concepts to reality. Experience and conceptual thought thus together constitute our single knowledge of reality. [1954]

3/ *The Growth of Experience into Knowledge: II*

On the one hand, experience presumes that *something* (an occurrence in nature and history, contact with another human being, etc.) is to be experienced; on the other hand, the experience of this occurrence presumes an interpretive framework which co-determines what we experience. Learning from experience comes about by bringing new individual experiences into connection with knowledge we have already gained and experiences we have already had. This brings about a dialectic. The entirety of previous experience becomes a new interpretive framework or "horizon of experience," within which we interpret new experiences. At the same time, however, new individual experiences subject this interpretive framework to criticism and correct it, or allow previous experience to be seen in a new connection. In other words, our experience always occurs within an already established interpretive framework, which in the last analysis is nothing other than cumulative-personal and collective experience, a tradition of experience. This interpretive framework, as the whole into which individual experience is taken up, gives this individual experience significance as an experience of meaning. Thereby we ought not lose sight of the fact that the interpretive framework itself comes about in the same way as all of our other experiences in the present. The earlier, more limited cumulative experience served as an interpretive framework or horizon of experience into which new experiences (which now belong to our interpretive framework) were taken up in a critical fashion. [1980]

4/ *How Experience Gains Authority*

Experiences of meaning have authority because they reveal meaning. To understand this, we must consider, however, different assumptions, in order to clarify whether we are creating meaning out of our own fantasy or whether meaning is revealing itself to us.

Human, experiencing consciousness, also insofar as it is the object of the revealing word of God, is not a *tabula rasa*. Revelation, therefore, never occurs in a psychic and social vacuum. Some aspects of this complex structure of human experience need to be illuminated here briefly.

(a) Human consciousness has the capacity to bring to expression what is experienced. This bringing to expression occurs in language, through the medium of images and concepts, connotations and emotions, which have already been part of a longer history, and form part of the heritage of the culture in which we live, carrying with them social and economic implications as well. World views and images of humanity already determined are active in language; language is really the first world project in which anyone is educated and lives. The expressions and forms which give shape to experiences (of faith), have their origin in the human repository of imagery which is itself dependent upon historical experiences. These experiences, for their part, have to do with each individual's personal situation and with the collective sociocultural and social emotional contexts of life. Without some kind of active articulation, there is no validity and no truth, and therefore no experience of revelation either. Experiences (of faith) cannot therefore bypass cognitive human activity as it expresses itself in language. Experiences brought to expression which create moments of alienation must therefore be analyzed critically, if experience, expressed in an already established language, wishes to manifest its authority.

(b) As we have learned from "masters of suspicion" such as Marx, Feuerbach, Nietzsche, Freud and others, human consciousness also has an ability to bring to expression things which, once brought to expression, obliterate precisely that which was supposed to be expressed. That which should have come to expression is, psychically or socially, "repressed." If experience is to be what it is supposed to be, then it must be examined in light of this possibility of repression.

(c) The claim to so-called immediate experience also needs to be critically examined. The concrete "objective form of society" in which, for example, we in the West live, does not exist only outside of us, but also has an effect on our interiority, and there becomes its own form of consciousness. Because experience is also socioeconomically mediated, experience can only become what it is supposed to be, be authoritative, and give direction, if it critically thinks through the conditions which gave rise to it. On the other hand, there is no basis for claiming that an analysis of the actual history of the origin of experiences as such is already a critique of, or denial of, their validity and their revelation of truth. Knowledge of a process of historical development and critique of logical coherence, of validity and truth, are methodically two distinct problems. However, the knowledge of how experiences and attempts at meaning came about can serve to eliminate elements which try to put them beyond criticism.

(d) As we said, experiences are mediated socially and politically. But one cannot be satisfied with this general statement. A precise analysis of the situation is necessary, if basic experiences are to manifest their own original authority. Such analyses have made evident that our actual socioeconomic culture is internally determined by bourgeois ideology which has shaped our society since the Enlightenment and has brought this society under the domination of a utilitarian individualism. Society in the East, on the other hand, is characterized above all by an antihistory of a historical-materialist dialectic. What is striking everywhere in our society is a facile speaking about *the* human subject, humanity in general, and universality, which upon analysis appears to mean either the bourgeois subject, who is already socioeconomically disenfranchised, or the communist comrade ("what is communist is human, what is human is communist"). Whoever is unaware of this ideological implication when analyzing basic human experiences (which is frequently the case in so-called humanistic psychology, e.g., that of Abraham Maslow) discovers a hierarchy of values in basic human experiences, values which are then called "universally human." In reality, however, they represent to a great extent the basic values of a bourgeois, economically disenfranchised society, a society in which the socially and economically oppressed can in no way recognize themselves. Moreover, one must realize that the dialectic itself is taken up into history. At the present time technical rationality is increasingly being fused with the rationality of domination in East and West, which is resulting in the great oppositions in the world shifting to an opposition between north (rich countries) and south (poor countries). This is all of fundamental significance for a praxis of faith within the horizon of experiences of the world.

(e) Experiences do not only interpret, they do not only use previously established concepts and images, to express what has been perceived.

Beyond that they work with models and theories, humanly created, which are to make the greatest number of experiential phenomena as simple and as clearly intelligible as possible. Statements (of faith) as expressions of experiences (of faith) are therefore not simply "pure" reproductions of certain "immediate experiences," but also products of human theory. Dogmatizations, either of immediate experience or of models, are therefore to be avoided.

(f) There exists in human consciousness beyond this an active relation between the (personal and collective) unconscious and reflective consciousness. This provides perceiving consciousness with a projective structure. Symbolizing activity, especially evident in experiences of transcendence, takes place not in the first instance on the conscious, reflective level, but rather at the transition from the unconscious to consciousness. Besides their value as expressive of reality, symbols also connect consciousness with the stream of the entire conscious world. Since the work of C. G. Jung one can hardly deny that unconscious forces are also at work in the interpretive articulations of religious experiences. But that does not in itself imply that that which is experienced as revelation is nothing other than the unconscious activity of the human mind. The projective aspect of human experiences can therefore be valued in a positive fashion. In doing so, one is properly distinguishing between "archetypal" symbols and "cultural" symbols ("historical master images"), however much the two may intermesh.

Symbols, such as the Reign of God, Black Power, La Grandeur française, and so forth, are ideas of power which also create a future. These archetypes and symbols are religiously neutral in themselves. They are indeterminant and undirected, and can therefore be the bearers of experiences of revelation. The presence of an influence of this flow of the unconscious says nothing as such for or against an authentic experience of revelation, which of course in no way needs to be completed solely on the level of reflective consciousness. But by the same token analyzing only the psychic presuppositions and implications of experiences of faith is equally incomplete and inexact.

(g) Finally, individual experiences are never isolated acts. They are taken up into a person's total psychic life. Seen in this manner, all psychic—also religious—experiences emerge from a dark and, for the most part, unconscious ground. "Purely" religious experiences (which are already experiences with experiences) are also for this reason an abstraction.

It is already evident from this brief description of the complex structure of human experiences that experience is in no way a one-dimensional phenomenon. And beyond that, precisely the contemporary and new insight into this complex structure, as well as the increasing consciousness of the mutability, and of the actual changes in our society, has caused a "new form of consciousness" to come about, which has been called "Dauerreflexion" (continuing reflection). Everything handed down is critically questioned.

Experience is completed therefore in a dialectical process: in an interplay of perceiving (within a certain interpretive framework) with thinking, and of thinking with perceiving. Experience gains authority first in a reflected experience. To be sure, reason does not stand at the beginning of this process as its genesis, but an authoritative experience implies reason and critical rationality. Thinking makes experience possible, and experience makes new thinking necessary. Our thinking remains hollow if it does not continually return to living experiences, which for their part remain irrational without reflective reason. The authority of experience is finally a competence arising *out of* experiences and *for* new experiences.

If they are critically reflected upon, human experiences have in fact authority and validity as revelation of reality or of that not conceived and not produced by human beings. They have a cognitive, critical and productive or liberating power in the enduring search of humanity for truth and goodness, for justice and human happiness. However, our experiences must occur under the condition of freedom, and also get space in our institutions. For institutional violence–as well as a one-track, purely technical-scientific civilization, which under societal pressure is appraised as the single dominant cultural value–can make people in that culture experience-poor and manipulate all their experiences. Of course, new experiences do not have authority solely and entirely on the basis of their being new: no reasoning person would claim such. For we have no guarantee anywhere in our history that the historical course of human experiences can only be progressive and not regressive. "Discernment of spirits," thanks to critical remembrances of experiences past among other things, is part of what is called experiential competence and the authority of experience. [1980]

2

Living in Human Society

COMMENTARY

These five selections situate human experience within society. While issues of society have concerned Schillebeeckx since the very beginning, they have become increasingly central in his thought since his reflections on secularization in the mid-1960s.

Selection 5 represents his thought on secularization from the late 1970s, and it also gives a good outline of how he sees religion functioning in a secularized society. It also touches upon how experience can be religious experience in such situations. Selection 6 focuses upon one theme within this complex: the issue of science and technology, and theology's relationship to it.

Selections 7 through 9 deal with a central theme in Schillebeeckx's thought: suffering in human experience. Suffering, as selection 7 points out, has both positive and negative aspects. As one of the most acute forms of human experience, it provides much for reflection on the human condition. Schillebeeckx also gives a response to the classical theological question of theodicy, or the problem of reconciling the idea of a good and all-powerful God with the presence of evil in the world.

Selections 8 and 9 focus on the revelatory moment of suffering, which Schillebeeckx calls the contrast experience.. This moment reveals the difference between what is and what ought to be or will be. The power of this moment, working out that difference dialectically, is in its negation of that difference; that is, moving away from what ought not to be (suffering in the present) toward what ought to be (a full sense of humanity, or humanum, in the future). The term "negative dialectics" is borrowed from the German philosopher Theodor Adorno, who was part of the first generation of the Frankfurt school of social critical theory. The second

45

generation of that same school, best represented by Jürgen Habermas, will be influential in Schillebeeckx's theory of society and theology from the 1970s on. The term "critical negativity" comes to replace "negative dialectics" in Schillebeeckx's later work.

5/ *Experience and Religion in Contemporary Society*

However, the disjunction between faith as it is actually practised and contemporary experiences becomes especially critical in a modern world in which religion is no longer the cement of society and is therefore no longer reinforced by social and cultural life. This new situation exposes religion to all kinds of new risks, such as the tendency to retreat into the limited sphere of privacy where it still seems to have a place; or the tendency to reduce religion to a school of social ethics (in terms of an ethical revival or a form of social criticism) in order above all to seek for society, particularly by means of macro-ethics, the integrating force without which no religion can survive; or, finally, the tendency to long nostalgically for the old view of the church in which religion was the all-embracing and integrating factor of society.

Nowadays the institutional aspects of all religions have been opened up to serious questioning, but not a single sociological analysis has shown that the religious and spiritual dimensions of human life have ceased to fascinate people. And although institutions and dogmatic positions are essential aspects of religion, they remain subordinate to religious experience, which is concerned with God, i.e., to the religious orientation of faith.

On the other hand, we must note that especially in a secularized world, the experience of alienation makes itself felt in a new and more urgent way, above all because secular belief in progress on the basis of science and technology has been dealt such a powerful blow in modern times. The consequence of all this is that experiences can seldom, if ever, be interpreted unequivocally as religious experiences. However, if it is not to perish, religion can never give up its efforts towards ultimate integration, even if they may take a different form from those of former years. The integrating effect of religion no longer serves the function that it once did; religion is no longer needed to maintain the basic values of a society or to legitimate social institutions which in former times did not seem capable of supporting themselves. Rather, we might say that the experiences which make modern people secular at the same time confront us with new experiences and new choices. In a secularized world, people no longer undergo religious experience in an exalted or passive way; it is no longer a kind of "high"—that is suspect from the start. As we know, the contemporary religious attitude reflects a personal and reflective response to experiences which can point in different directions, religious or non-religious. For all its appearance of immediacy, religion has, and always has had, a reflective element which does not necessarily do away with its spontaneity. What happens in a secular world is that this characteristic simply becomes more evident. Modern people reflect on certain experiences and interpret them, often tentatively, as religious. Our ambiguous experiences are both positive and negative: experiences of totality and joy, of finitude, suffering and liberation. These confront modern people with a choice, in other words, they are an invitation to an experience with experiences. Life in a void, which may come to an end at any moment, along with freedom as a permanent challenge and burden, together produce a feeling of the precariousness of our existence, which is perhaps more intense now than ever before. Furthermore, it is precisely in their social successes that people feel most threatened. The threat itself takes on a "transcendent" allure. Experiences of this kind are not in themselves religious (some poeple even give up their old beliefs as a result), but they do bring man up against a limit, against something infinite, whether this is a conviction that the naked and sheer factuality of existence is the infinitely sombre last word, or the positive belief that there is a merciful and transcendent reality. These ambiguous experiences confront us with a choice; not a cerebral choice, but an experience with these ambivalent experiences which cry out to be interpreted in a meaningful way. But the transition from vague, undirected and ambiguous experiences to a positive religious experience leads (in any religious interpretation) to an integration of the first ambivalent experiences into a new experience, of deliberately anticipated totality, i.e., religion. Anyone who undergoes this has an alternative, viz. religious experience with human experiences.

However, this experience-with-experiences never in fact takes place in the abstract nor through isolated individuals; it always happens through someone who lives in a particular culture and in a tradition of religious experience, for example, Christian or Buddhist. This religious experience with ambivalent human experiences only becomes an experience of Christian faith when someone, as a result of what he has heard from Christians, arrives at the conviction *in* his experience-with-experiences that, "Yes, that's it; it's like that." In the end, what is proclaimed by churches in their message as a possibility for life which can also be experienced by others, and what these can provisionally call a "searchlight," becomes *in* the experience-with-experiences (within the given search-light) a highly personal act of Christian faith, a personal conviction of faith with a specific content of Christian faith. In a modern world people will no longer accept Christian belief simply on the authority of others; it will have to happen in and through an experience-with-experiences, which is interpreted in the light of what the church proclaims on the basis of a long history of Christian experience.

It looks as though for many people this will become the way to religion and Christianity, rather than by people becoming Christians at birth. [1978]

6/ *Science, Religion, and Society*

The past decades have taught us, not without pain and grief, that this arbitrary and unbridled Western concern for self-realization has not brought men salvation either personally or in the social and political sphere. Furthermore, our unrestrained economic expansion nurtured on a nineteenth-century myth of limitless progress has been achieved at the expense of people from other parts of the world and has threatened the environment in which we live to such a degree that the whole of mankind is endangered as a result. The programme of a total liberation of man by man at present seems to be the greatest threat to all humanity. The "modern Western world" is in particular need of salvation today, for liberation and redemption precisely from those dark powers which modern man has himself called to life. The demonic in our culture and society has taken on a different name and content from the demons of the ancient world and the Middle Ages, but it is no less real and just as threatening. I am not criticizing science, technology or industrialization in any way here, but rather those who have these powers and use them for their own personal, national and continental profit—and so much the worse for those who do not have the good fortune to live in a prosperous country or who are at best tolerated as immigrant workers. Is it not a supreme irony of history that science and technology, which since the seventeenth century we have hailed as the cultural forces which will finally deliver mankind from all those things from which religion has failed to deliver us—hunger, poverty, tyranny, war and historical destiny—at this moment represent, in the hands of men, the greatest threat to our future? "Knowledge is power," said Francis Bacon. But our domination over nature has led to the beginnings of the destruction of fundamental elements of life; our unrestrained economic growth threatens our human survival; control over genetic structures and the manipulation of them conjure up disturbing prospects for the future; and finally, the nuclear arms spiral twists higher and higher above our heads and given that a strategy of deterrence makes sense only if one is determined to use nuclear weapons if need be, this necessary determination in itself is enough to make this strategy inhuman and ethically indefensible. Neither science nor technology is to blame, but man. Once one gives these means an absolute character; once one invests them with a sacrality and an immunity characteristic of our modern world, they cease to contribute towards our freedom and become a threat to man and society. The sciences are children of their time and in their own intrinsic autonomy reflect the hesitations, the blind spots and even the sicknesses of their time. Science is no more purely objective than the other forms of knowledge; so it certainly does not have any letters patent by which in a legitimate way it can lay claim to the dominant role which it in fact exercises in Western society, at the expense of other kinds of cognitive relations with reality. The applied sciences are also an instrument of human will and are thus subject to the same distortions which affect it. Knowledge is power, but power delivered into the hands of an unfree liberty, itself the slave of greed, lust for power and personal or collective egoism and the uncontrolled need for security, is in fact power on the way towards corruption. It is a fact that science and technology cannot bring men their authentic salvation: "holiness" and wisdom. What they can do is make us considerably more competent, and that in itself is a blessing. Science and technology work miracles when they are used to bring about the freedom of others, solidarity among men and women. But in fact the sciences function as an instrument of power: power over nature, power over society and also power over men and women, even extending to power over their masculinity and femininity. Science is the key to the military power of nations; it is the secret of their economic and social prosperity—also at the expense of others. The trust placed in verifiable and falsifiable knowledge and in technological know-how as unique ways of removing human misery dominates the present-day cultural world, whether we look at Europe and North America, Russia and India, Japan or China.

Towards the end of the eighteenth century science seemed to be announcing the end of all religions, which was innocently thought to be a period of childlike ignorance in the history of humanity. Now that the year 2000 is approaching it is in fact science and technology themselves which compel us to raise more necessarily and more urgently than ever the religious question—if the question of human salvation is to retain any meaning at all. It is not science and technology which make us anxious, but their absolute claim to bring us salvation. We have come to see that human creativity implies the possibility of self-destruction. Science and technology, once acclaimed as the liberators of mankind, have subjected us to a new kind of social and historical fatalism. This historical irony is biting when we see how the East is seizing hold of Western technology and science for its material prosperity, while the West is looking to the East for its lost inwardness. Is it then our creative power itself which threatens the meaning of our history? Or is it that the finite creature is never in a position to understand and free itself? Is not the acceptance of a living relationship with the transcendent the deepest dimension of our finite human creativity and, as a result, the deepest and most extreme possibility of all humanism?

Now it is theology which seeks to preserve this faith and this hope in a liberating and saving power which overcomes evil and therefore refuses to be hypnotized by a catastrophic vision of things, despite the inextricable mixture of sense and nonsense at the heart of which we live. History can teach us that a humanism which in any society is founded exclusively or at least predominantly on science and technology, poses the threat of inhumanity to human beings and their society.

But if religion here has its irreplaceable word to say, this must be a religion concerned for man in the world, a religion which begins from faith in a liberating God and is interested in the human being in his specific historical and social context. Might there be another humanism, neither dogmatic nor threatening, and more universal, more humanist than the humanism of God himself, a God concerned for humanity who wants men to be concerned for humanity as well? But if the religions and the Christian churches want to proclaim this message with some credibility, they should begin by confessing that they have often obscured and even mutilated the face of God's humanity. Where religion or science is made absolute, rather than God himself, not only the image of God but mankind itself is disfigured: *ecce homo*—on the cross and on the many crosses which men have set up and keep setting up. Theology has also played its part here in the past. But whatever one thinks of contemporary theologians, one thing should be granted them: by means of a historical praxis of commitment to mysticism and politics, they are trying to discover the human face of God and, starting from there, to revive hope in a society, a humanity with a more human face.

Because the main task of theology is to preserve the transcendence of the God who loves men, hidden and yet so near, in the face of the idols which human beings set up, it must always be opposed to the positivistic claims that might be made by the sciences, no matter how valuable or how necessary they might be, to be the only relevant cognitive relationship to reality, and their claims to provide the only effective solution to vital human problems. But this very theology must in turn accept that unless it adopts a truly interdisciplinary approach, it is reduced to being an ideology. [1982]

7/ *Human Experience and Suffering*

Taught by our own specific experiences, we can accept that there are certain forms of suffering which enrich our humanity in a positive sense, which can even mature men so that they become thoroughly good and wise personalities. A man who has become mature through suffering compels wonderment, deep admiration, and reduces one to silence; one finds oneself enriched by the experience of such gentle wisdom which has grown through life. A world in which there was no place for suffering and sorrow, even for deep grief, would seem to be inhuman, a world of robots, even an unreal world. In almost all languages, people rightly speak of the "school of suffering." In our human world, great things are evidently born only in suffering.

Furthermore, a certain dose of suffering undergone can make us sensitive to other men. Love and attractiveness, as openness towards others, are at the same time the capacity to suffer: vulnerability. We found it striking that the wise men of the Stoa, who felt themselves to be above true sorrow, consistently rejected sensitive compassion for suffering men. They knew no sorrow, but also . . . no love. But believing love of God also knows its own fragments of suffering. Not all suffering is meaningless. That is part of the sum of human wisdom, as the whole of human history bears witness.

Furthermore, a certain amount of suffering transforms men, ourselves and others; not only in lesser things, but above all when it is suffering for a good, righteous or holy cause which is close to a man's heart. At the same time, however, human experience shows that this is not suffering which man chooses or seeks for himself. What man does choose is the cause for which he gives himself wholly. That is vocation: obedience towards the good which summons us and which we think worth the trouble: man is better than the suffering which can bring this sacrifice with it. Thus suffering takes on significance as the *actual* implication of a call to, and a responsibility for, a true and good cause (fellow man, God). In *that* sense, this suffering is on the one hand not sought, and on the other freely accepted as an actual and possible consequence of a particular commitment. In this kind of suffering man is not concentrated on himself, nor on his own suffering, but on the cause which he takes up. All this is equally true of religious sacrifice. Such sacrifice is experienced as sacrificial love: for Christians that means "participating in the suffering of Jesus Christ" (2 Cor 1:5).

Despite all these true considerations, however, there is an *excess* of suffering and evil in our history. There is a barbarous excess, for all the explanations and interpretations. There is too much *unmerited* and *senseless* suffering for us to be able to give an ethical, hermeneutical and ontological analysis of our disaster. There is suffering which is not even suffering "for a good cause," but suffering in which men, without finding meaning for themselves, are simply made the crude victims of an evil cause which serves others. Furthermore, this suffering is the alpha and omega of the whole history of mankind; it is the scarlet thread by which this historical fragment is recognizable as human history: history is "an ecumene of suffering." Because of their historical extent and their historical density, evil and suffering are the dark fleck in our history, a fleck which no one can remove by an explanation or interpretation which is able to give it an understandable place in a rational and meaningful whole. Or does someone perhaps want to give Buchenwald, Auschwitz or Vietnam (or whatever else) a specific structural place in the divine plan, which, as Christians believe, directs our history? No man, at any rate, who thinks it important to be a man and to be treated as a man will do so. And then we have still not said anything about the unmerited suffering of so many of the nameless among us, in our immediate neighbourhood. Perhaps including our own suffering that we do not understand. *We* cannot justify God. Of course we are not God, and we think of God's omnipotence and goodness with petty human terms. Yes, but that does not make the scandalous history of human suffering which we have to bear, with all its negativity, any less real.

Thus suffering and evil can provoke scandal; however, they are not a *problem*, but an unfathomable, theoretically incomprehensible *mystery* (unless one reduces it—against all human experience of suffering—to a *particular* sector of human suffering which we clearly have within our grasp, both scientifically and technologically). One can objectify a problem and take one's distance from it; this makes a detached explanation possible. But suffering and evil in our human history are also *my* suffering, *my* evil, *my* agony and *my* death. They cannot be objectified. In a moving passage in *The Brothers Karamazov,* Dostoievsky makes Ivan say that if this great universe, with its wonderful realities and splendid events, is bought at the cost of the tears of an innocent child, then he will politely refuse to accept such splendour from the hands of the Creator. Human reason cannot in fact cope with concentrated historical suffering and evil. Here the human Logos, human rationality fails: it cannot give any explanation.

If the powers of human explanation and interpretation are incapable of giving a meaningful explanation of suffering and evil, might not logic and everyone's dreams suggest that perhaps human *action* can provide a solution? In connection with this, it must first be conceded that if we cannot justify evil and the unfathomable mass of innocent suffering, or explain it as the *unavoidable* obverse of God's fundamental plan in his will for good, then the only meaningful reaction to this history of suffering is in fact to offer resistance, to act in a way meant to turn history to good effect. That is also urgently necessary. For one can refuse to allow evil the right to exist, on the basis of the insight that it has no justification for existence, and therefore refuse to give a theoretical answer to what is experienced as the darker reality of evil in its specific historical proportions and distortions. However, that is only consistent and coherent if this refusal is linked with a powerful involvement in resistance against all forms of evil. That means that *in practice*, too, people must refuse to allow evil the right to exist: they must espouse the cause of the good and refuse to treat evil on the same level as good.

In theory, people may not be in a position to *explain* suffering and evil, but the *remembrance* of what has happened in very specific suffering in a particular historical context also belongs to the structure of human reason or critical rationality. The history of these specific remembrances therefore remains an inner stimulus for practical reason which seeks to be liberating and active. Human reason may not simply brush aside these admonitory remembrances if it still wants to remain *critical* reason.

The only question is whether at the same time this implies that the practical task with which men find themselves confronted as a result of the many accounts of contrasting experiences in our history of human suffering can also in fact be brought to a successful conclusion. For human action in resistance against evil is itself subject to criticism, at least in its claim to totality—not through any theory, much less through religious and Christian faith, but through a specific reality of experience, part of human life: the tension between "nature" and "history" which makes up man's transitory life and can never be removed, a dialectic of which death is merely an extreme exponent, the boundary situation. Thus at the deepest level, at the level of our outline of an earthly, human future, we are at the same time confronted with the final fiasco of our efforts at resisting evil. Death above all shows that we are deluded if we think that we can realize on earth a true, perfect and universal salvation for all and for every individual. However, human salvation is only salvation, being whole, when it is universal and complete. There cannot really be talk of salvation as long as there is still suffering, oppression and unhappiness alongside the personal happiness that we experience, in the immediate vicinity or further afield.

All this means that we cannot look for the *ground* of suffering in God, although suffering brings the believer directly up against God.

The Christian message does not give an *explanation* of evil or our history of suffering. That must be made clear from the start. Even for Christians, suffering remains impenetrable and incomprehensible, and provokes rebellion. Nor will the Christian blasphemously claim that God himself required the death of Jesus as compensation for what *we* make of our history. This sadistic mysticism of suffering is certainly alien to the most authentic tendencies of the great Christian tradition, at the very least. Nor can one follow Jürgen Moltmann in solving the problem of suffering by "eternalizing" suffering in God, in the opinion that in the last resort this gives suffering some splendour. According to Moltmann, Jesus not only shows solidarity "with publicans and sinners," with the outcast and those who are everywhere excluded; not only has God himself identified him with the outcast; no, God himself has cast him out as a sacrifice for our sins. The difficulty in this conception is that it ascribes to God what has in fact been done to Jesus by the history of human injustice. Hence I think that in soteriology or the doctrine of redemption we are on a false trail, despite the deep and correct insight here that God is the great fellow-sufferer, who is concerned for our history. [1977].

8/ Contrast Experiences

Contrast experience, especially in the memory of the actual human history of accumulated suffering, possesses a special epistemological value and power, which cannot be deduced from a goal-centered "Herrschaftswissen" (the form of knowledge peculiar to science and technology), nor from the diverse forms of contemplative, aesthetic, ludic, or non-directive knowledge. The peculiar epistemological value of the contrast experience of suffering as a result of injustice is *critical:* critical of both contemplative and scientific-technological forms of knowing. It is critical of the purely contemplative perception of the whole, because this form already lives out universal reconciliation in its contemplative or liturgical celebration. But it is also critical of the world-dominating knowledge of science and technology, because this form as such presumes that human beings are only dominating subjects and ignores the ethical priority to which those who suffer among us have a right. Whoever suffers comes into resistance against the purely contemplative person, or shall we say, Eastern culture. But whoever suffers also comes into resistance against the onesided economics of science and technology, which can put someone on the moon, but gives no priority to the resolution of sublunar suffering. In other words, those who suffer come into resistance also against the technocratic West. What is the meaning of this datum?

The epistemological value peculiar to suffering is not only its being critical of both positive forms of human knowing. In a dialectical way it can be the link between the epistemological possibilities of the human psyche: contemplative and active forms of knowing. I am personally convinced that it is the contrast experience of suffering (with its implicit ethical claim) which alone is in the position to connect the two internally, because it alone has characteristics of both. On the one hand, experiences of suffering just happen to a person, even though this form of experience is a negative mis-experience, thus completely different from the experiences which also just happen but are positive experiences of joy in contemplative, ludic and aesthetic occurrences. On the other hand, the experience of suffering in the sense of a contrast experience or critical negativity creates a bridge toward a possible praxis, which wishes to remove both the suffering and its causes. On the basis of this internal affinity with both contemplative and nature-dominating knowledge, albeit in critical negativity, I call the peculiarly "contemplative" epistemological power of suffering a practical-critical one, that is, a critical epistemological power which initiates a new praxis, which opens up a better future which it really wants to bring about (although it remains a question whether it will succeed). All this means, if I have seen things correctly, that given the "human condition" and our actual social culture, contemplation and action can only be connected internally, in a paradoxical but nonetheless real way, through the ethical critique of the accumulated history of humanity's suffering, if it is to lead to a possible realization of meaning. As a *contrast* experience, the experience of suffering presumes, after all, an implicit impulse toward happiness. And as an experience of injustice, it presumes at least a dim consciousness of the positive prospects of human integrity. As a contrast experience, it implies indirectly a consciousness of an appeal of and to the *humanum*. In this sense, activity which overcomes suffering is only possible on the basis of at least an implicit or inchoate anticipation of a possible, *coming* universal meaning.

In opposition to the goal-directed knowledge of science and technology, and also to the "non-directive" knowledge of contemplation, the peculiar epistemological value of the contrast experience of suffering is a knowledge which asks for a *future* and opens the way to it. Thus, the concept "future" makes its entrance into our considerations, alongside the concepts of "goal-directed" and "non-directive." For on the basis of its double-track peculiarity of being related to both contemplation and to action, and its ethical character of protest, the experience of suffering is a knowledge which does not ask for goal-directed or a non-directive form, but for a *future:* for a future of more humanity and the coming elimination of the causes of injustice. For precisely as a passive mis-experience, this experience implies in its negativity an ethical resistance to passive resignation. It has a *critical* epistemological power which appeals to a praxis which opens up the future, a mode of action which does not subject itself to a taken-for-granted pandomination of a goal-directed technocracy, which is one of the causes of suffering. The contrast experience of suffering is thus the negative and dialectical coming to awareness of a longing for and an asking for a coming meaning, and coming, real freedom and happiness. It strives for a reconciling, "non-directive" contemplation, which is a (believing) perception of universal meaning, for the sake of connecting the experiencing of contrast with a new praxis which overcomes suffering and creates a new future. To this end, science and technology must also be brought into the picture, but then in service of a genuinely human policy formation and a *political* project for the future. [1972]

9/ *Negative Dialectics and the Humanum*

Man's quest for meaning is in fact answered in many different ways. This has resulted in a pluriformity of positive views of man which are not, as such, representative of mankind as a whole and cannot therefore form the basis for the universal claim of the Christian answer. If we were to confine ourselves purely to this dimension of reality, theology would become little more than a fashionable imitation of the contemporary way of life. Any serious method of correlation is bound to fail if it does not preserve the critical distance that we learn to acquire especially by remembering the past with a better future in mind. Without this critical distance, the present functions as an uncriticised pre-decision with regard to the Christian faith.

All the same, it is possible to distinguish, in all these human answers to man's deepest question about meaning, something that is common to all of them and therefore universal. This is, however, negative, although it is clearly sustained by an unexpressed positive sphere of meaning. Despite all pluralism, then, there is, in positive views of man, the element of a common search to realise the constantly threatened *humanum*.

It is impossible to formulate the positive content of this *humanum* without reverting to many different, fragmentary and mutually contradictory views. There is, however, at least this one common basis in all these different views of man: resistance to the threat to humanity. This critical negativity, or negative dialectics, is the universal pre-understanding of all positive views of man. It is not really in the first place knowledge, but a praxis which is motivated by hope and within which an element of knowledge that can be formulated in a theory is discernible. There is, among men, a critical solidarity over the threat to humanity. There is no question here of a vague ideal of humanity. The *humanum* that is sought only becomes a universally recognised value via a negative and indirect mediation, that is, via a resistance to the inhumane. All resistance to inhumane situations reveals, if only indirectly, at least an obscure consciousness of what must be confessed positively by human integrity; it manifests in a negative and indirect way the call of and to the *humanum*. As soon as this humane element is positively articulated, either theoretically or practically in a definite plan of action, a great many theoretical and practical projects come about at once. I regard these negative dialectics coming within a positive sphere of meaning which is, however, in its universality only implicit (it is a call to the *humanum)* as the universal pre-understanding not only of the pluralist answers that man gives to this call, but also of Christian talk about God, in other words, of the gospel. In a pluralist society such as ours, these negative dialectics must be seen as a critical resistance to the threat to the *humanum,* without being able to define this *humanum,* the form in which a universal experience is mediated. If this is taken as the point of departure, the Christian message does not, in order to be understood, need first to place itself at the mercy of one definite philosophy or one definite image of man out of all the philosophies or views of man that we know.

In view of the fact that all positive images of man, both theoretical and practical, can be broken up into many different and mutually contradictory views and plans of action, the Christian message or *kerygma* can only be geared to what is common to all— an unceasing resistance to the inhumane and a permanent search for the humane, a search that man himself tries to solve in the praxis of his life (even though this often results in inhumane behaviour). Christian identity has to do with human integrity, and even though the latter cannot be theoretically and practically defined in one all-embracing system, man's existential problem is, in it, inwardly linked with the Christian revelation. Universal resistance to alienation, inhumanity and the absence of freedom assumes, in Christianity, the form of a redemption by God which can be realised in and through the faith of people in history. The Christian answer is at one with man's universal protest against the inhumane, but at the same time Christian faith refuses to postulate a secular or universal subject of history, in other words, to point, either theoretically or practically, to a secular principle which would give unity to man's history of emancipation. The Christian answer reminds man that such a universal subject of history, which everyone is seeking, really exists, but cannot be given from history itself. Neither the human individual, nor the community nor any part of society, but only the living God is recognised in Christian faith (man's answer to Jesus Christ) as the universal subject of history. This is why the Christian answer views very critically all theories and plans of action which postulate a positive principle of unity within and from history. A theoretical or practical system of unity of this kind potentially leads to the totalitarian rule of one man or group over other men. This is why I regard the fact that the Christian answer is geared to the universally human pre-understanding as a critical solidarity with man's resistance to the inhumane. This resistance to what is inhumane, negative dialectics, which can also be found in the Christian answer, is at the same time a resistance to any secular, theoretical or practical, system of unity and this is so on the basis of God's promise that has been revealed in the resurrection from man's ultimate impotence, death. A life without alienation, a realm of freedom without injustice, really is the prospect before us and exists already as a positive possibility (see 2 Pet 3:13; Rev 21:4). But even Christians can only formulate this future in a negative way, in the form of a contrast. No definite plan of action has been given to them in revelation. The answer is a promise and at the same time it is critically negative.

This, then, prevents the principle of correlation of critical resistance as a universal pre-understanding of Christianity from being misused. This is a real danger. In the name of and appealing to "the threat to the *humanum*," men in history have themselves often been a threat to the *humanum*. A very striking example of this is, of course, nazism in Germany, but there have been several modern theories claiming to protect the *humanum* which have in fact resulted in a degradation of humanity. Christian faith resists any premature identification of the *humanum*. In its resistance and its protest, which is joined to the universally human protest, Christianity remains critical and insists that it cannot accept any uniform positive definition of the *humanum*. The power to realise this *humanum* and to bring about an individual and collective peace is reserved for God, the power of love. This is the "eschatological reservation."

Individually and collectively, man needs emancipation and redemption. However this may be formulated and however inhumanly it may sometimes be expressed, this is undoubtedly man's deepest experience.

The answer which Christianity gives to this deepest human need is this: it is right to look for man's emancipation and, what is more, this emancipation is a positive possibility as the grace of God which has to be given definite form in history, a form which is peace, justice and love.

Christian talk about God is therefore only negatively and indirectly open to universal understanding and acceptance, in other words, it takes place via the experience that the *humanum* is always threatened, perhaps above all by its premature positive identification. To the question of the meaning that is contained within the radical historical question that man himself is, man himself gives a practical answer: on the one hand, resistance to the inhumane, though this, on the other hand, often causes the *humanum* to be even further degraded through false identification. On the basis of a more accurate analysis, this could be extended to a satisfactory method of correlation. Such a method would not give a religious or theological answer to a non-religious or philosophical question. It would also indicate the context of human experience in which Christian talk about God can be heard in a way which is both secularly meaningful and universally intelligible. There is indeed a convergence or correlation between what is affirmed in the gospel message as a promise, a demand and a criticism and what man experiences as emancipation in his resistance to the threat to the *humanum* that he is seeking. The Christian message gives a counter-answer containing a promise and a criticism to the living praxis of mankind insofar as man is seeking an inner and a social *shalom* or peace. Whether this Christian answer is accepted or rejected, it cannot be denied that it is, as an answer in the form of promise, possibility, perspective, strength and criticism, historically relevant and meaningful to any man who is seeking the meaning of human life, whether individually or collectively, personally or politically and socially. In this way, the Christian message can be made intelligible. All the same, these negative dialectics need to be supplemented. [1970]

3

Toward a Full Humanity

COMMENTARY

This section looks at what Schillebeeckx sees the negative dialectics as moving toward: the future, where the fullness of meaning and of the humanum lies. If suffering provides the most profound entry into experience, the future keeps it from lapsing into meaninglessness and despair.

Selection 10 spells this out, how salvation is the opposite of suffering. It draws together the strands set out in the previous section and draws them toward a theology of the future, or eschatology. There are many references to analytic philosophy of language, with which Schillebeeckx was concerned at the time: "language games" (use of language governed by a given set of rules about what is meaningful), and "category mistake" (mixing apples and oranges from a linguistic point of view). It provides a clear statement of the importance of eschatology in his thought.

Selection 11 is an early statement of his major concerns for a theory of knowledge and the meaning of truth. While cast in an encounter between Neo-Thomism and phenomenology, the themes he presents continue to be part of his theory of truth: the dynamics of truth, the need for historical concreteness, and perspectivism (always viewing from a certain perspective).

Selections 12 and 13 weave together the range of the themes addressed thus far: meaning, suffering, truth, concreteness of action, and the meaning of universal truth. Universal meaning is mediated concretely in history, and must be truth for all if it is to be universal—not just for the powerful and the victors.

Selections 14 and 15 conclude Part I by bringing together the themes of anthropology and history within the framework of an eschatology. Selection 15 points to some of the concrete issues within that quest for a future.

10/ *The Struggle for a Full Humanity*

Because man experiences so much that is meaningless in his own life, in society and even in the churches, it is quite impossible for him to be reconciled with his fate, with his fellow men and with society as a whole. It is only possible for him to be fully reconciled with the whole of reality, that is, to be in a state of justification, when meaningfulness and meaninglessness are no longer insanely interwoven and when fully realised meaning is actively experienced. This situation can be described as "salvation," being whole. It can also be called the *eschaton* or perfect fulfilment of meaning without any threat, and *shalom* or eschatological peace stimulating us to establish peace here and now in our history.

We cannot simply stand still once we have accepted negative dialectics. It is even possible to say that this critical negativity is impossible and unintelligible without the justified trust that perfect meaningfulness and an experience of this meaningfulness are not entirely beyond our reach. As the "believing atheist," Ernst Bloch, has rightly said, an "objective hope" which makes subjective hope possible must correspond to the subjective hope which expresses itself negatively in resistance to every threat to the *humanum*. There can be no doubt that the incomplete character of our being as men as such imposes on us the task of constantly transcending ourselves. But can this incomplete character itself be, as some scholars claim, the basis which makes this transcendence of self possible and which will even bring it about? Cannot the history of men fail? Indeed, there is no need to look very far around us in the world to discover that men do make history fail.

Man can certainly avoid the question concerning the ultimate meaning of being man theoretically, that is in thought, but he cannot avoid it in action. He has in fact already answered this question in his human praxis, in a positive or a negative sense or by a nihilistic or sceptical attitude to life. He acts in the conviction that life itself is or is not worth living. In this, an important part is played by the datum of evil, the datum of what is, from the human point of view, meaningless. Evil has clearly been a datum of such great proportions in human history that neither man nor society can offer us any guarantee at all that we shall ever be able to overcome it. . . . It seems to me undeniable that human life includes particular experiences which are signs or glimpses of an ultimate total meaning of human life. All our negative experiences cannot brush aside the "nonetheless" of the trust which is revealed in man's critical resistance and which prevents us from simply surrendering man, human society and the world entirely to total meaninglessness. This trust in the ultimate meaning of human life seems to me to be the basic presupposition of man's action in history. . . .

It is therefore both possible and meaningful to regard, even apart from revelation, human life as more than simply meaninglessness, but as a manifestation of essential goodness, even if this manifestation is often impotent. In this consideration of reality from the point of view of man's question about the authentic fulfilment of his life, about salvation, I see the only explicitly non-religious context within which it is meaningful to speak correlatively about God according to the criteria of the religious language game. It is certainly not meaningful to give a religious answer to a non-religious question, because, in this case, question and answer belong to two different language games and, according to the rules of linguistic analysis, a "category mistake" is committed. We can only say that this takes place in the case outlined above, however, if we lose sight of the profundity of our human existence—our being an *Ereignis* or "event" in the Bultmannian sense. Man's question concerning himself, which is apparently not a religious question, is in fact sustained by the reality of creation and is thus, implicitly, rooted in the soil of all religious experience: God's sovereign and unexpected act of creation which is not overcome by our sinfulness. The superior power of God's good act of creation arouses in us the quest for the real basis of the datum of experience that people, despite everything (and often without knowing about the redemption of Christ) continue their trust that goodness and not evil must have the last word. The Christian revelation extends this "must have" to "will have"; but without man's "must have," the Christian "will have" would be unintelligible. The ultimate fulfilment of man at the end of time, which all men are seeking but cannot formulate and can only partly realise, is the universal pre-understanding of the *humanum* that is promised to us in Christ. Eschatology and Christology coincide essentially here. Human reality, which can, despite everything, be meaningfully interpreted in secular terms and especially by realising meaning in praxis within a history of meaninglessness, receives from Christianity meaning in abundance: the living God himself, who is ultimately the abundance to which all secular meaning is indebted for its own secular significance.

I have not, of course, penetrated to the deepest mystery of the Christian message itself in this argument, but have remained at the threshold with man himself, for whom Christian talk about God must be intelligible. I should have preferred to speak about Christianity itself, but I believe that the first task of Christians today is to listen very attentively to the world in order to collect the material with which they will be able to make Christianity accessible to their fellow men, because it is precisely here that the greatest unsolved problems are still to be found. We cannot

avoid analysing man's alienations more fully and exposing the dimension
in our humanity in which Christian talk about God can be intelligible.
What is more, this does not exclude the fact that it will also imply a self-
denying *metanoia* on man's part to listen. Christian talk about God will
not be accessible to contemporary man if he does not experience, in his
actual life, signs and glimpses of transcendence, and does not come to
understand, that an exclusively scientific and technological interpretation of reality inevitably leads to many forms of inhumanity. It is true
that man will not at once experience the space which is made free, after
these alienations have been analysed, as a question about God, but it
does, on the other hand, seem as if only this context of human experience offers a sensitive point of resonance for Christian talk about God,
which can only there be meaningful and intelligible as good news. We
can in fact dispense less now than in the past with a natural theology
faithful to human experience.

I would personally not maintain that the question–answer correlation,
seen as the pre-understanding of Christianity and the basis of its universal
validity, could be interpreted as man asking a question and Christian
revelation being the answer to this question. This does not, in my view,
make revelation intelligible; it would be playing, as it were, according to
the rules of two different language games at the same time. I would rather
formulate the correlation in this way: man, who, despite everything, is
looking for meaning in the world, asks a question and he must first
answer this question himself. Something of the wonder of man's existence which he is trying, despite everything, to realise and which he,
despite Dachau, Buchenwald and Vietnam, and despite the hidden personal spiritual and social misery of so many of his fellow men, continues
to trust in and commit himself to, believing that good will prevail, can
be discerned in this human answer. What can, in fact, be observed in
very many men is that there is something in man that does not come
from him, something that is "extra" to him. The Christian calls this inexpressible element God the creator who, precisely because he is God,
throws no shadows over man's existence and can therefore be present
even though he may appear to be absent. Man's hesitant answer to his
own question, which is in the first place given in praxis, is identified in
Christian faith. Man's history, which is God's creation, is thus the condition for understanding Christian revelation and at the same time the
answer given by revelation. The abundance of meaning which is contained in the meaning man has already discovered in the world is
manifested in the light of revelation. It is therefore not really possible to
speak of "anonymous Christians," even though it is certainly necessary
to express in one way or another the fact that non-Christians are not,

because of their orthopraxis, deprived of salvation. On the contrary, Christians call themselves such in an explicit, conscious and justified way: with joy because of the identified mystery which still remains a mystery. In the man Jesus, man's question about himself and the human answer to this question are translated into a divine question put to man and the divine answer to this question: Jesus is the Son of God, expressed in terms of humanity. He *is* the question–answer correlation. [1970]

11/ *Truth in the Human Context*

Our present thinking is characterized by a critical attitude towards the rationalism of previous centuries. Long before even the emergence of existentialism, thought which, in the Hellenistic climate of Western civilisation, was to a very great extent orientated towards the consideration of abstract and universal and unchangeable truths had changed course and was moving in a direction whose motto was *vers le concret*, back to the concrete, shifting reality. It was from this background of modern thought that both existentialism and phenomenology emerged; but from it also emerged a great variety of attempts on the part of neo-Thomist thinkers to reassess human thought as a faculty of truth whereby reality could be meaningfully encountered, according to the way in which this reality discloses itself to the activity of human thought which both extracts and gives meaning. Conceptual, rational thought is contrasted with lived experience, *l'expérience vécue*. Present-day thought is clearly reacting on the one hand against idealism, according to which human thought itself creatively produces its contents and therefore truth, and on the other hand against the "representational realism" of scholasticism, which regards the content of our concepts as an exact reflection of reality without any reference to a human act which confers meaning. This reaction against these two trends of thought clearly moves in two directions. On the one hand, it tends in the direction of phenomenology, one of the basic affirmations of which is that the world is essentially a "world-for-me." In other words, reality has no independent, absolute meaning, but many different significations in relation to man, and these significations vary according to the standpoint from which man approaches or deals with reality. Indeed, according to many modern phenomenologists, the objective signification of a reality can be found only in the meaning that this reality has in relation to man. On the other hand, there is also the trend of thought followed by certain Catholic philosophers (especially De Petter and Strasser) who claim that, implicit in the relative meanings given by man, there is an absolute meaning in reality. This meaning is, in their view, independent of human thought and acts, in its absolute value, as the norm for all meanings given by man. This second movement attempts to gear what is true in phenomenological thought to what may be called the insights of the *philosophia perennis*, but this perennial philosophy is consequently placed in a perspective which is entirely different from that in which it was seen in scholastic thought.

The notion of truth has thus become much more "supple" in modern thought—so supple, in fact, that it has in many cases moved in the direction of complete relativism. The modern insight that the essence of man is inseparable from his historicity has, of its very nature, resulted in a more flexible view of truth than the traditional one, according to which man is seen in terms of a human nature that has been permanently defined once and for all time and is incapable of being inwardly conditioned by concrete, changing circumstances. In the modern view, insofar as it accepts an absolute reality at all, reality (as truth) is seen as the never-wholly-to-be-deciphered background of all our human interpretations. The ontological basis, as the mysterious source of a still-hidden fullness of meaning, remains the same and does not change, but the human interpretation of this basis, and thus man's possession of truth, grows and evolves. This is, however, drawn in one definite direction by this implicit ontological significance, so that truth is always approached more and more concretely, even though it is never completely apprehended.

If we disregard the relativist views, according to which no absolute truth exists (a view which is, of course, implicitly atheistic), we are nonetheless forced, by experience itself, to affirm—against the background of the absolute truth that determines our thought as a norm—the imperfection and the evolving and relative nature of our possession of truth, and consequently the fact that our earlier insights are capable of inexhaustible amplification. It is the fundamental orientation to the absolute implicit in all our knowledge which gives continuity to our human and constantly changing consciousness. From a finite, limited, constantly changing, and historical standpoint, we have a view of absolute truth, although we never have this in our power. In this sense, we cannot say that truth changes. We cannot therefore say that what was true before is now untrue, for even our affirmation of truth does not change or become obsolete. The standpoints from which we approach truth, however, are changing continuously and our knowledge is thus always growing inwardly. The whole of our human knowledge is, in its orientation towards the absolute, also coloured by these standpoints. It is, however, at the same time apparent from the fact that we are aware of the existence of these perspectives from which we view absolute truth that we rise above relativism. We do not possess a *conscience survolante*, an awareness that is able to transcend all relative standpoints and thus survey objective reality. Yet this is still the view held in many scholastic circles with regard to truth. The consequence of this is that differences of view are frequently confused with the relativist tendencies that are in fact present in modern thought.

It is at the same time clear, from this "perspectivism" of our knowledge (which is orientated towards absolute reality and also regulated by it), that man's insight into truth will never lead to complete unanimity. Our maintaining an open and receptive attitude in our affirmation of the truth towards what is true in the views of others is, anyway, a condition for the attainment of the highest possible degree of unanimity. [1954]

12/ *The Quest for Universal Meaning*

The question about universal meaning is not only for human thought but also from the point of view of historical reality itself *as question* rationally as unavoidable as it is insoluble. For real history occurs in all those places where meaning and meaninglessness run over and across each other, where they are mixed together in joy and suffering, laughter and tears. In other words, where there is finitude. The copresence of meaning and meaninglessness in our history—the warp and woof itself of this history—cannot be rationally set into a coherent *theoretical* design because of the continuing obstinacy of all meaningless suffering. However, one can assert that individual experiences as experiences of meaning are logically possible only on the basis of the unavoidably logically implicit question in them about total meaning. The logical implication of this questioning in no way means that universal history in reality has to have a definitive positive meaning. Nor can this logical question reason away logically and theoretically a remainder of meaninglessness and absence of salvation. Logos, meaning and facticity, histories of meaninglessness, of injustice and suffering are thus related to one another in a theoretically insoluble tension. Theoretical reason cannot therefore anticipate rationally a universal, total meaning of history. And because the historical process of coming into being is not yet completed, every individual experience of meaning is subject to a *theoretically* insoluble and fundamental doubt.

Meaning is therefore decided upon by *practical* reason. But how? History as history of meaning or history of salvation is not a total history without human subjects, who in reality have often been bowed by suffering and meaninglessness. Universal meaning of history cannot be subjected to a logical coercion to totality, at least if it wants to be *human* history, history of freedom. This meaning cannot be posited either idealistically or materialistically as a "logical development," as though in the last instance the concrete histories of suffering of human beings do not count. There always remains for human reason a remnant of suffering and meaninglessness which cannot be accounted for in a theory. To speak theoretically of a definitive total meaning of history implies, in reality, an insensitivity to the world-historical and personal dramas and catastrophes in our history. In this at least Hans Albert seems to be correct when he speaks of the "myth of total reason" (understood as theoretical reason). But in contrast to what Albert claims, the concept of totality itself is not thereby declared meaningless. The relationship between part and whole, considered logically unavoidable by a long hermeneutical tradition, as a rationally given problem in every individual experience of meaning can hardly be denied. The unavoidable difficulty with a merely theoretical thematization of the universal meaning of history, of the totality of meaning, implied in every individual experience of meaning, finds its basis in the historical process of experience itself. On the one hand, it is not finished, and on the other it confronts us with catastrophic meaninglessness. A thematization of universal meaning must therefore be completed in a practical-critical direction. Only a definite liberating praxis can open the way to total meaning. In other words, total meaning can only come about in an *historical experience;* it cannot be theoretically anticipated. That indicates that it is impossible to speak of a total, universal meaning of history if one fails to consider a definite praxis which wishes to make all people free subjects of a living history without disadvantage to any single one. The "refuse of history," which theoretical reason cannot get hold of, remains, as memory, a cognitive thorn in the side of "practical reason" which, if it wishes to remain reason, is thereby forced into liberating activity. [1980]

13/ *The Relation of Meaning to Truth*

The concept "universal truth" has, especially since the Enlightenment, lost its essential historicity, as well as its personal subjects. It became truth in itself, different from the Greek concept of truth. But universal truth can only mean that it holds for all human subjects, and not just for the socially and economically, and therefore intellectually, privileged. That has fundamental consequences for the concept of truth.

One can rightfully say with all of analytic philosophy that only a meaningful statement can be the object of truth or untruth. Meaning

and truth are therefore to be distinguished. But this conception requires
a correction. Wolfhart Pannenberg affirms this distinction out of his
own theological project. But he rightfully adds to that, that the question
about truth does not stand as some externally added-on relation to the
questions about sense and reference. Reality is only brought to expression by experiencing subjects, so that truth in its relation to reality also
includes a relation to subjects. It is directed toward universal consensus
if truth wants to be really universal; in other words, if it wishes to be
called truth at all. And then a totality of meaning which embraces all
experience coincides with the revelation of truth. For then it does not
exclude any experience which could make the truth of this experienced
meaning problematical. In the all-embracing totality of meaning, the
experience of meaning and the *experience of truth* coincide. Without wanting to speak against this definitive coincidence of meaning, relevance,
and truth, one must nonetheless introduce a clear differentiation. It was
already conceded earlier that individual experiences of meaning, when
reflected upon, logically include the question about total meaning, and
that, on the other hand, factual history in no way is subject to a logical
compulsion to totality. Actual history is the course of individual histories of meaning and many individual histories of meaninglessness,
which cannot be brought into harmony through any logical or theoretical
design. That implies that genuinely liberating and relevant truth, and
therefore the coincidence of the experience of meaning and the experience of truth, stands under the primacy of the cognitive, critical and
liberating power of memories of history of suffering which, first taken
seriously by practical reason, urge these to a very definite liberating
praxis. Through this praxis truth really becomes universal, valid not
only for some individually privileged persons—be they the privileged of
bourgeois or socialist society — but for each and every individual. For
that reason, one can say with Johannes Metz "that is true which is relevant for all subjects, including the dead and the defeated." This universally
liberating praxis is not some subsequent superstructure or mere consequence of a truth recognized theoretically as universal ahead of time.
Rather, it is the *historical mediation of the manifestation of truth* precisely
as universal truth, valid for all people. [1980]

14/ *Human Orientation to the Future*

Today we observe a basic shift in the way man looks at history. The
more or less explicit identification of history with the past, which
dominated the writing of history since the beginning of its modern

phase, is now yielding to a view which sees history more as events in the making, events in the process of arrival, and therefore as happenings in which we ourselves play an active part. The future is of primary importance in what we call "history." So the concept of man's earthly future begins to exercise a kind of polarity in man's thought and knowledge, whereas in the past—at least in the West—the future dimension of history was almost only considered as a matter of the *finis ultimus*, the ultimate end of man, beyond and after this earthly life.

Since the rediscovery of man's true historicity as a creature of time, that on the basis of its past sets its course of life in the present towards a future, eschatology is seen as a question which lies embodied in man's existence. Man's experience does not simply run on in time, with an undercurrent of "becoming," but implies an element of time-consciousness. This does not allow him to escape from time but it allows him in a certain sense to transcend the lived time (*le temps vécu*), although he cannot put this time-transcending permanence into words, at least not positively. This time-consciousness which makes man reach beyond experienced time into both the past and the future makes man's questioning about the beginning and the end particularly relevant.

It seems to me, therefore, that to inquire after the future is a natural process, and fundamental to our human condition. Although caught up in time and never outside it, man is not the prisoner of time in his historical growth; he transcends time from within. That is why he can never feel satisfied. Within this time-condition man is therefore free to achieve a certain openness with regard to time. He can do so because he can also indulge like an epicure in the short-lived joys of the temporary condition in which he lives. But if he takes this time-consciousness seriously, he cannot avoid facing the question of the meaning of human history. For every moment of his free existence implies present, past and future. His freedom indeed is exercised in the present but only insofar as this present sets its course towards the future. The pure present is always on the point of sliding into the past. Man's future-building freedom thus essentially presupposes an open eschatology, an expectation of the future, a will towards the future which, in itself, slips into the ambiguity of all history-making freedom.

When in our old culture, mainly concerned with the past, we thought and spoke about God's transcendence we almost naturally projected God into the past. Eternity was something like an immobilised or immortalised past—"in the beginning was God." We knew of course quite well that God's eternity embraced man's present and man's future; that God was both first and last, and as such also a present that transcended our human present. On this point the older theology developed marvellous insights which have by no means lost their relevance. In a culture which constantly looked towards the past there existed obviously a powerful mutual attraction between "transcendence" and eternity on the one hand and an immortalised "past" on the other. Today, however, our culture is firmly turned towards the future as something that our culture itself must build. So the Christian notion of transcendence, supple and capable of more than one meaning, has to go through the same process. The meaning of "transcendence" comes therefore closer to what in our time-bound condition we call "future." If divine transcendence transcends and embraces man's past, present and future from within, the believer will preferably and rightly link God's transcendence with the future as soon as man has recognised the primacy of the future in our time-bound condition. So he will link God with the future of man and, since man is a communal person, with the future of mankind as a whole. When we once accept the reality of a genuine belief in the invisible reality of God who is the true source of our understanding of God from within this world, this new understanding of his transcendence will lead to the new image of God in our culture.

In this cultural context the God of the believer will manifest himself as "He who comes," the God who is our future. This implies a far-reaching change: he, whom we formerly saw as the "wholly other" in our old outlook on man and the world, is now seen as he who is our future and who creates anew man's future. He shows himself as the God who gives us in Jesus Christ the opportunity to build the future, to make all things new and to rise above our own sinful history and that of all mankind. Thus the new culture becomes an inspiration to rediscover as a surprise the good news of the Old and the New Testament, the news that the God of promise has put us on the way to the promised land, a land which, like Israel of old, we ourselves must claim and cultivate, trusting in his promise. [1969]

15/ A Critical View of Orientation to the Future

In all this we must not forget that any rationally planned future is only half a history, a history understood along the lines of the model of a relationship between means and ends. For the rational "future" does not coincide with what will really happens. *On the one hand* "the future" is a wealth of possibilities, of which some in fact will be realized; some elements of this future can be calculated rationally with a greater or lesser degree of probability. Here the decisive question is already: which possibilities are men to take up and which not? This makes history a real adventure in which human decisions play a large part, quite apart from the fact that some imponderables will make the future turn out differently from what men had planned. *On the other hand,* mankind is not the universal providence of its own history. When the "wealth of possibilities," which is what the future is for us today, has really become present, only one complex whole out of these many possibilities will have been realized, and this actual totality cannot ever be derived from the momentary "historical trend" which we can in fact analyse. History does not evolve logically! But in that case past and present are interwoven with the future only through those thin threads of the particular complex event in which the future in fact becomes present in its foreseen and unforeseen, unexpected elements. The future is significant in determining the meaning of past and present only as it in fact comes to pass. *Future* is therefore in the last resort that which keeps *coming towards* men who are alive today, at once both thanks to and yet despite all prognoses, all projections of the future and all planning. The future can never be interpreted purely teleologically, technologically or in terms of the logic of development. The future transcends human rationality, not only provisionally, but in principle. From a purely human perspective (leaving religious views aside), man's future stands under the fundamental proviso of the *ignorantia futuri,* the unknown future (which may perhaps make men raise the question of God). The consequence is that a purely teleological conception of history in terms of the model of means and ends lands man in alienating frustrations, and in the last resort reduces him to despair and defeatism.

I said earlier that our relationship to the future which calls forth a particular practice is only possible as a result of our relationship to the past, whereas the (hermeneutical) relationship to the past already implies a decision for the future. . . . The question therefore is: of what challenging realities, which cannot be controlled or theorized about by critical reason, must man take account in his concern for a good, true and happy future, a future worth living, and what must he do to secure such a future? [1977]

Part Two

Interpreting
Christian Experience

1

Experience and Christian Revelation

COMMENTARY

Schillebeeckx's emphasis on the concreteness and historical character of truth, as well as the fact that we always approach it from a perspective, means that interpretation has to be a major theme in his work. Part II explores how Schillebeeckx understands interpretation theory, or hermeneutics.

The five selections in this first section deal with how he understands the interpretive process in terms of Christian revelation. Selection 16 summarizes the theology of revelation behind his doctoral dissertation. An early work therefore, but one which already exhibits themes and an approach that will continue in his work. He presents revelation as a dynamic event between God and humanity, not just the communication of content. Important here too is his treatment of mystery, a way of talking about God's encounter with us that we still find in his writings in the mid-1980s. Already the strong concerns for concrete encounter and for the meaning of salvation are evident. Selection 17 shows how these themes continued in his theology of revelation of the later 1950s.

Selections 18 and 19 address the relation between human experience and Christian revelation. The first of these deals with how people come to religious experience and then specifically Christian experience. The second takes up the relation of Christian tradition and contemporary human experience.

Selection 20, as a sort of footnote, puts this entire discussion into the context of interpretive frameworks, or thinking in models.

16/ *Revelation and Mystery*

Christianity is a religion of revelation and is therefore a religion of dogma. Quite often this is understood as God revealing to us a number of supernatural truths which we could not ascertain with our natural reason, which then supplement natural knowledge of God already achieved. The entirety thus forms religious doctrine; in other words, "revelatio" or revelation is understood in strongly intellectualist terms. Now it is certainly true that the moment of knowing is something formal. Revelation necessarily addresses a *consciousness*. However, when so presented, the richer insight into what revelation is, is restricted too much and too exclusively to the intellectual realm which, however formal and fundamental it may be, remains nonetheless but a moment in what we could call an existential event.

A consequence of this one-sided intellectualist conception of dogmatic Christianity is that revelation is understood too exclusively as simple preaching, in which Jesus comes to tell us what he has seen from the Father. In other words, revelation is exclusively a *word-revelation,* which we can now find in the books of the Old and New Testaments. This approach is likewise a typically Protestant conception of the pure and simple revelation of the Word, which resulted in the sixteenth century in the catechism concept of Christianity, which involved a methodical, abstract religious instruction concerning a number of truths. . . .

While we most often consider dogma to be an abstract doctrinal whole, the Old and New Testaments and the church fathers—and to a great extent well into the period of high scholasticism—on the other hand, saw revelation rather as the *revelation of a reality,* in which the *word-revelation* functions rather more as an explanatory guide. In other words, revelation is seen as an existential event, a salvation event, wherein within earthly visibility a divine reality touches human reality—in other words, a salvation history. To put it in reflective terms, Christianity certainly has to do with a theologia, but with a theologia which reveals itself in an oikonomia, that is, veiled in an economy of salvation in time. Already in the sacred scriptures, but especially in the patristic period, that revelation is called technically a *mystērion,* a "mystery," a "sacramentum"—that is to say, a completion in earthly, historical reality of a divine activity regarding the salvation of humanity. Revelation is not merely Christ and the prophets speaking about God's initiative of love. More fundamentally, it is the historical completion itself of the divine initiative of salvation within the structure of general human history. The word-revelation is an integrating and essential moment of this process, guiding it and clarifying its meaning. But it cannot fully express that which that reality itself has placed here among us. . . .

Ignoring some small nuances, we may say thereby that, according to the fathers, and still somewhat evident in high scholasticism, this visible aspect, that is, the historically visible completion of that divine reality of salvation is called "sacramentum." The invisible aspect, that is, the divine reality brought to expression in salvation history (or in the "sacramentum") is called "mysterium." The two together, the *historical completion of salvation* and the *transhistorical divine reality* which comes to us within it, I call *mystērion,* following the terminology of the Greek fathers. On the basis of this distinction Christianity as a religion of revelation is a *sacramentum mysterii:* a becoming visible of divine realities of salvation in *our* earthly world. Seen subjectively, that is, from the side of our attitude of faith or of our actual entry into this sacramental scheme of salvation, this means that faith also has a sacramental structure so that human experience, or being engaged in a salvation history, is informed from within by the actual supernatural moment of faith, as a saving act of God within us. "Vididit et credidit," "he *saw* and *believed,*" it says in the gospel. One *sees* via the "sacramentum" which is humanly experienced, in which one is involved: the "sacramentum Christi," for us also immediately the "sacramentum ecclesiae." One *believes* by the power of what St. Thomas calls "the inner instinct which urges and moves us to faith" (e.g., in *Ad Johann.,* VI, lect. 5); that is to say, through the attracting grace of faith into the divine reality and activity of salvation, which in veiled manner are revealed in that external "sacramentum."

On the basis of the sacramental structure of revelation, i.e., by the fact that the divine manifests itself in the forms and shapes of *our* earthly reality, it is immediately evident that the material object of revelation always is the divine reality, as a reality immediately relevant to us: God as *our* God, the "Deus salutaris," so that this aspect of salvation is *essential* for the constitution itself of the material object of faith. We believe in *earthly* realities as visible, tangible, audible mysteries or manifestations of supernatural realities of faith.

With this the complete meaning of revelation as *mystērion* is still not presented in its entirety. "Sacramentum" means, from patristic times until the time of St. Thomas (and even later), not only a historical intervention of a divine transcendental reality of salvation. It is at the same time a prophecy of a *future* fact of salvation. And here once again, it is not only or formally a prophecy in words, but especially also a prophecy in and through an historical fact of salvation, which becomes a "sacramentum futuri," a sacramentum of something in the future. Thus, for example, the *mystērion* of Christ's human experience is intended not only as the meaningful and efficacious external expression of God's concern for human persons, but also at the same time the sacramental anticipation of the final consummation.

This entire insight into revelation teaches us that God is certainly accessible to us in revelation, albeit in and through an economy of salvation. Therefore theology is certainly to be concerned with God's intelligibility, but then as this intelligibility manifests itself in a sacramental scheme of salvation. "Deus sub ratione Deitatis," God as God is reached immediately in faith through the supernatural act of faith that is given in the "light of faith," with the "ratio Deitatis," however, being made explicit only through salvation history. The way to the "Deus sub ratione Deitatis" is through the event of Christ, salvation history, inaugurated in the old covenant as "sacramentum futuri," *completed* in the historical, redemptive appearance of the human person Jesus, who is himself "sacramentum" of the eschaton, the final event, of the "kingdom of heaven." It is attained by us sacramentally, in and through the "mysterium ecclesiae," the mystery of the church, which is the "sacramentum Christi," the sacrament of the completed redemption which is assumed into the final consummation. [1952]

17/ *The Experience of Revelation*

Religion is essentially a personal communion between God and men. This personal contact with the living God cannot be established by human effort. It can only be established by the initiative of grace with the divine revelation that is implied in it. *Salvation* is the very act of the encounter between God and man, in which the first fundamental contact is established by faith. This divine revelation makes history. It would take us too far from our subject to discuss this question fully, and I must be content to summarise briefly the theme of saving history (or history of salvation). The history that is made by men becomes itself the material in and through which God makes saving history and through which he accomplishes his revelation. God's saving activity is revealed by becoming history, and it becomes history by being revealed. The prophetic word throws light on this saving activity and makes it present for us *as* an act of God. All this was ultimately expressed scripturally—in writing— in the Bible, under the divine guarantee that it was a faithful reproduction of the consciousness of salvation that God himself wished to realise in the whole of mankind in and through his chosen people, Israel and the church.

There are distinct phases in this historical self-disclosure of the God of redemption. The first was the *constitutive phase of revelation*, the *revelatio publica constitutiva,* the stage in which Christ appeared in human form as the public revelation of God, both in his prehistory of the Old Testament and in his personal completion in human action—the *mysteria carnis Christi* ("the mysteries of Christ's humanity"). In this phase, which closed with the end of the apostolic period, God revealed himself definitively and the eschatological age dawned: we are redeemed. This constitutive phase was followed by the saving history of the church, living from the constituted phase of salvation. Expressed in terms of revelation, it is usual to refer to this as the *explicative and continuing phase of revelation.* It is in this period that what has taken place for all of us in Christ as our prototype and representative is accomplished within humanity in and through the church, on the basis of the completed mystery of Christ. Faith is conditioned by this revelation, in which we are addressed by God. Faith is therefore a way of knowing. This knowing has a distinctive character in that it is a knowledge which comes about by our being addressed, by our being confidentially informed, through God's mercy. God speaks to us inwardly through the inward grace of faith, the *locutio interior,* and at the same time we are addressed from outside by the God of revelation—this last is the aspect of *fides ex auditu.* This "external address" is the Old Testament history of salvation, accompanied by the prophetic word, and its climax: the human appearance of Christ himself in word and deed as addressed to the apostles. Finally, it is the life of the church, in her activity and in her kerygmatic word, by which man living now is addressed and in which the glorified Christ really lives. Within the church, we believe in the mystery of Christ as the revelation of God—we believe in the Christian historical plan of salvation in which the trinitarian mystery of salvation which transcends history is realised for and in us. The entire theological method is determined by this structure of revelation. First of all, however, we must ascertain how faith in this revelation gives rise to a reflection which we have called theology. [1958]

But the whole problem is, what is the mode of this revelation? Is it simply a question of a communication of a knowledge of truths that are beyond our understanding, or is it primarily a question of sacramental revelation, a revelation in human and historical form? We should at the very outset be misinterpreting the data of the problem if we were to take the assertion that Christianity involves revelation to mean that God has revealed certain truths that are beyond our natural understanding only as a kind of addition to an already acquired natural knowledge of God. It is, of course, certainly true that the aspect of knowing in revelation is formal. Revelation of necessity addresses a *consciousness.* But the whole problem is, how does this revelation, this process wherein the human consciousness is addressed by the living God, take place concretely? We should not forget that the dispensing and receiving of grace, the supernatural order of life, by definition involves both salvation and history. Through grace, God becomes a person for us—*Theos pros hēmas*, the living God, as the Old Testament calls the God of revelation.

The God of creation is, of course, also the personal God, but he does not reveal himself in his creative concern with the world as a person for us, thus enabling us to enter into personal relationships with him. Personal relationships with God are, of their very nature, of a theologal kind, even though they are sometimes anonymously theologal. The act of creation is certainly a free act on the part of the personal God, but the true face of the living God does not emerge an existential dialogue with his people as man's partner, a dialogue in which he opens up his inner life to us. The whole history of the Old and New Testaments clearly shows us that man's life with his God is a historically connected, constantly developing dialogue between God and mankind. It is, then, the history of salvation and not creation (which is, of course, the starting point of the history of salvation) that reveals to us who God really is and his wish to be really our God, also for us men.

This revelation reached its culminating point in Christ. God entered into personal relationships with us in and through his humanity, of which the Logos is the person. A fellow man who treats us personally, then, is personally God. Jesus' human treatment of his fellow men is therefore an invitation to us to encounter God personally. Christ is the historically visible form of God's desire to confer grace and to do this in such a way that the gift of grace is essentially linked with something which is visible, a fundamental historical fact—the man Jesus. Grace therefore does not come to us directly from God's suprahistorical, transcendent will to love us, but from the man Christ Jesus. The gift and reception of grace, revelation, thus takes place within the framework of human intercommunication. Human contacts with the man Jesus, historically situated encounters, become, in other words, meetings with God, because it was God's plan to redeem us only in humanity. It is at the same time the perennial, lasting character of the mediation of grace through the man Jesus that demanded, from the moment of Jesus' pneumatic glorification, the introduction of the sacramental economy of salvation, the *sacramenta separata*. Social intercommunication between men, after all, takes place via physical nature. The glorified Lord therefore continues, as a man, to be the lasting instrument of salvation, and grace continues to be conferred within the terms of human intercommunication—between men and the man Jesus.

But, because the living Lord lives in a pneumatic (that is, spirit) situation which is therefore invisible to us and we, on the other hand, still live in an unglorified earthly situation bounded by time and space, the man Jesus, who is still living even now, is able to encounter and influence us directly, but is not able to make himself directly present to us *in propria carne.* The man Jesus still belongs to our earthly world, but at a point where this world is already glorified. As a result, then, a disproportion has arisen between us, as the unglorified world, and Christ, as the glorified world. It is only under sacramental symbols that God's eternally actual act of redemption performed in humanity can be made present to us in our earthly and historical world. Because of the perennial character of the man Jesus, as the only Mediator, "the same yesterday and today and for ever," the life of grace continues to take place, even after the closing of revelation, as a history of salvation, and our sacramental, historically situated encounter with the living Lord in the sacral sphere of Christ's Church is *the* encounter with the God of our salvation. [1953]

18/ *The Structure of Belief Experiences*

Religious experiences show a unitary structure. Religious experiences are a particular kind of experience along with worldly experiences. But their structure needs to be analyzed more closely. Religious experiences happen to people as do everyday individual human experiences, but in light of and on the basis of the respective religious tradition in which one stands and which serves as the interpretive framework bestowing meaning. Religious or faith experiences occur therefore in a dialectical process. On the one hand the content of faith, itself already the reflective expression of the experience of a group of people (concretely, of the Christian churches), is determinative for the religious, Christian content of certain modern human experiences. On the other hand it is not this content of faith in itself which brings me directly to a Christian experience of faith through its mere proclamation; rather, under the directing light of the content of faith presented to me from the history of Christian experience, I have in and through everyday human experiences a personal Christian experience in which here and now I experience salvation in Jesus. The church's story of the tradition of Christian experience is thus the condition which makes experiencing the Christian gospel possible for others. But people come to a personal Christian experience only through human experiences.

Faith comes from hearing, but is completed and mediated only in a personal experience. Only when the living story of a respective religious tradition is recounted and put into practice in a lively way can contemporary people have from, in, and with their present experiences Christian experiences. That is to say, they can either identify with this story or distance themselves from it. In this story, they can in and with their human experiences in the world discover themselves at the same time.

To be sure, the church's liturgy is the place where God is praised, thanked and celebrated for the content of Christian salvation. It is the place where the content of the tradition of Christian faith is recounted. But nevertheless one may not reduce the situations which can lead to experiences of faith to the proclamation of the Word and the liturgy—especially in a so-called secularized world. The church's liturgy and proclamation of the Word already presume the emergence of religious experiences in and with human experiences (for example, the concrete experience of a group of men and women with the person Jesus of Nazareth in Palestine). And these presume already a fundamental experience of symbol in and from our utterly human, created world. Without this fundamental creaturely experience no renewal or shaping of the liturgy and no unmediated proclaiming of the Christian content of faith can give us a deepened Christian experience which is a real experience of the present and not merely the experience of our own subjective reactions to what is happening liturgically in the church. We cannot suddenly experience God in the church's liturgy if we nowhere come across him outside the church in our everyday experiences with people and with the world. Of course the possibility that many people come to religious experiences in world events precisely through the church's liturgy and proclamation of the Word can never be ruled out.

Because people as a rule come to religion through experiences with other people and with the world, this worldly mediation also explains the distinctions between the different religions. The emergence of the multiplicity of religions can be explained as coming from the same source; namely, from the multiplicity of human experiences with people and the world within a very specifically situated history. Thus to speak of God from human experiences is essentially bound up with the ability to talk about worldly experiences in a religious way, even if this is always done in light of a specific religious (sometimes Christian) tradition of experience.

It follows from this that the living environment in which Christian faith is nurtured and transmitted is not only the living community of faith or the *church*, but at the same time also is the *world*, the everyday human experience of life in the concrete world and history in which people live. That the church is already a *constituted* church changes nothing of the fundamental structure of experiences, because this "constitution" in no way can or may mean that the church is not a living church in a continuing history and repristinates her first constitution only materially.

All this means that a Christian answer to the question, who is Jesus and what salvation can we experience from him in God in our times, cannot be a one-sided one. That is, it cannot be derived solely from the analysis and interpretation of biblical texts and church documents, nor solely from the analysis of contemporary basic experiences and of our society. Preliminarily we have therefore come to the conclusion that this answer (within a practical identification with or imitation of Jesus) can only be given in a *correlation* between these two poles. Later it will be shown that this correlation must be a *mutually critical* one.

We cannot learn who Jesus is solely from contemporary experiences, nor solely from scripture and tradition. In the first instance, we are, to be sure, dependent upon and must turn to the experiences of believers who, as Peter says in the Acts of the Apostles, "belonged to our company during the time when the Lord Jesus was among us, from the baptism by John up to the day when he was taken up from us, witnesses with us of his resurrection" (Acts 1:21–22). We rely therefore on the so-called apostolic experiences with Jesus, as they were presented by the New Testament witnesses. The New Testament Christians speak to us from their experiences: "We have heard it and seen it with our own eyes, we have seen it and touched it with our hands—of that we speak," "we have seen it and are its witnesses," "what we have seen and heard we proclaim to you also" (1 John 1:1, 2, 3). Our Christian faith is therefore not based on so-called heavenly voices, but on an entirely concrete earthly event in our history: the life of Jesus of Nazareth, which those who followed Jesus experienced in a definite way as salvation. Their reports of it become for others a message: an offer of a new possibility of life which can be experienced by all. The beginning of Christian tradition lies therefore in what we can call the witness of the *apostolic experience of faith*.

Experience is, however, always an *interpreting perception,* even by the first and New Testament disciples of Jesus. The opponents of Jesus also experienced and interpreted him. They, too, had for themselves an image of Jesus—an image which drove them to his execution. They experienced him as a threat, while his disciples experienced him as salvation and mercy. In this, not only were the interpretations of friends and foes different. Their experience of Jesus was itself qualitatively different, for the one group an experience of mortal threat, for the other group an experience of liberation.

Christian belief is based therefore in the first instance on the historical mediation of the experiences of faith of others who have followed after Jesus. But this mediation can only be considered to have been successful, that is, the appropriation of these ancient experiences is only possible, if they happen here and now in ever new Christian experiences. In this fashion a living tradition comes about.

The alternative between "faith from experiences" and "faith from hearing" is therefore a false dilemma. Experiences of others can never be communicated directly. It is also not possible to realize the romantic attempts of Schleiermacher and Dilthey to get inside the skins of the experiences of others. To make our own what others have experienced requires the mediations of a life praxis, namely, the mediation of the "sequela Christi": to become truly a disciple of Jesus anew, over and over again. In other words, the mediation of a practical identification with the life of Jesus who proclaimed the reign of God as the future for humanity, but in a way that it became already "present" in his action and words for those who believed in him.

Testimonies of experiences of salvation with Jesus (therefore also proclamation and catechesis) are therefore never simply witnesses of contemporary human basic experiences, they will always unfold as well, in a way as responsible and as suggestive as possible, what the Christian orientation of faith can mean concretely for people in our time and in this society. People must know, with which "search project" or interpretive angle they wish to involve themselves or will permit themselves. But if the churches communicate or "mediate" in their proclamation their long history of experience with a conceptual system and a view of humanity and the world which are alien to contemporary people, then the desire to reach out to *this* (Christian) search project as a possible way of giving shape to their human experience is lost for most people already before they begin. On the other hand, a "catechesis of experience" not guided by the story of Jesus is also not a Christian option. According to the Christian tradition of faith, God himself has shown us in a particular history who God is, and how God wishes to be experienced. He has shown that in an event, which has its basis within the totality of our human history in Jesus. This history will have to be recounted as faithfully as possible if people want to be able to make of and from their human experiences a Christian one. Experiences of God are therefore mediated through histories and stories which so engage their hearers that they are able to come with and in *human* experiences to *Christian* experiences. Christian experiences of faith can only be made as mediated *in* human experiences as a sort of "alternative experience" in light of the living memory of the story of Jesus of Nazareth as the Christ. [1980]

19/ *The Authority of Christian Experiences of Belief*

It is clear from the structure of Christian revelation, which comes to a certain articulation in and from experiences of faith and which, reflectively considered, is brought into language in a certain doctrine, that the authority of Christian experiences of faith is quite complex. It cannot lie one-sidedly in the concrete testimonies of faith of the apostolic experiences of faith (sacred scriptures and the biblical tradition of experience of Christianity), nor one-sidedly in what is called modern experience.

There is a tendency in certain forms of contemporary catechesis and proclamation to proceed from basic human experiences, for which one then seeks out "stories," especially in the Bible, and in all the great, especially religious, traditions of humankind.

With this approach there exists a danger that these stories often only serve as confirmations. They legitimate thereby the particular, personal and collective, autobiography. Without a critical aspect this procedure can genuinely move incorrectly, at least from a Christian point of view. To be sure, Christian experiences of belief are always *contemporary* events, but events which contain within themselves *tradition* and *promise*. They point to a past event in Jesus the Christ and to the tension for an eschatological future. A simple appeal to the present, to immediacy and to contemporary basic human experiences without *anamnesis* or memory, and without *prolepsis* or eschatological reference is not a Christian possibility. The concrete, living memory of the story of Jesus, as it is living in the entire history of Christianity from the scriptures, although in high points and low points, is co-constitutive for a relevant living Christianity today.

From the previous considerations here it is, on the other hand, already evident that contemporary people–as always—have *Christian* experiences *in* and *with* human experiences in and of this world, our world of human life.

The concern for contemporary human experiences in nature, history, with people in a very concrete society, also shapes the authority of "Christian experiences." Seen from a Christian perspective, "experiences" have authority therefore first of all in the living context of a mutual *theoretical-critical* and *practical-critical correlation* of the apostolic experiences of faith then and our experiences now, wherein the intervening period plays a special role. One must also realize that a crude contrasting of the claims to validity of a revelation handed on and the authority of new experiences is rather naive and precritical, precisely because of the structure of our historical experience. The critical question is this: to what extent is the historical identity of Christianity actualized in new experiences and in a new praxis, or to what extent is it thereby alienated instead? Contemporary experiences have a hermeneutical, critical and productive power with respect to the experiential and epistemological contents of the tradition of Christian experience. But conversely, Christian experiences also have a special original, critical and productive power of disclosure in reference to our general human exeriences in the world, providing they are reflected upon.

This problem of the historical identity of Christianity, as challenged by new experiences, can however not be resolved solely on a theoretical-hermeneutical level. This identity requires essentially a *practical identification*, that is, a self-identification with the praxis of Jesus who proclaimed the reign of God as the future for all, but in such a way that this future was already present in the activity of his ministry. [1980]

20/ *Thinking in Terms of Models*

The brief account of revelation, experience and interpretation which I have just given would leave us with a misleading picture of the actual process of revelation if it was understood that every experience goes along with conceptual or metaphorical articulations. Since Kant and contemporary discussions of epistemological theory centering on K. Popper, T. S. Kuhn, I. Lakatos, Feyerabend and the Erlangen school, the recognition has grown that the theory or the model has a certain primacy over the experience; at any rate, in the sense that on the one hand there can be no experiences without at least an implicit theory, and on the other, that theories cannot be derived from experiences by induction, but are the result of the creative initiative of the human spirit.

It follows from this that even biblical or ecclesiastical expressions of faith are not purely and simply articulate expressions or interpretations of particular "immediate, religious experiences" (e.g., experiences of Jesus which people had). More or less consciously they are also expressions of a theory. The so-called interpretative element of experience is itself in turn taken up into a more general context, that of theoretical interpretation. We can find such theoretical contexts in both the Old and New Testaments. Both sets of writings do not simply express direct religious experiences; they also work with theoretical models by means of which they try to understand the history of Israel's experience. Thus in the Old Testament the Yahwist interprets the experience of Israel in a different way from the Priestly or the Deuteronomic tradition. These work with different models of interpretation; to put it in modern terms, they work with different theories. The New Testament does the same thing—not perhaps as clearly, but in fact to the same extent; the dogmas propounded by councils have arisen within a particular pattern of thinking in models. . . .

To sum up: in faith and theology, the situation is not very different from what we find in the sciences and in everyday human experiences: articulated experiences are already conditioned by a theory (though this theory may not have been developed explicitly). In our time it has become clear from the controversy as to whether experience influences theory or theory experience that to be dogmatic about experience is as unjustified as to be dogmatic about theory. On the other hand, we cannot avoid acknowledging that even expressions of faith are never simply the presentation of a religious experience (whether with one's own or other concepts); they are also theory (which also needs to be tested). As a result, naive confidence in so-called direct experiences seems to me to be a form of neo-empiricism. It is said that a theory never comes into being as a result of inference from experiences; it is an autonomous datum of the creative spirit by means of which human beings cope with new experiences while already being familiar with a long history of experience. Consequently what people call a religious experience contains not only interpretation (in the sense of particular concepts and images) but also a theoretical model on the basis of which divergent experiences are synthesized and integrated.

An expression of faith—in other words, any statement of belief which talks of revelation—at the same time includes a theoretical model; as such, this model remains hypothetical, though at the same time it provides a specific articulation for what is experienced, and therefore for what is revealed in the experience. Expressions of faith are therefore also theoretical expressions and not simply expressions of experience. Like any theory, they set out to clarify or illuminate phenomena of experience as simply and as plainly as possible. One theory is more successful than another. Thus in the Old Testament the Priestly tradition presents quite a different interpretative model of historical experience—a model for which social stabilization is essential—from the prophetic model of interpretation, directed towards change and the future. The Priestly interpretation of the experiences of Israel's history pays homage to the model of an ideal, stable world, whereas the Deuteronomic model interprets elements of experience in terms of the exodus model: leaving stability for a constantly better future. Theories are human hypotheses, inventions, a "context" in which attempts are made to give facts an appropriate setting. As such, they are significant in the way that they can give a meaningful setting to data from a particular sphere as comprehensively and as simply as possible.

Thus the whole of revelation is interpreted in a long process of events, experiences and interpretations, and in terms of interpretations within particular divergent models or theories. In that case revelation, in its character as that which is inexpressible, and in particular as the foundation of faith which leads believers to act and makes them think, comprises not only the experience of faith but also the way in which it is interpreted within divergent models or theories. The Christologies of the New Testament are also clear evidence of this. What is revealed, as expressed by believers, becomes an utterly human event both through the interpretative element and through the theoretical element (as a consequence of thinking in models), though it is not indebted to itself either for its own content or its own particular act of faith. All this is secured by the revelation which does not have a basis in ourselves, but the manner of this revelation is at the same time a warning against any fundamentalist interpretation of either the Bible or church dogma. None of this makes it any easier for us to interpret our faith in a truly Christian way, since the interpreter in turn also thinks in models. However, insight into this structure of revelation and the act of faith corresponds more closely to the real datum of the actual process of revelation and therefore keeps us on a sure foundation. [1978]

2

Christian Theology
and the Theologian

COMMENTARY

This section presents selections from Schillebeeckx's writings on what it means to be a theologian, engaged in the critical correlating of Christian tradition and experience.

Selections 21 and 22 were written thirty years apart; both emphasize the interpretive nature of theological reflection, its conscious use of certain methods and philosophies to help clarify Christian experience, and the risk which this always involves. Selection 23 continues the theme of the theologian grappling with experience.

A major consideration for any Roman Catholic theologian is the relationship between scripture, tradition, and the teaching office (magisterium) in the theological process. This selection, written during the Second Vatican Council, states Schillebeeckx's own view, based on the documents of the Council. It is a view he would still espouse.

Selection 24 is Schillebeeckx's own response to the investigation by the Vatican of his Christology (1976–79). With considerable feeling he recounts his own experience with the investigation and speaks about the relation of theologian, magisterium, and tradition within that context.

21/ *Theology and Thinking*

Theology is, of course, a hazardous business, because the theologian establishes himself completely in the reality of revelation with the whole of his human spirit and thinking mind. Theology is faith itself, alive in a thinking spirit. This thinking on the part of the human spirit is never finished. The growth of human consciousness is always continuing, and something new is gained in every age. But every age without exception also has its own emotional and theoretical emphases, which result in other affective and intellectual aspects being thrust into the background. When, for example, the incarnational tendency made its appearance in the Middle Ages and Aristotle's *ratio* was placed in the centre of *Sacra Doctrina*, this led not only to a great theological synthesis, but also to the conviction that the integrity of human thought could only be protected by a religion which was capable of philosophical thought. To live at the same time from an authentic philosophy seemed to strengthen authentic religion. Religion had to be able to think clearly about itself, and philosophy seemed to be indispensable in this clarification, insofar as it was, for the believer, the synthetic principle that connected his "openness to the world" with his "openness to God." Without philosophy, theology would, it was felt, soon become diluted to fideism and illuminism and be incapable of dealing with contemporary problems.

But this emphasis on the use of philosophy in theology is inevitably accompanied by the danger of one-sidedness, the danger, in other words, that the aspect of mystery, the basic resistance to complete intelligibility that is present in the datum of revelation, may be forgotten. The contrary, however, is also true. In stressing this aspect of mystery and the saving significance of the reality of revelation, many modern theological movements also pay insufficient attention to the necessity of the *determinatio fidei*, the accurate definition of what enables the content of faith to be intelligibly understood within the mystery. This results in dogma becoming less clearly defined, and there is a serious threat that it may become emptied of content, or at least rootless.

The development of the synthesis between the tendency towards incarnation and the tendency towards disincarnation in theological thought will always be accompanied by painful conflicts. Harmony between nature and supernature, both at the level of human action and ascesis and at the level of theological thought, is not something that is automatically given; it is something that can only come about in a very laborious way. It is clear from the whole history of theology that reflection about the faith has in the end always followed the course of violent polemics and anathemas. In any renewal, what is authentic for Christian life is always mixed up with so much that is not authentic that the new aspects which again and again emerge must in the first place be purified. Every crisis is a crisis of growth, but what is taking form, throughout the course of time, in these constantly renewed birth pangs, is the sound growth of theology, which will continue as long as "we are away from the Lord" (2 Cor 5:6). [1953]

22/ What Is Genuine Theology?

Genuine theology comes about in two phases, which together form a dialectical whole.

First, any theological proposition must be able to be substantiated by an appeal to the tradition of Christian faith in which the theologian stands. This means that all theologians are in each case involved with *interpretation*. Theology is a *hermeneutical enterprise*. This entails that theologians use certain, in point of fact multiple and diverse, methods of interpretation, which are borrowed mainly from literary criticism. (Think of the historical-literary critical method, the structuralist and semiotic methods, so-called materialist exegesis, etc.). The method used must then be explained and substantiated. Each method has its own "philosophy" and is not "innocent"; they all have a very directed intention. Finally, the elaboration of criteria is necessary, on the basis of which certain interpretations of the Christian tradition can be critically and publicly judged. There has to be a criteriology of orthodoxy.

Second, any theological proposition must also be substantiated by an appeal to the analyzed and interpreted "contemporary situation." Otherwise there will be a short-circuiting between the categories of experience and thought of the past, and those of the present. These two steps, however, form but one dialectical whole. For we understand the Christian tradition really only from the questions which the contemporary situation in which we live puts to us. Understanding the past already implies an interpretation of the present. And conversely, our understanding of the present itself stands under the historical influence of the Christian tradition. [1983]

23/ The Task of the Theologian

One of the fundamental tasks of theology is to attempt to put into words new experiences, with their criticism of earlier experiences, to reflect them and to formulate them as a question to the religious tradition, the church, and to the social and cultural circumstances in which the church finds itself. By virtue of this activity the theologian becomes vulnerable, because here he is in a special way a searcher, and because he is experimental and hypothetical in his assertions. For it is by no means clear from the start which elements in new experiences are important and which irrelevant for Christian faith. The theologian looks for the cognitive and productive force and significance of new experiences, instead of simply working on the concepts used in the New Testament and during the course of church history, in which earlier experiences were expressed. On the other hand, this first attempt is not chaotic or arbitrary; for by discerning the spirits the theologian attempts to discover whether new experiences are really the present echo of the inspiration and orientation which, in the context of the recollection of the biblical mystery of Christ, present their identity anew in these experiences or prove alien to them. [1977]

24/ *The Magisterium, Tradition, and Scripture*

Revelation in word and deed is not handed down within the church in a mechanical way, like a dead thing passed on from hand to hand. It is, on the contrary, essentially linked with its living subject, the church, consisting of the living people of God headed by the ecclesiastical office, both of which are under the guidance of the spirit of the heavenly Lord. The entire church is subject to tradition—the church which prays and lives in faith, hope, and love, the church which celebrates the liturgical mysteries, the church which is apostolically effective in its office and in its people and the church which reflects on its faith. The entire church carries out this tradition, but each part of the church does this in its own place and in its own way, the laity as the people of God and the office of the church in its hierarchical leadership. In addition, the ecclesiastical office as a whole also has a critical function. Everything that comes about and is brought to light within the life of the church must be carefully considered according to its apostolic and biblical content.

It is true that this consideration is also the task of everyone in the church, both lay people and those holding office, but it is the exclusive function of the teaching office of the church finally to judge whether we are faced, in connection with any definite reaction on the part of the people of the church, with an infallible, apostolic, and biblical reaction, or with a human—and perhaps all too human—reaction. In this sense, the church's teaching office is the judge of our faith, but it is this because it is itself governed by the norm of scripture. The magisterium of the church does not, therefore, stand above scripture, but it does stand above our interpretation of scripture. According to the Catholic view, then, scripture has a critical function with regard to the concrete and empirical appearance of the church. It is fundamentally Christ himself who interprets scripture through his spirit, active in the entire church and in a special way in the office of the church. . . . It will consequently be clear that I regard as alien to Catholicism both any exclusive assertion of the *sola scriptura,* the *sola traditio,* or the *solum magisterium,* and similarly any affirmation of two or three parallel and independent sources. Both the scriptures and tradition are necessary to the life of the church. But, on the other hand, scripture and tradition also need the church and each other if they are to be recognised as canonical scriptures and as authentically apostolic tradition. Apostolic scripture is not scripture as, for example, Marcion interpreted it, but as it is interpreted in the church of Christ. The church's supervision of scriptural exegesis does not place it above scripture, but merely points to the church's recognition of the exclusively apostolic principle as the norm of Christian faith and of life in the church. And this recognition of the apostolic authority with regard to our faith means in the last resort a recognition of the *auctoritas,* the power and authority, of God as the only and the exclusive criterion of Catholic faith—the Father sent his Son and manifested himself in him, and Christ sent his apostles, who became the foundation of the church. [1963]

25/ Tensions between Theologians and the Magisterium

A certain tension between the pastoral magisterium and the "scientific" authority of the theologians is part of the normal life of the church. For on the basis of faith theology also has a critical function with respect to the concrete forms in which this faith and the magisterium's presentations of it appear. But if this tension takes on the overtones of too strong a tension or even a situation of conflict, then there is something awry in the church's life, be it on the side of the actual exercise of the pastoral authority, be it on the side of the theologizing taking place, be it in the dialogue between the two. There are various elements one can distinguish here.

1. In contrast to the modernist crisis at the beginning of this century, it is striking that whenever certain theologians now are called to give an account of themselves by the organs of ecclesiastical authority, we believe rather generally in, and largely rather spontaneously choose, the side of the "suspect theologian." This is caused by many different things: e.g., that theology is no longer done in a sealed-off Latin ghetto, and is accessible for many believers, and has become a public matter. The phenomenon also indicates a greater competence on the part of believers, who know how to sift the wheat from the chaff without need of any intervention from higher authorities. Considering that greater competence of believers, it is noteworthy that in the published dossier of the

"Schillebeeckx case," as well as that of Hans Küng and Jacques Pohier, the Roman Congregation of the Doctrine of the Faith gives as the main reason for its intervention precisely the disturbing of the faithful by theologians. Likewise in his official commentary on the *Nova Agendi Ratio*, the new rules for doctrinal investigation promulgated by Pope Paul VI on January 15, 1971, Bishop Jerome Hamer concedes this point expressly: "May not believers who feel disturbed or confused in their faith demand clarification from a priest, a bishop, or from Rome?" On the one hand, therefore, a fairly general support of the "suspect" theologians by believers, on the other hand an appeal by ecclesiastical authority to theologians' disturbing the faithful: against the historically determinable, non-anonymous believers who show their approval, an appeal to the anonymous masses. That is an appeal which we know from elsewhere as one to the "silent majority," without any sociological guarantee that correct information is being presented. That there are things "disturbing to the faith" no one will deny. I would count myself among those so disturbed, because as Augustine and Thomas saw it, being disturbed belonged to the essence of Christian faith. Behind that which is often unrightfully called "disturbing the faithful" are hidden all kinds of disturbing things: for example, being disturbed about the decline our culture is going through. Or being disturbed politically, because a politicized view of the gospel which holds for a preferential love for the poor brings with it a critique of "rightist positions." It is also striking that (insofar as there are sociological data on this subject) those being disturbed in their faith do not seem to be workers or in the lower classes, but in the well-to-do social classes, the industrialists and the "rich" of our society. Often these merely defend their acquired positions in which they do not want to be disturbed or made uneasy by a vision of the gospel which has come to life. Church doctrine as it has been taught to them in the last hundred years is for them a mighty support indeed. While previously they experienced their religion without much feeling as a component in a proper bourgeois way of life, without much *engagement*, they are now suddenly "disturbed" and mobilized. Alongside this group there are others indeed of deep faith, who are very much unsettled in their old concepts by all the rapid changes brought into traditional church life since the Second Vatican Council (whereas previously the life of the church was held up to them as an almost absolutely immutable whole). *These* people are victims of our previous absolutist conceptions and certainly have a right to our caution and care.

One can overestimate as well as underestimate the influence of theologians. Directly—and no doubt even more via pastoral ministers and workgroups—what are called "the new Christologies" were more widely spread than one assumes; they connect in more closely to the concrete world of experience of people. But this still in no way legitimates a populist appeal to the unnuanced principle of theologians' "disturbing the faithful." The uncertainty was already there before the theologian was, who tried to discover, to decipher, and to thematize, precisely in order to be able to offer the faithful some help and perspective. The appeal to the "silent disturbed ones" assumes a pre-modern society. There faith found social confirmation, and only now and again was disturbed by the deviant opinion of a theologian. At that time the principle of what was called the "maiores" and "minores" in faith was in force: the "maiores," those "in the know" in matters of faith, were the bishops, the priests, and the "lower clergy." The "minores" were the non-intellectuals, the believing masses who had to be protected against possible heresies of theologians. In a modern, pluralist society, on the other hand, every world view, including the Catholic world view, finds itself in a socially precarious situation, challenged by many different forms offered, from which a choice can be made. In that sense, the modern pluralist society is by definition "disturbing to the faithful," while theologians try to give some perspective and new security within the disturbance caused by society. A theology which tries to remain within the great Jewish-Christian tradition, however, cannot act as though in the last two centuries nothing has happened. Of course, "modern society" needs to be critiqued also, and both within and outside the church many people are busy doing so (for some *this* is precisely the cause of their being disturbed!). But one cannot act as though the modern world were not there and then consider belief only to be possible in a pre-modern society (the forms of which one then continues to defend). The purpose of what are called "modern theologies" is by no means one of accommodating the Christian faith to "modernity." One wants to allow faith to preserve its own productive and critical power in a modern world whose one-sidedness is transparent. And this approach does not permit one-way traffic only, neither (a) in the direction of a more intense decision of the will whereby one "positivistically" chooses for the tradition of Christian faith *against* the modern world; nor (b) in the direction of a mere accommodation of faith to "modernity," which makes the modern world normative for new theological formulation. Both directions are sterile—one could call the first a "positivism of tradition," while the second actually deserts the Christian position and is "reductionist." A third possibility of "two-way traffic" is necessary: a mutually critical confrontation of the tradition of faith and the critically analyzed and reflected upon "new" in contemporary experiences and conflictual social situations. To be sure, this seems to me to be the most difficult way, but the only right one.

In my opinion, there is already a large difference in the theological sensibility between what are called the new Christologies in comparison with the christological approach of the Roman authorities. The latter say that "modern theologians" are following the second path, while they themselves tread the first path and those "modern theologians" are in fact following the third path, certainly at least in their deepest intention. All kinds of misunderstandings arise from this situation, as well as differences in the establishment of norms. The third path requires critique and hermeneutics. The first path (followed by Rome) appeals only to the authority of previous councils (without any hermeneutical considerations). The second path leads along a way unacceptable for faith. The danger that an interrogation of theologians "in the name of the Congregation of the Doctrine of the Faith" pretty well becomes a dialogue of the deaf is then very close at hand; or rather, it has already moved into the "red salon" of the Holy office. (I must add, however, that this does not therefore hold for all the participants in the discussion present.)

2. If it had not already come to me from the dossier, something did become certainly clear to me during the so-called colloquium which, by the way, confirms that Rome is taking the first path. The Second Vatican Council expressly deleted a formula out of the preliminary first schema: the distinction between the sacred scripture as the remote norm (*regula remota*) of Christian faith and the church's magisterium as the immediate or proximate norm of faith (*regula proxima*). In practice it appears that the Congregation of the Doctrine of the Faith continues to use the discarded principle, and indeed as the main criterion for judging the orthodoxy in faith of a theologian. But the Second Vatican Council expressly has said, instead of this outdated principle, that "the task of interpreting God's Word authentically belongs to the living magisterium of the Church," but that this magisterium "does not stand above the Word of God." Moreover, it is said of this Word or of the gospel that it is entrusted "to the entire people . . . united with its shepherds." This theological and ecclesiological structure in which the pastoral magisterium lies embedded is completely absent in the actual procedures of investigation. The believing constituency, the actual reading public of the "suspect" author, are not listened to; neither the local bishop nor the grand chancellor of the Catholic University is asked about his assessment, nor even the theologian's religious superior (which also counts in the case of a religious). Even less is the mutual theological discussion allowed to do its work. Those most concerned and those with a primary interest in the matter (not to mention the "suspect" theologian himself) do not really get a chance. All of this makes a positive as well as a negative verdict unsatisfying and even ambiguous. The same holds if one lets the whole matter

"run out of steam," for in that case one needs to remember the words of Cardinal Alfrink: "The entire community of faith of the Church will wish that the Church, in carrying out its commission, will find ways to develop ever better methods, which breathe the spirit of the Gospel, which respect believing persons, which do not proceed from indictments of suspicion, and which make every effort to safeguard the good name of believing persons."

Catholic theology is indeed still a long way from coming to terms with Luther's objection that it cannot reconcile the primacy of the gospel (accepted by both the Augsburg Confession and the Second Vatican Council) with the primacy of the pope. For how is it concretely demonstrated and proven that the primacy of the pope is subordinated to the primacy of the gospel? There are problems here yet to be solved, problems which cannot be solved solely by an authoritative statement (as many implicit retractions and some explicit rehabilitations—sometimes after centuries—have shown).

3. In view of the dossier, it seems that "clarity" counts as the most important principle for the Congregation of the Doctrine of the Faith. What is meant is the clarity of the articulated dogmatic formulas in the past. First of all, one would have to remark that the clarity of a conceptual formula is of less importance than the allusive speaking of an ever metaphorical and "analogous" language of faith. In a halting fashion, this kind of language points to an ungraspable mystery that can never be caught in a clear formula, even though it brings to articulation (within a specific interpretive framework) certainly something of "the truth." Moreover, secondly, that clarity is very misleading. For insofar as there is clarity, to that extent it must be situated within thinking in models and the interpretive frameworks of a specific period of church history. I myself referred again and again both in my written "Response" as well as during my interrogation in Rome to the "unclarity" of dogmatic formulations (in the area of Christology), given the semantic developments around concepts like "nature" and "person." But this is an unclarity which has nothing in common with the vague but allusive character of the language of faith as such; the intended "clarification" is therefore misleading. No purely conceptual clarification (however necessary they sometimes can be) makes religious and thus metaphorical speaking superfluous, except for those who propose in a Hegelian fashion the absorption of the metaphor into the univocal concept.

For myself the most alienating thing in the Roman discussion was the certainty with which one of the three theologian-interrogators gave witness. He was convinced that alongside statements of faith needing interpretation there were also statements of faith which were clear and evident in themselves, without any "interpretation." As an example he gave "God" in the statement "Jesus is God," as though God is not in our time the most problematic concept of all. The word "hermeneutic" was therefore already *a priori* under suspicion in the discussion. I had to come to the conclusion that, while the Catholic Church has officially parted ways with biblical fundamentalism since *Divino Afflante Spiritu* in 1943, since that time a kind of "magisterial fundamentalism" has gotten back in through a back door.

The bottom line is: with all of this, it is still not clear what is "correct"! Considering the theological presuppositions which seem to underlie the pieces from the Congregation, it seemed to be a matter, at least implicitly, of whether I subscribed to "their" presuppositions (which I in no way did), rather than whether all participants in the discussion shared in the same one, catholic, and apostolic faith. So one can ask once again: what is the real ecclesiological and theological value of an eventual final judgment (in a negative or positive sense)? Personally I am inclined to answer: just about none whatsoever, although it is more pleasant for a theologian not to be officially "condemned" by his own church. [1980]

3

The Interpretive Task
of Theology

In the latter half of the 1960s Schillebeeckx undertook extensive studies in hermeneutics and philosophy of language. Hermeneutics, or the study of interpreting texts, originally dealt principally with the interpretation of the Bible. Since the beginning of the nineteenth century, and especially in Germany under the influence of Friedrich Schleiermacher and Wilhelm Dilthey, it was directed at any text in religion or the humanities.

Schillebeeckx took up the study of this German tradition, especially as it was then developed as the "new hermeneutics," that is, a reinterpretation of that tradition in light of Heidegger's philosophy. The older hermeneutics stressed the historical character of any text and saw the best entry to the meaning of a text in the reconstruction of the mind of the author of the text to discover the original intent of that text. Heidegger's contribution to hermeneutics lay in his development of a philosophy of being which stressed the historical character, or historicity, of being itself. From 1928 on he explored what impact such a view would have on our modes of knowing and understanding, our use of language, and of language itself as revelatory of the historicity of being. Heidegger was very influential in German Protestant theology, particularly upon the work of the New Testament exegete Rudolf Bultmann, and in the 1950s and early 1960s on the theologians Ernst Fuchs and Gerhard Ebeling, who synthesized the "new hermeneutics."

Schillebeeckx studied the new hermeneutics to see what might be appropriated for a Catholic hermeneutics. The stress on the importance of a philosophy of language led him to explore the

Anglo-American philosophies of language as well, especially those of Wittgenstein, Ian Ramsey, and their synthesis by the theologian John Macquarrie. By 1970, Schillebeeckx was moving into critical theory away from the new hermeneutics, but a number of the concepts from the new hermeneutics have remained part of his subsequent vocabulary and are presented in the selections here. Two important concepts he took away from the Anglo-American philosophies of language were "disclosure," a term which he uses extensively in talking about God's activity in human history; and "language game," which was explained already above. The study of philosophy of language gave him a finer sensitivity to how language is used than is often found among theologians.

Selections 26 through 31 present major insights into the new hermeneutics which he has retained in his later work. The first of these selections states the basic hermeneutical question: what is a faithful reading of the Christian tradition and experience? Selection 27 sets out his own program of what would need to be done to carry out the new hermeneutics.

The last four selections provide definitions, as it were, of concepts which Schillebeeckx has continued to use in his work. Selection 28 sets out what is meant by the historicity of being and why thinking about this is important: why the concept of historicity is essential to the process of understanding itself. Selection 29 looks at the concept of preunderstanding, that understanding we already bring along to the investigation of a text. Selection 30 describes the hermeneutical circle, or process of knowing peculiar to hermeneutics. The last selection looks at the tripartite structure of the language event: speaker, listener, and message.

26/ *Hermeneutics and Theology*

The "new hermeneutics" seeks to expose the ontological structures of the theological understanding of reality as a totality. It is an attempt to clarify the presuppositions of the theological quest for reality in a situation wherein man, estranged from history and nature, raises the question of the meaninglessness of a world which he himself has created by technical and scientific ingenuity and is inclined to regard as the only relevant reality. . . .

The hermeneutical problem—since time immemorial, the problem of bridging the gap between the text and the reader—has come to a head in our own times. Indeed, the identity of faith, the problem of the relationship between scripture and present-day preaching by the church, is at stake. Can we and may we simply go on repeating word for word the "old" material, the Bible and the traditional statements, including those of the official magisterium of the church in the present and the past, under the penalty of being unfaithful to the message if we do otherwise? Or is not just such a literal repetition itself unfaithful—is *development* in dogma, an interpretative contemporary translation of the "old" material of the faith, not essentially the fidelity that follows from man's historicity? If it is, how can this be done without being false to the gospel and to the church which lives from the gospel? What, then, are the hermeneutical principles for this interpretative translation, this reinterpretation? [1967]

27 / A Program for the Hermeneutical Enterprise

I should like to throw a little light on a number of requirements for a system of theological hermeneutics, dealing with them in order of increasing importance. Theology interprets God's word, but this is expressed in human words. Theology, as the hermeneutics of God's word, is therefore also concerned with semantics: it presupposes a concept of what language is. The theologian must therefore listen very carefully to those who have specialised in the study of language and have considered language from different points of view. This approach is based on a respect for the word of God, which, although it is only spoken and recognised in human words, cannot be confused with man's own inventions or imaginings. The theologian has therefore to concern himself with structuralist linguistics and with logical linguistic analysis and must study these not as philosophies, but rather as sciences. He must also carefully consider the phenomenological philosophy of language.

On the other hand, the theologian is above all concerned with the interpretation of a reality which is expressed through literary documents. He will therefore have to pay close attention to an ontology of language which analyses the expression of reality in human language and views human speech in its ontological dimension, that is, as the universal revelation of being in the word. Christianity is not gnosticism, however, or a theoretical doctrine of salvation, and the original confession of Christian faith was therefore the theoretical aspect of the sacramental praxis of Christian life (the creed used at baptism).

For these reasons we are bound to point out how insufficient any purely theoretical hermeneutics are, and how orthopraxis forms an essential part of any criterion used for verification in a credible interpretation of faith. [1969]

28/ *Historicity of Being as the Basis for Hermeneutics*

It is precisely this distance in time, the filled "interim" between, for example, the Council of Trent and our own period, which evokes the hermeneutical problem. Ultimately, it *is* the hermeneutical problem. How can a being, personally involved in history, understand history in a *historical* manner? Ricoeur has formulated the problem more clearly than anyone else: How can human life, expressing itself, objectivize itself (for example, in a text) and, consequently, how does human life, objectivizing itself in this way, call meanings into being which can later be taken up again and understood by another historical being in a different historical situation? Hermeneutics points to what enables us to listen to the meaning of the message which comes to us from the utterances of men in the past. As we have already seen, the distance in time is not something that has to be spanned, but a positive condition that makes it possible for us to understand the past precisely as the past. That is why, on generally hermeneutical grounds, scripture (which, as a text, also has a future dimension of its own) cannot be understood if the tradition of faith which has grown out of it is neglected. Biblicism is condemned in advance by the very historicity of our existence and our understanding. Historical objectivity is the truth of the past *in the light of the present* and not a reconstruction of the past in its unrepeatable factuality. Simply to repeat the earlier formulae of faith word for word is to misconceive the historicity of our existence as men and is therefore a grave danger to genuinely biblical orthodoxy. No one can dissociate himself from the spirit of the age in which he is living and from the living questions which arise from it. It is from his own period that a man questions the past. Hence every age rewrites history and sees the *same* past quite *differently*, and it is possible for the reader of history to savor the distinctive quality not only of the period being studied and interpreted but of the period in which the history is being written. The historicist or positivist, in whose view the texts should be allowed to speak for themselves—"objectively"—without any modern presuppositions, without being placed in the light of the present, sees a failure of objectivity in all this. [1967]

29/ Preunderstanding in the Hermeneutical Process

Everyone agrees that anyone who wants to understand a text must be ready to submit to the authority of that text and should not impose his own meaning on it. Textual interpretation should never become eisegesis. The text itself is binding and acts as a norm to understanding. This is based on general hermeneutical principles (and not on, for example, biblical "inspiration") and applies to every text—whether scriptural, conciliar or a passage from profane literature. A hermeneutically trained thinker must *a priori* be open to the deviation of the text from his own views, demands and expectations. What is thematically new in modern hermeneutics is our having come to realize that this openness is made possible not by our adopting a neutral attitude and putting our own background in brackets in an effort to exclude it, but only by our doing the direct opposite— quite consciously admitting the light that we can throw on the text in question from our own contemporary situation. The exclusion of the presuppositions and prejudgments (that is, prior judgments) which we all have because we are situated in history and live from the past in the present towards a future does not involve the elimination of these presuppositions altogether; on the contrary, we should remain *conscious* of the fact that we approach the text from a preunderstanding and that we must, in so doing, *confront* that text with our own preunderstanding. The process of understanding is accomplished precisely in the possible *correction* of our preunderstanding. In the understanding of faith, which is subject to God's speaking to us, this correction of our preunderstanding is of a very special nature, but in its formal structures it follows the general hermeneutical pattern. It is precisely those presuppositions which we have not made conscious (but which are nonetheless always present) which make us blind to, or screen us from, a right understanding of, say, the texts of the Council of Trent. Prejudgment does not in itself have an unfavorable meaning. Its positive content reveals it as a necessary structural aspect of all understanding. [1967]

30/ The Hermeneutical Circle

This Catholic interpretation of the "development of dogma" implies in a specific way what, on the basis of Heidegger especially, both Bultmann and his followers and, independently of this school, Protestant philosophers such as P. Ricoeur and H.-G. Gadamer and Protestant theologians such as Paul Tillich and K. Löwith have called the "hermeneutical circle." All understanding takes place in a circular movement—the answer is to some extent determined by the question, which is in turn confirmed, extended or corrected by the answer. A new question then grows out of this understanding, so that the hermeneutical circle continues to develop in a never-ending spiral. Man can never escape from this circle, because he can never establish once and for all the truth or the content of the word of God. There is no definitive, timeless understanding which raises no more questions. The "hermeneutical circle" thus has its basis in the historicity of human existence and therefore of all human understanding. The interpreter belongs to some extent to the object itself that he is trying to understand, that is, the historical phenomenon. All understanding is therefore a form of self-understanding. [1967]

31/ *The Triadic Structure of Understanding*

From the phenomenological point of view, then, speech always has a triadic structure, which has been called the "discourse situation" by John Macquarrie, in other words, the language situation as a human phenomenon. Represented in the form of a diagram, language as an institution is at the centre of a triangle, mediating between the subject speaking, the listeners or readers, and the content of the conversation. The whole, the language situation, is the verbal event in which meaning becomes clear. Any discussion about the meaning of a text or of speech has therefore to take this triadic whole of the language situation into account. Dissociated from this situation, language is simply an abstraction and the interpretation of a text is not a responsible undertaking. Because of the tension between language as an institution and language as a verbal event, the understanding of texts and of speech is only possible in the act of reinterpretation. The minimal requirement of this act of interpretation is structural analysis, but the whole language situation has above all to be analysed. It is important in this context to throw some light on each of the three aspects of the language situation.

In saying something, the subject speaking also expresses himself as a being in the world. This reflects the existential aspect of the linguistic event, "existential" here referring to the existence of man in general, in his environment and together with his world, not in the narrower sense of individual existence. This self-expression includes a range of possibilities, from expression related to the whole of reality, especially in religious statements, to the expression of objective knowledge or science in which the existential factor is on the verge of disappearing, although it never disappears entirely.

In addition to self-expression, there is the referential and representational aspect of language, as conveying a meaning, in its function of saying something about something. Leaving aside meta-language (a statement about a statement) speech always transcends itself by its reference to elements outside language which co-determine its use. Apparently under the influence of such extra-linguistic factors, for example, the Eskimos have some thirty different words for snow.

Finally, there is the aspect of communication. The person listening to the subject who is speaking or who reads that subject's text is also acting as a being in the world. Communication therefore only takes place in the act of reinterpretation and, as a passing on of what is said, is always defective if the partners do not share the same presuppositions and the same sphere of understanding. It is therefore essential that the presuppositions of the subject who speaks or writes and those of the interpreter should be analysed so as to make the offer by the subject of a definite meaning accessible to the person who is listening or reading and to prevent breakdowns in communication. [1969]

4

From Hermeneutical Theology
to Critical Theory

COMMENTARY

By the end of the 1960s, Schillebeeckx was turning away from the
new hermeneutics to the critical theory emerging from a group
around the sociologist Jürgen Habermas in Frankfurt. Habermas
had become the leader of the second generation of the Frankfurt
School of Social Research, succeeding the likes of Theodor Adorno,
Max Horkheimer, Herbert Marcuse, and Erich Fromm. The critical theory Schillebeeckx first appropriated in this period was still
markedly part of his theology in the mid-1980s.

What led to the shift away from hermeneutical theology to
critical theory? Schillebeeckx recounts some of those reasons in
selection 32. The debate between the philosopher Hans-Georg
Gadamer in Heidelberg and Jürgen Habermas certainly contributed
to the move. Habermas pointed out that Gadamer, the premier
theoretician of the new hermeneutics—gave undue prominence to
the tradition and its transmittal in his hermeneutics. The new
hermeneutics was only concerned about the transmittal and interpretation of the *meaning* found in tradition. Its ultimate concern
was the making relevant and present (actualization) of that past
meaning in the present. Such a procedure did not deal with the
fact that history is also full of non-meaning: untruth, violence, and
repression of competing meanings. The new hermeneutics neglected
that fact, and so perpetuated only one tradition—usually the one
which legitimated those in power: the tradition of the victors, not
the victims. Habermas's theory combined the work of those two

great masters of suspicion, Marx and Freud. The new hermeneutics only retrieved the tradition of meaning of the dominant group in society (Marx) for the sake of keeping the present society stable and in continuity with that past meaning (Freud).

Habermas saw, therefore, that the task of interpretation was not just to retrieve the meaning of the past in some theoretical way but to expose the totality of that history, thus also the repression, violence, and alienation which had marked the ascendance of the dominant meaning. Thus, interpretation has an emancipatory task, to free the consciousness of contemporary society from simply those meanings which only legitimate the current structure of society.

No doubt Schillebeeckx found this approach helpful in developing a hermeneutical approach and a way of doing theology which corresponded to his interests in plumbing the meaning of human suffering, the threats to the *humanum*, and the negative dialectics which lead humankind to eschatological freedom.

Selection 32 documents his understanding of the relation between hermeneutical theology and critical theory. It is a challenge to the domination of one way of reading history which concentrates only on the given meanings. It deals instead also with the non-meanings the alienation of human suffering and contrast experiences. It aims at including in the dialectic of history those who have been excluded or silenced. Critical theory becomes the basis for his writings on church and world, on ethics, and for his historical investigation into ministry in the latter half of the 1970s.

Selection 33 points up the task of critical theory: an emancipative praxis. More than the theoretical understanding of hermeneutical theology, this approach calls for a liberating of consciousness from a false understanding (ideology) which in turn calls for contesting the dominant view of society.

Selection 34 addresses that mode of contestation for the theologian: the critique of the dominant consciousness or ideology of a society or tradition. He explores especially what this means for theology: it is to be at work critiquing ideology within the church as well as in the world. Only then can the church come to that true transcendence of itself into an eschatological future via an orthopraxis. This is the subject of selection 35.

Selection 36 defines theology as "the self-consciousness of Christian praxis," which interprets the activity-and-reflection (praxis) of the community. Thus, the theologian needs to be in touch not only with the tradition but also with the living communities of the present. Later on, Schillebeeckx will single out especially those communities who live in the gaps between meaning and alienation: the critical communities who are seeking out an emancipative praxis (see selections 58 and 66 especially). The potential implications of this for the critical theologian are explored in selection 37.

32/ Hermeneutical Theology and Critical Theory

The contrast may be expressed in the following way: the hermeneutic tradition looks in history for what can be made present again, while critical theory looks for what cannot be made present again. Both approaches are fully justified, since history is an insane complex of sense and nonsense. Those who practised the hermeneutic sciences or the humanities had to some extent forgotten that our relationship with the past contains elements of division and justified opposition. Now, however, those who practise critical theory seem to forget that thought (one form or another of philosophical, reflective thought) has an original relationship with what comes to us through tradition in the form of meaning already acquired. This shortsightedness reminds one of Heidegger's "forgetfulness of being."

A first, provisional confrontation between the analytic tendency of critical theory and the hermeneutic tendency of theology (and of philosophy) is therefore already possible. This confrontation is inevitable for two principal reasons. In the first place, theology is essentially a hermeneutic undertaking, because it attempts to make the meaning that has been proclaimed in history present here and now in our contemporary existence, whereas critical theory opens our eyes above all to the elements of nonsense in our existence, those elements for which history is also responsible. The second reason for this confrontation is that modern theology prefers, rightly, to use the behavioural or social sciences as one of its points of departure. The principal question then is whether this point of departure is, in the terminology of critical theory, the sociology of the establishment or a social science which is "critical." It has, however, to be recognised that, if theology does not make use of the second (critical) form of sociology, it is always in grave danger of becoming an ideology, both by presenting and continuing the Christian message that has been expressed in history and by its appeal to the humanities in this process.

Since the Enlightenment theology has, by comparison with the earlier *hermeneutica profana* and *hermeneutica sacra,* become hermeneutic in a completely new way, having been made more sensitive by the loss of traditional authority. Spinoza was one of the first to evolve a form of critical hermeneutics by his deep awareness of the fact that our relationship with the past contains elements of division. In theology, however, the romantic reduction of the concept of understanding quickly gained the upper hand, with the result that critical hermeneutics soon became identified with Schleiermacher's "new hermeneutics." Later, Dilthey became the main exponent of this new hermeneutic science. He certainly inherited the critical spirit of the Enlightenment, but his main concern was to restore the meaning handed down by tradition to which full justice was no longer done because of the breakdown in modern communications. Closely related to these heremeneutics are the "new" hermeneutic projects of Rudolf Bultmann and his successors, Gerhard Ebeling and Ernst Fuchs especially. These heremeneutics are based on the one hand on the younger Heidegger and on the other on the older Heidegger and have been formulated in a classical manner by H.-G. Gadamer. There is certainly a connection between hermeneutics and criticism in these later "new" systems of hermeneutics, expressed especially in Heidegger's "hermeneutic circle" which has been given the better title of "hermeneutic spiral" by the French historian H. Marrou and the American theologian Ray Hart. After all, a circular movement is unending.

Within the hermeneutic circle, there is an interaction between our understanding of traditional relationships of meaning and the constant correction of our own preunderstanding. This critical, corrective impulse goes back in practice to the dominant claim of the tradition that we are aiming to make present. The apparent point of departure is the presupposition that what is handed down in tradition, and especially the Christian tradition, is always meaningful, and that this meaning only has to be deciphered hermeneutically and made present and actual. The fact that tradition is not only a source of truth and unanimity, but also a source of untruth, repression and violence is not forgotten in hermeneutics, but it is also not considered systematically. At least as a theme, this particular insight of the Enlightenment has found no place in the hermeneutics of the humane sciences as used by theologians. With its own special method, this form of hermeneutics can therefore discover the breakdowns of communication in the dialogue with history which are the result of original differences in the sphere of understanding, but not those which are the result of repressive and violent power structures that already exist as given in any society. With precisely this last category in mind, critical theory presents us with the possibility of an extension of hermeneutic reflection, which can be brought about especially by this critical theory in view of the particular orientation of its model of interpretation. It has in fact discovered a new dimension in the hermeneutic process of understanding. It not only takes into account the breakdowns in historical communication between men from case to case, but also gives a central place in its investigations to the analysis of the significance and the compelling logic of such breakdowns. It conducts a systematic analysis of the violent structural elements present in every social system.

In view of this model of interpretation, it is clear that critical theory does not aim to make the past present today so much as to provide a key for a hermeneutic understanding which is a criticism of tradition to the extent that we cannot find ourselves in it "as in a dialogue." This kind of hermeneutic understanding is not just directed toward pure communication, as the hermeneutics based on the humane sciences certainly are, but rather towards an emancipation from repression and domination, which are experienced as a failure and as an alienation and can therefore be criticised as "historically entirely superfluous." The hermeneutic process is really an "understanding of tradition *against* tradition" and is therefore an emancipation from tutelage in subjection to tradition insofar as this is a context of compulsion. This kind of understanding is at the same time also the condition for emancipation at the level of praxis.

This model of interpretation can be accused of one-sidedness, but it is certainly justified. In any case, why should this one-sided interest be any less important than an equally one-sided interest in the meaningful elements of tradition? It is problematic to attempt to make traditional meaning present and actual without having clearly in mind what cannot be made present—and vice versa.

We have already seen in these comments that the right of an actualising theology to exist is not violated by critical theory, because this theory implicitly, nonetheless really, presupposes that hermeneutics is meaningful. All the same, it is difficult to understand why the implicit hermeneutic circle of critical theory should be justified and why the explicit hermeneutic circles of the hermeneutic sciences are not justified. Critical theory correctly directs the attention of hermeneutical theologians in a systematic way towards aspects which they, in their preoccupation with making tradition present, tend to forget. Critical theory draws their attention to the contingent aspect of tradition which is often apparently hypostatised in theological hermeneutics. In the hermeneutics of the humane sciences, after all, a methodological abstraction is made of this contingent aspect and of the contestive criticism that is evoked by it. As a consequence, theologians, both in their historical investigations and in their "actualising" reflections, often have a barely concealed idealist concept of history. They tend to regard the history of the church's *kerygma* and her dogmas purely as a kind of history of ideas. This autonomous development of ideas remains enclosed within speculation about faith and perpetuates itself on the basis of purely internal *aporias* which can only be solved by a process of speculative thought and dialogue, which in turn give rise to new speculative *aporias* and so on. The whole of man's history thus takes place within a purely theoretical circle of thought. Reference to the classical manuals of the history of dogma confirms the suspicion that there is at least an element of truth in this judgment. There is no need to assert that those who specialise in the history of dogma have no feeling for the findings of critical theory—most of them have a strong enough sense of reality. On the other hand, however, it cannot be claimed that they have given enough deliberate and systematic attention to those aspects that particularly concern modern man, who consciously wishes to take his place in the history of emancipative freedom. No apostolically orientated theology can afford to ignore this or it will degenerate into an esoteric study which no outsider will understand.

In the light of the salutary challenge presented by critical theory to theology, I should like to state explicitly that hermeneutic theology must be inspired by a practical and critical intention. This implies that the orthopraxis that has been discussed repeatedly in previous chapters of this book is an essential element of the hermeneutical process. Although it is, of course, possible to dispute precisely what may be called *orthos* in our praxis, it is in any case certain, on the basis of both human and Christian motivation, that any praxis which manipulates human freedom and brings about alienation is both wrong and heterodox. If this criterion were taken seriously into account, we should make considerable progress!

It is therefore clear that a theologically actualising interpretation is not possible without a critical theory which acts as the self-consciousness of a critical praxis. If the unity of faith takes place in real history, in other words, if it is itself really history, then we must not hope to be able to attain unity in faith either purely hermeneutically or by means of a purely theoretical theological interpretation. History is a flesh and blood affair and what has come about in history—the divisions in the Christian church, for instance—can never be put right by purely theoretical means. History is an experience of reality which takes place in a series of conflicts, which can only be resolved if the theory used is really the self-consciousness of a praxis. I would therefore agree with J. B. Metz's contention that the historical identity which Christianity has lost cannot be regained by making Christian traditions present and actual again purely theoretically. Christianity is, in its very being and therefore also in its history, much more than simply a history of interpretation. A purely theoretical interpretation of Christianity, an "orthodoxy" based on an idealist view of history, will in our own times inevitably come into conflict with the problems with which the reality of history itself confronts us. The churches are really the "community of God" and the "temple of the Holy Spirit," with the result that we are bound to speak about this in the language of faith. At the same time, however, the churches are also historical and contingent. "The earthly church and the church enriched with heavenly things . . . are not to be considered as two realities" (*Lumen gentium* 8). [1971]

33/ *Critical Theory as Emancipative Praxis*

Critical theory aims at a theoretical understanding which essentially accompanies an emancipative praxis. The analysis of social relationships does not aim to collect a theoretical knowledge of "what is"—scientific knowledge of this is irreplaceable. Scientific analysis aims to collect knowledge of what can be and of what must be, though this may be negative, as will appear later. This analysis does in fact also produce knowledge of what is, but the aim of the analysis is above all an emancipative praxis. It explains its knowledge of what is in the formal sense of what can be and not, for example, in the sense of what must necessarily be or of what ought ethically to be or even of what is eternally valid.

In critical theory, then, the reconstruction of history is at the service of its interest in a reconstruction of contemporary social relationships and this interest functions precisely as a criticism of those relationships. In other words, the understanding that critical theory has in mind is a historical understanding of repressive relationships insofar as they are experienced as violent, and of the justification of coercion and domination insofar as this is experienced as untrue. The aim of this understanding is to clear these relationships out of the way. It is clear, then, that what is involved here is a model of interpretation which can be used to enable society to understand itself, above all in the sense of the alienations that are present in that society. The special characteristic of this model, however, is that it is not simply a model of interpretation. On the contrary, the interpretation is inwardly linked to a critical praxis of contestation of these social structures. The interest in knowledge is identical with the interest in emancipative praxis, which is an enlightened praxis determined by scientifically explanatory interpretation. [1971]

34/ *Ideology and Ideology Critique as Hermeneutics*

Especially since the 1960s, partly occasioned by the polemic between Hans-Georg Gadamer and Jürgen Habermas, many a theologian has come to the insight that a purely theoretical hermeneutical theology can lead to wrong actualization, or at least that such an undertaking can lose its contextual credibility. The purely theoretical approach forgets that there can be ideological moments in both the Christian tradition (as it comes to us en bloc) and the contemporary situation in which we live.

"Ideology" I understand in the first instance as something positive which, however, can come to manifest pathological traits. The negative or unfavorable meaning of ideology I see therefore as derivative, that is, as a pathology of something good. In a positive sense, I define "ideology" as an ensemble of images, ideas and symbols which a society creates to give an account of its own identity. Ideology is the reproduction *and* confirmation of one's own identity by means of "foundational symbols" (symbolic universe of meaning). This ideological function of identification and ensuring of one's own identity can take on pathological forms, however, and so one comes to various negative forms of "ideology," analyzed in divergent ways by Karl Marx, Nietzsche and Freud, and many others since them. The function of ideology becomes pathological, especially insofar as that legitimation is distorted, manipulated, and monopolized by dominating groups in society. In this way ideology becomes a means of maintaining dominant interests, and is as such the mirroring of a false group consciousness. But because the group cannot give a false view of itself if it is not first constituted on the symbolic level, unfavorable meaning of ideology is not original. Precisely *because* every community has a symbolic structure, these symbols can also become mendacious and pathological. That is how I understand ideology in this second, derivative sense.

"Ideologically critical hermeneutics" or de-ideologization means for me the unmasking of the naive idea that *being* and *language* (= thinking and speaking) are always supposed to be coextensive despite all the conceptual inadequation, recognized already in classical times. For whoever realizes that thinking and speaking are also dependent upon all sorts of interests will not celebrate such a naive conception with regard to "conceptually theoretical" knowledge. It is not infrequent that concepts and theories are used to justify systematically and guarantee social circumstances and positions of power. If Christian theologians thus try to do justice to the binding substance of faith of biblical and church statements in its authentic evangelical breadth, they will come to the realization that an ideology-critical analysis belongs to the essence of hermeneutical theology, precisely on the basis of fidelity to the Word of God. Often the history of theology is, too, a history of conquerors and powerful ones who marginalize evangelically possible alternatives or even, once conquered, silence them—although only for a time, because forgotten truths always work their way back to the surface.

Undoubtedly there are also always voices raised which have claimed and still claim that that history of the conquerors is concretely only the result of the saving activity of God's spirit in the leadership of the church and that therefore there can be no discussion of legitimate alternatives sanctioned by the gospel. No Christian will deny that the grace or activity of the Holy Spirit—soul of the entire ecclesiastical community of faith—while always transcending its historical forms of manifestation, nonetheless is only to be found *in* specific church forms and *in* specific personal or historical forms—never behind them or above them. But in those concrete historical and ecclesiastical forms the felicitous reply of the church with regard to grace is documented, but equally so her historically less adequate and even ideological response to the offer of grace. From the New Testament we hear that the Spirit of God guides the "community of God" through history and holds it fundamentally on the right course. But this promise is in no way a guarantee or alibi for the correspondence of every given historical decision of church leadership to the gospel. Alongside a Syllabus of historically successful decisions one can also set down an "ideologically critical" Denzinger of unsuccessful and, from the perspective of the gospel, even unfortunate Christian decisions. As a matter of fact, the Roman Catholic church itself has rightfully always resisted sectarian claims that the community of faith is only a "church of the pure" or a "church of the holy remnant." This holds, however, equally for the church's pastoral-doctrinal and disciplinary-governing authority. What the church calls "infallible statements" are really only a few, rare and sporadic "traffic signs" on its historical path through life, corrections of course in the many-sided moves of the church. Although I find a self-serving neo-modern triumphalist critique of the church wrong, this does not alter the fact that theologians, "mindful of their own situation," may not hold back their own ideology-critical findings. A church which does not positively permit this or at least tolerate it, shows itself to be weak and little sure of the power of the gospel of the powerless. It is a form of "little faith."

Without de-ideologization, any theoretical-hermeneutical theologizing may go right past the actual question in two ways.

On the one hand, the theologian may end up unconsciously accommodating the tradition of Christian faith to "modern times" in a false "aggiornamento," e.g., to our Western, privatized, technocratic consumer society so directed to the apolitical individual, and to this society's modern belief in progress. Such a theology would relieve Christian faith of its liberating power with regard to the enslaving instances in our modern societies. Faith is then accommodated to categories of thought and experience not critically analyzed of what is called "modern humanity."

On the other hand, the theologian then remains equally deficient with regard to the faith tradition of the past. For this tradition does not come to us in purely evangelical terms, but in categories of thought and experience of many cultures and periods of culture, which just as much need to be investigated from an ideology-critical perspective. The danger here is in positing outdated or ideologically freighted concepts as normative for Christian and theological thought under the guise of the gospel or church tradition, thus unjustly limiting Christians in their evangelical freedom. [1983]

35/ Orthopraxis as a Criterion of Critical Theory

Yet compared with the purely theoretical hermeneutics of the humanities, an essentially new element is introduced here into theological hermeneutics: orthopraxis or "right doing." It is not possible to affirm that we can interpret the past, in advance and purely theoretically, in the light of the present, in order then to interpret, for example, the one baptism, the one celebration of the eucharist and Christian commitment to man and the world as pure consequence of a unity of faith which is already firmly established in advance and purely theoretically verified. Those who practise purely theoretical hermeneutics (Gadamer, Bultmann, Ebeling and Fuchs) affirm, correctly, that the past must be interpreted in the light of the present. The object of Christian faith is, of course, already realised in Christ, but it is only realised in him as our promise and our future. But future cannot be theoretically interpreted, it must be done. The *humanum* which is sought and which is proclaimed and promised to us in Christ is not an object of purely contemplative expectation, but also a historical form which is already growing in this world: at least this is what we have to do, in the perspective of eschatological hope. Christianity is not simply a hermeneutic undertaking, not simply an illumination of existence, but also a renewal of existence, in which "existence" concerns man as an individual person and in his social being.

In interpreting the past in the light of the present, then, it should not be forgotten that eschatological faith imposes on the present the task of transcending itself, not only theoretically, but also as a change to be realised. Only the critical attitude towards the present, and the resulting imperative to change and improve it, really open access to the coming truth. The basic hermeneutic problem of theology, then, is not so much the question of the relationship between the past (scripture and tradition) and the present, but between theory and practice, and this relationship can no longer be solved idealistically, by a theory of Kantian pure reason from which consequences flow for the practical reason, but it will have to be shown how the theory appears in the praxis itself. How, for example, can religious freedom, as formulated by Vatican II, be deduced by purely theoretical exegesis from the church's past? The church's practice in the past at least contradicts this theory rather seriously. Only a new praxis in the church can make the new interpretation credible, namely as a theoretical element in effective practice here and now by the churches themselves. Without the renewal of praxis in the church, there can be no historical basis for the reinterpretation. Indirectly, via the new praxis, this can still be formulated in a theory. [1969]

36/ *Critical Theory, the Church, and Theology*

Insofar as they are empirical data, religion, Christianity and the church all belong to those social forms the structure and function of which merit specific analysis. A critical theory of Christianity can only be built up on the basis of analyses of the historical forms in which it has appeared, and these can be assessed scientifically. But even this does not mean that the critical theory of Christianity is a theology. What it shows, however, is that theology, if it be regarded as a specific form of theory (and this possibility cannot exclude critical theory, which is implicitly based on hermeneutics) cannot be really scientific, and therefore cannot really be theology, if it is not consciously independent of present society. If theology is not conscious of this need and has not assimilated critical theory into its own design, it may well become an unscientific ideology.

Critical theory therefore certainly has the right to criticise a hermeneutic theology which idealistically hypostatises its object of research

and reflection and gives its social infrastructures no place in its considerations. This last question has often been neglected by hermeneutic
theology, even though the results achieved by theology have been surprisingly good, perhaps because it has, in the course of history, been very
sensitive, one might almost say naturally sensitive to man's "sinful heart."
One is reminded here of the wisdom of the East: "however pure you may
be, on your way you will finally meet someone who is more pure and
who will purify you." To this we might add that this saying applies both
to the critic of society and to the theologian. . . .

My claim that theology cannot be traced back to the critical theory
of society or history does not bring the confrontation between the two
to an end. This claim leads to the further assertion that, if the intention
of the theology that continues and actualises the Christian interpretation
of reality is a practical, critical one, then theological hermeneutics are
inevitably correlative with critical theory.

It is quite clear that, if such a theology remains tied to a purely
theoretical form of hermeneutics and is not correlative with the critical
movement of emancipative freedom, it can play no part in bringing
about the history of the future. It will inevitably become a system of
thought, confined to a decreasing minority of thinkers without any
message of liberation for the world.

The relationship between theory and praxis as worked out by Habermas especially is, of course, of great importance to us if we want to
understand correctly the hermeneutic process of this actualising theology.
What is more, critical theory's understanding of itself as the self-
consciousness of a critical praxis is also undoubtedly correct.

The theological process of making the apostolic faith present and
actual in the world of today should not be a purely ideological process.
There should, in other words, be a firm basis in history itself for the
actualising interpretation of faith if this is to be at all credible. If this
historical basis is overlooked, the process of making present will become
purely speculative and theoretical and—as has so often happened—it
will give the impression that all that theologians do is to make use after-
wards of what has already been discovered and exploited. . . .

The theologian can, of course, defend himself, with good reason,
against this charge, by pointing out that his experience is not confined
to the contemporary church, but that it includes the past history of the
church's life of faith. Although there is a good basis for this attitude, it
is not entirely satisfactory because, despite the fact that it is certainly
possible to find initiatives here and there in the past history of the
church which correspond to what are now called movements of religious
freedom, as a general rule the practice of the church in the past points

in the opposite direction. Therefore, if we were now to speak, in an attempt to make the traditional Christian teaching present and actual, of religious freedom as the teaching of the church, very many people would regard this as an unfair adaptation to the present situation and devoid of any basis in the past history of the church.

We can moreover also ask whether the theologian practises theology simply for himself, or simply perhaps for a handful of initiates. I have always been of the opinion that theology ought to be practised for the whole community of believers. These believers may have to trust the theologian's knowledge of scripture and tradition, but should they also trust his authority? What should at least be clear from these questions, however, is that theology is valueless, whether it is progressive or conservative, as soon as it loses contact with the empirical basis of the praxis of the community of believers.

If theology is, as I believe it ought to be, the self-consciousness of Christian praxis, then it cannot, without coming to be regarded as an ideology tolerate a breach between a purely theoretical process of making present and a practical perpetuation and confirmation of earlier praxis. It is not the theologian who is the subject responsible for this process of making present, but the living community of believers. The theologian simply interprets critically their self-consciousness. Praxis, then, is an essential element of this actualising and liberating interpretation. In this sense, then, theology must be the critical theory (in a specifically theological manner) of the praxis of faith. Its point of departure is the contemporary praxis of the church. It analyses the models in which that praxis is presented and the attitudes on which it is based. In correlation with the critical theory of society, it also measures this praxis against its own evangelical claims and thus opens the way for new possibilities, which have, in turn, to be made a living reality in the praxis and faith of the church community. The relationship with praxis therefore forms an inseparable part of theological critical theory. What is more, the theologian, helped by his historical experience, has to express theoretically the theory that is implied in the new activities and patterns of behaviour of the believing community. [1971]

37/ Critical Theory, Faith, and the Theologian

The critical and hermeneutic contribution that the theologian can make to the present and future praxis of the church is above all an understanding of the past and an attempt to make it actual and present, so that we can discover, in our present situation, the direction that we should follow in living for the future.

Theology is the critical self-consciousness of Christian praxis in the world and the church. If we take this as our point of departure, then it seems to me that we should not be alarmed by the fact that the theologian is nowadays, as he has always to some extent been in the past, often suspected both by those who uphold the primacy of reason and by (uncritical) believers who insist on the primacy of faith. In the eyes of both groups of people, the theologian apparently denies the interpretation of reality which they advocate, so that he has to be regarded as heretical. The critical science of faith, which theology aims to be, is therefore condemned as heretical both by faith and by reason. But this is precisely the irreplaceable contribution which both faith and reason can make to the interpretation of reality, insofar as both tend inevitably to perpetuate themselves in establishing a system. The theologian is therefore the custodian of transcendence, but he does not guard it like a treasure. On the contrary, he prevents it from becoming a datum, because he is conscious of the fact that transcendence must be won again and again in the face of historical alienation and must therefore always be kept in mind in any critical praxis. Theology is the critical theory of the critical praxis which has this intention and it therefore does not hesitate to use the meaning and nonsense that have been discovered in man and society by the human, analytical and hermeneutic sciences. It will probably be clear, then, that theology without faith simply produces nonsense and is therefore the opposite of theology, although this does not mean that it cannot achieve positive results at a different level. At the same time, it should also be clear that faith without theology is hardly worthy of the name of faith. [1971]

Part Three

God's Salvation in Jesus Christ

1

Approaches to Jesus of Nazareth

Concurrent with Schillebeeckx's interests in critical theory was a period of study of the exegetical work on the New Testament. Schillebeeckx had shown an interest in salvation—the fundamental Christian experience—from almost the beginning of his theological career. Interest in the bearer of salvation from God, Jesus of Nazareth, was part of that. After addressing the reality of Christ in the sacramental encounter in the 1950s, he wrote a series of articles on Christology in the 1960s. These led him to go back to study the New Testament materials on Jesus of Nazareth and how the early Christian communities came to confess him as Lord.

This process of study culminated in the publication of *Jesus* in 1974, followed by a second volume in 1977. Part III explores the principal aspects of his Christology, concentrating on his thought from *Jesus* into the mid-1980s.

In this first section, preliminaries are explored. Selection 38 presents Schillebeeckx's own summary of *Jesus,* along with his reasons for undertaking that monumental task. The brief selection 39 reechoes a theme found throughout his Christology—the primacy of the experience of the salvation of God in Jesus as the starting point for any confession of Jesus as Lord. Selection 40 looks at the more technical issue of how one is to locate a point of departure in the New Testament materials, working as we do with historical reconstructions which are at best fragmentary. The interaction of the reality of Jesus and the confessions of the early communities is explored.

38/ *A Path Through the Book* Jesus

I have formulated the actual purpose of this book in two places, in about the same way: "I wish to look for possible signs in the critical historical reconstructed image of Jesus which could direct the human question of salvation toward the Christian offer of an answer which points to a special saving activity of God in this Jesus." This issue is thus (in the final redacting of the book) really about the *Christian* "unadulterated Christ." But at the same time (and in this lies the special character of the book) the concern is the disclosure of the pathway whereby modern people who have doubts about the "Christ of the church" again can come to the insight of faith that Jesus of Nazareth is not valued in his true identity if one does not ultimately identify him as the Jesus Christ raised from the dead by God, who is now with the Father, and therefore still living among us in a personal way.

On the basis of this purpose, disclosure of the pathway to Jesus as the way to open the possibility of belief in Christ, the question about the access of the believer to the historical Jesus of Nazareth gains a central significance in this book. This approach is all the more necessary because the offer of salvation from the earthly Jesus of Nazareth and the Christian response to it *come together* within very definite historical experiences and very concrete traditions of experience in the one story of the New Testament. A critical reflection on Jesus Christ requires therefore not only a historical study of what has really come to expression in Jesus of Nazareth, but also of the historical horizon of experience and expectation within which originally Aramaic- and Greek-speaking Jews, and then much later also "pagans," reacted positively to the historical phenomenon, Jesus of Nazareth.

In Part I, the question is asked about the criteria on the basis of which the critical historical study can be placed within a believing purpose. In the course of this, it is shown that, on the one hand, it is extremely necessary to seek out an "image of Jesus" that can withstand every historical critique; on the other hand, that every person in his or her own irreducible particularity escapes the scientific approach, for there is always a surplus which remains after the sum of all the critical results. . . .

If, therefore, the core of the Christian Jesus interpretation consists in Christians acknowledging that God has brought about decisive and definitive salvation for the liberation of people in the life history of Jesus of Nazareth, then the particular historical history of this person Jesus may not be allowed to evaporate, if this believing speaking about "Jesus Christ" does not want to run the chance of becoming an ideology. Therefore it is precisely from theological motives that I am interested in the historically ascertainable earthly appearance of Jesus of Nazareth. This interest in Part I is already prepared for by a long sketch of the so-called "christological situation" of the present in an extended Foreword, where I explain why I have written the book in *this* way and not another. The entire analysis is intended to be a way of extending an invitation to the reader, on the basis of the objectively studied material from the historical investigation, to undergo the same Christian experience or disclosure-discovery as the one the first Christians (Jews) were able to have with Jesus.

After this methodological analysis, I come to Part II, entitled "The Gospel of Jesus Christ." After an introductory analysis of the concept "euangelion" or good news, I wanted to make clear what Jesus preached and how his manner of life was his praxis. Point of departure was Jesus' baptism in the Jordan by John, which was given a prophetic meaning. Then the basic directions of Jesus' appearance as preacher are analyzed: his message of the reign of God mindful of humanity, interpreted as the radical trust and devotion of God to persons for whom he wishes to be the future. This is clarified and given content by means of Jesus' parables and the beatitudes. Then we hear how Jesus' own attitude about life and his communication with God and people are the concrete illustration of what he preaches. Then one after another I analyze Jesus' caring sojourn with people, which comes to expression in his wondrous freedom "to do good" (Jesus' deeds of power or miracles); in his association with his own and his (table) fellowship with rejected people, "tax collectors and sinners"; in his "pity for the flock;" and in his living community with disciples called to "come after" him. In this Jesus appears as the liberator of persons from an overly restrictive image of God (Jesus and the law), and moreover it becomes evident that his *Abba* experience is the source of his message and praxis.

The enthusiasm which all of this can evoke, and indeed did evoke among many, is countermanded however from a certain point, which is historically difficult to situate, by an emerging resistance (especially from the officialdom) to the "Jesus phenomenon" in Israel. The cleansing of the temple appears to have been only a catalyst which, on the one hand, evoked messianic expectations regarding Jesus, and on the other hand (via public opinion about Jesus) led to Jewish orthodoxy's mistrusting Jesus. Finally this led to a fusion (via public opinion) of what Jesus actually said with the expectations of salvation of a people grievously tired of foreign occupation and desperate social conditions, which in turn led to his being handed over to the Romans. The Romans condemned him as a political revolutionary to death by crucifixion, a punishment reserved for criminals and resistance fighters.

Next I investigate how early Christianity came to terms with the ignominious death of its venerated master. Then the question is asked about how Jesus, himself clearly confronted from a certain point with the fated termination of his life, experienced this approaching death, with an eye to his message of the imminent reign of God. That this historic failure upset his plans cannot be denied. The New Testament says very little, from a historically ascertainable point of view, about how Jesus himself made sense of his impending death by execution. Nonetheless, there are some signs to be found which, from a traditional-critical point of view, are all remarkably conjoined with the "Last Supper" tradition: Jesus' talk about "unconditional servanthood", the offering of the final cup, his (historically guaranteed) resolute certainty of salvation even in the face of a fearsome death. He continues to promise and to offer a communion of salvation to his followers despite the imminent "historic failure" of his life. Perhaps not understanding, but deep in his heart, he did not experience his death as a *divine* failure of his life mission.

After the death of Jesus, the christological interpretations begin, however not without *new* experiences. The last point is essential to the process. For death ended the life community of the earthly Jesus with his disciples, which was magnified by the fact that they had abandoned their master, in a number of different ways, by not "following after him," *the* most important charge to each of Jesus' disciples. The problem which arises out of this is the following: how is it possible that those disciples "of little faith" some time after Jesus' death were courageously announcing that the crucified one was rescued from the dead by God, raised up and glorified, and could proclaim him as universal salvation, first for the Jews, and then for all people? What happened in the time between Jesus' death and this proclamation of the church? Put another way, how did the disciples arrive at their belief in Jesus' personal resurrection? For that resurrection is something which happened to and with Jesus beyond the boundaries of death, something in which the disciples of course could not participate, if we may put it so. How could they speak then of Jesus' resurrection unless they in some way or other had an experience of the risen one?

For that reason I sought after idiosyncratic experiences of the disciples after Jesus' death. The first, immediately obvious fact presses forward and speaks for itself: whoever at first was scandalized by Jesus' arrest and death, and then after that proclaims him as the sole messenger of salvation, has had unavoidably on this point a *conversion experience*—at least from the disciple's point of view. Between Good Friday and the church's proclamation of Jesus' resurrection lies (from our point of view of reality) in any case the historical fact of a sort of "conversion experience" of the disciples, a conversion in which God himself takes the absolute initiative in Jesus, therefore out of sheer grace. That initiative is then finally thematized in a vertical fashion in the biblical story of "Jesus' appearances" (the story itself being supplemented from later occurrences).

With the graced character of the apostolic belief in the resurrection as a premise, I then set out in search, via the perspective of the life history of these disciples, of the historical events in which that grace found its form; that is to say, in the bringing back together of the scattered disciples on the basis of "repentance." A number of factors come together in this process: the memory of Jesus' basic message, of his mercy toward sinners and others; the earlier hunch that Jesus was the eschatological prophet; the reflecting on Jesus' death—would God identify himself with someone others have rejected? For that was a basic theme of Jesus' preaching and life praxis. Thus reflection on Jesus' life as a whole is part of this process. All of this grows, via a conversion process under the power of God's illuminating grace, to the conviction (perhaps first to Peter) that God identifies himself with those who are rejected by their fellow human beings, that Jesus' communion of life with the Father was stronger than death, and that God has made him rise from the dead (or, God took Jesus to himself). The resurrection of Jesus and the experience of faith (the "appearances model" points to grace-filled, divine *initiative* in this process of experience) cannot therefore be separated from each other.

In Part III, the diverse, though at base same, New Testament interpretations of the risen crucified one are analyzed in two phases. First, the entire New Testament is seen as written from the view of belief in the risen crucified one and thus from the certainty in faith regarding Jesus' identity. Then the salvific meaning of the Jewish expression "risen on the third day" (which does not carry a chronological meaning) is analyzed.

From this analysis it appears that four pre-canonical creed models have come together in the New Testament: "maranatha" Christologies, which confess Jesus as Lord of the future; "theios aner" Christologies, or more precisely, an interpretation which sees Jesus as the "miracle worker" in the line of the Solomonic son of David; wisdom Christologies, which see Jesus as sent by Wisdom on God's behalf (low wisdom tradition), or as himself personified as Wisdom, who proclaims God's mysteries (high wisdom tradition) and finally, different forms of "pascha" Christologies, in which death and resurrection are central.

Each of these creed models shows a special interest in certain historical aspects of Jesus' life; the proclaimer of the coming reign of God; Jesus who goes around Palestine doing good; Jesus who reveals God to people, and people to themselves; Jesus as the one condemned to death. From this it seems that all the creeds are normatively shaped most profoundly by the historical Jesus of Nazareth, measuring rod and criterion of each Christian confession, and that in a critical historical reconstruction we do nothing other than illuminate the *de facto* contents of Christian faith by the earthly appearance of Jesus.

That these four creed directions could come together in one basic view, albeit not without some mutual corrections, presumes that one can recognize one's own creed in the creed of other Christian communities. In other words, a prior communal identification of the *person* of Jesus by Jews become Christian must have taken place already before these creeds were set in motion. This original, first and oldest "confessing naming" of Jesus I see, under the impact of scriptural texts, in the name "eschatological prophet," the "other and greater Moses," a key concept that shows the inner connection between the earthly Jesus, the heavenly Christ, and the evangelical creed of the churches. . . .

This Jewish, primarily Judaic (intertestamental) key concept of the end-time prophet, under the historical pressure of Jesus' message, life praxis, and martyrdom, is the source of the *way* in which the oldest creeds were formulated and probably the chief source of the oldest Christian *use* of Old Testament (and intertestamental) titles such as *Christ, Lord, and Son.* However, in later reflection these titles get a condensed meaning also from other traditions, likewise from the pressure of what has been experienced in and with Jesus of Nazareth. From here the line continues on to the christological dogmatic definition of Chalcedon: one and the same, truly human and truly divine. Jesus Christ is given us from God as the eschatological presence of salvation among us.

The basic question here is how can Christianity remain credible and meaningful in the comtemporary world without losing its proper identity. And how can it preserve this proper identity without becoming a sect (ghetto) or, thus, losing the *universal* meaning of the *individual* person clearly recognizable in history, the Jewish man Jesus of Nazareth?

In the concluding part of the book (Part IV) I try to make the universal significance of Jesus—given by God for all people—intelligible and credible for comtemporary men and women. I do this within the universal human (although not able to be fully theoretically stated in a rational manner) horizon of experience of our human history of suffering in search of meaning and liberation. Within that horizon, the concept "revelation" is also clarified; namely, the saving activity of God in history as experienced and brought to expression in the language of faith (or proclaimed) by believers. This means that any separation of the "objective" (God's activity) from the "subjective" (experience of faith) in revelation will reduce revelation to a subjective experience or a secondary interpretation of an event which itself can never bear this objective meaning. [1975]

39/ *It Began with an Experience*

A particular experience stands at the beginning of Christianity. It began with an encounter. Some people, Jews, came into contact with Jesus of Nazareth. They were fascinated by him and stayed with him. This encounter and what took place in Jesus' life and in connection with his death gave their own lives new meaning and significance. They felt that they were reborn, understood and cared for. Their new identity was expressed in a new enthusiasm for the kingdom of God and therefore in a special compassion for others, for their fellow men, in a way that Jesus had already showed them. This change in the direction of their lives was the result of their real encounter with Jesus, since without him they would have remained as they were, as they told other people later (see 1 Cor 15:17). This was not something over which they had taken the initiative; it had happened to them.

This astonishing and amazing encounter which some people had with Jesus of Nazareth, a man from their own race and religion, becomes the starting point for the view of salvation to be found in the New Testament. This means that grace and salvation, redemption and religion, need not be expressed in strange, "supernatural" terms; they can be put into ordinary human language, the language of encounter and experience, above all the language of picture and image, testimony and story, never detached from a specific liberating event. And yet, divine relvation is involved here. [1978]

40/ *What Is the Starting Point?*

Within the New Testament as it stands there is to be found a motley whole of varying interpretations of Jesus that go back to the first local communities of Christians: the thing is done one way in Mark, differently in Matthew and Luke, differently again in the case of Paul and in the Johannine gospel. Via the gospels and Paul it is possible to reconstruct, with a fair degree of certainty, a number of yet more primitive variations: a Hebrew and Judeo-Greek Jerusalem Christology, a pre-Pauline Christology, a pre-Marcan, a pre-Johannine one and, finally, the Christology of the Q community, where the christological confession is often less developed though never totally absent. Of a non-dogmatic representation of Jesus there is no trace anywhere. To look in the synoptic or pre-synoptic material for an undogmatic, as it were totally "neat" historical core (what indeed is such a thing?), is to hunt a will-o'the-wisp. Jesus is to be found there only as the subject of confession on the part of Christians. Thus we are always coming up against the Christian movement. The question then arises: What is the constant factor that will create unity within this variegated whole? . . .

A (modern) christological interpretation of Jesus cannot start from the *kerygma* (or dogma) about Jesus, or indeed from a so-called purely historical Jesus of Nazareth; whereas a historical and critical approach, set within an intention of faith, remains the only proper starting point. As so far all these sallies have proved to be unsatisfactory, what in the way of a constant unitive factor is left? I would say (and this really is something): the Christian movement itself—in other words a Christian oneness of experience which does indeed take its unity from its pointing to the one figure of Jesus, while nonetheless being pluriform in its verbal expression or articulation. "You yourselves," Paul writes to the Christians at Corinth, "are . . . an open letter from Christ—written not on tablets of stone but on tablets of human hearts" (2 Cor 3:2-3). By unity of experience I mean not an individual or individualistic religious experience of Jesus, a sort of "revivalism," but a community experience, in the sense of an ecclesial or collective experience which obliges people to define the ultimate meaning and purport of their lives by reference to Jesus of Nazareth or, to put it in traditional and equally proper terms, which causes people to interpret Jesus' life as the definitive or eschatological activity of God in history for the salvation or deliverance of men and women. The constant factor here is that particular groups of people find final salvation imparted by God in Jesus of Nazareth. In other words, on the basis of and in that experience we see two aspects in the life of Jesus: (a) this life has an effect within the historical situation of the Christian congregations here and now, and (b) has a significance that is crucial for the fundamental option presented by life here on earth and so for the eschatological relation of fellowship with God. Next we see that determining in this way the final and definitive meaning of our own life by reference to Jesus of Nazareth is not something given or appropriated once and for all. It is a decision that a person must take, subject to circumstances, over and over again, and must then continually re-articulate. That is to say, one cannot formalize a *kerygma*, for instance, "Jesus is the Lord." One has to make Jesus the prescriptive, determining factor in one's life in accordance with changing situations, cultural, social and ecclesial: and in that context one will proceed to live out, experience and put into words what "making Jesus the determining factor" really entails at this precise moment. For Christians from a Jewish background the "words" in question included Lord (*mar*), son of man and messiah; and this had far-reaching consequences for their faith and life. It might be more accurate to say that because they felt these consequences to be meaningful for the life they lived from day to day "in Jesus," they describe him in that way. To Greek Christians those titles said nothing; but from their cult of Caesar they were familiar with the "*Kyrios*," so that for them it is not the emperor but Jesus who is the *Kyrios*. That meant a good deal.

Thus the Jesus event lies at the source of the "local congregation" experience to which we have historical access; and it governs that communal experience. To put it another way: the constant factor is the changing life of the "assembly of God" or "assembly (congregation) of Christ," the community-fashioning experience evoked by the impression Jesus makes and, in the spirit, goes on making upon his followers, people who have experienced final salvation in Jesus of Nazareth. Priority must be conceded to the actual offer that is Jesus; but this is embedded, vested in the assent of faith on the part of the Christian community we experience as being amidst us in our history. We might say: Jesus was such as to engender precisely that typical reaction of faith which was confirmed by the "local church" sort of experiences. . . .

Neither Jesus nor the earliest "church community" constitutes the fount and origin of Christianity, but both together as offer and response. No Christianity without Jesus, but equally none without Christians. This source event, the fashioning of the Christian congregation, does indeed have normative value: the primitive church reflects or mirrors, in its New Testament, the Jesus event in its effect on a group of people. Constantly repeated contact with the primary response to an initial offer in history remains normative, therefore, for its own response. In that sense, as the church's "charter" or foundation document, there can be no substitute for the New Testament's authority. If the Catholic interpretation that the church is the sole living relic of Jesus of Nazareth, and therefore the norm for our understanding of the faith, might be called a splendid intuition (being indirectly corroborated by historical criticism), the Reformation principle of the inalienable normative value of the biblical witnesses finds a like critical confirmation. The two interpretations merge into one: Reformed Christians acknowledge the Bible as the "book of the church" and the dogmatic constitution, *Dei Verbum*, of Vatican II recognizes that not even the church's magisterium is "lord" over scripture, but is "subject" to the revelation of God as articulated by Christians in the Bible. Because the congregation-based experiences deposited in scripture are the constant factor whereby the whole New

Testament is held together in its plural Christologies, the New Testament as a document—and in its totality at that—is to some extent part and parcel of this unitive factor. Thus the interpretative norm provided by scripture can only be rendered more specific via the method of systematic co-ordination: in that way the biblical text, insofar as it actually mirrors the life of diverse Christian congregations, is the interpretative norm. To that something else must be added. Despite internal tensions the New Testament affords a relatively coherent picture which on the one hand can be taken to be a result of the historical effect of the one Jesus at the source of the somewhat dissonant traditions, and on the other hand to be the expression of an "ecumenical" desire to marshal the original and diverse Christian traditions into a unity. For us too, therefore, this ecumenical desire for unification, which is noticeable in the synoptics and perhaps even in pre-synoptic traditions, is an indispensable element of the interpretative norm. [1974]

2

Basic Elements of
Jesus' Message and Praxis

COMMENTARY

Schillebeeckx devotes a significant section of *Jesus* to describing Jesus' message and praxis. For the two go together; one cannot understand the message without understanding Jesus' activity, and vice versa.

Selection 41 talks about the context in which Jesus' ministry took place, centering especially on Jesus' relation to the Pharisees. Schillebeeckx notes how increasingly important understanding that relation has become. The following selections explore Jesus' message of the approaching rule or reign of God (42), Jesus' use of parables as part of the praxis of the reign of God (43), his healing activity, and table fellowship (44), and his experience of God as *Abba* (45).

41/ *The Context of Jesus' Ministry*

Although Jesus' appearance reached its high point in Jerusalem, it took place principally in the triangle between Capernaum, Bethsaida, and Chorazin, at the uppermost point of the Lake of Genesareth, at that time an ideal place to bathe because of its clear and pure water. The climate there is subtropical, the area densely populated and known for its fertile agriculture: the grain (wheat) of Chorazin was renowned. From here fisherfolk set out onto the lake. Farther up lay the border area of the tetrarchy of Herod Antipas and the tetrarchy of his brother Philip: Caesarea Philippi and northwest of that, Tyre and Sidon, and at the same elevation to the northeast, Damascus. From Nazareth, Jesus therefore did not move in the direction of Jerusalem to make his appearance preaching and healing, but to the north, to the land which can be designated, with the prophecy of Isaiah 8:23 and 9:1–2 (see Matt 4:15–16) as "Galilee of the Gentiles," the boundary area between "Israel" and the "land of the Gentiles." In Jesus' time, one hour's walk from Nazareth, lay Sepphoris, the Galilean capital at that time, with its Greek theater and gymnasium. Sepphoris was destroyed in the year 4 B.C.E., but it was rebuilt by Herod Antipas, during the lifetime of Jesus, as a fortress. During Jesus' life, this Herod Antipas (4 B.C.E.–26 C.E.) was lord of Galilee and Perea. Pontius Pilate was the Roman procurator after 26 C.E. The emperor Augustus died when Jesus was about eighteen, and he was succeeded by Tiberius, under whose regime Jesus was crucified, as we also hear from the Roman historian Tacitus.

Politically, it was a turbulent time for Palestine. In the difficult days after the death of Herod the Great (4 B.C.E.) the emperor Augustus sent the general Sabinus to Palestine to arrange the succession. He groveled before the Jews, who therefore even attacked his troops in Jerusalem on the feast of Pentecost. This was the beginning of a vehement resistance. In the neighborhood of Sepphoris Judas the Galilean gathered like-minded people and confiscated weapons from the royal arsenal; thus began the Jewish Zealot resistance. When Varus, the governor of Syria, to which Galilee has been annexed, heard about this, he came from Antioch with two legions to restore order in all of Palestine. The capital Sepphoris was burned to the ground and its inhabitants sold off as slaves. From there the troops moved to Jerusalem, which was beseiged by the Zealots. The Zealots fled in the face of the Roman superior strength. Varus held a roundup in the entire country and had several thousand Jews crucified. Herod Antipas had Sepphoris rebuilt but also had a new capital built elsewhere, which he named Tiberias, after the emperor.

In the year 6 C.E. (Jesus was then about ten years old), the emperor sent his legate Quirinius with the first procurator of Judea, Coponius, to Syria with the charge to hold a census in Judea (not in Galilee). This amounted to estimating the incomes and holdings in those areas in connection with taxes. Judas the Galilean went into action again but without much success. Then the militant wing of the Pharisees split off to form a separate "zealot" party. The movement remained underground after that time, until the pent-up anger exploded in 66 C.E. in the Jewish War (66–72 C.E.).

After having been free of Roman troops for thirty-seven years, the enduring military presence exacerbated the political situation in Jesus' time. The high priests at the temple in Jerusalem were appointed by the Romans, and were corrupt. They were lackeys of the Romans and already for a long time had not formed the true center of genuine Jewish piety of which Ezra had dreamed. The synagogues, spread over the entire country, had taken their place. The synagogues were an invention of the "Pharisees," for thus were they called by their opponents the Sadducees, while they themselves preferred to be called "scribes" or "the wise ones." With regret the priestly elite in Jerusalem saw that the moral authority no longer lay with them but with the Pharisees and their rabbis, who, however, did not possess any political authority. In contrast to the Sadducees, who held to a "sola scriptura" principle (the law alone without commentary), the Pharisees accepted the halakah alongside the Torah; i.e., an actualizing hermeneutic or interpretation of the law, to be translated into new situations for the sake of changed circumstances. Certainly not a fundamentalism!

If the Sadducees were the part of the rich and powerful, the Pharisees were rather the party of the poor and disenfranchised. Following the prophets, they wanted the conversion of the heart to go hand in hand with justice and love in all social relationships. It was the Pharisees who had brought into Judaism a new concept of God and religion since the Second Temple. Justice and love, not the priestly cult, was the highest experience of religion. The reign of God could not come in its fullness if justice did not first reign in all social relations. The Pharisees were not antiliturgical, but the temple liturgy had to go hand in hand with social justice and mercy. Nonetheless, the Pharisees set themselves against the Zealot violent solution to situations of injustice, especially during a military occupation. The Pharisees were also rebellious against Rome, but pursued a quite different course from the Zealots, an approach that was a good deal wiser at that time, given Roman military superiority. Their tactic was to never attack the Romans directly, but rather the Roman collaborators in the country, especially the priestly caste in Jerusalem. By doing this they shifted the center of moral power. They established synagogues throughout the country. The institution of the rabbinate grew spontaneously out of the Pharisaic movement. In Jesus' time, the synagogues were the central religious institution of Judaism, in resistance to the corrupt temple in Jerusalem. Finally, the Pharisees also emphasized table fellowship in the homes as a symbol of the power of the people, a power called "priestly and kingly" in opposition to the priestly elite. This entire Pharisaic politic was supported by a new concept of God, which went back to the old covenant theology: God, Yahweh, is personally very close to the people and to each individual within it. "Our Father who art in heaven" was for the Pharisees, despite all distance and religious awe, nonetheless the one always close by: *māqôm*, the omnipresent.

The more I study the more I am beginning to appreciate that, safeguarding

Jesus' original, particular, and creative traits, the Pharisaic movement made the "Jesus phenomenon" *historically* possible. The unsavory name "Pharisee" in the New Testament has to be seen in light of the situation after the Jewish War (66–72 C.E.), when Pharisaic rabbinism had hardened somewhat into an orthodoxy, and synagogue and church were parting ways in many conflicts. After the year 72, the Sadducees disappeared from the stage, as did the Zealots (at least for a long period) and the Essenes (entirely). As a result of the fact that the first three persecutions of Jewish, though Greek-speaking, Christians did not come from the Romans, and that the first Roman persecution of the Christians (in Rome) under Nero was probably instigated by Jews, the New Testament writers took over from the recently disappeared Sadducees *their* anti-Pharisaic terminology, which at the time had nothing to do with anti-Semitism. However, the discussion of those anti-Pharisaic tendencies of the New Testament is not yet completed, since our knowledge of Pharisaism in the time of Jesus is very indirect.

The historical lesson we can draw from the attitude of the Pharisees in Jesus' time is this: the clearly anti-Zealot attitude of the Pharisees, and of Jesus, by no means says that the Pharisees and Jesus were "politically neutral" or apolitical. They were very conscious of the injustice of the occupation and the exploitation of the Romans, and were acutely concerned about it. Personality and situation are difficult to separate. The line of argument of Eisler, Brandon, Carmichael and Maccoby, i.e., that Jesus was Zealot, and that of Cullmann, Grant, Hengel and Yoder, i.e., that he was apolitical toward the Romans, are both severe distortions from a historical point of view. As a "political revolutionary" Jesus was clearly in the line of the Pharisees of that time, despite his differences with them. We have a clear echo of that in the synoptic writers: "Jesus said: 'You know that those who rule over the people do so with an iron hand and misuse their power over them. It must not be so among you'" (Mark 10:42–43; Matt 20:24–25; Luke 22:24–27). Not a Zealot approach, therefore, but also for Jesus the God of Israel is not a symbol of legitimation of situations of injustice and of the status quo, but a God of liberation. This Jewish belief in God itself contains an emancipatory solidarity. [1984]

42/ *The Message of Jesus*

As with John, the context of Jesus' living and speaking is the future purposed by God; and by virtue of this he, like his precursor, subjects past and present to a prophetic critique. As with John, so for Jesus that future is an exclusive potentiality of God's. All other orientations and projects that do not start from the priority of God's future for man are criticized by Jesus. The coming judgment is also part of Jesus' total message, but its function there is very different from what we find in John's case. And that bring us up against the question of the central core of Jesus' message.

The focus of Jesus' message is a *euangelion*, that is, in contrast to John, cheering news from God: "God's lordly rule is at hand." We find this in no fewer than five complexes of tradition, word for word: in that of the Q community, in the Marcan tradition, in the source peculiar to Matthew, in that peculiar to Luke and the Johannine tradition and again in the New Testament epistles. The kingdom of God is Jesus' central message, with the emphasis at once on its coming and on its coming close. In other words, "expectation of the end" here is an expectation of the approaching rule of God. And for Jesus this means the proximity of God's unconditional will to salvation, of reconciling clemency and sufficing graciousness, and along with them opposition to all forms of evil: suffering and sin. This calls for more detailed analysis.

God's "lordship" or rule and the kingdom of God are two aspects of what the New Testament contains within the single concept *basileia tou Theou*. Mark and Luke speak of the *basileia*, the kingly rule, of God. Peculiar to Matthew is "the kingdom of heaven," where "heaven" is the late Jewish abstract way of denoting God. *Basileia tou Theou* is the kingdom of God, the rule of God as Lord, the realm of God. It does not denote some area of sovereignty above and beyond this world, where God is supposed to reside and to reign. What Jesus intends by it is a process, a course of events, whereby God begins to govern or to act as king or Lord, an action, therefore, by which God manifests his being God in the world of men. Thus God's lordship or dominion is the divine power itself in its saving activity within our history, but at the same time the final, eschatological state of affairs that brings to an end the evil world, dominated by the forces of calamity and woe, and initiates the new world in which God "appears to full advantage"; "your kingdom come" (Matt 6:10). God's rule and the kingdom of God are thus two aspects of one and the same thing. God's dominion points to the dynamic, here-and-now character of God's exercise of control; the kingdom of God refers more to the definitive state of "final good" to which God's saving activity is directed. This present and future are essentially interrelated (in a manner still to be more closely defined): God is the Lord of history and by proxy, as it were, presents salvation to human beings as a gift. This is the gist of the biblical notion, to us rather strange, of the "kingdom of God."

God's lordship, therefore, is the exercise of his peculiar and divine function as sovereign creator: as "king" he is purveyor of salvation to that which he endowed with life. That this kingdom comes means that God looks to us men and women to make his "ruling" operational in our world.

Lordship or "dominion" was a central concept in antiquity, as also was power (i.e., potent authority). For us these ideas have no ready appeal. They sound authoritarian to people who are only now learning how to take advantage of the freedom gained by the French Revolution: *"Nous voulons une humanité sans (Dieu ni) roi"* (J. Ferry). For that reason we may indeed go looking for other words, provided always that the idea of God's sovereign rights as creator is not dissipated; for such reverence for God's exalted nature is fundamental to Jesus' message and to his ministry. Of course Jesus interpreted this exalted nature of God as an unconditional willing of good towards human beings, an unimpeachable quality of pure love for man. But for Jesus, therefore, God's lordship and exalted nature entail doing God's will. God's lordship is not a function of man's salvation in the sense that God is "of use" for the salvation of human beings. Jesus is about God's business; and the business of man, the *humanum,* is to search after God "for God's sake." In other words, God's lordship is reason enough, in and of itself; the rest is gratuitous. Jesus is the man whose joy and pleasure are God himself. God's lordship is God's mode of being God; and our recognition of that engenders the truly human condition, the salvation of man. For that reason God's lordship, as Jesus understands it, expresses the relation between God and man, in the sense that "we are each other's happiness" . . . .

Jesus presents God as salvation for man. His God is a God who looks after people. Thus God's lordship, by which Jesus lives and which he proclaims, tells us something about God in his relation to man and likewise about man in his relation to God. It is a theological and yet also anthropological reality grounded in experience. A reality indeed, because for Jesus himself God's lordship is not just an idea or theory, but first and foremost an experience of reality. His very life is given decisive shape by his expectation of the kingdom of God in surrender to God's lordship. Jesus is gripped by that lordship, is compelled by it, so that his whole life is on the one hand a "celebration" of that lordship and on the other it gives a lead in orthopraxis, the right conduct of the kingdom of God. It is what he lived for and what he died for: God's concern as man's concern.

Radical conversion, prompted by grace and constituting the visible, historical form in which the coming of God's rule is manifested, has for Jesus at any rate not the apocalyptical (messianic) significance of a "turnabout" of the ages by an abrupt act on God's part; rather it entails both a new mental outlook and a new way of behaving, based on faith in the approaching rule of God. In its fullness, therefore, Jesus' message of God's lordship and his kingdom is: God's universal love for men as disclosed in and through his actual mode of conduct, consistent with and consequent upon it, and thus as an appeal to us to believe in and hope for this coming salvation and kingdom of peace, "imparted by God," and likewise faithfully to manifest its coming in a consistent way of living; the praxis of the kingdom of God. This will become evident only from the analytical sections to follow. [1974]

43/ *Speaking in Parables*

For us modern people, used to the exigencies of the historical sciences, it is often difficult to understand a "story-telling" culture; in such a culture the deepest mysteries of life are interpreted in stories and parables. An illustration of our inability to understand a narrative culture is the reaction many of us have to the story of Jonah's being lodged for three days "in the belly of a whale." The early Fathers of the Church had difficulty with it too; but in our own day the lack of comprehension has sometimes reached laughable proportions. After much systematic research one learned man came to the conclusion that in point of fact the fleeing Jonah went to ground for three days in some sort of private retreat of his, a small cafe known as "The Whale." Obviously we have lost all our "narrative innocence"! Actually, the tale of a man being swallowed by a large fish is well known to many cultures. It is a story which can be made to express all kinds of profound truths about life. Jonah's prayer (Jonah 2:2-10) serves to show why this folktale—familiar in so many cultures— has been taken up into the Old Testament: God will never abandon his own, however hopeless their situation may be. That is what Jonah's prayer in the belly of the whale, surrounded by the all-engulfing deep—a crazy situation of utter hopelessness and total impasse—is really saying. Such a story can be repeated *ad infinitum.* It neatly enshrines the variety of wisdom accumulated in the course of history by peoples who well know the savage power of the water. But when the Old Testament takes over this age-old, familiar story, a situation of extreme despair is brought within the context of Jonah's very pointed prayer. Thus is a new story born: the story of unconditional trust in Yahweh's nearness and helpfulness when someone is at the end of their wits. Later on this story would be told again; but each retelling is entirely new: Christians cite the Old Testament Jonah story in a completely new context, namely, the death and resurrection of Jesus. A story like this is never-ending. It is continually being retold: the core of it persists and is reinterpreted again and again.

The New Testament too, which tells us the story of Jesus, is set in a "story-telling culture," not in one like ours that has replaced a narrative innocence with historical disciplines. However, we cannot ignore either. For us modern people the story—including the story of Jesus—is only to be well and truly heard if we arrive at a second primitive stage, a second narrative innocence, that is, when we have passed through the stage of the scientific pursuit of history and criticism and thus can return to a "story-telling innocence," which itself then recoups its critical power from scholarship and criticism.

Conscious then of the narrative culture of antiquity, we must turn first of all to the gospel texts with the question: what are these gospels really trying to tell us when for instance they report the miracles of Jesus? Only after that can we inquire regarding the hard core of history in these stories. Of course the historical question is not unimportant; but it is a constituent part within a wider whole.

Jesus is a parable, and he tells parables. Only parables are able to "explain" a parable. Why?

The telling of a parable, the way a parable actually takes place, is a marvelous thing. Usually it enshrines a paradox, some startling effect. In a few cases this is the result of our failing, as Westerners, to understand what in the East are the commonplaces in these parables. The parable of the Sower features a farmer who is obviously quite reckless: he scatters his seed not only over the field but also on the rocky ground, in places where the thorns are growing, and even on the pathway. But there is nothing disconcerting about that—it is understandable in terms of oriental custom. It is the effects intended to startle that I am getting at. Those who work for only the one hour get as much pay as those who have toiled right through the day; this shocks not only our social feelings but those of the bystanders who heard the parable at the time. To us the five so-called foolish bridesmaids seem to have the most appeal, whereas the other five, the "wise ones" who refuse to help the rest, are immediately branded by youngsters hearing the story nowadays as "rotters"—but so they were then. The fact is, a parable turns around a "scandalizing" center, at any rate a core of paradox and novelty. A parable often stands things on their heads; it is meant to break through our conventional thinking and being. A parable is meant to start the listener thinking by means of a built-in element of the "surprising" and the "alienating" in a common, everyday event. It is not every night that one is hauled out of bed to help a needy stranger in dire straits; and you are not continually losing a sheep or a coin. It never happens at all to a good many of us. And yet in the parable I am confronted with it, here and now. The parable obliges me to go on thinking about it. Parables are "teasers." The familiar event is set against an unfamiliar background, and in that way what is commonplace becomes a stimulating challenge. It gives us a jolt.

The idea behind it is to make you consider your own life, your own goings-on, your own world, from a different angle for once. Parables open up new and different potentialities for living, often in contrast with our conventional ways of behaving; they offer a chance to experience things in a new way. Parables can have a strong practical and critical effect that may prompt a renewal of life and society. Although derived from familiar things and happenings in everyday life, by slipping in the scandalous, paradoxical or surprising element they cut right across our spontaneous reactions and behaviour. The Good Samaritan is not just helpful; he does apparently witless things: he walks, lets the wounded man use the animal; he brings him to an inn, comes back the next day, pays for the board and lodging himself and puts all future expenses, if any, on his own bill (Luke 10:33–35). With a deliberate touch of piquancy, as the story comes to be retold, this helpful fellow is made into a Samaritan, whereas the two clerics (Levite and priest) pass heedlessly by. In the everyday character of the parable there is an element of existential earnestness. Within the concretely human, mundane life of every day it encloses a more profound appeal. Parables point not to another, supra-natural world but to a new potentiality within this world of ours: to a real possibility of coming to see life and the world, and to experience them, in a way quite different from the one we are accustomed to. On a conventional view the kind-hearted Samaritan did rather too much of a good thing. And yet that is precisely what the parable teller is getting at, the astonishing, "excessive" compassion of the "good shepherd." The story sets the new world it discloses in perspective as a concrete possibility in life, even for whoever is listening to the parable now. In the world of Jesus' parables, living and evaluating are not what they are in the world of the ordinary, daily round. With the exception of three parables (the Rich Fool, Dives and Lazarus, the Pharisee and the Publican) they are all "down to earth." God does not come into it, directly; and yet anyone who attends to them knows that through these stories he is confronted with God's saving activity in Jesus; this is how God acts, and it is to be seen in the actions of Jesus himself, if, at any rate, you see with a heart ready to be transformed.

The parable remains "suspended," therefore, so long as the listener has not decided for or against the new possibilities for living opened up in it—and eventually decides for or against Jesus of Nazareth. Shall he, the listener, also enter that new world? He is faced with a choice between two models for living. Is he to accept the new "logic of grace and of having compassion" which the parables disclose and undergo that radical change in his own life? Or shall he set aside the challenge and return to the life of every day? Jesus and his world in the end become the issue in the parables, which open up a new world, in which only grace and love can dwell, and which places under judgment and seeks to change this history of ours, the course of human suffering that is the outcome of our short-sighted actions. Evidently, therefore, the time factor in the parable has an a-chronic significance. This does not mean that the story becomes a-temporal or supra-temporal. On the contrary it suggests that what is being narrated always embraces a constitutive relation to my present, here and now; this address to me now is fundamental to telling and listening to the parable. Here are no problems of translation or re-interpretation: I myself, here and at this moment, must come to terms with the parable, must answer the question whether I will acknowledge this new possibility for living as mine. Thus a parable needs no reasoned commentary, no explanation drawn "from elsewhere," no interpretation. It interprets itself, that is to say, our life, our existence and our actions. What may clarify the meaning of a parable is not argument but, if anything, the telling of a second or third parable—through the recurrently paradoxical effects of shock and "estrangement" regarding our normal, everyday, conformist behaviour. . . .

But Jesus does not tell parables just like any anonymous popular wise man. They are (or insofar as Jesus simply took over existing parables current as folk-wisdom, they become) part of his whole ministry, characterized by the message of God's coming rule. It is within that whole that the point of each parable must be looked for. Furthermore, very concrete situations in Jesus' life may have given occasion for telling just this particular parable or telling it in that particular way (though the concrete circumstances to which Jesus reacts by telling this or that parable for the most part elude us). . . . But even if we admit our ignorance of the concrete occasion of each separate parable, we do not know the context of Jesus' life as a whole, within which they were told. Of course the parables of Jesus in their original tenor, not as yet developed by the New Testament on explicitly christological lines, remain indeterminate in content and meaning and often, in a literal sense, even secular: they speak directly neither of God nor about Jesus himself. But within the setting of Jesus' message and of his own conduct their real point is clear: it is God's offer of salvation, God's lordship and the inward *metanoia* it demands; clear too that in view of Jesus' own concrete mode of living, his actual behaviour, which is as it were a living illustration of what the parables he tells are all about, they pose the question: Who is this Jesus? For because Jesus is constrained by the coming rule of God and talks about it in parables, while at the same time his life is itself a striking parable of it, we cannot avoid the question: Who is he? Who is this teller of parables in his own person? In this sense Wilder's conclusion regarding the parables is right: "They should be understood in relation to the speaker (and the occasion)." Although we hardly ever know what concrete occasion led Jesus to tell this or that particular parable, his public activity as a whole does begin to provide us with a notion of who is addressing us here and of what depth-dimension these parables can acquire because of that. The "living parable" that Jesus is in his own person and the import of his parable-stories confront us with the question whether or not we also wish, venture and are able to see in Jesus' activities a manifestation of God's regard for people. Although on the surface and in their secular content these parables have an obvious theological significance when placed in their Jesus-context, they are not directly christological; but given the context of Jesus' whole ministry and actual conduct, of which they are an integral part, they are nonetheless also an expression of Jesus' self-understanding and therefore present us with a "christological question": whether or not we will allow goodness, love, mercy and grace to be extended to us by this Jesus and, in accepting that grace, will permit ourselves to be constrained by his unconditional demand for an "about turn" (*metanoia*) in the conduct of our own lives. [1974]

44/ *The Praxis of the Kingdom*

In the synoptic gospels there are only two places where Jesus speaks to people explicitly of the forgiveness of sins (Mark 2:1–12, parallels at Matt 9:2–8; Luke 5:17–26; and Luke 7:36–50). But everything points to the fact that in such an explicit form these logia are not authentic sayings of the historical Jesus, that is to say, they are early Christian affirmations on the part of the church about Jesus, already acknowledged as the Christ. But the ground of this power to forgive sins, of this tender of salvation or fellowship with God, which the Christian community ascribes to Jesus after his death, really does lie in the concrete activity of Jesus during his days on earth. Jesus' presence among the people, helping them with his deeds of power, offering or accepting invitations to eat and drink together, not just with his disciples but with the mass of people and especially with outcasts, publicans and sinners, turns out to be an invitation to enter in faith into a companionship with God: the intercourse of Jesus of Nazareth with his fellow men is an offer of salvation imparted by God; it has to do with the coming rule of God, as proclaimed by him. This we must now examine in its various aspects.

The fact is remarkable in itself that the profane Greek word for "miracle" (*thauma*) does not occur in the gospels; they say only that certain sayings and actions of Jesus aroused a *thaumazein* among the people, that is, made them feel surprise and amazement. In the gospels certain acts of Jesus are spoken of as being "signs" (*sēmeia*) and "mighty acts" (*dynameis*) or simply "works of the Christ" (*ta erga tou Christou*.) This implies that as in former times God was able "in a marvelous way" to help people who had faith in him, so he is doing that now in Jesus of Nazareth. Whether they are for Jesus or against him, what strikes the people with amazement at his behaviour is interpreted by anyone putting their faith in him as God's saving acts in Jesus of Nazareth. Jesus as it were underwrites God's help to people in distress. . . .

In the struggle between the good power of God and the demonic powers which afflict, torment and seduce people, therefore, Jesus assigns to himself an explicit function. Later on, Christians saw this well enough: as in the beginning at the creation God saw that everything was good, so now it is said of the eschatalogical prophet: "He has done all things well" (Mark 7:37), while Satan, the power of evil, is the one who makes people deaf, blind, leprous and dumb. The power of goodness on the other hand, as manifested in Jesus, delivers a man from all the trials of Satan. That is the ancient way, and the New Testament's way, of understanding what go by the name of Jesus' "signs and mighty acts." As for whether natural laws are being broken or respected, nobody has a thought about that, neither Jesus nor his auditors, participating in the event by approving or disapproving of it. The miraculous element that finds expression in Jesus is not a point for his opponents or for his supporters; but what does count is the ultimate interpretation of what both parties alike experience. . . . The early Christian tradition of "miracles of Jesus" must be seen in the first instance, therefore (apart from the likewise important question of the historical authenticity of "Jesus' miracles"), as evidence of a very ancient tradition that identifies Jesus of Nazareth with the eschatological prophet, as that notion had come down to the Judaism of the time from the "Isaianic tradition" (Deutero-Isaiah and Trito-Isaiah) and had acquired an even more pregnant significance in the more Jewish "Solomonic" wisdom literature. . . . The task of the earthly Jesus was to arouse an unconditional faith in God, albeit in relation to people who came into transient or continuing contact with him. After Easter the church, being conscious of the distance between the situation then and its prevailing faith in the exalted Lord, continues despite every attempt at re-presentation to respect this difference in its account of the gospel. This shows the church reflecting on the significance in its own right of Jesus' earthly life prior to Easter. In contrast to the post-Easter miracles in the church—comforting signs of the exalted Lord working for the good of those who are already believers—the marvelous and powerful acts of the earthly Jesus are an offer of faith; the synoptic writers, in spite of their post-Easter situation, remain conscious of this distinction. It reveals their historical concern with the proper significance of the earthly Jesus: he proffers to people God's help and fellowship with God. At the same time this historical consideration itself entails a christological concern: Who is this Jesus, who is able to extend to people the help of God? Who is this man who can arouse people's faith? In his earthly life Jesus shows himself to be the one who, through his very ministry, summons men to faith in God. That is the point and purpose of Jesus' mighty acts.

What turns out, therefore, to be the oldest core of what Mark 2:15-17 is telling us—and it goes back to Jesus himself— is Jesus' special care for sinners, firm in the conviction and knowledge that he has been sent to carry to the outcasts, and to them in particular, the message of restored communication with God and with other human beings: thus in actual fact he is bringing the message of God's coming rule. The very fact that Jesus seeks encounter with them, offering them this fellowship with Jesus, breaks through their isolation and gives sinners the chance "to repent and be converted," the possibility of hearing about the invitation from the kingdom of God, first and foremost in actual fact. The Christian community, therefore, has in no way distorted its picture of his life on earth when it explicitly ascribes "the authority to forgive sins" to the earthly Jesus.

Although colored by the gospel narrative, both the story of Jesus' meeting with the "woman who was a great sinner" and that of his having something to eat with a crowd of tax collectors derive from facts historically grounded in Jesus' life on earth, so that we catch sight here of a very important facet of that life. Then again, this feature of his life is of a piece with the profoundest intentions of many of his parables as also of his mighty acts, so that we are bound to conclude: in Jesus' earthly career and ministry we are seeing demonstrated the praxis of the kingdom of God which he preached and implemented. In his earthly, historical life the eschatological praxis of the coming rule of God is already coming into view within the dimension of our human history here on earth. More and more insistently the idea presses upon us: in this concrete Jesus-phenomenon, proclamation, praxis and person cannot, it seems, be separated. Jesus identifies himself with God's cause as being man's also. . . . Meal sharing in fellowship, whether with notorious "tax collectors and sinners" or with his friends, casual or close, is a fundamental trait of the historical Jesus. In that way Jesus shows himself to be God's eschatological messenger, conveying the news of God's invitation to all—including especially those officially regarded at the time as outcasts—to attend the peaceful occasion of God's rule; this fellowship at table is itself, as an eating together with Jesus, an offer here and now of eschatological salvation or "final good." The instances where Jesus himself acts as host bring home even more forcefully the fact that Jesus himself takes the initiative with this eschatological message, which in the fellowship at table shared with him becomes as it were an enacted prophecy. Once again it serves to demonstrate that Jesus' actual way of living is nothing other than the praxis of the kingdom of God proclaimed by him. It is only through the subsequent effect of this historical praxis on the part of Jesus that the significance of the fellowship meal among Christians in the primitive church becomes intelligible. The Christians take over this praxis of Jesus. Acts 2:42–47: "They devoted themselves . . . to the breaking of bread," that is, to the provision of such meals; the concern for widows and orphans (in Luke's time) is a remainder of that. "They partook of food with glad and generous hearts" (Acts 2:46). Conversions too were celebrated with a meal (Acts 16:34). Thence also the eventual decision to eat in company with uncircumcised Christians, after several clashes on the issue (Acts 11:3; Gal 2:1–14). The very pronounced interest in fellowship-meals in the early church is obviously grounded in Jesus' own practice when he was alive on earth. [1974]

45/ *Jesus' Relation to God*

Even without our willingness to venture on the hopeless enterprise of dissecting the psychology of Jesus (the data needed for that are not available to us), what he said (his message) and what he did (his mode of conduct) are enough to shed light on his self-understanding: his activities spring from his extraordinarily pronounced consciousness of a prophetic role, on which is grounded his message of the approaching rule of God, while in and through his own strangely marvelous ministry he sees clearly that this kingdom is drawing near.

The distinctive relation of Jesus to God was expressed in the primitive Christian churches more especially by use of the honorific title "Son of God" and "the Son." These were Christian identifications of Jesus of Nazareth after his death. Jesus never spoke of himself as "the Son" or "Son of God"; there is no passage in the synoptics pointing in that direction; what is certain is that he referred in a special way to God as *Abba*.

What we gather in the first instance from the certain knowledge we have of Jesus' praying to God as *Abba* is the unconventional style of Jesus' intercourse with God, its unaffected and natural simplicity, which must have been inscribed on the hearts of the disciples, because this kind of praying to *Abba* at once became generally current in early Christianity.

To sum up, one can say that in Jesus' time, what the *abba* signified for his son was authority and instruction: the father is the authority and the teacher. Being a son meant "belonging to"; and one demonstrated this sonship by carrying out father's instructions. Thus the son receives everything from the father. As failure to comply with the father's will is tantamount to rejecting the Torah or law, this afforded a connection between obeying one's father and obedience to God (Sirach 3:2, 6; 6:27; Prov 1:7, 8). The son also receives from the father "missions," tasks which in the name of his father he has to make his own.

If in contrast to the current usage of his day Jesus uses the familial term *Abba* in addressing God, it quite naturally expresses the very core of his religious life exactly as the Christians represented it after his death: "Not my will, but your will, Father" (Luke 21:42; Matt 26:42); for this is the Jewish *Abba* concept.

By what authority, on what basis is Jesus able to speak of God in this manner? That was the question raised by Jesus' fellow villagers (Mark 6:2–3). Jesus' experience and awareness of the Father in prayer was also manifested in what for his listeners was an astonishing way of speaking about God, so much so that some took offense at it. It was not in his use of *Abba* as a way of addressing God that Jesus showed himself to be forsaking late Judaism; but the *Abba* form of address (expressing a religious experience of a special color), when linked with the substance of Jesus' message, ministry and praxis, began to prompt theological questions. The *Abba* experience would appear to be the source of the peculiar nature of Jesus' message and conduct, which without this religious experience, or apart from it, lose the distinctive meaning and content actually conferred on them by Jesus.

All this goes to show that one of the most reliable facts about the life of Jesus is that he broached the subject of God in and through his message of the coming rule of God; and that what this implied was made plain first and foremost through his authentic parables and the issues they raised: namely, *metanoia* and the praxis of God's kingdom. And then this message was given substantive content by Jesus' actions and way of life; his miracles, his dealings with tax-gatherers and sinners, his offer of salvation from God in fellowship at table with his friends and in his attitude to the Law, sabbath and temple, and finally in his consorting in fellowship with a more intimate group of disciples. The heart and center of it all appeared to be the God bent upon humanity. Of this God's rule the whole life of Jesus was a "celebration" and also "ortho-praxis," that is, a praxis in accord with that kingdom of God. The bond between the two—God's rule and orthopraxis—is so intrinsic that in this praxis itself Jesus recognizes the signs of the coming of God's rule. The living God is the focus of this life.

Against the background of the apocalyptical, Pharisaic, Essene and Zealotic conceptions upheld by current movements which isolated them-selves into "remnant" communities, Jesus' message and praxis of salvation for all Israel without exception, indeed including all that was abandoned and lost—that in particular— are difficult to place in a historico-religious context. For that reason we are bound to inquire whether Jesus' message and praxis do not become intelligible only when we presuppose his special, original religious apprehension of God. For the question is: Whence does Jesus obtain the unconditional assurance of salvation to which his message of God's coming rule as final well-being for men so positively testifies?

In the calamitous and pain-ridden history within which Jesus stood it was impossible to find any grounds or indeed any reason at all which would serve to explain and make sense of the unqualified assurance of salvation that characterized his message. Such a hope, expressed in a proc-lamation of the coming and already close salvation for men implied in God's rule—now that we have uncovered the unique quality of Jesus' religious life in terms of his (historically exceptional) *Abba* address to God—in Jesus is quite plainly rooted in a personal awareness of contrast: on the one hand the incorrigible, irremediable history of man's suffering, a history of calamity, violence and injustice, of grinding, excruciating and oppressive enslavement; on the other hand Jesus' particular religious awareness of God, his *Abba* experience, his intercourse with God as the benevolent, solicitous "one who is against evil," who will not admit the supremacy of evil and refuses to allow it the last word. This religious experience of contrast is, after all, what informs his conviction and proc-lamation of God's liberating rule, which should and can prevail even in this history, as Jesus knows by experience in and from his own praxis. Thus the *Abba* experience of Jesus, although meaningful in itself, is not a self-subsistent religious experience, but is also an experience of God as "Father," caring for and offering a future to his children, a God, Father, who gives a future to the man who from a mundane viewpoint can be vouchsafed no future at all. Out of his *Abba* experience Jesus is able to bring to a man a message of a hope not inferable from the history of our world, whether in terms of individual or socio-political experiences— although the hope will have to be realized even there. [1974]

3

Rejection, Death,
and Resurrection

COMMENTARY

Central, of course, to the Jesus story is his abandonment by disciples and other followers, his death, and the experiences of him by his disciples thereafter. In selection 46, Schillebeeckx explores the reasons for Jesus' rejection and death, and tries to reconstruct how Jesus might have faced his impending execution.

If it is difficult to reconstruct events around the death of Jesus, the events which follow it are even harder to ascertain. Yet we know that within a fairly short period of time, disciples of Jesus were proclaiming him to be alive. Schillebeeckx offers a model for understanding what we call the resurrection, based on a model of the conversion of the disciples back to Jesus and their experience of his forgiveness. The model is based on some inferences about experience: such experiences would have helped the disciples identify this person as Jesus, since their experience mirrored his activity while carrying out his ministry.

46/ *The Rejection and Death of Jesus*

In present-day discussion about continuity and discontinuity between Jesus on this earth and Christ in the preaching of the church there emerges, it seems to me, a fundamental misunderstanding, namely, that the break comes with on one side the death of Jesus and on the other the church's subsequent preaching of the resurrection. One school would put the whole emphasis on the caesura provided by this datum, others think they should relativize it. What is overlooked here is that while there certainly is a "breakage-point," it is to be located within the

149

ministry of the historical Jesus, in the resistance to him and the rejection of his message. And the insistent question arising out of this is whether that rejection, as a broad fact of Jesus' earthly life, did not give him occasion in one way or another to interpret his approaching death prior to the event.

Time and again exegetes have considered the question of whether Jesus' preaching in Galilee ended in failure, at least in the sense that people did not receive his message.

"*But*, blessed is he who takes no offense at me" (Luke 7:18–23 = Matt 11:6). Obviously, this passage is not looking back over the whole ministry of Jesus (after his life had finished) but is concerned with a historical recollection of specific facts of Jesus' life and the reactions they evoked: the question whether Jesus is bringing salvation or has within him "a demon." We saw earlier on that Jesus rejected both the Aramean-Pharisaic exposition of the Law and the high-handed Sadducees' devotion to the cult. His preaching and praxis struck at the very heart of the Judaic principle of "performance" in the religious sphere. In particular his solidarity with the "unclean" and with "tax gatherers and sinners" was a thorn in the flesh of pious officialdom—it was contrary to "the Law."

If one wants to establish a theology of Jesus of Nazareth which is concerned primarily with his life, message and ministry, then the rift which contact with Jesus engendered within the Jewish community of his day must have a fundamental place in it. After all, even a pre-Easter faith and trust in Jesus had to meet this challenge. Essentially, the question whether Jesus is bringer of good or ill, curse or salvation, is a problem already relevant before Easter. His suffering and death are actually the consequences of a conflict aroused during his life. The problem does not arise only with Jesus' death. After all, he did not die in bed but was put to death.

The Marcan gospel clearly says that Jesus' preaching in Galilee met with initial success. But from Mark 7 on, the allusions to "a great crowd of people" diminish, as do the positive reactions. The rule of God was the glad news that Jesus had brought to Galilee; salvation was what was being proclaimed. Yet in the earliest Aramaic layer of the Q tradition the consciousness would seem to be present that the "Jesus phenomenon" might be rejected: this possibility of "being offended at him" (Luke 7:18–23) goes back, apparently, to pre-Easter memories. Thus the possibility of Jesus being rejected is part of the oldest "Christological package"; it evidently goes back to recollections of failure in Jesus' days on earth. The veiled, ambiguous character of Jesus' historical manifestation— sharing the ambiguity of everything one could call historical—is amplified by Mark; but the Marcan redaction only makes more plain what had already been consciously articulated in the pre-Marcan tradition: a historical opaqueness is cast over Jesus' life. "The divine" in him, his coming "from God," is not something given apodictically, with a compelling absence of ambiguity; it calls for a vote of confidence. Mark thematizes the rejection of Jesus' message and ministry as early as the start of his gospel (Mark 2:1 up to 3:5); and he concludes these first stories with his pregnant interpretation: "The Pharisees . . . immediately held counsel with the Herodians against him, how to destroy him" (Mark 3:6). Mark obviously wants to show how it could come about that the revered master was put to death. Elsewhere in Mark it is not "the Pharisees and Herodians" but in particular "the high priests and scribes" who contemplate destroying Jesus (Mark 11:18). But it would seem from the Q tradition that the rejection of Jesus' message extended beyond these schematic categories. From the "woes" uttered over the towns of Chorazin, Capernaum and Bethsaida (Luke 10:13-15 = Matt 11:20-24) it appears that Jesus' message was rejected also by whole cities. The asides also, to the effect that a prophet is without honor in his own country (Mark 6:4; Matt 13:57; Luke 4:24; John 4:44), as well as the typically Johannine "Will you also go away?" (John 6:67), point in much the same direction of historically concrete experiences of failure. Jesus certainly appears to enjoy popularity so long as no danger threatens; but in the outcome his preaching of the great "about turn" of events as a manifestation of the coming rule of God has only a limited success.

There are grounds for seeing in this experience of the failure of Jesus' preaching and proffer of salvation the reason why he decided to "go up to Jerusalem." Despite the admittedly heated and persisting arguments among commentators, one can detect a growing consensus with regard to a hard core of history in the New Testament record, according to which Jesus, during his lifetime, sent his disciples out "to every town and place" (Luke 10:1), there to proclaim his message of God's coming rule (Luke 10:1, 11; Matt 10:5b-7; besides Mark 6:7-13). The presence of this material in both the Q community and the Marcan tradition argues for its authenticity. In taking this action Jesus is evidently facing up to the very imminent approach of God's rule on the one hand, and on the other the possible definitive rejection of his message (see Luke 10:10-12). At the least we are bound to say that this proclamation of judgment ensuing upon the failure to accept Jesus' message can hardly be laid purely at the door of the Q community and have no basis in the latest phase of Jesus' own preaching, after experiences of rejection. That Jesus restricted himself in his message exclusively to Israel (see also Matt 15:24) is nowadays less and less matter for dispute. Apropos of this relatively large-scale dispatch of disciples to the whole of Israel by Jesus, exegetes are very probably right in speaking of a "final offer to Israel on the part of Jesus." Jesus here is giving exactly the same commission to the disciples, to do what he himself is doing; preaching the coming kingdom of God, healing the sick and driving out devils (Luke 10:1; Matt 10:5b-6; Luke 10:8-11; Mark 6:7-13).

After the disciples sent out had returned—apparently full of enthusiasm about their activities—Jesus probably concentrated on training a more intimate group of disciples—the subsequent "twelve" (or: the twelve already singled out by himself?). This change in apostolic strategy was apparently the outcome of a growing experience of failure where his preaching in Galilee was concerned.

After this incident the focus of Jesus' activity switches apparently from Galilee to Jerusalem—although the connection is difficult to reconstruct, historically speaking. What does become clear is that, according to the gospels, from then on Jesus regards his message as having failed in Galilee and so decides to make for Jerusalem. From that moment on, the gospels begin to make clear allusions to the path of suffering set before Jesus, in other words, to his definitive rejection. This path is described, "typically," of course, as an "exodus," a journey to Jerusalem. Whereas in the first phase of his public ministry Jesus traveled around the country proclaiming the approach of God's rule, now he is shown, according to the gospel record, as making "a journey towards suffering," a journey towards death. This is defined in part, no doubt, by the historical outcome of events; but perhaps also by historical reminiscences of the already admitted fiasco in Galilee.

One would have to declare Jesus something of a simpleton if it were maintained that he went up from Galilee to Jerusalem in all innocence, without any idea of the deadly opposition he was to encounter there. Every Jew in those days knew that the Romans had the power of crucifixion, Herod Antipas the *ius gladii*—the right to behead someone—and the beheading of John the Baptist must have been vividly present in the mind of Jesus; then lastly, the Sanhedrin was empowered to use stoning (see Stephen's martyrdom). None of this, in itself, is either here or there. It is relevant, though, when the question becomes urgent as to whether Jesus was conscious of doing things, committing actions or proclaiming a message which sooner or later would result in an inevitable collision with one or more of those authorities. When we are dealing with a rational and purposeful individual, and not with an unrealistic, fanatical apocalypticist (even they were anything but fanatical in late Judaism), the consciousness of doing or saying something which could and would cause a fundamental conflict with one of those authorities is at the same time a way of deliberately taking upon oneself responsibility for the legal consequences of such behaviour. One can hardly maintain that Jesus both willed and sought after his death as the sole possible way of realizing the kingdom of God. There would have been an element of play-acting about his commitments to his message of *metanoia* and the rule of God, if he had thought and known from the very start that salvation would come only in consequence of his death. That death only comes in prospect as a result of his preaching and mode of life, which constituted an offer of salvation, having been rejected. This is not re-scinded or nullified by his death. An opposite interpretation would fail to give full value to Jesus' real function of "pointing the way" by the con-crete course of his own life's history; in other words, it disregards the fact of Jesus' "being truly man" in a historical mode. Furthermore, it would simply formalize the actual significance for salvation of Jesus' death.

What can be said on the strength of the real evidence is that at any rate Jesus did nothing to escape a violent death. On the contrary, despite the growing certainty that his message had, broadly speaking, been re-jected, he deliberately made for Jerusalem. But it can hardly be said that to accord with Jesus' self-understanding his message of salvation took its meaning only from his death. The truth is: he died just as he lived, and he lived as he died.

That Jesus had to settle for himself what his attitude to impending death must be follows from his overall attitude to life in confrontation with this new situation. Hence the question whether he kept this final event and the possible meaning he gave to it to himself, remained silent about them, or whether in his very last days, at least within the intimate circle of his disciples, he spoke of them (in one way or another). Only that could make clear in what sense Jesus was able to feel his death to be a service performed out of love.

To the exegete it is evident enough that all allegedly obvious and explicit predictions of the passion are secondary, that is, have (at least in part) been worded in the light of the actual event of Easter. Yet there is more to it than that. It is hard to believe, bearing in mind the concern he is known to have had for his friends, that even in his last days Jesus would have said nothing at all to his disciples about his approaching violent death. Would he have failed to prepare his disciples in any way for the shock of his death, when he saw himself faced by it with the grave problem of reconciling that death and his message with each other and of coming to terms with them? As a matter of history, therefore, we must take seriously the likelihood that during the final meal with his friends Jesus will have said or done something to ensure that when he was dead his intimate disciples would not fall for good into despair and disillusion. On the other hand any public and patently obvious discussion of it would seem to run counter to the basic tenor of the preaching of Jesus, who never made himself a second subject (next to God or to God's rule) of his preaching: Jesus proclaimed not himself but the coming kingdom of God.

Within these limits, maximal and minimal, the gospel accounts of Jesus' blessing of the bread and cup during the Last Supper, although heavily overlaid by the eucharistic observances which the church had learned to practise in the meantime, display as their central core certain recollected facts of history. . . .

That the Last Supper was actually a Jewish Passover meal is disputable on many different grounds; so that we shall not consider that aspect here. What is beyond dispute is that a farewell meal was offered by Jesus to his disciples in the consciousness of his impending death. . . . In view of Jesus' assurance, even in the face of death, of salvation through the approaching rule of God, one cannot simply regard the murder of this innocent man as one case more in the long line of innocent victims of murder. His death would then be a reason for resignation or despair rather than for new hope, which has given birth to the whole Christian church. For in a purely historical perspective this death by crucifixion is the rejection of Jesus and of his message, and therefore the total failure of his prophetic career. But if Jesus was humiliated by his crucifixion, then this was, even historically, submission to God. "My God, thou art God. I will praise thee" (Ps 118:28). An experience of a historical failure and at the same time a passionate faith in God's future for man is for the religious person no contradiction, but a mystery eluding every attempt at theoretical or rational accommodation.

The conclusion would seem to be justified that Jesus felt his death to be (in some way or other) part and parcel of the salvation offered by God, as a historical consequence of his caring and loving service of and solidarity with people. This is the very least—albeit certain—thing about the "institution narrative" and the account of the Passion that we are bound to hang on to as a historical core. . . .

The active acceptance of his own death or rejection can only be understood as Jesus' active incorporation of his death into his mission of offering salvation, and not simply and solely as a "notwithstanding." This applies with all the greater force because even during his life Jesus' fellowship-at-table shared with sinners was the token of an immediate tender of salvation. Given all this, the fact that it is impossible to find a *verbum ipsissimum* or authentic saying of Jesus that tells us how he regarded and evaluated his death (excepting the first section of Mark 14:25a; Luke 22:18a) is really irrelevant. Jesus' whole life is the hermeneusis of his death. The very substance of salvation is sufficiently present in it, which could be and was in fact articulated later on in various ways through faith in him. Although the historico-critical method cannot produce knock-down arguments on this score, still less can it assert categorically that so far as history goes we do not know how Jesus understood his own death. Jesus' understanding of that death as part and parcel of his mission of tendering salvation seems to me, therefore, a fact preceding Easter—and demonstrably so, at least for Jesus' self-understanding in the final days of his life. [1974]

47/ *The Resurrection*

The death of Jesus put an end to the common life in fellowship, shared by the earthly Jesus with his disciples—an end reinforced by their leaving him in the lurch. What was it then that after a time gave these same disciples reason to assert that they were once more drawn into a living and present fellowship with Jesus, whom they now proclaimed to be the living one, risen from the dead, either presently operative in the Christian propagandists or soon to return as the son of man? What took place between Jesus' death and the proclamation by the church?

Nowhere does the New Testament say that the resurrection is itself this event. By way of contrast to the apocryphal writings, especially *Ev. Petri* 35–45, the resurrection event itself is never related. Not the resurrection but some sort of gracious self-manifestation of the dead Jesus is what leads the disciples, prompted now by faith, to proclaim: "Jesus is back, he is alive," or "He is risen." How do the primitive Christian churches themselves interpret the emergence of their faith in the living or returning crucified one? In other words: What happened to them? . . .

The question raised earlier on but so far left unanswered was: What brought the disciples who had left Jesus in the lurch at the time of his arrest and crucifixion together again—and together now in the name of Jesus, acknowledged as the Christ, Son of God, the Lord? We posited as a working hypothesis that there was a connection between the scattering of the disciples and their "Easter experience," so called, as the reason for their coming together again. In other words, did not the Easter manifestation of Christ derive from what we might call a Christian "conversion vision"?

Both the outcome and the starting point are important here. On the one hand, the group of intimate disciples disintegrates because they have betrayed the very thing that keeps them together, the person of Jesus of Nazareth; on the other hand, reassembled in Jesus' name they proclaim, a while after Jesus' death, that this same Jesus has risen. What occurred in the period between on the one hand their master's suffering and dying and the disciples' panic-stricken loss of nerve and, on the other, the moment when they were heard boldly and confidently proclaiming that Jesus was to return to judge the world or had risen from the dead? For even the historian must face the problem involved here: something must surely have happened to make this transformation at any rate psychologically intelligible.

The primary and immediate reply to this cannot be: the reality of the resurrection itself. The resurrection in its eschatological "eventuality" is after all nowhere recounted in the New Testament; nor of course could it be, because it no longer forms part of our mundane, human history; it is, *qua* reality, meta-empirical and meta-historical: "eschatological." On the other hand, a resurrection about which nothing is said is an event of which nobody knows anything, for us, naturally, "non-existent." Opening up the subject of a meta-historical resurrection, as in fact is done in the New Testament, presupposes of course experiential events which are interpreted as saving acts of God in Christ. It presupposes a particular experience and an interpretation of it. The question then becomes: What, after Jesus' death, were the concrete, experienced events which induced the disciples to proclaim with such a degree of challenge and cogent witness that Jesus of Nazareth was actually alive: the coming or risen one? If it cannot be the resurrection itself, or the empty tomb (even if this be a historical fact, theologically it could yield no proof of a resurrection; a "vanished corpse" is not in itself a resurrection, and an actual bodily resurrection does not require as its outcome a vanished corpse), nor yet "appearances," taken to be real, which within the history of tradition already presuppose belief in the resurrection—then, what?

Anyone who has at first taken offense at Jesus and subsequently proclaims him to be the only bringer of salvation has of necessity undergone a "conversion process." As a first reply to the question: What actually took place between the two historical events—Jesus' death and the apostles' preaching—we are therefore bound to say at once: the conversion of the disciples, who "notwithstanding" Jesus' scandalizing death came together again—and did so in the name of this same Jesus, through the recognition of their paucity of faith. It is a process of conversion that lies between the two historically accessible elements. Only then can we go on to ask about the circumstances making such a conversion possible and more especially about what the essential requirements would be for such a thing. A straight exegesis of the "empty tomb" and of the "appearance stories" bypasses, it seems to me, this primary and fundamental question of the conversion or reassembly of the disciples. . . . The central core of what took place is indeed lodged in the biblical accounts of the Christ appearances, but overlaid by later experiences of what was after all an already established church, from within which the four gospels and the Acts were written. Can the threefold Damascus story—in which the "Christ manifestation" to Paul is depicted initially as a "conversion vision" and then as a "missionary" one—perhaps provide a model for understanding a similar development in the tradition of the official appearances of Christ to the twelve? Admittedly, there is a fundamental difference: the disciples had not been persecutors of Jesus—quite the opposite; they had of course fallen short in their "going after Jesus"; but in the New Testament this would seem to be the essential demand put to Christians. Thus they are in need of conversion: to resume the task of "being a disciple" and "imitating Jesus." But the first condition for that is the experience of having received forgiveness from Jesus—a quite specific experience of grace and mercy, the result of which was that they were received back into a present fellowship with Jesus and confessed him to be their definitive salvation, which was not at an end with his death and through which they were brought together again and restored to fellowship with him and each other.

In some modern attempts to make the manifestation experience intelligible, people have seen in the Christ appearances a sort of condensation of various pneumatic experiences within the primitive local congregations. What is basically wrong with that, however, is that one is then postulating what has to be demonstrated. In fact one is presupposing the existence of the "gathered congregation" (in which the pneumatic experiences occur), whereas the very thing the appearance traditions in the gospels are meant to signify marks the point from which the bringing together of the scattered disciples begins, in other words the very earliest event constitutive of the church (albeit still, to begin with, as a fraternity within the Jewish religion). The reassembly of the disciples is precisely what has to be explained. Appearance stories and accounts of the empty tomb assume the fact of the reassembled community and its christological *kerygma*.

We must therefore look in the direction of the "conversion process" of the disciples. Fundamentally, "conversion" entails a relationship (a) to him whom the disciples had let down: Jesus of Nazareth, and (b) to him to whom they return: Jesus as the Christ.

The disciples (perhaps in panic) fell short in their task of "being a disciple" or "going after Jesus": at what was for him the very worst moment they left him in the lurch, and then especially were they "of little faith"—something against which Jesus had repeatedly warned them. Yet their relationship to Jesus of Nazareth, whom they had deserted, enshrines also their recollection of his whole ministry, of his message of the coming rule of God, a God mindful of humankind, who wills only the well-being and not the destruction of men; of his admonitions regarding lack of faith; but they had also come to know the "God of Jesus" as a God of unconditional mercy and forgiveness; he had helped so many people simply because they came to him in distress; they remembered Jesus' eating and drinking in fellowship with sinners, that is, his proffering salvation to sinners in particular. And then finally there was their recollection of the quite special temper prevailing at the farewell meal—memories of what Jesus had said at the time, however vague. These remembered aspects of their life shared in fellowship with Jesus and of Jesus' whole line of conduct are essential elements in the process of conversion undergone by these men who did indeed fail, but had not in the end lost their faith in Jesus. They had been thrown off balance rather than been deliberately disloyal.

On the other hand the relationship they have with the one to whom they have returned is quite new. They deserted a Jesus marked down for death; they return to a fellowship in the here and now with that same Jesus, acknowledging him now as the returning judge or the crucified and risen one. It is this second relationship that connects with what lies at the source of the appearance traditions in the gospels. What, historically speaking, occurred that was experienced by the disciples as a pure act of grace on God's part and through which they arrived at the christological confession of the crucified one, risen or coming?

What happens in the Christian resurrection vision (the Easter appearances) is a conversion to Jesus as the Christ, who now comes as the light of the world. Just as the "enlightenment" of the law justifies someone (see Gal 1:14; 3:2ff.), so the disciples are justified by the illumination of the risen one. In the "manifestation" or the "vision" the gracious gift of conversion to Jesus *as* the Christ (thanks to an enlightening revelation of God) is effected and expressed. It is Jesus himself who enlightens, who discloses himself as the risen Christ in and through the grace of conversion: he is the enlightening Christ; he "makes himself seen."

How and on what bases of experience and recollection the disciples after Jesus' death reassemble around the nonetheless deceased Jesus is therefore a question calculated to send us back to the point at which the disciples—not yet a "congregation of Christ"—constituted themselves a Christ community (even if initially within Judaism).

In pursuing this inquiry we must suppose it more than very likely that upon his arrest and at his death Jesus' intimate disciples failed in one way or another to stand by him. We must also take into account the fact that so long as Jesus was still living on earth it was altogether impossible to make any essential and constitutive connection of his person—not just one or more of his actions—with the coming of God's rule. So long as Jesus was living in human history, which is *ipso facto* contingent, God's saving revelation in him was after all "unfinished"—still in process of coming to be. At that stage, therefore, "Christology" was out of the question; for a "christological confession" is a (faith-motivated) statement about the totality of Jesus' life, not about a salvific power thought to be due to particular sayings or actions on his part; for that was certainly "self-evident" to his disciples, even prior to his death. If one accepts the actual historicity of God's revelation in Jesus and sees how the faith of Jesus' disciples responded to this temporal event—Jesus' whole ministry—one realizes that the disciples had an incredible enthusiasm for their master—and that, in their fundamental relationship to God—and yet had not come to recognize that he was in his person of constitutive, all-decisive significance for the dawning of the kingdom of God. Now the whole point of a christological affirmation lies—if words still bear their proper meaning—in the acknowledgment of that constitutive significance. The reason why, prior to Jesus' death, an implicit "christological confession" (in a full christological sense) was impossible is, in my view, the genuine historicity—here again any kind of docetism is out of place—of Jesus' self-understanding and of his message, which gradually made him rise to the inevitability of a violent death. The Christian disclosure experience, ground, source and release of a truly christological confession of Jesus, presupposes the totality of his life, up to and including its being ended by his execution. From a theological standpoint too, only this completed life is God's revelation in Jesus of Nazareth. Only with Jesus' death is his life story—insofar as his "person" is concerned—at an end; only then can our account of Jesus begin.

Of course the disciples felt the violent end of their master's life as a tremendous shock and so, understandably enough, fell because of their "little faith" into a state of panic; but that did not in consequence of these last events undergo a total lapse of faith. Apart from Mark, who (for reasons in my view not yet satisfactorily explained) is keenly critical of the conduct of the twelve prior to Jesus' death, the panicky defection of the disciples, their deserting of Jesus, is nowhere represented in the gospels as a total breach, in the sense of a loss of faith. It was *oligopistia*—a "being of little faith." These disciples did of course come to realize—in a process of repentance and conversion which it is no longer possible to reconstruct on a historical basis—something about their experience of disclosure that had taken them by storm: their "recognition" and "acknowledgment" of Jesus in the totality of his life. This is what I call the "Easter experience," which could be expressed in a variety of ways: the crucified one is the coming judge (a *maranatha* Christology);

the crucified one as miracle worker is actively present in his disciples; the crucified one has risen. And then we may indeed say: at that juncture there dawns the experience of their really seeing Jesus at last—the basis of what is being made explicit in the Easter appearances: Jesus "makes himself seen" (*ōphthē*); not till after his death does he become "epiphanous," that is, transparent; it is through faith that we grasp who he is. This acknowledging on the disciples' part is at the same time a recollective and yet new seeing of Jesus—of Jesus of Nazareth; not of someone different, nor yet a myth. Jesus as they had encountered him remains the sole criterion for their recollections as well as for their new experiences after his death.

Historically speaking, it is likely (and accepted more or less universally by scholars at the moment) that—apart from the appearances to women, who in that antique, primarily Jewish culture could not provide any "legitimate" testimony—the first manifestation of Jesus (protophany) was to Simon Peter (1 Cor 15:5; Luke 24:34; and, indirectly, Mark 16:7), that Peter was the first to experience what is called in the New Testament the "seeing of Jesus" after his death. This is correlative with the Marcan tradition (or more probably redaction) which in the context of the shock and dismay felt by the disciples generally attributes to Simon alone an individual denial of Jesus— something which in the Marcan redaction is interpreted in terms of "salvation-history," that is, as a "divine must" of salvific design, in that Mark quotes at this point a passage of scripture and puts it directly into the mouth of Jesus (Mark 14:27; see the connection made by Mark between Mark 14:27 and 14:28 with Mark 16:27).

Then there are strong indications (noticed by many exegetes) that the name "Kepha(s)," Peter or rock, acquired by Simon, has a link with his prime position in the Christ appearances. Apropos of this first "official-cum-hierarchical" appearance Luke simply calls Peter "Simon": "he . . . has appeared to Simon" (Luke 24:34); elsewhere he usually speaks of "Peter." Moreover, B. Gerhardson has shown (with the backing of many other commentators) that it is "extremely probable" that Matt 16:17-19 stems from a (now lost) tradition which tells of the first appearance of Jesus, specifically, to Peter. With some admittedly fundamental corrections A. Vögtle too sees Matt 16:18-19 as a fragment which originally formed part of an account of a Peter-protophany (although A. Vögtle denies that a christological confession by Peter was associated with this account of the official "first appearance" to Peter). An important point is that A. Vögtle also recognizes that the Jesus logion in Matthew: "You are Peter (rock)" is the initial introduction of the name Peter for Simon; and that this name was certainly not given to Simon by the earthly Jesus. The linking up of the designation "rock" and Peter's protophany therefore is now held by many scholars to be the best hypothesis. The pre-Pauline use of Peter instead of Simon points, within this short period after Jesus' death, to an already established tradition.

All these things give us reasonable grounds for postulating that after Jesus' death Peter was the first (male) disciple to reach the point of "conversion" and to resume "following after Jesus," and then other disciples as well, on Peter's initiative. Peter is therefore the first Christian confessor to arrive at a christological affirmation; by virtue of his conversion he takes the initiative in assembling a (or the) "band of twelve" (whether it was by them called that or not; see immediately below). This is how he becomes the rock of the primal core of the Christian community, "the twelve" who acknowledged Jesus as the coming or risen "crucified one," that is, the community of the latter days, of the final aeon, the new kingdom of the twelve tribes, the gathered "church of Christ" (Rom 16:16) or "church of God" (1 Cor 1:2; 10:32; etc.). This, we may suppose, is the hard historical center of the process that brought about the reassembling of Jesus' disciples as the congregation of Christ. Very probably Peter was not himself the founder of "the twelve"—rather, the group of twelve was already in existence before Easter (how otherwise could Judas Iscariot be called "one of the twelve," and—more particularly—how can we explain the technical term "the eleven"?). It would seem, rather, that the pre-Easter action of Jesus in sending the disciples out on their mission served to constitute the group of the twelve. It was then a consequence of Jesus' protophany that Peter had the credit for reassembling this twelve. An echo or recollection of this historical event I find in Luke 22:32: "Simon, Simon . . . when you have turned again [*epistrepsas:* converted], strengthen your brethren" (in this complex, Luke 22:31–33, the use of "Simon" is a striking feature). Thus a link is forged here between Peter's denial, his conversion and initiative in bringing the disciples together again; in constituting them disciples of Christ. Yet Peter's act of conversion is not something detached from that of the twelve: belief in the resurrection presupposes a process of reciprocal communication among the twelve. Hence the testimony of scripture to their "at first doubting." . . .

It should have become clear, now that we have examined the structure of the appearance stories, that they point to an event set within a context of salvation history, and that, like the appeal to scripture, the "vision" model is a means of articulating an event engendered by grace, a divine, salvific initiative—a grace manifesting itself in historical events and human experiences. In other words, the reporting of what occurred in the guise of appearances indicates that the process whereby Peter and his friends were brought together again after their dispersal was felt by them to be an act of sheer grace on God's part, as (set in a different context) appears from the gospels. . . .

In which concrete historical events this "grace and favor" or renewed offer of salvation in Jesus has been manifested the New Testament nowhere explicitly states; it only speaks of the character of this event as one of amazing grace. The objective, sovereignly free initiative of Jesus that led them on to a christological faith—an initiative independent of any belief on the part of Peter and his companions—is a gracious act of Christ, which as regards their "enlightenment" is of course revelation— not a construct of men's minds, but revelation within a disclosure experience, in this case given verbal embodiment later on in the "appearances" model. What it signifies is no model but a living reality. Understood thus, the ground of Christian belief is indubitably Jesus of Nazareth in his earthly proffer of salvation, renewed after his death, now experienced and enunciated by Peter and the twelve. It means too that this time Jesus is acknowledged by God: the man put to death by his fellows was vindicated when he appealed to God. This is brought out more especially in the formulae stating that God caused Jesus to rise from the dead.

The experience of having their cowardice and want of faith forgiven them, an experience further illuminated by what they were able to remember of the general tenor of Jesus' life on earth, thus became the matrix in which faith in Jesus as the risen one was brought to birth. They all of a sudden "saw" it. This seeing may have been the outcome of a lengthier process of maturation, one primary and important element of which was enough to make Peter take action and bring the disciples together again. About this initial element there was obviously a collective exchange of ideas— "they doubted"—until a consensus emerged. Even the oldest, pre-Pauline creedal formulae are the result of an already protracted theological reflection and not the instant articulation of the original experience. In the experience of forgiveness as a gift of grace— the renewed offer of saving fellowship by the crucified one—lies the venture of faith, which is not, after all, an obligatory conclusion from this, that or the other premise. It is the individual's experience of new being that imparts to faith the assurance that Jesus is alive or is the coming judge of the world. . . .

The question is, surely, whether the Christian interpretation, after Jesus' death, rests solely on experiences with the earthly Jesus or whether it is not partly undergirded by new experiences after his death. This is the crucial point, it seems to me. And I mean, not experiences of an "empty tomb" or of "appearances" (themselves already an interpretation of the resurrection faith), but experiences such as I have already enumerated: the "conversion process" undergone by the disciples, their "encounter with grace" after Jesus' death. That the New Testament bases itself on specific experiences after Jesus' death (however they might be interpeted) seems to me, on the strength of the foregoing analysis, undeniable. As opposed to W. Marxsen I would proceed from the "Easter experience" as reality, real experience and experience of reality, which nonetheless carries within it an element of articulation. [1974]

4

Shaping the Experience
of the Risen Lord

COMMENTARY

In the face of the overwhelming experience of the risen Jesus, the disciples of Jesus had to come to terms with what this event said about him. Schillebeeckx has maintained that the experience of Jesus as prophet was fundamental to that naming process we now see in the New Testament. Selection 48 summarizes Schillebeeckx's argument for this position, where he traces the Moses tradition within which he sees the disciples developing their creeds.

The development of those early confessions of faith led to a shift in perspective on Jesus: from what God has done with Jesus (a theology of Jesus) to the relation of Jesus to God (Christology). Selection 49 explores this shift from more functional namings of Jesus, using titles from Jewish tradition, to the beginnings of some profound new reflection on the reality of Jesus. These reflections set the early communities on the way to confessing the divinity of Jesus, which Schillebeeckx discusses in selection 50.

The significance of Jesus lies especially in soteriology, that is, God's saving activity in Jesus for us. Selections 51 and 52 explore some dimensions of that: what it means in terms of human fulfillment and how it relates to a recurring theme of Schillebeeckx, namely, eschatology.

48/ *Jesus as Eschatological Prophet*

One of the basic arguments in my first Jesus book is that the first Christian interpretation of Jesus in the period before the New Testament was more than probably in terms of the "eschatological prophet like Moses," and that this tendency can still be recognized from a variety of early Christian strata in the New Testament.

This early Jewish, intertestamental religious concept goes back to a "Deuteronomic" view (Deut 18:15-19; 30:15-20; 30:1-3). "Behold, I send an angel before you, to guard you on the way and to bring you to the place which I have prepared. Give heed to him and hearken to his voice, do not rebel against him, for he will not pardon your transgression; for my name is in him. But if you hearken attentively to his voice and do all that I say, then I will be an enemy to your enemies and an adversary to your adversaries" (Exod 23:20-22; see 33:2): "The Lord your God will raise up for you a prophet like me [= Moses] from among you, from your brethren—him you shall heed" (Deut 18:15).

The tradition of the eschatological prophet was not originally connected with an expectation of Elijah (Mal 4:5f.; see also Sir 48:10f.); it belonged in the Moses tradition, since it is clear that in Mal 4:5f. the forerunner, Elijah, is a secondary insertion (see Mal 3:1, which has links with the original prophet like Moses). In early Judaism the figure of Elijah took on the function of a forerunner of the Messiah. However, this secondary tradition is based on an earlier, Deuteronomic tradition where Moses is a prophet, a proclaimer of the word. Deuteronomy is essentially composed as a discourse of Moses (Deut 5:1, 5, 14; 6:1). Moses is a mediator between God and the people (Deut 5:5), at the same time he is a suffering mediator, because in addition to being a spokesman for his people (Deut 9:15-19; 9:25-29), Moses suffers for his people Israel (see Deut 1:37; 4:21f.). For Deuteronomy, Moses is the suffering prophet. Later prophets are therefore fond of presenting themselves with the prophetic aspects of Moses (see Jer 1:6-9; cf. Exod 4:10-12; see also Elijah and Elisha, 1 Kgs 19:19-21; 2 Kgs 2:1-15, cf. Deut 34:9 and Num 27:15-23: Moses and Joshua as a pair). In this tradition it is also said: "If there is a prophet among you, I the Lord make myself known to him in a vision, I speak with him in a dream. Not so with my servant Moses; he is entrusted with all my house. With him I speak mouth to mouth" (Num 12:6-8) "face to face, as a man speaks to his friend" (Exod 33:11). This tradition also says that the prophetic Moses is the Ebed Yahweh, the servant of God (Exod 14:31; Num 12:7f.; Deut 34:5; Josh 1:2, 7; Wis 10:16; Isa 63:11). Moreover, Moses is a suffering Ebed Yahweh, "who bears the burden of the people" (Num 16:47; see Isa 53:4).

Moses, the suffering servant of God and the prophet! Perhaps we can say even more. It seems probable that even the theme of the "innocent sufferer," which forms a separate motif, is fused in Deutero-Isaiah with the theme of "Moses as the suffering, prophetic servant of God": the suffering servant of Deutero-Isaiah (above all Isa 42:1-4; 49:1-6; 50:4-11a;

52:13-53:12). In the final redaction of Isaiah it is wrong to put Proto-, Deutero- and Trito-Isaiah in succession as three disparate blocks; it is necessary to look at the final redaction as a whole. In that case the prophetic and royal Moses who bears the burden of his people *is* the suffering servant of Deutero-Isaiah. So Deutero-Isaiah would have spoken about the suffering servant in a terminology which at least is strongly reminiscent of the developing picture of the "eschatological prophet" like and greater than Moses. Like Moses, he communicates the law and justice (Isa 42:1f.), but now to the whole world: the suffering servant-like-Moses is "the light of the world" (Isa 49:5-9; 42:1-6); and like Moses he is the mediator of a covenant (Isa 42:6; 49:8), leader of the new exodus, this time from the Babylonian captivity. The twelve tribes are gathered together again as a result of this exodus (Isa 49:5f.; 43:5f.). In this exodus the eschatological prophet greater than Moses will again strike water from the rock and offer "the water of life" to his people (Isa 41:18; 43:20; 48:21; 49:10; see the Gospel of John). The suffering servant is the Moses of the new exodus (Isa 43:16-21): expiating sins, suffering for his people, the Mosaic servant has all the marks of the figure who in early Judaism is in fact called the messianic eschatological prophet like Moses. Moreover, before the time of Jesus this theme often developed into a Moses-mysticism which was also called "Sinaitism" (see already Sir 45:1-5): the royal messianic prophet Moses, the *divus.*

Now it is striking that in quite divergent early Christian traditions there are clear signs of the presence of the concept of the Mosaic eschatological prophet: both in the earliest (Mark) and the latest (John) gospel, in Stephen's speech in Acts and in the Q tradition (etc., etc.).

Mark 1:2 begins the gospel with an implicit reference to the classical texts of the tradition of the eschatological prophet (Exod 23:20; Mal 3:1 and Isa 40:3): "Behold, I send my messenger before thy face" (Mark 1:2): "before you," i.e., before Jesus, John the Baptist is sent out to introduce "the prophet after and greater than Moses": "a prophet from your midst and from your brothers" (cf. Deut 18:15-18 with Mark 6:4). Moreover, in Mark 6:14-16 three misguided prophetic identifications of Jesus are rejected: Jesus is not John the Baptist risen from the dead (Mark 6:14; his body has already been buried, Mark 6:29); far less is he Elijah, who is still identified with the Baptist and not with Jesus (Mark 1:2 and 9:11-13); finally Jesus is also not "a prophet like the others" (Mark 6:15). The sequence is Elijah, then Moses, then Jesus (Mark 9:2-9), from which it follows automatically: "Listen to him" (Mark 9:7; see Deut 18:15 and Exod 23:20-23). In all the gospels we find the theme: Jesus is a prophet, but "not like the others." Nowhere do they present any polemic against the conception of Jesus as the prophet: it is against the idea that he is a prophet like the others. This original view of Christ as prophet, a concept which does not make other honorific titles superfluous, has almost vanished from our Christian preaching. Therefore Christ can be made into a heavenly icon, moved so far on the side of God, who himself has already vanished from the world of men, that as a prophet he loses all critical force in our world.

Some critics think that the "eschatological prophet" (which in no way means simply the "last prophet") is too low a christological title and that in any case it is incapable of supporting the other, perhaps heavier, New Testament honorific titles. In that case, people are not thinking hard enough about the significance of "eschatological." Certainly in the New Testament, the term eschatological prophet implies that this prophet is significant for the whole history of the world, and significant for the whole of subsequent history, no matter how Jesus and his followers may have conceived of this ongoing history. Thus echatological prophet means a prophet who claims to bring a definitive message which applies to the whole of history. It is clear from texts from the Q tradition that Jesus himself was convinced of this, and even more that he attributed world-historical significance to his person: there is every guarantee here that we have a historical echo of Jesus' own self-understanding: "Blessed is he who takes no offense in me" (Luke 7:23 = Matt 11:6); this is developed in another Q text: "And I tell you, every one who acknowledges me before men, the Son of man also will acknowledge before the angels of God; but he who denies me before men will be denied before the angels of God" (Luke 12:8f. = Matt 10:32f.; cf. Luke 7:18–22 = Matt 11:2–6; and Luke 11:20 = Matt 12:28), which is then developed further in the synoptic gospels (Matt 12:32; Luke 12:10; Mark 3:28f.). The affirmation of a real relationship between the decision which men make about Jesus and their ultimate destiny (which is stressed even more strongly by the Gospel of John) without doubt goes back historically, at least in germ, to Jesus' own understanding of himself. The first Christians expressed this self-understanding, which was presented in the whole of Jesus' career, in terms of the concept of the "eschatological prophet": the intermediary in the coming of the kingdom of God. That in the coming of Jesus God himself touches us is a Christian conviction which therefore in the last resort goes back to Jesus' understanding of himself.

If the future or the historical influence of a person is part of the identity of that person, then this is true in a unique way of Jesus, for today's living Christian communities are not just in an accidental way part of the complete personal identity of Jesus. In such a case the historical influence of a person begins to belong to his identity in a very special way. The first Christians used the term "eschatological prophet" to express precisely this. In and through what he is, says and does, Jesus points beyond himself to the whole ongoing history of mankind as the coming of God's kingdom. I see the concept of Mosaic-messianic "eschatological prophet" as a matrix which gave rise to four pre-New Testament creedal models which later came together in the New Testament under the all-embracing title of Easter Christology. These are:

1. *maranatha* Christologies, which confess Jesus as the Lord of the future, the one who is to come;

2. a Christology which sees Jesus as the "wonder-worker," not so much along the lines of the sporadic *theios aner* theories of the time but rather in terms of the good and wise wonder-worker reminiscent of Solomon, who does not do wonders for his own profit but for the salvation of others and precisely for that reason is reviled, though his honor is later vindicated by God;

3. wisdom Christologies, which see Jesus as sent from God by wisdom (low-sapiental) or as identified with an independent wisdom which proclaims the mysteries of God's salvation (high-sapiental);

4. finally, all kinds of forms of Easter Christologies in which Jesus' death and resurrection in particular occupy a central place.

Each of these four creedal tendencies shows a particular interest in certain historical aspects of Jesus' life: the proclaimer of the coming kingdom of God, the other side of which is the final judgment: Jesus, who went around Palestine doing good; Jesus, who reveals God to man and man to himself; Jesus as the one who was condemned to death. It emerges from this that all the early Christian creeds or views of Jesus are in any event most profoundly directed and governed by real, historically demonstrable aspects of Jesus' life. It is this particular aspect which has been especially welcomed by many exegetes who have discussed my book.

The fact that these four attempts at a christological interpretation of the historical "phenomenon of Jesus," corrected and filled out by one another, could come together in the one canonical writing within the one fundamental vision of the crucified and risen Jesus as seen in the gospels and the New Testament, is an indication that in all these interpretations of Jesus there must have been a common identification of his person which can be approached from many different directions. For me this is Jesus, the eschatological prophet, who in the prophetic "Christ" tradition is interpreted as "the one inspired by God," "filled with God's spirit," who brings "the good news that God is beginning to reign" (a fusion of Deut 18:15 with texts from Deutero- and Trito-Isaiah in Judaism), the eschatological prophet greater than Moses who speaks with God "face to face," "mouth to mouth" (Num 12:6–8; Exod 33:10f.). God's last messenger of all is his beloved Son (Mark 12:6): this is the eschatological prophet greater than Moses. When filled in by Jesus' own life and death, this key concept is in fact capable of supporting all other honorific titles and disclosing their deepest significance for salvation. One can say that the continuity between Jesus before his death and Jesus after it is established by the recognition that Jesus is the eschatological prophet, an early Christian interpretation of Jesus' own understanding of himself. [1978]

49/ *From a Theology of Jesus to a Christology*

The gospels relate how, starting from his *Abba* experience, as contrasted with the course of our human suffering, Jesus both announced and offered to people, in word and action, "salvation from God" and a real future. Confronted with the historical rejection of Jesus' message and eventually of his person, the first Christians were moved by the renewal of their own lives after the death of their master and, recalling the fellowship they had enjoyed with him during his life on earth, to confess this Jesus as the crucified and risen one, in whom they had experience of definitive and final salvation; in him God himself has brought about redemption, salvation and liberation. Using the religious and cultural key concepts already available to them, and in virtue of this salvific function, they called Jesus the Christ, Son of God, their Lord.

With all this we are still within the "theology" of Jesus of Nazareth: that is to say, within the area of reflection upon what Jesus himself had to say about the coming rule of God as salvation, liberation and redemption for man; that is, within the discourse of Jesus concerning God, which was clothed in flesh and blood by his own public ministry, mode of living and death: "For the kingdom of God does not consist in talk but in power" (1 Cor 4:20). Living contact with this person who proclaimed the kingdom of God was experienced as God-given salvation. This yielded, as the outcome of a primarily theological, faith-motivated reflection, the creedal affirmation: God himself, the God of salvation history, has acted decisively in Jesus for the salvation of men: "It is God who through Jesus reconciled us to himself" (2 Cor 5:18). In that sense all the honorific titles of Jesus, including "Son of God," are in the first instance functional, are elements within salvation history, even in the late sapiential Johannine gospel with its pre-existence idea. As a matter of fact, in the line of traditions within which John stands, the Torah too was pre-existent, with God prior to all creation, although no Jew would have regarded the preexistent Torah of the Wisdom tradition as a sort of "second divine person"—not even John in respect to his "preexistent logos," which he identifies with Jesus of Nazareth and calls Son rather than "logos." . . .

The thing to bear in mind, then, is that this scheme of ideas (which in late Judaism served to underwrite the divine authority of an earthly being) is applied by Christians to a quite concrete historical person, Jesus of Nazareth. That is something radically new and in a religious context unprecedented—at any rate if we leave aside the ascription of divine status to the Roman emperors (associated not with any religious interest but with "reasons of state"). Intertestamentary literature, before and after Jesus, does admittedly speak of the preexistent Enoch or Ezra, who after his life on earth is taken up to God and exalted. They are called son of man, son of God and Lord of the universe; and all the peculiar names of God are assigned to them. But though once historical beings in a remote and hazy past, they were now in fact abstract *theologoumena*. On the one hand this only goes to show that in the first instance the honorific titles given to Jesus in the New Testament are understood to be functional, in a context of salvation history; on the other hand, however, that in the historical life of Jesus certain things had become apparent—an obvious authority deriving from God—which invited people to apply this already existing model of understanding and inter-pretation—which, *qua* model, implies nothing more or less than that we are faced here with an earthly manifestation in and through which a personal relationship to God is decided.

Since the idea of using these existing models is to throw light on a function, more precisely, the crucial, salvific function, of Jesus—salvation in Jesus imparted by God—we cannot in the end dodge the question: Who then is this Jesus in himself, if all this is supposed to have happened in and through him "as from God"? Particularly among Greco-Jewish Christians, and more so later on among Christians with a background of pagan Hellenism (which inquires not only about what has happened in somebody but what and who that person really is), the question of *ousia* or "essential being," in the spirit in which one may speak of "iden-tification of the person" in an ontological sense, was bound to arise. Indeed the Aramaic and Greco-Jewish Christians, within their own on-tology, were least of all able to avoid this question. For them this became a profounder question: What does the individual person, Jesus, who talks in this way about God, his *Abba*, mean for God himself? A primary insight into the initial, peculiar nature of the "God of Jesus," the *Abba*, raises the question of the "Jesus of God," that is, how does this Jesus per-tain to God himself: "*my* son," "*my* servant," "*my* holy one" and so forth.

This "possessive relationship" of God towards Jesus—corroborated here, there and everywhere in the New Testament—was sooner or later bound to lead on to more pregnant questions, to a second stage of reflection. Who is this Jesus, who to this degree is the "exclusive possession" of God? It was above all their belief in the crucified and risen one—evidencing for the first Christians this exclusive title and possession on God's part— that compelled a further reflection. For Jesus was not an "organ of salvation," in the sense in which Moses with his staff had struck water from the dry rock. That definitive salvation from God had been encountered in the man Jesus, and not in some celestial being or other, for Jews would quite certainly point to God's act of election, "gratis and for nothing"; it expresses God's pure pleasure. Jesus for his part—such was their express impression—had not falsified or betrayed this election of his, but in love and loyalty to Yahweh had lived and moved among people, caring for them, until he was broken by it. From a religious standpoint and within the framework of a particular pattern of thought, that says everything. Yet in its attempts to determine the moment at which God's choice was concretely and effectively accomplished in the man Jesus we see within the New Testament some very subtle and delicate changes, pointing to a persisting process of reflection, all the time refining, correcting and deepening the first one. It turns out that identification of the person can be intensified without ever coming up against a conclusive "delimitation." This further reflection does not actually reveal any completely new insights; yet neither is it meant simply as a "meta-language," that is, as a way of discoursing about "faith-motivated discourse about Jesus," in a linguistic-analytical sense. It does not have to do (however necessary the analysis of it may be) with talk about the very act of identifying (the act of faith as such), but about the self identified: a deepening, in faith, of understanding of a Jesus already interpreted and identified. And then all that has already been said about Jesus of Nazareth can be reformulated from another standpoint, namely, from that of God's saving initiative. Of course, there are no new and different roads to revelation provided here—a sort of private access—that would let us know just how God sees Jesus. It is only via the "theology of Jesus of Nazareth," in his words and his actions, that we are able to find out what God himself is disclosing about this Jesus. But this second concern is orientated differently from the first. It was out of this inquiry, already under way in the New Testament, that the early church was eventually to give birth to the Nicene dogma of Jesus' "co-essential being" with the Father, with later on, as a counterbalance to that in Chalcedon, the nature of Jesus as co-essential with the humanity of us all: "one and the same person"—Jesus Christ—is "true God" and "true man," not in a hybrid blending, but *asynchytōs* and *atreptōs*, that is, without merging and without loss of peculiar substance and significance, and at the same time *adiairetōs* and *achōristōs*, that is, indissolubly one. [1974]

50/ *Is Jesus God?*

First of all, then, let me say that this can be a perverse question. It is of course true that Jesus' message becomes incomprehensible if its hearers do not already have in advance a certain concept of what and who God is. Even the Jews who came into contact with Jesus and "followed him" did in fact have a prior understanding of what "God" means. But according to the four gospels, in which we have a kerygmatic account of Jesus, the whole significance of the man Jesus, to his Jewish contemporaries a fellow Jew, lay in the fact that through his appearance as a man among fellow man, in a special way he showed who and what and how God is, as salvation for man, in the line of what I would now want to call "the great Jewish religious tradition." In the last resort, the New Testament is not concerned to adapt a strange concept of God to what happened in Jesus; it is concerned with the new view of God which is given in and through Jesus—in the context of this great Jewish tradition of Yahweh.

However, what Jesus did so that others began to experience decisive salvation in him, salvation from God, ultimately raises the question: Who is he, that he was able to do such things? If he passes on to us a new attitude to God and his kingdom, it is obvious that people should ask: What is his relationship to God and—by way of the answer to this question—what is God's relationship to him? In this sense, the question posed is not only legitimate but, in the light of the phenomenon of Jesus himself, even necessary.

It becomes clear from this that in his humanity Jesus is "given a name," i.e., is defined by his relationship to God. In other words: the deepest nature of Jesus lay in his personal relationship with God (moreover, this is connected with the concept of the "eschatological prophet" who spoke with God "mouth to mouth," "face to face," "as with a friend"). Without doubt our creaturely relationship to God is also essential for our humanity. But this relationship does not define our being man or woman in our humanity as such. It says only that human beings are creatures. Nothing—no creature—escapes this relationship, but that is not to say anything about the proper nature of this creature. With Jesus there is more. It is already evident from the New Testament, on the one hand that God can only be defined from and in terms of the human life of Jesus, and on the other hand that as a man in his full humanity Jesus can only be defined in terms of his unique relationship with God and man (this, too, was a well-known aspect of the eschatological prophet). According to the New Testament, God belongs in a very special and unparalleled way to the definition of what and who the man Jesus is.

However, God is greater even than his supreme, decisive and definitive self-revelation in the man Jesus ("the Father is greater than I," John 14:28). Thus the humanity of Jesus is an essential pointer to God the Father and to the coming of the kingdom of God, for which he himself had sacrificed his life, i.e., "had thought it to be of less value." For Jesus, God's cause—the kingdom of God, as human salvation—was thus greater than the importance of his own human life. No theology may minimize this fact through a direct reference to what might be called a human attack on God himself. Though men may have made an attack on Jesus and in so doing may be guilty before God, Jesus himself nevertheless thought his life to be of less value than the cause for which he stood: the coming of God's kingdom as salvation from and for man—and therefore less than God. The definition, i.e., the real significance, of Jesus lies in this way in which he points from himself to God, whom he called Creator and Father. For Christian belief Jesus is therefore the decisive and definitive revelation of God; and at the same time shows us in this what and how we finally can be, and really should be. The glory of God is visible in the face of Jesus the Christ. Just as this same appearance of Jesus reveals to us what a human being should be. This is the interpretation of Christian faith. It is clear from this that the transcendence of God cannot be separated from his immanence or his presence with us. God's nature is absolute freedom: his nature determines freely what he will essentially be for us—and viewed from the perspective of our history in which Jesus has appeared (for we do not have any other perspective)— that is salvation for man in Jesus within a greater saving event which embraces creation from beginning to end. We cannot separate God's nature and his revelation. Therefore in the definition of what he is, the man Jesus is indeed connected with the nature of God.

I do not know whether we can, need or may make this theoretically more precise. I am sometimes hesitant to attempt to describe the mystery of a person, above all the person of Jesus, in every detail. When people have more to say than they can express rationally in words, they begin to resort to parables and stories. Symbolic evocation transcends the impotence of conceptual articulation. This is not meant to indicate any christological agnosticism. However, defining (*horismos* or definition) is also delimiting, and in that case one runs the risk of reducing the mystery and distorting it; whether by understating it (Arianism, Nestorianism) or by overstating it (Monophysitism), or by moving in the direction of a timeless and pure paradox, and in so doing detaching the Jesus of Nazareth who lived a historical life among us from his historical and temporal appearing as a man among human beings.

In Jesus God reveals his own being by willing to be salvation for humanity. That is why in my two Jesus books I emphasize two aspects: (1) salvation for mankind lies in the living God (*vita hominis, visio Dei,*) and (2) God's honor lies in our happiness and liberation, salvation and wholeness (*Gloria Dei, vivens homo.*)

In the man Jesus the revelation of the divine and the disclosure of the nature of true, good and really happy men and women—as ultimately the supreme possibility of human life— completely coincide in one and the same person. This fully corresponds to the Christian tradition of Christ mysticism. This liturgical mysticism found an appropriate expression in Nicea and Chalcedon, albeit in terms of the conceptuality of the later period of the ancient world. [1978]

51/ *Human Fulfillment in Christ*

History teaches us that there has never been a perfect redemption, but that in Jesus there is a divine promise for us all, and that this is anticipated in any definitively valid act of doing good to our fellow men in a finite and conditioned world in which love is always doomed to failure and yet nevertheless refuses to choose any other way than that of loving service. Any attempt at totality which cannot recognize the non-identical, refractory suffering and failure of this doing good and is not content with it, leads to an illusion, has an alienating effect, or becomes unproductive. Christian belief in salvation from God in Jesus as the Christ is the downfall of any doctrine of salvation or soteriology understood in human terms, in the sense of an identity which is within our control and therefore can be manipulated. The Christian gospel is not an unmediated identity, but a practice of identification with what is not identical, the non-I, the other, above all the suffering and the injustice of others. Definitive salvation remains an indefinable horizon in our history in which both the hidden God (*Deus absconditus*) and the sought-for, yet hidden, *humanum* disappear. But if the fundamental symbol of God is the living man (*imago Dei,*) then the place where man is dishonored, violated and oppressed, both in his own heart and in a society which oppresses men, is at the same time the preferred place where *religious experience* becomes possible in a way of life which seeks to give form to this symbol, to heal it and give it its own liberated existence. As the intrinsic consequence of the radicalism of its message and reconciling practice, the crucifixion of Jesus shows that any attempt at liberating redemption which is concerned with humanity is valid *in and of itself* and not subsequently as a result of any success which may follow. What counts is not success, any more than failure or misfortune, above all as the result of the intervention of others. The important thing is loving service. We are shown the true face of both God and man in the "vain" love of Jesus which knows that its criterion does not lie in success, but in its very being as radical love and identification. In that case, reconciliation and liberation, if they seek to be valid for all, despite the limited aspect of an imperfect historical situation, are not a mere change of power relationships and thus a new domination. Redemption is a task imposed upon us: for us it remains a reconciliation to be realized, which will constantly be moulded by failure, suffering and death in the refractoriness of our history—by a love which is impotent in this world but which will never give in. It is based on a love which ventures the impossible and does not compel man to what he himself sees as liberation and redemption. In our time, above all, Christians only have the right to utter the word "God" where they find their identity in identification with that part of life which is still unreconciled, and in effective action towards reconciliation and liberation. What history tells us about Jesus, what the church tells and indeed *promises* us about Jesus is that in this way of life, which is in conformity with the message of Jesus and the kingdom of God, we are shown the *real possibility* of an experience of God. In Jesus the Christ, we are promised that this way of life will bring us particularly close to God. However, what final possibilities are contained in the eschatological consummation of this saving presence of God, which we celebrate and give thanks for in the liturgy, is God's mystery, which may be called the abundance of our humanity. Furthermore, we know from the same history of and about Jesus, that the promise of the inward presence of God rests on the futility and the historical failure of this way of life, as on the cross. This kind of liberation refuses ever to sacrifice a fellow man for a hoped-for better future, or to leave him out in the cold until better structures have been found. The practice of reconciliation and liberation, which nevertheless can also experience the nearness of God even in failure and suffering, is the sphere in which mystical experience of God becomes possible and in which, moreover, it can show its credentials. Because in the last resort the one who is experienced and can be known in this action of reconciliation, the living God, is always greater than our action, this experience, this experience of God, as an inner element of liberating and reconciling action, always discloses to us a new and greater future. Here the believer experiences that redemption is not within our power and that God

nevertheless *gives a future* to all our action towards liberation and reconciliation, a future which is greater than the volume of our finite history.

What, then, is salvation in Jesus from God? I would want to say: being
at the disposal of others, losing oneself to others (each in his own limited
situation) and within this "conversion" (which is also made possible by
structural changes) also working through anonymous structures for the
happiness, the goodness and the truth of mankind. This way of life, born
of grace, provides a real possibility for a very personal encounter with
God, who is then experienced as the source of all happiness and salvation, the source of joy. It is communicative freedom which is actively
reconciled with our own finitude, our death, our transgression and our
failure. It sounds almost inauthentic: reconciliation with oneself as a
useless servant, although we know that God says to us, "You may exist."
It is being justified freely through faith by grace. Even if there is no
human love in return, sometimes if there is even misunderstanding, the
believer knows in his sovereign freedom, which is at the same time
grateful humility, that there is love in return: God first loved us. Real
redemption or salvation always passes over into mysticism: only here can
the tension between action and contemplation be sustained. This is existing for others and thus for *the* Other, the wholly intimate and near yet
"transcendent God," with whom Jesus has made us familiar [1977]

52/ *Christology as Eschatology*

Although Christian salvation also includes earthly salvation, in an upward direction this salvation in Jesus from God is in fact indefinable;
earthly salvation is taken up into a greater mystery. We cannot tie down
God's possibilities to our limited expectations of salvation. Filling out
this definitive salvation in a positive way runs the risk of making men
megalomaniacs or reducing God's possibilities, and as a result making
man smaller than God dreamed that he should be.

Because this definitive salvation, that is, the perfect and universal wholeness of all and every person, living and dead, cannot be defined, the end
of this story of God in Jesus with man cannot be told completely or to
the end within the narrow limits of our history. The individual's death
breaks the thread perhaps of a liberating story. In that case, is there no
longer any salvation, not even for the one who has handed on the torch
of this story and held it alight among the living, and perhaps was mar-
tyred as a result? It follows that the final consummation of God's way
of salvation with man cannot be "of this world," while the liberating
involvement of God with mankind, whom he rescues and makes whole,

nevertheless may and must take on a recognizable content within our history in forms which will nevertheless constantly be transcended.

Although definitive salvation is eschatological, and as such cannot of course be experienced as an already present content of experience, the believer is nevertheless aware of the promise of a definitive perspective of salvation actually given in an experience now, especially in fragments of particular experiences of salvation, thanks to Jesus Christ. Only on the basis of partial experiences of this kind does the church's proclamation and promise of definitive salvation from the story of and about Jesus as the Christ take on real meaning for believers. Without this religious story about Jesus Christ, at most we would be confronted with a utopian liberation which might perhaps stimulate some chances of life and salvation for people who appear on the far horizon of our history but which has written off the rest of mankind from this "prehistory" for the benefit of a dreamed-of utopia to be realized one day. Of course definitive salvation utterly transcends our present experience—in the last resort, no one among us experiences being whole now—but insofar as the announcement and promise of salvation can and may be said to be valid now, it has its basis in a context of experience here and now; of Jesus and of those who follow him in this world, and also of all those who in fact do what Jesus did. This eschatological promise cannot simply be based on a revelation in words—of course, for the anthropologist "word" is an expression of human experience and practice—and cannot therefore be a mere proclamation of a definitive and complete salvation to come. On what basis would an "announcement" of this kind have real value? As an interpreter of God and one who acted in accordance with the life-style of the kingdom of God, Jesus did not act on the basis of a blueprint or a well-defined concept of eschatological and definitive salvation. Rather, he saw in and through his own historical and thus geographically limited practice of "going around doing good," of healing, liberating from the demonic powers then thought to be at large in the world, and of reconciliation, the dawn of a distant vision of definitive, perfect and universal salvation. "Behold, the dwelling of God is with men. He will dwell with them, and they shall be his people, and God himself will be with them; he will wipe away every tear from their eyes, and death shall be no more, neither shall there be mourning, nor crying, nor pain any more, for the former things have passed away" (Rev 21:3f.). Interpreted in this way, the Christian Apocalypse presents a true vision of Jesus' ministry: the kingdom of God in its final form, of which Jesus Christ is now the positive guarantor. [1978]

Part Four

The Church:
The Community of Grace

1

The Experience of Salvation
as Grace

COMMENTARY

The reality of Jesus and the salvation which God has given us through him we experience especially within the community of grace, the church. Schillebeeckx has written extensively on matters surrounding the church and life in the church throughout his career. Part IV brings together some of his more important contributions in this area.

This first section provides a link between his discussion of New Testament Christology and soteriology, and how that salvation is experienced today. The traditional theological word for this relationship and experience is "grace." In selections 53 and 54, Schillebeeckx spells out what that New Testament witness to grace means for us in the contemporary situation. In selection 55, he takes up the differences between how grace was understood in early Christianity and how it came to be understood much later in the churches. The value of this reflection is to keep us from reading our own categories back into the New Testament and, at the same time, to permit us to view the New Testament data freshly.

53/ The Concept of Grace and the Reality of Salvation

Corresponding to the key Old Testament concepts *ḥesed* and *ḥānan*, in the New Testament grace means the benevolent and merciful (and at the same time free and sovereign) love of God for men. This is not, however, to be understood exclusively in an internalized sense, as a benevolent disposition of God and in God, but rather as a benevolence of God

...rings salvation that manifests or reveals itself freely in the
..edemption and liberation shown forth in history and experi-
.. by men in faith (for Jewish Christians the Old Testament concept
..f *hesed* and *ḥānan* rules out any dualism between inwardness and its outward expression).

Grace is a *new way of life* prepared for us by God in Jesus Christ and
offered to us on the level of our own earthly history, freely (Paul) and
to make us glad (Luke) (see Heb 10:20; 2 Pet 2:15; John 14:6; a way of
salvation: Acts 16:17; 9:2; 19:23; 24:14; 1 Cor 12:31; "the way" is an oriental expression, also to be found in late antiquity, for a particular practice
and viewpoint which leads to salvation). Thus grace is a new human
possibility for life, a particular mode of existence through which and in
which man really experiences salvation and redemption, liberation and
renewal of life, happiness and fulfillment. For the New Testament, "the
way" means following the life of Jesus with God, expressed in his concern for men, in solidarity with our experience of God's care for all, a
way of life or mode of existence through which God's own concern, his
merciful love and faithfulness—*hesed* and *'emet*—on which we can rely
are continued by man in our earthly history. . . .

The concept of grace therefore points primarily towards a *call* to this
special living community with God: the Christian vocation as a consequence of a prior decision made freely and graciously by God, who
calls men to the way of the gospel (Gal 1:6; 1 Tim 1:11). On the other
hand, by virtue of this call, namely as the obedience of faith (Gal 3:5;
1 Cor 2:12; Rom 6:16; 5:15; etc.), the concept points to Christian life
itself, existence in grace, in being and acting, through which this responsible action is experienced as being supported, guided and directed by the
power of Jesus which, as divine *dynamis* (Acts 4:33; 6:8; 20:32; 14:26;
15:40; 18:27; 1 Cor 1:18; 6:14; 2 Cor 4:7; 12:9f.; 2 Tim 2:1; Rom 1:16;
Eph 2:7f.; etc.) "fulfills everything in us" (Col 1:6f.), "through faith
which is at work in our love (of neighbor)" (Gal 5:6).

This divine calling has appeared to us personally in Jesus and has taken
shape in his personal call: to be converted, to take a different course from
the one that we have been on, since the kingdom of God is now near
(Mark 1:14f.). Therefore for those who have not themselves heard this
historical call of Jesus, there is the good news of this event given by the
Christian community in the world which is itself grace and power (Acts
5:20; 20:24, 32; Luke 4:22; 1 Cor 15:2; James 1:21; 2 Tim 1:1; Eph 6:15;
etc.). . . . All the parts of the New Testament assert that the earthly
appearing of Jesus is the grace of God. But there are marked differences
of accent. In the four gospels the whole event of and around Jesus is a
sign of the grace of God. For Mark this is true from the baptism of Jesus

on, and for Matthew, Luke and John from the first moment of his coming into the world (John 1:14; 3:16; 12:46f.; see also 1 John 4:9, 14). Not only his death and his resurrection but also his message of God's kingdom, intended for mankind, and his whole way of life are gifts of grace; his dealings with people, above all in eating with them, his care and concern and especially his contact with sinners, the poor and the oppressed who were despised by the religious and suffered the social consequences of this discrimination. It emerges above all from the supposition to be found even before Easter, that to take up an attitude for or against Jesus has to do with a decision about one's own destiny: a decision for or against the coming kingdom of God.

The all-embracing sign of grace, however, both in the four canonical gospels and above all in the whole of the rest of the New Testament, is Jesus' love to the point of death: his suffering and dying as a breaking of the life which he entrusts to his God, in grief, but with all his heart (see Rom 5:9–11; 1 Cor 15:2f.; 2 Cor 3:17f.; Heb 10:29; 1 Pet 2:21; 2 Tim 1:10b, etc.): "He who did not spare his own Son but gave him up for us all, will he not *also give us all things* with him?" (Rom 8:32). "God so loved the world that he gave his only begotten Son that all who believe in him should not perish but have everlasting life" (John 3:16). Above all in Paul and in the New Testament traditions influenced by Paul, the grace of God in Christ is so strongly concentrated in the death and resurrection of Jesus that there is a tendency to concentrate and to limit *charis* as it has appeared in Jesus exclusively to his death and resurrection. So Paul himself never connects the term *charis* with the message and the appearing of Jesus of Nazareth, but only with Christ Jesus who has risen from the dead. Paul never associates *charis* with *Jesus* but only with (Jesus) *Christ*, the risen one (Gal 2:19; see 1 Cor 1:30; 2 Cor 5:21). Only the *Lord* Jesus is grace. Without the resurrection from the dead, the earthly appearance of Jesus in fact remains open, even problematical. However, the four gospels avoid this exclusively *kerygmatic* conception of the dead and risen Jesus; in their proclamation *of the gospel* they also recognize the grace to be found in the message of Jesus and his way of life (albeit in the light of the resurrection).

It is, however, true of the whole of the canonical New Testament that death and resurrection are the determinative climax of the grace of God in Jesus Christ. Only after Jesus, dying, has firmly held God's hand and in turn has known himself to be sustained in this impenetrable situation, is he confirmed by God: "By the grace of God Jesus tasted death for everyone" (Heb 2:9). Hebrews above all emphatically stresses that an exclusive divine act on the part of the Father gives "perfecting" constitutive significance to the reality of Jesus' sacrifice. This in no way removes

⌐ Jesus' own love to the point of death, indeed it even
⌐s it, as it is this that is confirmed and sealed by God in the
⌐ction or glorification of Jesus. Jesus' resurrection is thus a free and
⌐vereign action on the part of God, even if it manifests itself as already
beginning *in* Jesus' personal communion with God into which he has
incorporated his suffering and dying. From God's perspective, this very
communion is already a manifestation of *grace* to Jesus, a grace which
simply reveals its inner dynamic in his exaltation or resurrection and is
brought to a final consummation. Only at this final consummation—
which Phil 2:9 expressly calls a grace for Jesus himself: *echarisato*, see also
Heb 2:9, can one say that Jesus "is the cause (source) of eternal salvation"
(Heb 5:9). In connection with the historical Jesus, the Gospel of John
also says (while putting stress on the grace which already became manifest
through the earthly Jesus): "The Spirit was not yet because Jesus was not
yet glorified" (John 7:39, a text which radically excludes the possibility
that after his death Jesus again became a post-existent Logos *asarkos*, not
incarnate as in his preexistence).

Thus the New Testament conception conveys that only the risen Jesus
bestows eschatological salvation: the *pneuma*, his, God's own Spirit (Rom
8:14–18; 8:29; Gal 4:4–7; Eph 1:3–5; Titus 3:6, etc. see below): the Spirit
through which the Christian, thanks to the grace of faith and baptism
(Romans 6; Gal 3:26f.; Titus 3:5), is conformed to God, i.e., receives a
share both in his relationship to God and also in his "brotherly" (Rom
8:29) radical service and his dedication to his fellow man. [1977]

54/ *Basic Elements of the Gospel of Grace*

In the light of all that has gone before, we now arrive at *four structural
elements* which Christians must take account of in any contemporary
reinterpretation in which an echo of the gospel of Jesus Christ can be
detected, if they want to preserve this gospel in its wholeness while at
the same time making it speak to their own age in word and deed.

I.   God and His History with Men

The Christian experience of an originally Jewish group of people with
Jesus of Nazareth developed into the confession that for these people,
Christians, the bitter question, insoluble in human terms, of the meaning and purpose of human life in nature and history, in a context of
meaning and meaninglessness, of suffering and moments of joy, has
received a positive and unique answer surpassing all expectations: God

himself is the guarantor that human life has a positive and significant meaning. He himself has made it his concern and has put his own honor at risk: his honor is his identification with the poor wretch and exploited man, with the captive man, above all the sinner, i.e., the man who is so at odds with his fellow man that this sickness "cries out to heaven" (see Exod 2:23-25; 3:7f.). Then "God came down" (Exod 3:8): "God so loved the world that he gave his only begotten Son that all who believe in him should not perish" (John 3:16). In the last report—and at the same time that is "protological," from the beginning—God *decides* about the meaning and purpose of mankind, in man's favor. He does not leave this decision to the whim of cosmic and historical, chaotic and demonic powers, on whose crooked lines he is able to write, indeed whose crooked lines he is able to straighten. As creator, God is the author of good and the antagonist of evil, suffering and injustice which throw men up against meaninglessness. In their experience of the meaning of life and its fulfillment, the disciples experience salvation from God in their trusting encounter with Jesus. This determination of life as an unmerited gift, as grace, is experienced as the initiative of God which surpasses all expectations. Here Old and New Testaments are agreed: Yahweh is a God of man, he is the "He is" (Exod 3:14), i.e., "I am concerned for you" (Exod 3:16). God's name is "solidarity with my people." God's own honor lies in the happiness and salvation of mankind. God's predestination and man's experience of meaning are two aspects of one and same reality of salvation. Salvation is concerned with human wholeness and happiness, and this is in an intrinsic mutual relationship involving the solidarity of man with a living God who is concerned with mankind. This is God's history with man.

II. The Nucleus of God's History with Men Can Be Found in the Person and the Life of Jesus

The meaning or the destiny of man, prepared for and intended from of old by God, has been disclosed and thus been made known in an expeience of believers in the person, career and destiny of Jesus of Nazareth: in his message and his life, his life-style and the particular circumstances in which he was executed. Such a life and death have value *in and of themselves*. But for that very reason they also have a primary significance for God, who here shows his own solidarity with his people, their own calling and their own honor, and therefore identifies himself not only with the ideals and visions of Jesus, but with the person of Jesus of Nazareth himself. Thus the destiny of Jesus is fulfilled even beyond death in his resurrection from the dead, the Amen of God to the person of Jesus which is at the same time the divine affirmation of his true being: "solidarity with the people," "God is love" (1 John 4:8; 4:16).

In general religious terms and in individual religions God may have many names, but he shows his *true countenance* to Christians in the unselfish involvement of Jesus as the good shepherd in search of his wandering and lost sheep. True, the Father is greater than his coming in Jesus Christ— "the Father is greater than I" (John 14:28), but in Jesus "the fullness of God dwells" (Col 1:19). Anyone who sees him, sees the Father (John 14:9b). Jesus is God's countenance turned towards man, the countenance of God who is concerned for all men, especially and concernedly for the humble of the earth, all those who are crucified. "Therefore God has exalted him and given him a name above every name" (Phil 2:9), the Lord, "I am" (Exod 3:14; John 8:24; 8:58; 13:19), I am there for you. This can be followed only by a confession of faith, an affirmation "that at the name of Jesus every knee should bow" (Phil 2:10).

In Jesus we have a complete portrayal of both the predestination of God and the meaning of human life: furthering the good and resisting evil. Therefore his destiny lay under a special divine care. He is God's only beloved as a gift to mankind. His career is the fulfillment and execution of divine care for man, albeit in and through the free and responsible, human and religious initiative of Jesus himself, in conflict and resistance at the same time through the historical occasion for his appearance as a pioneer in the fight for man's cause as God's cause.

This destiny shows the impotence of the still-necessary word, message or vision "in itself." Messages can be rejected, visions can be mocked as unrealistic dreams. However, anyone who as a martyr endorses his message with the sacrifice of his life "for the sake of this message" "as the service of reconciliation" thereby proves the *impotence* of those who can establish their rights only by murdering and doing away with the witness to the righteousness and love. Their brief victory bears the visible marks of self-destruction, even if their frenzy becomes the more violent the more it smells corruption. For the dying torch which they have quenched is taken over by others.

Suffering is not redemptive in itself. But it is redemptive when it is suffering through and for others, for man's cause as the cause of the one who says that he is "in solidarity with my people," who has "conquered the world" (John 16:33b). The New Testament does not praise suffering but only suffering in and with resistance against injustice and suffering. It praises suffering "for the sake of the kingdom of God" or "for the sake of the gospel" (Mark 8:35; 10:29), for the sake of righteousness (1 Pet 3:14), "unmerited suffering" (1 Pet 3:17), "for the good" (1 Pet 3:17), "suffering although you do right" (1 Pet 2:20f.), in solidarity with one's brothers (Heb 2:17f.). Suffering itself goes with the crooked lines which men draw. "The hour is coming when whoever kills you will think that he is offering service to God" (John 16:2b). . . . "But be of good cheer. I have overcome the world" (John 16:33b). Therefore instead of a "divine must" or an apocalyptic necessity, Hebrews says in a more restrained way, more on a human than a divine plane, "It was fitting that he for whom and by whom all things exist, in bringing many sons to glory, should make the pioneer of their salvation perfect through suffering" (Heb 2:10). For the name of God is "the one who shows solidarity with his people," and this people suffers.

III. Our History, Following Jesus

In the sense of biblical *anamnēsis* (*zikkārōn*) or remembrance, remembrance of the history of God with man in Jesus Christ is not just a matter of reminding oneself what took place at an earlier stage. It is a return to the past in narrative with an eye to action in the present. God "reminds himself" of his earlier saving acts in and through new acts of liberation. So Christian faith is a remembrance of the life and death of the risen Jesus through the practice of becoming his disciples—not through imitating what he has done but, like Jesus, by responding to one's own new situations from out of an intense experience of God. In the church community the future of Jesus, endorsed by his resurrection, is at the same time a remembrance of his life. What we have is a living tradition directed towards the future. Christian life itself can and must be a *memorial* of Jesus Christ. Orthodox confession of faith is simply the expression of truly Christian life as a *memoria Jesu*. Detached from a life-style in conformity with the kingdom of God, the Christian confession becomes innocuous and *a priori* incredible. The living community is the only real reliquary of Jesus. "Not everyone who says to me Lord, Lord, will enter the kingdom of heaven, but he who does the will of my Father who is in heaven" (Matt 7:21; see 7:22f.)—often the attitude of those who rightly want to hold high the orthodox creed of the resurrection of Jesus, but destroy its credibility by their petty way of life. It is in Christian living that one sees who really believes in the risen Jesus, the future of a more hallowed world. The New Testament (above all Paul; also Colossians and Ephesians, John, Hebrews) shows us that the church community, the assembly of those who call Jesus to mind, is the public and living memorial to Jesus and is thus "filled with the fullness of Jesus" (Eph 3:19; 1:23), and therefore with the vision, the life-style and the readiness for suffering through and for others to which Jesus inspired them by identifying himself with the God whose name is solidarity with his people.

So in the man Jesus, the risen one, the history of God also becomes our history, above all in and through the practice of solidarity with a God concerned for humanity. By following Jesus, taking our bearings from him and allowing ourselves to be inspired by him, by sharing in his *Abba* experience and his selfless support for "the least of my brethren" (Matt 25:40), and thus entrusting our own destiny to God, we allow the history of Jesus, the living one, to continue in history as a piece of living Christology, the work of the Spirit among us, the Spirit of God and the Spirit of Christ. So the Christian works in free responsibility for the completion of God's plan to give ultimate meaning to human life. This is the means of achieving the correlation between God's will for universal salvation in Jesus and for human happiness or success for each and every individual.

Therefore we can only speak of the history of Jesus in terms of the story of the Christian community which follows Jesus. In particular, the Gospel of John (so often despised) is a model for such a history, in which the historical level of Jesus' own life is as it were fused with the history of the later community. Thus resurrection, the formation of a community and the renewal of the world in accordance with the life-style of the kingdom of God (in a particular set of circumstances) form a single event with a spiritual and a historical side. The present of the living Christ and his pneuma is at the same time the historical story of the community of faith in prayerful confession and action, in solidarity with man's cause as the cause of God.

IV. History without Historical End

The end of this history of God with man in Jesus, handed on and put into practice by the "community of God," cannot ever be completed or narrated right to the end within the narrow confines of our worldwide human history. The death of each individual keeps breaking the threads of history. In that case, is there no longer any salvation, not even for those who have handed on the torch of history and kept it burning among the living, and have perhaps met their death for that very reason? The final consummation of God's predestination and the realization of human meaning and purpose and thus of grace, redemption and liberation, is "not of and from this world," although this liberating grace which makes men whole must take a recognizable, historically demonstrable form on the level of our earthly history in figures who constantly fade into the past and are superseded.

Although the definitive salvation is eschatological, and as such is obviously not experienced as the content of present experience, the awareness of this final perspective—the promise—in faith is given in an experience here and now, namely in fragments of individual experiences of salvation which bear within themselves an inner promise, as was the case in and through Jesus. The church's proclamatory announcement and promise of *final* salvation—the eschatological promise—takes on real significance only in the light of such fragmentary experiences of salvation. In fact, final salvation goes beyond our present experiences—in the last resort we do not experience actual salvation here and now—but the validity of this announcement in promise has its basis in a context of present-day experience of Jesus and the Christian life in this world. It cannot merely rest on a revelation through the *word*—besides, anthropologically speaking, "word" is an expression of human experience and practice—nor on the *mere proclamation* of a final and universal salvation to come (on what basis?). Without the mediation of human experience and the realization of fragments of salvation transcending man's own limits, "the Word of God" is not only not a metaphor, it is sheer illusion. However, in the context of fragmentary experiences of salvation we may rightly—metaphorically and with real depth—speak of the word of God and his promise of eschatological salvation which transcends all expectations of experience and is yet recognized as what is familiar and evident:

> Behold, the dwelling of God is with men. He will dwell with them, and they shall be his people [a reference to the old name of Yahweh, the one who shows solidarity with his people], and God himself will be with them; he will wipe away every tear from their eyes, and death shall be no more, neither shall there be mourning nor crying nor pain any more, for the former things have passed away (Rev 21:3f.).

Conclusion

Put in the category of narrative—for the New Testament, that is the *euangelion, evangelium* or good tidings—these four fundamental perspectives seem to me to be the essential structural elements of the experience interpreted and thematized in the New Testament, the basis of the Christian confession of the experience of salvation from God in Jesus the Christ.

However, this report and the critical life-style to which it leads result in continually new consequences through and in the mediation of ongoing human history. The history of Jesus is not at an end when we have said what the New Testament tells us about it. At that point *we ourselves* have not yet been touched, we who here and now must hand on this history to coming generations. Or do we do this simply and solely by selling Bibles? The great question for many Christians is: Where is the model of identification? Christian personal identity and church identity are correlates: they need mutual confirmation. Where this is lacking, and where only partial identification is possible—whether of believers with the church, or of the great church with believers, or of the Christian churches with one another—history undergoes a moment of crisis. It is not as though mutual confirmation would inevitably result in a uniform model. Even the Johannine church recognized the authority of the twelve, but required that Peter should have confidence in his own destiny and that the Johannine community should have its distinctive Christian character (John 21:15-17, as compared with 21:20-23).

The way in which the New Testament has given specific form to the four structural elements which we have just analyzed is doubtless bound up with the views about life current in the ancient world, the historical circumstances and the specific possibilities of the time. Many consequences which the New Testament has drawn from this for the behavior of Christians (which are very varied indeed, even in the New Testament itself) are historically conditioned. And precisely because they are historically conditioned, they are not directly a norm for the contemporary *memoria Jesu*, even if they are models for the way in which we, in a different historical setting and with different possibilities, can add a chapter here and now to the history of Jesus, the living one. [1977]

55/ New Testament Grace and Theological Categories

Because he has been shaped by philosophy, Western man in particular finds it striking that in the New Testament, *charis* or grace is not set *over against* nature or creation (like "nature" and the "supernatural" in later scholastic theology), but over against sin and helplessness (Galatians and Romans); as what is established and permanent in contrast with what is unholy, earthly and transitory (the "first age," Heb 12:15, 28; 13:8f.); as rest and cheerfulness in comparison with fear and anxiety over life and death (Heb 2:14f.) or the fear of demons; in contrast to standing under the law (Rom 6:14; 5:2; Gal 5:4, 18); in contrast to all the taboos, "Do not touch, do not eat, keep away" (Col 2:20-23); in contrast to self-righteousness, autonomy by virtue of a self-confident nature on the basis of personal achievement or merits in the Pauline sense (Rom 1:5; 9:12; 9:16; 11:6; Gal 1:15; 2:21; 5:4; Eph 1:4; 2:8; 2 Tim 1:9; Titus 3:7); finally as an abundance of grace in Christ as opposed to the gentle grace of the

Tanach (e.g., Heb 13:9; John 1:17). Where grace is clearly contrasted with "the world" (above all in Johannine theology), the world is understood to be the hybrid, ambiguous and in the last resort sinful world which is deprived of the light (John 1:9; 3:19; 6:14; 9:39; 10:36; 11:27; 12:46; 16:28; 17:18; 18:37; 1 John 2:15-17; 4:9).

It emerges from this that in the New Testament grace is a moral and religious concept from the language of faith or religious speaking about reality. Grace is not thematized so that it becomes a metaphysical concept (this will be the preoccupation, above all, of medieval theology). Nevertheless, even in the New Testament grace is more than one particular, religious way of speaking, which only makes sense within an absolutely closed language system. Or more correctly: what we are concerned with is not only *speaking about* grace, but with an experience of reality which can only be expressed in the language of faith. As a living reality of and from God—which appears to us in Jesus and comes to us through the risen Jesus in the gift of the Spirit—grace in the New Testament is also a reality from and in us (the Middle Ages termed it "created grace," *gratia creata*, within a metaphysical frame of reference, as a *consequence of* and at the same time a *disposition to* uncreated grace or grace indwelling divine persons). For God's grace makes man a truly "newborn being" (John 1:13; 3:3, 6, 8; 1 John 2:29; 3:9; 4:7; 5:1, 4, 18; 1 Pet 1:3, 23), thanks to faith and the "bath of rebirth" (Titus 3:5; John 3:5; 1 Pet 1:3, 23; see 2:2; John 3:3-8; 1 John 3:9; 5:8; cf. Rom 6:4; 2 Cor 5:17). Grace makes us "new creatures," "created in Christ" (Eph 2:10; Col 3:10; 2 Cor 5:17; Gal 6:15; Rom 6:5f.; 7:6); it transforms life (Rom 6:5f.; 7:6), our whole *psychē;* our thought (Eph 4:23); our spirit (Rom 7:6; 12:2); our senses (1 Cor 2:12-16); it makes us "other men with a new outlook" (Rom 12:2), in short "new men" (Eph 4:24; individual, but at the same time collective; Eph 2:14). Finally, by grace we receive a new name (Rev 2:17; see 3:12); that is, only at the eschaton will we see what is the deepest identity of our being renewed through grace. It will even become manifest as identity, being ascribed glorified corporeality (*inter alia,* Rom 8:11, 23f.; 1 Cor 15:12-57), a public expression of perfect Christian identity.

Thus anyone who hearkens in freedom and the obedience of faith to this *charis* of God, lives in a *state* of grace "stands in grace" (Rom 5:1f.; 6:1-23; John 8:44; 2 Cor 1:24; Phil 4:1; 1 Pet 5:12), in which, however, the one who has been given grace has to persist (Acts 13:43; see Matt 10:22, repeated above all in Hebrews). For men can also "fall from grace" or "forfeit grace" (Heb 12:15; Rom 11:22; 2 Cor 6:1; Gal 5:4; see 2:21) and thus "abuse the spirit" (Heb 10:29), "quench the spirit" (1 Thess 5:19) or "grieve the spirit" (Eph 4:20; *lypein* is not so much "disturb" as "impair," "damage," cf. Isa 63:10; this is therefore a regular biblical theme). However, by persevering in grace, the believer personally accepts God's grace in Christ as reality which is consistently affirmed, which becomes the basis of hope for resurrection (Rom 8:11, 23f.) and eschatological consummation (Rom 8:17; 8:29; Gal 4:5; Titus 3:6; 1 Pet 1:7–10; 3:7; 4:10f.; 5:10; Rev 21:23; Eph 4:30).

At the same time the transcendence of grace appears, despite or precisely in, this realism of the New Testament conception of a grace which is not to be seen purely in forensic terms: "independently of human actions and only dependent on the one who calls" (Rom 9:12). "So it depends not upon man's will or exertion, but upon God's mercy" (Rom 9:16; cf. Eph 3:20f.).

However, this grace must become fruitful for us in moral and religious action (Rom 6:1–23; 7:4; 1 Cor 15:10; 2 Cor 6:1; Ephesians; Colossians; Hebrews, etc.). In a word, the theological and ethical life which man has to live is the work of God's grace through which "the spirit helps us in our weakness" (Rom 8:26). Even pleading for grace *is* already the work of the Spirit in us (Rom 8:6b). "Now to him who by the powers at work within us is able to do far more abundantly than all that we ask or think . . ." (Eph 3:20). "God is at work in you, both to will and to work for his good pleasure" (Phil 2:13). Thus to allow the thought, the "mind," of Jesus to come to fruition in us means to act and think like Jesus (1 Cor 2:16b), who, by emptying himself (see 2 Cor 8:9 in connection with the collection for the poor community in Jerusalem, also Phil 2:6–11), made others rich. Receiving grace always involves complete self-denial, openness to others, availability and readiness to learn, in joy at the value of the treasure that has been found, a pearl (the Eastern symbol for the mystery of life for which man surrenders everything else; Matt 13:44). Here the Christian acts in the spirit of Jesus, "who for the joy that was set before him endured the cross" (Heb 12:2). Grace, the kingdom of God, the rule of God, the source and foundation of human and worldly peace, therefore require fundamental *metanoia*, a transformation of our natural and all too human attitudes (see Mark 1:14f.; 2 Cor 7:10; etc.). The new life with God in Christ requires a life for and with God in service towards one's fellow men: to have a share in the abundance of the *ḥesed* and *'emet* of God which are personally present in Jesus (see John 1:17). [1977]

2

The Community of Grace

COMMENTARY

These three selections present three of Schillebeeckx's perspectives
on a theology of the church. Selection 56, appearing shortly after
his *Christ the Sacrament*, speaks of the church as visible grace in
human society. Selection 57 brings together Schillebeeckx's sacramental notion of the church as a sign of God's presence in the
world with the theology of church developed in the documents of
the Second Vatican Council. The two help mutually define each
other and lay a foundation for an understanding of church and
world.

Selection 58 discusses critical communities in the church, that is,
those small Christian communities using the methodologies of
critical theory to challenge injustice and oppression in society and
in the church itself. At the time of the writing of this piece (1973)
there were many of these in the Netherlands, and Schillebeeckx
followed their development closely. Today many of these communities continue, not only in the Netherlands but in many countries
around the world. This selection describes much of their motivat-
ing force. The language of critical theory is much in evidence, as
well as terms borrowed from such theologians as Johannes Metz
("deprivatization").

56/ *The Church as a Community of Grace*

We have said that Jesus as man and messiah is unthinkable without his
redemptive community. Established by God precisely in his vocation as
representative of fallen mankind, Jesus had by his human life to win this
community to himself and make of it a redeemed people of God. This

means that Jesus the Messiah, through his death which the Father accepts, becomes in fact the head of the People of God, the church assembled in his death. It is thus that he wins the church to himself, by his messianic life as the servant of God, as the fruit of the sufferings of his messianic sacrifice: "Christ dies that the church might be born." In his messianic sacrifice, which the Father accepts, Christ in his glorified body is himself the eschatological redemptive community of the church. In his own self the glorified Christ is simultaneously both "head and members."

The earthly church is the visible realization of this saving reality in history. The church is a visible communion in grace. This communion itself, consisting of members and a hierarchical leadership, is the earthly sign of the triumphant redeeming grace of Christ. The fact must be emphasized that not only the hierarchical church but also the community of the faithful belong to this grace-giving sign that is the church. As much in its hierarchy as in the laity the community of the church is the realization in historical form of the victory achieved by Christ. The inward communion in grace with God in Christ becomes visible in and is realized through the outward social sign. Thus the essence of the church consists in this, that the final goal of grace achieved by Christ becomes visibly present in the *whole* church as a visible society.

It was the custom in the past to distinguish between the soul of the church (this would be the inward communion in grace with Christ) and the body of the church (the visible society with its members and its authority). Only too rightly, this view has been abandoned. It was even, in a sense, condemned by Pope Pius XII. The visible church itself is the Lord's mystical body. The church is the visible expression of Christ's grace and redemption, realized in the form of a society which is a sign (*societas signum*). Any attempt to introduce a dualism here is the work of evil—as if one could play off the inward communion in grace with Christ against the juridical society of the church, or vice versa. The church therefore is not merely a means of salvation. It is Christ's salvation itself, this salvation as visibly realized in this world. Thus it is, by a kind of identity, the body of the Lord.

We remarked that this visibility of grace defines the whole church; not the hierarchical church only, but also the community of the faithful. The whole church, the People of God led by a priestly hierarchy, is "the sign raised up among the nations." The activity, as much of the faithful as of their leaders, is thus an eccesial activity. This means that not only the hierarchy but also the believing people belong essentially to the primordial sacrament which is the earthly expression of this reality. As the sacramental Christ, the church too is mystically both head and members. [1959]

57/ *The Church as the Sacrament of the World*

In the various documents of the Second Vatican Council, the statement that the Church is the universal sacrament of salvation is encountered again and again:

"Christ . . . has, through the Spirit, instituted his body, that is the church, as the universal sacrament of salvation" (Dogmatic Constitution on the Church, 7, 48).

"The church is the universal sacrament of salvation which manifests and at the same time realizes the mystery of God's love for man" (Pastoral Constitution on the Church in the Modern World, 1, 4, 45).

"In Christ, the church is as the sacrament, that is, the sign and instrument of the inner union with God and of the unity of the whole of mankind" (Dogmatic Constitution on the Church, 1).

"God has called together and made into a church the assembly of those who, in faith, look up towards Jesus, the bringer about of salvation and the principle of unity and peace, so that this church may be for all people and for each individual the visible sacrament of this unity which brings salvation" (ibid., 2, 9). "For it was from the side of Christ as he slept the sleep of death upon the cross that there came forth the wondrous sacrament that is the whole church" (Constitution on the Liturgy, 1, 5).

It will, of course, be clear to everyone that these statements about the mystery of the church which are to be found in various conciliar documents are extremely important and above all that they will, by their pregnant content, stimulate not only theological reflection, but also and especially the Christian life of future generations.

I will confine myself, in this brief introduction, to an analysis of two aspects of the content of these conciliar statements; on the one hand, the relationship between the church and the divine decree as expressed in the history of salvation and, on the other, the relationship between the church and the whole of mankind, since the church is, after all, the sacrament of divine salvation with regard to the whole world, the *sacramentum mundi.*

I. The Church as the Epiphany and Historical Completion of God's Plan of Salvation

Without denying the legitimacy of a more technical concept of sacrament that has become current since the theology of the Middle Ages, the Council nonetheless went back to the richer and more dynamic and

universal concept of the Bible and the church fathers. The Greek word
mystērion—in the Latin of the church *sacramentum* and *mysterium*—
denoted the divine decree, or God's plan of salvation, insofar as this is
and has been manifested in a veiled manner in time and is accessible only
to faith. In this sense, the concept of sacrament embraces the whole of
the Christian plan of salvation, visibly prepared in the Old Testament,
but given a completing manifestation in the life, death and resurrection
of Jesus, the Christ, of whom the church is the visible presence in this
world (ibid., 14, cf. 7), although "under shadows" and "under the assumption of constant purification" (Constitution on the Church, 8). According
to this concept, then, sacrament is the history of salvation itself as the
active manifestation of God's plan of salvation.

What the Council meant precisely by the word "sacrament" is most
profoundly expressed in the decree on missionary activity, although the
word itself is unfortunately not used in this context: "Missionary activity
is nothing other and nothing less than the revelation of epiphany of and
the completion of God's plan of salvation in the world and in the history
of the world, in which God, through the mission, visibly completes the
history of salvation" (9). But because "the church on the way is, by virtue
of her being, orientated towards mission" (ibid., 2), one is quite justified
in replacing words like "mission" and "missionary activity" in this conciliar text by the word "church." Consequently, the text that I have just
quoted might just as well have read: "The church is nothing other and
nothing less than the revelation or epiphany of and the completion of
God's plan of salvation in the world and in the history of the world in
which God, through the church, visibly completes the history of salvation." In yet other words, using the concept "sacrament": "In Christ, the
church is the universal sacrament of salvation which manifests and realizes
the mystery of God's love for man" (Pastoral Constitution on the
Church in the Modern World, 1, 4, 45), "God's love for man" being "for
all people and for each individual" (Constitution on the Church, 2, 9).
The church, then, is the universal and effective sign of the salvation of
all people. She is the epiphany, in other words, the active and historically
tangible form of God's plan of salvation, a form which makes the source
of salvation, Christ, present for us. The church is the "instrument of
redemption," because she is the "visible sacrament" (Constitution on the
Church, 2, 9) of this redemption on earth—"she is the germ and the
beginning of the kingdom of God on earth" (ibid., 1, 5). But the church
is this only "under shadows"—"she is always in need of purification."
Indeed, the *Relatio*, the justification of this text provided by the commission during the council, makes this even clearer: "This empirical
church . . . reveals the mystery (of the church), but she does not do this

without shadows" and the mystery in the Catholic church becomes visible "both in strength and in weakness" (*Relationes in singulis numeris, Relatio in* 8, pp. 23 and 24). Partly in her *metanoia* and conversion, the church is therefore the historically visible form of salvation, in other words, salvation itself becoming visible in human history and, as such, the way to salvation for all people.

II. The Church, Sacrament of Salvation for the Whole World

According to the first aspect that I have considered, the church is the active presence of God's salvation in the world, in a veiled, but nonetheless perceptible form. It is precisely in this quality that the church is the sacrament of salvation offered by God to the whole world. In other words, salvation, which is in fact actively present in the whole of mankind, is given, in the church, the completed form in which it appears in the world. What God has already effectively begun to bring about in the whole of mankind is an activity of grace that is not clearly expressed and recognized as such, is expressed and accomplished more clearly and recognizably as the work of grace in the world in the church, although this expression and accomplishment are to some extent always deprived of their luster because of our human failure.

The Council did not state explicitly that the church is the visible sacrament of that salvation which is already active wherever people are to be found, but so many conciliar texts point in this direction that it is even possible to say that a dialectical tension exists which is not resolved in the texts themselves and which consequently calls for further theological clarification. Indeed, the constitution on the church says, on the one hand, with reference to the church as the "messianic people," that "although this does not yet in fact include all men and often seems to be a small flock," it is nonetheless "the most powerful germ of unity, hope and salvation for the whole of mankind" (2, 9). This small flock, then, is the sacrament of salvation for all men. On the other hand, however, the same constitution also explicitly states that "the church on the way is necessary for salvation" (ibid., 14). Other conciliar texts intensify the dialectical tension between these two statements. This tension is illustrated, for example, by the statement: "Even those who, through no fault of their own, remain ignorant of the gospel of Christ and the church, but who are nonetheless honestly seeking God and, under the influence of grace, are really trying to do his will, which they recognize in the voice of their consciences, are able to achieve eternal blessedness" (ibid., 16). The pastoral constitution on the church is even more emphatic.

After having depicted the Christian as the "new man in Christ," it states explicitly that this new mankind is present "not only in Christian believers, but also in all men of good will, in whose hearts grace is active in an invisible manner" (1, 22). The Council's declaration on the non-Christian religions, moreover, says that Christianity is the "fullness of the religious life" for all these other religions (2), thus indicating clearly that the relationship between the church and the non-Christian communities is not a relationship between a religion and a non-religion, but a relationship between a fullness and something that simply does not possess this fullness. Finally, the decree on missionary activity states clearly: "God's all-embracing plan for the salvation of the whole of mankind is not only realized in, so to speak, a hidden way in the hearts of men or by initiatives, including religious initiatives, through which they seek God in many different ways, 'in the hope that they might feel after him and find him; yet he is not far from each one of us' (Acts 17:27)" (1, 3).

These texts—and there are probably others which could be quoted—show that the Council has made two fundamental statements which are to some extent dialectically opposed. On the one hand, we have the statement that the church is necessary for salvation and, on the other hand, that those who are "outside the church" not only are able to achieve salvation, but also frequently do in fact share in it. What, then, we are bound to ask, is the real meaning of the conciliar statement that the church is the "universal sacrament of salvation"? Does it mean that God's salvation cannot in any sense reach the world except in and through this world's gradual and historical confrontation with the church? Or does it mean that universal salvation, which has already been offered to the whole world on the basis of God's universal will to save all men, and which is already active in the world, only reaches its completed appearance in the church? It is, I believe, abundantly clear from the texts that I have quoted that the Council tended to think in the second direction. What God's grace, his absolute, gratuitous and forgiving proximity, has already begun to do in the lives of all men becomes an *epiphany* in the church, in other words, completely visible. There is no doubt that, because she is the completed manifestation of God's saving grace, the church is a very distinct and separate gift of grace and opportunity for grace. There is equally no doubt that the other, non-Christian religions are not, as such, special and distinctive in this sense, because they need this completing grace. In order to fill this gap, the church, as the "universal sacrament of salvation," is, by virtue of her very being truly missionary, orientated towards mission.

From this, then, a certain "definition" of the church according to the

Second Vatican Council becomes crystallized, namely, that the church is the completed and active manifestation, confessed explicitly in thanksgiving and praise to God, of that salvation which is already actively present in the whole world of men. In other words, the church is the "primordial sacrament" of the salvation which is prepared for all men according to God's eternal decree, the salvation which is, moreover, not a monopoly of the church, but which, on the basis of redemption by the Lord who died and rose again "for the sake of the salvation of the whole world," is already in fact actively present in that whole world. The church is therefore both the sacrament of herself, in other words, the visible appearance of the salvation that is present in her, and, at the same time, the *sacramentum mundi;* in other words, what is present "outside the church" everywhere, wherever men of good will in fact give their consent personally to God's offer of grace and make this gift their own, even though they do not do this reflectively or thematically, is audibly expressed and visibly perceptible in the church. The church is the "sacrament of the world" precisely as the sacrament of the salvation which is offered to all men—she is hope not only for all who belong to her; she is also, quite simply, *spes mundi,* hope for the whole world. The mystery of salvation which God is always bringing about in the whole history of mankind and which he will never cease to bring about—the enduring fact of the living prophecy of the church bears witness to this— appears fully in the church and is present in her as in a prophecy. It is possible to say that the church is the making public of existential salvation in the world. She reveals the world to itself. She shows the world what it is and what it is able to become by virtue of God's gift of grace. Because of this, she hopes not only for herself, but also for the whole world, which she serves.

Since the conciliar texts can only be interpreted in this light, the council has in fact, with its key statement, "the church is the universal sacrament of salvation," laid the foundation on which a new and practical synthesis can be built up, a synthesis which may help to banish "the discrepancy which exists in the case of many believers between the faith that they confess and their daily lives," a breach which "must be regarded as one of the most serious errors of the present time" (Pastoral Constitution of the Church, 1, 4, 43). This will be a synthesis in which the church and the actual world no longer confront each other as strangers. On the contrary—in this synthesis, the church, as the sacrament of the world, will clearly express, for the benefit of the world of men, the deepest meaning which men have already experienced, in tentative search and without being able to express it, in the world, even though this meaning does not have its origin in the world. The world will then see, in grateful recognition, its meaning and hidden inspiration fully expressed as a sign in the church.

III. Pastoral Consequence

This brief exposition of one conciliar theme leads to the following pastoral consequence. I have argued from the conciliar texts that the church is the visible epiphany or the effective sacrament of God's salvation which is active not only in the church, but also in the whole world, and that the church, in this capacity, has to show herself in the whole of her historically situated life as an active appeal to the conscience of all men, so that they, in grateful recognition of the gift of grace which God offers to them, "may know God and him whom he has sent, his Son, Jesus Christ." If this is true, then it is not only a grace bestowing a clear privilege, but also a task implying a grave responsibility for the church "to make God the Father and his Son, who became man, present and, as it were, visible, by constantly renewing and purifying herself under the guidance of the Holy Spirit" (ibid., 1, 1, 21). This special grace which is only given to the church, the grace to be the *sacrament* of the world, is, after all, partly concealed by the life of the church and is therefore shown "both in strength and in weakness," "in the situation of sinfulness and conversion." In a very special way, the church is *simul iusta et peccatrix*—sanctified and yet failing. Her enduring quality and her holiness do not have their origin in herself, but in the redeeming grace of Christ, the bringer of salvation.

It is quite clear from repeated statements made by Pope John XXIII that the real aim of the Second Vatican Council was the renewal, purification and conversion of the church. The success or ultimate failure of the Council will be measured by the successful renewal and purification of the church. [1966]

58/ *Critical Communities in the Church*

What is quite clear, however, is that, partly because of the influence of the speed of modern information services, which expose abuses in any part of the world to people everywhere, the spirit of contestation has become very widespread in recent years. We have become very conscious of the contrasts in world society—between groups in our own countries and between the prosperous and the underdeveloped countries. There have also been popular scientific prognoses concerning the year 2000 and the urgent need to take countermeasures now to avert disaster. Finally, there is a general anti-institutional and anti-ideological feeling resulting from a meaningless suffering imposed by bureaucracy. All these phenomena have given rise to a widespread malaise in society, a malaise made more acute by the fact that so many young people— "hippies" and others—have opted out of a society that seems to them to be meaningless.

Signs of a "counterculture" and a "new consciousness," an "anti-history" existing alongside the "official" history, indicate clearly enough that our society has in a sense reached a dead end. Criticism of this society in a spirit of sharp contestation has led to the development, at the level of systematic thought, of critical theories and, at the level of Christian praxis, of politically committed critical communities.

Whereas the church has, until quite recently, been judged only according to evangelical or theological criteria, it has now come to be regarded as one part of the whole complex establishment of society and as such subject to the same criticism as such institutions as parliament, the legal system, state education, and so on, all of which share in the evils of society. All these structures are so closely interrelated that remaining aloof from political contestation, especially in the case of any struggle between those in power and the "poor," is in fact a pronounced favoring of those in power. It is above all this situation which has made many Christian communities critical not only of society as a whole, but of the institutional church in particular. To regard this as an infiltration of un-Christian, even demonic, elements into the church is to be blind to the "signs of the times" and is attributable to a false ideology or to wrong information.

The specifically Christian aspect of this criticism of the church and society comes from a new understanding of Jesus of Nazareth and the kingdom of God, often stimulated by study at various levels. Although some recent popular works have provided an exaggerated and historically distorted picture of Jesus as a revolutionary engaged in political contestation, others are exegetically more sound in their presentation of the political relevance of the appearance of Jesus as a political figure.

Because of the present historical situation and a new understanding of the historical Jesus, these critical communities on the one hand long for freedom, humanity, peace and justice in society and, on the other, resist the power structures that threaten these values by repression or oppression. What J. Jüngel has called "a Kingdom of God mindful of humanity," a rule that has been handed down to us in the tradition of the Old and New Testaments, inevitably makes Christians feel at one with the contemporary emancipation movements, although they have a critical attitude towards their violent and one-sided tendencies and subject them to the criterion of the "life praxis of Jesus."

It would be quite wrong to accuse these Christian critical communities of being inspired by Marxist infiltrators, above all because there is so much Marxist criticism of the Marxist system and because there are social evils in Marxist communist societies just as there are under capitalism. What Christian critical communities have derived from Marxism are very valuable aids to the analysis of society. The Marxist system, however, is subjected to sharp criticism. It cannot, of course, be denied that there are Marxist-Christian student cells in many countries. It would, however, be a mistake to think that all student and other communities are of this kind and, especially in the case of Latin America, where all freedom movements are labeled as communist, it is important to take this idea of Marxist infiltration with a grain of salt.

In contemporary society, it is impossible to believe in a Christianity that is not at one with the movement to emancipate mankind. The reverse is also true—Christianity has also become incredible to those who, against all Christian reason, persist in maintaining their established positions in society. This is a distinctively modern form of the stumbling-block of Christian faith, the direct cause of which is not Christianity itself, but the evidence of these privileged positions of power that are accepted without question.

If this Christian solidarity with the modern critical emancipation movements is not to produce a replica of what is being done elsewhere in the world by Christians simply as men and by many others, then the Christian promise that inspires this solidarity has to be expressed and celebrated. The church is, after all, the community of God called out by Jesus Christ and its message is both promise and criticism—criticism and political commitment on the basis of God's promise in Jesus Christ. . . .

It is possible for a critical community to be politically committed, but to fail to provide this distinctively Christian perspective and to celebrate the promise in the liturgical language which prayerfully expresses the transcendent element. Such a community might achieve very fruitful results, but it would not be acting as a Christian community. It would be in danger of becoming a purely political cell without evangelical inspiration—one of very many useful and indeed necessary political pressure groups, but not an *ecclesia Christi*. . . .

I should like to conclude with a few words about the "deprivatization" of human subjectivity. There has been a good deal of criticism in recent years both of the privatizing tendency in the middle-class idea of man as a subject and of the opposite tendency to eliminate the subject. In this, the Christian critical community will recall the implications both of Jesus' message concerning the people of God and the kingdom and of Jesus' life praxis as directed towards the individual. The Christian deprivatization of the subject is clearly to be found in mutual recognition of man as a free subject situated within (changing) structures. Without the recognition of and respect for the personal freedom or subjectivity of the individual, criticism of social or political action is hardly credible.

The critical community must therefore be bold enough to risk involvement both in action to achieve freedom and to change society and also in counseling and consoling individuals who have got into difficulties, even if these Christian therapeutic functions at the same time tend to justify the existing social structures. The promise of salvation here and now extends to all men and, even if the structures of society still cannot be made more just, this salvation can be brought to individuals here and now. The Christian may be committed to the task of bringing salvation to the whole of society in the form of better and more just structures for all men, but, until these structures have been created, he cannot and should not, in the meantime, that is, during the whole of the eschatological interim period, overlook one single individual fellow man. Many contemporary expressions of Christian charity have social and political dimensions, but interpersonal charity practiced by politically committed critical communities of Christians is still relevant and meaningful even if it has been thrust into the background of the community's activities.

Precisely because it claims to be Christian, no critical community can ever become an exclusive "in group" refusing membership to others who think differently. It must remain open and reject discrimination. In the inevitable case of structural difficulties, it will always be necessary to seek provisional solutions, which will be plausible in the Christian sense and even officially recognized by the church. The critical community must, moreover, never forget that, in imitation of Jesus, it is seeking freedom not so much for itself as for others.

Jesus' apparently vain sacrifice of love arose from the contrast between his experience of the living God and his memory of the accumulated suffering of mankind. Yet this sacrificial death seems to contradict the message of the kingdom of God that Jesus brought to man and the praxis of the life that he lived. Nonetheless, his death on the cross is justified by God, in the prophecy of the Christian community, concerning Jesus' resurrection, as the norm for the "good life" lived in freedom and seeking freedom for others. [1973]

3

The Life of Grace
in the Church

If experience became a key category in Schillebeeckx's thought in the 1970s and 1980s, then sacrament would have been its counterpart during the 1950s and 1960s. It was Schillebeeckx's theology of sacrament which first brought him to the attention of the larger theological world, by moving away from a more mechanical and instrumental notion of sacrament to one of a saving encounter in grace. One can say that there is a continuity between his notions of sacrament and of experience: both are investigations of what happens to people as they come into the presence of God.

During the 1950s and 1960s, Schillebeeckx wrote extensively on the experience of grace within the church, in the life of the sacraments. Selection 59 summarizes the argument from his *Christ the Sacrament*, the book by which he first became known outside the Dutch-speaking world. In that book, Schillebeeckx presents the sacramental tradition of the church in the language of existential encounter, centering on Christ as the primordial sacrament, from which the sacraments of the church flow. Again, the primacy of exploring the experience is noteworthy here, as well as his emphasis on bodiliness and concreteness.

Selections 60 and 61 bring together his sense of sacrament along with other recurring concerns (suffering, life in the world, eschatology) into the realm of the public sacramental activity of the church, the liturgy. References to liturgy recur in Schillebeeckx's work, no doubt because it is the preeminent *action* of the church.

In the mid-1960s many efforts were being made in the Low Countries to reinterpret traditional doctrines of eucharistic presence in more contemporary terms. Of central interest was finding a way of talking about the presence of Christ in the eucharist which would not have to rely upon Aristotle's distinctions of form and matter to describe reality. Selection 62 represents Schillebeeckx's contribution to this discussion. He brings together here his understanding of sacrament with a phenomenological analysis of relationships to recapture the older, premedieval notion of eucharist as encompassing both the eucharistic elements *and* the worshiping community. He came under suspicion of the Vatican for his views, but was exonerated.

Schillebeeckx also became widely known for his book on Christian marriage, published in the mid-1960s. In this magisterial work of historical research, he used history to help free contemporary theologies—something he was to do again with theology of the ministry fifteen years later. Selection 63 summarizes the results of his study, stressing marriage as both secular reality and saving mystery.

59/ *Christ the Primordial Sacrament*

Because the saving acts of the man Jesus are performed by a divine person, they have a divine power to save, but because this divine power to save appears to us in visible form, the saving activity of Jesus is *sacramental.* For a sacrament is a divine bestowal of salvation in an outwardly perceptible form which makes the bestowal manifest; a bestowal of salvation in historical visibility. The Son of God really did become true man—become, that is to say, a human spirit which through its own proper bodiliness dwelt visibly in our world. The incarnation of the divine life therefore involves bodily aspects. Together with this we must remember that every human exchange, or the intercourse of men one with another, proceeds in and through man's bodiliness. When a man exerts spiritual influence on another, encounters through the body are necessarily involved. The inward man manifests itself as a reality that is in this world through the body. It is in his body and through his body that man is open to the "outside," and that he makes himself present to his fellow men. Human encounter proceeds through the visible obviousness of the body, which is a sign that reveals and at the same time veils the human interiority.

Consequently if the human love and all the human acts of Jesus possess a divine saving power, then the realization in human shape of this saving power necessarily includes as one of its aspects the manifestation of salvation: includes, in other words, sacramentality. The man Jesus, as the personal visible realization of the divine grace of redemption, is *the* sacrament, the primordial sacrament, because this man, the Son of God himself, is intended by the Father to be in his humanity the only way to the actuality of redemption. "For there is one God, and one mediator of God and men, the man Christ Jesus." Personally to be approached by the man Jesus was, for his contemporaries, an invitation to a personal encounter with the life-giving God, because personally that man was the Son of God. Human encounter with Jesus is therefore the sacrament of the encounter with God, or of the religious life as a theologal attitude of existence towards God. Jesus' human redeeming acts are therefore a "sign and cause of grace." "Sign" and "cause" of salvation are not brought together here as two elements fortuitously conjoined. Human bodiliness is human interiority itself in visible form.

Now because the inward power of Jesus' will to redeem and of his human love is God's own saving power realized in human form, the human saving acts of Jesus are the divine bestowal of grace itself realized in visible form; that is to say they cause what they signify; they are sacraments.

At the heart of all ecclesial sacramentality is obviously the encounter itself with God in and through the sacramental encounter with Christ in his church: sacramental grace. We must now briefly draw together the many aspects of this problem.

In general "sacramental grace" means that grace which is bestowed through the sacrament. In the nature of the case this means grace that comes visibly. This ecclesial visibility of the bestowal of grace is the general but fundamental meaning of what is called "sacramental grace." By this the problem of the anonymity of extra-sacramental grace is resolved. The gift of grace is made real for us while it is showing clearly the demands it makes on us.

Moreover sacramental grace is the grace of redemption itself, since the deepest meaning of the church's sacraments lies in Christ's act of redemption. This remains a permanent actuality in which we become involved through the sacraments. All turns upon a participation in the grace of Christ. This christological aspect of sacramental grace brings us to a personal communion with the Trinity. For in the sacraments we are taken up into the eternal Easter and Pentecost mystery of the *Kyrios*, in which the three persons in their unity and distinctness play an active part. The effect of the mystery of the man Jesus' sanctifying worship is that in the power of the Spirit of sonship the Father becomes our Father.

To encounter Christ is, as we have said, to encounter God. Sacramental grace is this personal communion with God. It is an immediate encounter with him, not an indirect meeting through creation. But an encounter with God is essentially an encounter with the Trinity, since there can be no participation in the divine nature which is not a communion with the three persons who alone are the Divinity. Therefore sanctifying grace, as immediate relationship with God, is essentially a divine relationship with the three persons in their distinctness and their unity; for this is what God is. Sacramental grace is incorporation into the mystical body or into communion in grace with Christ, and is thus the identification of the goal of our life with the death and resurrection of the Lord; in this way it brings about our own personal communion with the Trinity. The indwelling of God, of the redeeming Trinity, which inwardly re-creates us in Christ and makes us *filii in Filio,* children of the same Father, is the overwhelming effect of a fruitful sacrament, and it is faith that gives us a conscious and living awareness of this.

Furthermore, since the sacraments are the embodiment, in a sevenfold perspective, of Christ's eternal act of redemption, sacramental grace is the grace of redemption itself in its direction and application to the seven possible situations of a Christian in the church, according to the special symbolism and telling significance of each sacrament. Therefore sacramental grace is the grace of redemption having a particular function with reference to a particular ecclesial and Christian situation of life, and to a particular human need. . . .

Finally, grace is not something which, once given to us, we are expected to assimilate by ourselves. In our friendship God and I are both continually active. This implies something that is generally called actual grace. Because the sacraments, each in its own special way, give positive commissions which remain valid for the whole of life, they themselves are the basis of the subsequent actual graces which we need if the commissions are to be fulfilled. The permanent ecclesial effect of the sacrament (different in each case) is the permanent foundation of this subsequent bestowal of grace within the limits of the sacramental contact with the church, which may be absolutely unrepeatable, relatively unrepeatable, or repeatable. Therefore it is sometimes said legalistically that the sacraments also give the right to actual grace; this means that man living by the sacraments is never alone, but that, united with the God who is ever active, he is carrying out his commissions as a Christian.

The fruitfulness of a sacrament in grace, then, includes all the richness of Christian life in communion with the church, the visible sign of grace in which the fullness of Christ is present. The church, the *pleroma* of

Christ, fills us with the fullness of him who is filled with the fullness
of God. And this is man's encounter with God in full mutual availability.
[1959]

60/ *Liturgy and the Struggle for Humanity*

The conviction that the history of human suffering is not necessary, and
faith that suffering may not be final and thus must be overcome, are experienced symbolically and playfully in the Christian liturgy. For the
sacraments are anticipatory, mediating signs of salvation, that is, healed
and reconciled life. And given our historical situation, at the same time
they are symbols of protest serving to unmask the life that is not yet
reconciled in the specific dimension of our history. In the light of its prophetic vision of universal *šālôm*, accusation also has a part in the liturgy.

As long as there is still a real history of suffering among us, we cannot
do without the sacramental liturgy: to abolish it or neglect it would be
to stifle the firm hope in universal peace and general reconciliation. For
as long as salvation and peace are still not actual realities, hope for them
must be attested and above all nourished and kept alive, and this is only
possible in anticipatory symbols. For that very reason, the Christian
liturgy stands under the sign of the great symbols of the death and resurrection of Jesus. Here the cross is the symbol of resistance to death
against the alienation of our human history of suffering, the consequence
of the message of a God *who is concerned with man;* the resurrection of
Jesus makes it clear to us that suffering may not and will not have the
last word. Sacramental action therefore summons Christians to liberating
action in our world. The liturgical anticipation of reconciled life in the
free communication of a "community of Christ" would not make any
sense if it did not in fact help to realize liberating action in the world.
Therefore the sacramental liturgy is the appropriate place in which the
believer becomes pointedly aware that there is a grievous gulf between
his prophetic vision of a God concerned for peace among men and the
real situation of mankind, and at the same time that our history of
human suffering is unnecessary and can be changed. So if it is rightly performed, there is in Christian sacramental symbolic action a powerful
historical potential which can integrate mysticism and politics (albeit in
secular forms). In remembrance of the passion of Jesus which was
brought to a triumphal conclusion by God—as a promise for us all—in
their liturgy, Christians celebrate their particular connection with this
Jesus and in it the possibility of creative liberation and reconciliation in
our human history.

History teaches us that there has never been a perfect redemption, but that in Jesus there is a divine promise for us all, and that this is anticipated in any definitively valid act of doing good to our fellow men in a finite and conditioned world in which love is always doomed to failure and yet nevertheless refuses to choose any other way than that of loving service. Any attempt at totality which cannot recognize the non-identical, refractory suffering and failure of this doing good and is not content with it, leads to an illusion, has an alienating effect, or becomes unproductive. Christian belief in salvation from God in Jesus as the Christ is the downfall of any doctrine of salvation or soteriology understood in human terms, in the sense of an identity which is within our control and therefore can be manipulated. The Christian gospel is not an unmediated identity, but a practice of identification with what is not identical, the non-I, the other, above all the suffering and the injustice of others. Definitive salvation remains an indefinable horizon in our history in which both the hidden God (*Deus absconditus*) and the sought-for, yet hidden, *humanum* disappear. But if the fundamental symbol of God is the living man (*imago Dei*), then the place where man is dishonored, violated and oppressed, both in his own heart and in a society which oppresses men, is at the same time the preferred place where *religious experience* becomes possible in a way of life which seeks to give form to this symbol, to heal it and give it its own liberated existence. As the intrinsic consequence of the radicalism of its message and reconciling practice, the crucifixion of Jesus shows that any attempt at liberating redemption which is concerned with humanity is valid *in and of itself* and not subsequently as a result of any success which may follow. What counts is not success, any more than failure or misfortune, above all as the result of the intervention of others. The important thing is loving service. We are shown the true face of both God and man in the "vain" love of Jesus which knows that its criterion does not lie in success, but in its very being as radical love and identification. In that case, reconciliation and liberation, if they seek to be valid for all, despite the limited aspect of an imperfect historical situation, are not a mere change of power relationships and thus a new domination. Redemption is a task imposed upon us; for us it remains a reconciliation to be realized, which will constantly be molded by failure, suffering and death in the refractoriness of our history—by a love which is impotent in this world but which will never give in. It is based on a love which ventures the impossible and does not compel man to what he himself sees as liberation and redemption. In our time, above all, Christians only have the right to utter the word "God" where they find their identity in identification with that part of life which is still unreconciled, and in effective action towards reconciliation and liberation. What history tells us about Jesus, what the church tells and indeed *promises* us about Jesus is that in this way of life, which is in conformity with the message of Jesus and the kingdom of God, we are shown the *real possibility* of an experience of God. In Jesus the Christ, we are promised that this way of life will bring us particularly close to God. However, what final possibilities are contained in the eschatological consummation of this saving presence of God, which we celebrate and give thanks for in the liturgy, are God's mystery, which may be called the abundance of our humanity. [1977]

61/ *True Liturgy*

Is church liturgy than simply communal thanksgiving and homage? Yes, it is, but in such a way that reality is intensified and the accomplishment of man's mode of existence in the sign of Christ's resurrection is enhanced by it. The liturgy, after all, is carried out in the church which believes that God's promise is fulfilled in Christ. In the liturgy of the church, this promise is therefore accomplished in us, in me, because I enact, together with the church, the faith of the church and thus come, in faith, into contact with Jesus Christ, on whom the church places her hope. It is in the church's liturgy that God's grace in Christ is made publicly apparent—the promise is made true *now* in me, in the celebrating community. It is in this witness of faith that the *public* confession of the Christian conviction is made manifest—the *sacramentum fidei*, in other words, God's saving act in our sacramental, liturgical, visible activity of faith. God's grace thus manifests itself in our terrestrial history in a way that is most strikingly transparent to faith in the church's liturgy, as an integrating part of the whole to which our "secular worship" also belongs, that other worship in which the same grace manifests itself in a different way and thus makes itself felt in a different way. . . .

Not only the physical but everything else which belongs to humanity is experienced as the sacramental manifestation of God's presence. It is precisely for this reason that the celebration of the community is once again stressed in the liturgy and that the communication of the divine is conceived *less* in material categories than in the "real presence" of Christ in his assembled people, who demand justice and love for all men. It is precisely for this reason that the present-day believer can no longer experience the real presence in the eucharist "considered in isolation"—that is, experienced separately from Christ's real presence in the assembled congregation. It is not a question of denying one concept in favor of the other but of making the material world of *man in community* central, with the result that the *whole* becomes the sacrament of God's manifestation in Christ. The fact that the whole human person and his physical mode of existence are committed at the same time—a commitment in which the man Jesus has gone before us—prevents the liturgy from being one-sidedly either materialized or spiritualized. Human solidarity has therefore acquired its own sacramental form in the renewed liturgy, so that the breach between life and liturgy, a consequence of the change in the West from "cosmocentric" to "anthropocentric" thinking, in which the liturgy lagged behind, can once again be healed. Worship and life thus join hands more cordially, and the church's liturgy is again becoming the *sacramentum mundi,* or rather, the sacrament of the *historia mundi,* of the world of men which, in the sign of Jesus' resurrection, moves towards the eschatological kingdom in which terrestrial history is, by God's power, perpetuated in eternity.

All this will have inescapable consequences for the further renewal of the liturgy, both in its content and in its structure. The liturgical cult will not be able to ignore the total structure of secular worship and its epiphany in the church's liturgy. A liturgy which spoke only of the hereafter and ignored the concrete history of the world, which is precisely the place where the *eschaton* is mysteriously in the process of becoming, would be a liturgy which forgot the Johannine account of the washing of the disciples' feet, a *liturgia gloriae* which left out the period and the realm in which people are engaged with all their heart and soul. How could life and liturgy then form a unity, as the council asked, without making a division between the secular and the religious? If this division is not avoided, the church's liturgy will not survive; it will become estranged from the world—and then Christians will, of course, abandon it.

If, on the other hand, the church's liturgy were reduced to what presupposes and at the same time gives rise to liturgy—that is, "secular worship," in which God is only implicitly experienced in secular life, or brought down to the level of a pleasant little chat consisting of "good morning" and "have a nice weekend"—then this liturgy would be a serious misconception not only of the "spiritual sacrifice" implied by man's being in the world in the light of community with God but also of the profoundly human dimension which is expressed in the thankful celebration of all that gives our lives meaning and makes them worth living. And this is certainly no trivial commonplace, but the "seriousness of divine love," made historically tangible among us in Jesus' human love of God which had the form of a radical love of men "to the end." [1968]

62/ *Eucharistic Presence*

The basis of the entire eucharistic event is Christ's personal gift of himself to his fellow men and, within this, to the Father. This is quite simply his *essence*— "The man Christ Jesus is the one *giving himself*" (*ho dous heauton*, 1 Tim 2:6). The eternal validity of his history on earth resides in this. As I have already said, the personal relationship to the heavenly Christ is at the same time an *anamnēsis* of his historical death on the cross.

The eucharist is the sacramental form of this event, Christ's giving of himself to the Father and to men. It takes the form of a commemorative meal in which the usual secular significance of the bread and wine is withdrawn and these become bearers of Christ's gift of himself— "Take and eat, this is my body." Christ's gift of himself, however, is not ultimately directed towards bread and wine, but towards the faithful. The real presence is intended for believers, but through the medium of and *in* this gift of bread and wine. In other words, the Lord who gives himself thus is *sacramentally* present. In this commemorative meal, bread and wine become the subject of a new *establishment of meaning*, not by men, but by the living Lord *in* the church, through which they become the *sign* of the real presence of Christ giving himself to us. This establishment of meaning by Christ is accomplished in the church and thus presupposes the real presence of the Lord in the church, in the assembled community of believers and in the one who officiates in the eucharist.

I should like to place much greater emphasis than most modern authors have done on this essential bond between the real presence of Christ in the eucharist and his real presence as Lord living in the church. After all, there is ultimately only one real presence of Christ, although this can come about in various ways. It forms, in my opinion, an essential element in the constitution of the eucharist. In interpreting the eucharist, it is not enough simply to consider Christ's presence "in heaven" and "in bread and wine," like the scholastic theologians, who regarded Christ's real presence in the faithful only as the fruit of these two poles, the *res sacramenti*. By virtue of the meaning which is given to them by Christ and to which the church consents in faith, the bread and wine are really *signs*, a specific sacramental form of the Lord who is already really and personally present for us. If this is denied or overlooked, then the reality of Christ's presence in the eucharist is in danger of being emptied of meaning. Transubstantiation does not mean that Christ, the Lord living in his church, gives *something* to us in giving this new meaning, that he, for example, gives us incarnate evidence of love, as in every meaningful present, in which we recognize the hand and indeed the heart of the giver and ultimately therefore experience also the giver himself. No, in transubstantiation, the relationships are at a much deeper level. What is given to us is the giver himself. This gift of the giver himself is quite adequately rendered by the phenomenological "giving of oneself *in* the gift." "This is my body, this is my blood": this is not a giving of oneself in a gift, not even at a more profound level because the giver here is Christ, the personal revelation of the Father. No, what is given to us in the eucharist is *nothing other than Christ himself.* What the sacramental forms of bread and wine signify, and at the same time make real, is not a gift that refers to Christ who gives himself in them, but Christ himself in living, personal presence. The signifying function of the sacrament (*sacramentum est in genere signi*) is here at its highest value. It is a making present of himself of the real, living Christ in a pure, meaningful presence which we are able to experience in faith. The phenomenal form of the eucharistic bread and wine is nothing other than the *sign* which makes real Christ's gift of himself with the church's responding gift of herself involved in this making real to us, a sign inviting every believer to participate personally in this event.

The sacramental bread and wine are therefore not only the sign which makes Christ's presence real to us, but also the sign bringing about the real presence of the church (and, in the church, of us too) to him. The eucharistic meal thus signifies both Christ's gift of himself and the church's responding gift of herself, of the church who is what she is in him and can give what she gives in and through him. The sacramental form thus signifies the *reciprocity* of the "real presence." As the definitive community of salvation, the church cannot be separated from Christ. If, then, Christ makes himself present in this particular sacrament, the church also makes herself present at the same time. The presence of both Christ and his church is meaningfully expressed in this sacramental sign in common surrender to the Father "for the salvation of the whole world" and thus realized in a special way. This is why Augustine was able to say that "we ourselves lie on the paten" and the whole patristic and scholastic tradition was able to call the eucharist the "sacrament of the unity of the church with Christ." "This is my body" is "the body of the Lord," the new covenant, the unity of the church with Christ. "Because there is one bread, we who are many are one body, for we all partake of the one bread" (1 Cor 10:17). This does not do away with the real presence of Christ himself, which is, of course, the foundation of the church. The "body of the Lord" in the christological sense is the source of the "body of the Lord" in the ecclesiological sense. Christ's "eucharistic body" is the community of the two—the reciprocal real presence of

Christ and his church, meaningfully signified sacramentally in the *nour-ishing* of the "body that is the church" by Christ's body.

In the eucharist, then, the new, definitive covenant is celebrated and made present in the community. Priority must be given to Christ in the eucharist. In the Middle Ages, the really present body of Christ (*res et sacramentum*) was traditionally taken as the point of departure and the really present "body that is the church" was only considered in the second place. But Christ's real presence to his church and the church's real presence to her Lord are really "sacramentalized" in the eucharist, with the result that this reciprocal real presence becomes deeper and more intimate in and because of the sacramental form and that the *reciprocal* giving of self to the Father in the form of a gift of love to fellow men becomes, through this celebration, more firmly rooted in the saving event of Christ's death and resurrection. Thus the Eucharist is directed towards the *Father,* "with, in and through Christ," and towards *fellow men* in fraternal love and service. The eucharist forms the church and is the bringing about of herself of the church which lives from the death and resurrection of Christ.

All this has important consequences for the constitution of the eucharist and for transubstantiation. The presence offered by Christ in the eucharist naturally precedes the individual's acceptance of this presence and is not the result of it. It therefore remains an offered *reality,* even if I do not respond to it. My disbelief cannot nullify the reality of Christ's real offer and the reality of the church's remaining in Christ. But, on the other hand, the eucharistic real presence also includes, in its sacramentality itself, reciprocity and is therefore completely realized only when consent is given in faith to the eucharistic event and when this event is at the same time accomplished personally, that is, when this reciprocity takes place, in accordance with the true meaning of the sign, in the sacramental meal. [1967]

63/ *Marriage in the Life of the Church*

Marriage is a secular reality which has entered salvation. But this worldly quality of marriage as a human commission always closely linked to the prevailing historical situation is subject to development, since human existence is a reflective existence. And in just the same way God's offer of salvation to man always follows this human history, and so assumes certain characteristics which become increasingly clear with the passage of time. The history of salvation began in the misty dawn of man's existence. The mists were slow to clear because man was at first concerned with living, and only gradually grew into a self-questioning being who was concerned to discover the meaning of his life. This is why it is impossible for the Christian view of man and of human marriage and family life to be a pure datum of revelation; it is more the result of a reflective human existence illuminated by revelation. Our very living as human beings is in itself a view of life and of the world. This view is never contradicted by revelation. It is corrected by relevation where correction is needed, and received by it into a transcendent sphere of life.

The first light shed by divine revelation on the secular reality of marriage resulted in the human realization that God himself, the utterly transcendent being, was outside the sphere of marriage. Marriage is essentially a reality of the created world which has significance in life here and now, but which loses its inherently secular significance for individual man, and for mankind as a whole, on death and at the end of time. Marriage is a good gift of creation, but one which belongs strictly to this world. It is within marriage that the essential fellowship of man can be fulfilled in the most meaningful and human way.

As a dialogue, marriage has in itself such a deep power of expression that it became the prophetic medium through which the dialectic of the life of the people of God with God was most clearly expressed—the concrete married life of Hosea and Gomer became the prophetic symbol of the historical dialogue of love between God and his people, and this covenant of grace implied a moral message for married life in the concrete. (See Ezekiel.) Because salvation comes to us in a secular, historical form, marriage has—both in its interpersonal and relational aspect, and as the means of founding a family—a subordinate function towards God's activity within the covenant: "I will make of you a great nation." Marriage is intimately connected with the Promise, and therefore always contains a reference to Christ. Every marriage, even civil marriage, is Christian—whether in the full sense, in the pre-Christian sense (marriage as having an orientation towards Christ), in the anonymously Christian sense, or even in the negatively Christian sense (a deliberate denial of the Christian aspect of marriage).

Christ's appearance was a confirmation of the primarily interior significance of marriage which, for the believer, had to be experienced "in the Lord." Salvation in Christ gives an unbreakable solidity to the inner structure of marriage, a quality which can only be experienced within the community of grace with Christ. According to Jesus' *logion* on indissolubility, marriage is a consecration of oneself for the whole of one's life to a fellow human being, one's chosen partner—and, according to Paul's interpretation, doing this just as Christ gave his life for the church. The indissolubility of marriage is connected in the closest possible way with the definitive character of the community of grace with God in Christ, sealed in baptism. On the other hand, the New Testament achieved a second demythologization of marriage arising from its eschatological view of life. The Old Testament vision had already stripped marriage of its pagan religious elements and raised it to the level of a secular "good" of the created world which had to be experienced in the light of faith in Yahweh. The New Testament reinforced the relative value of this good gift of creation in the light of the kingdom of God. The dogmatic link between Genesis (the divine institution of marriage as a good gift of creation, explicitly confirmed by Jesus' *logion*) and Ephesians 5 (marriage as the image of the covenant of grace between Christ and his church) is 1 Corinthians 7 (complete abstinence as the eschatological "relativization" of marriage). The primacy of the kingdom of God, not only with regard to marriage, but actually in marriage, is a biblical fact which no dogmatic consideration of marriage can afford to ignore.

At the same time it is evident, especially in the writings of Paul, not only that social structures are experienced "in the Lord," but also that there is a danger of transforming these social structures into theological realities when they are viewed in an eschatological light. In other words, the biblical ethos of marriage bears clear traces of the prevailing view of the position of woman in society.

It is also clear from the history of the church in the first eleven centuries that marriage was experienced as a secular reality which, because of its moral and religious implications, required special pastoral care. Tertullian in the West and Clement of Alexandria in the East both testify to the fact that marriage contracted civilly within the family by baptized Christians was itself a "church marriage." From the fourth century onwards, a marriage liturgy evolved which existed alongside the civil form of marriage, but which was not made obligatory in the West until the eleventh century, and even then was not regarded as a condition of validity. Up to the eleventh century this liturgical form of marriage remained completely free. It was obligatory only in the case of clergy in lower orders—in other words, in the case of those members of the clergy who were permitted to marry. Not only was this marriage liturgy not obligatory for other Christians; it was reserved for those Christians whose conduct was blameless, and was refused to those who married for the second time. Until the eleventh century, then, marriage was contracted civilly, although it was accompanied by church ceremonies.

From the eleventh century onwards, however, civil marriage—in its native Germanic, Gallic, Longobardic, Gothic, and Celtic forms—was taken over by the church. At this period marriage was contracted *in facie*

Ecclesiae (i.e., by the priest at the entrance to the church), and the social elements peculiar to the earlier secular form of marriage contract were incorporated into the liturgical ceremony. In other words, what had previously been secular became liturgical; and what had previously been a civil contract, made within the family circle and supplemented by a priestly ceremony of blessing or veiling, became a single liturgical whole conducted by the priest.

From the eleventh century onwards, too, various circumstances led to the actual transference of jurisdictional power over marriage to the church's sphere. The Pseudo-Isidorian decretals of the ninth century were not the direct cause of this transference, but their "authority" certainly added impetus to it. In order to exercise this power of jurisdiction the church needed to have a precise idea of exactly what constituted marriage as marriage. She was confronted by three systems of law: first, the Roman theory of the *consensus;* secondly, the idea prevalent among the western European tribes, among whom the marriage contract was seen to be situated above all in the father's handing over of the bride to the matrimonial authority of the bridegroom; and, finally, the view that had existed since the earliest times among all peoples, namely, that marriage was consummated in sexual intercourse. The church—which had supported the *consensus* theory expressed in the letter of Pope Nicholas I to the Bulgars, but had found it difficult to persuade the Germanic and Frankish tribes in the west to accept this—came eventually, after a long period of controversy, to the point where she herself accepted the view that the partners' mutual consent to marry was the essential element in the constitution of marriage, but that this element could be situated in indigenous practices, in accordance with the principle that there were as many different customs as there were countries. Her adherence to the Roman idea of law, however, led the Church eventually to insist on a "formalized" marriage *consensus,* and this was included, together with other practices, in the liturgy, although this purely formal dialogue had none of the strength of the original indigenous secular forms of the *consensus.* Finally, sexual intercourse was regarded as the element which ultimately consummated the marriage contract and made it permanently indissoluble. This was the subject of a long controversy which was finally resolved at the end of the twelfth and the beginning of the thirteenth century by Pope Alexander III, whose decision was confirmed by Innocent III and Gregory IX. A valid but unconsummated marriage was in principle indissoluble (that is to say, it could not dissolve itself), but it could be dissolved by an appeal to the hierarchical power of the keys. A consummated marriage, on the other hand, was absolutely indissoluble.

Does this do violence to the unconditional, absolute nature of Jesus' *logion?* We have already seen how Paul actually formulated this in the light of baptism which he regarded as the basis of the radical indissolubility of marriage. But now an (unconsummated) marriage between two baptized Christians could be dissolved! But it is important to bear in mind that, although Christ declared that marriage was indissoluble, he did not tell us where the element that constituted marriage was situated—what in fact made a marriage a marriage, what made it the reality which he called absolutely indissoluble. This is a problem of anthropology, since it is concerned with a human reality, the essence of which man must try to clarify in its historical context. And this human reality can be approached from various directions—it can be seen as a legal institution within human society and as an existential fact of human life. The Catholic Church took her stand—in her assertion of the indissolubility of marriage, at least—on the existential point of view, maintaining that marriage in the full sense of the word (that is, marriage that came within the authority of the unconditional pronouncement of God's word) was a community of persons which had been entered into by mutual consent and which was consummated in sexual intercourse. This was also the Jewish view of marriage which Christ had taken as his point of departure. Although I do not deny that, though it was less explicit than that of the church fathers, the scholastics had a certain antipathy towards sex and sexuality (this is something which will be discussed in a later volume), it is also impossible to dispute that the great medieval popes, on whose pronouncements the church's legal practice in connection with marriage is still based, included sex and sexuality in the "one flesh" of which Christ said that it was indissoluble. This constituted a complete contradiction of the one-sided, spiritual view expressed by Hugh of St. Victor in his theology of marriage. On the other hand, it remained possible for a virgin marriage to be experienced as a fully interpersonal relationship without sexual intercourse. Nonetheless, the fact that such a union was bound to be constantly threatened by real dissolution robs the assertion that the church regarded virgin marriage as the ideal realization of marriage as such of all its real force. Such a realization of marriage is a real possibility in the light of the kingdom of God, and, viewed in this light, it can even be a stronger intrinsic bond than marriage in which sexual intercourse plays a part, as was the case with Mary and Joseph. It cannot, however, be regarded as the ideal of married life itself, but only as an indication of the limits set by the kingdom of God around the "ideal marriage" (which is naturally celebrated as a physical union). Sexual intercourse is by definition the expression of a personal decision to serve the kingdom of God in a secular way, not in a directly eschatological way. This decision—by which man opens himself, through the other person, to the kingdom of God—is irrevocable, since it is in this decision that the mystery of the *henōsis*, or the union of Christ with his church, is completed. Love—the personal decision of the partners to be faithful to each other—is the natural soul of the community of marriage. [1963]

4

The Church's Ministry

Schillebeeckx has written with some regularity on church ministry since the mid-1950s. His understanding of ministry has evolved with his understanding of the church. Some of his views became widely known on the basis of his book on clerical celibacy in the latter part of the 1960s. But it was especially his book *Ministry* which brought his views to world attention.

Ministry is directed toward responding to the worldwide shortage of priests, which has resulted in many Christian communities being deprived of the eucharist. The six selections in this section all come from this book.

In selection 64, Schillebeeckx summarizes, in thematic fashion, the results of his historical research on the question of ministry. He sees the consolidation of an important change in the Middle Ages, and suggests that future forms of ministry might better look to the first millennium of the church for guidance.

Selection 65 tries to define what it means to be in apostolic communion or succession. Most commonly, apostolic succession has been defined by Roman Catholics as flowing from the twelve in the New Testament. Recent research has shown that categories of the twelve, the apostles, and the disciples were much more fluid in the New Testament than we had believed. Thus what it means to be apostolic needed to be reconsidered. In his attempt to develop criteria here, Schillebeeckx defines both the apostolicity of communities and their ministers.

Selection 66 takes up the thorny problem of alternative practices in critical communities. Schillebeeckx makes a distinction here between practices which are contrary to the law and those which try to respect what the law is trying to safeguard or protect. Since alternative practices are a fact in many communities, the problem has to be addressed.

Selection 67 represents a shift from Schillebeeckx's position on clerical celibacy taken in his book *Celibacy*. Historical research has shown him that the connection of celibacy with priesthood (as opposed to connection with religious life) has really been based on the pagan concept of ritual impurity rather than some Christian theological principle. He does not say that many priests have not incorporated a theological concern—only that the legislation has actually followed the pagan principle.

Selection 68 addresses the question of the exclusion of women from priesthood, in which he responds to the 1976 Vatican declaration on that question. The final selection sketches out the coordinates for ministry in the future, a ministry which will serve both the needs of the church internally and aid it in carrying out its mission in the world.

64/ *Ministry in the Church*

It can be seen from the preceding analysis that, generally speaking, in church history it is possible to recognize three views of the priest (which are partly socially conditioned): patristic, feudal or medieval, and modern. Because views of human nature and social sensibility have changed, present-day criticism is principally directed at the modern view of the priest, and in its reaction this criticism shows a clear affinity to the image of the priest in the ancient church.

Although the theology of the ministry which has developed since the end of the twelfth and the beginning of the thirteenth century has its own Western, Latin features, in theological terms I can see two submerged lines of continuity in the great tradition of two thousand years' experience of the Christian ministry. On the one hand, not only the ancient and medieval but also the modern church opposes any celebration of the eucharist which denies the universal *communio ecclesialis;* and on the other hand, there is an ancient and modern awareness that no Christian community can call itself autonomously the ultimate source of its own ministers. Of course it has to be conceded that the first Christian millennium—above all in the pre-Nicene period— expressed its view of the ministry chiefly in ecclesial and pneumatological terms, or better pneuma-christologically, whereas the second Christian millennium gave the ministry a directly christological basis and shifted the mediation of the church into the background. In this way a theology of the ministry developed without an ecclesiology, just as in the Middle Ages the so-called treatise on the sacraments followed immediately on Christology without the intervention of an independent ecclesiology (which at that stage had not yet been worked out). Although Thomas, at least, still always talks of "sacraments of the church" (*sacramenta ecclesiae*), the sacrament will later be defined in a technical and abstract sense as *signum efficax gratiae*, in which the ecclesial dimension remains completely unconsidered. Its sacramental power is founded directly on the "sacred" power (*sacra potestas*) which is the priest's personal possession. In this way the ecclesial significance of the ministry with its charismatic and pneumatological dimensions is obscured, and the more time goes on, the more the ministry is embedded in a legalistic cadre which bestows sacred power.

At many points Vatican II deliberately referred back to the theological intuitions of the ancient church, but its view of the church's ministry, above all in the terminology it used, is unmistakably a compromise between these two great blocks of tradition in the church. The churchly or ecclesial dimension of the ministry is again stressed, and instead of *potestas* the Council prefers to use the terms *ministeria* and *munera:* church service. However, *potestas sacra* also occurs several times, though the classic difference between *potestas ordinis* and *potestas iurisdictionis* cannot be found anywhere in *Lumen Gentium*. Rather, a break is made with this division, since it is stated that the essential foundation of the jurisdiction is already given with "consecration" itself. Thus at least in principle, the old view of the *titulus ecclesiae* of the ministry is restored to favor, and at least a beginning is made towards breaking down the legalism which surrounds the ministry,

By contrast, however, in 1976, especially in the declaration by the Congregation of the Doctrine of Faith on women in the ministry, this conciliar equilibrium which had been regained is again distorted. Granted, the declaration concedes that the priest is the figure with which the community identifies, but it immediately adds that he has this status because first and foremost he represents Christ himself and also represents the church simply because he represents Christ as the head of the church. Here the ecclesial and pneumatological standpoint is abandoned and the priesthood is again given a direct christological foundation.

On the basis of theological criteria I think that preference must be given to the first Christian millennium as a model for a future shaping of the church's ministry—albeit in a very different, modern historical context—and in particular to the New Testament and the pre-Nicene period. In arguing in this way I am also taking account of the Agreed Statements which have been put forward by official ecumenical commissions of theologians over the last ten years. In the community of Jesus Christ, not everything is possible at will. The self-understanding of the Christian churches as the "community of God" is the all-embracing principle. Therefore I shall first sum up the basic Christian view of the ministry in the church in a number of key concepts, taking account generally of modern, theological criticism of the ministry.

(a) The specific character of the ministry within other services performed by and in the community

Given the responsibility of all believers for the whole of the community, which also involves a whole series of other ministries and charismata, in the church there are also official ministerial services with their *own specific* feature, which is that they are different forms of pastoral *leadership* of the community or presiding over the community. Following an appropriate procedure, these ministers are themselves chosen by the community for this ministry, or are in fact confirmed by the community in their already existing position on the basis of their actual function in the community, a function marked by charismatic gifts. The call by the community is the specific ecclesial form of the call by Christ. Ministry from below is ministry from above.

After the apostolic period, but still within the New Testament, the custom already begins to arise in some communities of giving this calling by the community a liturgical form: in the last resort, the church does not make appointments as they are made to Unilever or General Motors, nor is this appointment like an appointment in the name of the civil authority. Hence the laying on of hands by leaders who at that time were still charismatic (first "prophets," and later presbyters), with prophetic prayer, the later *epiclesis* to the Spirit. In short, it is the liturgical and sacramental expression of the sense of the community that what happens in the *ecclesia* is a gift of God's Spirit and not an expression of the autonomy of the church. Thus the *pneuma hēgemonikon* was called down on the real leader of the pastoral team of a local church (in the ancient church, historically speaking, this was the bishop): the Spirit which directs the church community and also brings to mind what Jesus said and did, as it has been handed down to the communities as a heritage to be preserved in dynamic form through the apostolic tradition. It follows from this that as leader of the community the minister is the president at the eucharist, in which the community celebrates its deepest mystery and its own existence, in thanksgiving and praise to God.

The team leader is assigned fellow workers in his ministry, who are similarly appointed through the laying on of hands and prayer, in which it is said in rather vaguer or more specific ways to what specialized ministry they have been summoned. The charisma which they need for their particular ministry is called down on them. However, by virtue of the spiritual charisma which they have been given, in emergencies all ministers can take the place of the team leader and perform his ministry without supplementary "ordinations" being needed. It is often difficult to define where official and non-official ministry begins or ends in the specific life of a community. However, to put it briefly, the concepts of leadership, instruction, liturgy or diaconate show what the great Christian tradition understood as official ministry. Still, the New Testament allows the church every freedom in the specific structures of the ministry; even the choice of an episcopal or presbyteral church order is not a schismatic factor in the light of the New Testament. Church history also points in the same direction. Apart from the fact that the mono-episcopacy of the Ignatian writings must now be put much later than people had hitherto thought, many medieval theologians, above all the Thomists, did not see the distinction between episcopate and presbyterate as a difference in the power of consecration but only in the power of jurisdiction, while Thomas at the same time could nevertheless say that the episcopate "is the source of all church ministries." This question remained a focal point of vigorous controversy for a whole century, until on 20 October 1756, in his letter *In Postremo*, Pope Benedict XIV allowed the theologians complete freedom. Furthermore, it cannot be said that the Second Vatican Council settled this question in principle. On the contrary, this council gives a synthetic theology of *de facto* church order, in which the episcopacy is assigned "the fullness of the priesthood." In actual church order, then, the presbyterate is a matter of sharing in the priesthood of the bishops; presbyters are "auxiliary priests." However, we cannot say that this is actual dogma.

According to the New Testament, in the first place it is Christ and the church who are priestly; nowhere in the New Testament does the minister in the church take on particularly priestly characteristics. Even Augustine, who recognizes the priestly character of the minister, opposes a theology which sees the minister as a mediator between Christ and humanity. As a consequence of the priestly character of Christ and his church it is also correct to apply the adjective "priestly" to the minister in his service to Christ and his church; he is the servant of and in the priestly community of, and in association with, Christ the priest. However, at this point we should not forget that even the Second Vatican

Council did not explicitly want to use one formula proposed, viz., the priest as the mediator between Christ and the faithful.

(b) Clergy and laity

At a very early stage after the New Testament, with Clement, a distinction arose between *klērikos* and *laïkos*, analogous to the Jewish distinction between "high priest and the people" (Isa 42:2; Hos 4:9), but this terminology in no way indicates a difference of status between laity and clergy. A *klērikos* is someone who has a *klēros*, i.e., a ministry. What we have here, therefore, is a distinction of function, not in an official civic sense, but in an ecclesial sense; however, there were charismatic functions in the church which were of a specific kind compared with other ministries in the community. In this light, given the whole of the church's tradition, the insertion in *Lumen Gentium*—which is in fact a quotation from an encyclical of Pius XII—in which it is said that the ordained priesthood is "essentially different" (*essentia differunt*) from the priesthood of the believing people of God (the Reformers' phrase "universal ministry" also seems to me to be inappropriate terminology) must be interpreted as the confirmation of a specific and indeed sacramental function and not as a state. Because of this, and in my view correctly, the term hierarchy is not used in an ecumenical context to denote ministries; however, this is in no way to undervalue the function of leadership and authority in the church. Even the great medieval theologians refuse to speak of the ministry in terms of *praelatio* and *subiectio:* "this is not meant by the *sacramentum ordinis.*" The tension between an ontological-sacerdotalist view of the ministry on the one hand and a purely functionalist view on the other must therefore be resolved by a theological view of the church's ministry as a charismatic office, the service of leading the community, and therefore as an ecclesial function within the community and accepted by the community. Precisely in this way it is a gift of God.

(c) Sacramental ministry

The sacramentality (which is non-sacral) of the ministry emerges from what has just been said; it is normally coupled with initiation through a liturgical celebration. Although at present the ecumenical discussion of the technical meaning of the word "sacrament" is certainly not finished, in point of content all Christian churches which accept the ministry in the church are agreed over what may be regarded as the essential elements of *ordinatio:* calling (or acceptance) by the community and appointment to or for a community. The normal, specific form of this laid down by church order is the laying on of hands by other ministers with the offering of the *epiklēsis* by all concerned; in this respect the Catholic Church is not alone. At present, therefore, ecumenical theology rightly no longer connects the question of mutual acceptance at the eucharist with the question of the recognition of each other's ministry. As, for example, the analysis by the Greek Orthodox theologian J. D. Zizioulas has shown, the sacramental ministry is the action in which the community realizes itself; for him too, the charisma (without any contrast between "ministry" and institution) is essentially the *ordinatio*, but as something which concerns the community of the church, as a gift of the Spirit with both a sacramental and legal dimension. Here the validity of consecration is bound up not so much with one isolated sacramental action of the church, i.e., the liturgical laying on of hands seen in itself, as with the action of an apostolic church community as a whole. Within this view, "extraordinary forms of ministry" as expressed in the Bible and the early church are to be given a positive evaluation by the church in special circumstances.

(d) Sacramental character

For some Christian churches the sacramental character of the ministry still remains a stumbling block. This should not be the case. The first official church document which mentions a character dates from 1201 (the character of baptism, in a letter written by Pope Innocent III): "the priestly character" appears for the first time in 1231 in a letter from Gregory IX to the Archbishop of Paris. In its doctrine of the character, from the beginning of the thirteenth century on, high scholasticism had above all stressed the link between the "sacrament of ordination" and the "church," following the ancient church, though using a new conceptual category. Of course the sacerdotalist-ontological conception of the ministry which had grown up in the meantime was also connected with the character, which after a number of centuries would have to support all the weight of the ontologizing view of the ministry. From a dogmatic point of view, however, all that had been formulated was the existence of the character; of course, Trent wanted to leave open all precise explanations of it, even the view of some that it was merely the *relatio rationis* or logical relationship (Durant de Saint Pourçain). In other words, the ontologizing approach cannot be based on the councils which speak of character. In the last resort "character" seems to be a particular medieval category which expressed the ancient church's view of the permanent relationship between the minister and the gift of the pneumatological charisma of ministry in the church. In the Middle Ages a distinction was then made in this charisma of ministry between the authority of the entrusted office (expressed, moreover, in terms of *potestas sacra*) and the sacramental grace appropriate to it, which equipped the minister to exercise authority in a personally holy and truly Christian way. This distinction played into the hands of ontological sacerdotalizing. According to 2 Tim 1:6, however, the minister receives a charisma of ministry in the service of the community; here all the attention is focused on the charismatic and spiritual character of the ministry. In this the minister follows Jesus: in the spirituality and ethics of the gospel.

(e) The community and its celebration of the eucharist

The ancient church and (above all since Vatican II) the modern church cannot envisage any Christian community without the celebration of the eucharist. There is an essential link between local *ecclesia* and eucharist. Throughout the pre-Nicene church it was held, evidently on the basis of Jewish models, that a community in which at least twelve fathers of families were assembled had the right to a priest or community leader and thus to the eucharist, at which he presided. In the small communities, these originally episcopal leaders soon became presbyteral leaders, pastors. In any case, according to the views of the ancient church a shortage of priests was an ecclesiastical impossibility. The modern so-called shortage of priests therefore stands to be criticized in the light of the ancient church's view of church and ministry, because the modern shortage in fact has causes which stem from outside the ministry, namely the conditions with which the ministry has already been associated *a priori*, on not specifically ecclesiological grounds. Even now there are more than enough Christians, men and women, who in ecclesiological and ministerial terms possess this charisma, e.g., many catechists in Africa, and men and women pastoral workers in Europe and elsewhere; or who are at least prepared for appointment to the ministry if they do not feel that that means being clericalized and having to enter the service of a "system." According to the norms of the early church they meet every requirement.

(f) Local and universal church

Finally, there is the relationship between ministry in a local church and ministry in the "universal church." In the ancient world, the universal church was not an entity above the local churches. To begin with there was no supra-regional organization, though patriarchates and metropolitan churches soon developed, in which various local churches were brought together in a supra-provincial unity. As time went on, increasing recognition was given in the course of the first five centuries to the patriarchal *Sedes Romana,* the seat of Peter, as a result of the "primacy of the bond of love," even the other great patriarchates.

Vatican II once again took up the ancient notion of the universal church. The Council speaks of the local church communities "in which the one, holy, catholic, and apostolic Church of Christ is truly present and operative." The universal church is present in accentuated form in the local church. The view of Karl Rahner, who sees the universal church in the "higher, supra-diocesan personnel in the church," who form the College of Bishops, has no basis either in the factual history of the church or in Vatican II. Rather, people belong to the universal church because they belong to a local community. For this reason, however, no single community can monopolize the Spirit of God; as a result, mutual criticism on the basis of the gospel is possible within the local communities. Christian solidarity with other communities is an essential part of even the smallest grass-roots church communities. This ecclesial concern cannot be referred to higher authorities. It is a concern of every church community, but that should not include *a priori* self-censorship, in the sense that people exclude from the start everything that would not be welcome to higher authorities, though they themselves see it as legitimate Christian practice and as possible and urgently necessary within the context of their own church life. Within an "integrated leadership" ultimate responsibility is left to the person who in fact bears it; otherwise an obstructive vicious circle develops within the collegial leadership in the church. It was to overcome such introversion that the spokesmen of neighboring communities were required to be present at the liturgical institution of ministers in a particular local community.

All confessions in fact accept a supra-parochial and supra-diocesan ministry, in the sense of a synod, in a personal *episkopē,* in conferences of bishops, and even in the papacy. However, the structure is such that local ministers, as critical spokesmen of their churches, at the same time concern themselves with the management of the "universal church," the bond of love, along with the one from among them who fulfills the function of Peter. I think that a growing ecumenical consensus has emerged in all this. [1980]

65/ *Criteria of Apostolicity*

1. "Apostolic" first of all signifies the awareness of the community that it is carrying on the cause of Jesus. What is this cause? Jesus was the eschatological prophet of the kingdom of God, i.e., of God as salvation for mankind: of God's liberating action. Where God "reigns," communication prevails among men and women and brotherhood develops. This is a proclamation which, moreover, can be seen and experienced in the action of Jesus, in his life-style which is in conformity to the demands of this kingdom. Thus the coming of the kingdom of God as salvation for men and women is at the same time intrinsically bound up with the emergence of Jesus and his whole person. In the New Testament this is all expressed in the technical term "the gospel of Jesus as the Christ, Son of God." Thus in specific terms "apostolic" already implies the apostolic proclamation of Jesus' own message, from which the person of Jesus, and therefore also his death and resurrection, may not be separated. The apostolic interpretation of Jesus' rejection and death is part of the heart of the gospel. Thus what we have here is in the end "the gospel of God" (Mark 1:14), first of all because Jesus' message had as its content the coming rule of God, but also because God also clearly has something to say to us in and through the death of this "divine messenger." Jesus is therefore an essential constituent of the gospel as "the gospel of God."

2. The apostolic mediation of the faith of the Christian communities also has as a specific consequence the permanent importance of the foundation document in which the "gospel of Jesus as the Christ" is told in kerygmatic form: the New Testament interpreted against the background of what was called the Old Testament. This is where the inspiration of the Christian community lies: this book "is inspired" because it inspires us, just as God inspired Jesus and his movement. Thus the way in which the community stands under the norm of the New Testament is also part of what I call the "apostolicity" of the community (despite the necessary but precarious task of any biblical hermeneutics).

3. The fundamental self-understanding of the Christian community becomes clear from this: it is a "community of God" through being a "community of Jesus": the community stands under the apostolic norm of "discipleship of Jesus" which is to be realized again and again in new historical circumstances.

4. Proclamation, liturgy and *diakonia* (i.e., concern for suffering humanity and human society) are apostolic characteristics of the communities of God.

5. This community has an apostolic right to a minister or ministers, and also a right, on the basis of the New Testament mandate, "Do this in remembrance of me," to the celebration of the eucharist or the Lord's Supper.

6. From an apostolic perspective the communities are clearly not isolated entities but bound together in love (although in New Testament times there was not as yet an organization which extended beyond a particular region); a great *koinōnia* or brotherly community in which mutual criticism, grounded in the gospel, must be possible if all communities are to be maintained in apostolic lines. For the New Testament, this bond of love seems to be maintained in its apostolicity by the collegial leadership and *koinōnia* of all ministers, in which the function of Peter is a binding unitive factor in maintaining the bond of love.

7. Ministry in the church is not a status or state but a service, a function within the "community of God" and therefore a "gift of the Holy Spirit." Suffering solidarity with the poor and insignificant is an essential mark of the apostolicity of the ministry, since it is an apostolic mark of the whole community of Jesus.

8. Finally, the specific, legitimate contemporary forms of the apostolicity of the community and therefore of the ministry (which are constantly changing) cannot be discovered in purely theoretical terms, but only in a mutually critical correlation (which must be both theoretical and practical) between what the New Testament churches did and what the Christian communities do now.

This survey shows that as far as the New Testament is concerned the community has a right to a minister or ministers and to the celebration of the eucharist. This apostolic right has priority over the criteria for admission which the church can and may impose on its ministers (see already 1 Tim 3:1-13). Of course some criteria are attached to the purpose and content of the ministry in the service of a community of God. However, the apostolic right of Christian communities may not be made null and void by the official church; this is itself bound by this apostolic right. Therefore if in changed circumstances there is a threat that a community may be without a minister or ministers (without priests), and if this situation becomes increasingly widespread, then criteria for admission which are not intrinsically necessary to the nature of the ministry and are also in fact a cause of the shortage of priests, must give way to the original, New Testament right of the community to leaders. In that case this apostolic right has priority over the church order which has in fact grown up and which in other circumstances may have been useful and healthy (this is a point to which I shall return in detail later). [1980]

66/ Alternative Practices in Critical Communities

The alternative practice of critical communities which are inspired by Jesus as the Christ is (1) possible from an apostolic and dogmatic point of view (I cannot pass judgment on all the details here). It is a legitimate way of living a Christian life, commensurate with the apostolicity of the church, which has been called into being by the needs of the time. To talk of "heretics" or those who "already stand outside the church" (on grounds of this alternative practice) seems to me to be nonsensical from the church's point of view. Furthermore, (2) given the present canonical church order, the alternative practice is not in any way *contra* (against) *ordinem;* it is *praeter ordinem.* In other words, it does not follow the letter of existing church order (it is *contra* this letter), but it is in accordance with what church order really set out to safeguard (in earlier situations). It is understandable that such a situation is never pleasant for the representatives of existing church order. However, they too should take note of the negative experiences of Christians with church order and above all be sensitive to the damage which these do to the formation of communities, to the eucharist and to the ministry. Otherwise they are no longer defending the Christian community and its eucharistic heart and center, but an established system, the purely factual dimension. At a time when people have become extra-sensitive to the power structure of a system, a hardening of attitude in the existing system to the luxuriant upsurge of all kinds of experiments (even if some of them are perhaps frivolous) would be a very painful matter for all those who are well disposed towards the church.

Given that the alternative practice is not directly *contra ordinem,* but generally speaking merely *praeter ordinem,* in difficult circumstances in the church it can also be defended in an ethical respect (of course no one can pass judgment on subjective intentions). In this connection, too, to talk of "members who have placed themselves outside the church" is not only a distressing phenomenon which has no place in the church, but also smacks of what the church itself has always called heresy. Even the Second Vatican Council had difficulty in defining where the limits of church membership really lie. Of course they can be found somewhere; but how can they be defined precisely? Furthermore, talk like this makes posthumous heretics of authentic Christians of earlier centuries and above all condemns the New Testament search for the best possibilities of pastoral work.

I also want to say here that no one may pursue this alternative practice in a triumphalist spirit: this also seems to me to be un-apostolic. It remains a provisionally abnormal situation in the life of the churches. Personally (but this is simply a very personal conviction) I think that there is also need for something like a strategy or "economy of conflicts." Where there is clearly no urgent necessity for an alternative practice because of a pastoral need felt by the Christian communities, ministers must not put into practice everything that is possible in apostolic or dogmatic terms. In that case, of course, there is a danger that, for example, in critical communities, the communities are again put in second place after the problems of the ministry and begin to be manipulated on the basis of problems arising from the crisis of identity among ministers themselves. In addition, we must not turn alternative forms of ministerial practice into a mystique. We need a degree of realism and matter-of-factness. Of course renewals in the church usually begin with illegal deviations; renewals from above are rare, and are sometimes dangerous. Vatican II is an illustration of both these points. In its Constitution on the Liturgy, this Council largely sanctioned the illegal liturgical practice which had grown up above all in France, Belgium and Germany. On the other hand, when after the Council the Vatican programme of renewal was put into effect in other matters, largely on promptings from above, many people proved to be unprepared, so that there was resistance in many communities.

One often hears the objection that changes or an alternative practice are not justified by the fact that they are different or new. That is quite correct; but the implicit presupposition here is wrong. In changed circumstances this is equally true of the existing church order. It too cannot be legitimated on the basis of the inertia of its own factual existence. When views of man or the world change, it too can come under the suspicion of deterioration, i.e., of actually falling short of authentic Christian and church life. Even the old and venerable does not enjoy any priority because it is old and venerable.

Some people will criticize my views for being too one-sided and seeing the church in "horizontal" terms, exclusively in accordance with the model of a social reality which can be treated in sociological terms, and not as a charismatic datum "from above." I must reject this ecclesial dualism, on the basis of the New Testament. Of course we may not speak about the church only in descriptive empirical language; we must also speak about the church in the language of faith, of the church as the "community of Jesus," as "the body of the Lord," the "temple of the Spirit," and so on. And this language of faith expresses a real dimension of the church. However, in both cases we are talking about one and the same reality: otherwise we should split up the church in a gnostic way into a "heavenly part" (which would fall outside the sphere of sociological approaches) and an earthly part (to which all the bad features could evidently be transferred). Vatican II already reacted against this with the words: "We may not see the earthly church and the church enriched with heavenly things as two realities" (*Lumen Gentium* I, 8). In my view, the obstacles to the renewal of the official ministry in the church are grounded above all in this dualistic conception of the church (which is often described in pseudo-Christian terms as "hierarchical"). The consequence of this is that because of the shortage of priests Christian laity are allowed to engage in pastoral work as much as possible but are refused the sacramental institution to the ministry which goes with this. The question is more whether this development in the direction of pastoral workers (whose existence can only be understood in the light of historical obstructions which have been placed in the way of the ministry) who are not ministers and have not been appointed sacramentally is a sound theological development. It maintains the exaggerated sacral view of the priesthood, as will emerge even more closely from what follows. [1980]

67/ Celibacy for Priests

The law of celibacy, at first implicit in the Latin church at the First Lateran Council (1123) and then promulgated explicitly in canons 6 and 7 of the Second Lateran Council in 1139, was the conclusion of a long history in which there was simply a law of abstinence, applying to married priests. This earlier history extends from the end of the fourth century until the twelfth century. This history shows that the fundamental matter was a law of abstinence: the law of celibacy has grown out of a law of abstinence and was promulgated with the intention of making the law of abstinence effective.

In the New Testament period and in the early church there were from the start both married and unmarried ministers. The reasons why some of them remained unmarried might be personal, social or religious. Of course in the biblical post-apostolic period it is constantly stressed that ministers must be "the husband of one wife" (1 Tim 3:2; 3:12; Titus 3:6), i.e., that they must love their wives devotedly. But there is no mention here of the impossibility of remarrying. At that time we often find on epitaphs, "he was the husband of one wife," i.e., he loved his wife.

However, in the first centuries there was an increase in the number of priests who remained unmarried of their own free will, inspired by the same motives as monks. Only towards the end of the fourth century did there appear in the West completely new, ecclesiastical legislation concerned with married ministers (here bishops, presbyters and deacons). However, we have to wait until the Second Vatican Council before the church mentions Matt 19:11f. in one of its canonical documents (which to begin with discuss a temporary law of abstinence and later a permanent law of abstinence and finally the law of celibacy, in connection with the clergy). This passage talks of "religious celibacy," i.e., "for the sake of the kingdom of God," without any reference to ritual laws of purity (which were, of course, completely alien to Jesus). . . .

It appears from these official documents that the dominant reason for the introduction of a law of abstinence is "ritual purity." In ancient times the Eastern and Western churches of the first ten centuries never thought of making celibacy a condition of entering the ministry: both married and unmarried men were welcome as ministers. Originally, i.e., from the end of the fourth century on, church law, which was at that time new, contained a *lex continentiae* (see e.g. PL 54, 1204). This was a liturgical law, forbidding sexual intercourse in the night before communicating at the eucharist. Furthermore, this custom had long been observed. However, when, in contrast to the Eastern churches, from the end of the fourth century the Western churches began to celebrate the eucharist daily, in practice this abstinence became a permanent condition for married priests. A law to this effect became necessary for the first time at the end of the fourth century, and there was canonical legislation accordingly. What we have, then, is not a law of celibacy, but a law of abstinence connected with ritual purity, focused above all on the eucharist. Despite this obligation to abstinence, married priests were forbidden to send away their wives; not only an obligation to abstinence but also living together in love with his wife was an obligation for the priest under canon law. . . .

Furthermore, when in the twelfth century the ritual law of abstinence was turned into a law of celibacy, this theme continued to remain the chief reason behind the actual law of the celibacy of ministers. The Second Lateran Council, in which this law is officially promulgated, puts the emphasis here: "*so that* the *lex continentiae* and the purity which is well-pleasing to God may extend among clergy and those who are ordained, we decree . . .*"; the law of celibacy is explicitly seen as the drastic means of finally making the law of abstinence effective. It emerges clearly from the Councils between the fifth and the tenth centuries that the law of abstinence was observed only very superficially by married priests. The church authorities were aware of this. After a variety of vain attempts to make it more strict by sanctions and "economic" penalties they resorted to the most drastic means of all: a prohibition against marriage. Only from that time (1139) does marriage become a bar to the priesthood, so that only the unmarried could become priests.

Even after the Second Lateran Council, the law of abstinence, and thus ritual purity, therefore remained the all-decisive and sole motive in the question of the "obligatory celibacy" of priests. There is all the less mention here of a "religious celibacy for the sake of the kingdom of God." "One does not approach the altar and the consecrated vessels 'with soiled hands'": so went the pagan view which had now been taken over by the Christians.

Historically speaking, it can therefore no longer be denied that even the relatively recent law of celibacy is governed by the antiquated and ancient conviction that there is something unclean and slightly sinful about sexual intercourse (even in the context of sacramental marriage). This is not to deny that in the first ten centuries there were many priests who practiced celibacy much more "as monks," viz., for the sake of the kingdom of God (even Thomas makes a sharp distinction between the celibacy of the religious and that of the clergy "because of considerations of purity"). . . . The new motivation for the celibacy of the ministry given by Vatican II also raises new questions. What is the precise meaning of "religious celibacy," i.e., celibacy for the sake of the kingdom of God? This can have two meanings which, with some theological justification, for the sake of convenience I shall call "mystical" and "pastoral" (or apostolic), without being able to distinguish the two aspects adequately. The mystical and apostolic (and also the political) aspects are the two intrinsically connected aspects or dimensions of the one Christian life of faith. It is indeed justifiable and legitimate that someone should remain unmarried in order to be completely free for the service of church work and thus for his fellow human beings, just as others also do not marry (though that does not in fact imply "celibacy") in order to devote themselves wholly to science, to art, to the struggle for a juster world, and so on. Sometimes it amounts to an existential feeling that no other course is possible. In other words, not to marry is seldom, if ever, the object of a person's real choice. The real object of the choice is "something else," and this something else preoccupies some people to such an extent that they leave marriage on one side. Not marrying is usually not a choice in and of itself, but one "for the sake of . . .": in religious terms, for the sake of the kingdom of God. As a result, we may not consider the negative and exclusive aspect of this choice, which is really for some other reason, in isolation and on its own. Of course in the life of any culture it so happens that a particular existential "I cannot do otherwise" in the long run becomes ritualized. Thus, for example, the fact of "not being able to eat" because of a death, or because, in a religious context, one is looking forward excitedly to the feast of the Passover, developed into a ritual: penitential fasting, or fasting for forty days. People then fast even though they may perhaps have a great longing to eat. We must not underestimate the ritualizing of life, though in every culture in the long run there is the threat of a formalized evacuation of the content of this ritualization. It becomes narrow and rigid, when it was originally meant to serve, or at least to evoke, an existential experience.

Here the Second Vatican Council also introduced some important qualifications. Earlier, it was generally accepted that there was a kind of competition between love of God and married love, for reasons already given by Paul, namely, the need "to please one's wife," which would detract from undivided love of God (1 Cor 7:32–34). This alleged competition, too, can no longer be justified theologically. For this reason Vatican II explicitly rejected a prepared text which said that "undivided love" and "dedication to God alone" must be seen as the real characteristics of religious celibacy. This competitive opposition between love of God and love of a fellow human being (including sexual love) was deliberately rejected. The definitive text runs: "That precious gift of divine grace which the Father gives to some men . . . so that by virginity, or celibacy, they can more easily devote their entire selves to God alone with undivided heart" (*Lumen Gentium*, no. 42). It was thus conceded that total and undivided dedication to God is the calling of all Christians; according to this text from the Council, celibacy simply makes it to some degree "easier" to realize this spirituality, which is in fact enjoined upon all Christians. If we purify the law of celibacy from all antiquated and incorrect motivation, which is what this Council wants to do, some basis in fact does remain, but it is a very narrow one, viz., an abstract and theoretical "greater ease." I call this "abstract and theoretical": that is because in practice it can be easier for one person to arrive at a greater and more real and undivided love of God in marriage, whereas for someone else this only happens through an unmarried life. This, then, is the way in which the Tridentine view that unmarried life for the sake of the kingdom of God is a "higher state" than the "married state" has generally been interpreted in the theology of the last twenty years. The alleged superiority is dependent on the person in question, and cannot be established generally in purely abstract terms. What is better for one is less good and perhaps even oppressive for another, and vice versa. (In this connection a choice should be possible between "a provisional celibacy in the service of the kingdom of God" and a celibacy intended to be "perpetual," especially as in the course of a lifetime someone may arrive at the discovery that a perpetual celibacy undertaken as a convenience has in fact become a deep-rooted hindrance. However, we cannot discuss these problems here.)

If all this is correct, a universal law of celibacy for all ministers would at least be a serious exaggeration, on the basis of an abstraction, and therefore without concrete pastoral dimensions. At all events, one cannot interpret "the new law," by which I mean the new motivation which Vatican II has given to the old law of celibacy, as a principle of selection, in the sense that the church chooses its ministers exclusively from Christians who voluntarily embrace celibacy. Given the earlier history of the existing law and the official custom of speaking of a law of celibacy, despite new motivation, the canonical legislation persists in seeing the celibacy of the ministry as a kind of *statutory obligation* on the basis of an abstract and theoretical superiority of celibacy. Despite many affinities between ministry and celibacy, however, there are also unmistakable affinities between marriage and ministry, and the New Testament texts about "the husband of one wife" point precisely in this direction. . . . As a result of the present coupling of celibacy and ministry, at least in the Western church, in many places the apostolic vitality of the community and the celebration of the eucharist are endangered. In such a situation, church legislation, which can in any case be changed, must give way to the more urgent right to the apostolic and eucharistic building up of the community. (Finally, it is obvious that the pastoral authorities in the church must also, and above all, make a decision here.) However, one would be naive to think that the so-called "crisis situation" among the clergy will be of short duration, or is even over. That is to underestimate the force of the old spirituality which made many young men accept celibacy because they in fact thought that marriage was indeed something of less value. This idealism, mistaken though it was, led many people in fact freely to accept the celibacy of the ministry. If marriage is given its full value (and it should be remembered that for Catholics, it is a sacrament), the vocations to a religious celibate life will of course decrease. One could say: earlier, people in fact chose not to marry because marriage was a lesser, indeed almost a mistaken "good." In that case celibacy can directly be an object of choice. Nowadays a direct choice of celibacy (apart from the real choice of some other good which proves utterly demanding) is in fact ambivalent. Often it is even suspect.

At this point I should also indicate the "ideological element" that can be present in an appeal to "prayer for vocation." No Christian would deny the value and the force of prayer, even for vocations; but if the reason for the shortage of priests is "church legislation" which can be changed and modified in the course of time for pastoral reasons, then a call to prayer can act as an excuse; in other words, it can be a reason for not changing this law. [1980]

68/ *Women in Ministry*

In connection with all this, something must also be said about women in the ministry. The church's resistance to this is very closely connected with the way in which the ritual laws of purity led to the celibacy of males.

In 1976 the Congregation for the Doctrine of the Faith produced a declaration on the question of women in the ministry. The fact that this was not a *motu proprio* from the Pope but a document produced by a Congregation, albeit with the approval of the Pope, indicates a certain hesitation on the part of the Pope to make a "definitive" pronouncement on the question; this is the Roman way of keeping a matter open, though provisionally a kind of "magisterial statement" on the issue has been made. According to its own words, this document sets out to make a contribution to the struggle for women's liberation. However, as long as women are left completely outside all decision-making authorities in the church, there can be no question of real women's liberation. Nevertheless, this document says that women are excluded from leadership in the church on grounds of their sex, because they are excluded from presiding at the eucharist. Here, in a pre-conciliar way, the connection between church and ministry is again broken in favor of the relationship between eucharist (sacred power) and ministry. In particular, all kinds of feminine "impurities" have unmistakably played a part throughout the history of the church in restricting women's role in worship, as also in the Levitical legislation and in many cultures. What were originally hygienic measures are later "ritualized." All this is in no way specifically Christian.

But why must the fact that, given the culture of the time, Jesus only chose twelve men as apostles suddenly acquire a theological significance, while at the same time the similar fact that this same Jesus for the most part (perhaps even entirely) chose only married men for this task, along with the fact that Paul demands the apostolic right to involve his own wife in the apostolic work (1 Cor 9:5; though Paul renounces his own claim to this right), is not allowed any theological significance, and moreover is interpreted in the opposite direction through the law of celibacy? Two standards are used, depending on the particular interest. This mutually conflicting, arbitrarily selective biblical hermeneutic (or method of interpretation) shows that here nontheological themes unconsciously play a decisive role, while being presented on the authority of the Bible. (I am reluctant to express this sharp criticism, but honesty compels me to speak out.) As a Catholic theologian I know that magisterial pronouncements can be correct even when the arguments used in them are unsound. But in that case something meaningful must be said somewhere about the exclusion of women from the ministry. That is not the case here, and all the arguments tend, rather, to converge on the insight that this is a purely historically conditioned cultural pattern, understandable in antiquity and even until recently, but problematical in a changed culture which is aware of real discrimination against women. All the arguments in favor of "another attractive task" for women in the church, on the basis of "her own feminine" characteristics and intuitions, may sound fine, but they do not provide any support for the exclusion of women from leadership in the church. On the contrary. Of course we must allow on the other hand that the church authorities must not take any over-hasty steps here while their own church people (does sociology support this view?) are perhaps still some way from this awareness; however, this is quite different from looking round rather desperately for arguments which do not seem able to stand up to any criticism and are simply concerned to legitimate the *status quo*. . . . Thus the hindrances in the case of both priestly celibacy and women in the ministry seem to me at root to be of a pseudo-doctrinal kind, and are to be found especially in the ontological and sacerdotalist conception of the ministry in the setting of worship in the Western Latin church. In many religions and, in ancient times, even in the Christian church, for once to put it bluntly, "taboos" were associated with this sacralism: both feminine and sexual taboos. [1980]

69/ *Ministry in the Future*

What is the particular contribution of perhaps a small Christian grassroots community in the building up of a life of solidarity which is of a pluralist kind (and in which sooner or later people will feel the need to use the word "God")? The more time goes on, the more this is the particular situation of a Christian community.

As in the early church, this coming community is a community of brothers and sisters in which the power structures which prevail in the world are gradually broken down. All have responsibility, though there are functional differences, and here at the same time there is a difference between general concern for the community and specific tasks of the ministry, above all that of the team leader(s) who coordinate(s) all charismatic services.

Only when an overall plan of the situation has been outlined can we see what kind of differentiated pastoral team is needed for smaller and larger pastoral units within a limited area. The model of the pastor who is capable of doing everything is clearly out of date. The agenda of a Christian community, the questions with which it should be concerned, are here for the most part dictated by the world itself. This gives a four-fold direction, dynamic and task to the inspiration of faith and in the light of this to the Christian action of a community (seen generally and schematically).

(a) A practical and hermeneutical or prophetic task

By this I mean that the community along with its ministers places the Christian tradition of practice and experience within the experiential and conceptual horizon (analyzed and interpreted in a critical way) of those who live within a pastoral unit: i.e., preaching which relates the gospel to the present, catechesis within the context of particular experiences, interpretation of the meaning of existence and history, an indication of the way the community must go, and so on.

(b) The task of a Christian criticism of mankind and society

In the light of the liberating gospel, an attempt is made to trace out those points where particular structures and prevailing attitudes obstruct rather than further freedom and humanity, and thus hold back the coming of the kingdom of God. This includes a political responsibility for the salvation of the community, and of the community for the wholeness of the world.

(c) A diaconal task of Christian education

Here the building up of a community, as a catalyst in a pluralist society, is experienced as a growth process which takes its secular, human starting point in Christian participation in the various forms of communal life which already exist outside the church, in the neighborhood of the pastoral unit. In this way it is possible to avoid the formation of a ghetto or too much looking inwards. Thus, there should be critical Christian solidarity with the work of social restructuring which is already present, political involvement, and so on. Here the individual pastorate should not be forced out. For all the specialization, differentiation and restructuring of the ministry it would be an ominous thing if there were no longer any pastors who helped people in their desperate questions about meaning and their perplexity in the face of the anonymous and official bureaucracy of our modern life. Concern above all for the happiness of particular people in their everyday lives is a task for the whole of the church community, but especially for its minister. In that respect the minister still remains a jack-of-all-trades, and not someone who can hide behind his "pastoral specialization" or his legitimate demand for a reform of the structures.

(d) A task of celebrating the liturgy and ultimately the eucharist

"How shall we sing the Lord's song in a strange land?" asked the first despairing people when they lived in captivity in Babylon (Ps 137:4). Must we not first liberate men and only later, when they are freed, celebrate and sing of their liberation? With the prophets in captivity in ancient times and also with today's Latin American grass-roots communities, communities and ministers can overcome their doubts in the light of very specific experiences, namely that joy and prayer, singing and liturgy, while having their own intrinsic value and character of grace (so that they cannot be reduced to their effect on society), nevertheless also have a subversive effect in a world of disaster and oppression. Oppressors look to anxiousness and fear, bowing and scraping, to keep them in power, and not to happy songs of hope and love. In an evocative "symbolic interaction" the liturgy expressly remembers and celebrates that in which the community has the basis of all its language and action. Secular and symbolic or liturgical forms of communicating meaning need one another and provoke one another. This means that the community, and thus its leaders, no longer locates the meaning of life and religious need so exclusively and so massively in the liturgy and the sacraments. In that case liturgical celebrations are more the obvious *kairoi*, privileged moments in the forming of groups and communities, and no longer an obligation; in fact they are spontaneous and nevertheless intrinsically necessary celebrations of the Lord's day, the day of men and women set free. [1980]

Part Five

The Church in
the World Community

1

The Christian and the World

To speak of the church in terms of its life as a community cannot prescind from the fact that the church is in the larger human society, the world. Schillebeeckx's first published articles in 1945 already take up the question of what it means to be Christian in a humanist society.

The four selections in this section represent the development of Schillebeeckx's thinking over a period of twenty-five years. Selection 70, from 1958, uses vocabulary out of the French church-world discussions, notably that of laicization and laicism. The point was to find the authentic role of the Christian (lay person) in the world.

Selection 71, ten years later, exhibits the framework out of which Schillebeeckx will continue to discuss church and world questions: eschatology. This approach allows for more than dialogue between church and world, but sees the church deeply engaged in the transformation of the world.

Selection 72, again ten years later, continues those themes, under the eschatological proviso (that is, while we work toward bringing about the reign of God, it is ultimately God who will work the final transformation). Selection 73, from the mid-1980s, works out the meaning of that eschatological framework in terms of the great guiding symbols of the end-time.

70/ *Dialogue with the World*

We have already spoken earlier in an oblique way about man's dialogue with the world, but only insofar as God wishes to draw man's attention to his offer of grace by means of man's changing confrontation with this world. Seen thus, human dialogue with the world is the way in which God attempts to gain man for himself through the circumstances of human life. Thus the intramundane is already a dialectic element of this divine interplay of love, an element contributing towards theologal intersubjectivity.

We must now investigate the meaning proper to this dialogue with the world within the dialogue with God. For it is part of the factual essence of man that he participates in a dialogue with the world of people and things in which he stands. God calls on us to actively contribute meaning with respect to this world and to do so on the basis of our experience of God, which is not only a partial aspect of our human life but an integral attitude to life which also comprehends our being-in-this-world. For human freedom, which is personally addressed by God, is also a culture-creating freedom. We Christians tend rather easily to leave the ordering of temporal society to the non-believer. We forget that the so-called profane, the acknowledgment of mundane reality, is only one part of a total religious attitude to life. Laicization or secularization is in itself an intra-Christian and intra-ecclesial event, an event within the life of the people of God. These are ambiguous words. But their meaning lies in this, that within his dialogue with the living God the believer comes to the recognition of secular reality as calling for his commitment to its tasks. In this way Christian "laicization" is completely different from atheistic laicism, which experiences secular reality as its only horizon in life. Seen objectively, exclusively secular or atheistic laicization is an *hairesis*, a tearing away of profane or secular reality from the whole into which it fits, the existential relationship of faith with the living God. Only outside this connection is secular reality "profaned." For, although the intramundane possesses independence to a certain extent, through which it has of itself a certain intelligibility, it remains a question whether this secularity (in which the personal essence of man finds himself) can find a complete intelligibility *within its own boundaries*. The secular point of view is always circumscribed by temporality, and it is valid only when it remains open to the higher whole into which it is integrated in God's plan.

With regard to God, *coram Deo*, man will take up his personal responsibility in secular history together with God. On this level he lives out his immediate, intersubjective relations with God in the secular sphere, which has its own structure and immediate meaning. Although they are situated on completely different levels, the supernatural or religious and the intramundane or secular dimensions are not without influence on each other: despite the fact that the secular has a certain autonomy in its own sphere, dialogue with the world becomes a moment in our dialogue with God. The value and significance of secular life in itself remains untouched within the consciously experienced relationship with God. But all this calls for clarification.

(a) In itself this dialogue with the world runs according to a secular law of reality. In this sense we may really speak of a secular dimension of the task of human life. To be sure, this secular element is only human when it is given its place in the actual plan of a human person. It is a question of the achievement of authentically human values which, as such, are realized *diesseitig*, in this life, by the power of human capacities. On this level one meets general aspects of human life which are in no sense the exclusive property of Christianity and in which believer and atheist cooperate: the humanization of the world and of man. In its inward structure this task is therefore non-Christian; that is, not supernatural but purely and simply human. This whole area has an autonomous human value and its own sphere of activity in which anyone who is sensitive to general human values can participate. On this level the Christian can claim nothing as exclusively his own.

If we wish to talk about the Christianization of this intramundane task of life or of the "profane," we must definitely begin by recognizing the secular character of this calling. It is, of course, true that man is affected in his humanity by the repercussions of sin, and that sensitivity to general human values has received a blow thereby. Personal communion with the living God will give us a particular sensitivity towards human values. Thus the Christianization of the intramundane task of life may certainly be considered a restoration of general human values. Nevertheless, these remain truly human values, so that we do not leave the intramundane point of view hereby; in themselves they remain recognizable by man as man, independent of his theologal experience of God. This situation means only that under this aspect personal communion with God has a remedial significance even with regard to intramundane reality; in other words that, at least in principle, humanism and the secular stand their best chance within personal communion with God. But on the other hand it must be admitted that however much communion of grace with God may make us more sensitive towards recognizing general human values, it does not of itself, as Professor R. C. Kwant has rightly pointed out, make us concretely aware of given historical facts: for instance, of particular examples of deficiencies in the humanization process. Hence Christians may be late in recognizing the necessity for structural reform as the condition of a more personalized existence for the worker—or later, at any rate, than non-believers. But under this aspect, Christianizing our secular undertakings amounts to no more than fully recognizing human reality and human values as such. This is not specifically Christianization, except in a supplementary sense.

(b) However, for the person living in communion with God through grace—that is, man as we defined him theologically—this means that the secular sphere or lay task in life does not involve *laicism:* in this world the secular becomes a mode of incarnation, of personal communion with God, the taking up of the intramundane into our theologal relationship with God; and from God's side it becomes a thematic appeal. With God, and supported by his security in God, man stands in the midst of the secular world, which thus becomes the free space in which, as a child of God, he takes an active role in creating culture. Although remaining of this world, this reality becomes a moment in his presence with God, and thus the secular is present with God. Although the distinction between the secular and the sacral remains, the two spheres form real aspects of human presence with God. Being-in-this-world is a part of man's total religious existence.

In this way there is also a Christian "laicization," which is completely distinct from atheistic laicism—with which, moreover (taking into account a prudential assessment of the historical context), a cooperative dialogue is possible on this, its own level. As believers we live with God in this world, which we construct into a home worthy of human habitation in which, moreover, the incarnation of our personal communion with God is expressed. This expression takes place in the secular order itself; non-believers work at it too, from an exclusively secular standpoint, but on a common basis. In this way the biblical theme that the world is for man and man for God is given its ultimate significance. Were we to express this in classical terminology, we should say that the *finis operis,* the aim proper to the activity of secular life, is immediately intramundane. It is the humanization of man through humanization of the world, the construction of an earthly home for the glory of man. But men are there for God: the personal meaning of life is superhuman, non-intramundane, and cannot be gained on the basis of man's own human and mundane powers. Only in a self-transcending act can man receive the personal meaning of his life as a grace from the hand of God. This means that human dialogue with the world finds its ultimate sense only within the religious attitude to life. The "intrinsic aim" of the intramundane is orientated via man towards the *eschaton.* To contend that this introduces into the question only an extrinsic, supplementary end to man's activity (*finis operantis*) seems to me a failure to grasp the full implications of this fact. For the secular world has a meaning only inasmuch as it constitutes a *demand for meaning* over and against which man appears as a *giver of meaning:* man grants to it its human meaning. Because man's bodiliness relates him essentially and inextricably with the secular world, the ordering of the secular towards personal community with God, a relation not of necessity so far as the secular in itself is concerned, becomes of necessity owing to the orientation of the secular towards man. In virtue of the complementarity which exists between man and the world the destination of man living in dialogue with God may to some extent be termed the "proper end" of the secular itself. Hence the Christianization of work and of secular undertakings means giving full value to the secular— that is, fully recognizing the reality of the world, but as part of the integral communion of life with God. It means standing with God in the world.

In this manner the secular task of giving meaning becomes the embodiment of authentic love of God and authentic love of mankind: concrete charity or a theologal approach to existence. In and through the faithful, the secular task becomes an expression of God's redemptive love for humanity in the historically visible form of secular readiness to serve mankind. For it is a partnership in the creative activity of the God who saves, and not only in that of an abstract "creator God." Hence the intramundance order of life differs considerably, according to whether it is the incarnation of the man who is in communion with God or of one whose life is attuned exclusively to an intramundane wavelength. The two forms differ, even though, so far as their structure in itself is concerned, they are subject to the same laws. We might say as a rough comparison to illustrate this point that an animal and a human being each have a face, but we should only speak of a facial expression, the reflection of a deeper sphere of life, in the case of man. In the secular sphere we cannot speak of monopolies by Christianity, nor, on the other hand, by exclusively secular humanity. The secular task is an appeal directed to man as such, and anyone sensitive to human reality can participate in it. The man bound in grace to God is still a citizen of this secular home: he may not permit this to be taken over by a purely intramundane mankind. Both stand on their own ground; neither the believer nor the atheist is an outsider here. [1958]

71/ The Church and the Secular City

Jesus' death was, after all, not a "liturgical cultic mustery," set aside from the world, but a personal offering of his own life, made in a historical context, a coming together of conflicting situations in this world with the leaders of his people. This secular event, an incident in Jesus' complete life in the world, was later expressed, in the letter to the Hebrews especially, in themes taken from the Old Testament liturgy of sacrificial worship, but this should not cause us to forget that this event was not in the first place a liturgical sacrifice that took place alongside real life in the world, but a sacrificial act in a concrete, living situation. Christ's death, in other words, was not a liturgical flight from the world, but in the deepest sense, his immersion to the very depths of his being as a person in human life in the world, a radical love for men, only intelligible in its completely radical character in the light of the love of God himself for men. We celebrate and give thanks for this event in Jesus' life that was accomplished so radically in the world in the liturgy of the church, but we do so in order to draw from this celebration the strength to be able to experience our life in this world in giving ourselves radically and caring radically for our fellow men in a radical love that is only intelligible in the light of God's absolute love for us. This is the basic intuition of the pastoral constitution, clearly revealed by the fact that, in the middle of a discussion of the "church in the modern world," the eucharist is seen as the earnest money given to Christians in their commitment to the building up of life within this world (38).

Another perspective is revealed by the fact that Jesus' followers did not themselves choose the name of "Christian." It was non-Christians who discussed something of that which had inspired Christ himself in certain people and therefore called them "Christians." Authentic Christians are people in whose lives the Spirit of Christ himself is visible— "See how they love one another." In the early church, this visible love functioned within the early image of man and the world. How must it function today? In other words, what is the relationship between Christian love and the building up of a better world for men to live in? Quite correctly, the pastoral constitution warns us of two dangers; firstly, the danger of our not taking, as Christians, the building of a better future on earth seriously and, secondly, the danger of our identifying, in an un-Christian way, a self-made future with the kingdom of God. Because of the promise of the kingdom of God, the Christian is, in his commitment to this world, placed in the very center of the mystery—every result achieved in this world is always questioned because of Christian hope for the *eschaton*, yet this commitment to the world is never in vain. There is a tension between relativization and radicalization in the Christian commitment to the building of a better future on earth. I should like to conclude by throwing some light on this tension.

Every project to build a better future for man on earth has to come to terms with the problem of death, otherwise a utopia is planned without regard to real facts. The fact of death makes relative all attempts to build a better world for man to live in. On earth, humanization has no definitive shape or form which can ultimately be called Christian in content. The Christian hope for the *eschaton* and faith in an eschatological "new world," in which death no longer has any place, makes all humanization here on earth and all man's building of a "secular city" relative. It is clear that the council understood this from the section in the pastoral constitution referring to the need to include all activity within the world in the mystery of Easter (38). The ultimate world that is fully worthy of man can only be given to us as a gift of God beyond the frontiers of death, that is, in the act in which we ultimately confess our impotence to make this world truly human, in our explicit and effective recognition that the "new world" cannot be the result of human planning, but must be a pure gift of God. It is only when man surrenders completely to God that any real future lies ahead of him.

But, however fundamentally Christian this view may be, it is still not the whole of Christianity. If this—authentically Christian—aspect alone is emphasized, the objection raised by all those who are ready to lay down their lives in order to banish injustice and discrimination from the world of men still remains valid, namely, as Merleau-Ponty observed, if it ever comes to the point where there must be a revolution in order to banish injustice from the world, we can never rely on Christians, because they relativize every commitment to the world. This is a very real objection and, what is more, one which is not closely examined in the pastoral constitution.

Any attempt to answer this objection would in the first place have to throw a much clearer light on the fact that the Christian relativization of man's commitment to this world is not inspired by a flight from this world, nor is it prompted by a conviction that grace enjoys an absolute priority. The Christian makes this commitment to the world relative precisely because he hopes for an eschatological completion, in which man will possess himself and the world completely in a radical giving of himself. This hope for a "new world" makes every result achieved on this earth in the process of humanization relative because the result achieved is not yet and cannot be this hoped for "new world." In the past, Christians drew the wrong conclusion from this correct assumption, namely, that they had to be indifferent or even hostile to the building of a better world on earth. In fact, however, the only correct conclusion is that Christians can never reconcile themselves to an already "established order" in the world, because it can never be Christian in content. In this sense, there is no such thing as a "Christian" social order, civilization or policy. What is precisely Christian in this context is the constant striving to go beyond the result achieved, the refusal to say, "the result is satisfactory and everything is now in order." Christianity is therefore the confirmation of a future which always remains open and this openness is not a static datum or a purely theoretical statement, but an active commitment to a better future.

The change that was made in the original text of the pastoral constitution from "the form of this world, insofar as it is characterized by sin, *will* pass" into the final version, "is already passing," was quite justified. This passing of the form of the world does not, however, occur automatically, but through eschatological hope, which is already working for a better world here on earth. This may seem to some people to be an unjustified leap in the train of thought. But in this case they are forgetting the precise content of the "veiled relationship" between man's future on this earth and the eschatological future as affirmed by the Council. This relationship certainly cannot be determined more precisely. Precisely because the Christian believes in an absolute future, the future which is God himself for man, he cannot describe the precise shape of this future meaningfully—any more than the non-Christian can—and he can never confuse or identify the result of man's historical striving on earth with the promised "new world." After all, if God is the intangible, incomprehensible mystery and man is embraced by this mystery, then man's being is, by definition, also a mystery that cannot be comprehended by faith. But Christian hope in God, which is man's future, is not a theory, but an active hope, which only becomes a reality in man's working for a better future on earth, in other words, in his care for his fellow men in concrete situations in this world. This radical commitment to our fellow men is an incomprehensible love and this love, because it is incomprehensible, makes the commitment completely radical. We do not know where this love is leading us, but we do know that it is not ultimately meaningless and will not be in vain. This makes Christian love incomprehensible for the world. It makes our commitment to this world thematically incomprehensible even to us Christians—we are a mystery even to ourselves and have, in all simplicity, to confess this to our "non-Christian" fellow men when they ask us why we are committing ourselves to life in this world. This thematic incomprehensibility, however, does not mean that we commit ourselves any less to the world. On the contrary, it makes this commitment completely radical. Our commitment as Christians to our fellow men is completely radical because it is the other side of the coin of God's personal love for man. This commitment is radical because, even though it is not possible to realize here on earth a world that is truly worthy of man, it continues to work, in complete surrender to faith, towards a situation that is more and more human. It is hope against hope, a hope against all despair that comes from our human experience, which continues to suggest that all our attempts to build a better world are in vain. The radical character of this Christian commitment and of the surrender to faith cannot be justified in the light of purely human experience. It is, of its very nature, a hoping in God (explicitly or implicitly) as the future for man. It is possible that many Christians have not yet drawn all these conclusions from the radical nature of this view and that they are consequently still hesitant in their attitude towards the social and political dynamism of the modern age and the struggle to build a world that is more worthy of man. They may therefore feel too satisfied in their own welfare state, while more than half of the world is still hungering and thirsting for a strict minimum of human dignity.

Nowadays, Christianity is discovering the "political" dimension of Christian charity and the worldly dimensions of Christianity. The inspiration here comes from the present situation in the world and from contact with the Bible and especially with the Old Testament. In the past, Christians tended to live in a separate little world of the spirit, where God and the "soul" of man made asides to each other. The Bible, however, teaches us that God is active in the whole world of men and that the church is called to share in this activity of God in the world itself. In this age, God seems to be accomplishing more through men like Martin Luther King, for example, than through the church. As Harvey Cox so rightly said, "We Christians have been a very talkative people, talkative to the point of verbosity." We Christians used to interpret the world differently from non-Christians, but we did not transform it—and this is what really matters. The church must show what the future world will be. And here we are confronted with the mystery of Christianity, which relativizes and at the same time radicalizes man's work for a better world here on earth. The church therefore has to stimulate us continuously to transcend ourselves. In her liturgy, she has to celebrate the unnamed future, while, in the world, she has to prepare for this future. Non-Christians often leap into the breach to bring the biblical *šālôm* into the world, while Christians are conspicuous by their absence. On the other hand, those Christians who are actively beginning to make this secular dimension of Christianity really true are quickly characterized as "social gospel" Christians. Of course, their emphasis is often one-sided because of their reaction to the "unworldly" church, just as, in the past, a one-sided stress was placed on the cultic aspects of the church. It is above all the task of theologians to draw attention to every one-sided emphasis, whether his words are welcome or not. He has, for example, to warn Christians if the radicalization of their commitment to this world is correctly taken into account, but the relativization of this commitment is suppressed, so that the absolute character of man's history here on earth is disregarded and man himself is ultimately misrepresented. On the other hand, however, every period in human history calls for its special emphases. And then we may ask ourselves whether Christians ought not to be on the side of the great social, economic and political revolutions which are taking place in the modern world, not simply going along, as critics, with the revolutions, but as people taking (a critical) part in them. In this case, the real demand made by the present situation in the world may be for Christians to stress, perhaps one-sidedly, this worldly dimension of Christianity. The dangers inherent in such a necessary, but one-sided emphasis must therefore be obviated by an equally one-sided emphasis on contemplative monastic life (in a new form), which is also equally necessary to the totality of Christianity.

Both its relativization and its radicalization of all commitment to man in this world characterize Christianity as a radical self-emptying. In this sense, Christianity is a radically committed love which cannot justify itself, which has again and again to transcend its achievement in this world and which has again and again to give itself away in profound darkness in a self-emptying which often seems to be in vain in this world, but which is nonetheless so radical that it is precisely in this giving away of itself for the benefit of others that the very essence of the kingdom of God breaks through into our world. But this is already the kingdom of God itself—only the form of this present world passes, nothing of what has been achieved in the world by man's radical love for his fellow men. All this implies faith in the absolute God, whose being is the negation of everything that seems to be in vain. Everything that seems, from the human point of view, to be in vain is made mean-ingful and not ultimately in vain by faith in the absolute God and, in this faith, man is not an anonymous element in history and does not, as is affirmed by an authentically atheistic commitment to a better world, pass forever into oblivion. But, for man, this Christian attitude is a mystery that cannot be rationalized. It is an active surrender to the mystery of God and therefore to the mystery of man. It is a mystery which, as God's "Amen" or "Yes" (2 Cor 1:20) to man, appeared in a veiled form in the man Jesus, the Christ. The Christian does not flee from the world, but flees with the world towards the future. He takes the world with him towards the absolute future which is God himself for man. [1967]

72/ *Redemption and Human Emancipation*

Now it is essential for Christianity oriented on the gospel that it should encounter any culture (even its own—and even the cultural expressions of its own content of faith and church organization) in the light of the eschatological proviso (implication of faith in Jesus as an eschatological event). However, it is precisely this proviso that has its own special influence on culture. In Christianity, which people rightly experience as a unity of the religious and the secular, there is nevertheless an essential tension between the specifically religious focal point which is expressed in appropriate symbols (and in so doing is an essential element in forming a church and, in this sense, even forming a particular culture, for every specifically human expression is of a cultural kind), and the so-called derived religious element (i.e., the whole life of man in the world and society), whereas the whole forms a single integrated life. This double aspect cannot be avoided.

Without being specifically Christian, an emancipatory process of liberation can still be essential for Christianity, i.e., it can be a specific and historically necessary form of Christian love, faith and hope. Indeed, at a particular historical moment it can be a criterion of Christian authenticity, namely as a historical form of one of the fundamental criteria of the Christian religion: love of men. Whatever feature of empirical Christianity contradicts the demands of collective and personal human liberation must therefore be rejected in the name of Christian faith itself. Furthermore, the (critical) solidarity of Christians with the emancipating process of liberation must not be made dependent on the real chances of Christian proclamation or evangelization. Even when the church itself has no use for it, it has the duty to espouse the cause of men deprived of their rights, to press for a minimum of human salvation. The believer and the Christian may see the limits of such self-liberation *in principle*, but this is not to deny the Christian legitimacy of the process of emancipatory liberation. However, every believer will oppose in principle any totalitarian claim to emancipatory self-liberation. In view of men's transitoriness and the fact that "as humanity," they can only be the *theme* and *not the universal subject* of history, total liberation is, moreover, suspect and alienating for them, and at best only partial liberation. It limits and reduces humanity, and this *ipso facto* has an alienating effect. In contemporary situations, the impossibility of a total, universal and final liberation through emancipation is the context in which the *question* of the ultimate meaning of human life can be put. Thus a fundamental question mark is set against the project of emancipation, a question mark which goes with the dynamics of any historical process of emancipation. It is not a question of temporary limitations, but of impassable ones. In this situation there are no longer any alternatives apart from the *religious* answer: redemption or salvation from God.

Of course even non-believers must recognize the absoluteness of this basic question, but for them it is more in accord with human dignity to recognize its limitations with open eyes (when they do this), rather than exceeding them in the direction that they call the illusion of religion. However, it is striking that this theory of life is put forward by people who "fortuitously" live on this, the Western side of our world, where people enjoy the greatest prosperity and where there is abundant possibility to transform the experience that our history is a mixture of meaning and meaninglessness above all into personally meaningful experiences. "Fortuitously" they do not live on the other side, where meaninglessness, slavery and suffering determine the existence of many people. In other words, one can ask whether such a project, which "reconciles" itself with our history as a mixture of meaning and meaninglessness, of sorrow and happiness, adequately takes into account the *suffering of others*. Does it not remove an essential part of our real problem of suffering? The question then arises whether such a concept of life, whether deliberate or unconscious, is not a egotistical view of life. At all events, the human experience of the mixture of meaning and meaninglessness which makes up our life raises the question whether in the last resort we can trust life. Is not our history cause for lament? Is there any kind of total meaning? For to evade the question of meaning, redemption and total liberation is certainly not liberation. The history of human suffering, our human experience, compels us to put this question. The nonbeliever rejects the *religious* answer to this question because he sees a projection in the answer: the wish as father to the thought. But he himself does not give any answer. The believer has the experience of religious affirmation, an interpretative experience. So in present circumstances the religious problem stands very urgently in the center of the emancipatory process of self-liberation, as a liberating human impulse which can only lead to partial, non-universal and provisional results, and in the last result finds itself confronted not only with the failure of any liberation which seeks to be total and universal, but also with the *alienating* character of any claim to total liberation. Such a total project unleashes enslaving and irrational forces.

Therefore the history of emancipation *cannot be identified* with the history of redemption from God, nor can the latter be detached from human liberation. For salvation from God is always salvation *for men* with all that that implies for truly human life—given the anthropological constants. Here the fundamental problem remains the reality of the human history of suffering, which even *remains* firm in an allegedly successful process of emancipation and is not just an ingredient of the "pre-history" of mankind before emancipation (an aspect to which J.-B. Metz in particular has rightly called attention). Salvation cannot therefore be found *outside* suffering. Emancipatory liberation outside a perspective on religious redemption therefore takes on problematical and dangerous dimensions because it becomes blind to real aspects of human life and in this way reduces men. The history of freedom *remains* a history of suffering. That is a reality of being human which is taken seriously by religious soteriologies. Christian redemption is something more than emancipatory liberation, though it shows critical solidarity towards that. [1977]

73/ Church, Religion, and World

Religions, and the church, are not salvation, but "sacrament" of the salvation which God completes in the world of his creation. Precisely because one does not put the church "in its place," and then in the place where it belongs, and forget the basic datum about salvation being carried out in the world, the churches often become sectarian, clerical and apolitical. Religions and churches are in the order of sign or sacrament of salvation. They are an explicit naming of this salvation. They are themselves places of concentrated salvation. In that sense the church is the truth of the world, not its substance. Churches are places where salvation coming from God is thematized or put into words, expressly confessed, prophetically proclaimed, and liturgically celebrated. They are the hermeneutical key or code for reading world history and for bringing it to greater completion. Thus there is an indissoluble bond between religion and world. God cannot be reached outside his own manifestations and he never coincides with any one of them. Thus there is a necessary conjunction between appearance and obscurement. That is why it is indeed possible to forget God and to be silent about him. Now religions and the church are precisely the *anamnēsis*, the memory of this universal salvific will and saving presence of God, ground of all hope. The churches keep that universal saving presence from lapsing into oblivion, thanks to their religious word and sacrament.

But if religion is then dependent upon world history and what happens there, then it cannot itself exhibit God outside that history. God's absolute saving presence in the story and praxis of human history is thematized, proclaimed, practiced and celebrated in religions, in the churches, as grace. The condition upon which the church's language about God is possible is therefore the veiled appearance of God in world events, and the obscurement of that presence makes this religious language necessary. Churches understand themselves incorrectly if (a) they do not understand themselves as related to the experienced events of the world, and (b) they think they can neglect the specific religious forms of word and sacrament because they have interpreted the world event.

Churches do not possess any "autarchic" independence; they live from the salvation which God brings about in the world. Their religious symbols mediate for us the veiled saving presence of God in history. But the godness of God is that God's proviso holds therefore for the world, as it does for the church as sacrament of the world. Church is the thankful welcoming of the coming God. The religious word and sacrament do not make the experience of the events of the world superfluous, just as the so-called events happening outside in the events of the world do not make speaking in the language of faith superfluous. Historical praxis in the world is therefore not to be separated from proclamatory, sacramental, and ecclesial activity. To speak as confessing is therefore not a speaking on one's own accord, but rather a grace-filled response to that which precedes all speech: God's activity in history. God himself is the pre-given source of all speaking about God. We have God to thank for our confessing him, a God who has spoken to us. That is why the churches are in essence churches which speak *to* God, praying communities of faith, and not just one or the other protest group. The praxis of the church is the doing of the story it tells, especially in the liturgy. It may also be called characteristic that Jesus, who emphasized this universal salvific will the most forcefully, was himself condemned to the cross by a worldly, profane judgment. In that sense the central point of reference of the Christian churches is a historical, profane event which they, with right, celebrate liturgically. Thus the free being of God is inexhaustible promise for humanity. His name is promise.

The indefinable aspect of definitive salvation and eschatological freedom, i.e., of a *humanum* or humanity sought, but ever found only partially and continually threatened, can therefore only be brought to words in symbolic language: in speaking in parables and metaphors, which reach further than the acute pitifulness of our defined concepts. Three great metaphors, expressed in many sounds and tongues in the Jewish and Christian Bible, suggest to us the direction this *humanum* will take: (a) the definitive salvation or radical liberation of humanity to a brotherly and sisterly community of life and society where master—slave relationships no longer reign, where every pain and tear are wiped away and forgotten is called there *the reign of God*. (b) The complete salvation and happiness of the individual person (called body or flesh in the Bible) are called the *resurrection of the body* by the Christian tradition of faith, i.e., the resurrection of the human person even in human bodiliness, the visible orchestration, the individual melody of a person which others enjoy as well. (c) Finally, the completion of the unblemished "ecological life environment" vitally necessary for people is suggested by the great metaphor of *"the new heaven and the new earth."*

These three metaphorical visions of the human future prepared by God give orientation already now to the activity of Christians in the world. And it is not unspecific or undirected, but is given a very definite direction by the dynamic of those symbols and metaphors: concern for a better society for all, especially for the outcast, the marginalized, the oppressed; both a pastoral strategy of communication and an unrelenting critique of where injustice is evident in society; concern for human bodiliness, for psychic and social health; concern for the natural living environment of people; concern for the integral attitude of Christian faith, Christian hope and Christian love; concern for meaningful liturgical prayer of thanksgiving and praise; concern for the genuine Word and the meaningful sacrament; finally, concern for individual pastoral care, especially for the lonely and those "who have no hope." In short, a church truly remains a gathering of people around Jesus Messiah and thus, as a human community at the same time, a "community of God." [1983]

2

Christian Praxis in the World

This section continues some of the themes of the previous one, focusing now on the issue of individual and collective behavior in the world. Selection 74 is a complex discussion of ethics. It begins by looking at the nature of ethics in general, what can be religious in ethics, and to what extent the New Testament can be a source of Christian ethics. From there it moves into the eschatological framework and questions of God's proviso as a basis for looking at political activity.

Selection 75 picks up this concern about politics and tries to explore it further. Selection 76 returns to a theme often found in Schillebeeckx's writing about Christian praxis: the relation between inner holiness and political activity. In this selection Schillebeeckx proposes a "political holiness" as a way of being Christian in the world.

74/ Religions and Ethics

I am of the opinion that *ethical* as well as *religious* life is grounded in the same general human primal faith or primal trust for which the philosopher can adduce *good cause* on the basis of human experiences, but nevertheless in such a way that the primal trust cannot be accounted for purely rationally or theoretically. *In humanibus humaniter!* To wish for more than that seems to be human megalomania to me. An ultimate theoretical grounding would be, in a Hegelian sense, the *Aufhebung* or rational annihilation of all religiosity in the *concept* or in philosophy, so that the symbolic, metaphorical and narrative *representations* of religious language of faith would be definitively surpassed. This is neither philosophically nor theologically acceptable; it would rob our life also of its character of risk and adventure.

Believers would add that, if we are creatures of God, then the mystery of reality is the ground, the source and also the condition of possibility of all our rationality, but as such never fully accounted for. And philosophically we have good reasons for saying the same thing, even if not with the explicitly religious, metaphorical concept of creation, then with consciousness: that in our human experience something is shown to us which is not the product of our own planning, defining and projecting, but stands over against all our planning, defining and projecting, and can even knock these to pieces or give them a new direction. *Summa summarum:* we have good reasons to consider ourselves ultimately bound to live ethically: for the sake of the good, even if that which we call good here and now is accounted for not *a priori* but "empirically" within a concrete struggle for a hierarchy of values. Concretely, the final concern is not so much the ultimate grounding of our entire ethical behavior (all the participants in the discussion accept at least some value), as it is above all the question of which value shall have priority over the others. That absolute knowledge cannot be attained still does not give occasion to deny the possibility of reasoned speaking about ethical questions and conflicts of value. . . .

Ethics is concerned with both the inner attitude as well as the concrete activity of people, which is intended to be the concrete embodiment of this basic attitude or ethical dispostion. Two categories of ethical norms follow immediately from this: (1) *formal norms,* that is, general, dynamic directives which tell us we must promote the *humanum* and not try to slow it down; (2) *material norms,* that is, norms through which—that is, through the mediation of a culturally previously given image of the human and through the historically conditioned activity of people with the many-sided situation of the world—this formal ethical intention is embodied in time and space, and receives its concrete context.

One can say (with the entirety of human history in mind) that the "formal norms" are, and have been, always and everywhere valid. For example, even in the most primitive society, the principle of being just to one's fellow human being holds. Therein lies the absolute, immutable character of those formal norms. Because of the prevailing image of the human, for example, in a primitive clan, this principle has an absolute validity for the fellow human being. However, only a member of the clan is such a human being, not anyone else. The latter is "not human" in this sense, much as at one time colored people did not count as human for white people, in the white sense of the word. The material concretization of a formal norm, which is held to be unassailable, is therefore itself already relative; it is historically and culturally conditioned. But within this cultural relativity the fundamental human ethical pathos is indeed at work. Precisely for this reason I call this a formal norm, that is, the *forma*, the soul and energy of every basic ethical attitude, always and everywhere. But in concrete sociohistorical formation, this absolute claim appears historically conditioned and relative, that is, contingent on the prevailing image of the human and contingent historical situations.

In contrast to the absolutely valid "formal norms," all concrete material norms are therefore relative, historically conditioned and mutable. Although the formal norm only gains validity concretely in the material norms, which thereby participate in the absolute character of the formal norms, namely, promotion of the *humanum* and the checking and avoiding of all those things which do it damage, these material norms count only as conditioned. Why? Because our concrete human activity is *ambivalent*. This activity has to do with a reality in which premoral values and dysvalues are the order of the day. On the one hand: life, physical and psychic health, social well-being, eros, friendship, art, science and so on; on the other hand: hunger and thirst, illness, suffering, death, war, violence, ignorance, pollution, and so on. These values and dysvalues are premoral, with the accent on both the "pre" and the "moral." They are (1) *pre*-moral, because they—in or from themselves—are not moral activities and therefore cannot be called either moral or immoral (being sick or poor is not a personal vice); (2) pre-*moral*, because it is of decisive moral importance how we, in our disposition and our activity, comport ourselves toward these values and dysvalues. . . .

The ethical has essentially to do with the question: "What really is human being?", and because of this, with the question "How does one want to ultimately live out one's being human?" or "For which way of being human does one finally decide?" But in spite of the pluralism in religion and world view one must respond, here and now, to the concrete inner claim and to the call of the ethical situation: this human, here and now, and in our times: this humanity must, in view of its situation of need, be helped forcefully and immediately (directly intersubjectively and through structures). Ethics has for this reason the character of the utmost necessary urgency which cannot wait until a unanimity about ultimate questions of life has been reached. This ethical commission is for this reason not an abstract norm, but historically a challenging *event:* our concrete history itself—people in need, humanity in need. Ethics has to do concretely with redemption and liberation.

As to the specific content of the New Testament ethical norms, nowhere can one actually find a unitary concept in the New Testament, as is the case for the New Testament conceptions of soteriology and grace. Nonetheless ethical guidelines and exhortations take up a good deal of space in the New Testament literature, so much so that, were the ethical texts taken out of the Pauline corpus, it would only be half as long as it now is. But the ethics there comes out only from a religious and eschatological background.

Religion is "not only" ethics and cannot be reduced to ethics. On the other hand there exists an inner connection between religion and ethics.

Ethics needs a different language game from that of religion. The understanding of good and evil precedes logically the understanding of God and the doing of his will. That means that we cannot, in the first instance, define our moral duties in concepts of God and his will. On the other hand, what one has learned to perceive as good and evil can and may be seen by the believing person as the will of his or her God. . . .

The ethical possesses a certain autonomy, although the believing or religious person sees the deepest grounding, source and basis of the ethical in the reality of God. Beyond that the Christian sees autonomous morality in the context of the praxis appropriate to the demands of the reign of God: of the God mindful of humanity, whose honor lies in the happiness of people, that is, it lies in people mindful of him and of humanity.

Even when their fundamental inspiration comes from a religious belief in God, ethical norms—that is, norms promoting human dignity in an intersubjective discussion accessible to all reasoning people—must be rationally grounded. None of the participants in the discussion can hide behind an "I can see what you don't see" and then require others to accept this norm straight out.

If we speak of a specifically Christian ethics, we do not mean an ethics specific alone and only to Christianity. One perhaps goes from a Christian interpretation to a certain judgment and ethical praxis. But this ethical insight can be mediated and universalized, that is, the ethical content itself is then accessible to non-Christians as well.

But cannot one say that love is the basic ethical principle of the New Testament? Certainly. But this love is precisely *theologal* love, that is, the love of God and of neighbor as one and the same divine virtue. *Agape* in the New Testament is actually love of neighbor as grounded in faith in God (*pistis tou theou*) and experienced in Christ. "Be doers of the word and not just hearers" (Jas 1:22) "who will be blessed through his works" (Jas 1:25c). "Those who believe in God must strive to be the first in every good work. That is a matter of honor for them, and the world will profit from it" (Titus 3:8). But the factual and material norms in the Bible have only a historical significance for us; that is, to help discover the state of moral insights and judgments in New Testament Christianity.

This does not always make them suitable for a hermeneutical or actualizing interpretation. That would be a biblical fundamentalism. The Bible does not know any autonomous ethics in our sense of the word; that we have to concede. The New Testament *theologal* basic principle and principle of unity, love, is concretized in the New Testament through the mediation of the prevailing ethics of that time, which was of Old Testament and Stoic origin. . . .

The ethical life in its microethical dimension is concretely the *recognizable* content of salvation, the historical manifestation or becoming visible of the approaching reign of God. The religious is manifested *also* in the ethical, and transforms then the merely rational meaning of the ethos. The reign of God becomes present, therefore, also via the prevalent ethic, in our history, in non-definitive, ever to be superseded forms. Ethical betterment of human life and the world *is* not the reign of God (any more than the church is), but it is however its anticipatory form. Salvation in the sense of "what makes 'whole,'" universal and complete, needs (as a minimal presupposition) social, societal and political institutions, which do not make one group "whole" at the cost of another. If these minimal presuppositions are not granted in the Christian concept of salvation, then there exists no possibility of establishing eschatological salvation *positively* in relation to human efforts for justice and peace between social groups. The Christian concept of salvation loses its rational sense; i.e., it cannot be a concept of *salvation* from a rational perspective, if no *positive* relation exists between (to put it biblically) "justification through faith alone" and the human ethos, that is, finally, between justice and the peace of the world. . . .

Earlier, but also modern ethics of natural law presupposes that "order" is naturally pre-given; that therefore we discover it and from this follows the commandment not to do it injury. This conception proceeds all too matter-of-factly from an order already established in the good, which then may not be disturbed. But if we look more closely, we see that the concrete historical point of departure of every ethic is not some previously given order, but an already damaged human condition: disorder, both in one's heart as well as in society. The threatened *humanum*, in point of fact already damaged, leads concretely and historically to the ethical challenge and to the ethical imperative in confrontation with very definite, negative contrast experiences. The "ethically good" is consequently—concretely—that which overcomes evil; it is that which "makes good," in the double sense of the word: (a) what brings about the realization of the good, and thereby (b) straightens out the old, the bad, the crooked, bringing it again into order and renewing it. In other words, making good in the sense of liberation and reconciliation.

Orthopraxis in this sense is a fundamental hermeneutical principle, a preunderstanding, in which the actualizing interpretation of the Christian message becomes concretely and meaningfully possible. The religious position is, as a matter of fact, subject to suspicion of ideology if it is socially, politically and personally neutral in ethical matters. If therefore that which is pre-given to faith—namely, the human as a subject who hears the gospel in a concrete situation—is not reflected upon and kept in mind in theology as such, Christian faith becomes unworthy of credence and unintelligible. An ethic, as the situation of the (believing) person, has therefore also a hermeneutical or interpretive function in the theological self-understanding of Christian faith. . . .

If one were only to attend to the proviso of God, without considering along with it the concrete content of belief in God, especially the content of Christian belief in God, directed to Jesus Christ, the eschatological proviso could acquire an extremely reactionary function, to the detriment of human persons. For God's proviso lies over our entire human history and over all which humanity brings about within it. All political options are hereby relativized. But that means then, that if this real aspect of the revelation of God is taken *in* itself, without taking into consideration what has been brought about for us in Jesus, this eschatological proviso can relativize every worldly activity in such a way that a conservative social policy as well as a policy calling for more justice for all can both equally be neutralized. Christian faith would then not only desacralize human justice and take from the threat its absolute character— herein lies the special right and the meaning of the eschatological proviso or the freedom of God's being God—but it would of itself be unable to give any inspiration at all, and above all any *orientation* (pointing in a very *definite* direction) in the choice of a socioeconomic policy to promote a growing and realizable humanity. God could then just as well—that is, equally—appear as "salvation" in the maintaining and the renewing of the world as in its suffering, its enslavement and its demise. The correct Christian confession—that for believers (looking up to the cross of Jesus) demise, disaster and suffering can in fact be the *form of salvation*, sign of the silent presence of God—can then in reality be misused politically to shore up and continue actual oppression. With a merely formal eschatological proviso the humanitarian impulse present in freedom movements would be snuffed out from the very beginning, while at the same time because of keeping quiet God's proviso would obviously not be allowed to prevail against the status quo. That is then the political consequence (and silently often the intent) of calling upon the eschatological proviso in social and political questions.

The *content* of the confession of God codetermines therefore the concrete directed activity of Christians in the world. If one actually proceeds from what is the case in primitive and many other religions, that God is ground and source of all positivity as well as all negativity—a God who causes things to die and makes them alive—then religion indeed does not possess any critical and productive power at all for acting toward the salvation of people in personal, physical, medical, economic, social, educational, etc., areas. Human life and history are indeed ambivalent, so that seldom can it be conclusively said what lies on the side of life and what on the side of destruction, death, and decline. But ambiguity is not the same as neutrality. If justice as well as injustice, joy as well as anxiety *equally* had their ground and source in God, it would be futile and meaningless for a believing person to want to change anything about this. But precisely because of the special critical and cognitive power of human experiences of suffering, many true believers would reject such a concept of God. Such a concept of God has, however, as a consequence that "God has willed the structures of society as they are," then he has willed equally masters and slaves, oppressor and oppressed, and has held the family of the holy hierarchy together in the universe through command and obedience. In any event what proceeds from this is that religion is *always* politically relevant. But this relevance is not being discussed here. The sole decisive question is: Which kind of sociopolitical relevance does religion assign to itself, which kind of social and humanly relevant politics does it want to advocate and which kind does it want to hinder?

But the God of Christians is "not a God of the dead, but a God of the living" (Matt 22:32). In other words, *this* concept of God ascribes to him only and solely positivity: "God is love" (1 John 4:10, 16), who is according to his being a promotor of the good and an opponent of everything evil. And then for the believer who wishes to follow after God the *orientation* for all activity can only lie in the promotion of the good and in the resistance to evil, injustice and suffering in all its forms. This conception of God, which is not given to us in a general concept of God derived from the study of religions, but from and in Jesus of Nazareth, mediates to the Christian a very definite orienting direction for action (within what I have called the seven anthropological coordinates). Then the believer has the duty in faith to promote that which is good and true for realizable humanity, and to fight energetically against everything which does harm to persons in their bodiliness, which weighs down their psychic lives, which humiliates them as persons, which enslaves them in social structures, which through irrationality drives them into irresponsible adventurism, which makes the free exercise of their religiosity impossible, and finally, everything which curbs their human rights and, through working conditions and bureaucracy, turns them into objects. This productive and critical impulse of Christian belief in God, for both activity healing to humanity as well as for a goal-directed sociopolitical praxis for a better future for humanity, does not, for its part, neutralize the eschatological proviso. The eschatological proviso even then remains critical and productive because humanity is not the subject of a universal providence; so therefore the illusions, disappointments and failures can, despite all efforts and resistance, finally be entrusted to God, the sole subject of universal providence. God's proviso shows itself precisely in humanity itself not being the universal subject of history, and that in humanity's temporal providence being transcended by the Lord of history. . . .

Grace gives to the human ethos, which becomes the historical form of a praxis commensurate to the reign of God, an even greater, better future. No matter how serious it may be, Christian ethics will never become grim if it is to remain Christian. Ethics as such often has a difficult time in *forgiving;* powerlessness to forgive. There are in fact cases in which our feeling for what is human is so fundamentally injured that we are ethically powerless to grant forgiveness. Peter Berger says "There are deeds which cry out to heaven, and therefore to hell." A fundamental, non-restitutable transgression of humanity does not permit any relativity: then there exists the "impossibility of forgiveness." But the question is whether this judgment and this condemnation are permitted to *us*. Damnation—*if* it is to be concretely realized—is more than the deed of people closed to love and even to forgiveness than it is a positive act of God, let alone that *we* can or dare pronounce a definitively condemning judgment. God loved us *"even when we were still sinners"* (Rom 5:8). That is why God's mercy is greater than all evil in the world. Ethics disappears into the religious, finally into the mystery of God "who is love" (1 John 4:8, 16). Through this elevation of the ethical into mystery the manifold human concern for the future of a good, true, free and happy humanity in the most just social structures possible is in no way neutralized; on the contrary, it is radicalized. At the same time this elevation is a critique of all schemes to identify salvation exclusively with political self-liberation; to identify salvation exclusively with "being nice to one another"; exclusively with the ecological efforts; exclusively with either micro- or macro-ethics, or with mysticism, liturgy and prayer; exclusively with pedagogical, adult learning, or gerontological techniques of education, etc. And yet all these belong to the concept of salvation or being made whole *of people* and therefore have essentially to do with *salvation coming from God,* which may be experienced as grace.

What the elevation of the ethical into the religious will involve—in consideration of the spiritual openness and human self-transcendence yet to be historically realized, in consideration of the "in addition to that" of the absolute freedom of God as the "God of human beings," a God whose honor lies in human happiness—cannot now be defined in positive terms on the basis of our situation. Every positive definition runs the risk of either becoming humanly megalomaniac or curbing the possibilities of God. The Greek fathers especially spoke of a "divinization" of humans, in the sense of a grace-filled participation of humans in God's own life. But with that only the positive undefinability of the definitive future of human life from grace was brought to expression in other words. For we have no concept we can draw out of our continuing history of what *being human* can ultimately mean; nor an unhistorical workable concept of what God's *being God* (as salvation for human beings) precisely means. "Divinization of human beings through grace" therefore means nothing other than the positive undefinable fact that God is the *salvation of human beings*. Because of this the Old and New Testaments said: These are things, of which the scriptures say: "Eye has not seen, ear has not heard, nor has it entered into the human heart, what God has prepared for those who love him" (1 Cor 2:9; Isa 64:3; 65:17b). [1978]

75/ *Religion and Politics*

However, the key question is whether believers and non-believers do not in fact *do the same thing*, namely renew the world. Perhaps the believer is simply giving another *interpretation* of this common action which *qua* interpretation has no consequences for what is done. For religion cannot of itself make any contribution to a practice which is indifferent to *religious* or *non-religious* interpretations. It follows from this that the claim of a religion to perform a unique and irreducible service for the world becomes problematical and seriously ambiguous to the degree that this service is understood in terms of *non-religious* goals. And vice versa, the claim of religion to offer its *own* interpretation of the world becomes just as problematical and seriously ambiguous to the degree that this interpretation remains irrelevant for *action*. Thus when we have a course of action which is common to believers and non-believers, and moreover with different theoretical interpretations of the world, we have mistaken the particular critical impulse which issues from the religious consciousness. For religion is not an interpretation of the world which remains alien to practice, any more than it is a practice without any reference to a particular interpretation of man and the world. Therefore in reality we often have the following experience. To begin with, people talk of inspiration provided by the gospel which stimulates them towards solidarity with liberation movements (which are in fact socialist). In a second phase, people see more accurately the particular rationality of this emancipation. In a third phase, they recognize the priority of emancipation in their own rationality over the proclamation of the gospel; and in a last, fourth phase all this often ends up with the rejection of orientation on and inspiration from the gospel, as being irrelevant to liberation movements. This development, which can in fact often be noted, indicates that—although it is in fact possible to misuse religion, for anything at all—religion is *not usable* by nature, for anything at all. God cannot be used as a means for human ends, any more than man can be used as a means for divine ends. Religion and mankind transcend the category of the usable and the functional—which does not prevent religion in this respect being "highly functional" for the advancement of human dignity generally. For religions are not inner dispositions; they *bring salvation.* They bring *salvation for men.* Only if we recognize the particular critical and hermeneutical force and impulse of religion as religion, can religion (as inner fullness, implication and consequence) show a service to the world which is both *specifically religious* and *practically effective* in the world (in politics as well). If specifically religious interpretation-and-criticism is lost sight of, in other words, if religion is made to serve non-religious ends, then *either* religious means are offered as means for non-religious ends and in fact religion becomes magic, *or* religion is merely forced into the role of being a teacher and instructor in morality. (At an earlier stage, this morality was seen primarily as individual ethics, but now it is the macro-ethics of political and social society.) In other words, if religion enters the service of tasks imposed *from outside,* say by economic, social or political needs, it degenerates into magic, or it is undermined and reduced to mere ethics (though here it must remember that its specifically religious interest can be maintained only *within* the five *other* anthropological constants which were analyzed earlier). True, religion implies an ethically good attitude, but it cannot be reduced to ethics. The only difference from the earlier position would then be that the alien service of religion to the world formerly showed a right-wing and reactionary tendency, whereas now it follows a left-wing and revolutionary course. In both cases, then, we have forms and manifestations of an out-dated "Constantinian theology." In that case, the appeal to Christian faith is often to serve the ends of a right-wing or left-wing policy, or to benefit a shriveled, faceless party of the center; it is merely an alibi for the lack of *rational arguments.* Therefore theology must stress the *specifically religious* form of the criticism of man and

society; religion can do a service to the world in this respect if theologians do not just repeat and duplicate what critical sociologists have
already said (perhaps rightly), but draw on *an experience of the holy.*
Religions seek to bear witness to the holy, to God; it is there that they
find a legitimation for their language and action. In their *service to God,*
religions are also a *service to men.* If not, what we have is no more than
a mere idealistic duplication. For when we speak of religious consciousness (and its special critical force), we are speaking of a particular form
of human consciousness. And the question then is, "What is the *religious*
element in this consciousness?" In other words, we then ask what
knowledge and what reality so determine our consciousness that this
consciousness becomes a religious consciousness. And at the same time,
that means: how are we to judge the reality of man and the world in the
light of the religious consciousness? Religion is concerned not only with
God, but also with the *totality,* the support and hope of which is God.

Religion judges man and the world in the light of its experience of the
holy or the divine. Every religious statement about the holy is in fact
a statement about man and his world, but in the sense that every
religious statement about man and the world is in reality also a statement about the holy, about God. In other words, the religious understanding contains—as it were from the start—a particular, i.e., religious,
understanding of the world and of man. The question of God cannot
be separated from the question of the nature of man, which in the last
resort must also have a religious determination, so that man can be
wholly and completely man. Religion does in fact express the existence
of man and the world, but as an ambiguous manifestation of the holy,
and not otherwise (though this does not mean that we can reject non-
religious talk about the same phenomena). For the believer, man in the
world is the fundamental symbol of the holy, of God as the champion
of all good and the opponent of all evil, and therefore a manifestation
of God as grace and judgment. In order to be able to appear, the holy
must always conceal itself in images; it reveals itself in a veiled form in
such a way that the holy cannot be attained outside these manifestations,
although it is never itself identical with these manifestations. Therefore
there is a *necessary identity* between *manifestation* and *concealment.*
Religion under the aspect of a religious understanding of man and the
world is indebted to this structure for a particular religious symbolism
which, despite its special character, again points to the historical reality
of man in the world.

From this critical-hermeneutical relevance of the religious consciousness there emerges: (a) the impossibility for a believer in any way to
idealize any particular form of the world—past, present or future—giving

it the status of a healed or reconciled world. For everything is only a *manifestation* of God, and is never identical with the holy, as man's salvation. But (b) at the same time religion forbids any escapism, because for the believer everything, everywhere, can be a manifestation of the divine. Because of that, nothing can be underestimated: reality is never completely outside salvation, as long as God is still there. So religion opposes *any theory of identity,* any sacralizing or absolutizing of any politics, right-wing, left-wing or center, although political action is at the same time a *manifestation* of God among us for the good of men: indeed, concealment and manifestation are identical. In other words, religion, even Christian faith, is politically relevant, in that it opposes a *complete identification* of human salvation with politics. God's proviso, which for men takes the form of an eschatological proviso, makes it impossible for the believer to absolutize politics. Christianity *desacralizes* politics. For if the ground of the possibility of all existence lies in God, and on the other. hand our human existence is threatened, not only from outside (by nature, by fellow men and by society), but also most profoundly from within (through one's own permanent possibility of being able not to be), then salvation in the full sense of the word is possible only where man can entrust himself to the ground of the possibility of his existence, that is, to the renewal of life through the holy, which is veiled in this permanent crisis of existence. The critical consciousness peculiar to the religious consciousness knows the validity of everything secular, and at the same time its radical crisis. That makes it possible to turn to man and the world *without* divinizing the world or idealizing and making absolute any particular policy of liberation: it makes possible radical criticism of man and society and the furthering of their good *without* recourse to a dreamed-up state of salvation and without the fiction of a healed or reconciled world in the limits of our history: in part, present or future. Thus religion criticizes both the *status quo* and also the absolutizing of a mere political and social renewal which men must undergo whether they want to or not. Nevertheless, following the God who is concerned for humanity, it seeks to support and further *men who are concerned for men,* and therefore also structures which make this possible, support it and further it.

This criticism based on religion is in fact religion's contribution to the world, but it is a contribution in and through *service to God.* We shall have to keep this firmly in mind in subsequent analysis, if we want to be able to talk meaningfully in *theological* terms about human liberation and not repeat like Christian parrots (under the flag of theology) what people worth taking seriously have said long before. [1977]

76/ *The Christian Connection between Mysticism and Politics*

What at the moment is being discussed is not whether we are able to come to a view of transcendence from the cosmic world (nature) rather than from human subjectivity (which moreover is not a pure interiority). It seems to me that this position was clarified already by modernity. The question now is whether the praxis of liberation is not the preferred context in which a view of God, of transcendence is illuminated, especially of we mean by this "the God of Jesus."

Concepts such as mysticism and politics are ambivalent, even suspect. Let me therefore give a general definition for working purposes. "Mysticism" is an intense form of experience of God or love of God. "Politics" is an intense form of social engagement (thus not restricted to the political doings of professional politicians), an engagement accessible to anyone.

Political love, I have said, is a form of Christian love of neighbor alongside other possible and necessary forms of love of neighbor. Holiness is always "contextual." Given the current situation of *suffering humanity* which has now become conscious universally, political love can well become the historically urgent form of contemporary holiness, the historical imperative of the moment, or in Christian terms, the contemporary *kairos* or moment of grace as appeal to believers.

In the Jewish and Christian traditions of faith God is experienced as a God directed to human beings, who also wants human beings to be oriented to humanity. He is the advocate of the good and the opponent of evil. Christian talk about God corresponds, therefore, with talk about the universal ground of hope, a speaking about God's universal salvific will for the benefit of all people and—precisely in this matter—a preference for people at the greatest distance from this salvation, people kept small by their fellow human beings or by oppressive structures—the one lost sheep of the parable. And there are many of these. The memory of the life and execution of Jesus, and belief in his resurrection are therefore not only a liturgical act; they are at the same time a political deed. With the Jewish and Christian tradition of faith as a compass or divining rod, as it were, we can check out whether our profane history squares with salvation history as God intends it. And precisely in this contrast experience lies the possibility of a new experience of Transcendence. There are two facets to such an experience: (a) on the one hand, a person, especially someone poor and oppressed, and someone who has declared him- or herself in solidarity with these, experiences that God is *absent* in many human relationships of property and power in this world. Thus they experience alienation, the distance between God, the reign of God, and our society.

(b) On the other hand, the believer experiences precisely in political love and resistance against injustice an intense contact with God, the *presence* of the liberating God of Jesus. In modern times authentic faith by preference seems to be able to be nourished in and by a praxis of liberation. In that grows the realization that God reveals himself as the deepest mystery, the heart and soul of human liberation. To bring into concept or "understanding" that mystery, first enshrouded in every form of genuine activity liberating human beings, receives then its first expressed wording in its naming in the declaration of faith: You are the liberating God, not a God of the living and the dead, but a God who wants to give life! The discovery (also made possible by the searchlight which is the Jewish-Christian tradition) that God himself is the heart and source of all truly human liberation evokes praise and thanksgiving, a liturgical celebration of God as liberator, even before we are completely liberated and redeemed, for the basis and source of universal hope always precedes our activity. Thus the story went already in Israel, and the New Testament picks up this thread of the story again.

This form of political love and holiness gets its best chances precisely in our time. The times call for it, as it were, although we ourselves must interpret that voice. For "signs of the times" do not speak; we must cause them to do so. That political form of Christian love of God and neighbor, albeit in another area of experience, knows the same conversion and metanoia, the same ascesis and detachment from self, the same suffering and dark nights, the same losing of oneself in the other as was the case in contemplative mysticism in times past. Political holiness has today already even its own martyrs for the sake of justice among people as the cause of God—for that is precisely the meaning of the mysterious term "reign of God." A difficult ascetical process of purification not inferior to the ways of purification of classical mysticism lies in the *disinterested* partisanship for the poor, the oppressed, the exploited, as a demand for Christian love precisely in its societal and political dimensions.

It cannot be denied that the political, as worldy reality, is also filled with ambiguity, is full of temptations and threats, especially because politics deals with power. Those who are engaged in it know better than those who stand on the sidelines. The classical ascetical and mystical love also was and is full of threats and temptations, to which many have succumbed. Indeed because of these dangers politics itself asks for holiness and humanization; it must legitimate itself as disinterested love. But a praxis of liberation supported by political love is, in its emancipation, at the same time (through every metanoia) a bit of Christian redemption.

Of course, Christian redemption is more than emancipatory self-liberation. But real human liberation, borne up by political love, refers concretely to the worldly fruitfulness of Christian redemption. It is an interior ingredient of it. The experience of God is here the animating aspect of guidance of a concrete praxis of liberation in which this praxis is transcended at the same time: it is active testimony of the God of justice and love. And it is experienced thus in, e.g., many Latin American Christian liberation movements. And because salvation does not completely coincide with our consciousness that this salvation *came from God*, we may say that everywhere where good is done and injustice is opposed by a praxis of love for one's fellow human being, the *very being of God*, which is love for human beings, is imitated and brought into force. Not "Lord, Lord, Alleluia" but praxis is decisive.

Politics without prayer or mysticism quickly becomes grim and barbaric; prayer or mysticism without political love quickly becomes sentimental and irrelevant interiority. [1983]

Part Six

The Experience of God: Spirituality

Spirituality

Someone so preoccupied with Christian experience in its most concrete form is bound to deal with issues of spirituality. This is true in the case of Schillebeeckx. For most of the 1950s he edited a journal of spirituality and contributed many articles to it. He has continued to write in this vein.

Selection 77 talks very directly about our access to God, an access which Schillebeeckx calls here a "mediated immediacy." Selection 78 is a sermon on Matthew 25, which expresses the spirituality of the emancipative solidarity which he sees as characterizing Christian praxis in the world. Selection 79 was an address for Dutch Radio, which addresses first-world spirituality as it faces the third world.

Selection 80 is also a sermon, first given on the feast of Thomas Aquinas in 1965. It is a fitting piece to conclude the *Reader.* It not only speaks of a theologian who has been most influential in shaping Schillebeeckx's theology. One can also not escape the intuition that it also says much about the life project of one of Thomas's greatest students in this century.

77/ *Our Access to God*

The heart of the problem therefore seems to be: Does the believer have a *direct* relationship with God or not? The decisive question here is whether both the men of the past and the so-called moderns have clearly formulated the scope of this problem. Perhaps both have seen part of the truth, and in each case have interpreted it in a one-sided way. Having carefully examined both the—let us say—traditional Western, Augustinian expressions and the newer Western Christian statements, I would

277

venture to make the following comments. If by talking of the death of the "immediacy of God," one means that man has *no unmediated* relationship with God, then I fully agree. However, things look different if we consider this same, i.e., mediated, relationship from the other side, for in my view there certainly is an unmediated relationship between God and us. The objection that immediacy on only one side of a mutual relationship amounts to an inner contradiction is untenable in this particular case. What we have here is not an inter-subjective relationship between two persons—two mortal men—but a mutual relationship between a finite person and his absolute origin, the infinite God. And that has an effect on our relationship to God. In other words, we are confronted with a unique instance, an instance in which the immediacy does not do away with the mediation but in fact constitutes it. Thus from our perspective there is *mediated immediacy*. Between God and our awareness of God looms the insuperable barrier of the historical, human and natural world of creation, the constitutive symbol of the real presence of God for us. The fact that in this case an unmistakable mediation produces immediacy, instead of destroying it, is connected with the absolute or divine manner of the real presence of God: he makes himself directly and creatively present in the medium, that is, in ourselves, our neighbors, the world and history. This is the deepest immediacy that I know.

"Mediated immediacy" seems to me to be the most appropriate way of expressing the mystery of God as the salvation of man, and also of coming as near as possible to the nature of prayer and liturgy; at the same time it can give us some insight into the relationship between the mystical and the political aspects of Christian belief in God. Here one can say that on the one hand the mystical element does not branch off into gnosticism, and on the other, that political involvement is realized, not on the basis of humanism, but on the basis of real belief in God. . . .

That leads us to a second aspect of mediated immediacy. It is not that we could now do without this mediation, but in the mediation the accent now lies on the God who is immediately near in it, since this is a *divine* absolute nearness. At this point it becomes clear that "man's cause" is in fact "God's cause," expressed in the biblical concept of the kingdom of God as human salvation, in other words, the kingdom of God concerned with humanity. Jesus experienced his sacrifice for his fellow men as God's cause. The recognition of the deity of God is at the same time the recognition of the unexpected humanity of man. Even M. Horkheimer doubts whether a human ethic which has detached itself from its religious basis can in the last resort have any meaningful effect. In that case the expectations which ethics arouses are too great, and it cannot give us what it promises. To be aware of a religious foundation in God provides the strength constantly to begin again in working for man and the world and carrying on the struggle, because in that case no single historical event is the eschatological final event, and by the same token a fiasco is not ultimate failure. Religious faith gives us confidence that what is impossible for men is possible nevertheless, because God's nature is the benevolent power of the one who is against evil, an undefinable gift.

However, it also emerges from these considerations that we need a liturgy in which we *transcend* both personal and individual intimacy, and also critical, socio-political concerns, from within (that is, not through an alienating rejection). One can call this the mystical aspect of belief in God in the wider sense, in which we represent to ourselves that God is near to us only in mediated form, yet nevertheless in real immediacy; that therefore we are never alone, even in our greatest loneliness; and that despite everything, goodness and mercy have me, all of us, in their grasp. This awareness of being grounded in God, of persisting when every empirical foundation and every guarantee have been removed and one weeps over the fiasco of one's life, is the mystical power of faith. When we lose all our supports, even those which can be experienced empirically with some degree of positiveness, the immediacy of the presence of God is in fact experienced as a "dark night." All the mystics have experienced this immediacy of the presence of God as a *nada*. One might say that they have experienced it, not as a nothingness (*nada*) of emptiness, but as a nothingness of fullness: God's presence as a pure experience of faith, even if this is communicated in a negative way. There are many ways or situations in which believers can experience such moments. I have often come across them with people who have seen a loved one die in the most grievous and most incomprehensible circumstances, and have been able to accept this only as believers, and even then not without profound sorrow. In that case this belief is not simply a theoretical conviction—were that so, it would be shattered. No, in that case it is an *experience* of the real presence of God, not in the mediation of positive support but in the mediation of extreme negativity, a dark night. And this does in fact imply "mediation."

However, this mystical depth in which the immediacy of God is the essential element, because in this case the mediation is experienced as "pure negativity," does not reveal itself only in negativity or "dark nights," but also in joyful experiences. In one saying, the substance of which certainly comes from him, Jesus thanks God with trembling joy after the triumphant return of his disciples. He had sent them on a mission and they have come back telling him that their task has been accomplished successfully (Luke 10:17-21). There are experiences in the life of a believer in which he has a disclosure: if this man is already so disarmingly good, how much better must God be! Here, too, there is a change in perception from mediating to mediated, namely towards God's real, immediate presence. Therefore alongside the implicit life of prayer in the secular, human manifestations of God, I see *explicit prayer* as man's attempt to see this dimension of immediacy, an attempt to which the believing life of the everyday world as it were drives him, because the believer is aware of the *real* (though mediated) nearness of God. However, the attempt continually fails because this nearness, divine and absolute as it is, is as inward as it is incomprehensible. At the very moment when we turn our attention from mediation to look towards God's real presence itself, with the shedding of the mediation God himself also vanishes into nothing. Prayer is as it were a game of hide-and-seek between God and man. In fact there is always something extremely playful in prayer. Prayer has its supreme significance as a kind of game in the normal, everyday practice of our praying. *Si vere Deum quaeris,* if you really seek God, said the old monks, then come to us. Praying means looking for God. We need to understand that God is a living being who knows how to disappear now and then so that we keep on looking further for him, and how to appear for a moment now and then so that we do not get tired of looking.

That brings us to a last and very difficult question. Is praying an "*I-thou relationship*" between God and man? It is hard to answer this all too naively in the affirmative; but it seems to me to be too subtle to deny the relationship. Of course a mutual relationship between God and man is an extreme analogous instance of what we call "inter-subjectivity" or an I-thou relationship. If the immediacy is always mediated, and nevertheless constitutes mediation through its immediacy, we must answer this question with a paradox: yes, and at the same time no. We just need to remember that this mutual relationship between God and man falls outside the human category of inter-subjectivity because it transcends it, not because it falls short of it. On the one hand that makes explicit praying the most difficult *metanoia* or conversion in our life, yet on the other hand we cannot dispense with prayer without in the end grounding our life on idols, ideologies and utopias, and not on God himself. Prayer is therefore not so much mediation as conversion. Therefore prayer—and I think only prayer—gives Christian faith its most critical and productive force. The most critical element in belief in God does not come from a political theology but fundamentally from the articulation of faith in prayer, from prayer as an act of faith. It is precisely this faith which becomes effective indirectly in activity which takes a political shape, thanks to the mediating analysis of our particular social structures.

All this must be given a theoretical basis by means of a "political theology." [1977]

78/ A Glass of Water (Matt 25:31–46)

The gospel to which we have just listened presents us with the Last Judgment: the real end. In the form of a country shepherd's story (to which we find it very difficult to attune ourselves) we are given a religious vision of the future. However, if we look more closely at Matthew's composition of this vision it is striking that it can really also be seen as a retrospect. Matthew simply tells us who Jesus has been—someone who spoke in the midst of our history about the divinity of God—expressed in the Jewish concepts of that time with the words kingdom of God; moreover, a man who had acted in the spirit of this God, i.e., had accomplished the works of the kingdom of God. He had gone about doing good in the service of people in need, the outcasts, for whom he opened up communication. What Jesus said and did is projected into the future by Matthew as a standard for the Last Judgment. Even he cannot say more about the future; but he knows that in Jesus the divinity of God appeared as the achievement of more humanity between fellow human beings: giving a glass of water to thirsty people in the desert, their lips chapped by the desert drought; providing clothing as protection in the day against the searing heat and in the night against the sudden bitter cold (that's the way things are in Palestine). He attempted, then, to fulfill everyday needs, in situations in which the most insignificant people suffer the most. So Matthew's story of the Last Judgment is evidently focused on purely human concerns; indeed, it seems even to be atheistic, since the name of God is not mentioned in it except when the matter is settled: "Come, blessed ones of the Father." The key here is the needy person, the person in distress. Our attitude towards these people, the humble and the needy, is what is at stake in the Last Judgment, i.e., it is the standard, the criterion by which the significance and content of our life is to be judged. The main criterion is therefore not whether we have lauded and praised God liturgically as the king of the universe, or have supported the church and its organizations. No, the question in the judgment is simply: Have we—personally or structurally—helped those in need? This need not simply be a matter of people in the abstract, all those who belong to the human race. Rather, it is a matter of our attitude towards the lowly and the insignificant, the oppressed, those in any kind of need, whether material or spiritual; the neighbor who may be distant or close, who is in any kind of need, who lacks something, perhaps a bit of your own life that you love and find indispensable.

So at first sight there is nothing Christian about Matthew's story. The story itself stresses this, since the club that we call "Christian" is left out of account: this is the judgment on *panta ta ethnē*, i.e., all peoples, without any distinction between the people of God and Gentiles (25:32). All will be judged on the giving of a glass of water, not from the surplus out of a water tank—which is something that people in the desert would never have heard of then—but out of the little remaining in a few water bottles. The physical conditions envisaged here are more critical. This is precisely the situation that Matthew has in mind in his vision of the end of all things. The end of all things is to be found in the midst of our daily life.

And yet! On closer inspection this is still the external aspect of Matthew's story; even this is not the specifically Christian element that he has in view. His vision of the judgment is anything but atheistic, despite all the modern so-called "Christian atheism." Matthew has not forgotten what he had said a few pages earlier: "What reward do you have? Do not Gentiles do the same?" (Matt 5:46). Furthermore, we find all kinds of literature from the same period—from pre-Christian Judaism, Egypt and neighboring countries, in which what people should do as humane beings is described with just the same imagery: giving a glass of water, clothing the naked, visiting those in prison. So this is ancient Eastern, very human experiential wisdom, though even there it is not just something that is taken for granted.

However, anyone who hears only this in Matthew's account misses the real point with which he is particularly concerned, on the basis of the remembrance of his community of Jesus' own proclamation of the divinity of God as salvation of and for insignificant, oppressed people. For what we do not find in Jewish and Egyptian texts comes into the foreground in Matthew, namely the identification of the judge of the end-time, who makes the judgment, with the lowly person in need: "Inasmuch as you have done it for one of the least of these you have done it for *me*" (25:40). *Me*, that is the Son of man who is mentioned at the beginning of the story: "The Son of man comes in his glory surrounded by his angels (the corona of the eschatological court of judgment), and will take his place on the judgment seat, before which all nations will be summoned." By means of this identification of the final judge with the lowly person in need Matthew interprets the Christian significance of giving loving help to the needy in a very special way. He does this in a twofold sense. First of all, it is the oppressed of the world who will judge us by the standard of the suffering which has been inflicted on them. That is perhaps why the final judgment on those who find themselves on the wrong side (Hebrews called it the left hand side) is such a harsh one: "Depart from me, you cursed ones." They have kept so accursedly far from these needy people during their lifetime that one can now well understand their reaction. However, such an identification is perverse. The lowly person is at the same time the Son of man who utters the judgment. And for Matthew this is Jesus, the Christ who identifies himself with the lowly, with any member of the human race, all the sons and daughters of men. To take the side of those in need is to follow God himself, God as he has shown his deepest compassion towards humanity in Jesus. "He loved us when we lowly Christians were still in misery" (see Rom 5:10). God's concern for man becomes the criterion, the standard and at the same time the boundless measure of our concern for the needy. This boundless sensitivity towards human needs only develops fully out of a personal experience of God's own gracious "Yes" to all men: "Yes, you may live," the expression of God's being, described by theologians as "justification through grace," a learned phrase for God's love for mankind. This divine boundlessness is not so obvious to us human beings; it transcends what we call co-humanity. Of course it is obvious to all those who have experienced God's mercy themselves, in other words to religious men and women; it is also the test of the authenticity of our liturgical prayer, which praises Jesus as Lord of the universe.

This boundlessness becomes clear from the first reading to which we listened in this celebration, that from Ezekiel. The prophet asserts that people who by virtue of their office are made shepherds and pastors of the needy in our society are in fact letting them come to grief. For that reason God pronounces his judgment. "I the Lord will myself look after my sheep and care for them." God is more human than any human being. With the Gospel of John we can say: "God so loved the world." I believe that we human beings find it difficult to understand the love of God for all men who are in want, who fail, and are oppressed. It *is* impossible to understand; but the great vision of the Last Judgment which Matthew sets before our eyes shows us something of the unshakable and incomprehensible love of God for man. This also explains the harshness in the divine judgment on all those who in whatever way ensnare fellow human beings or hurt them to the depths of their souls, even if this is simply as a result of doing nothing. At that very point we come up against the sensitive concern of God for what is closest to his heart: human beings, and above all human beings in need. According to Vondel and all kinds of apocryphal writings, even angels were offended by this love of God for man. Finally, Jesus, whom we may call his onlybeloved son, is also a man like you and me—except that he is more human. Human love, as the liturgy teaches us today, is a religious happening.

There is just one more thing to say to end with. We may not detach the story of the Last Judgment according to Matthew from the whole of what we are told in the Old and New Testaments. If we do, we risk reading into this text a cruelty which is alien to it. Furthermore, the preference for the needy should not make us forget the others. In Ezekiel we heard, "I the Lord will myself look after my sheep and care for them"; after that there follows not only, "I will bring back the lost and stray sheep, bind up the wounded and strengthen the sick," but also "I will look after the fat and the strong sheep." The Good Shepherd does not leave the ninety-nine healthy sheep in the lurch. Where this is said elsewhere in scripture, it is only a way of stressing a total concern for the lost sheep. In Christian terms, you cannot deny deeply emotional feelings for the ninety-nine remaining sheep for the sake of the one lost sheep. Christianity is thus a *complexio oppositorum*, that is, a very complex, evidently contradictory and yet simple matter, but it calls for creative imagination in which priority for the needy and the lowly does not result in any inhumanity towards the ninety-nine fat sheep, even if in our society these are only one-third of the world's population. What must happen as a result, I don't exactly know. However, I gather from the readings for today that the call for a partisan predilection for people in need must be reconciled with solidarity with the equally precarious men and women represented by the "fat and strong beasts" among us, as Ezekiel put it, without distracting attention from this partisan concern. The readings are not a law book, but critical reminiscences of already old and proven experience of religious people. They summon us to combine, with some creativity, concern for the oppressed with a universal compassion on all human beings, even on those who have made a mess of their humanity, I believe—and I say this with some hesitation—that at the Last Judgment perhaps everyone will stand on the right side of the Son of Man: "Come, all you beloved people, blessed of the Father, for despite all your inhumanity you once gave a glass of water when I was in need. Come!"

> "For he himself has gone before,
> Faithful shepherd is his name."
> [1979]

79/ The Gospel of the Poor
(Luke 6:17, 20-26)

Jesus does not call any virtuous people happy, nor does he say that poverty and misery are a good thing. He calls poor people happy: poor people who cry out aloud for hunger. He calls them happy because with him the kingdom of God has come among men. God is concerned for humanity, and in particular is in search of people in distress, the weak, the lonely, the insignificant members of our society, people who have dropped out, or have been thrown out, of the normal processes of communication. These poor marginal people usually seek comfort from one another. They come together like the clochards in Paris, gathering together under a bridge somewhere to find whatever scant warmth they can from one another, bosom companions in shared misery.

It was the same in Palestine. As Jesus was coming down from a mountain with the twelve, at the halfway stage he came across a crowd of people. In Israel at that time a meeting with such a person always aroused the vague expectation that God would bring about some great miracle. There was a dulled certainty that there is also a future for the poor, a future in which the powerful and the prominent no longer oppress the poor, the weak and the insignificant among us. For that was the old message: it lived on in Israel only among the poor, searching and looking out for a better life. They had already heard of a man from Nazareth who talked of a mysterious new future: it was called the kingdom of God. This was a new, happy life, a kingdom for poor fishermen, joy for those who weep, fullness for those who are hungry. And here was this Jesus, suddenly large as life before them, surrounded by his fishermen who had left everything to follow him.

Then something happened that always happens in a crowd of people who suddenly begin to move. The whole crowd tried to touch him, for a power went out from him which healed them all. There were the impotent gestures of close-packed people who are looking for contact, begging: "Just speak one word and salvation, communication, will be restored." Jesus sees this crowd and the crowd knows it all: in Jesus, God is concerned for them. Then the great saying suddenly rings out over the plain. Jesus says, "Happy are you poor who weep for hunger. Congratulations, you lucky people, because the kingdom of God has come to you, and everyone will be so satisfied that they laugh for joy." On hearing that, these poor people must have had a vision of a laden table with pots of meat, fine bread made of meal and oil, everything that goes to make up a festive meal, in which communication is established and laughter becomes infectious.

A first reaction to Jesus' message is still very ambiguous. Hungry people are listening to Jesus; you could hardly object to that. They have not yet understood that Jesus does not want to be the fulfiller of unfulfilled daydreams. Yet Jesus outlines a new future for the poor by means of the image of the rich who laugh and are satisfied round a laden table. "Is this misleading the people?" you might ask, for Jesus calls people happy who do not feel happy by human standards and indeed are not happy. In many respects this Gospel of Luke is an irritating text for us; of course it is inspiring, but in addition it is rather irritating. We do not know what to make of it, whether we are rich or poor. Either way we are stuck after hearing the gospel for today.

It was just the same for the three evangelists, Mark, Matthew and Luke, who wanted to bring their community new and topical inspiration by this old recollection of Jesus' gospel for the poor. Sometimes it becomes rather different, but sometimes it reflects Jesus' own original purpose. For us now these differences are also a challenge, an incentive not to treat this text romantically, but to let it speak to us here and now. This text is concerned to give a direction to our action. So let us look rather more closely at what Luke means by it.

When Luke wrote his gospel, he was thinking of a very particular Christian community, somewhere in a great city of the Roman Empire outside Palestine. And it emerges from this gospel that this Christian community consisted of a prosperous middle class with all kinds of major or minor social conflicts between the properous and the less important members of the community. It was on the basis of these social conflicts, and with an eye to them, that he wrote his gospel. In it he described the new conditions which Jesus had promised earlier. First, Luke makes Jesus pray all through the night. Then Jesus chooses from his many disciples just those twelve of whom Luke says that they had left everything or had sold all their possessions to serve the kingdom of God. In between, Luke also tells us about a failed calling. There was a deeply religious, rich young man, who could not, however, bring himself to give everything to the poor in order to follow Jesus. Surrounded by the twelve, who have actually accepted the call to voluntary poverty, Jesus comes down from the mountain and appoints his twelve poor fishermen, his poor fellow-workers, to serve the crowd. In Luke, the crowd was already his own Christian "middle-class church." Jesus then praises these apostles, in the presence of the Christian church, for having willingly given up all their possessions in the service of God's concern for the poor.

Luke's Christian community found this hard. His Gospel begins to fill in the details. Following the example of Jesus' apostles who left everything, Luke gives a guideline to the rich people in his church. Like Zacchaeus, you must give half your possessions for the poor in your church: fifty percent. At the moment we haggle whether we should give two or four percent of our own income for the Third World. Luke says fifty percent. The whole of his gospel and the Acts of the Apostles suggest that Luke is building up a very specific utopian society, at least for the Christian community. Here at least it is possible to realize what at that time was impossible in the bourgeois world. In the Christian community there is to be no difference between rich and poor, between the powerful, the important and the unimportant. This Christian, Luke, has understood Jesus' message very well. To take the part of those in need is to follow God himself, God as he has shown his deepest concern for people in Jesus with his twelve poor men who went round doing good in Palestine, God's concern for the unimportant becomes the criterion, the standard and at the same time the boundless measure, of our concern for the needy and the oppressed. This boundless sensitivity to human need only develops fully from a personal expreience of God's own gracious Yes to all men. Yes, you may live: you here in church and you there looking at the television screen. You may live. This divine boundlessness in particular is not so obvious to us human beings. Of course it is obvious to all those who themselves have experienced God's mercy, in other words to religious believers. God is more human than any human being. I believe that we human beings find it difficult to understand the love of God for all men, who because they are human, fall short, fail and above all are oppressed. And according to Vondel and all kinds of apocryphal writings, even angels argued over this predilection of God for human beings, for the humble, the wretched and the lonely, man or woman.

Finally, Jesus too, whom we may confess as the one beloved Son, was a human being like you and me, but more human. This gospel from Luke teaches us today that human love is a religious, Christian event. Luke does not leave this vague. Within the church he is clearly concerned that possessions should be shared, so that there will not be poor Christians alongside rich Christians. For Luke the beatitudes of Jesus are praise of the rich who give half their possessions to the poor in the community. From a social perspective, that, and only that, is life according to the gospel. It is not the whole of Christian life, but it is also Christian life. Furthermore, it is striking that Luke deliberately but consistently changes the familiar liturgical words at the celebration of the eucharist in his community, "Drink you all of this," into "Share this cup with one another." Everything is to be shared with one another. Luke translates Jesus' gospel for the poor into a gospel for the rich, since in his day the original church of the poor and the underdogs had become a community of both poor and rich. And Luke wants to exploit this new situation. In almost every chapter of his gospel his demand for the social solidarity of rich Christians with poor Christians has a prominent place.

Translated for today's world, above all in its beatitudes, the gospel of Luke is a direct indictment of our bourgeois existence, our bourgeois behavior and our bourgeois society. That bourgeois character has also attacked the hearts of Christians and of the church itself. Of course we cannot derive any suitable social programme for our time from the gospel. But the plan that Luke sketches of a truly Christian community in accordance with the gospel— half of what you possess for the unimportant among us—remains a challenge which can make us lie awake at nights worrying whether we are taking Christ's gospel seriously. At all events this message of Luke does not let present-day Christians get off scot-free.

In terms of the modern world, what Luke says to us describes precisely the scandal in which the present church is involved. How is it possible for defenders of oppressive systems and those they oppress, all of us and the Third World, to celebrate the one eucharist together as Christians? We drink from our full cups but do not share the one cup among one another. The great scandal among us is not intercommunion among Christians of different communions: that is a sign of hope. The scandal is the intercommunion of rich Christians who remain rich and poor Christians who remain poor while celebrating the same eucharist, taking no notice of the Christian model of sharing possessions; the sharing of the one cup of salvation among one another. For this salvation also has social and economic consequences. Everyone, not just an elite group, has to be full enough to be able to laugh because salvation has happened to him or her. Jesus said, "Today salvation has come to the house of Zacchaeus," because Zacchaeus gave away to the poor half of what he possessed.

Is not all this more urgent than our petty problems within the church, however real they may be at the time? God does not want human suffering, he wants life, and life in abundance. And he wants it for all and not simply for one-third of the world's population.

What about our abundance? That is Luke's critical question, a concrete challenge to all of us, here and now. [1980]

80/ *Thomas Aquinas: Servant of the Word*

Rarely has human thinking been a liturgical service as it was with Thomas Aquinas. We can see this clearly from two typical events from Thomas's life, and from his expressed declaration of his own program.

On a Holy Thursday, while his confreres were carrying out the services of Holy Week in choir, Thomas was editing his little work "Declaratio questionum ad Magistrum Ordinis." On another occasion when he was sojourning outside his priory due to a question of inheritance, he wrote his book *De Substantiis Separatis,* and accounted for it as follows: "I must make up through study and writing for the time which I cannot devote to the singing of psalms." These individual facts become meaningful and are only then not misunderstood when we put them against the background of Thomas's expressed life program. Writing by way of exception in the first person singular (albeit in the form of a quote), Thomas formulated boldly in his first great work, the *Summa contra Gentiles,* how he saw the mission of his own life. This is what he said: "I see clearly as the very primary task of my life, that I am indebted to God to let him see-and-speak (loqui) through all my words, thoughts-and-feelings (sensus) (I, 2)." Thomas sees the general vocation of serving God concretized for him in the form of serving God by speaking about him to other human beings. The reasons for the existence of his life lie in that service of charity or servanthood to his fellow human beings, which consists of being *ex professo* involved with God, and to share these experiences and reflections about him with others. The *thinking* religious activity with God and human beings as being of service to humanity: that was for Thomas a liturgical action. Thinking itself becomes here liturgy and apostolate; thinking is for Thomas the matter he sanctifies and offers to God, and at the same time that with which he would be of service to his fellow human beings.

As a theologian, Thomas Aquinas is a servant of God and human beings. He experienced the reality of this word "servant" in its feudal context of the poor who stood to wait on their lord, on whom they were dependent in all things, as people who felt themselves to be a gift from another to another in complete self-expropriation and absolute appropriation by their feudal lord. Thomas called this lordly service and subservience the ministry of truth (*ministerium veritatis*). His *principium* or inaugural address on the occasion of his promotion to *bacchalaureus biblicus* is concerned exclusively with "serving the truth." He is a doctor of truth (*doctor veritatis*).

I would like to consider the life of Thomas as a priestly doctorate, a priestly service of the word in a thoroughly thought-out form of expression appropriate to its time. As a theologian, Thomas abides *in* the faith with the whole power of his human reflection. He is aware of the fact that theology is a scientific study of a non-scientific datum, of a datum that is not subject to scientific verification, of a datum offered only to those who believe, to those who in thought can rise above thought to a childlike acceptance of God's self-evidence that for us, problematic people, is of course a mystery and may even become a problem. It is remarkable that this consummate theologian admits that he daily prays to God *that*

he not lose the faith, as he says explicitly in one of the prayers which we
have from his own hand.

Not to lose the faith! For Thomas this has a twofold meaning. It means,
on the one hand, that his theological thinking ought never to diminish
or adulterate the word of God's revelation. It means, on the other hand,
that he ought never to present as God's commanding word what is in
fact its human and ephemeral expression, so as not to burden others with
a yoke that is not of God, but has been prefabricated by theologians.

First of all, the theologian ought never to diminish or adulterate the
faith. The liturgy of the *opus divinum* that is the service of the truth
implies for Thomas that he accept the Other—God—as other, so that
the datum upon which he reflects as theologian not be distorted by his
own creative imagination, but rather that he mold his thinking according to the self-revealed image of God. As servant of the truth, Thomas
is attached to the Other, God, precisely as he has manifested himself to
us. Thomas has no patience with a blind spot that would cause us to be
selective in the face of divine truth. To gloss over a single facet of that
truth would mean being unfaithful to his priestly doctorate.

Secondly, the theologian ought never to present as God's word something that is not. For Thomas, this is also a form of not losing the faith.
In this respect he has an unusual sensitivity which found expression in
the phrases *derisus infidelium* and *articulus fidei.* I have encountered the
former expression at least twenty times in Thomas's writings and he
means by it that we should not present the faith in such a way that it
appears naive, passé and ludicrous to the non-believer. In modern terms,
this indicates the necessity of a continual reinterpretation of dogma in
line with the dogma itself, and thus of a certain measure of demytholo-
gizing demanded by loyalty to the truth. Thomas is also careful to ascertain whether or not he is dealing with an *articulus fidei,* that is, a religious truth that can be known only through revelation and cannot be
arrived at by human thought alone. This shows his concern for not
offending the thought of others, for allowing human thought freedom
in its own domain, and for making clearer distinction between God's
revealing word and human speculations.

Thomas's perceptive solicitude for not losing the faith explains also
the fact that he battles equally on two fronts in order to preserve this
faith, in order to accept God as the Other.

On one front, he fights against various forms of *conservative integralism* that would make a farce out of genuine confrontation. His library
is full of works considered suspect by the theologians and hierarchy of
his day: the latest novelties of pagan philosophers and of Jewish-Arabic
thinkers. This amounted to a medieval modernism, in reference to which

Thomas's no less holy but more excitable confrere, Albert the Great, had written:

> Our opponents are too lazy to study these works; they merely leafed through them in order to charge us with whatever heresies and errors they may run across, and so they feel that they are doing Christendom a service. They are the ones who have murdered Socrates, who have driven Plato away, and whose machinations have banned Aristotle from the universities.

Thomas thought the same, but said nothing; he worked and constructed a new Christian synthesis from these modernistic writings.

But there is yet a second front on which Thomas struggled for the purity of the faith. He entered the lists against all kinds of *excessive progressivism*, the excesses of Siger of Brabant and his associates, which brought discredit to the progressivism of Thomas himself. And because this cast suspicion on his life work of service to the truth, the usually serene and imperturbable Thomas suddenly became fierce. It is only in this context of an excessive progressivism that threatened any authentic renewal, and almost inevitably brought about a reactionary integralism that we find Thomas, remarkably enough, using the uncommon epithets *stupidum, absurdum* and *stupidissimum. . . .*

When we look for the key to the life of this man of study, we find it in his own words. At the time of his last reception of the eucharist, just before his death, he called out: "Jesus, *for the love of whom* I have studied, have stayed awake nights, have preached and taught." "*Jesus . . . pro cuius amore!*" No ivory-tower scholarliness, no ambition or intellectual curiosity explains his life of study, but the generous love for a living person, the Lord Jesus Christ. On his way as *peritus* to the Council of Lyon where he was to be made a cardinal along with his colleague Bonaventure, Thomas asked God that he might rather die than reach Rome as a cardinal. Bonaventure arrived in Rome and became a cardinal. Thomas died on the way. If being a cardinal meant the end of his priestly doctorate, it was better for him to die, for his task was accomplished. For us, however, his unfinished *Summa* is a constant reminder that the task of the priestly doctorate is always an unfinished life work, that every generation must begin again and press forward.

"*Jesus, pro cuius amore*"—because he loved. Love is the form of the priestly or ministerial doctorate. That is why Thomas is a saint, and an unusual one. It is for that reason that we gratefully celebrate his life as a glowing example for all theologians. [1965]

Sources of the Selections

Christ: The Experience of Jesus as Lord (subtitled in the U.K. *The Christian Experience in the Modern World*). Translated by John Bowden. New York: Crossroad/London: SCM, 1980. Copyright © 1980 by The Crossroad Publishing Company.

Christ the Sacrament of the Encounter with God. Translated by Paul Barrett. London/New York: Sheed and Ward, 1963. Copyright © 1963 by Sheed and Ward Ltd.

"Critical Theories and Christian Political Commitment," *Concilium* 84 (1973) 48–61. Copyright © 1972 by Herder and Herder, and Stichting Concilium.

"Erfahrung und Glaube." In *Christlicher Glaube in moderner Gesellschaft*, vol. 25, pp. 73–116. Freiburg: Herder, 1980.

The Eucharist. Translated by N. D. Smith. London/New York: Sheed and Ward, 1968. Copyright © 1968 by Sheed and Ward, Inc.

"Glaube und Moral." In *Ethik im Kontext des Glaubens*, 17–45. Fribourg: Universitätsverlag, 1978.

God Among Us: The Gospel Proclaimed. Translated by John Bowden. New York: Crossroad/London: SCM, 1980. Copyright © 1983 by John Bowden.

God and Man. Translated by Edward Fitzgerald and Peter Tomlinson. New York/London: Sheed and Ward, 1969. Copyright © 1969 by Sheed and Ward, Inc.

God the Future of Man. Translated by N. D. Smith. New York: Sheed and Ward, 1968. London: Sheed and Ward, 1969. Copyright © 1968 by Sheed and Ward, Inc.

Interim Report on the Book Jesus and Christ. Translated by John Bowden. New York: Crossroad/London: SCM, 1980. Copyright © 1980 by The Crossroad Publishing Company.

"Jerusalem of Benares? Nicaragua of de Berg Athos?" *Kultuurleven* 50 (1983) 331–47.

Jesus: An Experiment in Christology. Translated by Hubert Hoskins. New York: Seabury (Crossroad)/London: Collins, 1979. Copyright © 1979 by William Collins Sons & Co. Ltd. and The Crossroad Publishing Company.

"Kritisch geloofsdenken als eredienst en apostolaat." *Neerlandia Dominicana* 20 (1965) 77-80.

Marriage: Secular Reality and Saving Mystery, 2 vols. (subtitled in the U.S. *Human Reality and Saving Mystery*). Translated by N. D. Smith. London: Sheed and Ward, 1965. New York: Sheed and Ward, 1966. Copyright © 1965 by Sheed and Ward Ltd.

Ministry: Leadership in the Community of Jesus Christ (subtitled in the U.K. *A Case for Change*). Translated by John Bowden. New York: Crossroad/London: SCM, 1981. Copyright © 1981 by The Crossroad Publishing Company.

The Mission of the Church. Translated by N. D. Smith. London: Sheed and Ward/New York: Herder and Herder, 1973. Copyright © 1973 by Sheed and Ward.

"Naar een 'definitieve toekomst': belofte en menselijke bemiddeling." In *Toekomst van de religie—Religie van de toekomst?*, 37-55. Brussels: Desclée de Brouwer, 1972.

Revelation and Theology, vol. 1 (Theological Soundings I/1). Translated by N. D. Smith. London: Sheed and Ward/New York: Herder and Herder, 1967. Copyright © 1967 by Sheed and Ward Ltd.

Revelation and Theology, vol. 2 (Theological Soundings I/2). Translated by N. D. Smith. London: Sheed and Ward/New York: Herder and Herder, 1968. Copyright © 1968 by Sheed and Ward, Inc.

"De sacramentaire struktuur van de openbaring." *Kultuurleven* 19 (1952) 785-802.

"Theologische overpeinzing achteraf." *Tijdschrift voor Theologie* 20, no. 3 (1980).

Theologisch Geloofsverstaan anno 1983. Baarn: H. Nelissen, 1983.

The Understanding of Faith. Translated by N. D. Smith. London: Sheed and Ward/New York: Seabury, 1974. Copyright © 1974 by Sheed and Ward.

"Verrijzenis en geloofservaring in het 'Verhaal van een levende.'" *Kultuurleven* 42 (1975) 81-93.

"Was Jezus een christen?" Lecture to be published.

1 *Christ*, pp. 731, 733-43.
2 "The Concept of 'Truth,'" in *Revelation and Theology*, vol. 2, pp. 18-20.
3 "Erfahrung und Glaube," p. 80.*
4 "Erfahrung und Glaube," pp. 86-90.*
5 *Interim Report on the Book Jesus and Christ*, pp. 4-6.
6 "Speech of Thanks on Receiving the Erasmus Prize," in *God Among Us*, pp. 250-53.
7 *Christ*, pp. 724-28.

8 "Naar een 'definitieve toekomst': belofte en menselijke bemiddeling," pp. 45–47.*
9 *The Understanding of Faith*, pp. 91–95.
10 *The Understanding of Faith*, pp. 95–100.
11 "The Concept of 'Truth,'" pp. 5–8.
12 "Erfahrung und Glaube," pp. 103–4.*
13 "Erfahrung und Glaube," pp. 106–8.*
14 *The Understanding of Faith*, pp. 3–5.
15 *Christ*, pp. 669–70.
16 "De sacramentaire struktuur van de openbaring," pp. 785–87.*
17 "What Is Theology?" in *Revelation and Theology*, vol. 1, pp. 93–95. "Salvation History as a Basis for Theology: Theologia or Oikonomia?" in *Revelation and Theology*, vol. 2, pp. 88–91.
18 "Erfahrung und Glaube," pp. 81–85.*
19 "Erfahrung und Glaube," pp. 93–94.*
20 *Interim Report on the Books Jesus and Christ*, pp. 17–19.
21 "What is Theology?" pp. 84–85.
22 *Theologisch Geloofsverstaan anno 1983*, pp. 12–13.*
23 *Christ*, pp. 42–43.
24 "The Lord and the Preaching of the Apostles," in *Revelation and Theology*, vol. 1, pp. 19–20, 23–24.
25 "Theologische overpeinzing achteraf," pp. 422–26.*
26 "Toward a Catholic Use of Hermeneutics," in *God the Future of Man*, pp. 4, 20.
27 *The Understanding of Faith*, pp. 22–23.
28 "Toward a Catholic Use of Hermeneutics," pp. 24–25.
29 "Toward a Catholic Use of Hermeneutics," pp. 25–27.
30 "Toward a Catholic Use of Hermeneutics," pp. 7–8.
31 *The Understanding of Faith*, pp. 27–29.
32 *The Understanding of Faith*, pp. 128–33.
33 *The Understanding of Faith*, p. 114.
34 *Theologisch Geloofsverstaan anno 1983*, pp. 17–19.
35 *The Understanding of Faith*, pp. 66–67.
36 *The Understanding of Faith*, pp. 140, 142–44.
37 *The Understanding of Faith*, pp. 154–55.
38 "Verijzenis en geloofservaring in het 'Verhaal van een levende,'" pp. 82–88.*
39 *Interim Report*, p. 10.
40 *Jesus*, pp. 52–53, 56–57, 58–59.
41 "Was Jezus een christen?"*
42 *Jesus*, pp. 140–43.
43 *Jesus*, pp. 156–58, 169–71.
44 *Jesus*, pp. 179, 183–84, 187–88, 199–200, 212–13, 218.
45 *Jesus*, pp. 257–58, 261–63, 266–68.
46 *Jesus*, pp. 294–97, 299, 306–8, 310–11.
47 *Jesus*, pp. 331, 380–84, 386–92, 394.
48 *Interim Report*, pp. 64–68, 69–70.
49 *Jesus*, pp. 545–50.
50 *Interim Report*, pp. 140–43.
51 *Christ*, pp. 836–38.
52 *Interim Report*, pp. 122–24.
53 *Christ*, pp. 463–68.

54 *Christ,* pp. 638–44.
55 *Christ,* pp. pp. 530–32.
56 *Christ the Sacrament of the Encounter with God,* pp. 47–49.
57 "The Church, Sacrament of the World," in *The Mission of the Church,* pp. 43–50.
58 "Critical Theories and Christian Political Commitment," pp. 47–49.
59 *Christ the Sacrament,* pp. 15–17, 179–81, 183–84.
60 *Christ,* pp. 835–37.
61 "Secular Worship and Church Liturgy," in *God the Future of Man,* pp. 110, 111–13.
62 *The Eucharist,* pp. 137–41.
63 *Marriage,* pp. 384–90.
64 *Ministry,* pp. 66–74.
65 *Ministry,* pp. 35–37.
66 *Ministry,* pp. 82–85.
67 *Ministry,* pp. 85–94.
68 *Ministry,* pp. 96–98.
69 *Ministry,* pp. 135–37.
70 "Dialogue with God and Christian Secularity," in *God and Man,* pp. 223–28.
71 "Christian Faith and Man's Expectation for the Future," in *The Mission of the Church,* pp. 83–89.
72 *Christ,* pp. 767–70.
73 "Jeruzalem of Benares? Nicaragua of de Berg Athos?" pp. 344–46.
74 "Glaube und Moral," pp. 31–44.*
75 *Christ,* pp. 774–77.
76 "Jeruzalem of Benares?" pp. 336–38.*
77 *Christ,* pp. 809–10.
78 *God Among Us,* pp. 59–62.
79 *God Among Us,* pp. 175–79.
80 "Kritisch geloofsdenken als eredienst en apostolaat," pp. 77–80.*

*Translated for this volume by Robert Schreiter.

A Bibliography of the
Writings of Edward Schillebeeckx
from 1945 to 1983

The bibliography of the writings of Edward Schillebeeckx given here was first published in *Tijdschrift voor Theologie* 14 (1974) 491–501, and continued in H. Häring, T. Schoof, A. Willems (eds.), *Meedenken met Edward Schillebeeckx* (Baarn: H. Nelissen, 1983) 320–25. That bibliography was based upon the list of Schillebeeckx himself, further researched by a number of students, and put in its final form by T. M. Schoof. For this edition, R. Schreiter made some corrections which had become evident, and has added further bibliographic information on the books and translation of books where that was available. Where there are routinely multiple translations of an article (as in the case of the *Concilium* articles), the Dutch original and the English translation in the American edition are the only ones cited.

Only material written by Schillebeeckx himself is listed here; thus, interviews are not included. All the translations known have been included as well, except for those instances noted above. In some instances, the translated text differs from the original because of corrections made by or on behalf of Schillebeeckx; these are noted by the notation "corr."

The numbering system used here follows the Dutch edition of the bibliography. The gaps in the latter part of the numbering system do not indicate omitted titles; rather, they allow an opportunity of filling in additional items, usually translations or smaller pieces, which may be discovered in the future.

I wish to thank Ben Berinti, C.PP.S., who patiently typed the versions of this bibliography.

Abbreviations

Conc.	*Concilium*
DB	*De Bazuin*
KL	*Kultuurleven*
OG	*Ons Geloof*
TGL	*Tijdschrift voor Geestelijk Leven*
Th	*Thomas* (Ghent)
TvPh	*Tijdschrift voor Philosophie*
TvT	*Tijdschrift voor Theologie*
VS(Suppl)	Vie Spirituelle (Supplément)
col.	column
corr.	corrected translation

summ.   summary
tr.   translation
→   article included in this book (see the number indicated)

1945

1. "Christelijke situatie," *KL* 12 (1945) 82–95, 229–42, 585–611.
2. "Technische heilstheologie," *OG* 27 (1945) 49–60; →143.
3. "Kloosterleven en heiligheid,"*OG* 27 (1945) 49–60; →143.
4. "Schepselbesef als grondslag van het geestelijk leven," *TGL* 1/I (1945) 15–43.
5. "De akte van volmaakte liefde," *TGL* 1/I (1945) 309–18.
6. "Hoe komt bij zwakte de sterkte tot haar recht?" *TGL* 1/II (1945) 277–80.

1946

7. "Kultuur en godsdienst in het huidige Frankrijk," *KL* 13/I (1946) 220–32; →168.
8. "De Heilige Communie als menselijkgodsdienstige daad," *OG* 28 (1946) 283–88.
9. "Volmaakte liefde en zuivere liefde," *TGL* 2/I (1946) 62–64.
10. "Considérations autour du sacrifice d'Abraham," *VS* 75 (1946) 45–59.

1947

11. "De ascetische toeleg van de kloosterling," *TGL* 3/I (1947) 302–20.
12. "Toeëigening van de verdiensten der heiligen," *TGL* 3/I (1947) 346–47.

1948

13. "Theologisch-metafysische grondslagen van het christelijke geweten," *Sacerdos* 15 (1947–48) 684–701.
14. "Beschouwingen rond de 'Geestelijke Oefeningen'" *TGL* 4/I (1948) 202–11.
15. "Kloosterlijke gehoorzaamheid en zedelijke vorming," *TGL* 4/I (1948) 321–42.
16. "Beschouwingen bij een 'Guide médical' voor het klooster- en seminarieleven," *TGL* 4/I (1948) 350–55.
17. "Guardini's 'De Heer,'" *TGL* 4/II (1948) 54–57.

1949

18. "Nederig humanisme," *KL* 16/I (1949) 12–21; →168.
19. "Bedenkingen rond het christelijk progressisme in Frankrijk," *KL* 16/I (1949) 221–29; →168.
20. "Rozenkrans, bidden in nuchtere werkelijkheid," *DB* 33 (Oct. 1, 1949) 4–6.

21. "Theologische grondslagen van de lekensprirualiteit," *TGL* 5/I (1949) 145–66; →200; →223.
22. "Zien en getuigen zoals Christus," *TGL* 5/II (1949) 145–54.
23. "Sacramenteel leven," *Th* 3 (1949–50) no. 3, 5ff.; no. 4, 3ff.

1950

24. "In memoriam E. P. Van Hulse, hoofdredakteur van T.G.L.," *TGL* 6 (1950) 433–34.
25. "Ik geloof in de levende God," *TGL* 6 (1950) 454–67.
26. "De gezinsrozenkrans," *TGL* 6 (1950) 523–32.

1951

27. "Gij zult het aanschijn van de aarde vernieuwen," in: *Het geestelijk leven van de leek,* Tilburg: H. Giannoten, 1951, 7–27; →168.
28. "Het hoopvolle Christusmysterie," *TGL* 7 (1951) 5–33.
29. "Beschouwingen rond de Misliturgie," *TGL* 7 (1951) 306–323.
30. "Eucharistische literatuur," *TGL* 7 (1951) 381–84.
31. "Het mysterie van onze Godsliefde," *TGL* 7 (1951) 609–26.
32. "De dood, schoonste mogelijkheid van de christen," *DB* 35 (Nov. 24, 1951) 4–5.

1952

33. *De sacramentele heilseconomie: Theologische bezinning op St. Thomas' sacramentenleer in het licht van de traditie en van de hedendaagse sacramentsproblematiek,* I, Antwerpen: 't Groeit/Bilthoven: H. Nelissen, 1952.
34. In *Theologisch Woordenboek,* I, Roermond/Maaseik: J. J. Romen en Zonen, 1952: (a) "Censuur," col. 753–54; (b) "Depositum fidei," col. 990; (c) "Dogma," col. 1078–81 (→143); (d) "Dogmaontwikkeling," col. 1087–1106 (→143); (e) "Eclecticisme," col. 1282; (f) "Eschatologisch," col. 1399–1400; (g) "Ex cathedra," col. 1480–81.
35. "Kunt gij niet één uur met Mij waken?" *DB* 35 (Apr. 5, 1952) 4–5.
36. "Spanning tussen Misoffer en Kruisoffer," *DB* 35 (June 28, 1952) 2.
37. "Reikhalzend uitzien naar de komst van Gods dag," *DB* 36 (Dec. 20, 1952) 6–7.
38. "Diocesane spiritualiteit," *KL* 19 (1952) 144–53.
39. "De sacramentaire struktuur van de openbaring," *KL* 19 (1952) 785–802.
40. "Het sakrament van de biecht," *TGL* 8 (1952) 219–42.
41. "De broederlijke liefde als heilswerkelijkheid," *TGL* 8 (1952) 600–19.
42. "Pogingen tot concrete uitwerking van een lekenspiritualiteit," *TGL* 8 (1952) 644–56.
43. "Het niet-begrippelijk kenmoment in onze Godskennis volgens St. Thomas," *TvPh* 14 (1952) 411–54; →143.
44. "Is de biecht nog up to date?" *Th* 6 (1952/3) no. 3, p. 5ff.; no. 5, p. 3ff.

1953

45. "Le forme fondamentali dell'apostolato, de apostolatu moderno," *Acta Congressus Internationalis O.C.D.*, Rome 1953/4, 1-15.
46. "Investituur tot meerderjarigheid," *DB* 36 (May 23, 1953) 4-5.
47. "Het opus operantis in het sacramentalisme," *Theologica* (=jaarboek van het Vlaams werkgenootschap van theologen), I, Ghent, 1953, 59-68.
48. "De evangelische raden," *TGL* 9 (1953) 437-50.
49. "Recente literatuur over de priester-, klooster- en lekenheiligheid," *TGL* 9 (1953) 695-98.
50. "L'amour vient de Dieu," *VS* 38 (1953) 563-79; tr. "Love comes from God," *Cross and Crown* 16 (1964) 190-204.

1954

51. *Maria, Christus' mooiste wonderschepping,* Antwerpen: Apostolaat van de Rosenkrans, 1954, cf. 60.
52. "De heiligmakende genade als heiliging van ons bestaan," *TGL* 10 (1954) 7-27.
53. "Evangelie en Kerk," *TGL* 10 (1954) 93-121; also in *Carmel* 6 (1953/4) 129-57.
54. "Het geloofsleven van de 'Dienstmaagd des Heren,'" *TGL* 10 (1954) 242-69.
55. "Dogmatische Marialiteratuur," *TGL* 10 (1954) 386-88; 392-95.
56. "Het gebed, centrale daad van het menselijk leven," *TGL* 10 (1954) 469-90.
57. "Het wonder dat Maria heet," *Th* 7 (1953/4) no. 7, 5-7.
58. "Maria onze hoop," *Th* (1954/5) no. 1, 4-6.
59. "De zware strijd van Maria's geloof," *Th* 8 (1954/5) no. 3, 6-7.

1955

60. *Maria, moeder van de verlossing,* Antwerpen/Haarlem: Apostolaat van de Rosenkrans, 1955 (revised edition of no. 51); tr. (a) *Marie, mère de la rédemption,* Paris: Cerf, 1963 (corr.); (b) *Mary, Mother of the Redemption,* London/ New York: Sheed and Ward, 1964 (corr.); (c) *Maria, madre della redenzione,* Rome: Catania, 1965; (d) *Maria, mare de la redempció,* Barcelona: Edicions, 1965 (corr.); (e) *Maria, maê de redençaô,* Petrópolis: Vozes, 1966; (f) *Maria, Madre de la redención,* Madrid: Cristianidad, 1969 (corr.).
61. "Het offer der Eucharistie," *DB* 38 (June 4, 1955) 6-7.
62. "De dood lichtende horizont van de oude dag," *DB* 39 (Dec. 10, 1955) 4-5.
63. "De bruid van de Heilige Geest," *Th* 8 (1954/5), no. 3, 3ff.
64. "Christendom als uitnodiging en antwoord," *Th* 9 (1955/6), no. 3, 4-5.
65. "De dood van een christen," *KL* 22 (1955) 421-30; 508-19; tr. "Death of a Christian," *Life of the Spirit* 16 (1962) 270-79; 335-45 (corr.); →130.
66. "Rond het geval 'Konnersreuth,'" *TGL* 11 (1955) 52-63.
67. "Priesterschap en Episcopaat," *TGL* 11 (1955) 357-63.
68. "Turbaris erga plurima: over de geest van het streven de volmaaktheid," *TGL* 11 (1955) 495-516.

69. "Betekenis en waarde van de Mariaveschijningen," *Standaard van Maria* 31 (1955) 154-62.
70. "De christelijke hoop, kernproblem van de huidige christelijke confessies," *KL* 23 (1955) 110-25.

1956

71. "Kloosterlijke gehoorzaamheid," *TGL* 12 (1956) 352-65.

1957

72. In: *Theologisch Woordenboek*, II, Roermond/Maaseik: J. J. Romen en Zonen, 1957: (a) "Geloofsbelijdenis," col. 1749-50 (→143); (b) 'Geloofsbepaling," col. 1750; (c) "Geloofsgeheim," col. 1750-52; (d) "Geloofswaarheid," col. 1755-58; (e) "Geschiedenis," col. 1838-40; (f) "Gezagsargument," col. 1908-20 (→143); (g) "Handoplegging," col. 2300-2302; (i) "Kerkvader," col. 2768-72 (→143); (j) "Kerkvergadering," col. 2773-76; (k) "Kerygmatische Theologie," col. 2779-81; (l) "Ketterij," col. 2784-85; (m) "Lex orandi lex credendi," col. 2926-28 (→143); (n) "Loci theologici," col. 3004-6 (→143); (o) "Maria, theologische synthese," col. 3078-3151; (p) "Merkteken," col. 3231-37.
73. "Op zoek naar Gods afwezigheid," *KL* 24 (1957) 276-91; (→168).
74. "Mutua correlatio inter redemption obiectivam eamque subiectivam B. M. Virginis," *Virgo Immaculata* (Acta Congr. Mariologici-Mariani, 1954), IX, Rome: Academia Mariana Internationalis, 1957, 305-21.
75. "Sakramente als Organe der Gottesbegegnung," *Fragen der Theologie heute*, Einsiedeln: Benziger, 1957, 379-401; revised Dutch version: (a) "De sacramenten der Kerk," *Theologisch Perspectief*, III, Bussum: Paul Brand, 1959, 165-92; also: Hasselt: De Heideland, 1960; (b) "The Sacraments, An Encounter with God," *Christianity divided*, London/New York: Sheed and Ward, 1961, 245-75; (→241 corr.); (c) "Los Sacramentos como organos del Encuentro con Dios," *Panorama de la Teología Actual*, Madrid, 1961; (d) *Katorikku Shingaku* 2 (1963) 3-26; (e) *I Sacramenti punti d'incontro con Dio*, Brescia: Queriniana, 1966.
76. "Het apostolisch ambt van de kerkelijke hiërarchie," *Studia catholica* 32 (1957) 258-90.
77. "God in menselijkheid," *TGL* 13 (1957) 697-710.
78. *De Christusontmoeting als sacrament van de Godsontmoeting*. Antwerp/Bilthoven: H. Nelissen, 1958. See no. 90.

1958

79. *Lexikon für Theologie und Kirche*, vol. II (1958²): "Begierdetaufe," col. 112-15.
80. In: *Theologisch Woordenboek*, III, Roermond/Maaseik: J. J. Romen en Zonen, 1959; (a) "Mysterie" col. 3387-92; (b) "Mysteriëncultus," col. 3392-95; (c) "Nouvelle Théologie," col. 3519-20; (d) "Obex," col. 3523; (e) "Overlevering," col. 3683-93; (f) "Priesterschap," col. 3959-4003 (→80x); (g) "Reliquiënverering," col. 4118-23; (h) "Sacrament," col. 4185- 4230; (i) "Sacramentale,"

col. 4231-32; (j) "Schat der Kerk," col. 4247-48; (k) "Scheeben," col. 4248-49; (l) "Schisma," col. 4270-71; (m) "H. Schrift," col. 4294-99; (n) "Simulatie," col. 4334-35; (o) "Symbolum," col. 4449-60 (→143); (p) "Theologie," col. 4485-4542 (→143); (q) "Verijzenis," col. 4741-48; (r) "Voorgeborchte," col. 4830-34; (s) "Vormsel," col. 4840-70; (t) "Wijding," col. 4967-82; (u) "Zalving," col. 4997; (v) "Zegening," col. 4999; (w) "Zekerheid," col. 4999-5001; (x) tr. of (f). *Síntesis teologica del sacerdocio,* Salamanca: Calatrava, 1959; 1964².

81. "Maria 'meest-verloste Moeder,'" *De Linie* 13 (July 23, 1958).

82. "God en mens," *Theologische week over de mens,* Nijmegen: Dekker en van de Vegt, 1958, 3-21; (→155).

83. "Het katholieke ziekenhuis en de katholieke gezondheidszorg," *Ons Ziekenhuis* 20 (1958) 317-25; tr. (a) "L'hôpital catholique et le service de santé catholique," *Hospitalia* 4 (1959) 29-35; (→168).

84. "De predicatione dominiciana ad academicos quid doceat historia Ordinis nostri," *Acta conventus internationalis O.F.P. de predicatione,* Rome, 1958, 57-63; tr. (a) "Dominican Preaching," *Dominicana* (Washington) 52 (1958) 390-99; →155.

85. "De roepingsverantwoordelijkheid van de katholieke intellektueel," *Roeping* 34 (1958) 390-99; →155.

86. "De theologische zienswijze nopens het probleem van de menselijke verantwoordelijkheid," *R. K. Artsenblad* 37 (1958) 361-63.

87. "De Maria-gestalte in het christelijk belijden," *Studia Catholica* 33 (1958) 241-55.

88. "Het Lourdes-dossier," *TGL* 14 (1958) 256-60.

89. "De kyriale waardigheid van Christus in de verkondiging," *Vox theologica* 29 (1958) 34-39; →143.

1959

90. *Christus sacrament van de Godsontmoeting,* Bilthoven: H. Nelissen, 1959 (revised edition of 78); tr. (a) *Christus, Sakrament der Gottesbegegnung,* Mainz: Matthias Grünewald, 1959 (corr.); (b) *Le Christ, sacrement de la recontre de Dieu* (Lex orandi, 31), Paris: Cerf, 1961vv; id. (Foi vivante, 133), Paris/Brussels: C. E. P./Office générale du livre, 1970 (corr.); (c) *Cristo, sacramento dell'incontro con Dio,* Rome: Paoline, 1962 (corr.); (d) *Christ the Sacrament of the Encounter with God,* London: Sheed and Ward, 1963 (corr.); (e) *Christ the Sacrament of the Encounter with God,* New York: Sheed and Ward, 1963 (corr.); (f) *Cristo Sacramento del Encuentro con Dios,* San Sebastian: Dinor, 1964 (corr.); (g) *Jesu Crist, sagrament entre Déu i l'home,* Barcelona: Edicions, 1965 (corr.); (h) *Chrystus, Sakrament spotkania z Bogiem,* Krakow, 1966; (i) (*Christus Sacrament*), Tokyo, 1966; (j) *Cristo Sacramento do Encontro com Deus,* Petrópolis: Vozes, 1967.

91. *Op zoek naar de levende God,* Nijmegen: Dekker en van de Vegt, 1959; →155; →223.

92. "De genade van een Algemeen Concilie," *DB* 42 (Feb. 7, 1959) 4-6; tr. "The Grace of a General Council," *The Advocate* (Melbourne), (March 15 and 22, 1962); →144.

93. "Nieuwe theologie?" *KL* 26 (1959) 122-26.

94. "De plaag van onchristelijke toekomstverwachtingen," *KL* 26 (1959) 504–13; →168.

95. "Godsdienst en sacrament," *Studia Catholica* 34 (1959) 267–83.

96. "De kerkelijkheid van de godsdienstige mens," *TGL* 15 (1959) 108–131; →168.

97. "Wat is heiligheid?" *TGL* 15 (1959) 221–25.

98. "God op de helling," *TGL* 15 (1959) 397–409; →155.

99. "De leek in de Kerk," *TGL* 15 (1959) 669–94; tr. "The Layman in the Church," *Doctrine and Life* 11 (1961) 369–75; 397–408; and *The Thomist* 27 (1963) 262–83 (corr.); →130; →200.

100. "Hemelvaart en Pinksteren," *Tijdschrift voor Liturgie* 43 (1959) 161–80; tr. (a) "Ascension and Pentecost," *Worship* 35 (1961) 336–63, and *Word and Mystery*, Westminster, MD: Newman, 1968, 245–72 (corr.).

101. "Tendances de la sensibilité religieuse contemporaine," VS(Suppl) 48 (1959) 5–9; summ.: (a) "Sources of Current Religious Attitudes," *Theology Digest* 9 (1961) 137–39.

1960

102. "De zegeningen van het sacramentale huwelijk," special number of *DB* 43 (Feb. 7, 1960); tr. (a) *Le mariage est un sacrement*, Brussels: CEP/Paris: Office générale du livre, 1961; (b) *Il matrimonio e un sacramento*, Milan: Ancora, 1963; summ. (c) "El matrimonio es un sacramento," *Selecciones de teología* 4 (1965) 121–31.

103. "Het gesprek tussen de levensbeschouwingen," *Het gesprek* (Nederlands: Gesprekscentrum publikatie, I), Kampen/Utrecht/Antwerpen/Den Haag, 1960, 11–16; →168; →223.

104. "De kloosterlijke gehoorzaamheid," *De kloosterling*, supplement 1960, 19–32.

105. "Priesterlijke Narcissus of mislukte theoloog?" *KL* 27 (1960) 24–29.

106. "De zin van het dier voor de mens," *R. K. Artsenblad* 39 (1960) 59–63; →168.

107. "Het komende concilie als opdracht voor de gelovigen," *TGL* 16 (1960) 365–76; →144.

108. "De goede levensleiding van God," *TGL* 16 (1960) 571–92; →155.

109. "De dienst van het woord in verband met de Eucharistieviering," *Tijdschrift voor Liturgie* 44 (1960) 44–61; tr. (a) "Parole et sacrement dans l'Eglise," *Lumière et vie* 46 (1960) 25–45; (b) "Revelation in Word and Deed," *The Word: Readings in Theology*, New York: Sheed and Ward, 1964, 255–72; "Word and Sacrament in the Church," *Listening* 4 (1969) 25–38; →143.

110. "Verschillend standpunt van exegese en dogmatiek," *Maria in het boodschapsverhaal* (Verlagsboek der 16e mariale dagen 1959), Tongerloo, 1960, 53–74.

111. "Derde Orde, nieuwe stijl," *Zwart op Wit* (Huissen) 30 (1960) 113–28.

1961

112. *Catholica*, 's-Gravenhage: A. M. Heidt, 1961²: (a) "Jesus Christus," II, col. 675–80; (b) "Maria," I en II, col. 1040–44.

113. "Het gebed als liefdegesprek," *De Heraut van het Heilig Hart* 92 (1961) 163–65.

114. "Gebed als daad van geloof, hoop en liefde," *De Heraut van het Heilig Hart* 92 (1961) 186–88.

115. "De betekenis van het niet-godsdienstig humanisme voor het hedendaagse katholicisme," (W. Engelen, ed.), *Het modern niet-godsdienstig humanisme*, Nijmegen: Dekker en van de Vegt, 1961, 74–112; →155; →223.

116. "Wijsgerig-theologische beschouwingen over man en vrouw," *R. K. Artsenblad* 40 (1961) 85–93.

117. "Roeping, levensontwerp en levensstaat," *TGL* 17 (1961) 471–520; →200.

118. "De nieuwe wending in de huidige dogmatiek," *TvT* 1 (1961) 17–47; →143.

119. "Het bewustzijnsleven van Christus," *TvT* 1 (1961) 227–51.

1962

120. "Exegese, Dogmatik und Dogmenentwicklung," *Exegese und Dogmatik*, Mainz: Matthias Grünewald, 1962, 91–114; tr. (a) "Exegese, dogmatiek en dogma-ontwikkeling," *Exegese en dogmatiek*, Bilthoven: H. Nelissen, 1963, 92–114; tr. (b) "Exegesis, Dogmatics and the Development of Dogma," *Dogmatic vs. Biblical Theology*, Baltimore/Dublin: Helicon, 1964; 115–45; →143.

121. "Theologische reflexie op godsdienst-sociologische duidingen in verband met het hedendaagse 'ongeloof'," *TvT* 2 (1962) 55–77; tr. (a) "Theological reflections on Religio-Sociological Interpretations of Modern 'Irreligion'," *Social Compass* 10 (1963) 257–84 (corr.); →200; →223.

122. "Ter school bij prof. A. Dondeyne," *TvT* 2 (1962) 78–83.

123. "De zin van het mens-zijn van Jezus, de Christus," *TvT* 2 (1962) 127–72; expanded tr. (a) "Die Heiligung des Namens Gottes durch die Menschenliebe Jesu des Christus," *Gott im Welt* (Festgabe für K. Rahner), II, Freiburg/Basel/Vienna: Herder, 1964, 432–91 (corr.); tr. (b) "La santificazione del nome di Dio nell'amore di Gesu Cristo per gli uomini," *Orizzonte attuale della teología*, II, Rome, 1967, 9–67.

124. "Dogmatiek van ambt en lekenstaat," *TvT* 2 (1962) 258–94; →200.

125. "Hoop en bezorgdheid: Op de vooravond van een concilie," *DB* 46 (Oct. 6, 1962) 1–2.

126. "Het waarheidsbegrip en aanverwante problemen," *Katholiek Archief* 17 (1962) 1169–86; also, *De katholieke kerk en de oecumenische beweging* (Do-C dossiers, 2), Hilversum: Paul Brand, 1964, 91–118; tr. "Notion de vérité et la tolérance, *La liberté religieuse* Paris: Cerf, 1965, 113–54; →143 ("Waarheid"); →168 ("Tolerantie").

1963

127. *Het huwelijk: aardse wekelijkheid en heilsmysterie*, I, Bilthoven: H. Nelissen, 1963; tr. (a) *Marriage, Secular Reality and Saving Mystery*, 1 & 2, London/Melbourne: Sheed and Ward, 1965 (corr.); (b) *Marriage, Human Reality and Saving Mystery*, 1 & 2, New York: Sheed and Ward, 1966 (corr.); cf. 241; (c) *Le mariage, réalité terrestre et mystère de salut*, I, Paris: Cerf, 1966 (corr.); (d) *Il Matrimonio, Realtà terrena e mistero di salvezza*, Rome: Paoline, 1968 (corr.); (e) *El matrimonio: realidad terrena y misterio de salvación*, I, Salamanca: Sigueme, 1968 (corr.); (f) *O matrimônio: Realidade terrestre e mistério de salvacao*, Petrópolis: Vozes, 1969 (corr.).

128. "Indrukken over een strijd van geesten, Vaticanum II," *DB* 46 (Jan. 5, 1963) 1-5; tr. (a) "Vatican II: Impressions of a Struggle of Minds," *Life of the Spirit* 17 (1963) 499-505 (corr.); (b) "Impressions sur Vatican II," *Évangéliser* 17 (1963) 343-50; →130; →144.

129. "Misverstanden op het concilie," *DB* 46 (January 19, 1963) 1-5; tr. (a) "Misunderstandings at the Council," *Life of the Spirit* 18 (1963) 2-12 (corr.); (b) summary, *Theology Digest* 11 (1963) 131-34; →130; →144.

130. *Vatican II: the Struggle of Minds, and Other Essays,* Dublin: M. H. Gill, 1963 (includes: 65, 99, 128, and 129); (a) *The Layman in the Church,* Staten Island, New York: Alba House, 1963 (corr.).

131. "De stem van Elckerlyc over het concilie," *DB* 46 (March 16, 1963) 1-3; →144.

132. "Wederwoord (aan W. K. Grossouw, 'Evelyn Waugh en de Anawim')," *DB* 46 (March 30, 1963) 5.

133. "Johannes XXIII en Vaticanum II," *DB* 46 (June 29, 1963) 1-5; →144.

134. "Aan de vooravond van de tweede sessie," *DB* 44 (Oct. 12, 1963) 1-2; →144.

135. "De natuurwet in verband met de katholieke huwelijksopvatting," *Jaarboek Werkgenootschap van Katholieke Theologen in Nederland,* Hilversum: Gooi en Sticht, 1963, 5-61; →155.

136. "Het niet-begrippelijk moment in de geloofsdaad volgens Thomas: kritische studie," *TvT* 3 (1963) 167-95; tr. (a) "L'instinct de la foi selon S. Thomas d'Aquin," *Revue de Sciences Philosophiques et Theologiques* 48 (1964) 377-408 (corr.); →143.

137. "De heilsopenbaring en haar 'overlevering,'" *Kerk en theologie* 14 (1963) 85-99; also, *Jaarboek 1962 Werkgenootschap van Katholieke Theologen in Nederland,* Hilversum: Gooi en Sticht, 1963, 137-62; also, *Schrift en traditie* (Do-C dossiers, 8), Hilversum: Paul Brand, 1965, 13-20; →143.

138. "Het moderne huwelijkstype: een genadekans," *TGL* 19 (1963) 221-33.

139. "Bezinning en apostolaat in het leven der seculiere en reguliere priesters," *TGL* 19 (1963) 307-29.

140. "Communicatie tussen priester en leek," *Nederlandse Katholieke Stemmen* 59 (1963) 210-222; →200.

141. "Evangelische zuiverheid en menslijke waarachtigheid," *TvT* 3 (1963) 283-326; tr. (a) *Personale Begegnung mit Gott: Eine Antwort an John A. T. Robinson,* Mainz: Matthias Grünewald, 1964 (corr.); (b) Polish tr. *Spór o uczciwość wabec Boga* (Biblioteca), Warszawa: Wiezi, 1966, 339-410; (c) summ. *Selecciones Teologicas* 6 (1967) 171-84; →155.

142. "Een uniforme terminologie van het theologische begrip 'leek,'" *Te Elfder Ure* 10 (1963) 173-76; →200.

1964

143. *Openbaring en Theologie* Theologische Peilingen, I), Bilthoven, 1964 (includes 2, 34c and d, 43, 72a, f, i, m, and n, 80o and p, 89, 109, 118, 120, 126, 136, and 137); tr. (a) *Révélation et théologie* (Approches théologiques, I) Brussels: C. E. P./Paris: Office général du livre, 1965 (corr.); partial reissue: (b) *Le message de Dieu* (Foi vivante, 123), Brussels: C. E. P., 1970 (ch. I/1, 3, 2, 4, and II/3 and 4); (c) *Offenbarung und Theologie* (Gesammelte Schriften, 1), Mainz: Matthias Grünewald, 1965 (corr.); (d) *Rivelazione e teologia,*

Rome: Paoline, 1966 (corr.); (e) *Revelation and Theology* (Theological Sound-ings, I/1), London/Melbourne: Sheed and Ward, 1967; also, New York: Herder and Herder, 1967 (corr.); (f) *Revelation and Theology* II (Theological Soundings, I/2), New York: Herder and Herder, 1968 (corr.); (g) *Revelación y teología* (Verdad e imagen, I), Salamanca: Sigueme, 1968 (corr.); (h) *Revelació i teologia* (Tempteigs teologics, 1), Barcelona: Nova Terra, 1970.

144. *Het tweede Vaticaans concilie,* Tielt/Den Haag: Lannoo, 1964 (includes: 92, 107, 125, 128/9, 131, 134, and 146); tr. (a) *Die Signatur des zweiten Vatika-nums,* Vienna/Freiburg/Basel: Herder, 1965 (→169 partial; corr.) (b) *L'Eglise du Christ et l'homme d'aujourd'hui selon Vatican II,* Le Puy/ Lyon/Paris: X. Mappus, 1965 (→169 partial; corr.); (c) *La chiesa, l'uomo moderno e il Vaticano II,* Rome: Paoline (→169; corr.); (d) *L'Església i l'home, segons el Vaticà II,* Barcelona: Edicions, 1968 (→169); (e) *La Iglesia de Cristo y el hombre moderno según el Vaticano II,* Madrid: Herder, 1969; corr.).

145. "K. Rahner 60 jaar," *DB* 47 (Feb. 29, 1964) 1–2.

146. "De tweede sessie van Vaticanum II," *KL* 31 (1964) 85–99; →144.

147. "Herinterpretatie van het geloof in het licht van de seculariteit: Honest to Robinson," *TvT* 4 (1964) 109–50; tr. (a) *Neues Glaubensverständnis,* Mainz: Matthias Grünewald, 1964 (corr.); (b) *Spór o uczciwość wabec Boga,* War-szawa: Wiezi, 1966; summ., *Selecciones Teologicas* 6 (1967) 171–84; →155.

148. "Kardinaal Alfrink en het tweede Vaticaans concilie," *Vriendengave Bernard Kardinaal Alfrink,* Utrecht/Antwerp: Het Spectrum, 1964, 217–27.

149. "De ascese van het zoeken naar God," *TGL* 20 (1964) 149–58; →200.

150. "Theologische bezinning op de geestelijke begeleiding," *TGL* 20 (1964) 513–27.

151. "De gestalte van de kerk in de toekomst," *Utopia* (Eindhoven) 3 (1964) 18–31; →155.

152. "Kerk en wereld," *TvT* 4 (1964) 386–99; published separately, Hilversum: Gooi en Sticht, 1964; also, *Kerk en wereld* (Do-C dossiers, 10), Hilversum/ Antwerp: Paul Brand, 1966, 7–21; tr. (a) "Church and World," *The Catholic World* 200 (Jan., 1965), 218–23; (b) "Kirche und Welt: Zur Bedeutung von 'schema 13' des Vatikanums II," *Weltverständis im Glauben,* Mainz: Matthias Grünewald, 1965, 127–42; →168; →223.

153. "De waarheid over de laatste concilie-week," *DB* 48 (Dec. 23, 1964); also, Michael van der Plas (ed.) *De paus van Rome,* Utrecht: De Fontein, 1965, 147–66.

154. "La théologie de l'efficience en apostolat," *La responsabilité universelle des chretiens* (Congress Pro mundi vita, 9–10 sept., 1964), Leuven: Pro Mundi Vita, 1964, 231–49.

1965

155. *God en mens* (Theologische Peilingen, 2), Bilthoven: H. Nelissen, 1965 (con-tains 82, 91, 98, 108, 115, 135, 141, 147, and 151); tr. (a) *Dieu et l'homme,* Brussels: CEP/Paris: Office Genéral du livre, 1965 (corr.); (b) partial reissue (chaps. 1, 2, 5, and 6): *Dieu en révision,* Brussels: CEP, 1970; (c) *Dio e l'uomo,* Rome: Paoline, 1967 (corr.); (d) *Dios y el hombre,* Salamanca: Sigueme, 1968

(corr.); (e) *God and Man,* New York: Sheed and Ward, 1969; also London & Sydney: Sheed and Ward, 1969 (corr.); (f) *Deus e o homem,* São Paulo, 1969.

156. *Cardinal Alfrink* (The Men Who Make the Council, 24), Notre Dame: Ave Maria Press, 1965; (a) abbreviated Dutch version: *Bernard kardinaal Alfrink, vragen aan de kerk,* Utrecht/Baarn: Bosch en Keuning, 1967, 5–28.

157. "Kerk en mensdom," *Conc* I (1965) no. 1, 63–86; tr. (a) "The Church and Mankind," *Conc* I (1965) no. 1, 69–100; (b) "The Church and Mankind," *The Sacred and the Secular,*Englewood Cliffs: Prentice-Hall, 1968, 14–40; also, *Readings in the Theology of the Church,* Englewood Cliffs: Prentice-Hall, 1970, 10–38; summ. (c) "Iglesia y Humanidad," *Selecciones Teologicas* 4 (1965), 161–69; →223.

158. "De derde sessie van Vaticanum II," *KL* 32 (1965) 21–38; tr. "Die dritte Sitzungsperiode des Zweiten Vatikanischen Konzils," *Der Seelsorger* 35 (1965) 31–45; also, *Vaticanum secundum,* III/2 *Die dritte Konzilsperiode: Die Verhandlungen,* Leipzig: St. Benno, 1967, 901–17; partially in *Glauben heute,* II: *Ein Lesebuch zur katholischen Theologie der Gegenwart,* Hamburg: Furche, 1968, 106–14; →169.

159. "Wij denken gepassioneerd en in cliché's" *DB* 48 (Jan. 23, 1965), 4–6.

160. "Een nieuwe visie op het rechtvaardigingsdecreet van Trente," *Conc* I (1965) no. 5, 173–76; tr. "The Tridentine Decree on Justification: A New View," *Conc* I (1965) no. 5, 176–79.

161. "Christus' tegenwoordigheid in de eucharistie," *TvT* 5 (1965) 136–73; →188.

162. "Het celibaat van de priester," *TvT* 5 (1965) 296–329.

163. "Ecclesia semper purificanda," *Ex auditu verbi* (Feestbundel G. C. Berkouwer), Kampen: J. H. Kok, 1965, 216–32; →200; →223.

164. "L'université catholique comme problème et promesse," *Recherche et culture: Taches d'une Université catholique,* Fribourg (Suisse): Presses universitaires, 1965, 33–48; tr. (a) "Die katholische Universität als Problem une Verheissung," *Forschung und Bildung,* Freiburg: Universitätsverlag, 1965, 35–51 (corr.); (b) summ. "Considerazioni teologiche sull'Università Cattolica," *Studi Cattolici* 70 (1967) 3–10; (c) tr. "Problems and Promise," *The Catholic University: A Modern Appraisal,* Notre Dame/London: University of Notre Dame Press, 1970, 58–73; →168.

165. "De Godsopenbaring en de heilige boeken volgens het tweede vaticaans concilie," *TGL* 21 (1965) 461–77.

166. "De wisselende visies der christenen op het huwelijk," *Kerk en wereld* (Do-C dossiers, 10), Hilversum/Antwerp: Paul Brand, 1965, 91–114; tr. (a) "Det kristne syn på aeg teskabet gennem tiderne," *Lumen* (Kopenhagen) 9 (1966) 69–91; (b) "Cambios en los conceptos cristianos respecto al matrimonio," *Iglesia, población y familia* (Estudios doctrinales), Santiago (Chile) 1967 (corr.).

167. "Kritisch geloofsdenken als eredienst en apostolaat," *Neerlandia Dominicana* 20 (1965) no. 3, 77–80; also, *Nijmeegs Universiteitsblad* 14 (1964/5) no. 20, 3–4.

167.1 (with Karl Rahner), "Waarom en voor wie dit nieuw internationaal theologisch tijdschrift?" *Conc* I (1965) no. 1, 5–7; tr. "General Introduction," I (1965) no. 1, 1–4.

167.2 (with B. Willems), "Ten geleide," *Conc* I (1965) no. 1, 9–10; tr. "Preface," *Conc* I (1965) no. 1, 5–7.

1966

168. *Wereld en Kerk* (Theologische Peilingen, 3), Bilthoven: H. Nelissen, 1966 (contains: 7, 18, 19, 27, 73, 83, 85, 94, 96, 103, 106, 126-II, 152, 157, 164, 171, 184, and an unpublished article); tr. (a) *Le monde et l'Eglise,* Brussels: CEP/ Paris: Office générale du livre, 1967 (corr.); (b) *Il mondo e la Chiesa,* Rome: Paoline, 1969 (corr.); (c) *El mundo y la Iglesia,* Salamanca: Sigueme, 1969 (corr.); (d) *El mon i l'església,* Barcelona: Edicions, 1970; (e) *O mundo e a Igreja,* São Paolo, 1971; (f) *World and Church,* London, Sydney, and New York: Sheed and Ward, 1971 (without 7, 19, and 73) (corr.).

169. *Het tweede Vaticaanse concilie,* II, Tielt/Den Haag: Lannoo, 1966 (contains 158, 182, and an unpublished article); tr. (a) *Besinnung auf das zweite Vatikanum: Vierte Session,* Vienna: Herder, 1966 (partial) (corr.); (b) *L'Eglise du Christ et l'homme d'aujourd'hui selon Vatican II,* II, Paris: Le Puy, 1966 (partial) (corr.); (c) *Vatican II: The Real Achievement,* London/Melbourne: Sheed and Ward, 1967; (d) *The Real Achievement of Vatican II,* New York: Herder and Herder (corr.); (e) *A zsinat mérlege: Zsinati Bizottsag,* Rome, 1968 (Hungarian) (corr.). See 144.

170. *Het Ambtscelibaat in de branding,* Bilthoven: H. Nelissen, 1966; tr. (with some revisions): (a) *Der Amtszölibat: Eine kritische Besinnung,* Düsseldorf: Patmos, 1967 (corr.); = (b) "Der Amtszölibat," in *Um Himmelreiches Willen* (Pastoral-katechetische Heften, 37), Leipzig: St. Benno, n.d. (1968); (c) *Autour du célibat du prêtre: étude critique,* Paris: Cerf, 1967 (corr.); (d) *Clerical Celibacy under Fire: A Critical Appraisal,* London/Melbourne: Sheed and Ward, 1968; (e) = *Celibacy,* New York: Herder and Herder, 1968 (corr.); (f) *Il Celibato del ministero ecclesiastico. Riflessione critica,* Rome: Paoline, 1968 (corr.); (g) *El celibato ministerial: Reflexión critica,* Salamanca: Sigueme, 1968 (corr.); (h) (partial edition) "Le Celibat sacerdotale," VS(Suppl.) 79 (1966) 514-47.

171. "Het leed der ervaring van Gods verborgenheid," *Vox Theologica* 36 (1966), 92-104; a slightly different version: (a) *Kerygma* 9 (1966) no. 4, 5-34; and (b) "Christen-zijn nú," *Christendom en wereld,* Roermond/ Maaseik: J. J. Romen en Zonen, 1966, 37-61; (c) tr. *Christentum im Spannungsfeld von Konfessionen, Gesellschaft und Staaten,* Vienna/Freiburg/Basel: Herder, 1968, 7-35; →168.

172. "Apostolat des religieux et épiscopat," *Vie Consacrée* 38 (1966) 75-90; tr. (a) "Religiosos y Episcopado," *Selecciones de Teologia* 6 (1967) 239-44 (corr.).

173. "Faith Functioning in Human Self-understanding," *The Word in History: The St. Xavier Symposion,* New York: Sheed and Ward, 1966, 41-59; tr. (a) *Theologie d'aujourd'hui et de demain,* Paris: Cerf, 1967, 121-38 (corr.); (b) *Künftigen Aufgaben der Theologie,* München: Herder, 1967, 61-85; (c) *La parola nella storia,* Brescia: Queriniana, 1968, 45-62; original version: (d) "Het geloof functionerend in het menselijk zelfverstaan," *Het woord in de geschiedenis,* Bilthoven: H. Nelissen, 1969, 49-66.

174. "Zijn er crisis-elementen in katholiek-kerklijk Nederland?" *Katholiek Archief* 21 (1966) 340-353; tr. (a) "Crisis en la Iglesia Catolica de Holanda?," *Palabra* 1966, no. 14 (Oct.) (corr.); (b) "The crisis in Dutch Catholicism," *The Catholic Messenger* (June 2 and 9, 1966): (c) "Kirche nach dem Konzil: Ausblicke für Holland," *Diakonia* 2 (1967) 1-15 (corr.); (d) "Osservazioni sulla 'crisi' in Olanda," *Rassegna di teologia* 8 (1967) 287-94; (e) "In Olanda le cose stanno

così," *Famiglia Cristiana* 37, no. 47 (Nov. 19, 1967), 32–42 (corr.); also, *I grandi teologi respondono*, Rome: Paoline, 1968, 255–87.

175. "In Memoriam Bisschop W. M. Bekkers," *Katholiek Archief* 22 (1966) 632–39; also, *Bisschof Bekkers, negen jaar met Gods volk onderweg*, Utrecht: Ambo (1966), 54–64; summ. (a) *Conc* 2 (1966) no. 6, 157–59.

176. "Transsubstantiation, Transfinalization, Transfiguration [*sic*] (Transsignification)," *Worship* 40 (1966) 324–38; also, *Living Bread, Saving Cup: Readings on the Eucharist*, ed. by R. Kevin Seasoltz, Collegeville, Minnesota: Liturgical Press, 1982, 175–89; tr. (a) "Transustanciación, Transfinalización, Transignificación," *Sal terrae* 54 (1966) no. 1, 8–24; (b) "Una questione attuale di teologia eucharistica: transustanziazione-transfinalizzazione-transignificazione," *Revista di pastorale liturgica* 4 (1966) 227–48; (c) "Transubstanciaçâo, transfinalizeçâo, transignificaçâo," *Revista Eclesiastica Brasileria* 26 (1966) 286–310; summ. (d) "Transubstanciación eucharistica," *Selecciones teologicas* 5 (1966) 135–41.

177. "Het huwelijk volgens Vaticanum II," *TGL* 22 (1966) 81–107; also, *Kath. Artsenblad* 45 (1966) 33–41; also, *Verplegenden en gemeenschapszorg*, 1966 no. 2, 111–31.

178. "De kerk op drift?" *TGL* 22 (1966) 533–54; →200; →223.

179. "Persoonlijke openbaringsgestalte van de Vader," *TvT* 6 (1966) 274–88; summ. (a) "Cristo revelación personal del Padre," *Selecciones de teologia* 11 (1972) 170–77 (corr.).

180. "De eucharistische wijze van Christus' werkelijke tgegenwoordigheid," *TvT* 6 (1966) 359–94; →188.

181. "Het concilie en de dialogale strukturen," *De concilieboodschap voor de kerk in Vlaanderen*, Leuven, 1966, 43–62.

182. "De typologische van de christelijke leek volgens Vaticanum II," *De kerk van Vaticanum II*, Bilthoven: H. Nelissen, 1966, 285–304; →200; →223.

183. "Bezinning op het eindresultaat van Vaticanum II," *Oecumene* 5 (1966) 12–22; also, *KL 33 (1966) 84*–108; tr. (a) "Besinnung auf das II. Vatikanum," *Der Seelsorger* 36 (1966) 84–96 (corr.); →169.

184. "Neutralité technique et professionnelle et perspectives spirituelles du travailleur social," *Service social dans le monde* 25 (1966) 103–13; →168.

185. "Nieuwe bloei van integralisme: Rome-brief gevaarlijk," *De Volkskrant* (Nov. 23, 1966).

186. "Ecclesia in mundo huius temporis," *Angelicum* 43 (1966) 340–52.

187. "De leken in het volk van God," *Godsvolk en leek en ambt* (Do-C dossiers, 7), Hilversum/Antwerp: Paul Brand, 1966, 49–58 (tr.)

187.1 (with B. Willems), "Ten geleide," *Conc* 2 (1966) no. 1, 5–6; tr. "Introduction," *Conc* 2 (1966) no. 1, 1–4.

1967

188. *Christus' tegenwoordigheid in de eucharistie*, Bilthoven: H. Nelissen, 1967 (contains 161 and 180); tr. (a) *Die eucharistische Gegenwart: Zur Diskussion über die Realpräsenz*, Düsseldorf: Patmos, 1967 (corr.); (b) *La presenza eucharistica*, Rome: Paoline, 1968 (corr.); (c) *La presencia de Cristo en la Eucharistia*, Madrid, 1968 (corr.); (d) *The Eucharist*, New York/London/Sydney: Sheed and Ward, 1968 (corr.); (e) *La présence du Christ dans l'Eucharistie*, Paris: Cerf, 1970.

189. "Het nieuwe mens- en Godsbeeld in conflict met het religieuze leven," *TvT* 7 (1967) 1-27; tr. (a) "Das Ordensleben in der Auseinandersetzung mit dem neuen Menschen- und Gottesbild," *Ordens-Korrespondenz* 9 (1968) 105-34 (corr.); (b) summ. "La vida religiosa en conflicto con la nueva idea del hombre y de Dios," *Selecciones de teolosgía* 8 (1969) 141-52; →200.

190. "Christelijk geloof en aardse toekomstverwachting," *De kerk in de wereld van deze tijd* (Vaticanum II, 2), Hilversum: Paul Brand/Antwerp: Patmos, 1967, 78-109; tr. (a) *Gaudium et spes: L'Eglise dans le monde et son temps,* Paris: Cerf, 1967, 117-58; (b) *The Church Today,* Westminster: Newman, 1968, 60-94; (c) *A Igreja no mundo de hoje,* São Paolo: Liberia Sampedro, 1969, 95-125; →200; →223.

191. "De a.s. synode der bisschoppen is nagenoeg even belangrijk als het tweede vaticaans concilie," *DB* 50 (April 8, 1967) 1-3.

192. "Deconfessionalisering der universiteit?" *Universiteit en Hogeschool* 13 (1967) 428-34; also, *Onze Alma Mater* (Leuven) 21 (1967) 211-18.

193. "Un nouveau type de laïc," *La nouvelle image de l'Eglise: Bilan du concile Vatican II,* Tours: Mame, 1967, 172-85 (tr.); summ. *Spiritual Life* 14 (1968) 14-24; →200; →223.

194. "The Spiritual Intent of Indulgences," *Lutheran World* 14 (1967) no. 3, 11-32; also, *The Reformed and Presbyterian World* 29 (1967) 255-82 (corr.); (a) German version: "Der Sinn der Katholischen Ablasspraxis," *Lutherische Rundschau* 17 (1967) 328-53 (corr.).

195. "Pastoraal concilie: óók teologisch beluisteren van Nederlandse situatie; op zoek naar een 'fundamenteel document,'" *Kosmos en Oecumene* I (1967) 181-92.

196. "Die Sakramente in Plan Gottes," *Krankendienst* 40 (1967) 278-81; tr. (a) "De sacramenten in het heilsplan Gods," *Ons Ziekenhuis* 29 (1967) 294-98 (corr.); (b) "Les sacrements dans le plan de Dieu," *Presences* no. 102 (1968) 25-34.

197. "Naar een katholiek gebruik van de hermeneutiek: Geloofsidentiteit in het interpreteren van het geloof," *Geloof bij kenterend getij* (Feestbundel W. van de Pol), Roermond: J. J. Romen en Zonen/Maaseik, 1967, 78-116; tr. (a) "O katolickie zastosowanie hermeneutyki: Tożcamość wiary w toku jej reinterpretacji," *Znak* 20 (1968) 978-1010; (b) "Auf dem Weg zu einer katholischen Anwendung der Hermeneutik," *Neue Perspektiven nach dem Ende des konventionellen Christentums,* Freiburg: Herder, 1968, 69-119; (c) "Hacia un empleo católico de la hermenéutica," *Fin del Cristianismo convencional,* Salamanca: Sigueme, 1969, 61-103; (d) "Verso un impiego cattolico dell'ermeneutica," E. Schillebeeckx and P. Schoonenberg, *Fede e interpretazione,* Brescia: Queriniana, 1971, 25-81; →201; →240.

198. "Werkelijke eredienst en kerkelijke liturgie," *TvT* 7 (1967) 288-302; tr. (a) "Skal man aere Gud midt i verden eller gennem kirkens liturgi?" *Lumen* (Kopenhagen) II (1968), 125-41; (b) "Glorifier Dieu en plein monde," *Liturgies et communautés humaines,* Paris: Cerf, 1969, 103-28 (corr.); (c) "Culto profano e celebrazione liturgica," *Rivista di pastorale liturgica* 7 (1969) 215-324. See 241; →201.

199. "Zwijgen en spreken over God in een geseculariseerde wereld," *TvT* 7 (1967) 337-59; →201.

199.1 (with B. Willems), "Ten geleide," *Conc* 3 (1967) no. 1, 5-6; tr. "Preface," *Conc* vol. 21, 1-2.

1968

200. *De zending van kerk* (Theologische Peilingen, 4), Bilthoven: H. Nelissen, 1968 (contains 21, 99, 117, 121, 124, 140, 142, 149, 163, 178, 182, 189, 190, 193, 213, and two unpublished articles): tr. (a) *La mission de l'Eglise*, Brussels: CEP/Paris: Office genérale du livre, 1969 (instead of 121, no. 210; corr.); (b) *L 'Església enviada*, Barcelona: Edicions, 1971; (c) *La missione della Chiesa*, Rome: Paoline, 1971 (→210; corr.); (d) *La misión de la Iglesia*, Salamanca: Sigueme, 1971 (instead of 121, no. 210; corr.); (e) *The Mission of the Church*, London/Sydney/New York: Sheed and Ward, 1973 (partial; →210; corr.).

201. *God, the Future of Man*, New York: Sheed and Ward, 1968; also, London/ Sydney: Sheed and Ward, 1969 (contains 197, 198, 203, 204, and 205; corr.) tr. (a) *Gott, die Zukunft des Menschen*, Mainz: Matthias Grünewald, 1969 (corr.); (b) *Dio, il futuro dell'uomo*, Rome: Paoline 1970 (corr.); (c) *Dios, futuro del hombre*, Salamanca: Sigueme, 1970 (corr.). See 240.

202. "Katholiek leven in de Verenigde Staten," *DB* 51 (Jan. 21, 1968) 4-8; tr. (a) "Catholic Life in the United States," *Worship* 42 (1968) 134-49 (corr.).

203. "Het nieuwe Godsbeeld, secularisatie en politiek," *TvT* 8 (1968) 44-66; tr. (a) "Dio è colui che verrà," *Processo alla religione*, Milan: Mondadori, 1968, 139-59; (b) "Per una immagine di Dio nel mundo secolarizzato," *La secolarizzazione*, Bologna: il Mulino, 1973, 279-92; (c) "Nový obraz Boha a sekularizace," *Křestanství dnes (Eseje)*, Prague, 1969, 125-49; (d) summ. "La nueva imagen de Dios, secularización y futuro del hombre en la tierra," *Selecciones de teología* 8 (1969) 305-12. See no. 215; →201.

204. "Theologische draagwijdte van het magisteriële spreken over sociaal-politieke kwesties," *Conc* 4 (1968) no. 4, 21-40; tr. "The Magisterium and the World of Politics," *Conc* vol. 36, 19-39; →201.

205. "De kerk als sacrament van dialoog," *TvT* 8 (1968) 155-69; tr. (a) "L'unique témoignage et le dialogue dans la recontre avec le monde," *Oecumenica 1969*, 1969, 171-87; →201.

206. "De kerk en haar problemen," *DB* 51 (Aug. 25, 1968), 1-2.

207. "Woord vooraf," T. M. Schoof, *Aggiornamento: De doorbraak van een nieuwe katholieke theologie*, Baarn: Het Wereldvenster, 1968, 7-12; tr. "Introduction," in *A Survey of Catholic Theology*, New York: Paulist Newman Press, 1970, 1-5.

208. "Theology of Renewal talks about God," *Theology of Renewal*, I, Montreal: Palm, 1968, 83-105; also, *The Spirit and Power of Christian Secularity*, Notre Dame: University of Notre Dame, 1969, 156-79; also, *Theology* 71 (1968) 256-67; 298-304; tr. (a) "La théologie du renouveau parle de Dieu," *La théologie du renouveau*, I, Paris: Cerf, 1968, 91-109 (corr.); (b) summ. "Il silenzio cristiano e il discorso sul Dio," *Rocca XXVIII* no. 4 (Feb. 15, 1969) 26-29; (c) "Sollen wir heute noch von Gott reden?" *Theologie der Gegenwart* II (1968) 125-35.

209. "Kleingelovigen!" *Accent* I (1968) no. 43, 41.

210. "Theologische kanttekeningen bij de huidige priestercrisis," *TvT* 8 (1968) 402-434; tr. (a) "Réflexiones théologiques sur la crise actuelle du prêtre," *Collectanea Mechliniensia* 54 (1969) 221-57; (b) "The Catholic Understanding of Office in the Church," *Theological Studies* 30 (1969) 567-87 (corr.); (c) "Reflexiones teológicas sobre la contestación y la crisis actual del sacerdote,"

312   *Bibliography*

Seminarios 17 (1971) 45–80; (d) summ. "Theologie des kirchlichen Amtes," *Diakonia/Der Seelsorger* I (1970) 147–60 (corr.); (e) "Towards a More Adequate Theology of Priesthood," *Theology Digest* 18 (1970) 105–13 (corr.); →200 a, c, d, and e; →223; also, *Evangelium, Welt, Kirche,* Frankfurt a. M., 1975, 245–306.

211. "Wijsgerig-antropologische beschouwingen over de medische manipuleerbaarheid van het sterven," *Katholiek Artsenblad* 47 (1968) 361–69; (a) in a different place, "De grens tussen leven en dood: I. Wijsgerig antropologische beschouwingen," *KL* 37 (1970) 119–26.

212. "Le philosophe Paul Ricoeur, docteur en théologie," *Christianisme Social* 78 (1968) 639–45.

213. "De Ecclesia ut sacramento mundi," *Acta congressus internationalis de theologia concilii Vaticani II,* Vatican City, 1968, 48–53; →200; →223.

214. "Il rapporto tra sacerdozio e celibato: Appunti teologici," *C'è un domani per il Prete?,* Milan: Ancora, 1968.

214.1 (with B. Willems), "Ten geleide," *Conc* 4 (1968) no. 1, 5–7; tr. "Preface," *Conc* vol. 31, 1–2.

1969

215. "Kritische beschouwingen over het 'secularistatie'—begrip in verband met allerlei thema's van het pastoraal concilie," *Pastoraal concilie van de Nederlandse Kerkprovincie,* V, Amersfoort: Katholiek Archief, 1969, 114–39 (expansion of 203).

216. "Enkele hermeneutische beschouwingen over de eschatologie," *Conc* 5 (1969) no. 1, 38–51; tr. "The Interpretation of Eschatology," *Conc* vol. 41, 42–56; →240.

217. "Kulturele en kerkelijke revolutie," *St. Lukas Tijdschrift* 41 (1969) 5–19; also, *De Maand* 12 (1969) 426–36.

218. "Préface," J. Sperna Weiland, *La Nouvelle Théologie,* Paris/Brussels: Desclée de Brouwer, 1969, 11–14.

219. "Preface," I. Berten, *Histoire, révélation et foi,* Brussels/Paris: Desclée de Brouwer, 1969, 7–8.

220. "Het 'rechte geloof,' zin onzekerheden en zijn criteria," *TvT* 9 (1969) 125–50; →223.

221. "Synode, gouvernement collégial et Eglise locale," *IDOC-International* no. 8 (Nov. 15, 1969) 75–86.

222. "Hermeneutiek en theologie: Schematische proeve van een totaal concept," *Interpretatieleer* (Annalen van het Thijmgenootschap 57/I) Bussum: Paul Brand, 1969, 28–56; →223; →240.

222.1 (with B. Willems), "Ten geleide," *Conc* 5 (1969) no. 1, 5–8; tr. "Preface," *Conc* vol. 41, 1–2.

1970

223. *Gott-Kirche-Welt* (Gesammelte Schriften, 2), Mainz: Matthias Grünewald, 1970 (translation of selections from 155, 168, and 200; contains: 27, 91, 103, 115, 121, 152, 157, 163, 178, 182, 190, 193, 210, 213).

224. "De nederlandse katholieke partijvorming," *DB* 53 (Jan. 4, 1970), 6–8.
225. (with G. C. Berkouwer and H. A. Oberman): *Ketters of voortrekkers? Vier gesprekken over de geestelijke horizon van onze tijd,* Kampen: J. H. Kok, 1970; also, *Rondom het woord,* vol. 12, no. 1 (Feb. 1970), 3–39.
226. "Het christelijk huwelijk en de menselijke realiteit van volkomen huwelijksontwrichting," *(On)ontbindbaarheid van het huwelijk* (Annalen van het Thijmgenootschap 58/1), Bussum: Paul Brand, 1970, 184–214; tr. (a) "Die christliche Ehe und die menschliche Realität völliger Ehezerrüttung," *Für eine neukirchliche Eheordung: Ein Alternativentwurf,* ed. by P. Huizing, Düsseldorf: Patmos, 1978, 41–74.
227. "Profetas de la presencia viva de Dios," *Revista de Espiritualidad* 29 (1970) 319–21.
228. "Christelijk antwoord op een menselijk vraag? De oecumenische betekenis van de "correlatiemethode,'" *TvT* 10 (1970) 1–22; →223; →240.
229. "Leven ondanks de dood in heden en toekomst," *TvT* 10 (1970) 418–52.
230. "Na twintig eeuwen schijnen we gewend te zijn aan Gods bezoek," *DB* 54 (Dec. 20, 1970) 4–5.
231. "Ten geleide, openingstoesprak en slottoespraak wereldcongres 'Concilium,'" *De toekomst van de kerk* (Proceedings of the *Concilium* world congress), Amersfoort/Bussum: Paul Brand, 1970, 6–14, 24–27, and 155–59; tr. (a) *Die Zukunft der Kirche,* Einsiedeln: Benziger, 1971; (b) *El futuro de la Iglesia,* Madrid, 1970; (c) *L'avvenire della Chiesa,* Brescia: Queriniana, 1970; (d) (Japanese version), Tokyo, 1971; (e) *L'Avenir de l'Eglise,* Paris: Cerf, 1970; (f) *Materialy Kongresu przyslość Kościyola,* Poznan, 1971.
232. "Het kritisch statuut van de theologie," *De toekomst van de kerk,* Amersfoort/Bussum: Paul Brand, 1970, 56–64 (translation of no. 231).

1971

233. *Glaubensinterpretation: Beiträge zu einer hermeneutischen und kritischen Theologie,* Mainz: Matthias Grünewald, 1971 (contains translations of 220, 222, 228, 235, 236; one previously unpublished article); see 240; tr. (a) *Interpretación de fe,* Salamanca, 1973; (b) *The Understanding of Faith,* London: Sheed and Ward, 1974; New York: Seabury, 1974.
234. (with S. L. Bonting, J. M. G. Thurlings, and S. F. L. baron van Wijnbergen), *Katholieke universiteit?* (Annalen van het Thijmgenootschap, 59/1), Bussum: Paul Brand, 1971.
235. "Naar een verruiming van de hermeneutiek: de 'nieuwe kritische theorie,'" *TvT* 11 (1971) 30–51; →223; →240.
236. "Kritische theorie en theologische hermeneutiek: confrontatie," *TvT* 11 (1971) 113–40; →223; →240.
237. "De schok van de toekomst in Amerika," *DB* 54 (July 11, 1971) 4–8; tr. (a) "Future Shock in America," *The Critic* 31 (1972/3) no. 2, 12–29 (corr.).
238. "Dualisme tussen boven, en basis nog hardnekkig: Bericht van de synode," *DB* 55 (Oct. 17, 1971) 1.
239. "Synodalen zijn duidelijk niet representatief," *DB* 55 (Oct. 24, 1971) 1.
239.1 (with B. Willems), "Ten geleide," *Conc* 7 (1971) no. 1, 5–6; tr. "Preface," vol. 61, 1–2.

1972

240. *Geloofsverstaan: interpretatie en kritiek* (Theologische peilingen, 5), Bloe-mendaal, 1972 (contains: 197, 204, 216, 220, 222, 228, 235, 236; one pre-viously unpublished article. See 201 and 233).

241. *Theologians Today: Edward Schillebeeckx, O.P. An Introductory Selection of His Writings,* London/New York: Sheed and Ward, 1972.

242. "De toegang tot Jezus van Nazaret," *TvT* 12 (1972) 28–60; tr. (a) *L'approccio a Gesù di Nazaret: linee metodologiche,* Brescia: Queriniana, 1972 (corr.).

243. "Christendom en kerk: opgaven voor de toekomst," *KL* 39 (1972) 4–15.

244. "Jesus-Movement, exponent van een ontwrichte samenleving," *KL* 39 (1972) 231–43.

245. "Toelichting bij het rapport Katholieke Universiteit," *Katholieke universiteit? II. Reacties en meningen* (Annalen van het Thijmgenootschap 60/1), Bussum: Paul Brand, 1972, 8–15.

246. "L'Eglise catholique aux Pays-Bas," *Septentrion: Revue de culture néerlandaise* 1 (1972) no. 1, 25–39.

247. "De christen en zijn politieke partijkeuze," *Archief van de kerken* 27 (1972) 185–99; also, *Politiek perspectief* 1 (1972) 19–33; "De progressieve christen en zijn politieke partijkeuze," *Socialisme en Democratie* 29 (1972) 68–78; tr. (a) "The Christian and Political Engagement," *Doctrine and Life* 22 (1972) 118–27.

248. "Naar een 'definitieve toekomst': belofte en menselijke bemiddeling," *Toekomst van de religie—Religie van de toekomst?* Brugge/Utrecht: Desclée de Brouwer, 1972, 37–55; tr. (a) "Hacia un 'futuro definitivo': Promesa y mediación humana," *El futuro de la Religión,* Salamanca: Sigueme, 1975, 41–68.

249. "Ik geloof in de verrijzenis van het lichaam," *TGL* 28 (1972) 435–51.

250. "De priester op de synode van 1971," *Aaan mensen gewaagd: Zicht op de iden-titeit van de priester,* Tielt/Utrecht: Lannoo, 1972, 241–86; summ. (a) "The Priest and the Synod of 1971," *Doctrine and Life* 22 (1972) 59–70.

251. "Magnificat," *Reliëf* 40 (1972) 9–17.

252. "Jezus de Profeet," *Reliëf* 40 (1972) 194–210.

253. "Religieuze herleving," *Voorlopig* 4 (1972) 109–12.

254. "Heel Jeruzelem schrok," *DB* 56 (Dec. 24, (1972) 2–3.

255. *Maatschappijcrisis in wereld en kerk* (University Anniversary Speech), Nij-megen: Katholieke Universiteit, 1972; also, *Archief van de kerken* 27 (1972) 1091–1103.

255.1 "Ten geleide," *Conc* 8 (1972) no. 1, 5–8; tr. "Editorial," *Conc* vol. 71, 7–11.

255.2 "Kromme lijnen met Gods schoonschrift erop," *DB* 55 (July 2, 1972) 2–3; →380.

255.3 "Jezus, de anti-messias," *DB* 56 (Oct. 29, 1972) 4–5; →380.

1973

256. "Godsdienstige herleving in conflict met sociale inzet," *Politiek of mystiek?* Brugge/Utrecht: Desclée de Brouwer, 1973, 9–29.

257. "Stilte, gevuld met parabels," *Politiek of mystiek?* Brugge/Utrecht: Desclée de Brouwer, 1973, 69–82.

258. "Jezus: de parabel van God," *Schrift* No. 26 (April, 1973) 68–72.

259. "De vrije mens Jezus en zijn conflict," *TGL* 29 (1973) 145-55.
260. "Heer, naar wie zouden wij gaan? (Joh. 6, 68)," *Kosmos en Oekumene* 7 (1973) 58-67; tr. (a) "Seigneur, á qui irions-nous?" *Le service théologique dans l'Eglise* (Mélanges Congar), Paris: Cerf, 1974, 269-84 (corr.).
261. "Het onfeilbare ambt in de kerk," *Conc* 9 (1973) no. 3, 86-107; tr. "The Problem of the Infallibility of the Church's Office: A Theological Reflection," *Conc* vol. 83, 77-94.
262. "Kritische theorieën en politiek engagement van de christlijke gemeente," *Conc* 9 (1973) no. 4, 47-61; tr. "Critical Theories and Christian Political Commitment," *Conc* vol. 84, 48-61.
263. "Crisis van de geloofstaal als hermeneutisch probleem," *Conc* 9 (1973) no. 5, 33-47; tr. "The Crisis in the Language of Faith as a Hermeneutical Problem," *Conc* vol. 85, 31-45.
264. "Ons heil: Jezus' leven of Christus de verrezene?" *TvT* 13 (1973) 145-66.
264.1 (with B. van Iersel), "Ten geleide," *Conc* 9 (1973) no. 3, 5-6; tr. "Editorial," *Conc* vol. 83, 7-8.

1974

265. *Jezus, het verhaal van een levende,* Bloemendaal: H. Nelissen, 1974; tr. (a) *Jezus, Die Geschichte von einem Lebenden,* Freiburg/Basel/Vienna: Herder, 1975; (b) (partial) "Jesus angesichts der Nahe seines Todes," *Theologie der Gegenwart* 18 (1975) 151-56 (tr. of *Jezus,* 245-48; 251-56); (c) *Gesù: Storia di un Vivente,* Brescia: Queriniana, 1976; (d) *Jesus: An Experiment in Christology,* New York: Seabury, 1979; London: Collins, 1979; (e) *Jesus: La Historia de un Viviente,* Madrid: Cristianidad, 1981.
266. "Jezus, het licht van de wereld," *DB* 59 (March 1, 1974) 4-5; in a separate edition by the Catholic University at Leuven, 1974.
267. "De 'God van Jezus' en 'de Jezus van God,'" *Conc* 10 (1974) no. 3, 110-15 (tr.) (a) "Der 'Gott Jesu' und der 'Jesu Gottes,'" *Was haltet ihr von Jesus?* Leipzig: Sankt-Benno, 1975, 227-42; (b) "The 'God of Jesus' and the 'Jesus of God,'" *Conc* vol. 93, 110-26.
268. "God is klein begonnen," *Weerwoord: Reacties op Dr. H. Berkhof's Christelijk Geloof,* Nijkerk: G. F. Callenbach, 1974, 62-72.
269. "Toespraak over het eeuwig leven," *Als je zoon je vraagt,* Bilthoven: Ambo, 1974, 238-43.
270. "Arabisch-neoplatoonse achtergrond van Thomas' opvatting over de ontvankelijkheid van de mens voor de genade," *Bijdragen* 35 (1974) 278-308.
271. "Hij is 'de koning van het heelal,'" *Getuigenis* 18 (1974) 289-94.
272. "Ergernis van onze lijdensgeschiednis en mysterie van heil," *Schrift* no. 36 (1974) 225-31.
273. (with B. van Iersel) "Ten geleide," *Conc* 10 (1974) no. 3, 5-11; tr. "Editorial," *Conc* 10 (1974) no. 3, 5-11; tr. "Editorial," *Conc* vol. 93, 7-14.

1975

276. (with H. Kuitert) *Jezus van Nazareth en het heil van de wereld,*Baarn: Ten Have, 1975.

277. "Mysterie van ongerechtigheid en mysterie van erbarmen: Vragen rond het menselijk lijden," *TvT* 15 (1975) 3–25; tr. (a) "The Mystery of Injustice and the Mystery of Mercy," *Stauros Bulletin* 3 (1975) 3–31.

278. "Pasen, bevrijding uit paniek," *DB* 58 (March 28, 1975) 1–2; →380.

279. "De toekomst van de kerk," *Rondom het Woord: Theologische Etherleergang* 17 (1975) no. 1, 36–41 (with discussion, 42–48).

280. "Fides quaerens intellectum historicum: Weerwoord aan H. Berkhof," *Nederlands Theologisch Tijdschrift* 29 (1975) 332–49.

281. "Kritische bezinning op interdisciplinariteit in de theologie," *Vox Theologica* 45 (1975) 111–25; summ. (a) "Interdisciplinarity in Theology," *Theology Digest* 24 (1976) 137–42.

282. (with B. van Iersel) "Ten geleide: Demonen zijn 'nietsen,'" *Conc* 11 (1975) no. 3, 5–6 (tr.); *Conc* vol. 103, 7–8.

283. "De mens Jezus: concurrent van God?" *Wie zeggen de mensen dat Ik ben?*, Baarn: Ten Have, 1975, 51–64.

284. "Gesù, storia di un vivente," *Rocca* (Jan. 1, 1975) 46–48.

285. "Dominicaanse spiritualiteit," *Dominicaans leven* 31 (1975), 242–246; 32 (1976) 2–7, 54–59; tr. (a) "Dominican Spirituality," *Veritas, Dominican Topics in Southern Africa* 16 (1975) Feb., 3–6; May, 3–8; Aug., 5–9; Nov., 3–5.

286. "Verrijzenis en geloofservaring in het 'Verhaal van een levende,'" *KL* 42 (1975) 81–93.

287. "Dood en christendom," *Intermediair* 11 (1975) no. 8 (Feb. 21, 1975), 3–5; also, *Het naderend einde* (ed. E. v. d. Valk), Meppel: Intermediar Boom, 1975, 249–54.

1976

291. "De vraag naar de universaliteit van Jezus," *Moderne theologie, Congres 1975* (Radar peiling); Utrecht, 1976, 15–26.

292. "Glauben in der Erfahrung des Scheiterns: Die universale Bedeutung Jesu," *Evangelische Kommentar* 9 (1976) no. 76, 402a–405b.

293. "God als luide kreet," *DB* 59 (April 9, 1976) 4–5; tr. "Gott—ein lauter Schrei," *Publik Forum* 24 (March, 1978) 3–4; →380.

294. "Die Frage nach der Universalität Jesu," *750 Jahre Dominikaner Worms, 1226-1976*, Worms, n.d. (1976), 26–42.

295. "Salut, rédemption et émancipation," *Tommaso d'Aquino nel suo settimo centenario, Atti del Congresso Internazionale*, no. 4 *Problemi di Teologia*, Naples: Edizione Dominicane Italiane, 1976, 274–78.

296. "Korte theologische bezinning op het conflict in het Midden-Oosten," *Het beloofde land?* (Annalen van het Thijmgenootschap, 64/1), Bilthoven: Ambo, 1976, 77–84.

297. (with B. van Iersel), "Ten geleide: De falende mens," *Conc* 12 (1976) no. 3, 3–5.

298. Schoonenberg en de exegese," *TvT* 16 (1976) 44–55.

299. "Jezus en de menselijke levensmislukking," *Conc* 12 (1976) no. 3, 86–96.

300. "'Wie geloof heeft, beeft niet': Het kerkbeeld van B. kardinaal Alfrink," *Alfrink en de kerk*, Baarn: Ambo, 1976, 144–76.

301. "Jézus: Parabole de Dieu, paradigme de l'homme," *Savoir, faire, espérer: Les limites de la raison*, Brussels: Facultés Universitaires St. Louis, 1976, 797–812.

1977

305. *Gerechtigheid en liefde: Genade en bevrijding,* Bloemendaal: H. Nelissen, 1977; tr. (a) *Christus und die Christen,* Freiburg/Basel/Vienna: Herder, 1977; (b) (partial) "Der Sieg über den Tod," *Theologie der Gegenwart* 30 (1978) 109–10; (c) *Il Christo, la storia di una nouva prassi,*Brescia: Queriniana, 1980; (d) *Christ: The Christian Experience in the Modern World,* London: SCM, 1980; *Christ: The Experience of Jesus as Lord,* New York: Crossroad, 1980; (e) *Cristo y los cristianos, Gracia y liberación,* Madrid: Cristianidad, 1982.

306. "Jèsus, le récit d'un Vivant," *Lumière et Vie* no. 134 (1977) 5–45; →365.

307. (with B. Iersel), "Ten geleide," *Conc* 13 (1977) no. 3, 3–5; tr. "Editorial," *Conc* vol. 103, 7–8.

308. " 'God is groter dans ons hart en ons verstand': Dank- en afscheidsrede voor prof. Schoonenberg," *DB* 60 (March 18, 1977) 2–3.

309. "Waarden en normen binnen de wetenschappen en de schoolvakken," *Waarden en normen in het onderwijs* (Annalen van het Thijmgenootschap, 65/1) Baarn: Ambo, 1977, 9–25.

310. "Rahner vertelt ons over de afgronden van het menselijk bestaan," Introduction to K. Rahner, *Wat is een christen,* Tielt: Lannoo, 1977, 5–9.

311. "Waarom Jezus de Christus?" *TGL* 33 (1977) 338–53.

312. "Godsdienst van en voor mensen," *TvT* 17 (1977) 353–71; tr. "Religion of and for men," *Servartham* (St. Albert College, Ranchi) 4 (1979) 3–20.

1978

316. *Tussentijds verhaal over twee Jezusboeken,* Bloemendaal: H. Nelissen, 1978; tr. (a) *Die Auferstehung Jesu als Grund der Erlösung: Zwischenbericht über die Prolegomena zu einer Christologie* (Quaestiones Disputatae, 78) Freiburg/Basel/Vienna: Herder, 1979; (b) *Interim Report on the Books Jesus and Christ,* London: SCM, 1980; New York: Crossroad, 1980; (c) *La quaestione cristologica: Un bilancio,* Brescia: Queriniana, 1980; (d) *El Torno al problema de Jesus: Claves de una cristologia,* Madrid: Cristianidad, 1983.

317. "Op weg naar een christologie," *TvT* 18 (1978) 131–57 (part of 316).

318. "Society and Human Salvation," *Faith and Society: Acta Congressus Internationalis Theologici Lovaniensis 1976,* Gembloux, 1978, 87–99.

319. (with B. Iersel), "Gezag van openbaring en van nieuwe ervaringen," *Conc* 14 (1978) no. 3, 3–5; tr. "Editorial," *Conc* vol. 113, vii–ix.

320. "Een nieuwe aarde: Een scheppingsgeloof dat niets wil verklaren," *Evolutie en scheppingsgeloof,* Baarn: Ambo, 1978, 167–76.

321. "De toekomst van de wereld en van onze samenleving," *Politieke Documentatie* 9 (1978) 213–31.

322. "Ik geloof in God, Schepper van hemel en aarde,"*TGL* 34 (1978) 5–23; →380.

323. *Bevrijdingstheologieen tussen Medellín en Puebla* (University anniversary speech), Nijmegen, 1978; *Bevrijding en christelijk geloof in Latijns-Amerika en Nederland* (Annalen van het Thijmgenootschap, 68/1) Baarn: Ambo, 1980, 18–34; tr. (a) "Befreiungstheologien zwischen Medellín und Puebla," *Orientierung* 43 (1979) 6–10, 17–21; (b) "Liberation Theology Between Medellín and Puebla," *Theology Digest* 28 (1980) 3–7 (summ.).

324. "Evangelische inspiratie en politiek," *Schrift* no. 56 (1978) 43–48.

325. "God, Society and Human Salvation," *Toward Vatican III: The Work that Needs to be Done*, New York: Seabury, 1978, 27–44; tr. (a) "Cuestiones sobre la salvación cristiana," *Hacia el Vaticano III* (Concilium 138 bis), Madrid, 1978, 164–83; (b) "Problemi sulla salvezza cristiana dell'uomo e per l'uomo," *Verso la chiesa del terzo millennio* (Giornale di teologia, 120) Brescia: Queriniana, 1979, 15–38.

326. "Gij zijt het licht van de wereld," *Reliëf* 46 (1978) 65–67; →380.

327. "Glaube und Moral," *Ethik im Kontext des Glaubens*, Fribourg/Freiburg i. Br.: Universitätsverlag, 1978, 17–45.

1979

331. *Menschliche Erfahrung und Glaube an Jesus Christus: Eine Rechenschaft*, Freiburg/Basel/Vienna: Herder, 1979; →365.

332. "Openbaringsdichteid van menselijke ervaringen," *Verbum* 46 (1979) 14–29.

333. "Basis en ambt: Ambt in dienst van nieuwe gemeentevorming," *Basis en ambt*, Bloemendaal: H. Nelissen, 1979, 43–90 (see 345).

334. "Creative terugblik als inspiratie voor het ambt in de toekomst," *TvT* 19 (1979) 266–93 (see 345); tr. (a) "A Creative Retrospect as Inspiration for the Ministry in the Future," *Minister? Pastor? Prophet? Grass Roots Leadership in the Churches*, London: SCM/New York: Crossroad, 1980, 57–84.

335. "Ik geloof in Jezus van Nazareth," *TGL* 35 (1979) 451–73; tr. (a) "I Believe in Jesus of Nazareth: The Christ, the Son of God, the Lord," *Journal of Ecumenical Studies* 17 (1980) no. 1 ("Consensus in Theology? A Dialogue with Hans Küng and Edward Schillebeeckx"), 18–32; also, *Listening* 15 (1980) 159–71 (based on an incorrect French translation); (b) "Ich glaube an Jesus von Nazareth," *Glaube an Jesus Christus*, ed. by J. Blank and G. Hasenhüttl, Düsseldorf: Patmos, 1980, 11–27 (expanded with 380, 10); →380.

336. "Kreling en de theologische situatie van zijn tijd," *Kreling, Het goddelijk geheim*, Kampen: J. H. Kok, 1979, 47–68.

337. "De apostolische constitutie 'Sapientia Christiana,'" *Tegenspraak* (Nijmegen) 3 (1979) no. 11, 20a, b, and c.

338. "Hoe zouden wij voor God zingen in een vreemd land? (Ps. 137, 4)," *TGL* 645–57; →380.

339. "Jezus voor wie vandaag gelooft," *KL* 46 (1979) 887–901.

340. "Discours d'Edward Schillebeeckx à l'occasion du doctorat honoris causa de Gustavo Gutiérrez (Université Catholique de Nimègue, May 7 1979)," *Liaisons internationales* 21 (1979) 12–15; tr. (a) "Discurso de Edward Schillebeeckx," *Paginas* (Lima) 4 (1979) no. 23, 6–10; (b) "Gustavo Gutiérrez recebe em nimega o título de Doutor Honoris Causa," *Revista Eclesiastica Brasileira* 39 (1979) no. 155, 502–5.

341. (with B. van Iersel), "Ten geleide," *Conc* 15 (1979) no. 3, 3–5; tr. "Editorial," *Conc* vol. 123, vii–ix.

1980

345. *Kerkelijk ambt; Voorgangers in de gemeente van Jezus Christus*, Bloemendaal: H. Nelissen, 1980 (333, 334, 350, and 352); tr. (a) *Ministry: A Case for Change*,

London: SCM, 1981; *Ministry: Leadership in the Community of Jesus Christ,* New York: Crossroad, 1981; (b) *Le ministère dans l'Eglise,* Paris: Cerf, 1981; (c) *Das Kirchliche Amt,* Düsseldorf: Patmos, 1981; (d) *El Ministerió eclesial,* Madrid: Cristianidad, 1983.

346. "Wederwoord van Schillebeeckx," *De zaak Schillebeeckx: Officiële stukken,* red. en inl. T. Schoof, Bloemendaal: H. Nelissen, 1980, 53-92 (with French text); tr. (a) "Answer of Edward Schillebeeckx O.P. dated 13 April 1977, to the Questionnaire No. 46/66," P. Hebblethwaite, *The New Inquisition?* San Francisco: Harper and Row/London: SCM, 1980, 129-53; (b) "Schriftelijk verweer van Schillebeeckx," P. Hebblethwaite, *Rome, Schillebeeckx en Küng,* Bloemendaal: H. Nelissen, 1980, 126-50.

347. "Erfahrung und Glaube," *Christlicher Glaube in moderner Gesellschaft,* 25, Freiburg/Basel/Vienna: Herder, 1980, 73-116.

348. "Het 'evangelie van armen' voor rijken," *TGL* 36 (1980) 356-62; tr. (a) "Das Evangelium der Armen für die Reichen," *Wort und Antwort* 22 (1981) 46-49; →380.

349. (with J. B. Metz), "Inleiding," *Conc* 16 (1980) no. 3, 5-6; tr. "Editorial," *Conc* vol. 133, vii-ix.

350. "Albertus de Grote," *Reliëf* 48 (1980) no. 12, 369-376; →380.

351. "Offenbarung, Glaube und Erfahrung," *Katechetische Blätter* 105 (1980) no. 2, 84-95.

352. "Christelijke gemeente en haar ambtsdragers," *Conc* 16 (1980) no. 3, 77-103; see 345; tr. "The Community and its Office-Bearers," *Conc* vol. 133, 95-133.

353. "Plezier aan God beleven," *Menselijke verhoudingen in de kerk (Liber amicorum Petri),* Hilversum: Gooi en Sticht, 1980, 69-77.

354. "Zukunft der Gemeinde," *Sein und Sendung* 12 (1980) 63-78.

355. (with H. Albertz), "Ist Protestantismus noch eine Kraft?" *Radius* 25 (1980) no. 4, 13-17.

356. "Het theologisch zoeken naar katholieke identiteit in de twintigste eeuw," *De identiteit van katholieke wetenschapsmensen* (Annalen van het Thijmgenootschap, 68/2), Baarn: Ambo, 1980, 175-89.

357. "Wereldijke kritiek op de christelijk gehoorzaamheid en christelijke reactie op deze kritiek," *Conc* 16 (1980) no. 9, 17-29.

358. "Der Völkerapostel Paulus und seine Nachwirkung," *Paulus, in 114 Farbbildern erzählt von Erich Lessing,* Freiburg/Basel/Vienna: Herder, 1980, 40-72; (tr.) *Paul the Apostle,* New York: Crossroad, 1983.

359. "Theologische overpeinzing achteraf," *TvT* 20 (1980) no. 3 ("De zaak Schillebeeckx: Reflecties en reacties"), 422-26.

360. (with J. B. Metz], "Inleiding," *Conc* 16 (1980) no. 3, 5-6; tr. "Editorial," *Conc* vol. 143, vii.

1981

365. *Expérience humaine et foi en Jésus Christ,* Paris: Ed. du Cerf, 1981 (306 and tr. of 331).

366. "Père Chenu; Een profetisch 'natuurgeweld,'" *Studio-KRO-gids* (Jan. 24-30, 1981) 18-19.

367. (with J. B. Metz), "Inleiding," *Conc* 17 (1981) no. 3, 5-6; tr. "Editorial," *Conc* vol. 153, vii-ix.

368. "Een leefbaar religieus huis," *TGL* 37 (1981) 40–48; →380.
369. "Het blijde nieuws verkondigen," *TGL* 37 (1981) 512–18; →380.
370. "De ontmoeting van het Westen met de Aziatische spiritualiteit," *TGL* 37 (1981) 652–68; →380.
370.1 "God, the Living One," *New Blackfriars* 62 (1981) no. 7, 357–69.
371. "Kritische gemeente en traditie," *Uittocht* 8 (1981) no. 7, 8–9.
372. "Can Christology Be An Experiment?" *Proceedings of the 35th Annual Convention of the Catholic Theological Society of America (1980),* New York: Catholic Theological Society of America, 1981, 1–14.
373. "Op zoek naar de heilswaarde van politieke vredespraxis," *TvT* 21 (1981) 232–44; tr. (a) "Auf der Suche nach dem Heilswert politischer Friedenspraxis," *Atomrüstung: Christlich zu verantworten?* Ed. by A. Battke, Düsseldorf: Patmos, 1982, 78–97.
374. "Alla ricerca del valore salvifico di una prassi politica di pace," *Il regno* 26 (1981) 664–69; see 373.
375. "Kerklijk ambt in schijndiscussie," *DB* 64 (Dec. 4, 1981) 1–2.

1982

380. *Evangelie verhalen,* Baarn, 1982; contains 230, 254, 251, 258, 252, 259, 326, 293, 266, 322, 335, 271, 278, 249, 255.2, 255.3, 382, 370, 348, 338, 368, 369, 350; 10 niet eerder gepubliceerde bijdragen; tr. *God Among Us: The Gospel Proclaimed,* New York: Crossroad, 1983; London: SCM, 1983; *Das Evangelium Erzählen,* Düsseldorf: Patmos, 1983.
381. "De sociale context van de verschuivingen in het kerkelijk ambt," *TvT* 22 (1982) 24–59.
382. "Christelijke identiteit en menselijke integriteit," *Conc* 18 (1982) no. 5, 34–42; →380.
383. "Kerkelijk spreken over samenlevingsvraagstukken," *Tijd en taak* no. 2 (Jan. 23, 1982) 8–11; no. 3 (Feb. 6, 1982) 11–13.
384. "Befreit die Welt von Atomwaffen! Der soziopolitische Impuls der christlichen Hoffnung," *Lutherische Monatshefte* 21 (1982) no. 5, 226–28; see 373.
385. "Van Praags pathos voor het humane," *Rekenschap* 29 (1982) 77–78.
386. "De fysiotherapeut is ook een mens," *Nederlands Tijdschrift voor Fysiotherapie* 92 (1982) 136–40.
387. Speech at the awarding of the Erasmus Prize, *DB* 65 (Sept. 24, 1982) 3, 8; tr. (a) "Erasmuspreis für die Theologie," *Orientierung* 46 (1982) no. 18, 193–95; →380 (English translation).
388. "The Magisterium and Ideology," *Journal of Ecumenical Studies* 19 (1982) 5–17 (*Authority in the Church and the Schillebeeckx Case,* ed. L. Swidler and P. Fransen, New York: Crossroad, 1982).
389. (with J. B. Metz), "Jezus als Zoon van God," *Conc* 18 (1982) no. 3, 5–7.
390. "Christian Conscience and Nuclear Deterrent," *Doctrine and Life* 32 (1982) 98–112; see 373.
391. "Kerkelijk spreken over seksualiteit en huwelijk," *Het kerkelijk spreken over seksualiteit en huwelijk,* Baarn: Ambo, 215–38.
392. "Vorwort," in Tadahiko Iwashima, *Menschheitsgeschichte und Heilserfahrung. Die Theologie von Edward Schillebeeckx als methodisch reflektierte Heilserfahrung,* Düsseldorf: Patmos, 1982, 15–18.

395. "Het 'onze vader' van Johannes 17," *TGL* 58 (1982) 563–68.

1983

396. "Theology and Nuclear Weapons," *Before It's Too Late: The Challenge of Disarmament*, Geneva: World Council of Churches, 1983.
397. *Theologisch Geloofverstaan Anno 1983*, Afscheidscollege gegeven op vrijdag 11 februari 1983, Baarn: H. Nelissen, 1983.
398. "Jeruzalem of Benares? Nicaragua of de Berg Athos?" *KL* 50 (1983) 331–47.
399. "Bereid tot het Evangelie van vrede," *Conc* 19 (1983) no. 4, 96–105.
400. "The Right of Every Christian to Speak in the Light of Evangelical Experience," Nadine Foley (ed.), *Preaching and the non-Ordained*, Collegeville, MN: Liturgical Press, 1983, 11–40.
401. "Het 'Projekt Katholieke Universiteit' Geen stok om te slaan maar een staf om te gaan," *Democratisering en identiteit*, Baarn: Ambo, 1983, 11–23.

Indexes

Subjects

Authors

Scripture References

Books by Randall Wallace

SO LATE INTO THE NIGHT

THE RUSSIAN ROSE

SO LATE INTO THE NIGHT

Randall Wallace

DOUBLEDAY & COMPANY, INC.

GARDEN CITY, NEW YORK

1983

All the characters in this book
are fictitious, and any resemblance
to actual persons, living or dead,
is purely coincidental.

Library of Congress Cataloging in Publication Data

Wallace, Randall.
     So late into the night.

     I. Title.
PS3573.A429S5   1983   813'.54
ISBN 0-385-18440-9
Library of Congress Catalog Card Number 82–45625

To my parents, Evelyn and Thurman Wallace.
And to Christine.

So we'll go no more a-roving
So late into the night,
Though the heart be still as loving,
And the moon be still as bright.

For the sword outwears its sheath,
And the soul wears out the breast,
And the heart must pause to breathe,
And love itself have rest.

Though the night was made for loving,
And the day returns too soon,
Yet we'll go no more a-roving
By the light of the moon.

—Lord Byron

Part One

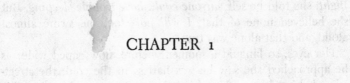

CHAPTER 1

Even the trees were featureless, lines of black chalk rising against the gray luminescence of the night fog which hid a feeble moon. It was past midnight; the houses sitting back from the tree-lined street threw no light across their wet lawns. She thought she was alone.

In taking her strolls through the midnight streets of McLean, she had never doubted her safety; if she had doubted, she would still not have stopped. Of all the reasons for not doing something she wanted to do, fear—even for her physical safety, even this close to downtown Washington, D.C.—was not a reason she would allow. She walked with her hands jammed deep into the pockets of her raincoat.

She moved slowly, keeping to the side of the street; no cars passed this late, and she preferred the blacktop to the concrete of the sidewalks. She stared at the pavement ahead of her, looking up rarely because she knew the way. Ornamental streetlamps, spaced at wide intervals to preserve the country-lane flavor of the street, were smothered in the mist, and she slid into and out of their globes of light.

She saw him before she heard him. She was sighing deeply, as if to exhale the thoughts that drove her on these walks of hers, when she looked up and caught the silhouette coming toward her, framed by the light of the streetlamp a hundred yards away. Breath caught in her throat and her legs jerked but she kept moving, refusing to be afraid and yet spiked alert.

The man—his silhouette was tall, too broad—moved toward her slowly, and she toward him. *Anyone could go for walks at night,* she told herself, *anyone could have trouble sleeping.* But she believed none of that. *I will not stop,* she swore almost aloud, and that alone was true.

Her eyes, so languid a moment before, now gaped wide: as he approached she saw he was hatless in the cold, the street-lamp behind him making his hair an aura around an invisible face; his arms hugging his sides, with his hands pressed into the pockets of his coat, gave him the width that at first made him look so huge, and there was some detail on his shoulders—epaulets? He kept coming directly toward her, thirty feet away, now twenty. She touched the house keys in her pocket, wedged them between her fingers and closed her fist. She kept walking as the blood burned her cheeks.

Ten feet away, she could see the tautness of his neck, could almost make out his eyes.

Just as she was ready to scream and thrust the sharp ends of her keys into the black shadow of his face, he jerked, stopping dead still. The suddenness of the move stopped her too.

In the slowly unfolding instant that they stood there frozen she sensed everything: that he had been out walking the streets at midnight himself, that he had looked up just now to find he was not alone beneath the fog and the trees.

The realization rang in her brain before her body could react. She was still standing with her elbows locked at her sides, her feet poised in half-step, when the soft, almost whispered words came to her across the heavy air.

"I'm sorry . . ." he said, and moved past her into the night.

The darkness, which before had been a dead space about her, an encasement of her private thoughts, was quivering with life. She listened breathlessly to the noises all around—crickets, the clash of bare tree branches blown together by the wind, the rattle of leaves along the street. She whirled once and looked behind her; no one was following. New sounds caught her ears and new sights filled her darting eyes.

But when she reached the light of the porch of the two-story brick Colonial house, she looked back no more, and her raw senses went suddenly back to sleep. She opened the front door, went in, bolted the locks automatically behind her, hung her coat on the hall rack, and climbed through the overheated air straight up the staircase to the second floor.

She stopped at the first doorway on the right and looked into the darkened room. In the light filtering in from the hallway she saw Jamie asleep on the bed. The front of his University of Maryland T-shirt was spotted with the food he had had for dinner. The drawstring sweat pants that served as his pajama bottoms were also stained. His legs stretched to the end of the bed, his feet, splayed out, were bare. His neck bent at a right angle where the back of his skull rested against the headboard, pushing up a tuft of hair in back, and the blond strands gathered in thick locks all over his head except for the bare spots around the pink scars at the temples, where the bullet had gone in and come out.

She stood in the doorway and watched him for a moment, and then went down the hallway to the next room, hers now, and went to bed.

That night she dreamed of a faceless lover who came to her in a trench coat with epaulets on the shoulders and whispered gentle words in a soft, strong voice.

CHAPTER 2

The eastern edge of the United States lay on the brink of daylight, and John Livingstone rode in the back of a chauffeured limousine along the George Washington Parkway into the heart of the city.

Livingstone loved Washington at dawn. He had been to Greece eight times in his life, and he knew the capital of the United States in no way resembled the modern Athens; and yet there was something classical about Washington to him, something Athenian, when the granite and marble edifices glowed pink in the first blush of sun, and then, growing ever more stark and white, seemed to rise to full height against the cobalt sky—like the American republic against the barbarous void—filling granite torsos to shout, "Civilization!"

Livingstone smiled to himself at the way his mind, freed to thoughts he knew he would never tell another living soul, would soar. He told himself such reflections were pretentious, even silly. But as he looked back again at the city, something within him argued.

Washington.

It was a city whose contradictions, mundane yet timeless, sang with the clashing voices of myth: at the Library of Congress, uniformed guards who watched over the greatest assemblage of knowledge in history were themselves semiliterate; through the halls of the Senate passed personages whose hold on power spanned decades and influenced the world, yet whose grip could be broken forever by a change of favor over a single issue sweeping through some isolated heartland; like temples to the gods, monuments to the saints of Democracy rose over the city, holding up noble words etched into their stone, while every day oceans of ink printed forms, regulations, documents no one would ever read, conflicting reports, gossip, lies. *Washington is the Nation's heart*, Livingstone thought. *It pumps words.*

The city belonged to America; it was America.

At midday, full of gawking tourists and numb bureaucrats, its architecture made it brag. At night, floodlit in gold, it looked a bit gaudy. But Livingstone loved it in the dawn, when his mind was most private, and for some reason he loved the sunset. America at the edge of darkness always looked brave.

As they reached an exit and the driver swung the Cadillac onto city streets, Livingstone turned from the window. Mounted in the center of the car just behind the front seat was a telephone; below that was a radio with two rows of push buttons. Livingstone switched on the radio and punched through channels until he found the news. The reporter was talking about the *Constellation*'s story on Bortchers. Livingstone listened. He found another channel with the same report and listened to that. When he looked up again they were passing through the south gate of the White House.

Livingstone walked along a West Wing hallway, directly to the Oval Office. Every administration creates its own jargon, and in the parlance of this one Livingstone had *high octane*—that is, he could enter the Oval Office without knocking. Livingstone himself detested such jargon; it was in-groupish, it seemed to him self-consciously clever, and besides all that it was meaningless. He could enter without knocking, all right, but this President was hardly ever in the Oval Office.

But Mrs. Kerley was always in the anteroom. With the precision that only a seventy-year-old, ninety-pound woman can show, she nodded and said, "Mr. Livingstone."

"Good morning, Mrs. Kerley. Is he awake?"

"Not yet. I'll ring him at eight."

"Did you reach all four of my writers?"

"They'll be at C.R. Four of the E.O.B. at eight-thirty," she said, meaning a conference room in the Executive Office Building, across the street from the White House.

"Thanks for calling them, Mrs. Kerley. And for calling me."

She nodded again, and went back to work on the schedule book open upon her desk.

As Livingstone turned back out into the hallway, Forbis, the chief of staff, always alert to voices coming from the Oval Office, stepped from his doorway across the hall and said, "Traitor."

Livingstone walked up to him and Forbis said, "That's what he is, doing this to us now. *Traitor!*" He spat the word with a forward jerk of his head.

Still Livingstone answered nothing, only moved in and stood in the middle of the office until Forbis stalked back to his desk and sat. Livingstone then took one of the unpadded wooden chairs Forbis used for guests. Forbis glanced down at Livingstone's suit; he always did that. Forbis liked to brag that he could buy a perfectly fitting 38-regular off the rack of any J. C. Penney store in the country; Livingstone's suits were hand-made. Forbis was forty-five, lean, and kept his hair dyed auburn. His face was a disk, the features muted, as if purposely. Forbis's desk faced the hallway; he always kept his door open. But his voice seemed to flatten again walls, to reach the center of a room and die; no one passing ever heard him speak. Livingstone, on the other hand, had a broadcaster's baritone, resonant and rebounding even when soft. Livingstone had wondered if it was his voice alone which made Forbis so often look uncomfortable when they spoke.

"I know the leak was intentional," Forbis said. "Bortchers never could avoid shooting off his mouth. But was it calculated, that's the thing." He said "calculated" the same way he said "traitor."

"The Secretary of Defense has never been intimate with the *Constellation*," Livingstone said.

Forbis's eyes darted toward the open doorway, through which the words spilled, and in an even flatter voice he said, "So if he wanted the leak of his opinions to seem uncalculated, he couldn't have chosen a better forum."

Forbis picked up a pencil and, holding it exactly upright, tapped its point on the blank legal pad in the center of his desk. "If the *Constellation* didn't print—correctly—every internal dispute of this administration, we wouldn't have this problem."

Livingstone made no response.

"The President's been in office not two years and Bortchers is already running for next term," Forbis went on.

"For the Secretary of Defense to spout off about NATO being impotent just before he goes to a European defense conference is dumb, but within his charter. For him to say we're going to reinstate the draft is altogether improper. If that's what really happened," Livingstone added, to Forbis's scowl. "But Bortchers's opinions are highlighted mainly because we haven't expressed our own. So I'm having the writers start on a speech today."

"Based on what?"

"I'll need something from you."

"We've been working on the military manpower plan for

weeks! You know that!" Forbis snapped. "It's full of problems. The hawks, the doves, the women's question, the minorities issue. Our plan can't be released piecemeal, it would be doomed."

"Then give me parameters. We don't need exact numbers, just a guide."

"When do you meet?"

Livingstone checked his watch. "Forty-five minutes."

"I'll have something for you in thirty. I'll send it down."

On Livingstone's way out the door, Forbis's dead voice fell in his path and stopped him. "Say. When you do get the speech ready, would you please send me a copy right away? I'd like to see it before it appears in the *Constellation*."

There were times when John Livingstone felt oddly out of place in the Stern administration, and as he left Forbis and walked downstairs to his own office, it was one of those times. The sense of not belonging had the power to haunt him: were it not for Livingstone, there would never have been a Stern administration, and everyone in America knew it.

Two and a half years before, Livingstone was a network news commentator, having already become a legend as an anchorman. The reports he filed daily on the national evening news pierced the rhetoric of all political views. He created a universal tableau of American life with situational studies of everyday people. One major news magazine called Livingstone "the Norman Rockwell of broadcasting." The same magazine had described him as "the stuff of which living legends are made: eyes a phosphorescent blue, hair oak riddled with silver. He is a tall man whose size is less noticeable than his warmth, his elegance less apparent than his dignity." Such publicity became commonplace when Livingstone began to consider an early retirement—he was fifty-eight—and rumors circulated about the huge amounts the network was offering him to stay on to cover a particularly crowded presidential campaign. It was at the height of the speculation that Livingstone stunned the country.

Mired down among the special-interest Congressmen and ex-generals who were trying to assert themselves as serious candidates for the job being vacated by a President who had decided not to run for a second term was an old friend of Livingstone's named Baxter Stern. Stern was foundering in inattention—until John Livingstone announced that he had decided to leave the network to run Stern's campaign.

Stern's problem was image; not a bad one to overcome, simply no image at all. He was thin but not wizened, his eyes small but not beady, his voice tenor and thin but not shrieking, his hair wispy but not entirely gone. Hardly anyone outside of his home state had ever heard his name. His original announcement of candidacy was a surprise only for its unlikeliness, and it was taken generally as a joke, made more cruel by the apocryphal but ubiquitous story that at Harvard (he and Livingstone had lived in the same dormitory) his stated ambition had been to be a doctor—more specifically, a proctologist. Though checks into his records showed that he had actually majored in political science, the title "Stern the Proctologist" still followed him, and through most of his campaign more bumper stickers urging "Vote Stern For Rear Admiral" appeared than did legitimate slogans.

The first press conference Livingstone held after assuming leadership of Stern's campaign (with the title "Policy Coordinator"; he was never called the campaign manager) drew five times as many newspeople as had ever appeared for anything else Stern had done in his life, including the announcement of his candidacy. Initially the tone of the conference was charged but playful, a media event; one of the first questions directed to Livingstone was, "Are you aware that, if he were to win, Baxter Stern would be the first bald man elected to the presidency since Dwight D. Eisenhower?"

After the first chortles Livingstone said, "Since my own hair has begun to thin, I have viewed baldness as the mark of maturity and intelligence." There was more laughter, but then Livingstone said, "The truth is, Baxter Stern does not make a good caricature, and it won't be easy for a political cartoonist or a television comedian to portray him. A major newspaper recently referred to him—in passing—as 'the most boring man in Washington.' That's an interesting commentary, isn't it? His colleagues have known him for years as capable and fair. And honest. Maybe that's uninteresting. But is it unpresidential? Does his lack of a bushy head of hair mean that he can't be a serious candidate, because professional electioneers, and professional newspeople, believe the public won't respond to him? Ladies and gentlemen, I am here today because I believe you have underestimated the man. And underestimated the American people."

The first preference poll taken after that news conference showed Stern jumping from seventh place to fourth among voters of his own party. Two weeks later he was third.

Livingstone selected and personally supervised a new speechwriting staff weighted toward younger people with journalistic training. It was one of several changes Livingstone made, and no one imagined how critical that single step would be, until fate in all its unpredictability threatened not simply to wipe out the Stern campaign, but to destroy Baxter Stern himself. Two weeks before the party convention, Stern's wife, Lenore, finally went to the hospital for the stomach pains she had suffered for months but never mentioned. They cut her open immediately, found cancer, and five days later she was dead.

Stern vanished from the race. His only public appearance for a week was his somnambulation through the funeral of his wife. And since he was not the leading party candidate—he was still second in delegate votes—and the other party had already nominated a man considered invincible because of his charisma and long-established name, everyone expected Stern's withdrawal. The press reported it as imminent so many times that most people believed it already confirmed.

Then Stern delivered a speech.

In it, he did not refer to his wife by name, and at no time did he use the word "nevermore." But in the press and in the popular memory, the speech Stern made after a week of pining over his lost Lenore was dubbed forever the "Raven Address."

Four months later, Baxter Stern was elected President of the United States.

John Livingstone was not made a member of the Cabinet; he had said all along that he lacked the expertise for any such post and would not accept one. But Stern kept him on as Presidential Policy Coordinator.

And now, in situations that drove the President's younger and politically more experienced men, professionals like Forbis, into fits of crisis intensity, Livingstone found himself brooding, strangely apart.

When the messenger brought down the briefs from Forbis, Livingstone rose from his desk and walked upstairs and out into a cold morning grown fully bright. He crossed from the White House to the Federal-baroque Executive Office Building, and suddenly realized that he had walked right in front of an oncoming limousine without ever noticing its approach. He stopped on the sidewalk, and stared back across Executive Drive, where the cars bringing Cabinet members in for a meeting with Forbis pulsed along in their morning rush.

Do I do that all the time? he thought. *Do I not see the danger until it's passed?*

CHAPTER 3

She had walked through the central room of the office without speaking to anyone and without being greeted herself. Once inside her cubicle, she paced aimlessly. Four strides took her from plastic wall to plastic wall. She moved slowly. The partitions, opaqued by bureaucratic gray paint, were sounding boards more than mufflers for the typing on one side and the mad shuffling of notes on the other, but the noises made no ripple through the blankness of her face.

On one corner of her metal desk lay ten newspapers, waiting to be read and passed along for ten more. In the center of the desk stood a manual typewriter. Beside it lay a white block of paper, but she had not loaded a sheet into the typewriter in days.

She continued pacing as a sharp rap on the glass door of the adjacent cubicle sounded through hers as well. Three seconds later the demanding knuckles rapped for her, and then moved on down to Sherwood. Even secretaries who are obsequious—and civil service stenographers never are—become demanding to their bosses when a greater boss calls, and the knocks that morning were belligerent. All typing and shuffling in the next offices stopped.

She heard the silence more than she had heard the noise. Her gaze floated up from the floor. She reached to the shelf, where her empty notebook rested, and walked out into the central room of the suite. Kurtz and Sherwood were waiting at the main door. As she joined them she gave a nod of greeting. They nodded back.

Virginia Anne Longstreet's reluctance with the spoken word was an unsurprising and yet remarkable trait.

Part of the unsurprising quality was physical; there is something forbiddingly self-sufficient about someone who is beautiful and has never thought of herself that way. Hers was not the pretty kind of beauty, that which a little girl's cuteness becomes. In fact, in growing up with a single older brother she had made no distinction between herself and boys; the other children in school, even in the later grades, never counted her —in the rigid castes of youth—as someone attractive. But as she matured the close-cropped, almost colorless yellow hair grew out and mellowed into the color of sunlit honey, the narrow face looked less hungry, more finely cut, the hard boy's body surged in spots that made it unmistakably female, and yet it kept a leanness, as if something angry inside kept everything extraneous burned and beaten away.

But the statement of self-sufficiency that her physical presence made was punctuated most by her eyes. In the hills of the Virginia Piedmont, where she was born, there occurs a slate-green stone which the natives use to build churches, banks, and patios, and her eyes were that exact color. "Virginny

Greenstone," her schoolmates had once called her, because of the name of the stone, and those eyes. Hard, opaque, they often defocused and she seemed to drift; then her attention would come back with a suddenness that many people found unsettling.

Her presence, her glance, made spoken words seem redundant. But to the men she worked most closely with, the power of her solitude went beyond the physical. They knew, or thought they knew, the calamity that had occurred in her life and, each having settled on his own understanding of it, they expected her to be withdrawn.

So the men who worked with Virginia Anne Longstreet did not find her habitual silence surprising.

And yet it was remarkable, because Ginny Longstreet was an artist with words, a master wordsmith. She wrote speeches for the President of the United States.

Adam Kurtz and Malcolm Sherwood were both short men with slender bodies and taut faces; both wore rimless glasses, both, like the President and Livingstone, were Ivy Leaguers. Both had curly hair which they never combed. Kurtz's locks were black, Sherwood's a deep red. Kurtz was from New York, Sherwood from Boston, and they thought of themselves as totally dissimilar. With Ginny, they waited at the doorway, fidgeting in matching rhythm, until Thayer wheezed up from his office at the far end of the suite, and then all four started down the hallway.

The procession to the conference room moved oddly, like a mismatched harness team. Kurtz and Sherwood always let Ginny into the hallway first, flanking the doorway to bow and motion her between them in a style that said, "Gentlemen after ladies." They would then surge up and fall back all the way along the corridor, knocking against the pace she set. Neither Kurtz nor Sherwood would lead the group himself, and they masked both their impatience and the agitation they felt when approaching a staff meeting by nudging elbows, exchanging grins, rolling their eyes, and looking toward Ginny's muscled behind as she walked ahead of them. In fact, Kurtz and

Sherwood had each decided that relationships with females, like friendships, must belong to some future time when career development was not so demanding; and as they had no real physical intimacies, their references to anything of a sexual nature were always strained and unnatural.

So Virginia Longstreet walked down the corridor ahead of shallow breaths and frustrated sighs as Kurtz and Sherwood tried to hurry, and the smell of nervous sweat.

Thayer, at sixty more than twice the age of any of his counterparts, drifted along behind them, falling back as they went.

Livingstone, who had lived for years exactly on the deadline, was just arriving at the conference room from the other direction as the delegation turned a corner and approached. He stopped and waited. "Ginny," he said.

"John." The first-name greetings were not totally informal. From him the use of her nickname had always seemed fatherly; and since Livingstone had been known for two decades by millions of Americans as "John," the first name still could sound respectful.

As the others filed by he said, "How are you doing?"

At the last staff meeting, three days before, Livingstone had assigned each of them to turn in a list of issue guidelines, topics they considered most timely should the President encounter an unexpected speechmaking situation. Ginny had submitted nothing. But Livingstone's face showed no reproach; his question was genuine. She raised the corners of her mouth in the joyless smile that was her answer for everyone. Livingstone smiled back; her smiles, however pallid, had always been infectious to him. They moved inside.

At the table there was a shuffle. Kurtz and Sherwood, having proven their team spirit by arriving together, had now rushed unrestrainedly to opposite seats, framing the chair Livingstone always took at the end nearest the door. But Sherwood, positioning his notes just before sitting, turned, glanced at Ginny entering with Livingstone, and then stepped to the next seat over. But Ginny took a spot at the far end of the table, and Thayer, who stopped just inside the doorway to clean his pipe

over an ash stand, shambled obliviously to the seat Sherwood
had vacated.

Livingstone, sitting down at the head of the table, stared for
a moment at Sherwood, who sat self-consciously squaring his
stack of notes. Then, glancing around the table, Livingstone
said, "Nothing strident. Remember that before anything else
as you work on this speech. Stridency projects worry and antag-
onism. We want neither. Remember that."

Livingstone always sat erect at the table, but he had the ability of making that posture seem relaxed. It was the tone of his
voice that made the urgency of his words match the import of
the meeting. "I'll fill you in as best I can, because there will be
rumors and I don't want you influenced by them. We have
sent a cable to the Secretary of Defense asking him to confirm
or deny the views printed in the *Constellation* and ascribed to
him. He has not yet responded."

"The communications from Berlin must be a problem,"
Kurtz said, knowing, as all of them did, that Washington
could communicate with Berlin as easily as with Philadelphia.
Kurtz even snickered.

Livingstone barely glanced at him. "The *Constellation* has
printed remarks which purport to be Bortchers's plans for the
Administration's military manpower priorities to restructure
our armed forces. Whatever Bortchers's response to the publication—denial, support, resignation—the whole situation only
highlights the fact that the *Administration's* policy is as yet
unannounced. So—"

"Once again the *Consternation* forces our hand," Kurtz interrupted with a cool smile.

Livingstone popped his index finger into the air. "This is no
press issue! The Administration's relationship with both the
press and Secretary Bortchers is sure to be discussed in the next
few days, but don't miss the crucial aspect, which is this: the
President has not yet announced his own program. If we have
not made a positive stand, then we have no room for arrogance, animosity, or negativism toward anyone."

With that Livingstone withdrew from his inner pocket four
folded briefs covered in blue paper and dealt them around the

table. "This document contains the parameters of the plan the President will present to Congress soon. The final tuning of the program is not complete, but it will follow the guidelines set forth in this document." Livingstone paused and said more slowly, "Please remember how delicate an issue this is. This document outlines the Administration's plans concerning staffing the military, and contains projected numbers, but the numbers will not be in your speech. The concept of military obligation is an economic, political, even racial, sexual, most of all *patriotic* issue—we need to address that larger aspect in this speech. Later the President will announce *numbers* to Congress. Please remember, this affects the Administration's relationship with foreign governments as well as with the Congress and the American people. I cannot overemphasize the importance of avoiding leaks. These documents are not to leave your offices."

More casually Livingstone said, "Your speeches are for the American people. You need to know the specifics so that our rhetoric matches our policy. But the public at large needs to know our rhetoric." Livingstone's brows bunched together in the broody reflectiveness that the discussion of a speech's purpose always brought upon him. "You see . . . speechwriters are not supposed to create policy, they are to express it. And yet we do create it, because how a policy is expressed is part of the policy."

He frowned at the tabletop a moment, then looked up and smiled. "Any questions?"

"Yes, I—" Kurtz and Sherwood both said at the same time, and Kurtz, his black eyes darting, dropped his chin and peered over his glasses at Sherwood, who said, "I've jotted down some phrases that I thought might be appropriate to—"

"Keep them," Livingstone said sharply, before Sherwood had gotten his notebook half open. Quickly softening his shortness Livingstone added, "Put into your speech any catchphrases you feel are appropriate. But I want to see them only in the context of the message you plan to get across." Sherwood sucked in his upper lip, closed the binder with a snap, and tried to sit still, but rubbed unconsciously with his right thumb at the red callus on his middle finger, where his pencil had rubbed since six that morning. Kurtz managed to keep from smiling; he too had several pages of notes, believing as Sherwood did that the writer who came up with the best phrase had the best chance of getting his speech, or most of it, used. Kurtz felt superior now to have found out at Sherwood's expense that Livingstone was in an extremely businesslike mood today.

"Any questions," Livingstone said again and looked around the table. When there were none he said, "We need a good speech. A really good one." And then, without meaning to, Livingstone looked directly at Virginia Longstreet. It was a strange moment and an instant only, but as everyone looked up just as Livingstone said "a really good one," they noticed it all together, and their shared attention froze time.

Livingstone looked away from the slate-green eyes, toward each of the others around the table. "Well . . ." he said, and stood.

But why shouldn't I look to Ginny Longstreet when I need a good speech? he thought.

Virginia Longstreet had written the Raven Address.

The walk back to the speechwriters' suite was different in that it was the same; usually Kurtz and Sherwood returned from a meeting at their own frantic pace, but this time they followed her again, only there was no surging forward, no broad leering. They walked at a constant speed, staring at the back of her head.

But as they entered the central reception area of their suite the procession shattered. "A pot of coffee!" Sherwood yelled at his secretary, and rushed into his office.

"Camels. Three packs," Kurtz said, slapping a bill down onto his secretary's desk and rushing into his.

But inside her own office Ginny Longstreet moved slowly through the cross fire of sound—the uneven spitting of Kurtz's typewriter on one side and the grinding of Sherwood's electric pencil sharpener as he broke leads on the other—and sagged down in the chair behind her desk. With her elbows propped on the desk top she ran her fingernails into the hair at her temples, then closed her eyes and pressed the sides of her skull with her palms.

She sat that way for perhaps five minutes and then forced herself to stand. She started to pace around the office, but slowed to a stop. She stood at the window and watched the winter coming over the city.

During lunch hour she slept at the desk. Afterward she paced or stood at the window until late that afternoon, when she sat down at the typewriter.

MEMO

To: John K. Livingstone
From: Virginia A. Longstreet
Dear Mr. Livingstone:

I am grateful for the recognition, opportunity and guidance that you have given me. You have treated me as someone with perspectives to value and talent to nurture. You have validated the admiration I have always held for you. You have been my friend.

It is with regret that I resign my position on your staff, effective immediately.

This action is not reflective of any disagreement with the Administration's policies, or lack of them.

I'm just sick inside.

And so empty.

She stared at the page and then wrote:

And so

Her fingers stopped on the keys, hovered, quivered. She snatched the page from the typewriter, wadded it into a tight ball, threw it into the trash can, and went home.

Maybe she had come to expect the disgusting, to approach the house with her senses alert with dread, and that was why she smelled it so soon. The odor caught her instantly, the sour stink of vomit in the draft of overheated air that hit her in the face as she pushed open the door. There was a moment, so brief she could deny it ever existed, in which she wanted to turn and flee, to leave this house and everything in it forever. But it was her home. She went inside.

"Mary?" she said.

A Black woman, with a girl's breastless body, stalky as a mantis, came rushing down the stairs. She held a damp towel in one hand, a can of aerosol air freshener in the other. She whined, "I tried to clean it up. I didn't want the house to be smelling this way when you got home."

"It's all right, Mary. What happened?"

"I made a chocolate cake this afternoon. It was . . .." Suddenly crying, Mary threw her willow arms around Ginny's neck and squawked, "Happy birthday, honey!"

Ginny felt displaced, as if she had stepped into a moment of someone else's life. For one thing, though she and Mary were always comfortable with each other, they had never before hugged. But more odd . . . yes, she was sure of it—it was not her birthday.

As Mary released her Ginny thought, *When? When?* before collecting herself. *Last week,* she remembered.

Frowning at the look on Ginny's face, which must have been dazed or, at the least, distant, Mary stuck out her florid lower lip, like a pouting child. Tears welled in her eyes as she said, "I wanted for you to be happy!"

"I *am* happy, Mary! Of course!" Ginny smiled as broadly as she could. When Mary smiled back she said, "Now what happened?"

The corners of Mary's mouth sagged with amazing elasticity. "I had you a chocolate cake, all iced up and sitting on the table waiting to decorate." Mary's tears were already drying with the explanation. "And then Alice called . . ." Alice was Mary's sister; she kept Mary's children.

"I wasn't on the phone that long," Mary pleaded. "I was just looking out the window, and Alice kept talking and talking, and when I turned around he had gobbled up that whole cake."

One of the more subtle peculiarities of Jamie's condition was that the cells which control the sense of smell in a normal brain no longer existed in his, so that his perception of taste was greatly altered. He could still experience flavor but it was independent of the normally attendant aroma, and Ginny could never tell which foods he would ignore and which he might devour. "He drank almost a half-gallon of milk, too," Mary added, shaking her head. "Made a terrible mess. I'm so sorry . . ."

"Mary. Please. It wasn't your fault. And it was really sweet of you. Really, really sweet. And I appreciate it so much."

Mary smiled.

"Where's Jamie now, in bed?"

"Yeah. I just . . ." Mary broke off and sighed.

"Come on, I'll help you clean it up."

On the way down the hallway, for an instant as intense as it was brief, Ginny fought off the memory of another time she had approached the same doorway to find another mess Jamie had made in the kitchen.

Together they washed down the kitchen table, the legs of the chair, the floor. When they finished, and Mary hurried around the house spraying the chemical equivalent of fresh mountain breezes into the stale air, Ginny washed her hands in the kitchen sink and glanced at the calendar beneath the telephone on the cabinet. Yes—a week ago. She had not marked the date on the calendar, but the square, like the rest of the page, bore Mary's jottings of phone numbers and telephone-talking doodles. Mary made herself at home.

When Mary had first come to the house to interview for the job, she had worn a snow-white nurse's uniform and explained that she had just come from a Wednesday night prayer meeting at her church. Ginny understood that Mary was not a registered nurse (no one else the agency sent her was either), but the uniform did sway her; she felt that if Mary was game enough to spend evenings catching those who toppled in the swoons of faith, she could handle whatever came along with Jamie. Secretly, too, Ginny had liked the fact that Mary was a churchgoer. The churchgoing had not lasted long: two months after she started with Ginny, Mary became a Rastafarian ("Oh no, Miss Ginny, I won't *ever* use the ganja in *your* house!") and spent a week's salary having her hair braided into cornrows. But whatever her current mystical fascination, Mary remained thoroughly trustworthy, often cheerful; and most of all, she had never flinched at the idea of caring for Jamie.

For the first few months after Mary moved into the guest room, Ginny had not known about her children. (Ginny found out one weekend, when Alice called, angry and wondering where Mary was.) And though Mary often spoke lovingly of her "babies" after that, she still asked for no nights off to see them and would even stay over some weekends, having her dates pick her up right at Ginny's front door.

The flaw in Mary, as it seemed to Ginny, was the thing that enabled her to spend all day with Jamie. Mary did not take life seriously.

Ginny dried her hands on a kitchen towel, hung it on the refrigerator handle, and stopped to look at the photograph Mary had taped to the door. Ginny was one week past twenty-five, and Mary was about the same age, but her daughter and son were eight and seven. Both had their mother's chocolate-milk skin and her huge, expressive eyes. Beneath their smiling faces Mary had written, "My love-children—Mai Desire & K-Poppa."

On her way up the staircase, Ginny realized that Mary must have confused her birthdate since the day she asked for it so she could do Ginny's astrological chart. Ginny wondered if that meant all the celestial insights, predictions, and confirmations Mary had so excitedly told her about since then were miscalculations even in Mary's own system. It occurred to Ginny that there was humor in that, but she could not laugh.

At the head of the stairs she passed Mary going back down and told her once more how much she appreciated being remembered on her birthday and that the thought really did matter. Mary seemed pleased.

Jamie was sitting up on the bed. The front of his T-shirt was still wet and clung to his broad, muscular chest. The top of his jeans was unsnapped, and a white bulge of soft hairy lower belly showed through. Mary had sprayed him with Lysol, too, and it was not cruel: Jamie got upset whenever they made him wear fresh clothes—because they were stiff, because the detergent irritated his skin, of for some other reason they could never figure out and he could never tell them. As she stood there his eyes batted slowly open, and he gave her a slack smile. She walked to his side, placed her hand on his head, leaned, and kissed him on the cheek. He did not move. She walked to the door and smiled back at him until his eyes drifted shut again, and when they did she went down the hall to her own room and closed the door softly, but with a rush.

She did not go out for a walk that night. But once, standing at her window in the darkened room, she thought she saw a slender figure moving ghostlike beneath the trees that lined the distant street.

CHAPTER 4

Kidd was sitting in a wing chair in the corner of the restaurant foyer, staring away from the book that was open on his lap, when Collier walked in. Collier stood at the door for a moment before he went up and, purposely abrupt, said, "Jeff. Good to see you."

Kidd stood quickly, and the book was suddenly at his side with a marker closed in it. *Habitual reader,* Collier thought. *And he still has those fluid hands.* With one of them—surprisingly slender—Kidd shook the hand Collier offered.

"Thank you, Walter. It's good to see you again."

Collier noted that Kidd still held himself erect. When he had first met Jeff Kidd two years before, Collier had formed a theory which he still trusted: that Jeff Kidd's posture derived from the fact that he was exactly six feet tall if he did not slouch at all. Kidd was the kind of man who would want to be six feet tall.

And as Collier reached up (he was five foot eight himself) and put his hand on Kidd's shoulder, guiding him into the restaurant's main room, he noticed Kidd was still knotty and lean —had maybe even lost five pounds.

They chatted about the weather until the waiter brought the menu. As Kidd read it, Collier had a chance to study his face.

Kidd was twenty-nine, exactly half Collier's age, and his tan hair, in need of trimming, was almost collegiate, but his face was a bit drawn, so all in all he looked his age. Kidd's appearance—like his hands—had always had a fluid quality to Collier. He was handsome, and because he was often direct and especially because he spoke with a slight Southern accent, he tended at times to seem boyish and naïve. He wore glasses for reading—he had had them on since Collier first walked into the restaurant—and they made him look bookish. Physically he could appear slight; his motions had the deftness of a much smaller man's. But when he took his reading glasses off, as he did now, folding them into the pocket of his sport coat, his face had an entirely different quality. His eyes were gray—a gray like a blue with the softness drained away. When he was crossed a light came into those eyes that made you feel you were several steps too close to him. Without his glasses on he could look dangerous.

But he did not look hostile now, only wary. As soon as the waiter had taken their order and left them alone Kidd said, "I'm anxious to find out what you want, Walter. What do you want?"

"I have a job for you."

"You told me that over the phone. What kind of job?"

"I should have said a position. It's something more or less permanent."

"If you're not going to tell me what the job is, then how am I going to tell you if I want it?"

"Once you get into it, you'll want it."

"Then maybe I should turn it down now. While I still don't want it."

Both men smiled, each wishing he was enjoying himself more than he actually was.

"So how's school?" Collier said.

"School is . . . fine," Kidd said in a way that seemed to mean school was neither good nor bad nor mediocre. It seemed to mean that school was nothing at all.

"You're bored," Collier said, more statement than question.

Kidd's gray gaze swung over Collier's face, as if searching for the answer there, or for a different question. "I don't know, Collie," Kidd said slowly. "I never thought of it as action. Not like a war, or a boxing match. Or even action like a chess game. But after I got out, I realized it was action. And . . . yeah, I missed it. I was never sure I should have, though—that it was good to miss that kind of thing."

With increasing frequency Collier was meeting in young men—the promising ones, with experience—the same kind of professional misgivings he saw in Jeff Kidd. He hoped that the deep wrinkles of his own face appeared to Kidd as lines of wisdom rather than weariness as he said, "It's getting better for us. I know. And if you take this job I might have for you, you'll see its importance. And that'll feel good."

"What is the job?"

"I'll tell you after lunch." Collier grinned. "Tell me about school. I want to hear all about it. I may go back when I retire."

"Would you at least give me an idea of what I'd have to do in the job?"

"Yes, I can do that," Collier said. "You'll have to wear your glasses."

The restaurant shared the bottom floor of an office building with a bank branch, a gift shop, and several small stores, one of which sold books. On their way out Collier glanced at the bookstore window and saw a display of the newest novel from a British master of spy thrillers. "Oh, he's got a new one out!" Collier said, and excusing himself he popped into the store. With his new purchase under his arm he rejoined Kidd outside the door and said, "Now I've got a book to carry too. See? Now I don't look so unintelligent beside you."

Kidd smiled.

"You know, I met Kim Philby when he first came to Washington as the new head of M.I. Six," Collier perked, referring to the infamous English double agent whose treason had been the inspiration behind one of the British writer's best-known works. "I met him in Washington. He stuttered, chain-smoked, and wouldn't look anybody in the face. Dawley, the man he replaced, covered for him, though, said Philby had nerve damage from an interrogation he went through during the war. The good-ol'-boy system, British version—if you went to the right school, you couldn't be a traitor. Mr. Hoover decided, as long as they weren't any more careful with their people than that, they weren't getting anything else from us."

It had always amazed Kidd that professionals in the intelligence field—Kidd considered his six years in the CIA to be a dabbling—loved to read spy novels, and that the real characters could display such traits as chain-smoking, stuttering, and inability to meet the eyes of the men they were betraying. The British writer might have been thought of as a hack, had he given such obvious traits to his fictional characters; and yet the real traitor had them (and was not caught by the men who loved to read spy novels!).

Kidd had just confused himself. He seemed to be doing that a lot lately.

They walked outside the building, onto a veranda. Their coats were not enough in the wind, but they leaned against the railing anyway, their shoulders a foot apart, and Collier said, "We've decided to adopt a global strategy against terrorism."

"I thought we always had a global strategy," Kidd said.

"In theory. But two separate organizations."

"Collie, I never knew an FBI agent who wasn't happy to work with the CIA, and happier still that he wasn't a part of it. You're telling me there's going to be a combined force?"

Collier turned to Kidd with a slow grin. "You're pretty sharp. You really are. Yeah, there was some . . . *discussion* about the combining of forces. As it is now, the Bureau will administer and train here in Washington, but we'll use Langley, too, and draw men from both agencies. We're a separate unit, but part of both. We're looking for global capability—instant response to terrorism, anywhere, by experts."

"Why me, then? I'm no expert on terrorism."

"You're an expert on people—personalities, tendencies, the subtle signs. We see intelligence as a central aspect to the whole unit—studying the terrorist groups around the world, even key individuals, so we have more intelligence when something happens, or better yet, so we can anticipate."

Kidd stared out at the flat gray clouds of winter. "Collie, I'm not sure that I'm somebody you can rely on to anticipate what other people will do."

There was a silence between them. Collier said, "Jeff, women come and go. A lot of good, solid, fine, virile men have been—"

"Wait a minute!" Kidd said hotly, straightening and turning to face Collier full on. Collier's expression went murky, as Kidd glared at him. "Listen, Walter," Kidd said with forced control. "I know you've checked me out. You'd have to if you want me for a job like this. I don't blame you for that. But I'd appreciate it if you didn't bring up Linda. Not to me." Kidd took a deep breath, said, "We can discuss my appropriateness for a job without bringing up my personal life," and turned back to the rail.

"Sorry, Jeff," Collier said. "I didn't mean to pry. I thought you brought her up."

Kidd's glance sprang back at Collier, but Collier was staring away. *What?* Kidd thought. All he had said was that he didn't feel like any expert in predicting human behavior. But . . . Collier thought he must have been referring to Linda?

Maybe I was, Kidd thought.

When Jeff Kidd reached his sister's house he felt both comfort and fear—comfort because it was a warm place of home-cooked meals, clean sheets, crying, squealing, laughing babies; and fear because he ached with an uneasiness about himself, a vague and powerful feeling that something had gone wrong with him and he did not belong in a place that was so much a home. He was not so much haunted with his loneliness as he was disturbed by the sense that he might somehow spread it. As he parked on the street and walked up the driveway, he actually smiled, telling himself that through determination alone he could be pleasant.

He entered through the side kitchen door and found his

sister Carol wearing a jogging suit and standing over the stove, supporting the diapered bottom of a fat baby in one hand and stirring a pot of boiling vegetables with the other. He kissed his sister on the back of the neck and said, "Hi!" Whether she felt uncomfortable with the unusual show of affection from her younger brother or was just so distracted as to be indifferent he did not know, but it seemed to him a long time that he stood there. "Uh, smells great, what is it?" he said to her back.

"Soup," she said, capping the pan, shifting the baby, and turning down the heat, all in one motion. "Jeff, can you . . . oh, she's wet," she said as her hand hit the cold spot on the diaper, and she turned quickly and went into the hallway and lugged the baby up the stairs.

He followed her to the foot of the staircase. "Can I what?" he called up, and after a moment she appeared at the balustrade.

"I'm going jogging. Can you watch the kids?"

"Well sure . . . Great!"

Starting into a doorway, she stopped, turned back, and said, "Linda called." Her eyes were still a moment. Then, disappearing back into the baby's room, she yelled, "Just until Bobby gets home! Or I may get back first if they keep him at the hospital!"

"That's great!" he yelled.

"What?!"

"That's great! You jogging! How far do you go?"

"Just a couple of miles," she said, carrying the baby back down the staircase. "I'm gonna increase next week."

"That's great, Carol, I didn't know you were doing that. But listen, don't push yourself too much. The main thing is to just do it enough that you feel good about it."

"Yeah, I know, 'Go every day until you don't ask yourself if you will anymore,'" she said as if to parrot him. "I'm making it a habit."

"That's really super," he said as she handed him the baby. "How long have you been doing it?"

"This is my first day." She laughed. Then she ran into the kitchen.

"You sure make nice babies," he said to her as she rushed back out.

"Yeah," she said, grabbing and shaking the baby's dimpled knee. "Listen, the carrots are . . . what's the matter, Davey?"

The older of his sister's blond cherubs walked from the den into the hallway, crying tentatively, the way children do when they are worried more than hurt. There was a dark spot in the center of his blue corduroy trousers. "Oh Davey! Crap!" Carol blurted, and Davey began to cry in earnest. The baby Kidd was holding decided to join in.

"When?" Carol moaned. "When am I going to jog?" Taking the baby from Kidd she snatched the screaming Davey by the wrist and half-carried him up the stairs yelling, "You wanna wear big-boy pants? Big boys wear big-boy pants, but big boys use the potty!" Reaching the bedroom she continued, "You're gonna wear diapers even when you're in *college!*"

Kidd waited, astonished and a bit horrified, until Davey, naked now except for a T-shirt that stretched tight and ended at his plump belly, came waddling back down the stairs, crying quietly. As Carol stayed upstairs trying to put her daughter to bed, Kidd took his nephew in his arms and sat down with him on the stairs. The boy's wet eyes shone with the same gray as Kidd's, his fine hair was the same blond Kidd's was when he was a boy, and Kidd could not shake the impression as he held his nephew that he was looking back at himself. "What's the matter, Davey?" he said softly.

"I gotta use the potty!" Davey sobbed.

"Davey. Hey Davey. Let me tell you something. You'll learn to use the potty. You're learning right now. Everybody pees in his pants sometimes. You have. And your Uncle Jeff has. And you know what else?" He leaned very close to the boy's face and whispered, "I happen to know that your mama has peed in her pants, too."

The still-crying child lifted his arms and cried out, "But I gotta learn to use the *potty*, Unca Jeff!"

Fifteen minutes later Kidd sat in an easy chair in the den, holding the infant niece who had refused to sleep in a crib but had grown suddenly quiet in his arms. Like so many men who are childless, he held the baby clumsily, with his elbows spread, feeling off-balance and nervous. His sister was gone. His nephew, in dry diapers, pushed a plastic car slowly and distantly across the carpet with his finger. At that moment Kidd felt a desolation, but did not think of it as his own; he looked at the boy and hurt for what he was sure his nephew must be thinking, for the feelings he imagined but could not lift. His niece, sleeping now, stirred in his arms, and he bent his head to her, tasting the sweet smell of a freshly powdered baby. He pressed his lips slowly against her round, full cheek, and a warmth came over him, a longing so nearly sexual that it suddenly disturbed him to have such a feeling with a baby in his arms. He raised his head and looked away, out the window, before he realized what the feeling was: the painful longing a man feels, even a hard man such as Kidd imagined himself to be, when he has gone too long without holding another human being.

That night after everyone else had fallen asleep, he slipped out of the house again and walked through the neighborhood. For some reason he found that he could not think about the problems and the unmade decisions that kept him awake at night. When he was out on those dark empty streets, alone, he kept looking for the woman he had seen the night before, but tonight no one else, not even she, was there.

CHAPTER 5

The outer office had gotten strangely quiet moments before the knock, but Ginny, who at home heeded the slightest nuance or sound, had not noticed now, had only said, "Come in." So as Livingstone stepped through her door she faltered, "John . . . ?"

"Good morning, Ginny!" Livingstone said in a tone so bright and resonant that Kurtz, standing over the secretary who was typing the first page of his speech, looked up in spite of himself, and watched the door of Ginny's office close.

"Good morning," Ginny said, feeling the bareness of her office—the desk uncluttered by notes or newspapers (already passed along unread), the empty typewriter, not even any wads of paper in the trash can the janitors emptied every night.

But Livingstone glanced all about as if pleased with some way she had redecorated. He suddenly seemed particularly fascinated by the green metal bookshelves against the side wall, and the works by and about Thomas Jefferson which stretched across the top row. "Oh! Have you added to your collection?" he said.

After a pause she said, "No."

Her pause and the quiet in her voice broke his rhythm, and he turned to her. "How are you doing, Ginny?"

If for a moment her face was open, it was again stiff before he could be sure. "Fine!" she said.

"I just—" he began.

"I'm sorry I'm late, I should have sent you a note or something before, but I—" she blurted.

"Wait! Please wait!" he said, even lifting his hands to stop her. "I didn't ask what happened to your three-pointer or your outline, Ginny. I asked how you were." And then he sat down in the chair across the room from her, his eyes looking old.

She tried to smile but immediately abandoned the effort. "I'm fine. I really am. Lately I've . . . had a little trouble getting down to work. That's all."

"With the job part of your life, are you happy?"

"Of course!"

"Do you need a vacation?"

She stared away from him, and Livingstone noticed how her face had lost its last color, as if the idea of a vacation had never occurred to her and the suggestion of it now left her chilled. "Are all the preliminaries getting to you?" he said. "By that I mean, I thought you might need to know that *I* know the outline and three-pointer are bullshit."

Her chin came up slowly, her mouth slightly open. Livingstone had suspected he might surprise her: not only had he always followed Stern's speechwriting procedures enthusiastically, but Livingstone's propriety of speech, in public and private, was legendary. Suddenly Ginny laughed so loud Sherwood heard it next door.

Livingstone guffawed too, looking at her with his eyebrows raised, as if he had just told a secret that surprised himself.

As their laughter faded, they were once again staring at each other. Livingstone's gaze dropped toward the floor.

Slowly he said, "I think people should have their private lives. Not just because they have a *right*, but because we have a need, each of us, to keep some part of ourselves . . . all to ourselves, to show it or not show it solely by our own choice. There's something in us we have to preserve to be human beings. That part we can show, when we're ready, and still keep secret. So I don't—and I won't—pry. But . . . Well I guess I just came to ask you . . . Do you need to talk?"

At that moment Ginny wanted desperately to tell him something deeply personal, to spill her darkest thoughts. But inside she was one seamless dun mass, without words. "I . . . John . . . Thank you. It's just that right now I don't . . . I can't really talk about it."

He nodded, with the firmness of having expected no other answer. He stood. "If you ever want to . . ."

He stopped at the door and, turning back, said, "How long has it been since . . ."

She helped him quickly: "Twenty-two months."

He nodded. "I couldn't remember. I couldn't place just when it was that it happened. You see. It's not just that I don't want you to be isolated. I don't want to be so isolated either. Especially not from someone like you."

At some point in saying that he had looked at her and now was smiling. He nodded and was halfway through the door when she stopped him by jumping up, taking a few quick steps around her desk, and saying, "I've not gotten you in trouble with the Boss, have I?"

"He used to look through every three-pointer and every outline. But if we've already decided that all four writers will submit a speech, he's started having me summarize the preliminaries. You're covered." Livingstone was still smiling. "So don't worry about your job—we need somebody who reads Thomas Jefferson instead of the newspaper. And no one's ever going to forget the Raven Address. But . . . this is an important speech we've got coming up. We need something from you, if you have something to give us."

The outer office was already growing quiet as Livingstone strode through it. "John!" Livingstone halted, and he and everyone else turned to see Ginny, who had hurried to the doorway of her cubicle. Aware of the eyes and the silence, she said, "Mr. Livingstone. Thank you."

Livingstone smiled again, like grimacing, and walked without speaking through the outer office and down the hallway, buoyed by a sudden irrepressible energy.

Ginny, drawn in his wake, walked with slowing steps into the center of the suite and finally stopped at Maggie's desk.

Maggie, the senior stenographer, was one of those women who, having never been the object of a sexual proposal, suspected that all other women, especially attractive ones, received and accepted such proposals constantly. There was the arrogance of confirmed suspicion in her voice when, without looking up from her office supply inventory list, she intoned, "Coffee, Ms. Longstreet?"

"No, thank you, Maggie."

Ginny was back to the door of her office before Maggie's tone really caught up to her. She stopped and turned. "I would like some orange juice though."

Maggie's head pivoted more than raised; her eyes swung up to meet Ginny's. "They sell it at the shop in the basement," Ginny said, and after staring at Maggie for another moment she stepped into the cubicle and retrieved her wallet. "Here are two dollars," she said, going back and setting the bills on Maggie's desk. Then she turned and walked away.

She felt Maggie's stare on her back, but did not hear her rise until she reached her office doorway. She fought back the urge to add, "Keep the change," and closed the door behind her.

She had been staring for five minutes at a blank sheet of paper in her typewriter when there was a soft knock at her door. "Come in," she said, expecting Maggie.

The door swung open. "Uh, Virginia Longstreet?"

Ginny looked up to see a man's head poked around the door. "I'm sorry," he said, "there was no one at the desk outside your door and the other secretaries are grafted to their typewriters."

"I'm Virginia Longstreet. Come in," she said, and stood.

"Peter Pugh," he began, as Ginny shook the hand he offered and nodded him toward the chair, and as they sat he said, "with Internal Security."

Instantly he held up both hands. "Please! Don't get that look that everybody gets on their face when I tell them who I'm with. Do you know what it's like to meet people, especially beautiful women, when the first thing they think is, *Oh God, what do they want to see me about?*"

Pugh's accent was crisp Bostonian, the pace fast. He was youthful, probably thirty, with strong features. His black straight hair was carefully trimmed, his face triangular, his eyes brown and sharp beneath heavy brows. A silver pin squeezed his broadcloth collar and lifted his tie. His skin, a clouded beige that would have tanned easily, was a shade lighter around the jaw, as if he had finished a close shave with talc. Maybe it was the extra care in his dress, or maybe it was the way he talked; maybe it was just that he had closed the door behind him. "What *does* I.S. want to see me about?" she said.

His smile was broad and easy. "Nothing, actually! I'm just trying to get by and talk to everybody here, and there's nothing formal about it and that's why I didn't call for an appointment. The President asked us to see that everybody who works in the executive branch who has direct contact with policy matters be reminded of the responsibilities regarding the release of information. He didn't want to send out some formal statement—and can you see that getting into the papers:

'Presidential Memo Demands Secrecy!'—but he did want everybody personally reminded. I got the job!"

Pugh looked at his watch and stood. "That's all I dropped by for. Watch the leaks! Maybe I should write it on the walls!"

Write it in the toilet, Ginny was tempted to say, but did not.

"Say, those guys you work with, do they ever stop working?" Pugh said with a grin. "I was by here last night, I thought I might catch some people in. You were gone, and that— Thayer, is it?—he was gone, and all the secretaries, but they were here with signs on their office doors saying 'Do *not* clean.' And when I got here this morning they were already at it again."

Ginny was still staring at Pugh when the door opened and Maggie walked in with a carton of orange juice. "Here it—oh, I'm *sorry*," she said.

"No, come in, Maggie," Ginny said, standing. "Mr. Pugh was just leaving." Maggie swayed fully inside as Ginny said, "Maggie Archer, Peter Pugh. Mr. Pugh is with Internal Security," she added, and Pugh rolled his eyes at Ginny and smiled as if the two of them shared some joke.

Maggie nodded to Pugh and set the juice on the desk. "Two dollars bought four cartons. I put the other three in the refrigerator in Mr. Livingstone's office. He never uses it anyway."

"Which, the refrigerator or the office?" Pugh said, grinning.

"Neither!" Maggie said. "He—"

"Thank you, Maggie," Ginny broke in. "Would you see if Mr. Kurtz or Mr. Sherwood could see Mr. Pugh for about two minutes, please?"

"What?" Maggie said, frowning. "Yes. Okay."

As Maggie waddled out Pugh said, "Thank you for your time. I hope I didn't interrupt anything."

Again Ginny said nothing and Pugh looked at her and then looked away. He turned toward the door, stopped, and turned back again. "You know, I have to tell you. I heard about you over in Justice. They say you're the best-looking woman in Washington. They're right."

Ginny's face was so set that even a small change would have seemed large, but Pugh could see nothing different on it as she said, "Thank you."

"Listen, uh, you wouldn't want to have lunch, would you?"

"I'm going to have to work through lunch," she said.

"Well, what about—"

"I'm also married."

"Oh, I'm sorry. I didn't know."

After he was gone Ginny sat at her desk but did not turn back to the typewriter. She waited a minute and then picked up the telephone and hit the intercom buzzer. "Maggie, could you step back in here, please?"

Maggie entered with a robot stiffness, stunned to have received so many directives in one day. Ginny motioned Maggie to a seat, then said quietly, "Maggie, I.S. is free to interview anyone in the executive branch . . ."

"What do you mean?" Maggie interrupted.

Ginny looked at Maggie's demanding face and felt herself losing patience—for nigglers like Maggie, frantics like Kurtz and Sherwood, liars like Pugh. (He knew she was married—four different men from the Justice Department had asked her to lunch during the last year.) "If I.S. is interested in Kurtz's or Sherwood's work schedule, they can ask Kurtz or Sherwood. If they want to know if Mr. Livingstone uses his office in this suite more or less than the one in the White House, they can ask Mr. Livingstone."

Maggie knew Ginny was right. In fact, months ago there had been a universal memo announcing that any executive branch employee's responsibility for disclosure to the White House's Internal Security department was limited strictly to that employee's specific job function, and no one else's. Maggie resented anyone else reminding her of rules; but it was mention of Livingstone's name that broke the haughty righteousness on her face. "That Mr. Pugh seemed like such a nice young man," she sighed.

Avoid him especially, Ginny wanted to say; but for at least the third time in an hour, she did not say what she felt.

Out in the central suite, Pugh stepped from the office where Kurtz had listened silently and with darting eyes to his little lecture. Pugh glanced to Maggie's desk, seeing it again empty, and then to Virginia Longstreet's door, where on the translucent glass he could see Maggie's silhouette as she stood to leave. Virginia Longstreet did not seem to like the obviously pompous old secretary, and needed her so little that she could send her out for orange juice, and yet had called her back into the office as soon as he had left.

Pugh wondered.

Ginny Longstreet wrote nothing that day and went home early, hoping her mind would clear after dinner.

CHAPTER 6

Kidd sat, as he had for the last three evenings, on the couch in his sister's den, across from the television set where his nephew was switching channels. Next to Kidd the baby lay sprawled; he turned idly toward her, picked up a bright orange piece of molded plastic she had chewed into some indiscernible shape, and made noises as he shook it at her. The baby ignored him, and Kidd put the toy down and fumbled with the laces of his running shoes.

When the phone rang he did not move but listened hard to his sister in the kitchen and heard her say, in a polite voice, "Uh yes, yes he is. Just a moment, please," and as he got up and met her in the doorway she said. "It's for you. A Mr. *Al Fredo*." She pronounced the name as if unsure she had heard it correctly.

"Thanks, Carol, I'll take it upstairs."

As he took long, swift strides up the staircase, Kidd thought, *Collie hasn't changed.* The day before Collier had ordered fettuccine Alfredo for lunch.

In his brother-in-law's office, Kidd picked up the desk phone; a sticker on the dial said *Anesthesiologists Do It While You Sleep*. "Al! Hello!" Kidd said, and heard the receiver in the kitchen click as his sister hung up.

"Ah, Mr. Salad! Do you mind if I call you 'Shrimp'?"

"Knock it off, Al," Kidd said, and realized crazily that he had instinctively followed the game. "What's up?"

"Oh, I was just wondering if you had any answer for me on that real estate deal."

"Uh, yeah . . ." Kidd said. "I'm . . . getting close."

"Well, sure, okay," Collier said in a voice that could have belonged to a real estate agent. "I do hope you'll be able to decide soon." And in a tone appropriate to both his real and assumed characters Collier added, "My clients need to know something right away."

Kidd was just reaching the foot of the stairs when the phone rang again. This time his sister's voice was different, from the very beginning familiar yet tentative as she said, "Oh hi! Yes, fine, how are you?" She turned around slowly, as if she already knew her brother was standing in the kitchen doorway, and with both pairs of gray eyes locked together, joined by both heritage and conspiracy, she said, "No, Linda, I'm sorry, he's not here . . . Yes. Yes. I'll give him the message . . . Okay . . . Take care . . . Yes, they're fine . . . I'll tell them . . . Okay, take care, bye-bye." She hung up the phone, turned back to the stove where she began to stir a pot harshly, and as Kidd started to fade from the doorway she said, "Really, Jeff, that's terrible for me. The only reason I can get myself to lie to her like that is because I know how she'd feel if I told her you just wouldn't speak to her. But it doesn't matter anyway if you're not going to call her back."

"I'll be out of here in a few days. Then you won't have to be bothered with it," Kidd said, not without cruelty, and turned away.

CHAPTER 7

Livingstone went into the kitchen, filled a chilled glass with
the single measure of white wine he allowed himself per day,
and carried the drink back through two rooms, one filled with
Italian art, the other with French. Livingstone had owned an
estate in northern Virginia for ten years, but had leased this
town house as an alternative to commuting. He had tried last
year to induce his son to attend law school at Georgetown by
offering him the town house as a residence, but the son had refused ("Jeez, the place is a museum!") to Livingstone's secret
relief: the Virginia estate was so large it required servants, even
when mostly empty—his wife and son were now in Holland
collecting more art they would put God-knows-where—and the
town house was Livingstone's real retreat. It was where he
stayed when he needed to sort his thoughts.

There was a gala at the White House that night, a reception
for the visiting Presidente of a South American country, and
Livingstone had begged off; there was only so much posturing
Livingstone could take. He had already changed into his smoking jacket and slippers.

Reaching his study he plopped down into his favorite chair,
lying back more than sitting. He took a sip of wine and stared
at the ceiling. *Stern,* he thought. *Forbis. Bortchers. The* Constellation *and Sam Emmett, its star columnist,* whom everyone
in the Administration considered a mortal enemy. Livingstone
was troubled by that kind of absolutism, by the sharpness of
the lines people in Washington continually drew. Bortchers
seemed to disagree with the President's plan, though the plan
was unstated. To Forbis that made Bortchers a traitor. Or did
it? Did "traitor" to Forbis simply mean "competitor"? Where
was the proportion of it all? Gone, for sure, but whose fault

was that, the press's? Livingstone, as a broadcast journalist, had always thought of himself as having responsibility but not power. Now that he was involved with power, he wondered if he took the machinations of politics too seriously, or not seriously enough.

His immediate task was to get a speech together, and he was confused.

The process of preparing speeches for Baxter Stern had been so carefully simplified that it was now virtually impossible.

The paradox originated with Stern himself. Stern would not have been President had it not been for certain key speeches, most notably the Raven Address; but knowing the power of speechmaking, he was cautious of it, as if believing it political hucksterism. Making a distinction between what he called "leadership by administering and simple public posturing," that is, between what is done and what is said, he installed his staff of scribes not in the White House basement, according to precedent, but in the Executive Office Building across the street, and yet he kept four writers rather than three, as previous Presidents had done. He refused to discuss with Livingstone for longer than five minutes at a time an impending speech, yet whenever possible he would order preparations begun weeks in advance, in specific stages which he reviewed at every step. A speech would not be written without an approved outline, the outline preceded by a stage called "flow notes"—jottings on the speech's development—and none of that was ordered before the three-pointer was endorsed.

The three-pointer was the phase Stern actually enjoyed. He had not used it during his campaign, but instituted it upon taking office, based on a personal observation which he expressed to Livingstone: "People, all of us, remember only the most basic phrases of anything—a speech, an ideal, or even an experience. Every American reveres the Declaration of Independence, but all anybody can quote of it is 'all men are created equal,' 'unalienable rights,' 'life, liberty and the pursuit of happiness.' So why not look first at any key phrases we might like to express? You know then if you have the substance of a speech!"

Livingstone found himself in the odd position of following the logic of everything Stern said and yet considering his conclusions total nonsense.

But Stern was adamant about his revelation and the procedure he derived from it. First of all the number three had a dialectical perfection—only two points in a speech would be unsubstantial, four would be confusing. Hence Stern called for his writers to submit three-pointers on a regular basis. But he went a step further; to give his speeches what he called "balance of approach," he wanted the points tailored to include three elements: an incisive jab at the central political issue, a moment—however brief—of humor, and some reference to Divine Providence. Kurtz and Sherwood referred to the order of a three-pointer as "the Poke, the Joke, and the Holy Smoke." Every time Livingstone heard that he winced.

Stern might take the poke from one speechwriter and the joke from another, without regard to context or style; in fact he seemed to favor the mixing. He would send Livingstone back to his staff with an approved master three-pointer, from which they made outlines, which underwent further mixing and revision. Then Stern and Livingstone might select the writer who had contributed most during the preliminaries to finish the speech. For bigger addresses, or when haste blurred the steps, they all submitted final drafts.

This procedure had not won Stern the presidency; during the campaign his writers labored furiously, under Livingstone's direction, to provide fresh words for every forum, and before that Stern the Senator had spoken little, merely standing "on my record, which is public." To Livingstone, this new process eliminated any opportunity a speechwriter might have to create something of vitality and power. What surprised him was that of the four people on his staff, all but one thrived on the process.

Kurtz and Sherwood loved catchy phrases like "nattering nabobs of negativism" and "moral equivalent of war." Thayer was a specialist in acronyms: he thrilled to slogans like "WIN —Whip Inflation Now!" To Livingstone such phrases and acronyms were vulgar, as well as dangerous; what went out clever always came back mocking.

Virginia Longstreet, Livingstone thought, sipping the wine that had grown tepid in his hand. Now there was a speechwriter.

Livingstone sat still another minute, then got up, walked to the shelves surrounding the television, and found a cassette of video tape. It was marked in black: "The Raven Address." He slipped the cassette into its player, switched on the set, and sat down again, this time on the edge of his chair.

The tape came from the broadcast made by Livingstone's old network. The friends at the network who had sent the tape to him had included, with a sense of shared irony, the introduction by the network's star anchorman—Livingstone's replacement—who said, ". . . We go now to the headquarters of the Stern campaign, where Baxter Stern is expected to announce his withdrawal from the presidential race . . ."

The picture cut to a scene of somber disarray at the Stern headquarters. The faces of the workers, flat, drained, brought back in Livingstone now all the emotions he had been feeling at the time. There was even a quick shot of Livingstone on the screen—*Do I look that old?* he thought now—and then Stern stepped to a battery of microphones set up upon an otherwise bare folding table.

His face was ashen, but his voice was steady.

"I would like to thank all of you for the sympathy and shared grief you have shown over the loss of my wife. Expressions have come from people everywhere, of all political outlooks, and they have left me profoundly grateful.

"The death of my wife was sudden, and completely unexpected. And, as we had no children, and . . ."

That was the only point at which Stern's voice weakened. He looked down for a moment and then continued.

"The loss of someone so central calls all plans into question. I have faced a decision, a question not of political commitment, which we politicians seem never to doubt, but of private commitment, the kind of steadiness in the heart-of-hearts required of any man who would hold the reins of this nation. In the aftershock of the loss of my wife, I have had to reconsider this private commitment.

"My wife never campaigned publicly for me, she never made appearances or speeches, never raised funds—frankly, she did not have a talent for that. But she was always there, always with me. She did not always believe that I was right, but she always believed that I would do my best, and when I had, she was satisfied with the outcome, whatever it was. That very faith of hers gave me a confidence, made me dare to believe, enabled me to accomplish what I would not, and could not, have attempted without it.

"Now my wife is gone. And as I have asked myself what I will do, I find I still have a kind of faith. I believe that, somewhere, she still believes. When I contemplate a withdrawal from a great challenge, when I sense the urge to make anything less than a total commitment, I feel her silent disapproval, wordless as it was when I could turn and see her face. And I believe that when I do my best, I will feel her still with me, approving—wordlessly—regardless of the outcome.

"And I . . . do not . . . withdraw." Stern's voice rang. "I will continue to seek the office of President of the United States."

Emotion staggered through that room on the screen, surging to a fervor that built from the plane of defeat and exhaustion, and fueled by surprise—for until Stern spoke no one but Livingstone and Ginny Longstreet knew the text of the speech they had given up, and even they were uncertain Stern could utter the words. But he had, and his supporters were suddenly throbbing. The contingent of journalists, caught off guard, were groping through the melee.

Quickly Livingstone switched off the set, as if he hated the scene, but for the opposite reason. The emotions Livingstone had felt then were a kind of elation and faith unique in his public life; they were a memory he wanted to keep precious, not weakened through repetition.

But as he sat back again in his chair, he thought of Virginia

Longstreet. Two years ago Livingstone had ordered each of his four writers to draft Stern's withdrawal, and he had gotten three solid, dignified resignations. He had given the best of those—Kurtz's—to Stern, along with one other speech—the draft Ginny Longstreet had written while sitting in the corner of the staff's headquarters workroom—and then he had left Baxter Stern alone to make his decision.

The Raven Address. A speech. A choice.

And something else, Livingstone thought. No three-pointer could have guided that speech, in Stern's choice of it or Ginny's creation. What eloquence and power Ginny Longstreet had found within herself to write of the loss of a loved one and the crisis it presents to the partner who remains.

Livingstone lurched forward in his chair, where he poised on the edge of the seat, stung by the realization of a fact that had been before him constantly, always obvious, but which had never struck him before.

Ginny Longstreet had reached inside herself and found the Raven Address, those bravest of words about bereavement, five months *before* what had happened to Jamie.

CHAPTER 8

After she had put Jamie to bed (he would shower himself, grinning and grunting as if his teammates were still around him, oblivious to her standing by waiting with a towel, but he grew upset whenever she did not tuck him in) Ginny went to her bedroom and the writing desk in the corner.

She sat there with her pencils and paper, her typewriter ready if she needed it, but even when she tried to force herself to jot down notes she felt soaked in a strange mix of restlessness and indifference. Some nights a malaise gripped her; tonight she had a physical craving to get up and move around.

In the next room, the one that had once been the master

bedroom, Jamie lay asleep silently, for he never made noise. From down the hall and the guest room that was now officially Mary's came a long, regular snoring. It was a peaceful house.

And Ginny Longstreet felt she did not belong in it. She walked softly down the stairs, pulled on the long coat she kept hanging by the door, and slipped outside.

The street was still and quiet as always, and she strode out into its undisturbable darkness with a surge of energy, moving without thought or conscious purpose. The lanes of her neighborhood ran roughly parallel and were cut at intervals by short connecting roads, so that she could have varied her path endlessly, but because she was not after a change in scenery, and did not want to make even the smallest decision, she always walked the same way, up one lane, across to and down the next.

The night was less misty, less damp than the last time she had walked, but the late fall air still had an edge of cold. As she began her route, stalking beneath the gnarled oaks and hickories that spread against the star-sprinkled blackness of the sky, she kept her head down and bore on. But as she walked her rhythm changed; as she turned corners, rose and fell with the pavement that lay like a blanket on the rolling northern Virginia terrain, she began to slow. Moving along the street in the darkness she felt a quiet that was almost like peace.

She did not try to think. Thoughts did occur to her; they were not pleasant thoughts but they were clear, separate from each other, and when they came like that and she could feel one emotion at a time—the fear, the loneliness, which she recognized and admitted to herself, or the disgust, which she did not—they brought a bittersweetness that was not so much pleasant as it was . . . *real*, she decided. *The middle of the night is real.*

The houses she passed were substantial, brick and wood, most often Colonial. She knew them all and yet she could not have described a single house individually, recognizing each only in the pattern of her passing. Mostly the lights were out. Occasionally she saw the glow from draped windows of lamplit bedrooms or the flickering that meant late-night television. But the people who slept or watched TV or talked or made love in the houses, or the rare jogger or dog walker who passed her, were part of a different universe, a world parallel but totally apart from the one in which she walked.

When she turned onto the fourth long street and passed the white house that she knew was the halfway point, she would not have admitted that she was looking for anybody. But when she turned down the last cross lane that led back toward her house she began to be afraid, and this time it was not the heart-racing physical sensation she had felt when last on this street, with the realization that she was not alone. Now she felt a fear that came with a draining away of hope, a hope that until now she was not aware that she had.

Consciously denying that hope—that there was anything for her to expect, that she could accept anything new in her isolated world—she walked along the pavement from streetlamp to streetlamp, looking from one puddle of light to the next. She passed the section of trees and shadow where she had seen the silhouette before—the place to which she had returned in her dream—but he was not there, and she walked on without slowing, her breath coming now in defeated sighs.

The disappointment raced with self-disgust far ahead of her loneliness. She was already giddy as she saw the form sitting beneath the hickory tree on the bench where the county bus stopped to pick up the government commuters. A streetlamp glowed twenty paces beyond, dampening him with light; he sat tilted forward, his elbows propped on his knees, his legs barely flexed and pushed out before him. His spine was too straight; his shoulders and head sagged, as if to spite the rigid effort. She kept moving forward, her steadiness unreal. As she neared, his head made a startled twist, and then he sat upright very slowly, as if to be sure not to alarm her.

She stopped, ten feet away.

They looked at each other, and in the brief moment she stared at him she felt the sensation of watching herself from a distance. Then that unmistakable, strong, gentle, familiar voice that she had heard only once said, "Hi, I . . . didn't scare you again, did I?"

She thought at first the word was not going to come out, and then it came stronger than she wanted. "No."

He laughed—a bit nervously she thought—and said, "I really . . . I hope I didn't scare you the other night. It was you I almost ran into, wasn't it?" His voice was quiet, but not calm— more like he was having trouble speaking and the words when pushed came out softly. Whether it was this softness or something else that drew her closer, she did not know, but she drifted forward a few steps.

"Yes."

"I'm not dangerous at all." He laughed, then stopped again quickly.

"Oh don't tell me that, I was hoping you were."

Ginny was stunned, not just by the flirtatiousness of the remark but by the completely natural manner in which it had come out. In the wash of light from the streetlamp she could see the right side of his face: the straight line of his nose, the lean jaw, the chin lifted toward her. The entire left half was black shadow except for the glint where the light caught his eyelashes; she was staring at him that closely, realized she was, and could not stop.

"I was just a little startled, that's all," she said, her voice sounding to her strangely bright. "I guess I thought I was the only one who came out for walks at night." His eyes—at least the one she could clearly see—were wide open, maybe as startled and expectant as hers must be as she waited for whatever might come next.

"I'm sorry, would you like to sit down?" he said suddenly, and as she hesitated he slid to the end of the bench. There had been plenty of room already for her to sit; but it was midnight, and they were alone in the dark. Still, when he moved away and gathered himself up so that his knees were together and his hands folded, the knuckles of the left hand pressed into the palm of his right, he looked so nervous himself, so concerned that she not feel threatened, that she simply sat, as if automatically.

"You live in the neighborhood? We're . . . neighbors?" he

said, in a voice that sounded uncertain. His face, except for a thin aura around the silhouette, was now totally in shadow.

"Oh, you live here too?" she said, with that surprising brightness.

"Yes. Well," he said, as his shadowed face turned fully to her for an instant, "I'm really just . . . staying for a while at my sister's."

The next day Ginny would try to avoid mentally reliving these events, consciously afraid of distorting and secretly afraid of deadening what had happened. But whatever force it is within the human heart that casts up involuntary echoes would make an odd selection in Ginny's: the memory of this moment, when she sat on the cold bench, and the bare tree branches overhead bobbed in the wind beneath the stars, and the stranger next to her had asked if she was his neighbor and then admitted nervously that he was not hers—this memory, and the unshakable conviction that it was at this exact moment when she ceased to feel alone.

The pause that set off the moment was brief, as she, to save him, rushed to say, "But you are from around here, aren't you," making it more a statement than a question. "You're a Southerner, I mean."

"Does it show?"

"Only to my ears, I think," she said, and smiled. "You've got that kind of Southern accent that's been mellowed by education, and maybe travel." Jokingly she added, "You didn't try to lose it, did you? I mean, some of us do, when we've been away too long."

He turned his head again and stared through the darkness. "I wanted to once. Not any more."

"Really? I understand that, but . . . tell me why."

"Well . . . You're a Virginian, aren't you?"

"Yes," Ginny said, surprised that he had nailed her own accent so easily.

"Well, you being a Virginian, this may surprise you—but there are people who think a Southern accent shows a *lack* of culture and brains."

"*Shame* on them, sir," she said.

He laughed, then said, "Actually, I don't know if it's trying to hold on to something I'm afraid I'm losing, like some ideal of chivalry and honor, or wanting to find something like that that I never really had. I mean, some of the basest words I've ever heard were spoken in a Southern accent, and some of the noblest, too. I don't mean aristocratic and lofty so much as just plain honest. I guess most of the people I've known who said exactly what they meant were Southerners. But it isn't that honesty is limited to the South, maybe it's just that I'd like to be more . . . that I could *know* more who I am, and be that, no matter who likes it, or doesn't."

He blew out a short laugh and said, "What about you?"

It was her turn to stare through the darkness. "In Washington . . . I work in government . . . and in the political environment in Washington everything is calculated, as if everything—the way you talk, and dress, and cut your hair—is for a label. I don't think it goes as deep as what you're talking about, and that's the point to me—it isn't deep here. And I wish it were—as deep as you seem to feel it. I mean . . ." As she was speaking she felt the energy in her voice, and an odd confidence that seemed in direct contradiction of the fact that for the first time since before she could remember she was starting sentences with no idea how she would finish them. ". . . Washington is the center of power, national and international. It's full of all kinds of people playing very sophisticated games by constantly changing rules. But a hundred miles, ten miles from here, you find communities of people whose values aren't at all sophisticated, but they hold them with a profound strength. And it's such a funny thing . . . When I grew up, in a little town not far from here, I hated so many things about it and I was dying to get away. I'm not saying I could ever go back now, I really couldn't. But still there's something . . ." She trailed off, and they sat in the silence that neither hurried to break.

And suddenly Ginny, who had written tens of thousands of words but had not spoken that much at one time in years, now said, in that voice grown strangely bright, "Tell me. Tell me something. What do you think of the country? America right now?"

"You mean . . . what? Politically? The state of the government right now, or . . . ?"

He stopped and waited, and she stammered, "No, I'm—I'm sorry. I didn't mean any specific aspect. I was just wondering how you, as a man on the street"—she forced a tinkle of laughter—"perceived America, in a broader sense. How you feel about being an American. Patriotically."

He hesitated. His gaze seemed to drift down to his lap. He wet his lips and said, "Well, I—"

"Wait."

She spoke so suddenly that his head snapped around toward her, and the eyes which she could not see seemed to be looking at hers. "I didn't mean that," she said. The tinkle was gone from her voice. "I don't want to know what you think because it relates to my job. I want to know what you think because . . . I want to know."

He turned his head away finally and raised his face toward the trees and the sky. "I've thought about that a lot, actually," he said. "Thinking about it now, it relates to what we were just talking about. I don't think you can understand a Southern mind unless you talk about the question of honor. I don't mean honor like pride, dueling at dawn, or nuking some pompous dictator somewhere because his people have burned an American flag. I mean the motivation that makes a common person decide that if his country needs him, that need is imperative. It's honor to respond to it, and honor is more important than survival. It's always drawn Southerners toward war. To really answer your question, to make it personal . . . Right now, everything in my life has turned into"—he laughed, and said—"garbage. I know it's natural for a person in a time like that to doubt everything he's always assumed, and thought, and believed in. I'm no different, I'm . . . right now I guess I'm pretty cynical. I hate politicians. I don't think much of the press. There's hardly an organization of any kind that I don't consider hypocritical and ludicrous. But one thing I've never doubted is my country. Does that sound funny to say? It does, but it's true. I've never doubted the country. My country." He turned to her and with the wisp of a laugh he said, "That's strange, isn't it."

"No."

"What's your name?"

"Virginia . . . Ginny Longstreet. What's yours?"

"Jeff Kidd."

"I have to go," she said, standing before she thought about it. He nodded and stood slowly, six feet away from her.

Not looking at him, she hesitated, pressing her hands down tightly into the pockets of her coat. Then she turned to him, started to smile—though she was never sure if the smile actually reached her face—and turned and began to walk away.

She heard his steps start in the opposite direction and then heard, "Ginny?" She spun around, much too quickly, though she did not move toward him again. In that quiet voice of his that for the first time actually quivered he said, "Do you come for walks here often?"

Finally she nodded. "Yes."

She did not go home intending to write the speech. She had thought, when she had begun her walk, that she would rise before dawn the next morning and, goaded on by absolute necessity, would write and submit whatever came to her then. Even when she stepped from the cold, fresh night into the warm staleness of her house and moved with habitual stealth up the staircase and down the long hallway, she felt no sense of purpose or duty, and her mind was vibrating, but not with words.

Nor did she, once inside her room, discover a sudden verbal torrent. Locked within her bedroom (it was strange: when she had brought Jamie home from the hospital and ensconced him in the master bedroom, she switched the locking hardware of his door with the unlockable knobs from the second bedroom, and now she used her lock secretly and with guilt, but always) she lay down fully clothed upon the bed and remained totally motionless, experiencing an odd and not entirely welcome sense of energy and buoyance. Sleep, she realized, was out of the question, and with that realization came another: that she had once seen every assignment as an opportunity for self-expression, and excellence as something she owed herself.

That was when she got up and began to write the speech.

CHAPTER 9

Along one perimeter of the White House's West Wing is the Oval Office, central workplace of Presidents, famous or infamous for the decisions and discussions that have gone on there. Every President since Teddy Roosevelt has used it. Its design, like that of the rest of the mansion, is Federal, its carpet is inlaid with the seal of state, its walls are hung with portraits of great chief executives, and Baxter Stern was so uncomfortable there that he used it only when he absolutely had to.

So Livingstone, when he left his office in the White House basement for his appointment with the President, did not stop on the first floor, but went straight to the living quarters on the second. He walked on a thick rose-blush carpet down a long quiet hallway, until he passed the door of the presidential bedchambers, through which filtered the faint strains of classical music from a record player. Livingstone stopped at the next door he came to and then entered without knocking.

The room was dimly lit, and Livingstone could barely see for the blue haze of cherry-maple tobacco smoke hanging in layers below the mahogany paneled ceiling. But he knew right away from the electronic pings and whistles that Baxter Stern was huddled in the corner, and a tenor voice mumbled, "Hi, Livver," through the smoke.

Livingstone picked his way through the room—there were dark leather chairs strewn about in no particular order—and looked at the screen over which the President crouched. There, superimposed upon a pink and purple alien landscape, ranks of electronic ghouls marched back and forth dropping straight and squiggly bombs upon a crumbling row of forts. At the bottom of the screen, dodging the bombs, was a counterattacking cannon; Stern moved it back and forth with the buttons at his left hand, and with his right jabbed at another button, which shot green bolts upward on the screen, exploding the ghouls with a pop.

Livingstone stood watching over Stern's shoulder. "I wonder what kind of statement I'll have to make when the public finds out the President likes to play Space Invaders."

"Wait. This is a five-hundred," Stern said as a flashing yellow spaceship appeared in the top right corner of the screen and floated over the ranks of ghouls. He crouched lower, his chin almost touching the buttons, and fired; the spaceship exploded in the top left corner and the machine gave off a chortle. "Ha!" Stern exclaimed, and then said, "Tell them nothing gets my mind off my frustrations as effectively as the knowledge that the Martians are about to overrun my laser bases."

Stern risked a quick glance over his shoulder at Livingstone, and Livingstone said dryly, "Somehow I don't think they'll be reassured."

The ranks of glowing crabs, becoming depleted, began raining bombs faster and accelerated their march. Stern slid his cannon beneath them, firing as he went, and the ominous droning music the machine emitted grew faster. Stern, raising himself up a little, but still jabbing frantically at the buttons and never blinking, said, "You could tell them I don't rent this machine! I bought it with my own money!"

Livingstone stood still for a long while and finally said, "I'm not sure that knowledge would be a comfort."

Stern, maneuvering to catch a ghoul in the upper row before the ranks changed direction, got caught in the corner by a rain of bombs, and his cannon blew up with a dull crash. "Crud! Those squiggly ones'll get you every time," he said.

He still had two cannons left to throw into the fray, but flipped on the hold switch he had had the White House electrician install, and rose up, wincing and grabbing at his back as he bent past vertical. He snatched up the pipe which had smoldered its way out in an ashtray and darted to the opposite corner of the room, where he began to scatter the mounds of paper stacked a foot deep on his desk.

Stern, in the privacy of his lair, in the presence of a lifelong friend, might have struck an observer as a Dickensian eccentric. Forbis had once suggested a careful publicizing of this hidden side of Stern's as a way of stemming the sag of his popularity. Livingstone vetoed the idea for two reasons. One was that the American public found odd mannerisms lovable rather than disturbing only when the country did not seem to be in crisis, and the sense of crisis in one area or another had existed since before Stern took office. The other reason was that Stern's habits were coldly purposeful. The letters which lay on his desk, for example, were a random grab from the stacks of mail which arrived at the White House daily, and every morning an aide would bring in a new bunch and cart the old pile away, whether the President had looked through it or not. Stern, by open declaration, distrusted tallies and summaries of calls, telegrams, and correspondence. The tone of one letter, which he might jerk from the stack at any time of the day or night, could influence him more than any "counting of noses that are temporarily out of joint," he had once told Livingstone. So Stern's brusqueness in pushing aside wads of these letters, even knocking some to the floor, implied no disrespect; he simply felt that for his system to work he had to remain random.

Finally finding his humidor, Stern filled his pipe and sat down in the nook that his desk and the corner created. Livingstone pulled up one of the chairs and sat in front of the desk. He was just about to say something when Stern blurted, "Congress!"

Stern's tenor was scratchy with disgust. He sat quietly as if that one word summed up everything, and leaned back in his swivel chair. But then the words spilled out. "Two days from now I'm going to present my military manpower plan to Congress. But now Congress has decided not to wait for me, and today they've started debating their own program. They're out-and-out telling the public they think my program will be worthless before they ever hear it!" Stern stopped jabbing the stem of his pipe into the air and instead stuck it in his mouth. "Did you know about that?"

"The congressional liaison people told me to expect it," Livingstone said. "I briefed my staff by memo yesterday."

"It's always a war," Stern said. "Congress and the President are supposed to fight, but we don't have any credibility. Congress ought to be ashamed of doing this, but there's no shame in Congress, and no fear. With things like this Bortchers incident we look disorganized. We aren't, but we look that way. A year ago the press was after Congress. Now it's me. If I scratch my butt in public, they call for a full investigation."

"Except in your case, Mr. President. They know that when it comes to the investigation of—"

"Wait a minute, is this going to be another proctologist joke? Then save it. Good lord, Livver, they ought to impeach me for surrounding myself with guys like you."

"How do you feel about Bortchers's denial of the *Constellation* article?" Livingstone said. After waiting a full day, an assistant at the Department of Defense had issued a statement that, whereas Secretary Bortchers had expressed the opinion, publicly and on many occasions, that the United States needed to return to a peace-time draft, the Secretary at no time implied that he held any power beyond recommendation; all decisions rested with the President, to whom Secretary Bortchers remained thoroughly loyal, and whose authority he respected.

"Oh, that was perfect," Stern said. "He got in his licks for the draft, showed himself to be a good team player, though an overzealous loudmouth, and he put the whole hot potato back into my lap."

"Are you nervous about the speech tomorrow night?"

"I won't be, if you'll come up with something good for me to say. The speeches you sent me last night aren't right. This military thing is tricky."

"Yeah. Thayer's past his time. Kurtz and Sherwood are sharp, but those brilliant phrases they insist on writing just don't sound right coming from you." Livingstone knew without looking up from the floor that Stern's small brown eyes had cut over to him. He hesitated a moment, suppressing a smile, and said more thoughtfully, "Thayer's going to retire soon. I think I may speed him along, replace him with someone more in-date."

"No. Not yet. Don't let go of anybody until I tell you."

Now Livingstone did look up, and quickly, but Stern was staring away from him, into the cloud of smoke he had blown toward the ceiling.

Livingstone waited for something more, but got nothing. Breaking what was for him an awkward silence, he pulled a folded sheath of papers from his suit pocket. "Virginia Longstreet gave me this about thirty minutes ago. You'll be pleased." Livingstone dropped the freshly typed manuscript onto Stern's desk, but still the President did not move.

"Ginny Longstreet . . ." he mumbled, still staring away. "That husband of hers . . . His name was Jamie, wasn't it?"

For the second time that morning Livingstone felt the uncertainty that is common when men are confronted with the reticence of a friend grown more powerful than themselves. Stern had always been a realist in speech as well as thought; since assuming the presidency his practicality had become almost obsessive. Livingstone now wondered for an odd moment if Stern's brain had not already written Jamie off as dead.

"Yes. Jamie," Livingstone said. And then he added, "He's not getting any better."

"Is she going to quit?" Stern said to the blue clouds rising against the ceiling.

"You mean . . . her job? I don't know. I haven't had any indication of that." Livingstone thought back over the last two days, wondering if there was something he had missed about Ginny, or something Stern knew about her that he did not. "But this speech is good," Livingstone said. "It's really good."

"I'll read it when you're gone. You and I will go over the final version tomorrow."

"Don't change too much, Baxter."

"Go to hell, Livver."

"You're the most boring man I know. The whole country knows it. Do you think it's easy trying to keep them from finding out you're also illiterate?"

"Boring? Tell them I can play Space Invaders. They won't think that's boring. Tell them I'm great at it."

"I'm better."

Stern was up and clearing the old game off the machine before Livingstone stood. "You know," Stern said in a shrill, suddenly animated voice, "I hear some kid got eight hundred thousand on this thing. Can you imagine that? *Eight hundred thousand!* I wonder how he did it."

"Practice," Livingstone said, bending his big frame down over the controls.

Stern stared at the screen filling up with new ranks of invaders. "No. Youth," he said. "Watch out for the squiggly ones."

Outside the President's study after the game (Stern had thrashed him), Livingstone paused. Faintly through the door he heard the sound of the desk chair creaking back. Stern was settling in to read what Virginia Longstreet had written.

It was another anomaly of his friendship with Stern—a relationship so intimate yet speckled with warm mysteries—that Livingstone was unsure of Stern's attitude about Virginia Longstreet. Stern inquired about her—it was unusual for him to ask about the personal life of anyone—and he paid special attention to her drafts of speeches. But Stern had restricted his speechwriters, all of them, through what Livingstone knew was a fear of becoming a mere figurehead, a mouthpiece of his minions. Livingstone, in that moment outside Stern's door, thought again of the Raven Address, and he again felt amazement that Stern could have trusted enough to accept the words someone else had given him, and to say them without abridgment at that darkest of times.

There could be only one reason: Ginny Longstreet had a special place somewhere in the secret self of Baxter Stern; and that position was gained through the unique place she held in relation to Lenore Stern.

No one had ever been close to Stern's wife, not even Livingstone. She was always around, but apart; through the campaign she went everywhere, but kept a cassette player with earphones with her constantly and buried herself within it, varying her routine only with an occasional book. She did watch Stern's most important campaign performances—press conferences, speeches, national interviews—but she never went "on parade," as the campaign sages liked to say, never smiled, and they kept the cameras away from her. But after any important campaign encounter, Stern would demand that he be left alone with her; if there was nowhere more private they would step to a corner and hold a hushed conversation. Everyone in the Stern campaign understood that Lenore Stern was off-limits, by Baxter's choice and her own, and she had no personal encounters at all —except for one time, with Ginny Longstreet.

They were on the campaign plane, flying back to Washington after a storm of effort in California. Everyone was exhausted but tension was driving them on. Livingstone remembered that Forbis had called a powwow in the conference section of the plane, and fifteen people were arguing about how well they had done; some felt they would carry California, others thought they would lose. In fact no one had any idea, and the professional debaters were spouting heated opinions that they changed in mid-sentence. Ginny sat through the whole discussion, typically silent. Livingstone, in his own frustration with the uncontrolled waggling, noticed that Lenore Stern and Ginny were looking at each other—they seemed to have caught random glances—and Livingstone realized for the first time that they were the only two women in the twenty-member campaign inner circle. While the arguments swirled about them, Livingstone watched, unnoticed, as Lenore Stern took the headphones off and handed them to Ginny.

People who are together nineteen hours a day talk about everything, especially each other, and one of the gossip intrigues of the campaign was just what Lenore Stern listened to. Some said it was tapes of Stern's old speeches, others said no, it was a collection of Hitler's speeches. One aide even swore the tapes were copies Stern had obtained when he was a member of a

Senate freedom-of-information subcommittee, and that they were clandestine recordings of a noted civil rights leader making love. Ginny Longstreet was about to find out.

She took the earphones from Mrs. Stern and put them on. At first no one but Livingstone was aware of what was happening, but attention filtered into the whole group. The discussion died. The plane's engines hummed like an echo. Ginny's face was intent, even excited. Her eyes widened at first, then closed. Slowly her expression grew placid; she smiled. She opened her eyes, looked at Lenore Stern—and suddenly both women burst out laughing.

Ginny handed the headphones back, and she and Lenore continued to laugh. The press secretaries, advance men, other writers and advisers all around chuckled too, asking, "What? What?" But neither woman would look at anyone else. Finally Baxter Stern, with just the hint of a smile, said, "I think there's nothing to do or talk about or settle, gentlemen. Let's get some rest." Everyone got up, including Ginny, and went back to the main section, leaving the Sterns alone.

As far as Livingstone knew, Ginny Longstreet and Lenore Stern never actually exchanged words, then or at any other time, but whenever they encountered each other, the light smiles they exchanged were always knowing. And when Ginny was besieged by everyone hungry to know what Lenore Stern was listening to, she never seemed to hear the questions, and her stare was so stony people quickly ceased to ask.

But two weeks later they won the California primary, and Stern came out to the party at the Washington hotel where the campaign workers had watched the returns. He waved at the crowd, and then took Lenore, feeling ill, home. The party continued, but Ginny wanted to get home herself, and Livingstone walked her down to her car. It was more than gallantry that made him offer; no one in the campaign really knew Ginny beyond work, but Livingstone felt close to her even then. She seemed the only one besides himself who realized that only something very serious could make Stern miss a chance to celebrate the most important primary victory of his campaign. They rode the elevator down to the parking lot, walked together to her car, and Livingstone said abruptly, "What is it she was listening to, Ginny? What's on those tapes?"

Ginny was silent a moment, and then spoke just as abruptly. "Vivaldi," she said. "That's what it was when she let me listen."

Livingstone stared, motionless. Ginny looked away and said, "All that talk, all that pressure, her husband after the most powerful, important position in the world, and she his anchor. While he muddles through the politics, she listens to Vivaldi."

Three weeks later, Lenore Stern was dead. And Virginia Longstreet wrote a speech so simple and personal and *intimate* that Livingstone could never have even submitted it to Stern at that awful time, had it not been for that one simple secret that had passed between Ginny Longstreet and the only person Baxter Stern ever fully trusted.

Livingstone turned from the study door and walked down the hallway, past the doorway to the presidential bedchamber, where the Vivaldi still played, music for the dancing of ghosts.

CHAPTER 10

The central newsroom of the *Constellation* was not an impressive place. Its desks dated from the 1930s and broken plaster webbed the beige paint in all its corners. Mounds of paper lay around the new word processor terminals which sat like hi-tech mushrooms sprung from verbal humus. An outsider would never have been able to pick out whose desk was whose, or even exactly where one desk top ended and another began; reporters talked on each other's phones, hacked at ancient typewriters, and chain-smoked.

Physically Sam Emmett was as unimpressive as his newsroom. He was stocky, pale, not tall. He had black hair in big thick Harpo Marx curls, and his nose was flat and small. It was Sam Emmett alone who had taken the newspaper from obscurity to the position of euphemism; as Kurtz and other members of the Stern administration would say, Emmett worked for the *Consternation*. He sat now with his feet propped on one of the desks, his hands folded atop the potbelly that should have belonged to a man fifty, not thirty-five.

The editor of the *Constellation* was Brooks Barker, who, as the reporters who worked for him said, was two years ahead of retirement and two years past caring. Barker had cataracts, well advanced on one eye, just starting on the other, and was leaning very close to an unedited piece of hand-typed copy which lay flat on his desk. His face was without expression. He sat back, picked up the telephone, dialed Emmett's com number, and said, "Come here."

Emmett, out in the thicket of paper, ink, and Marlboro smoke, hung up the phone without speaking. He withdrew a manila envelope from his desk and dodged toward Barker's office. His uneven gait was not from a limp, as it at first appeared; he hopped on his left foot and skidded on his right whenever he hurried, which was all the time.

Barker did not look up from the copy when Emmett walked in, closing the glass door behind him. "I want to see your source on this," Barker said.

Emmett thrust the envelope beneath Barker's nose. Barker undid the clasp and drew out the document. The stationery was from the White House. Barker peered at the text, noting especially the numbers.

"All right," Barker said, turning his clouded pupils up toward Emmett. "The speech is tomorrow night. We'll run this the morning after."

As Emmett skipped out of the office, Barker turned in his chair to put the document into his safe.

CHAPTER 11

As Kidd drove through the northern Virginia countryside, he thought of Stonewall Jackson, hemmed up in the Shenandoah Valley and facing what seemed certain annihilation from three separate Union armies, any of which might have crushed him. Jackson wrote to his wife almost daily, though he was a fire-and-brimstone Presbyterian and refused to post any correspondence if it would have to travel on a Sunday. In one desperate hour, the night before a critical battle, he wrote his wife that he was being sorely pressed, and events were preventing him from writing her as often as he wanted, but she must never forget his love and never doubt that she was always in his thoughts and in his prayers. The next day Jackson went out, and, with his blue eyes glowing with a fire that his adjutants took to be an unearthly fury, shattered the Union army before him, then wheeled, maneuvering his infantry more swiftly than anyone thought possible, and drove his other former pursuers like chaff before the whirlwind. Union reinforcements, intended to be sent to Richmond to crush Lee and the Confederacy forever, were withdrawn by Lincoln to defend Washington itself.

Jeff Kidd was aware of these facts, having written a master's thesis analyzing the interplay between a man's private self—his personality, beliefs, emotions at a given time—and his actions as a leader; he had used Confederate generals as the objects of his study. Kidd knew countless anecdotes about men in battle and in the shadowy, stress-filled limbo that surrounded it. As he drove along the Washington Beltway that morning, seeing the signs that pointed the way to Richmond and Fredericksburg, and especially as he saw the one that said "Manassas," he recalled the history in which he was steeped. He stared out at the rolling fields and wondered what the men who fought and died upon them thought.

But most of all, for reasons he did not understand at first, he thought of Stonewall and how he had loved his wife, and missed her.

It seemed such an odd thing to think about, but the phrases and images of the anecdote kept coming to Kidd as he drove, like a melody that lingers so stubbornly that it becomes obnoxious. Kidd was hunting for an apartment; he kept trying to think about where he should live, what furniture he would pull together, how far from central Washington he should be. But he kept thinking of Stonewall.

Off the highway he saw a building, square, squat, and new, with a banner draped along its roofline declaring: "Now Renting." Kidd drove to it, was shown by a too-heavy divorcée in a too-tight sweater to a one-bedroom apartment. The walls and ceilings were covered with the white spray texturing that modern builders use to cover shoddy construction; the floor was a concrete slab covered with lime-green shag carpet. The bathroom and kitchen had the same wallpaper—green tropical trees printed on something that looked like tin foil. And it rented for a sum that Kidd had thought would get him something tasteful and roomy. "Do I have to sign a lease?" was the only thing he asked the woman.

"Yeah. And you should do it quick," she said sleepily. "These are renting fast."

"I'll let you know as soon as I can," Kidd said.

As he drove away he thought of Stonewall again, and began to ask himself why he should be hounded by the recollection. The anecdote was easy to misunderstand; it seemed to be about a great general who had time to think of his wife. But Kidd had seen and analyzed that story in reverse—it was about a man who had all sorts of inner struggles, including loneliness, and was able to focus himself to be a great general. Kidd was almost back to his sister's house before he realized why the Stonewall story was tormenting him. It was very simple. Kidd did not have an army to lead, or history to make; he had very small things to do, things as simple as deciding on a job, or finding an apartment. And yet he could not do them well, could hardly face the tasks at all. He had to force himself to go out driving, had stopped at the first place he had seen, then gave up the search as too depressing.

Stonewall had one advantage, Kidd thought: his wife loved him. But that, to Kidd, was no excuse, and as he thought of Stonewall Jackson as a great man, he felt his own impotence. Not only was he aware of a huge gulf between himself and all men of greatness, but he doubted, in a kind of black fear, that he had any worth at all.

And later that night he felt stupid for going to the bus stop bench, looking for Virginia Longstreet, and thinking she would come back.

CHAPTER 12

The same morning that Jeff Kidd went apartment hunting, John Livingstone played Space Invaders with Baxter Stern, and Sam Emmett received a bootlegged White House memo, Ginny Longstreet had gone early to the office. There she made her final revisions, gave the manuscript to Maggie to type up a clean copy, and sent it by the messenger shuttle so that it would arrive at Livingstone's office in the White House basement exactly on the deadline. Then she sat down again at her desk. She expected the energy that had kept her wide-eyed until five that morning, and barely let her sleep at all, to suddenly drain away; instead she felt restless, anxious for more work. So she dug into the mounds of printed matter that had been stacking up in her office—newspapers, news magazines, political commentaries, polls and analyses, survey data from the census bureau—and worked away for hours, until she had sorted everything and made reference notes for anything worth keeping. She even thought of going into the television cubicle and catching up on the news broadcasts banked there on video cassettes, but she checked her watch and saw that it was almost seven o'clock.

When she stepped from her own office into the outer secretarial suite, its vacantness shocked her—the empty desks, the typewriters covered in gray vinyl blankets. Only one of the four ranks of fluorescent strips still glowed overhead, and the door panes of all the offices were dark, except the one to Sherwood's silent cubicle. Ginny thought he must have left last, even after Maggie, for Maggie would never have left allowing energy to be wasted like that.

She crossed the suite quickly and tapped on the lit panel. Hearing nothing, she swung open the door, reached at the light switch, and gasped as she saw Sherwood lying across his desk.

He was pitched forward from the chair, his arms spread wide, his thin neck stretched out, and one side of his face pressed against the desk surface as if he awaited the executioner's ax. Ginny stood with her hand to her mouth, and then realized in solitary embarrassment that he was asleep.

Post-natal depression—that's what old Thayer called the state that both Sherwood and Kurtz always found themselves in after their herculean exertions. Once they had submitted a speech (which they always did before the deadline, to Ginny's bewilderment, considering their common perfectionistic obsession), they fell into physical and emotional exhaustion. Kurtz would often not come into the office at all; Maggie said that he would go bar-hopping, drinking himself into oblivion, but Ginny had never heard that confirmed. Sherwood would come in, merely to drift zombie-like around the office, not having slept in days.

Ginny left the light on and slipped out silently.

Back home Mary had already started Jamie on his dinner. Ginny sat down and began hurrying through her meal, as Mary, freed of solitude with Jamie, got up and began washing dishes.

Ginny ate silently; Jamie, the doctors had said, was physically capable of speech, but his mental capacity for it was gone. Still he followed her, not with his eyes or with his hearing, but she felt distinctly that he was latched onto her, with some invisible strength, from some unseen appetite. She turned to watch him as he ate, was surprised at his speed, and then realized, with a weakening low in her guts, that he had quickened his own pace so that he was shoveling food into his mouth as fast as she was into hers.

Mary, noticing the silence, turned from the sink and said, "The macaroni all right?" She stuck her chin out further in Ginny's direction and said, "You feel okay, Ginny? You're white! More than usual." Mary laughed.

"I'm fine," Ginny said, putting down her fork.

Jamie put down his fork, too.

Ginny closed her eyes. Her fingertips moved to the center of her forehead. The silence in the kitchen was unbroken until Jamie stood; Ginny looked up and saw him walking in his viscous pace out into the hallway. Ginny sat stiffly; she and Mary both raised their faces upward as they heard his heavy tread moving up the staircase. "Well . . ." Mary declared, mildly puzzled. "I guess he's ready for bed."

Ginny started to stand, but before she could get up Mary had dried her hands, patted Ginny's shoulder, and said, "I'll put him to bed. You just rest tonight."

Left sitting alone at the table, Ginny felt the energy that had driven her all day—since, in fact, the night before—shattered against the impenetrable wall that was Jamie. The collision left an emptiness like a ringing echo, soon deadened by a feeling thick and pervasive as Jamie's presence. *Betrayal.* Now, drawn up short by what seemed to her Jamie's perception and mirroring of her moods, she was overwhelmed with a guilt of having dismissed him, and confessed to herself, with the rapid openness of the criminal caught red-handed, that she had been rushing all day as if to hurry to that one time, *midnight*, when she could walk out again to the darkness, and freedom, and Jeff Kidd.

She stood and went out of the kitchen, through the hallway, up the stairs, and into Jamie's room, where Mary had just cleaned his macaroni-slicked fingers with a wet towel and was smoothing the covers around. Ginny leaned, kissed him on the cheek, smoothed her hand over his forehead, and walked slowly from his room to her own.

Behind her closed door, which she refused this time to lock, she lay down on the bed and closed her eyes, letting in the kind of tense fatigue that has no location.

There on the bed she argued with herself. A voice inside her, with the swiftness and pleading of a young girl, said that she had been going for late night walks for weeks, months even. She liked it, it helped her; why shouldn't she go? Why shouldn't she look forward to it? There was nothing different about that.

And then the other voice, that seemed so much older, and wiser, and more powerful, asked quietly, if there was nothing different, then why had she planned all day to allow herself extra time to shower, wash her hair, and to put on fresh clothes before she went outside?

She could argue no further with that voice; and yet the younger, weaker side refused to die. She set her alarm clock for 11:15 and dropped off to a shallow sleep.

The alarm rang for a half second before she shut it off. The house was deadly quiet.

She did shower and wash her hair, but that was not a commitment; it was preparation for tomorrow anyway. But then she got dressed and still did not feel she had made up her mind.

She sat on the edge of the bed in her room, until the clock read 12:30, then 12:45. At 12:55 she rose suddenly, went down the stairs and out of the house, and though she walked straight to the bus stop bench and then stalked quickly up and down the route she always walked, he was no longer there, if he had come that night at all.

CHAPTER 13

For the first eight minutes Stern had wrestled through the charts which showed Soviet military manpower levels in surging stalks of sinister red and American resources in declining stubs of true blue. Forbis had briefed him well for this section of the speech, and though Stern ad-libbed, he fumbled only a little. But the statistics, however simplified, were numbing. Ginny, Livingstone, Kurtz, Sherwood, and Thayer watched the screen in the video room of their suite, and each knew that if Stern did not change his pace soon, fifty million Americans would be switching him off.

Finally he twisted away from the last chart to face the camera fully. He pushed his glasses back up on his nose. As a transition from the statistics to the heart of his address, he said, "To summarize, the manpower levels of our military are extremely low." His eyes rounded out, and his head tottered from side to side; the writers tensed, feeling it coming. "My advisers in the Pentagon tell me that what we need is a"—Stern's eyebrows soared—"A Stern Approach!"

Livingstone sat stiff with embarrassment; Ginny's eyes closed with a shamed ache. Kurtz and Sherwood winced. Then from the back of the room came Thayer's chuckle. So he had contributed the Joke.

Stern made the moment even worse by pausing, as if allowing the laughter to die down in living rooms all across America. But at last he picked up his notes. (He refused as a hypocrisy the broadcaster's TelePrompTer, and read openly from large sheets.)

"The question of military obligation strikes at the most fundamental issues of a democracy.

"The laws of this nation declare that the President and the Congress work together to establish the nature of military obligation, and in the next few days we will be taking up the specifics of the question. I am coming before you tonight to discuss the issue because the power of your commitment transcends the power of the presidency or the Congress. You are the nation.

"The question of a citizen's responsibility to defend the nation is so basic that it alters our simplest understandings. We speak, for instance, of a 'volunteer army'; yet enemy bullets never ask how a person was inducted, and the death of a draftee is no less a sacrifice than the death of a volunteer. Ultimately, all who serve have made a choice. And so have those who do not.

"The nation has the power to compel a choice; not what the choice will be, but that each individual make one. To consider the exercise of this power raises complex problems: who could be called first, would burdens be borne equally among age groups, races, sexes, economic classes?

"The program I will submit to Congress will not call for an immediate resumption of the draft, but will suggest a commitment to certain personnel levels, and the identification of factors which would set in motion the machinery for the reinstitution of the draft. The program is not a rhetorical exercise. It carries no inspirational title. It is a blueprint, a schedule of numbers worthless as a document alone, and even dangerous if viewed out of context. The debate, in and out of Congress, will be vigorous.

"It may also be divisive. To explore any possibility on the question, to take any stand, is to risk charges of war-mongering or cowardice, of racism, of stupidity. But it is our strength that permits such debate, and the preservation of freedom that is at the heart of the discussion."

Finally Stern paused, and with a handkerchief he wiped the perspiration from his upper lip.

"As I reflect on the problems that face us today, I become increasingly aware that we, as Americans in a free society, are constantly offered, by various groups and individuals within our society, widely differing definitions of what it means to be

American. This deluge of ideas is a result, and in fact one of the privileges, of being free.

"The very deepest principle upon which our democracy is founded is not only the idea that all men are created equal but also the belief that each of us has an inner integrity, an inner dignity which gives his point of view worth. I do not believe that you have elected me, or cast your vote for someone else, because you want me or anyone else to define for you what it means to be an American. I believe my duty as President is to respect each person's opinion and to protect the right to hold and express those individual convictions.

"Sometimes it is easy to doubt your country's leadership. It is in fact a duty of each citizen within a republic to try to view the leadership with a critical and yet responsible eye. But many of you—I think most of you—can say honestly that you have never doubted your country. You *have never doubted your country.* Think of that for a moment—the faith that expresses, the willingness to take responsibility that it implies. I only want to tell you tonight that I believe in you who have that spirit for your country.

"The next days and months and years will tell whether you consider me a good leader. Sometimes any person who would be a leader must step before his people and tell them, as clearly as possible, what he believes, and that is what I have done.

"Finally let me say that there are times when being President of the United States is bewildering and baffling, when no decision seems the right one and no outcome seems positive. At these times I find the job that I sought, and you have given me, extremely hard.

"But there is not a night that goes by that somewhere in my heart of hearts I do not thank God Almighty that I am one of you.

"Thank you. And good night."

"Mmmm," Livingstone intoned, nodding his head slowly.

The President's face faded out on the screen before them

and the picture flickered as the network news commentators came on for their instant recaps and analyses.

"Ginny, that was—Oh, you arrogant . . ." Livingstone broke off in the middle of his soft words, and pointed a finger at the screen. "Listen to that! He presumes to tell the American people what they just heard! Only *his* version! Come on, Waldo! No wonder the network's slipped to third place." Livingstone leaned forward and switched off the sound. Then he turned back to Ginny, put a hand upon her forearm, and squeezed.

Sherwood, who had written the "Rebirth of Confidence" speech, and Kurtz, whose offering had twice repeated the phrase "a Time for Daring," now stood together at the back of the room. They were very still.

"Did he have to linger so, over that last bit about the Almighty?" Ginny said.

"You know how he is," Livingstone said.

"Who, God or the President?" Sherwood said, and Kurtz joined him in a sharp laugh.

"You mean that's two different things?" Kurtz blurted, and laughed again.

"Everyone knows the President is a devout man," Livingstone said quietly. "The lines about him praying at night were legitimate. He lingered over them because they *were* true, and he was legitimately moved by the entire speech."

Livingstone stood and, thrusting his hands into his pockets, began to pace the room. Except for the obvious quality of his suit he looked like a distinguished university lecturer. "Today we had a speech about what? About nothing in one sense, about everything in another. About nothing in that no specific policy was announced, only promised. We were denied the use of hard substance with which to work."

Livingstone stared at the floor as he said this, pacing back and forth slowly. Kurtz and Sherwood watched him closely. Thayer looked out the window. Ginny's gaze floated down to her feet. "But . . . But . . . ." Livingstone went on, "it was also a speech about everything, because when a President goes before the American people he can't always tell them the complex details of the governmental process that baffle, and bore, even U.S. Senators. Sometimes the President has to remind us of our"—now his voice took on that quiet, resonant boom for which he was famous—"*greater traditions*. Lincoln, Lincoln at Gettysburg! What did he come to do? Dedicate a battlefield. And the day after the dedication the papers neglected his speech almost entirely! Like, like Waldo there they liked to discuss flowery orations, like the polemic some Congressman nobody can remember delivered during the same ceremony with Lincoln. But later, people—even the media—realized what great words they had heard, written while Lincoln rode the train to Gettysburg." Then, in a moment of self-parody, Livingstone grinned and stretched his arms wide. "And that, my friends, is great speechwriting."

Livingstone walked out of the room. But as he passed Ginny Longstreet he stopped for a moment and said very quietly, "That's what you did. Thank you."

CHAPTER 14

Kidd tried to work out every day. It was not that he had a problem finding the time—time was all he had—but rather that he could not seem to push himself the way he liked when exercising. Instead of doing a hundred sit-ups and a hundred push-ups straight through he broke them into sets of twenty-five each and alternated. He thought of that as cheating, and tried to atone for it in his rope jumping, but his rhythm was off and he could not maintain a steady pace until his legs cramped; he kept speeding up in sprints, and had to stop repeatedly to ease his scalding lungs. He believed he had lost his will.

Once hot and restless within his sweat clothes, he felt guilty to return from the backyard into the house, where his sister seemed always swamped by the tasks of homemaking and mothering. So today when he saw a can of spray paint sitting beside the faded base of a stone birdbath that stood just off the patio, he took on the job, and had the surface a glossy white in ten minutes. Then he surveyed the yard, went into the tool shed beside the patio, found a rake, and began scraping leaves into neat piles. There was a half acre of grass and hardwood trees behind the house; he was nearly done when his sister stuck her head out the back door and said, "Jeff, the phone's for you."

"Look, Jeff," Collier said at his end of the line. "I don't want to press you, but I will need to know something soon."

"I know that, Collie," Kidd said, relieved they were talking straight, that Collie had dropped the "Mr. Fredo" bit. "I'll let you know as soon as . . . I know myself."

"Well, let me ask you this. If you did take the job, who would be the first man you'd hire?"

Kidd did not respond, not for lack of an answer but because of the commitment that giving one would be. "I mean," Collier said, "the thing has to start with key people, to choose the others. You're the one I called before the paint in my new office dried. I'd just like to know who you'd call. Give me some direction to think in."

"There's no question about it," Kidd said at last. "You need a man who's a top interrogator. Who's tough and smart and can take a lot of heat, outside and in. I met a guy when I went through a refresher at Quantico in hand-to-hand. He's FBI. You may—"

"Tennyson Dooley," Collier said.

Kidd hung up, but not before promising to come down to Collier's office the next day for another discussion. Kidd agreed to the meeting with reluctance, and in that reluctance saw his own hypocrisy. He liked being wanted. He wondered if he were not abusing a good man and friend to be acting so damn demure.

When he got back out to the yard his sister was heaping stacks of leaves into polyethylene bags; Davey, sacked in a too-large sweater and a red stocking cap that said "Redskins" on the front, was waddling around behind her, kicking up leaves. "Hey, the birdbath looks great! Thanks!" his sister called.

"You stole my job, Carol! Do you get nervous when anybody does any work around here besides you?" Kidd said, feeling his joke fall flat because it was true.

"You think I'm going to let you have all the fun?" she said. "I love the leaves. And I thought Davey wanted to be outdoors a little. But here!" she said, tilting the rake toward him.

"No, no, I'll find something else," he said, and walked back toward the tool shed.

"Get *away* from that, Davey!" he heard her yell, and glancing up from the clutter of hoses, tools, empty jars, and broken toys, Kidd looked out the window to see his sister shaking a finger at her son as he tottered near the newly painted birdbath. "Don't you touch that!" she said severely. "If you touch that, you're gonna get paint *all over* your *new sweater!*"

She turned back to her pile of leaves, and Davey, to Kidd's delight, reached immediately toward the birdbath, and touched it with a mystic softness, as Midas might. He then gazed at his finger—there was nothing there, the paint having hardened in minutes—and took a slow look down, even spreading his elbows a bit to get a full view of his sweater. Then he stared toward his mother's back.

That's it! Kidd thought, in awe. *He's just understood what I couldn't tell him, that day he peed in his big-boy pants!* Kidd imagined the revelation that had just occurred within his nephew, a new-dawned awareness that was wordless, perhaps even without consciousness; but if it could be described, Kidd knew the words would be: "I get it. *I get it!* Mama's all bluster! It doesn't mean anything! I'm not covered in paint. And . . . and I won't have to wear diapers even when I grow up!"

As the boy staggered off happily, to hang on to his mother's legs and play with the leaves at her feet, Kidd thought, *At what age do we forget how to grow past the wretchedness we gather to ourselves in trying to live with others?*

CHAPTER 15

As Kidd left his sister's house and walked down the dark street that sloped until it joined another tree-lined lane, he felt the sharp cold on his face but nothing more. Everything else around him was blocked out by the turbulence of his emotions, and the effort to control it. He walked stiffly, with his arms pressed to his sides, and his face was rigid, but not from the cold.

In trying to crush the impulses that were bumping inside him, Kidd told himself a lot of things, but the main one was: Ginny Longstreet had never said that she would come back the *very next night*. So he had no reason, and certainly no right, to have expected her to. Because of her, he was subject to flights of anticipation which he tried to suppress. But he did admit her impact on him. He consciously labeled it an infatuation. He reminded himself that this infatuation could have twisted his perceptions. But what he found most unacceptable within him, and tried most to deny, was anger that she had not come. As he stalked along, he said to himself over and over that she had never said she would come back the very next night, so how could he possibly feel anything approaching anger that she had not come? He was afraid, almost physically shaken by the fear that he would show that anger in some subtle, or even not-so-subtle way, and thereby ruin everything.

He came to the spot where the lane bridged a narrow stream. He pressed the dial light of his wristwatch, saw that it was eleven forty-five, and berated himself; both times he had seen her just after midnight, and now he felt misplaced. Either he would barge up to the bench early and wait like an overeager schoolboy, or he would walk stupidly around the unfamiliar streets, trying not to get too far from the spot where he hoped to meet her. Either way he knew he would feel ridiculous, and settled for slowing down, and walking directly toward the bench. So just after the bridge he turned right, onto the narrow road that bisected the suburban lanes and led to the bus stop.

There were no houses built along this road, and while the lanes had streetlamps, this road had none at all. But it was short, and Kidd could make out the light near the bench a hundred yards ahead. He could see from where he was that the bench was empty, but as he drew nearer he thought he saw a shadow pass rapidly before it, and then after a moment he saw the same fleeting form move back the other way. He walked on, peering ahead into the darkness, until he made out clearly the unmistakable figure of Ginny Longstreet.

She was pacing.

Kidd felt a lightness, an elation that he struggled to contain just as he had tried to grip the darker, sinking emotions seconds before. The sight of her—beautiful, nervous, strong somehow in her energy—waiting for him, pacing and even expectant, made him pause. He even considered retreating unseen and waiting, afraid that he might embarrass her now. But then he stepped forward, walking into the light.

She was pacing away from him as he came, and then pivoted, walking back several steps toward him until she drew up and said, "Oh."

"Ginny," he said.

She was embarrassed; her eyes fixed on him restlessly, not looking away but wanting to, and then they settled, and she smiled. "I was hoping I would see you here tonight," she said softly.

Ginny saw the smile break out on his face, and to her the smile seemed disbelieving, a little afraid, but uncontrollable.

"You're early," he said. "Earlier."

"So are you," she said. "Or do you sit on the bench all the time?"

"No. No, I don't," he said, and he grinned. "Would you like to walk? Could I take a walk with you?"

For all the thinking she had done that day about meeting him there tonight, she had not once pictured them walking together. Maybe he saw the surprise and confusion on her face because he said suddenly, "Or if you can't, if you'd rather sit . . ."

"No. Please. Walk with me."

The sky was full of broken clouds and the night breezier than the last one had been. The wind that pushed the clouds brought the smell of wet leaves and dying fireplace blazes. She felt—or maybe only heard—him take a deep breath beside her. They walked awhile without speaking.

They passed through irregular patterns of darkness and light. They met the glow of streetlamps at steady intervals and the darkness in between was now and then mottled by the light of a full white moon which, breaking between the clouds and through the tree limbs, would bathe the street in gray-blue sheen.

"Were you sure that I would come?" he said.

"You said you would," she said. "Should I have doubted you?"

"No. But . . . a stranger on a dark street. Might be a hard person to trust."

She looked up at him. She caught his full profile in the moonlight. "You said you weren't dangerous."

That smile—this time she was sure he tried to hold it back but it came anyway—broke out on his face again and he said, "I lied."

But the smile vanished just as suddenly and they walked on together in silence. They reached a corner and he said, "Which way?"

Ginny pointed, and with a sudden hollow feeling in her stomach, that feeling of betrayal, she realized that she was leading him along the exact path that she had walked so often alone.

"Did you hear the President's speech tonight?" She said it a bit quickly, as if to make conversation, and she was surprised to hear that strange brightness back in her voice.

"Yes. Some of it."

"What did you think of it? I mean, I heard it too, and some of the things he said . . . remind me of you."

He turned and looked at her. They were in shadow and she could not really see his eyes, but she saw his head turn and stay very still for a moment, and then he looked away and said, "Hmm. Well! I don't know. I didn't hear it all, really, just the last half, and the commentary at the end. I liked what the President said. But I get really sick of hearing the commentators say later that a President's speech is calculated to do this or that. I think sooner or later you have to accept that he said what he wanted to and you have to decide whether you believe it or not. What he said this evening was . . . Well, he said some good, brave words. Maybe words are just words. Maybe talk's cheap. But I've always liked brave words. Just wanting to say words like that says something about the man, I think."

She had caught her breath while he was speaking; she felt herself almost gasping when he was through. And when he said, "What did you think?" she responded a little too quickly.

"Me? Oh, I thought it was . . . good."

She was uncomfortable in the pause after that, and hurriedly added, "I think the President is a good man and he's trying. I believed in what he said, but . . . sometimes I wonder if it's not a little empty. Patriotic words, but . . . it all seemed a little bland."

"I guess you can't really hold that against the President."

"What do you mean?"

"Oh, I don't know, coming across as bland, even if what he said was good and right. I mean . . ." Kidd was warm to the topic, remembering her question at their last meeting of how he felt about the country. "I wonder sometimes—I'm sure you do, too—how we compare with people in the past. What they faced, and how they responded. We seem so pale, though people then must have been as subject to gossip and lying and sensationalism as we are. But take the great ones, like Lincoln. Take his speech at Gettysburg . . . I'm getting carried away with this, am I going to bore you?"

"No."

"Well, you take Lincoln at Gettysburg. He made that speech at the exact middle of the Civil War, and that war— most Americans today don't have any idea of the depth of that war. More Americans died in that war than have died in all other wars in our history—*combined*. That includes both world wars, Korea, Vietnam! Did you know that?" He did not wait for her answer, feeling the question was pedantic, and quickly added, "More Americans killed each other with bayonets and musket balls and grapeshot and sabers than died from dive bombers or machine guns or panzer shells. And that was at a time when the population of this country was a fraction of what it is today.

"So when Lincoln made that speech about whether government by, of, and for the people would perish from the earth, he had to mean it. He had to. And when he talked about a hallowed ground, he was standing on a place where thousands of men had fought, with enormous courage and suffering. So . . . Well, I am getting carried away. I just mean that the times took the measure of the man." He rattled out a laugh and said, "I'm sorry, I really do get carried away."

"No, please! I love history," she said quickly.

"Really?"

She nodded. "And yes, I did know about the Civil War statistics," she said, smiling. "You don't grow up in Virginia and not know about that. But my favorite period is the Revolutionary/Federal. I'm a Jefferson freak."

"Quite a pick."

When they reached the corner, and Kidd paused for her to show him the way, the moment's hesitation gave room to a small nasty urge within her, that made her turn from her normal route and lead him in a shortened circuit, back toward the bench. She cursed herself instantly, that she had cut off the time.

As they came to a section where the trees sat back further from the pavement, exposing the street to the open sky, he turned as they walked, and studied her face in the moonlight. She did not feel self-conscious, and looked at him openly.

"You're a handsome man," she said.

He mumbled something, the same thing, three times, and she did not catch what it was until the last: "My God . . ." he was saying.

They drew toward the bench and began slowing, as if by silent agreement it would mark the end of their conversation. In the nimbus of the streetlamp they looked at each other, closer than they had been all night but still feet apart.

"Jeff," she said, and noticed as she felt that hollow feeling again that she had just spoken his name for the first time. "You said last night . . . I mean night before last, that you're staying with your sister."

"Yes."

"Are you married?" It came out so easily, with surprising firmness.

"I have a wife. But I don't have a . . . marriage."

She felt a rush of things when he said that. Soberness, for one, because she had just heard what she knew was the truth. Relief for another, because it was what she had expected and the confirmation was a comfort. There was also a fear which she could not explain, but that had been with her since she first saw him.

And floating to the surface of that swell of other feelings was a stirring she immediately, instinctively knew but misnamed in a dozen ways, a warm, soft, and yet commanding feeling that spread through her when she heard the pain in his voice and the silence of his hesitations. She felt understood, though he hardly knew her. And in his wanting to explain, his desire for her to understand that he was—available?—she felt . . . *reached out to.*

"I have to go," she said suddenly.

He stopped, dead still. He seemed to want to speak but did not. She had never been nearer than three feet at any time, and she moved no closer to him now; but standing in front of him with her hands in the pockets of her coat, she looked directly into his eyes and said, "No, there's nothing wrong. Nothing the matter with me because you're married or . . . whatever it's like. I want you to tell me about it, I want to hear everything you feel. I want to come back here. I will, can you, tomorrow? I just don't want to hear too much right now."

"Yes. Okay," he said, and nodded very slowly. "Okay. But

tell me just . . . one thing before you go. You're married too. Aren't you."

"Yes."

Walking alone across the bridge and back up the slope to his sister's house, Jeff Kidd understood what had been behind his anger and his fear. He had accepted wanting her, but what he had been blind to was the need—the absolute, desperate need. He had known it for the first time in himself when he had watched her then, and saw how much she needed him.

CHAPTER 16

That night she did not think about the strangeness of what she had felt and said. But the next morning when she awoke out of a sound and dreamless sleep she did begin to think about it and was baffled. People meet strangers—on business trips and vacations, in airplanes or restaurants—and sometimes will, within a shockingly brief time, tell a stranger everything: dreams, failures, secrets. The anonymity makes it easier to talk about some of the things that are hard to bear alone. That was understandable to her. But something about this was different.

It was during breakfast when she was feeding Jamie warm cereal with bananas that it came to her exactly why she had so abruptly broken off her talk with Jeff Kidd the night before. People on airplanes talk freely because they expect never to see the other person again. They say everything at once, in an unfettered gush, because the other person does not really share in the intimacies, he only hears. That talk is the cheap kind. But with Jeff Kidd it was different. Everything he said meant something, seemed to come from something important inside him and reach something special in her. That kind of talk was not cheap. It had to be unraveled carefully.

And yes, she realized, she meant to unravel it. She had an expectation—more than that, a determination, a compulsion—to share those secrets with Jeff Kidd.

She looked at Jamie sitting there with milk-wet banana clinging to his chin, and she almost cried.

The office suite, first thing in the morning, had a certain smell—the aroma of coffee from the drip percolator in the corner mixing with the undertone of the lemon-scented cleaner the janitors used at night. *And in ten minutes,* Ginny thought as she walked toward her cubicle, *the whole place will bloom with perfume.* Ginny had always thought the secretaries wore too much scent, but today the idea seemed pleasant. Maggie, always the first to arrive, looked up as Ginny walked past with a "Good morning!" Maggie scowled.

The fluorescent lights of her office came on with a hum she had never noticed before, and the air smelled thickly of newsprint; Ginny sat down at her desk, realizing that today she was aware of the smallest details.

The knock on her door was sharp, more frantic than angry. Frowning at the door for a moment, she said, "Come in," and Adam Kurtz hurried inside. As soon as he closed the door he stopped and took several breaths.

Ginny could not take her eyes off him. Her stare clearly made him more nervous, and it was that edginess itself that was hypnotic. He was pale, and his eyes, always magnified by his glasses, were glaring white. "Virginia, I want you to tell Livingstone that I had nothing to do with it."

Very slowly Ginny said, "Adam, you definitely have my attention. But I don't know what you're talking about."

"Have you seen the papers?" He held up a newspaper and shook it at her.

Since she shared with the other speechwriters a circuit of forty papers every day, Ginny did not have a morning paper delivered at home, and even after a presidential address tended to approach printed reports systematically and analytically, reacting not to the news, since for her it was often not news at all, but to the selection and presentation of the particular journalist. Kurtz too was a reader of vast amounts of reportage, and Ginny assumed he was angered by a slant, not shocked by a revelation. "No, no I haven't," she said. "It's not about the speech, is it?" She reached for the paper on top of the stack that Maggie had squared at the corner of her desk.

"Not that one!" Kurtz said, bouncing forward. "The *Constellation!*" He opened the copy of the paper he was holding and shoved it at her. The headline read: "Stern Restructures Draft."

Kurtz stepped back from the desk and began to pace, pressing the edge of his thumbnail between his teeth as Ginny skimmed the paper.

It was another leak.

The article trumpeted the bootleg character of its information in its very first sentence. "Sources near the President" had disclosed the "closely guarded plans" Stern had hinted at in his address. There followed an itemized list of the steps the President contemplated to reorganize the nation's defenses, with particular emphasis on utilizing women in the military and on unshackling the intelligence networks. The article did not include any context for the steps; it simply outlined the areas the President's reorganization would affect, and added wild speculations on the "philosophy behind these radical moves." For good measure, the writer threw in the impassioned comments of well-known figures, from a celebrity attorney to a Hollywood actress/activist, "reached at home with this news."

When Ginny looked up, Kurtz jerked to a halt, as if staggered by her attention. Quickly he resumed pacing, lurching back and forth in the small room. Ginny glanced down again to the paper, checked the by-line she already knew, and said, "Okay. Another of Sam Emmett's leaks. It looks like a lot of trouble for the Administration, but we've been through these leaks before. What makes you take it personally?"

Kurtz whirled and almost screamed, "Per—I'm not taking it personally!"

Ginny realized that she was staring at him, and wondered if her gaze seemed accusing to Kurtz. "No, Adam, I just mean that . . . personally, for all of us in this department. You seem to be trying to tell me the leak came from here."

"Look at the numbers!" he said, stabbing his finger toward the paper spread on her desk. "The exact numbers!" Ginny looked down to read again but before she could, Kurtz said, "The specific steps, listed bare-bones. And the exact target numbers—percentages of wage increases, programs cut, programs increased. It's the exact information that was in the confidential brief Livingstone gave us."

Ginny knew immediately that Kurtz was right. Not only did the facts and numbers coincide with their brief but the information was listed in almost identical order.

"All right, Adam. That's serious. And it might create fallout but I don't see why you think it's going to land on you. Or on any of us. We got the information after it was discussed on lots of different levels. Any one of—"

"They think the leak is in this department already!" Kurtz broke in.

"Who told you that?"

"Rumors."

"Rumors are a plague in Washington."

"Not just rumors, Virginia! You talked with that guy from Internal Security, that Pugh!"

"Yes, I did." Ginny's eyes defocused for a moment in the direction of her desk top; Kurtz stood in the center of the room spitting shards of thumbnail. Then Ginny looked up and said, "All right. Suppose they are taking a hard look at our department. There are two things you haven't told me: why you think suspicion might center on you personally, and why you want me to speak to John Livingstone in your behalf."

For the first time since Kurtz stormed into the room his eyes were still. "Both questions have the same answer. I'm not Livingstone's—the *President's*—star speechwriter. You are."

"Adam," Ginny said slowly. "You know how the process works with the President's speeches. He did use some of what I wrote the other night. Some. He—" Kurtz started to protest and Ginny held up her hand to keep from being cut off and said more deliberately, "He takes from all of us and he takes what he wants. But that's not the point. The point is that a person's trustworthiness doesn't have anything to do with some temporary appraisal of his success."

"In Washington it does," Kurtz shot back. "The I.S. department goes after only the little fish." Kurtz grinned as he paced and shook his head, as if denying that he could be fooled. "Internal Security is a department of the executive branch, and that makes it a part of the bureaucratic machine of politics and power. Its function is to make its agents tend to pick on the little guys and to leave the big ones alone. The press, the press is the opposite! It's just a part of the fabric of fad and publicity! The average newspaper reader doesn't know and doesn't care about the small fry of government, so the press doesn't either! But the big guys, the ones everybody knows, they're the ones the *press* and the *public* love to hang. I.S. doesn't want the press coverage. They want any little jerk they can hang out to dry."

Ginny had the unsettling sense of hearing a man she knew was crazy wildly declaring what she suspected was the truth. "Listen, Adam," she said. "I don't see what I can promise you except that I'll do everything I can to see that nobody in our department gets leaned on disproportionately. I hate snooping around anyway."

"I know you do," Kurtz said, with a smile that looked soft and strangely genuine. "Your secretary told mine the other day to keep her mouth shut around Pugh."

Ginny smiled back and said, "There we already have proof of a cover-up."

"That's right," Kurtz said, ceasing to smile.

As he stood there motionless, lost-looking, in the center of her office, Ginny said, "I'm . . . a bit flattered that you said all this to me."

"Yes. Well." Kurtz's eyes, behind his lenses, grew glassy as he stared out the window behind her. "This job is really . . . really important to me. I write the best speeches I possibly can. You write better ones. John Livingstone loves you for that. I hate you for it. But I respect you. I have talent and energy. You have a gift of words."

"Whether that's true or not, Adam, it's nice of you to admit it." Ginny listened to the strange sound of laughter spilling from her own throat.

"Whether it's true or not—it's nice that I *admit* it! You see what I mean?" Kurtz laughed too, a light, fast chuckle, and then the life drained away from his face. Without speaking again, he turned and left the office.

Ginny sat thinking for a few moments, and read again the paper Kurtz had left with her. Then she turned to the stack of newspapers beside her and read through them all; there was no mention in any of them of the hard facts that Sam Emmett had reported.

Ginny had already left the papers and was starting to scan a news magazine when she stopped and looked up as if a voice had called her name. She closed the magazine, put it down, and opened the desk drawer, the second on the right, where she kept all her important material and where she had placed her copy of the policy guidelines Livingstone had given them four days ago.

It was not there.

CHAPTER 17

"We have no comment on the report appearing in the *Constellation*," Livingstone said into the telephone.

The man on the other end of the line said, "You don't deny it?"

"We have no comment."

"Oh come on, John," said the television reporter, who had worked for years on the same network as Livingstone. "A no-comment is a nondenial. A nondenial on an exclusive like Emmett's is as good as a confirmation."

"I suppose that's right. But that supposition is off the record." That morning Livingstone was taking only the calls of people whom he could trust off the record. One hundred thirty journalists had called his office that morning, and so far Livingstone had talked with twelve.

"Then you're telling me Emmett's information is accurate," Livingstone's old colleague said.

"I'm telling you we aren't denying it, but I don't want you to broadcast that as if we'd confirmed it." The reporter started to say something but Livingstone overran him. "It's a leak—or claims to be. This administration has its own timetable for revealing everything in the right order to the right people. It's protocol if nothing else. We aren't trying to hide anything from the press or the public."

"John," the reporter said, his voice grave, "do you remember what it was like when somebody else had a story you didn't have? Well that's what's happened to me, to all of us except Emmett."

"Of course I remember."

"Well what am I supposed to think? Emmett has exclusive stuff! Consistently! So consistently it looks intentional."

"If you're suggesting we're manipulating Sam Emmett, I deny that publicly. Put *that* on the air if you want to."

"So are you plugging the leak? Give me a story about that then, John. Christ, give us something!"

In the voice Livingstone himself hated, the mechanical voice of a man mouthing what he must say, Livingstone droned, "All leaks are unintentional and disruptive, but we have no vendetta against Sam Emmett or any members of the press. Discretion is expected of every person in this administration, and breaches of informational security are investigated as a matter of routine. Our main concern is to develop the best programs and implement them effectively, and that is how we focus our attention."

When his friend had hung up, Livingstone raised his hand to his secretary, who could see him through the open door, and she blocked the next call he would have taken. Livingstone sat back in his chair and sighed. It was hard answering the same questions over and over, but he had long ago gotten used to that. He felt sapped now, and not from effort, but from uncertainty.

Stern and Forbis had met for an hour that morning in the Oval Office, but neither had told Livingstone what they had discussed. Ordinarily that would not have bothered Livingstone, but for some reason it troubled him now.

CHAPTER 18

To Kidd, the central file room of the FBI headquarters in Washington created a perfect example of subjective perception. Almost anyone seeing the room for the first time would be struck by its enormity, by the endless rows of shelves bearing stack after stack of information, bound and numbered, on every known bit of criminal activity falling under the Bureau's jurisdiction. The sheer mass of it all suggested to most minds that everything knowable was there. Anybody sliding open one of the legions of card catalog drawers and seeing a name, then an entry, such as "*Student at Berkeley. Known to be follower of Y. A. Farks; See RADICAL PROFESSOR,*" followed by a string of reference numbers, might easily imagine the FBI knew too much.

But experience, Kidd knew, shaped perception. To anyone who had seen a child molester set free on a legal technicality, and wanted to know the cities and types of neighborhoods in which he might settle; to anyone who had seen the aftermath of an amateur bomb set off in a crowded airport; to anyone who knew of a professor at a major school who had explained in great detail to his students how LSD could be introduced into the water supply of a large arid city—to anyone charged with the prevention of such crimes, the files looked small.

Kidd understood the workings of the file room, it being similar to many others he had used before, but the plump spinster whom Collier had asked to conduct the private tour took her charge seriously. She walked Kidd down tunnels of shelves, singing out numbers and rattling off, from memory, the subject of each grouping. She stopped at a large collection, one whose final letters ran from A through BBB, and picked up its master shelf reference. She took ten minutes demonstrating to Kidd how any book could be opened anywhere, any document selected, the red lines traced through every name cross-referenced, or through every pertinent location mentioned, and the numbers written in beside it used to find all the other information pertaining. She did not speak with pride; it was more with watchfulness, as if she were ready to uncoil at any mistake, to pounce on any omission and correct it.

Kidd, bleary after a thirty-minute tour, went back to Collier's office and found him going over personnel files. "What'd you think?" Collier said, grinning.

"You're not going to like it," Kidd said.

"Give it to me."

"For what you're talking about, instant response information accessing, the current system is useless. It's great for criminal investigation, when you need to probe and mull through everything to try to find what you're not even sure you're looking for. But for instant response in a crisis . . ." Kidd squinted, pinched the bridge of his nose. "The files go from the general to the specific. That's how they're designed, according to their exact function. But we have a different function." Kidd realized he had just said "we," but Collier did not smile at him.

"If I understand what you're trying to set up," Kidd went on, "you want to go the other way, specific to general. You've got a terrorist incident. Hostages, or a whole city held hostage. You want to take everything you know and get an instant line into all your possible adversaries. I mean, specifically—you get a threat that a man has a bomb. You don't know if it's conventional, nuclear, if it exists at all. You send in a negotiator, somebody who's trained in minute observation, physical and psychological. Your negotiator comes out and says, 'The guy's got red hair. He's left-handed. He has an accent—Spanish.' Now, our people usually know a bomber's signature—whether a guy wires with a left- or right-handed twist, things like that.

You want to find out, as soon as your man comes out with the information, what left-handed, red-headed, Spanish-speaking bombers you know about."

Kidd smiled and pushed his glasses back up. "Okay, there should be only one. But what if there are two? And one has nuclear experience, or say he's been sighted recently in South America, talking with reactor people. The CIA might have that information. So let's say it's summer in South America, so you say to your negotiator, 'Did this guy have a tan?' I mean, 'Was he sunburned?' Then you can make a better guess whom you're dealing with. Of course odds are you won't know the guy anyway. But if you really worked, developed a system based on a fine enough subset, you'd have all you could have."

"And how do we do this?" Collier looked pleased.

Kidd hated being asked a question by someone who already knew the answer. "Study, first. Train agents based on the observational criteria you're using to establish your subset. Most of all you've got to computerize. It's all got to be in a computer bank instantly accessible by a team in the field."

Collier grinned slowly.

"I don't know a damn thing about computers, Collie."

Collier picked up the two files on his desk and handed them to Kidd. They were the personnel dossiers on the best computer men the Pentagon had. "We can have them on loan to set up the program. After that they rotate, until they've trained our own computer personnel."

"Computers are worthless unless you know what to tell them."

"That's right," Collier said. His grin kept getting bigger.

They walked down the hall together and turned into an empty corridor. Collier opened the first door, revealing a huge empty room. "This is ours," he said. "What do you think?"

The door on the opposite side of the room opened and a man walked in. Kidd looked at Collier, then back to the man, who walked all the way up to them and stared down into Kidd's face. "Collie," the man said, never taking his eyes from

Kidd's, "do you know how you can tell if your neighbor is from Virginia?"

"No," Collier said.

"If he's only got enough paint to cover one side of his fence, he paints the side that faces the house, because that's the side *he* looks at. *That* arrogant bastard is a Virginian."

"Collie," Kidd said, "do you know how Arkansas was settled?"

"Tell me," Collier said.

"People from Tennessee were trying to go to California. When they crossed the river into Arkansas, there was a sign: 'This way to California.' The ones that could read went to California. The ones that couldn't stayed in Arkansas."

"I'm really from Texas," the big man said.

"That's what everybody from Arkansas claims," Kidd said.

"Good to see you, Jeff."

"Good to see you, Tennyson."

Collier, Kidd, and Dooley sat in a conference room that was stripped out for security: no drapes, no rugs, no place to hide a microphone. The room was as bare as their beginning.

Collier knew everything he thought had to be done; therefore he said nothing, letting his subordinates direct the meeting.

Kidd said, "The task is so big we can't do anything but cut it in two, half for each," meaning himself and Dooley. "The problem breaks down to us and them—forming the guidelines for establishing potential perpetrators, and for choosing which agents we'll consider possible trainees to counter them."

"Sounds right to me," Dooley said. "I don't know which half is bigger. There're five thousand agents we can choose from, but God knows how many bomb brains we got out there."

When Collier still said nothing, Kidd said, "Tenny, you're the man for the agents. We'll establish some general criteria to narrow the field down—good performance in the behavioral sciences classes and good *hos neg* skills. We won't make the final choices until I've soaked in the *ter pro* charts."

"The terrorist profiles of the Bureau?"

"And the Company."

"That's a tall job," Dooley said.

"Can't pick the men till we know the enemy," Kidd said.

CHAPTER 19

She left the house at a quarter past eleven, and when she reached the corner she did not make the familiar turn that would take her around to the bus stop, but went the opposite direction, for a short, slow stroll around a different route. The streets were still familiar, but she would have to make choices in her route in order to gauge her arrival at the bus stop. But that was all right; this was a night when she thought she ought to be making decisions.

She blew out a cloud of breath and watched it dissipate, she listened to her own footfalls in the crisp air, she tried to hear the wind and could not. She tried to imagine his face when she told him what she felt she had to say. She could not focus her mind on what he looked like.

She turned a corner and started back up another lane. It was part of her usual route, but she had always walked it in the opposite direction. On one side of the lane and parallel to it ran a creek, which during the late winter and spring became swollen. Then the bridges across it were good places to stand and watch the water pass. Without wanting to, she thought of herself standing on that bridge on a spring night, looking down at the polished surface of the flowing water, and turning to say something—to Jeff Kidd.

She topped the rise in the street and was moving down the other side when she saw him passing through the intersection a hundred feet ahead. He was walking slowly, drifting really, into the light of the lamp that stood on the far corner of the inter-section. He was slanting into the crossing, as if unsure of his direction, and there was something about the way he walked that struck her as she stared across the distance, watching him with anonymous intensity. His spine was straight, he was holding himself upright, but as before, the uprightness appeared a struggle; his head, his shoulders, seemed to want to fall, and he braced them up as a tired man might.

She had stopped walking to watch him; in a moment he had disappeared around the corner, toward the bench.

She did not know which house was Jeff Kidd's sister's, if she had passed it many times or if it was not along the way she normally went. But it did not seem to her that Kidd had just come from there; he had been out walking earlier, to think. She felt strangely distant and strangely close to him all at the same time.

When she reached the bench he was sitting there. "Ginny?" he said, looking up and smiling.

He stood and joined her. They began walking without preamble, as if both had already accepted it as habitual.

"You were here early, weren't you?" she said.

"Yes! I was." He seemed in good spirits.

"I saw you on the next street," she said, intending that as an explanation and realizing it explained nothing.

"I like to walk," he said. "Some of the psychology people I've known would say that 'ambulation helps anxiety.' Meaning you feel better walking."

"You don't think much of psychologists?" she said.

"Psychologists' kids and preachers' kids are the most damning examples of their parents' philosophies. If you were the son of a preacher *and* a psychologist, they may as well just drag you off and hang you when you're twelve, 'cause you won't be worth shooting."

They walked a half block in easy silence.

"Say," he said brightly. "I've got to make sure about something that hit me after our conversation last night. Just to make sure I haven't been a complete fool. I was rattling on about the Civil War, and it hit me later . . . Please reassure me that I wasn't giving a Civil War lecture to a direct descendant of one of Robert E. Lee's generals."

"No," she said, smiling. "That Longstreet was a South Carolina aristocrat."

"That's right, he was!" Kidd said, delighted.

"I'm a Virginia Presbyterian preacher's daughter."

"You're joking. You're not. Oh great." .

She grinned. "As far as I know there's no connection between us and the Civil War Longstreet. Of course I did have to learn about him, growing up in Virginia. And I remember getting hissed in the seventh grade when we studied about him disagreeing with Lee's strategy at Gettysburg."

Kidd's laughter rang through the street. "They took it out on you, huh?"

"Yeah. And the teachers didn't bother to tell us that Gettysburg was the one place Lee blundered."

"That's right. That's right. You know . . . I'm not sure I like having you know as much about all this as I do." He glanced at her, and she lifted her chin arrogantly.

"But tell me something," Kidd said. "That really interests me that your father was a preacher. I want to ask you about that as soon as I get my foot out of my mouth."

She smiled, kicking out at the leaves blown into rivulets on the street. "My father wasn't a happy man," she said easily. "He was *respected*, that was for sure, the *Reverend* Mr. Longstreet fit him perfectly. His church was just outside Charlottesville. There were a lot of members from the University faculty and a lot of the landed gentry from the horse country. I say, 'his church,' my father's church, because he ran it just the way he thought it ought to be, and he preached exactly as he believed, and he was always historically accurate and scholarly, so whenever his sermons were harsh the congregation felt they were being criticized on good authority."

They turned a corner. Tonight she took him the long way.

"Our mother died when I was six—I have a brother, a year older. Mama was the soft side of the family. She liked us to play, Daddy liked us to study; I could read when I was four. She died from spinal meningitis, they said she caught when visiting some of the sick church people in the hospital. I don't know if that's true. But she died. And after that my father was

more distant. Whenever he would try to show us affection—
You see," she interrupted herself, her speech faster, her gestures animated, "he understood that he needed to be support-
ive to us, so that was his *duty*, and he would *do* it, but . . .
whenever he tried to talk to us, to give us any kind of softness,
he got disoriented. He would start out trying to talk to us
about school, and he'd get uncomfortable, you could see him
falter, and he'd end up preaching us a little sermon about per-
severance and all things working together for good. I think he
just . . ." She paused. "He never was able to face what he felt.
I believe, I honestly believe he thought he would lose his faith
if he ever really took the time to think about losing my
mother."

Ginny turned to Kidd with a look that was both surprised
and bewildered; but her voice was calm. "I'm not sure I ever
really realized that before."

"Are you close to your brother?" Kidd said at last.

"I was then." She was speaking much more slowly now.
"We were pretty much alone. The church gave my father a
string of housekeepers, all spinsters, all ancient. We got a new
one every time the old one died." She laughed.

Giddy with the draft of long-fermented secrets, Ginny began
spilling words again. "My brother was very shy and inward. I
got shy later in school, rigidly shy, but then, at seven or eight,
I was just quiet. People would pick on my brother, and he
wouldn't fight back, but I would. I could beat up any boy in
his class. Partly they were reluctant to hit me, but I was a terror anyway. I'll never forget the first time one of them actually
hit me with his fist. It was the fifth grade. I just stood there,
wiping at my nose. I'd never had it bleed before. At recess I
went up behind him and hit him in the back with a softball
bat. I never fought anybody else. And nobody else fought me.
Nobody in school."

"I guess not."

"No. I guess not."

"I knew I was right," Kidd said.

"About what?"

"That first night we almost ran into each other. You would have shoved those keys into my eyes."

She held her hand up to her mouth. "I couldn't really have done it," she said.

"Of course you could have. I saw it right off, that first night. There was never any question of it to me."

Her brow was wrinkling when he interrupted the question she was forming; "So you're not still close to your brother?"

"No, no," she said, called back. "Not since college. I went to Maryland, for their journalism program. He went to U.Va. Grew his sideburns till they met at his chin, got drunk three times a week, barely graduated though he had great ability, and now sells real estate."

"Mmm."

"How did you know they were keys?"

"They were keys, huh?" Kidd said, and paused, neither in surprise nor satisfaction, simply letting it register in his own thoughts that he had been right. "Oh, I just assumed that later. When I almost ran into you everything happened so quickly, and I sort of realized everything at once, and I was past you before some of it soaked in. I was sure you must have had a weapon of some kind because of the way you held your right arm cocked, and your attention, your body attention, seemed all focused on your right pocket. Anyone with a weapon tends to fixate on the weapon and forget about everything else. That's until the fighting starts, and then it's target fixation. In Vietnam, the gunners in helicopter gunships . . . that's off the point, I'm sorry.

"I just mean that even most trained professionals can't have a weapon, like a gun or a knife, and still be ready to hit with the other hand or kick or whatever. All the security is centered in the weapon. Now you didn't have a gun, I mean I didn't think so because first of all you wouldn't have been out walking around alone in the middle of the night if you thought you needed a side arm, and besides that, if you had had one, you would have been juiced just by having the gun and you would have drawn it out of your pocket a long time before I almost fell over you. The same with Mace—you might have had that, but you would have had it out, and covered me with it probably, before I ever got so close. It might have been a knife, but not with a well-dressed woman in a neighborhood as good as this one.

"Besides all that, my impression was . . . it was somewhat stronger than an *impression*, but—you didn't seem like someone who'd have a weapon at all, and I don't mean because you looked too tame for it, I don't mean that at all. You were walking. You had to have seen me first. But you kept walking. And you were ready to fight if you had to. And if you then latched onto something, it would be something common that you had with you normally. You wouldn't leave a house at night without locking the door, so . . ."

"Keys."

"Yeah," he said.

They turned again, walking down another street where the lights of the distant houses winked off across silver lawns. Their breath ghosted in clouds before them but she felt no cold. "Jeff . . . what do you do? I'm sorry, I don't want to pry. But I wonder."

"No, Ginny, it's not prying! I'll be glad to tell you, but first . . . I don't mean to be coy, but I'd like you to tell me what you think."

"Well, sometimes you've seemed like a soldier, and sometimes like a . . . teacher."

"A teacher because I'm full of irrelevant facts, but—"

"No, no!" she interrupted. "A teacher because you're literate. Very literate. But I know you're not a teacher because you're not pedantic, just the opposite, actually. You know more than you pretend to. You seem embarrassed sometimes to show how well read you are."

"You're starting to sound like me."

She smiled. "I'm sure I can unravel your case."

"Okay. Okay! Why a soldier?"

"The way you walk. Your posture."

"Ah."

"No, please, I don't mean it's rigid, I just mean most people slouch."

"Yeah," he said; friends had kidded him about his posture before. "So what do you think now?"

She stared at him for a moment. "I think you're in some kind of intelligence work. I think you're a spook."

He cut his eyes back toward her; they both seemed to smile at the same time. "That's damn good," he said. "A little bit frightening though, if I ever want people to think I'm an accountant. I should wear my glasses, I guess. They say I look harmless in my glasses."

"You never have looked harmless to me."

He slid a look over at her again, but let the comment pass.

"I'm not actually a spook," he said, "though that's been something of a problem for me. I always wanted to be more active. But yeah, I've been in intelligence work. I spent six years with the CIA."

"Did you . . . were you . . ." she groped, wanting to hear all about it and not being sure just what to ask.

"I was recruited out of college," Kidd began, wanting to tell her everything and knowing he would get it all out of sequence. "Vietnam was almost over. We were already getting ready to pull out, that is. I never had felt completely right about not being involved more in everything that happened about Vietnam. When I started school I was actually secretly gung ho, in that Southern way. I mean I had that urge to do my duty, that affinity for glory and disgrace that haunts every redneck boy. I actually thought I'd sign up for the Marines' Platoon Leader Corps, and come out of college as a second lieutenant, until the day a cab driver, just back from Vietnam, told me Marine Corps second lieutenants had the shortest life expectancy in the war—two weeks—because they were so likely to be shot in the back, intentionally, by their own men." He looked toward her and smiled. "It dawned on me fairly shortly after hearing that that we weren't talking about being a cavalry officer at the Battle of Bull Run."

Kidd kept his hands in the pockets of his coat, and as he walked, speaking in a calm, resonant voice, she could see why he stood so straight; she could see that he was, in a sense, the man he had dreamed of being.

"It wasn't any sudden realization for me that Vietnam was a cesspool for us, that we weren't there trying to win anything, that we weren't committed, that our leaders were misleading us. I knew that pretty much all along, I just hated . . . to admit it. I still admired somehow the men who were going, maybe I envied them, as long as I didn't know what it was really like. And the people in college seemed so righteous, and smug—because the ones who stayed in school never really had to go. Nineteen-year-old soldiers dying in that gore over there, and back here we're marching and playing music and talking about free love. Free love—that's quite a concept, isn't it?

"So anyway, in school I started to pursue formally something that had always fascinated me. That was the question of what actually went on inside people when they were in critical situations. Mainly I was interested in men in battle: foot soldiers in actual combat, but generals, too, spies, politicians. I remember"—Kidd had withdrawn his hands from his pockets so he could gesture—"when I was in high school, doing a term paper on the Civil War, I had come across this picture of a Confederate soldier, dead in the trenches around Petersburg. A Union photographer had taken the picture after the battle, and there was some meaning just in that fact, in that the fall of Petersburg meant the fall of Richmond, and Lee surrendered just days after that. But this soldier was lying on his back. So he'd been killed facing the enemy. He was barefooted —in the end, Lee's army didn't have any more shoes. In one hand he had a muzzle-loading musket—that's a single shot, while the Union troops had breech-loading rifles, and could fire five times to his one—and in the other hand he was clutching a ramrod. That meant that in the face of overwhelming numbers, after four years of desperate war, he had fired off a volley, and then stood there before the bayonets and tried to reload. God, I thought that was courage! Maybe too, of course, it was desperation. Maybe courage is a kind of desperation. But the point is, he didn't run.

"And Lee had known how his troops would stand up that day. Looking over the battle lines just before the Federal assault he told one of his adjutants, 'You will see a brave defense today.'

"Anyway, in college I worked out a special program, I called it 'Crisis Dynamics.' I guess the head of the history department found that a catchy name, because he helped me arrange the whole thing. I took history, psychology, even some theology, and a lot of literature. I stayed on after graduation and did a master's thesis. And then I got this phone call. One of my professors happened to be a recruiter for the CIA. That is, he recommended people who might have useful knowledge or skills. They contacted me. I thought, *Intrigue. Adventure. Excitement . . .*"

"And a chance to be a patriot," Ginny broke in.

"Yes," he said slowly. "That's right."

He put his hands back into his pockets, and looked down at the pavement as they walked. "I got into analyzing people. Foreign agents, our own agents, even some foreign political leaders. Some of it was behind a desk—they'd just bring me the data, and mostly it was just an academic problem. But there was some resistance to my work. The Agency has staff psychiatrists, and since my background was different from theirs, I didn't quite fit in with the bureaucratic format. Also, my opinions usually differed from theirs. I had only a master's degree, which added to the problems when some of the Ph.D.s ended up working under me. So I tended to work a lot in the field, encountering people directly in one way or another and predicting who might be turned as a double agent, what approach to take, or which of our people might be vulnerable. So . . . that's what I did."

"You don't do that now?"

"No. I came up to Washington to look into some new work, actually, but I left the CIA a year ago. Partly it was the rape of the intelligence services in this country. Again, I understood the reasons for it, a democracy has to be aware of the potential for governmental abuse, but there was incredible hypocrisy involved in that. It was even worse for the FBI. I've worked with them, I have friends there. Sometime I'll tell you the horror stories. But that was only the precipitator. I had some personal problems. And also I was restless, I'd always wanted to be that unambiguous soldier. Jeb Stuart, maybe. Or that guy in the trench. So I left and went back to school."

"To study . . . what? The same thing?"

Kidd smiled, but did not look at her this time; it was really a grin of embarrassment. "I went in on a history program, for a Ph.D. But what I really wanted to do was to write a book. I wanted to call it *American Heroes*. I just thought that we'd grown so cynical, and so ashamed really, that we needed that. We all go around talking about losing in Vietnam, as if someone else beat us. But, but I'm not just talking about military heroes. I didn't want to write any handbook for the American Legion. Those stories deify people anyway, separate a 'hero' from a common person. That's bullshit—pardon me, madam. A man who isn't scared, who's more powerful than all the rest, who has no misgivings, is no hero, he's Superman. I . . . I'm sorry, I am getting carried away, I keep doing that with you. Anyway, most of the time now I think the idea is just maudlin."

They walked for a long way, up a rise, around a corner onto the cross lane that led back to the bench, without speaking. Then Ginny said slowly and quietly, "Do you analyze me?"

He was staring toward the trees, and the stars that moved with them as they walked. "I try not to. I don't think of you during the day. I don't trust myself. I enjoy talking with you a great deal. I look forward to it. But yes . . . I do think of you, and I just sort through things, almost unintentionally, like I did the keys. It's not that I analyze, it's just that from the first I've felt I understood things about you." He paused as they turned the final corner before the bench. "Like now," he said. "I think you have something else you want to ask me, that you were thinking about when you got here tonight and have thought about at different times while we've been walking."

They stopped at the bench. She looked directly into his eyes. "You're right. I want to know something else."

He waited, ready to answer anything.

"Did you wait for me?" she said. "That first night, I mean when you were sitting on the bench and we first talked. Were you there hoping to run into me again?"

"Yes."

"Why?"

"It's not the easiest thing to explain, though I know exactly why, or now I do, and it seems I couldn't have done anything else, though at the time I called myself crazy and was kind of baffled. But what it was . . . When I first ran into you, that first night, and just looked up and saw you, it was . . . there was this big impact for me. I'd never seen anybody more beautiful. But it wasn't just that that haunted me. I mean, beauty can be intimidating, even forbidding. But also it was your eyes. I'd never seen eyes like that. So wild and fierce."

Ginny was smiling. She could not help it, her lips were curling up. It seemed completely inappropriate, but she was beginning to smile. And also, inside, she was trembling.

"But there was something else too about the whole thing—the surprise and the fierceness, the beauty, the keys, and the hint of panic. I found something compelling about a woman with the courage—or maybe it was the despair—to walk alone out here."

The night was deathly still.

"I'll see you tomorrow night, Jeff," she said.

As she was turning he said, "Ginny . . ." She stopped. "You weren't going to come back, were you? You had made up your mind, before you came, that this was the last night we would talk."

She looked at him for a very long time. "I'll be back tomorrow night," she said again, and felt her eyes misting but that strange smile curling her lips as she turned and walked back toward home.

CHAPTER 20

Mary cooked the breakfast steak but did not cut it up for Jamie. Ginny liked to do that; feeding him was something she could do and it made her feel better to do it. His hand-eye coordination was adequate for him to feed himself, but he was often so slow that during the course of a meal he would lose interest altogether.

Mary took two steaks from the oven broiler, forked them onto separate plates, and put both before Ginny. Ginny began to draw a knife through the steak closest to Jamie and said to Mary, "Aren't you going to eat?"

"I ate," Mary said, arching her eyebrows into the high curve of her forehead and rolling a wide-eyed stare toward the ceiling; Mary never showed displeasure in subtle ways.

"What's the matter with you?" Ginny said.

"Red meat make a man aggressive," Mary said.

Ginny paused and looked at Mary, at the flawless black skin stretched tight over a perfect skull, the hairline on the very summit, leaving a long arc of forehead. Mary liked to say that her ancestors had been Somalians, and Ginny could see something primordial and instinctive in her sometimes, especially when she said something like she just had. And Ginny wondered if it was true, if red meat did have some chemical or psychological effect on a person, or if the very expression was an indication from Mary that Jamie was getting too much for her to handle. But Mary's face was set and Ginny could not read it. "He's getting fat," Ginny said at last, "and I think more protein and less starch will help him."

Mary shrugged broadly. Ginny turned back to Jamie and noticed for the first time that she had been holding the fork poised in the air, the steaming morsel of meat not eighteen inches from Jamie's slack mouth, and still he had not moved, had not even batted his heavy eyelids.

"What? What is it?" Mary asked.

"Nothing, nothing," Ginny said, realizing Mary had noticed her staring at Jamie. She poked the piece of steak into his mouth.

"I don't think the meat'll really hurt him," Mary said.

"No, he'll be all right," Ginny said.

But the thought had flashed through her mind and she could never call it back. *A baby would yell. Even a dog would*

*bark or whine or lurch at the meat. But he just sits there worse
than a baby, worse than a dog. Like a dead man,* she thought.

She tried to squeeze the thought and its memory from her
head by cutting more meat. Mechanically she fed him one
piece after another, overloading him. She jerked to a halt,
snatched up a napkin, and wiped away the excess that fell
from his lips.

She sat back and waited as he slowly chewed the meat.

Like worse than a dead man, she thought.

When the phone in Ginny's office rang the first thing that
morning, she had a premonition. She answered and a voice
said brightly, "Ms. Longstreet?" with too much emphasis on
the *Miz.* "This is Peter Pugh. I need to speak with you."

Her premonition was right.

She hesitated, then said, "Yes?"

He fumbled a moment, and laughed. "Oh, no! Not over the
phone. I mean I'd like to see you and I wanted to make an appointment."

She flipped open her desk calendar and there was nothing on
it; there seldom was. "All right. I'm free at ten. Or two."

"I was wondering about lunch. Are you busy?" When she
did not answer immediately he said, "It's business, not pleasure. But why shouldn't it be as pleasant as possible? Can you
meet me?"

Ginny hung between her instinct to avoid Pugh altogether
and her sense that it was best to meet trouble head on.
"Where?" she said.

Pugh was waiting for her at the entrance to the Marriott,
whose coffee shop was a popular spot for lunch. But when,
after stiff greetings, Ginny started through the lobby, Pugh
caught her arm and grinned. "No, this way." He pointed to
the elevator, open beside a sign on an easel advertising *The
View,* the restaurant on the top floor.

From their table they could see white boats upon the distant
gray expanse of the Potomac. "What's the matter?" Pugh said.

"This is a little rich for routine government business, isn't it?" she said, as the starched waiter who had seated her went to fetch their menus.

Pugh smiled. "If I put in for your share and pay cash for my own, I can almost stay under my expense limit. Wine?"

"I don't drink."

"*Wine?*"

"With strangers. What do you want?"

"A polite conversation! I told you I wanted to take you to lunch. I told you it was business. I don't understand your sudden defensiveness."

"It makes me nervous when people spend too much money on me. Tell me the business now. Maybe I'll be able to enjoy the meal."

Pugh stared at her, and looked away only when the waiter returned with two menus bound in red leather. Pugh asked for the wine steward. The waiter retreated. When Pugh looked back to Ginny, sitting with the menu folded on her plate, he said, "The President's furious about the leaking of information to the press. He thinks the leaks have come from within your department."

"Why does he think that?"

"What do you mean?"

"You said, 'The President thinks.' If the President thinks anything about those leaks he thinks it because you told him. It's not a national security leak, if it were the FBI would be in this instead of you. It's a leak that makes him mad because it upsets his timing—important timing, I completely agree, but timing that concerns political, not security matters. So I.S. is in it to plug a leak and the President knows what you tell him. So don't tell me what he thinks, tell me what you think."

Pugh's eyes got something like mean, but only for an instant. Calmly he said, "All right. We think the leaks are coming from your department—the speechwriters specifically. The details of the news stories are consistent with the details of briefs given out by the President for the preparation of speeches."

"That's nothing. It doesn't mean a thing," Ginny said, and it sounded stronger saying it to Pugh now than it had the afternoon before, with Kurtz. "We're not the only ones who get information."

At an expensive restaurant in any other city, the wine steward, approaching a table where the conversation was growing tense and a bit loud, would have interrupted, and cooled the scene by the measured calm of his manners. But in Washington, where restaurants teem with journalists and lawyers for whom abrasiveness is a matter of professionalism, the wine steward backed away.

Pugh, his eyes bright and locked onto Ginny's, said in a lowered voice, "You're right. Some of the leaks in the past that Mr. Emmett has reported in his newspaper have contained information that was available to several departments. But in this most recent case, the brief made available to the speechwriters was unique in one particular way."

He paused, savoring. "It was inaccurate regarding one small but very specific detail. All the information briefs issued to other departments were the same, except that they listed the President's projected intelligence reorganization as going into effect in *two* months. Your department's briefs all said seven. And Sam Emmett . . ." Pugh took out a cigarette, lit it, and blew out a puff before he said, ". . . reported the changes for 'mid-summer.' Seven months away."

"*Monsieur-'dame*, what is your pleasure?" said the wine steward, taking advantage of the new quiet.

"A carafe of rosé. Well-chilled," Pugh said immediately, holding his cigarette like a scepter and rapping its ash into a silver Chesapeake Bay oyster shell.

As the steward glided away Ginny said, "Okay. I don't agree that your evidence is conclusive. Emmett's report on that figure was vague. But I agree the evidence is suggestive. So what do you want from me?"

Wordlessly Pugh pulled a paper from his inner coat pocket, unfolding it as he passed it across to Ginny. She glanced at it quickly. It was a questionnaire. The first article was: "List all persons associated with the print media—columnists, wire journalists, reporters of any kind—that you have seen and/or with whom you have communicated within the last seven days."

"I'm supposed to fill this out?"

"No. You're supposed to ask your people to fill it out. Kurtz, Sherwood, Thayer, all four secretaries. Tell them it's your own request."

"Baxter Stern," Ginny began in a measured voice, "said specifically during his campaign that he was going to eliminate the periodic loyalty pledges required during the previous administration."

Pugh smiled, amused that any speechwriter should be surprised at a politician's broken promise. Ginny, attacking that smile, said, "This isn't going to catch anybody, anyway."

"I didn't say we had to catch anybody. The point is to stop the leak. Maybe we can do it through intimidation."

"Yes. I see," Ginny said, with extreme politeness. "Well, Mr. Pugh, I don't believe in loyalty oaths, or questionnaires like this." She slid the paper between the matched pewter candle holders in the center of the table. "They don't shame the guilty, and they offend the loyal." She reached for her purse and shoved back from the table.

"Just a minute," Pugh said, reaching out his hand but not touching her. "You're right. It's offensive. But sometimes digging is more offensive. We don't like to dig. It uncovers too much."

"Mr. Pugh," Ginny said, with her politeness so cold now it had edges, "that begins to sound like a threat. I think you'd better tell me exactly what you mean."

Pugh did hesitate, but only for an instant. He withdrew from his pocket another paper, and handed that to her. At first glance it looked crumpled, but it was not. It was a photocopy of an original that had been wadded. The original was the resignation Ginny had typed and thrown into her wastebasket.

Pugh watched her very closely now, and when her eyes came off the page they were bright green and hard, steady as stone.

"That phrase," Pugh said, " 'not reflective of any disagreement with the Administration's policies, or lack of them

. . .' Now would you assume that the person who wrote that had some, uh, *secret criticism* of the President? Maybe some private resentment?"

"I don't feel I owe you an explanation, or a damn thing. But I'm going to tell you this, and then I'm going to leave. When a person writes anything . . . I won't say 'from the heart' because you wouldn't understand that, but anything . . . that is a stretch of effort and caring, then that person opens up all sorts of private thoughts. When I write, and I'm stuck, I sometimes sit down and try to get out the things that are blocking me. I throw away what I *don't mean to keep*. And if you want to go through people's garbage, then I can't stop you."

She stood up, and Pugh stood too, talking. "Come on. That sounds nice and righteous. It's not as simple as that. I mean digging. Personal stuff."

Ginny turned, took two blind steps, and then stopped to look for the door. "Take you, for instance, Ms. Longstreet!" Pugh said in a voice so loud that people at adjacent tables were turning to watch. Ginny began stalking away, and Pugh called after her in a voice both unabashed and bitter. "What about your husband? He had a problem, didn't he? Tried to kill himself?"

Ginny hurried, passing the stunned wine steward, who was approaching the table with a chilled carafe on a silver tray. And then Pugh, as if to include all the dumbfounded patrons of the restaurant, boomed, "Would you like to tell us *why?!*"

Ginny ran toward the door, but stopped as she reached it. She turned, strode back to the frozen steward, snatched the crystal carafe from the tray, and hurled it twenty feet across the room, straight toward Pugh's head.

He ducked—had he not the carafe would surely have hit his face—and the crystal shattered against the thick safety glass of the outer window. The wine sheeted down in the sunlight, like watery blood.

Only a few of the people in the restaurant looked back from Pugh and the window in time to see Ginny Longstreet pull a twenty-dollar bill from her purse, slam it on the desk at the entrance, and disappear through the door.

The head waiter and the wine steward both rushed to Pugh at the same time, apologizing profusely and wiping at his shirt and coat, though the only splashes were on his shoes. Politely he pushed them both away, grinned, and said, "Make the next carafe a bordeaux."

CHAPTER 21

The basement of the White House was impressive more for where you were, what you knew you were under, than for any appearance of its own. The offices were small, packed tight, and were fed by narrow hallways. Ginny was led by a male aide with a military haircut through one of these corridors, and she stopped at the door she knew was Livingstone's.

"No ma'm, right this way," her guide said.

"Mr. Livingstone . . ."

"Yes ma'm. Right this way, please."

So she followed him to an office two doors away. He opened the door for her and she walked in to see Livingstone sitting behind a bare oak desk in an otherwise empty office. "John. You've moved," she said.

"Yes I have, Ginny, but not here." He stood and walked around to the front of the desk and then sat down on it. "This is your office," he said. He laughed at whatever her face showed. "Yours. Would I joke with you?"

"I don't know, John. You would surprise me though, yes."

"The President liked—no, he loved—your speech. He started giving me credit and I told him the only credit I deserve is for being smart enough to have found you. He wants you closer."

Livingstone explained to her that he would retain some authority over the speechwriters as a unit, but that she would take up the daily supervision. The others would function more as backups now, anyway; the President wanted her close, to be his voice. Livingstone told her that he was being given a broader authority—being "kicked upstairs," as he put it. In anticipation of the fight over the military manpower legislation, the President was drawing the wagons into a circle.

So on the same day that Ginny met Pugh for lunch she got a promotion into the White House. Livingstone had already left her alone, standing still stunned in the middle of the carpeted floor of her office, when she recalled that Pugh, in suggesting that she pass a security questionnaire off on the other speechwriters as her own request, had already treated her as the new head of the department.

CHAPTER 22

Kidd rented the lime-green apartment, but never felt it was home. He slept there, but even then the scattered dreams took him away. Sometimes the intelligence reports and psychological profiles he read all day at Langley would flash again through his brain in stark though jumbled clarity. At other times a woman's vague presence would drift with him in his sleep, but these dreams were more emotion than image—the weightless warmth of union, or the clammy stiffness of isolation and betrayal. And these slumbered feminine spirits bore no faces, but Kidd, who remembered and gave waking thought to his dreams, knew they were not the same woman.

Kidd's bed was new, a frameless box spring and mattress resting on cinder blocks. Large and inexpensive, it had been his only housekeeping purchase. Collier, however, with the same obsessive professionalism that made him needlessly disguise his identity when telephoning Kidd at his sister's, had sent over at odd times various furnishings: a used portable television, a mismatched group of stereo components, a mixed set of dishes, even a fake-leather sofa. Collier figured that this close to Langley, a man alone should seem to his neighbors, or even to a random burglar, like a newly separated husband, which Kidd

was, rather than a spy in training, which he was not. Not
exactly, anyway.

Kidd's sister was surprised, after he had moved out, to have
him accepting her standing invitation for dinner. All his life he
had been aloof to her attempts at mothering him; but now he
would show up promptly at seven-thirty, often directly from
"the office," as he put it. He told them he had gone back to
work in Langley's foreign news analysis section, where he had
never actually worked in the first place. After dinner he would
talk idly with his brother-in-law or play with the children until
they went to bed. His sister would then retire herself, leaving
Kidd dozing before the murmuring television. She would hear
him leave at eleven forty-five.

What she did not know was that on the nights he did not
come to dinner, he would still drive to her neighborhood, parking along the deserted streets to wait for midnight.

CHAPTER 23

At exactly five forty-five Sam Emmett emerged from the *Constellation* Building and turned toward the heart of Georgetown. He walked with his feet shuffling rapidly, hardly lifting
them above the sidewalk, while his arms jerked at his sides,
and that odd gait, plus his shape—a husky trunk tilted backward in support of a protruding belly, all perched on legs so
thin that the knees showed through the trousers—made him a
distinctive figure in the crowd of lawyers, students, and bureaucrats hurrying through the cold. Keeping him in sight was no
trouble for Pugh. He had only to be careful, in rushing to keep
up with Emmett, that he did not make himself conspicuous.

After two blocks Emmett turned into the first of three bars
that he would go to that evening before dinner; afterward he
was to hit four more. But at this first bar he ordered only one
drink, and did not finish that; he stood with one Gucci-moc-

casined foot on the polished brass rail and talked and laughed with a dozen different men and a handful of professional women who bounced up to him for a few words and then swirled away. Pugh did not go in. He stood casually on the sidewalk, as if waiting for a friend, and watched through the amber windows of the bar. Even then, Emmett was easy to pick out: while almost every man around him wore a three-piece suit, Emmett wore a tweed sport coat over an open-collar shirt and a deep-red sweater, which stretched over his belly and made it a beacon. Pugh planned to become exasperated with the lateness of his imaginary friend and enter the bar himself after Emmett ordered again, but Emmett suddenly set down a half glass of whiskey, yelled a general good-bye, and, leaving no money, hurried out.

Emmett scurried past Pugh without looking up. He walked for two more blocks and went into another tavern.

Emmett again stationed himself at the bar, this time on a stool. Pugh came in behind a congressional aide and a woman pretty enough to be a lobbyist, and sat down alone at a table in the dark corner nearest the door.

This bar was so much like the first that Pugh could not have told the difference. There was the same wood-paneled darkness, the same jaded barman tending an array of bottles in ordered ranks, the same conspicuous lack of the tiffany and hanging plants that tourists took as Georgetown atmosphere. This was a place for insiders only, for those who flowed through the arteries of power.

Emmett did the same thing here, swiveling back and forth from the bar to exchange quick words with passing clusters of acquaintances. This time he had two drinks. As he finished the second a woman who looked twenty came up with a man much older on her arm and began to flirt with Emmett. He glowed in her attention. When she left, he sat grinning at the bar, smoothing out the thatch of hair she had mussed with her vermilion fingernails.

He's vain, Pugh thought.

At the next tavern Emmett had another whiskey, but Pugh,

watching again from a side table, could tell no difference in his manner. He was still loud, but no louder. He was still in constant motion, jerky but not sloppy. His eyes too were always moving—to the faces around him, to the walls, to the mirrors behind the bar—but it was not as if he was looking for anything; it seemed more that he listened and thought with his eyes, and they were greedy and gleaning as his mind.

On leaving the third bar, Emmett took his longest walk of the day, four blocks into Georgetown's most fashionable section. He turned into a short alley and stepped down a stairway which led to the door of a restaurant.

There Pugh hesitated. He had no ridiculous expectation that anyone would publicly pass Emmett information; in the zeal of inexperience and frustration, Pugh was simply studying the enemy. But he had warmed to the role of spy. Emmett had not noticed him in the crowded bars and streets, and his confidence had grown. The night before he had sat all night long in a car outside Emmett's apartment, just to see if anyone came or went. That was not fun. This was. Pugh went inside.

The restaurant was smaller than he had expected, with eight tables, and only two were occupied besides the one against the back wall where Emmett sat. Pugh took a table near the center of the room. The cheapest entree on the menu was halibut for $22. Pugh ordered crab legs.

Emmett dined slowly, and alone. Pugh had bought a newspaper outside the third bar he had followed Emmett to, and at dinner he remembered it gratefully, withdrawing it from his coat pocket and reading the international news. Emmett knew all the waiters, addressing them by their first names as he ordered dessert and then coffee.

Pugh decided to leave first. He had just folded his paper when he looked up and saw Emmett directly before him. "All right," Emmett said, smiling and sitting down, propping his elbows on the table and leaning toward Pugh. "Uncle Sam, or Uncle Larry?" He was smiling.

Pugh said, "What?"

"Come on, who sent you after me?" Emmett looked amused.

"Who's Uncle Larry?" Pugh said.

Emmett kept smiling, but his eyes darted about. "Who are you?" he said definitely.

Pugh struggled to look more offended and less shocked. "My name is Peter Pugh. Who are you, and why are you asking me these questions?"

"Come on, come on," Emmett said, rapidly rotating a thick finger, then leaning back and calling to the waiter, "I'll take it over here, Julio." The waiter left the coffee and Emmett said, "Cut the crap. You've been following me since I left my office." He took a tiny sip of the black brew. "Rather badly, too. See, I check from the second floor every day before I leave the building. I look for people waiting. It's an old habit from the Nixon days. Of course then the guys were pros, they'd switch off, never send the same guy after me into three straight bars. So what do you want?"

Pugh felt like an utter fool and was angered because that was exactly what Emmett intended. He struggled to improvise, and said without thinking, "I wasn't following you. I was trying to make sure you weren't being followed."

"You're doing me favors?"

"I'm doing myself a favor. I wanted to talk with you alone."

Emmett seemed to half believe it. "You've got me alone," he said, and took another gourmet sip.

"I work for the President's Department of Internal Security," Pugh said.

"Ooo, a plumber."

"That's Nixon White House jargon," Pugh said, and felt he had the indignation just right. "We don't use that term at all."

"A plumber. What do you want?"

"I have information. I come across it. Things I can't use, but things that bother me, do you understand? I can't use information from a wiretap that doesn't officially exist, for example. But maybe I find out things about the system, about people in it, that I think the public has a right to know."

"Yeah?" Emmett said, and his eyes got sleepy with caution.

"I wondered if I could pass things along. But I'd have to be able to do it safely. I have a career." *When you lie, make it close to the truth,* Pugh had once heard. The mention of his career brought fervor to his voice.

"Yeah. Well. I think you know I can be trusted."

Pugh was unsure if Emmett had bought any of it. He said, "All right. I'll be in touch." And then he called to the waiter, "Check, please."

"That's okay," Emmett said. "I'll take care of this."

"No need," Pugh said. "I have a rich father."

Pugh left the restaurant and walked straight back to the first bar, where he had stood on the sidewalk and watched Emmett without going in. Now he went inside.

It was just like the second and the third; but the crowd was thinner now. Three men at a table were arguing loudly about tax reform, and several others were scattered about, privately, sullenly drunk.

Pugh went to the bar, obtained a drink from the tired bartender, and sipped it pensively.

Ten minutes later he walked down to where the bartender was adding receipts at the cash register. The bartender looked up and said, "Oh, excuse me, sir, that'll be two-fifty."

"Put it on Sam Emmett's tab," Pugh said. "He told me to have a drink on him."

The bartender shrugged and reached for his tab cards. Pulling out a well-fingered one he added the $2.50. "Okay, sir, thank you," the bartender said.

Putting a two-dollar tip on the bar, Pugh said, "Thank you. I just love drinking on Sam."

As Pugh walked down to the corner to look for a cab, he felt exuberant. With that improvisation he had just seen that Emmett's bill for the week at that one bar alone was thirty dollars. He could make calculations from that to estimate what Emmett spent on food and drink. The information was totally useless—Emmett lived in a shabby place and spent all his money on drinking and circulating; so what? But Pugh had learned something by wits and stealth. He felt invincible.

But in the cab he fell once again to stewing over the question that he had gone to the bar to think about: Who, or what, was Uncle Larry?

CHAPTER 24

Dooley was an inch taller than Kidd, with wide hard shoulders and long loose hands. He had fine brown hair that looked sometimes red, sometimes blond, and a high square forehead he had gotten from his Cherokee Indian grandfather. (Like most Texans, Dooley claimed to be "part," "a little," or "mostly" Indian, depending on his mood.) He was handsome, but only when he wanted to be, and he had a redneck accent he liked to lay on, as he did now, leaning one elbow on the bar, winking at Kidd, and saying, "Since we're *oh*-ficially off duty, ah'll have me a Black Jack on the rocks! What'll yew have?"

"Nothing right now."

"*Hay*-ell, boy, I thought yew said yew wanted to drank!"

"I said I wanted to talk."

"Same thang."

The bartender fetched Dooley's Jack Daniel's and glanced at Kidd, but Kidd never looked at him; intelligence agents, who so often use bartenders and waitresses for gathering and passing information, feel a natural lack of obligation to buy what they do not want.

They were in the Washington National air terminal, in one of the bars open to the main corridor. There were three tables, all empty; Kidd and Dooley took the one on the left side, and both of them sat facing the streams of people.

"So they decided not to prosecute Collie, huh?" Dooley said

in a voice as normal as he ever got. "I hear he's supposed to feel grateful."

"I think part of him wanted to be prosecuted. How else could he prove his point?"

Dooley sipped his whiskey and waited for Kidd to tell him why he had suggested they come there.

Kidd stared at the crowd. Finally he nodded toward the corridor and said, "That guy there, with the briefcase and the Earth Shoes. How do you make him?"

Dooley instantly spotted the right man, hopping along through the crowd. "What do you mean?"

"I say he's a professor. Some small college, not a university because he'd have the money to fix those bent-up steel glasses —and a guy like that wouldn't scrimp on his glasses unless he had to. In fact, I'd say he's even gone down in the world, gone to a dead-end school, because he's still wearing those Earth Shoes. They were with-it for eggheads when I was in college."

"Okay," Dooley said, playing, though it was no game. "No money. But a pompous ass. Look at how he holds his head." And the subject in question did have his head tilted back, and almost tiptoed along the corridor in his thick-toed shoes. "Probably teaches political science. And got cockier as soon as he landed in Washington."

"We're sure he's not local?"

"Looked tired to me. Nobody starts a trip that way."

"I agree," Kidd said. "And he *did* look cocky. That's a weak spot in him: his ego gets battered because he doesn't make much, so he compensates with intellectual arrogance. Probably here to lecture to some shoestring conference. Or maybe to research. Probably let it slip to one of his classes that he was going to the Library of Congress because there are still a couple of facts he isn't sure of." Kidd and Dooley both smiled at their own arrogance, and Kidd said, "So how would you break him?"

The smile left Dooley's face. His eyes looked hungry. "Anything he'd be involved in would be political. Some goons might rob a bank but they'd have some cause. He'd be the idealogue. The *justifier*. He couldn't handle the hardware, he'd have other people with the guns because he wouldn't trust himself with them, but he'd make thorough plans. Plans, of course, suck. But he'd believe in them. And the ideology.

"So I'd play to his inclinations. I'd make the son-of-a-bitch feel more righteous. If I had him for interrogation, I'd take the lead myself. I'd let him know, before I heard anything from him, that I personally hate Blacks, Jews, handicapped people—my only fear is to be reincarnated as Sammy Davis, Jr. Haw! Haw!" Dooley laughed with such glee—and beyond that, confidence—that Kidd could imagine the little professor hating the big Texan's guts.

"See, they guard their minds," Dooley said, intense again, the smile vanishing before it could look like artifice. "In an interrogation, the subject thinks you're trying to trick him. He *knows* you're trying to trick him. So he's preoccupied with his own thoughts. But you break his emotions, you cut out his core. Every crook, even an amateur, expects the good-guy/bad-guy routine, but I'd make my backup man worse than me, play to what the subject would like to believe of every FBI man. Maybe I'd get the professor to spout off his ideology: no plans in that, so what would it matter? Either way I'd have him feeling good and righteous, like his opinions were crucial to the survival of humanity.

"But then I'd put the wedge between him and the *doers!* I'd tell him we're going to cut his people up when we catch them, not take them alive. But him we'll probably let go because he's done nothing *dangerous*. He won't even get to be a martyr. And nobody will ever hear his ideology." Dooley took a triumphant sip of whiskey. "Not long after that, he'd tell me everything."

Kidd sat with one elbow propped on the cocktail table, holding his chin. He knew all the techniques of interrogation sanctioned within the Bureau, and many that were not. But techniques were dead without a performer, and Dooley was an artist.

"I tell you what we've gotta do, Tennyson," Kidd said. (He had a habit of addressing people he liked by their proper names.) "You've got some good interrogators, I've got some good men from the CIA's training center."

"Voodoo U.?" Dooley broke in.

"Yeah." Kidd grinned. "They can learn a lot from each other and I think this is the way to do it. We'll get them in twos, or small groups, and send them to public places like this and have them do what we just did. Look at random strangers. Do rundowns."

Dooley tugged a red ear. "Film might be better. We could show the whole group a tape, have them write out profiles and breakdown procedures, and discuss it in a class. Don't get me wrong, I ain't hooked on the classroom, it just might be more efficient."

"No," Kidd said, surprising himself by his sharpness. "It's got to be live. Tapes like we use in training, even if they're tapes from the field, just confirm existing theories. We've got to do this live."

Kidd could feel Dooley's attention on him—not his eyes but his mind, wondering at Kidd's sharpness; Kidd said, "Look, Dooley. Sometime not too long from now—two months, ten weeks, whenever they think we're ready—we're going to get a phone call, and one of us is going to walk into someplace where people are gonna die. It'll happen, I know it. Did you . . . did you ever see the recruits come through training, trying to learn karate, and they get so full of theories—blocks, positioning, balance—that they forget *combat* is one man knocking the shit out of another? We're teaching subtle stuff. Finesse. And maybe it's all bullshit. They won't call unless it's a media event. Pressure. And people die."

"All right," Dooley said slowly. "But how do we confirm any of our assumptions? Like—that professor. I mean, for all we know the guy's a placekicker for the Redskins and our profile is a mile off."

"Right. That's what I mean."

The people shuffled by in the corridor, the bartender clinked glasses, and somehow Dooley understood a point Kidd was unsure of himself.

"Say, tell me something though," Dooley said, his accent all but gone. "Our mad-bomber professor. Those Earth Shoes. Thicker at the ball of the foot than at the heel, right? And trendy ten years ago. You took that to be that the guy was poor, couldn't afford better. What if he's just got a bad back?"

"The shoes were old."

"More comfortable."

"He didn't walk like he had a bad back. Did he." Kidd made it a statement.

"I tell you, padnah. I'm impressed."

"Don't be. Hell, I didn't notice how he walked."

Suddenly they were laughing.

"For all I know," Kidd said, "that fat lady over there has heroin in the pink suitcase."

"Naw. Porn for sure."

"And that sailor. The one with the pimple on his nose. How do you make him?"

"Sex change. No question."

Kidd decided it would be nice to have a drink with Dooley —maybe two—and he turned toward the bartender just as Dooley said loudly, "Now let's see. Which airline is it *she* works for? TWA? American?"

Kidd looked back around to see a stewardess stopped in front of them just out of the flow of traffic, adjusting the flight bag on her shoulder. She was pretty, had on a trim uniform, and around her slender neck was a silk scarf that had "United" printed all over it. She looked up, found the source of Dooley's voice, and smiled.

"Pardon me," Dooley said happily. "We're just working on our powers of observation, and we're trying to decide which airline you're with."

"Is this a game you two always play in airports?" Her voice was warm molasses.

"This is no game," Dooley said with gravity. "We're a couple of FBI agents, sharpening our powers for a dangerous mission. If you could spare us just a moment of your time, your country will be forever silently grateful."

"My patriotic duty?" she said with a smile.

"We don't like to use those terms," Dooley said. "We don't

lay a guilt trip on anybody." With a gesture he included Kidd, who smiled and felt stupid. "We only ask that you let us study you for a moment."

The girl struck a pose like a high-fashion mannequin, in profile.

"If we could only see you sitting down . . ."

She hesitated. "I assure you, miss, you are safe with us. We are gentlemen." Dooley said it in an antebellum style full of such elegance that it was not the least bit threatening.

The girl sat. Her back was to the crowd.

Dooley sucked on an index finger knuckle, studied the girl grimly, and said, as if to Kidd, "I don't know. Could be Pan Am. But there's only one sure test."

The girl's eyes shone.

"Do you know the test, miss?"

"I'm sorry, I don't."

"Well. They were having a contest. 'Miss Stewardess U.S.A.' And the three finalists were from Eastern, Delta, and United. So to choose the winner they asked them each the same question: 'Your plane goes down. You're in a life raft alone. You row toward a tiny island and when you get there you see men. Thirty men. No one else. What do you do?' So the stewardess from Eastern says"—and here Dooley used a dead-on Boston accent—"'I'd stay out in my raft until help came.' They asked the one from Delta and she said"—here Dooley's voice dripped magnolias—"'Ah'd just go right in and tell those thutty men that ah'm a Suthun *Bab*tist, and en*gaged*, and they just better leave me *alone!*'" Now Dooley leaned very close to the stewardess and said, "So they came to the girl from United, asked her the same thing, and she said, 'I understand the question . . . But I don't see the problem.'"

The girl roared. Dooley leaned toward Kidd and said, as if confidentially, "See. I told you she was from United."

It took Kidd twenty minutes, refusing drinks and laughing, to excuse himself. He left Dooley with the car and took the train back into the heart of the city. He stared at the windows, at the images reflected harshly on the brightly lit inner panes against the falling night, and mixed among them he saw

Dooley, taking the girl into his apartment, still entertaining her with his wit and grace, and then removing his coat, so she could see his gun. She would be wide-eyed, and Dooley would look at her as she tingled in awe and excitement, and with only his expression he would say, "Yes. I *am* a federal agent. Secretive, complex, sad . . . living with danger. Alas! But that's how it is, and I accept it . . ."

CHAPTER 25

It was too late and too brief to be Indian summer, just one evening when a front moved up from the Gulf of Mexico and covered Washington with warm air. The wind, for one day, lost its edge and children stayed up to play in the streets and late that night Ginny Longstreet met Jeff Kidd at the bench. Maybe it was the warmth of the night that calmed her, or maybe it was the interruption in the march of seasons that gave her a sense of suspension in time and space. He stood easily as she came up, falling in wordlessly at her side.

They walked along quietly for two blocks, he with his hands in the pockets of his jeans, mostly staring down at the pavement. He wore a checked shirt beneath a pullover; it was the first time she had ever seen him in less than a long coat or a thick sweater, and she noticed, without self-consciousness, the edges of his shoulders, the tautness of his legs and arms. She wanted to take his arm, but she did not. She kept her hands folded together behind her back as she walked.

But the urge to touch him was the only urge she denied. In a quiet voice which sounded neither abrupt nor startling she said, "Jeff . . . Tell me about your wife."

He accepted the question as he accepted her presence—without defense. She knew, somehow trusted completely, that however shocking the question would have seemed to her if she had anticipated it or might seem to her when she reflected on it the next morning, it was absolutely natural now, and the pause that followed it did not come from reluctance to answer.

Again she wanted to wrap her fingers around his arm. Again she did not, but she watched him as they walked. A few steps later he said, "She isn't . . ." He faltered. "My wife, who isn't my wife. I don't know where to start to tell you this story."

Then, withdrawing his hands from his pockets and folding them behind his back like Ginny, he began.

"When I was a freshman, my first year at the university, we were having fairly regular demonstrations on campus. About race, the war. In those days I guess every demonstration was a protest about everything.

"I went through that whole time pretty wide-eyed, I guess. I remember this distinct awareness I had when I first went to college of how little I actually knew about anything. So when it came to making some dramatic statement for or against something . . . well, I was never that sure about how I thought the world was, or ought to be.

"But you know, it was a pretty self-righteous age, and I never felt altogether comfortable with my lack of fervor for—the brotherhood of man? I don't mean to be facetious. I thought a lot of the activists were sincere. And I watched, and I . . . questioned.

"So one week, we had had a full-scale riot on campus. It had to do with the university's pay rate for nonacademic employees, but . . . it was a basic early seventies riot. Yelling, not much bloodshed. But it precipitated this enormous demonstration, that they called the 'Vigil.' Students camped out in the middle of the campus, and said they wouldn't go to class until their demands were met, though the demands weren't really formulated for a day or two. They sang all day, or listened to speeches. They slept out under the stars. So many students were there, and so many professors sympathized, that almost all the classes were suspended.

"I met Linda at that Vigil. I can't say I participated in it, but I didn't oppose it either. I didn't make a stand either way. It was just that people felt passionately about what was happening, they seemed desperately committed to me, and I wanted to find out what was happening, so I went out to the Vigil—it was right on the campus lawn in front of my dorm—and started talking with the people. Linda was there. She was beautiful. She had this long dark hair, absolutely straight, and a beautiful face, which looked tragic to me, against the patched-up jeans and denim jacket she wore. She was in this heated political discussion—'strategy meeting'—with some friends of mine, and she was intelligent, and had this air of thoughtfulness and confidence about 'the only productive course.'

"She didn't go to the university, she went to a small college about a hundred miles away, a super-liberal place where the students didn't have to go to class, and set their own requirements for graduation. See, the Vigil was a big event and drew people from all over.

"I got to know her. When the Vigil was over—with some settlement that the students considered a victory, raising the salaries of the university's cooks and janitors but getting half of them laid off, because the school couldn't afford their wages—we began to date. We didn't call it 'date,' of course. I'd drive up to her school and we'd spend hours talking about politics and life. It was funny, after every discussion she would come to a conclusion, a certainty, which I never had. I thought conservatives *and* liberals were all self-righteous hypocrites.

"I became obsessed with how she thought and felt about things. What went on in her affected me. I figured that was love.

"I was terribly jealous about her. I only saw her on weekends, but we would write letters and call a lot. And she was always surrounded by men, boys I mean, but she was actually aloof. And she wasn't comfortable with sex.

"I liked that about her. To really explain that, or to try to, I have to go back a little further. To when I was twelve."

Kidd suddenly looked up and laughed loudly. It was a brief interruption.

"When I was twelve my family moved from Richmond to Roanoke. It wasn't that big a change, really, but the point is that it hit me squarely at puberty. I mean it was as if at my old school we were all children, but when I got to the new one, people were starting to comb their hair, have acne, have their first girl friends and boyfriends.

"I hit a class where everybody had known each other for years. They were having their first kissing parties—you know, with the contests of who could kiss who the *longest*. I was the new kid. And of course there was an in-group. They made it clear that I could be in if I understood my place. Whose girl was whose, who the top people were.

"For some reason, I can't say exactly why, I didn't want to be in their group. I mean I *did*, a lot I guess. But I didn't. And I wasn't. Whatever the reason, I was a loner that first year in junior high school. And that lasted for me.

"I did become popular enough, eventually. But I developed this incredible secret thing about waiting for exactly the right person.

"I was elected to the homecoming court my senior year. But I had never kissed a girl.

"I have to say, for the sake of my own ego now, that I never considered myself a nerd. I thought of myself as romantic. And tragic.

"The summer before college I relaxed my stand somewhat, and got in some necking practice. And had my heart broken at least twice. But Linda was the first one I really took . . . seriously. So her aloofness, what I took as aloofness toward sex, fit with what I expected. An attractive woman, with restraint.

"We went together through college. When we graduated, we weren't going to get married, we were just going to experience life and see what we felt like doing later. I wrote my master's thesis, got the offer from the CIA, and went to Washington. She worked in a string of social activist jobs that always petered out. We saw each other every few months, and it was the same broody romance. In the intervals I tried to date other women, and nobody I met seemed at all . . . important.

"Then she came to Washington, too. She was going to study in a free-form law school—Virginia is one of the five states in the union that allow admission to the bar based strictly on passing the state exam, not on graduation from a Bar Association–approved school.

"She had always disapproved of my working for the CIA, but she was also intrigued. I think too she was jealous. I found the work challenging.

"She started being depressed. I didn't call her all the time, and when she moved up—this was the big thing—I didn't ask her to move in with me. She had problems with her money. She didn't like to work. She couldn't pay her rent one month, and I got her an office job through some friends of my sister's. Linda worked three days, made enough for the rent, and then quit. We had our problems. I wanted to understand what was happening to her and couldn't.

"I came to her apartment one day after work and found her in her bathtub with her wrists bleeding."

Those words went through Ginny with a jolt; she actually staggered.

Kidd, thinking her reaction came from his narrative alone, said quickly, "No, no, it wasn't a serious attempt, she wasn't really even trying. But she was depressed, and what do you do for a person like that? I thought she saw life more deeply than I did. Hell, I was depressed too. I didn't know how far my depression could go. Maybe I thought helping her would help me. I was confused.

"I married her. I don't know what else to say about that. For a few years it was . . . no worse than a lot of marriages are. She was restless and unhappy. So what? So was I. When I left the agency and went back to school, at Charlottesville, I was somewhat more pensive, I guess. And we had very little money.

"Anyway, this is getting too long," Kidd said, and casually dropped the leaf he had pulled from a tree and rolled and crushed between his fingers. "She met this guy at a party we went to, a 'minister' doing work in Harlem. Linda talked about how thrilling his work sounded, and he told her that he thought she had 'just the species of sensitivity' they needed there in his project.

"He invited her to come up to New York to see the project —he was flying back that weekend. She went. When she came back she called him frequently. Not when I was home—I got the phone bills.

"Anyway, she fell back into the bouts of depression and eventually started going to a therapist. One day she comes home and says that her therapist says that total honesty is good for intimacy, and so she tells me that she and this minister spent the night together. One was all she admitted. But you know, she didn't come back and just say, 'Here was a man and I was attracted so I did it.' What she told me, I just —I can't believe this now, she said that when their flight was landing in New York, the plane developed some kind of trouble with the landing gear, and they had to circle for about thirty minutes before they actually went in. But in that thirty minutes—do you believe this, God, it's so stupid!" Kidd wiped his face with his hands. "In that thirty minutes, when she really *faced death for the first time,*' she was struck with the shortness of life. Apparently the minister had the same revelation, and they suddenly had this bond with each other, this need to hold and be held. They were drawn together in their existential moment."

His voice had grown harsh, openly venomous. But then he calmed. "I felt I had to forgive her. I expected myself to be that . . . big.

"But now comes the sick part, the part of the whole thing that I really . . . that just . . ." Kidd shook his head, showing disgust, and Ginny saw that the disgust he indicated was all directed at himself. "I knew it would be hard for any man to learn that his wife had been unfaithful. It destroyed me. I kept trying to fight my way up from it, but God, it ate my guts out. I thought it might be ego, and it certainly was a blow. I mean, I was always proud of my ability to read people, not to be deceived. And here I was, a professional, and I had been absolutely blind. That was a big thing, and it bothers me now, but that's just a question, it wasn't an emotional thing. The emotional thing was that I'd failed.

"Nothing in me was worth it. I couldn't give her something worth keeping—although she swore later that what she did with him was 'no negation of what we had together.' I even tried to accept that. But why is it, when human beings are betrayed, that it's the one betrayed, not the betrayer, who feels the most untrustworthy, the most dishonored?

"Okay. It ate me up. And it got worse. One day I took the flight they took, the same one, and rode up to New York. I took a cab into town, just as they would've, and I stood on the street in front of his apartment—I got the address from her book—and I tried to imagine it all.

"I know that sounds sick, but it was something I thought might help me, to try to confront what was real, to get past it! The images kept eating me up, of her . . . giving herself to him, and I knew there were all sorts of pains and jealousies involved in that, and I thought if I could just face it, see it as real as it was, then I could maybe feel all the pain at once, and be done with it. And I'd always had the most vivid imagination; I think that's where my skill, or the skill I thought I had, comes from. I could go to a battlefield and see everything that happened there, and once I knew where everything happened, where the troops were, saw the road where the infantry held or where it ran, then I could envision everything, and I could understand why. Well that apartment in New York was a battlefield to me, the scene of a defeat and a loss, and I went."

"Did it help?" Ginny's words were barely whispered.

"No. Or maybe it did. I stood there for a couple of hours in the rain, wanting to be as miserable as I could be, and then I went back to the airport. I still didn't understand anything. I still don't. But when I got back I told my wife that it was over." With a light toss of the hand Kidd added, "The next day I moved into a boardinghouse by the campus and went to see a lawyer. The divorce is final in two months."

They had returned to the bus stop bench. With the pauses they had made, with all the talk that had passed and the times they had stopped to look at each other and exchange something in the wordless silences, the walk had taken them much longer than normal. But though it had gotten very late, neither felt the night was over. And so they sat down on the wooden bench, and he took her hand, and they sat there together until the sky went from black to gray and the dawn birds began to sing.

CHAPTER 26

The obvious assumption was that Uncle Larry was nongovernment: "Uncle Sam, or Uncle Larry?" Of course there were foreign governments that might have a nickname to contrast with Uncle Sam, in a journalist's slang—Uncle Ivan, Uncle Pierre with some stretch—but Uncle Larry?

Pugh knew it might not be important at all, but he had a feeling it was; Emmett had been trying to psych him out, and for all the composure he had shown, Emmett seemed to have regretted the comment when Pugh pursued it. And if Uncle Larry was someone who might want Emmett followed, he had to be some kind of nemesis. It was worth finding out.

If it was vendetta, it was either personal or professional, and Pugh thought personal vendetta was unlikely. For one thing, Emmett was a man who cultivated a kind of popularity; people could despise his ethics, his journalistic tactics, his willingness to ruin reputations and political strategies, and yet they could respect him. He was courtly, oddly charismatic. He ran up, by Pugh's estimate, $100 every week in bar bills, buying drinks for friends or enemies. Anyone who took offense at him could personally punch him in the nose (there were stories, which Emmett himself told, of that happening).

The government had plenty of reason to hate Sam Emmett, but who else did, for professional reasons?

Other journalists.

Pugh sent a request through the Justice Department computer records section, asking for a printout on every top newspaper editor or columnist whose first or last name was Larry or Lawrence.

Because of Pugh's junior standing, his request was not run until a large batch of more pressing queries was answered. He did not receive his reply until past noon. It took him four hours to compare the biographical information of the more than twenty names on his list with what he already knew of Emmett's background. There turned out to be two Lawrences currently in high positions in domestic print journalism whose careers or schooling had coincided closely with Emmett's. Both were women.

Pugh went back over to the computer section and gave a clerk his two tickets to the Redskins game that weekend, and asked him to run the same check on broadcast journalists. Later that evening he got a call.

CHAPTER 27

Their conversation that night was thin; both of them felt it from the beginning, and they grew edgy as their stroll wore on. They talked in generalities, of books they had read or places they had been or wanted to visit. When they parted he asked her, as he had not done since their first night together, if she would be coming back the next evening.

Ginny told herself that she had a great deal going on in her life and some distraction was inevitable; she tried hard to accept this as the sole cause of the distance they both felt, and yet she looked for other reasons. She was tired, or maybe their lack of connection stemmed from turmoil in Kidd's life. As she left him, promising that she would return and almost begging the same pledge from him, she passed through the streets, walking the two dark blocks back to her house, feeling insecure and afraid and never knowing the reason.

The next day she threw herself into the chore of transferring her office, and even had time for a crisp meeting with Kurtz, Sherwood, Thayer, and the secretaries. Without explaining the reorganization (which Livingstone had already announced in a memo the previous afternoon) or apologizing for her own promotion, she took charge, laying out the new logistics. She offered to answer any questions en masse or in private. There were none.

At home that night after feeding Jamie and **putting** him to bed she took a nap (through hard experience she had learned to refresh herself with quick respites) and rose about ten to exercise intensely for an hour and then shower.

She met Kidd at midnight. He brightened at the sight of her; the smile he gave her made her chest go warm and she felt tension she had not been aware of suddenly draining away.

But she had not found the answer to the distance; not in organizing her work, not in rest, not in giving herself a physical pounding. As they walked, she found that stiffness between them she had felt the night before.

He tried at first to chat. He made a few casual comments and laughed as if he had said something funny. But then he fell silent, and they walked nearly a mile until she said, "I know what it is."

"What . . . is what?"

"It's me. It's my fault we can't communicate."

He started to protest that they were having no trouble, and besides, how could it be her fault? He got tangled, and grew quiet.

Walking slowly, hanging her head, Ginny said, "You can't just hold your ground and keep things as they are. You can't be half honest. You've told me about yourself. I wanted to know." She stopped, turned to him, and said, "I haven't told you about me."

She reached and took his hands, and held them together between her own.

Her head sagged. Her hair fell off her shoulders and into the wind and pressed across her face like a veil. When she looked up her eyes were rimmed in tears.

"My husband . . ." she began. "My husband . . ." She could not find a next word. "He's . . . an invalid," she said.

Kidd said nothing; his face was wrenched, but had been that way all along, as he watched the struggle it took for her to try to tell him some truth she could not utter.

"I want you to meet my husband," she said with no voice. "I want you to come to the house, my . . . our . . . house, and see where I live, and see . . . my husband."

Kidd's mouth formed the start of several words, none spoken, until he finally said, "When?"

"Tomorrow," she said at last. "Tomorrow night."

CHAPTER 28

"All right, kid, what is it you want to know?" Douglas lit up his pipe and stared out the window.

"What is it between Sam Emmett and Lawrence Hanrahan?" Pugh said.

"Why do you ask me?"

"There's an entry in the computer about Hanrahan. You either approved the entry or made it yourself, since you were head of the team checking out journalists during the last administration. If you know Hanrahan's nickname, you must know if there's anything between him and Emmett."

Douglas's red eyes focused for the first time on Pugh. "Most of these guys around here don't know that," Douglas said. "They don't know the goddamn computer's not the brain of God Almighty. Somebody, some flesh and blood, has got to feed it, and what they feed it is all it has."

"Yes," Pugh said, "that's why I wanted to come to you." Pugh saw he was flattering Douglas, and was relieved; Douglas was in the national security section, and Pugh was stepping over protocol to have approached him at all.

"There was more in that file. I mean, that *computer entry,*"

Douglas said, with some derision. "I wrote all I know under 'background.' But when invasion of privacy became the Unpardonable Sin, all of that stuff got purged. Excuse me, *deleted*. We don't purge in this country." Douglas smiled, much more broadly than he would have had he been amused.

"You mean there's something heavy between Hanrahan and Emmett?"

"Heavy? Is that what they say now when they mean important? No, no it wasn't *heavy*, not heavy enough to stay in the computer."

Douglas relit his pipe and immediately coughed. Pugh thought he could feel smoke-born influenza soaking through his suit. Douglas gained uncertain control of his lungs, and sat back. "Hanrahan and Emmett started their careers at the same time, in New York. Emmett was a newspaper reporter and Hanrahan was working for a television news department. They knew each other because they drank together. But they were never friends. Rivals. That's standard. There's a war, see, between print and broadcast. Networks love to do stories about a Pulitzer Prize being awarded for fabricated stories, and papers jump on anything that shows the networks stinking. It's trench warfare that only they care about. The public doesn't. That's why this information is not heavy. Not important. It's only about how the news gets reported." He trailed off.

"So, Emmett and Hanrahan?" Pugh prompted.

"Yeah," Douglas said, quickly back to life. "Just two young pups, aggressive, chafing on their own ambition and taking it out on each other. So they start to follow each other around, as if they mean to do an exposé on the other's medium. So, one day Hanrahan is tailing Emmett, and Hanrahan has a camera tucked in his coat. And he sees Emmett talking with a girl who looks exactly like Patricia Hearst—when she was missing. Hanrahan shoots pictures. His station runs them on the news. The FBI shows up wanting to know the source. But Emmett shows up at the station too, just after the pictures went over the air. With Emmett is the girl. *Not* Patty Hearst."

"A setup?"

"Burn. They call it, 'burn.' Emmett acted like it was a joke.

But to Hanrahan it was more serious than that. A journalist without credibility is like a pitcher without arms."

"So they've been bitter enemies ever since," Pugh said, smug with the confirmation of his instinct that "Uncle Larry" was an important lead.

"Were enemies, I guess. Hanrahan's dead."

"What?"

"Car wreck, couple of years ago. He was working as a cameraman at a station in Podunk."

"Well . . . why then would Emmett ever mention 'Uncle Larry' in conversation?"

"He treats it as a joke. Slowed down a little when Hanrahan died, but still uses it, maybe to say he's not responsible for Hanrahan. But what the joke means, when he says, 'Are you Uncle Larry?' he means, 'Are you snooping around me?' He's telling you, nobody gets to Sam Emmett."

"He didn't say that to me. I just overheard it."

"Watch your step with Emmett, boy."

Pugh stood. "Thank you for your time."

"He asked me about you."

"Who?"

"Emmett." As Pugh stared, Douglas said, "We drink at the same bar."

"What did you tell him?"

"That your father's rich. A rich *liberal*. Contributor to the Stern campaign. So when Sonny didn't pass the bar exam he got him a job in a department where nobody expects anything from him."

"You told him right," Pugh said, and even smiled.

But when he got back to his office he closed his file on Sam Emmett, and did not speak or think about him for five months.

CHAPTER 29

Ginny sat alone in the living room, her hands folded in the center of her lap. She wore a white lace dress, once her favorite, that she had not worn in two years.

The doorbell rang dry and hollow through the house. She rose slowly and walked out of the living room, through the hallway, and up to the heavy Georgian door. She opened it to Kidd, who stood stiffly erect on the porch. He wore a sport coat and had on a tie. There was a quickness in his smile and nod, as he stepped into the foyer.

Full light shattered from the chandelier directly overhead, and they both drew up short and stared at each other. He looked away first, looked back up, and started to speak but did not.

"Did you have trouble finding it?" she said.

"No. No," he said quickly. "We've passed here lots of—" He stopped himself, as if he should not speak at all of their walks together.

"It's all right," she said, and led him into the living room.

They sat down across from each other in chairs placed before the empty fireplace. Kidd's eyes kept darting back toward the hallway. "I would have made a fire," Ginny said. "But I can't have them because of Jamie." He looked at her—at least his eyes were trained in her direction—but he seemed not to see or to have heard.

She felt she had already lost him.

She glanced around the room, and ached more than she had thought she would at its stained-wall dinginess, and its bareness. In shame she looked back at Kidd. His gaze had grown steadier. "I've never seen eyes as green as yours," he said.

"Jeff," she said. "I know how . . . in the dark I've left you

. . ." *In the dark,* she thought. "And I'm sorry. I haven't meant to make this . . . mysterious, as it must seem to you now. I couldn't describe him to you, it would seem so . . . But I wanted you to see him because . . . I want you to know the truth about me. Only I couldn't tell you, I had to show you."

Kidd's head moved up and down.

She took a deep, slow breath. "Before I get dinner ready, maybe we should go see Jamie." She stood. He followed her out of the living room and down a long hallway to the den.

The swollen figure slumped in the soft chair before the television looked at first like an old man. An instant later, when Kidd got a glimpse of the simple face with the round white cheeks and the bloated belly, he thought Jamie was a teenager. When the fragments finally rushed together in Kidd's brain, he jolted. He did not know if he actually wobbled but he felt no weight in his knees, no knees at all. Ginny's hand, without pressure or force, with touch alone, steadied him, and guided him to the sofa. She sat down beside him, and said, in a voice soft as milk, "Jamie, this is Jeff Kidd. He is a very good friend of mine."

Jamie's head turned slightly, but very slowly and only halfway around. There was a remote smile on his wet lips.

Ginny, seeing the quiver of Kidd's fingers and the tapping pulse of the veins in his neck, looked down to her lap and said, "I should never have asked you to come."

"No," Kidd said sharply. He turned to her and said again, "No. You were right." He turned back toward Jamie.

For the first time now Kidd saw details. The room, the whole house, was battered and stark. The walls had been scrubbed often enough to make yellowed blotches where paint was rubbed away, but smudges still clung everywhere about the height of a man's head. The shelves behind the television were jammed with books, but there were no delicate conversation pieces, no lamps, none of the prints or hanging plants that might have made the room more pleasant.

And Jamie. His biceps, large and flaccid, pressed flat against the armrests of the chair he sank within, his legs stretched straight out over a faded ottoman. His knees were locked, his heels together, the feet slewed, his pants hiked up to mid-calf. The ankles, Kidd noticed, were swollen, not in the low, liquid way of obese old ladies, but in the high, hardened-calcium way of someone who has experienced countless sprains. Kidd stared at those soft feet and the swollen ankles, and thought they made the ugliest sight he had ever seen—until he brought himself to look at the hairless purple scars on the sides of Jamie's head.

"How long . . . ?"

"Two years," Ginny answered, her voice steady.

"Does he . . ." Kidd began. "Is he dangerous to you?"

Ginny paused for a long moment and said, "No. He isn't completely docile. A lot of his intelligence is gone, but some of it is still there, too, we don't—"

Jamie's head wrenched around as if someone had shouted his name. Kidd saw the whole movement—the apparently purposeless, mindless jerk, the body's awkward lifting that kept the legs straight and made the feet snap over like windshield wipers suddenly switched off. The face stared toward Kidd with a blankness he found unsettling, even frightening.

Ginny felt Kidd go rigid beside her. And as Jamie's face began to dissolve from starkness into a lopsided look of anger, she saw Kidd's hands go hard.

Ginny's hand went over the backs of Kidd's fingers, and she squeezed them into her palm. "Jeff. Listen. He draws from the people around him. I don't know how, but he does. He gets emotion, and . . . everything he seems to feel. Maybe he saw something in your face, when you asked me if he was dangerous." Kidd squeezed her hand. When he turned from Jamie to her, she said, "I don't understand it, but he looks to me for . . . life."

Kidd turned back to Jamie and saw a face grown completely placid. It could have been the visage of a monk. Jamie's languid eyes drifted down to the spot between Kidd and Ginny, where her hand covered his and pressed it into the cushions of the couch. Jamie stood.

Ginny did not move. And because she did not, or perhaps

because he could not, Kidd did not move either. Jamie stepped —plodding, swaying—to Kidd's side and, sitting down, he took Kidd's free left hand, and wrapped it within his own huge, sweaty palm.

Jeff Kidd was a man who in his secret heart judged the smallest of his actions against the absolutes of the qualities and loyalties he most revered. As Ginny disappeared, leading her grunting husband upstairs to put him to bed, Kidd felt nausea in waves, and he fought not only with the physical urge to vomit but also with the sense that to give in to it would be a betrayal through cowardice of Ginny Longstreet. He sat on the sofa, where she—and Jamie—had left him, and closed his eyes and lowered his head against the sick confusion.

After a few seconds he raised his head, and took several deep breaths. The fingers of his left hand, which had lain so lifelessly inside Jamie's slick grasp, now felt unbearably foul. He stood and walked to the half-open door of the bathroom adjoining the den. He stepped to the sink, switched on the faucets, and stared into the jet of water. Rubbing the thumb along the fingertips of each hand, he could still feel Jamie's touch in his left, Ginny's in the right. He pressed his palms down onto the cold porcelain of the sink and sagged.

And then the hot bile spilled into his throat, and he whirled and bent over the toilet, choking and gagging as nothing came from his empty stomach.

Ginny returned to find Kidd standing straight and pale in the center of the den. She stopped in the doorway and after a moment said, "I have our dinner in the oven. Let's go into the kitchen."

Again he followed, and sat down at a sturdy table, laid out with a new cloth and old dishes. Perhaps because his forehead was beaded with sweat she said, "I'm sorry the house is so hot. We have to keep it that way, Jamie won't keep shoes on, or a sweater. 'We'—that's Mary and I. She helps me, I gave her the night off."

She went to the oven, fiddled with the controls, switched on the light, and peered in, fiddled with the controls again. She walked to the center of the kitchen, stopped, and said, "I'm sorry. Nothing is ready."

He watched her so intensely that she knew he was not listening.

"Would you like something to drink?" she said.

"No. Thank you."

"The food will be ready soon."

She stopped in the center of the kitchen, and lowered her eyes to the floor. "I'm sorry, Jeff," she said. "I had to tell you. I wanted . . . you to know. I didn't know this would be so wrong."

"No. This was right."

She came and sat down next to him.

There had not been another moment in all the time he had known Ginny Longstreet when he wanted more to reach for her. But he did not, and the longer he waited the more he knew he could not. It was a helplessness which he did not yet understand.

She sat with her hands folded on the table, the thumbs pressed and purple. Her body was so carefully erect that she looked fragile. But her eyes, when they lashed up to his, were clear and demanding.

"We met in college. Like you and Linda. We had a class in economics together. I was a very quiet sophomore, and he was this big star freshman athlete . . ."

"Basketball?" Kidd interrupted.

"Yes," she said. "You recognize him?"

"No, the ankles . . ."

"Oh. Yes. I forgot you could do that."

"Recognize him? Should I? Jamie . . . Longstreet?"

"Whittaker. Jamie Whittaker."

Jamie . . . *Whittaker!* Kidd had seen his picture in the newspapers, maybe even on the covers of magazines. Though Kidd had never followed sports that closely, he had a memory of a robust, handsome All-American, brimming with prodigious self-assurance. While Kidd was still reeling, struggling to connect that person with the degenerated mass of flesh he had seen a few minutes before, Ginny added, "I kept my maiden name." She said the words as if admitting to a crime.

Staring away from Kidd, into the whiteness of the Dutch tile that covered the kitchen wall, she said, "I hardly knew who he was when I met him, or if the team won or lost. I think he liked that about me. I liked him for liking that about me.

"I studied journalism. I was a good student. In my first year of graduate school I entered a contest sponsored by a television network, for a news commentary apprenticeship program, to be judged by their staffs. I won. A few months later I got a phone call from one of the judges, who was working on a political campaign and wanted a youthful approach in the speechwriting." She did not mention that the judge was John Livingstone, though she had no reluctance to tell Kidd that, and had in fact intended to tell Kidd all about her job at the White House. But now she was trying to get out a story that even she was smothered by. "I got a job in a presidential campaign.

"Jamie thought it was just great at first. He was enthusiastic and I think maybe a little . . . relieved. You see"—she had stopped looking at Kidd; it was as if she were pleading before an unseen jury, as if she were not already convicted—"at the time I got the job offer he was just graduating, and had signed a huge contract to play professional ball."

Kidd seemed to remember that. For years pro basketball had been dominated by Blacks, and national sports magazines made open references to the "Great White Hopes," the players to whom middle-American audiences might relate, the potential stars who promised to restore the crowds that had dwindled in the last decade of Black-dominated games.

"He had always told me, through the three years we went together in school, that he wanted to marry me at graduation. I had never agreed, but . . . I liked him saying that. But when he got the pro offer, he started saying . . . I don't think I ever brought marriage up, I believe it was always him . . . but he said that it would be good for us to take some time to 'get our heads together.'" She looked toward Kidd then, but her eyes were glazed. It was as if she had seen for the first time the irony in that phrase.

Looking down and tracing a fingernail across the tablecloth she said, "The first team he signed with, out in Los Angeles, put him on the bench at the start of the season. He demanded to be played or traded, and a month into the season he just left the team. He told them they could tear up his contract, but he wasn't going to sit on the bench."

All the time she spoke, Kidd's imagination filled in the gaps. Jamie's frame—maybe six-foot-five when he had stood up straight—would be small in a world of seven-footers. And the complex zone defenses and corresponding offenses, in which a finesse player might excel in college, were outlawed in the freewheeling pros. Kidd could understand Jamie's difficulties. And his frustration.

"He sat out the rest of that first season," Ginny said. "His father was successful in the insurance business and tried to get him to work in the agency, just to give him something to do, to take his mind off . . . but he couldn't.

"I didn't see him much then, I was working, and traveling a lot. But we talked by phone. And then one day—we were in Chicago, it was fall, toward the end of the campaign, and we were getting ready to catch a flight to New York. And thirty minutes before we were going to take off, Jamie came in. He had a man with him. I was shocked to see him there, of course. He was ecstatic. He said the Washington Bullets had just picked up his waivers, and he was going to play for them. The man with him was a minister. He wanted to get married right then."

She paused. The juices of the roast sizzled in the oven.

"We never had a honeymoon. We just had the ceremony there in a corner of the waiting room, and I flew off to work, and Jamie came back here and bought a house. This house."

Ginny's face had paled, but even as the blood had left her face her voice had grown more calm. "A few months after that . . . He still wasn't playing . . . I was . . ." She stared down. Her chest went up and down in a slow breath. "I was working. And I came home one night. It was late, but that never mattered, because his games kept him out until midnight."

Now for the first time since she started her narrative, she really looked at Kidd. "I smelled a fire in the fireplace as soon as I walked in the door, you know how it is when you first come home. And I could hear it crackling in the living room.

"I called to him. I remember that. No one answered, just, just music came on, disco-type beat music that blared out and then went down suddenly, very faint. I walked in. The lights were all dim, and Jamie was standing by the stereo, swaying. He had on a new robe, thin and shiny, and he turned to me and sort of spread it open to the waist, as if he thought it very . . . sexy."

Images pulsed in flickering firelight through the heat of Jeff Kidd's brain.

Ginny faltered, as unready now as then to admit that Jamie, in his sleazy robe above his wide calves, shaved ankles, and bare feet, both repelled and frightened her. She pressed on firmly: "He was watching me, staring toward me from the time I walked through the foyer into the room, and it was like . . . I'd never seen his face before, like he didn't know me. Or I didn't know him.

"I don't remember if I said hello, or said his name. He didn't speak. He just smiled and started toward me."

Kidd could see Jamie's mass—not the soft bulk he was now, but the muscled, angular figure he must have been then—lumbering toward her in an ugly parody of men's magazine sensuality. Ginny, almost whispering now, said, "He was swaying as he walked, and was all out of rhythm, making these strange twitches, jerky and slow all at the same time. He staggered when he stopped. His eyes were . . ."

Ginny's interruption suddenly brought Kidd back to seeing her before him, her face imploring, brittle. "I can't say I didn't know he was starting to use drugs," she said. "Back in college he wouldn't even drink beer. But over the last few months he had gotten so he'd come home very late, after I'd gone to bed, and would bang around and wake me up, and talk, talk really fast. Not about basketball—he hated the practices and never got into the games—but about new cars or stereos or something, at three in the morning. Then he'd take pills to sleep, and others when he had to get going early, and . . .

"So when he came toward me, in that robe, and I saw in his hand he had . . ."

She paused again, and did not resume until she had lowered her head. "Physically, the attractiveness in our marriage was . . . And it wasn't just his fault, it was mine, too. I didn't know what to do about it, any more than he did. But you have to understand that he was important to me." She looked up. "Like you and Linda. I saw it myself, when you told me about her. You were trying to explain why you married her, and you felt you couldn't, but you said you had dated other people, and no one else ever mattered. That's what it was to me. Jamie . . . mattered."

Kidd wanted to say, *You don't have to tell me you loved him.* But his throat was too tight, his chest too swamped, for him to speak.

"He had a bottle of pills and poured some out into his hand and held them to me, like candy. I said, 'Jamie, what . . .'" Her voice faltered, as Kidd was sure it must have faltered then.

"'I thought we'd have a little party,' he said, and when I didn't move or say anything he kept staring at me, smiling and swaying as he waved the pills at me." She lifted her own hand, and lowered it quivering back to the table. "'Ludes, baby,' he said. 'Come on. Come on!' Then he stopped and said, 'What's the matter? Are my parties not *good enough* for you?' I remember that—he emphasized 'good enough.' And then he grabbed my head and was shoving the pills against my lips and teeth, and shoving, until I slapped the bottle and they all fell."

The house was so quiet the pills still seemed to be bouncing on the hardwood floor.

"And then I said, 'Jamie, get those things out of here.' And he said, 'What did you say?' And I screamed, 'Get them out of my house!'"

She said those words now as if they were the most unforgivable words that any human being could utter to another.

"And then he hit me."

Kidd winced, the pain sudden in his face. Ginny saw she had no need to tell him her nose was broken. He seemed to know everything already.

And she was right. Kidd could see her flying backward, her head snapping back and carrying the rest of her with it, her feet scattering in the air, until she hit on the polished parquet of the entrance foyer, and slid.

Ginny stared off now into a memory: the vague surprise that she was still conscious, an awareness of very little pain, a feeling that she was under water, water warm, thick, and red. "I saw Jamie turn and walk back toward the fireplace. I got up. I ran upstairs."

She paused and took a full deep breath. Her voice was steady now, resigned. "I had been locked in the bedroom for about five minutes when I heard the shot. I wasn't sure that's what it was. It was just once, and faint. I had a wet towel pressed into my face, and I was confused, trying to decide what to do next, and I thought it couldn't be a shot. But Jamie had a pistol, he usually carried it in his car. I had found it there a few weeks before when I was looking for a road map and he said he'd just gotten it because 'some fans are crazy,' and he had to drive home late at night.

"So I heard this one bang, nothing more, no sound at all. I thought of calling the police . . ."

She lowered her face into one hand and began to cry. The last thing she said was, "He was in the kitchen."

And Kidd could see her, that night two years ago, going to the door of the bedroom, opening the lock, and calling, "Jamie?" Then stepping into the hallway, walking down the stairs, through the empty living room, finally into the kitchen, where she found her husband, shrunken on his knees on the linoleum, the pistol clutched in a hand twisted at his side, his forehead pressed into a widening pool of blood—and spattered against the snowy white of the kitchen wall, a major portion of what had once been Jamie Whittaker's brain.

They sat there at the table for perhaps another half-hour, during which time she told him, in a matter-of-fact voice, of the next-door-neighbor doctor who had administered the immediate first aid, the medical analysis of the path of the bullet that had obliterated so many brain cells and the shock waves and swelling that had destroyed so many more, and of the surgeon who had said that, "because so few people have expertise with suicide," such survivals were not uncommon.

They had dinner, dessert, and coffee. They talked more. But something had passed, and they both felt it.

It was as if a moment had come and gone, leaving before either of them knew it had arrived, an instant when she had expected something of him, something which he had not delivered.

Even more than expected; she had demanded something of him, and it was to that purpose that she had invited him in the first place, to declare who she was and what she was and how she lived. To test him.

Neither of them had known the test was going on, and yet both of them felt somehow that he had failed—failed, perhaps, in wanting something from her that she would not, or could not, give.

When he looked at his watch and said woodenly, "Well, I guess I really should go," she let him stand, without argument.

They walked back up the hallway to his eager chatting about the tastiness of the dinner. But when he stopped at the door, he felt the defeat, a battle lost that he had not known he was fighting.

He stared at her and said, "I love you, Ginny." His voice was hoarse. He even had to clear his throat, and might have said it again, had it not sounded so artificial the first time.

Her lips moved, but shaped no sound or words; her head floundered in something that might have been a nod or a shake.

He turned and shoved the door. It felt ponderous as he stepped around it, closed it behind him, and left into the night.

Ginny, who from the beginning had understood everything, went back to the kitchen table, sat down, and began to weep.

CHAPTER 30

She got home early, before six o'clock. The house was quiet as she walked in the front door. She went into the living room and found Jamie asleep upon the couch. The portable television, which Mary sometimes rolled into the living room to keep Jamie occupied while she cleaned some other part of the house, was playing softly in front of the fireplace.

Ginny walked back into the foyer. "Mary?" She heard a noise upstairs and stepped to the foot of the staircase and called up, "Mary?"

"Yeah!" Mary said loudly, appearing at the bathroom door.

"Oh, hi! Anything the matter?"

"No, no . . . Aw, *shit!*"

Ginny rushed upstairs as she heard the sound of bottle breaking and a clunk that seemed to be Mary staggering against the bathroom cabinets. She found Mary hunched over shards of glass on the tile; the room smelled of Campho-Phenique. "You okay?" Ginny said, and then saw the dark welts on Mary's calf, foot, and ankle. "What happened?!"

"Scalded," Mary said.

"How did you do that?"

"I knocked . . . Jamie knocked over a batch of my potato soup I was making up. It was sticky. Before I could get it off it burned . . . ."

"Oh God, what's the matter with him?"

Mary knew what she meant. "He didn't mean to, he . . . You know how he kinda stumbles sometimes."

Together they wiped the bathroom floor, Mary insisting that her leg did not hurt at all though she winced each time she stepped. "Come on, I want you to lie down," Ginny told her.

But Mary said, "I can't, I gotta make supper. Besides that I gotta look at Jamie. I've got to clean him up."

Ginny had a stab of concern before she remembered Jamie sleeping so peacefully on the couch. When they found him still asleep they decided to clean him up after supper.

Ginny did the cooking, then went and woke Jamie. He smiled at her, grunted, and followed her into the kitchen.

Mary had used Ginny's absence to disobey orders and get up to serve the plates with baked chicken and salad. Ginny sat Jamie down, got Mary to sit, and took a place herself.

As she reached to Jamie's plate to cut up his meal, she noticed his flannel shirt. She had seen the left sleeve when she woke him; it was soiled with dried flecks from a light spatter. Now she saw for the first time that the right sleeve was sticking to his forearm. But the potato paste was thick, and she thought only of the wetness, the stickiness of it as it dried rather than how much heat a boiling slosh of it would transmit. "Here, let me see, Jamie," she said as a mother might to a child, and Jamie turned slowly toward her as she unbuttoned his cuff. He let out a low moan.

The moan threw her off. He often moaned when he was touched, but he made a different, higher sound when he was upset. She opened the cuff and in a quick casual movement pulled up the sleeve.

The redness of the craters stood out against the white flesh of his inner forearm—blisters torn open, sticky tops adhering to the sleeve, white fragments clinging to the edges of the sores.

A scream ran backward into Ginny's throat; she bit a half-clenched fist. "Lord God!" Mary yelled and jumped up from her seat.

Neither Ginny nor Mary realized it, but it was not the pain that set Jamie off. For him the sensation in his arm was a dull ache that had no particular location in his body. But the sight of the burn was, somewhere in his ruptured brain, a symbol of something horrible—not necessarily to himself, for he no longer had the capacity to make connections like that, but a suggestion of horror in general. And the reaction of Ginny and Mary, the two who made up his whole world, was a confirmation of the terror for him. He bellowed; not a cry of vicious rage but something like an echo of it, a soulless pantomime that was more unsettling than real rage might have been. They gaped at him in horror, and then he bellowed again, standing and knocking over the table, a doll-house toy against his bulk.

Ginny reached to take hold of him, and then jerked her hands back as she realized she was about to grab his arm. It might have been better if she had taken him there; he could not feel the pain much and it might have calmed him if she had acted as if the wound were nothing. But he saw her pull her hands back—his eyes, slow and bulging, dumb but observant, never left her face—and when she reached for him again he hit her.

The blow was slow, an open-handed slap that caught her midway between breasts and throat and threw her backward. Her head hit the corner of the china cupboard and she heard the crash of dishes.

Somehow she saw that he was not coming at her—she must have opened her eyes before the pain caught her and squeezed them shut—and she dipped to her knees and felt the back of her head. Her fingers got warm and wet.

When she opened her eyes again she saw Jamie standing in the center of the kitchen, a giant towering above the wreckage. His face bore only the hint of confusion, of pain, of anything like anger; in its blandness it was surreal. Behind him, backed all the way to the kitchen sink, with both hands wrapped around the wooden handle of a butcher knife, stood Mary. The end of the blade danced in the air, Mary's eyes were huge. Her arms were extended but not fully; terror kept them contracted. "Ah . . . Ah . . . Ah . . ." she moaned. "Ah'm gonna kill him."

Ginny stared up at Jamie's cowlike eyes. "Listen to me, Mary," she said as calmly as she could. "Listen now. Put that knife down. Go call the doctor. Just tell him we need him right now, that's all you've got to tell him. Then bring me the syringe and the sedative." She never took her stare from Jamie's eyes.

"He's gonna kill you, Ginny!" Mary cried sloppily through her tears.

"No he's not. Go get the syringe. Call the doctor first. And put that knife down. Put it in the drawer. Don't even let him see it."

Finally Mary obeyed, returning in two minutes. She edged along the wall where Ginny still knelt, handed her a full syringe, and then stood by in spasms of dry weeping as Ginny stood, moved to Jamie very slowly, and in one continuous motion pushed the needle into his shoulder, right through the shirt.

Ginny's head bled profusely, wetting a patch of her sweater between the shoulder blades; the sight of the blood as she pulled the sweater off made her come closer to passing out than either the shock or the pain had. But the doctor found that the actual cut was very slight—he had to explain twice to Mary that wounds in the scalp, where there are so many capillaries, always create quick, heavy bleeding, and Ginny was not, as Mary had screamed over the phone, "gashed right through her skull." The wound did not require stitching, though the doctor did try to insist on X rays. As with other of the doctor's insistences, Ginny refused this too.

Jamie was another matter. The circulation was normal in his arm, if the sensitivity to pain was not, and his burns, the doctor said, would heal routinely if the bandages were kept clean. But Mary was still quivering long after the doctor had arrived, and Ginny, though she maintained a rigid calm, was shaken. The doctor agreed with Ginny's theory that Jamie had been reacting to their reactions, but to him that was just the point.

"Ginny," he said, sitting beside her on the bed, where she lay on her stomach and felt at the puffy cut he had coated with antibiotic cream, "how can you expect to take care of a full-grown man like this, just you and Mary? He's a grown man, Ginny, not a child, not a clinical lobotomy patient who might at least be predictable. Yes, your anxieties may upset him. Do you think you can keep from having anxiety in a situation like this?"

Ginny did not turn her face from the pillow.

"Violet Ridge is a quality place, Ginny. In twenty-five years

I've never seen a better one. I don't know what the image of an asylum conjures up for you, but you've got to understand it is not cruel. I would have never told you about it if I didn't approve of the care they give. Why do you keep refusing to even consider it?"

Still Ginny did not turn around.

The doctor left around midnight. Ginny went into the kitchen and cleaned it. Then she sat down, propped her elbows on the table, and pressed her face into her hands. But tonight she did not cry. Now she was sure she could not feel anything.

But she was wrong. When she went upstairs and checked in on Mary—still quivering—and on Jamie—still asleep—and went back to her own bedroom and lay down, her head throbbing, and she finally looked at the clock and saw 1:12, she did feel something: an aloneness deeper than any she had ever thought possible.

He stood up. He walked back and forth from the streetlamp to the bench. He looked at his watch.

He waited until 1 A.M., and then he went back to his apartment, to the big bed on the cinder blocks, but he did not sleep at all.

CHAPTER 31

Ginny awoke at seven, her alarm clock screaming her from heavy slumber.

The back of her head was tender and sore, but the swelling was almost gone and the cut was closed. Her habit was to exercise and shower before she left her room, but this morning she went first to check on Jamie.

He was still sleeping soundly, his face serene. The bandage on his arm was undisturbed.

But as she walked back toward her room, Ginny had the

sense of something wrong, something out of place or absent. There was no sound coming from the kitchen, where Mary normally would be making breakfast.

Ginny walked to the head of the staircase and looked toward Mary's room, where the door was ajar and the light off. "Mary?" she called. Hearing no answer she descended the stairs and walked to the kitchen. "Mary?" she said again, and switched on the light. The kitchen was clean and silent, exactly as Ginny had left it the night before. "Mary!" she said again loudly, and looked out the window over the sink, as if, in the dead of winter, Mary might have strolled into the backyard.

She was wandering with the vague notion of going back to look in Mary's room when she halted at the hallway entrance and turned to look at the refrigerator door. The picture of Mai Desire and K-Poppa was gone, and Ginny knew, without having to go back to her bedroom, that so was Mary.

Jamie sat beside her in the car, reflections of the Maryland countryside racing across the surface of his eyes.

In forty minutes they were pulling into the curved driveway of a five-bedroom ranch-style house in the country-club suburbs of Baltimore. She shut off the engine, took a deep breath, and sensed—perhaps only imagined—that the house itself had grown suddenly quiet, as if someone within had paused, with the kind of hesitation one makes before rushing into a storm. Then, like one who believes it is possible to outrun the rain, Jamie's mother opened the door and hurried into the winter morning.

Her hair was the dull ooze color of yellow gone gray; of that same shade was her face, the older, female version of Jamie's. Her eyelids were jittering, her fingers shook as she tried— blindly, Ginny thought—to help Jamie from the car. She was mumbling something that sounded like, "Dear, precious, precious . . ."

Ginny walked around to the side of the car where Jamie sat immobile as his mother's pressureless fingers quivered upon the slab of his right forearm as if it might dissolve were she to tug at all. Stepping gently between mother and son, Ginny put one palm on Jamie's chin, pulling his face around toward her, and then tugged at his upper arm with the other. Facing the open door, Jamie came out easily, and stood.

"Ginny. Hello," a male voice said, and Ginny turned around to see Jamie's father. Darker than his wife or his son, broad and trim, he had the physique to be commanding; and yet his face, stained shallow by the smile habitually upon it, was timid. He had drifted from the house in his wife's wake.

"Good morning, Mr. Whittaker," Ginny said. "I'm really sorry to ask you to do this. On such short notice," she added, though she had never before asked them to keep Jamie at all, on any notice. Mr. Whittaker's lips stretched into a smile, broad and thin; his head bobbed.

"Please, please! Let's get him into the house!" Mrs. Whittaker pleaded, her hands now on Jamie's shoulder. "Precious . . . precious . . ."

In the less than an hour she had had since Ginny's call that morning, Mrs. Whittaker had transformed one of her guest bedrooms into a hospital ward. She had closed the blinds, stripped the flowered spread off the bed to put on a plain wool blanket, placed a pitcher of water and glasses on the bedtable, even rolled in a television set. Ginny allowed herself the cruel thought that if Mrs. Whittaker had had more time she would have forced her husband to mount the set on the wall.

"There's really no need for you to . . . he doesn't have to stay in bed all day . . . unless you want . . ." Ginny mumbled. Jamie lay down obediently as his mother got him to the bed.

Turning to Mr. Whittaker, Ginny said, "I'm really sorry to have this happen this way. I'd stay out of work except that we've just reorganized and I have to be there right now. I'm sorry this came up so unexpectedly."

"She left you with no notice whatsoever . . ." Mr. Whittaker said gravely.

"Those people!" his wife hissed, beginning with great effort to unbutton the new shirt Ginny had dressed Jamie in before they left.

"I've got the employment agency looking already," Ginny

said. "It's not easy to find the right person, but I hope we'll get lucky in just a day or two."

Mr. Whittaker, obviously relieved, said, "There's no hurry at all. We want to help."

"If we only could afford to we'd hire a person ourselves and help more," Mrs. Whittaker said.

The dues the Whittakers paid annually to the North Baltimore Golf and Tennis Club were more than Ginny had paid Mary, and Ginny knew it. Mr. Whittaker, she was sure, knew it too. Was it possible that Annabelle Whittaker did not? Ginny stared at her for a moment, and then looked back to Mr. Whittaker. "I'll be back tonight after work, to pick him up," she said.

"You don't have to do that," Clarence Whittaker said. "That's a lot of driving. We can keep him overnight."

From the corner of her eye, Ginny saw Annabelle Whittaker's face whip toward them.

"No. Thank you. But I'll take him home with me."

"Well," Mr. Whittaker said. "Well. Won't you have a cup of coffee with us before you go?"

"No, thank you, I—"

A screech tore through the room, and Ginny spun around to see Mrs. Whittaker backing away from the bed, her hands going to her mouth as her bulging eyes stayed locked on the white bandage she had just uncovered on Jamie's arm.

"It's all right! All right!" Ginny said as she rushed to Jamie, cutting off his view of his mother, and she smiled at him until she was sure he had not reacted. Turning slowly to the far wall, where Clarence Whittaker was trying to calm his shivering, sobbing wife, Ginny said, "He burned himself a little, that's all."

Annabelle Whittaker's eyes rolled toward her, vibrant with accusation and hate.

Back out in the entrance foyer, Ginny explained to Mr. Whittaker that Jamie's burn caused him no pain and was healing properly, and along with her new number at the

White House she left them Dr. Wimbly's number, if for any reason they should need to call.

As she left, Ginny could hear the faint murmur from the other room, as Annabelle Whittaker sobbed to her son, "Oh Precious . . . Precious . . . What has she done to you?"

CHAPTER 32

She got to the bench at 11:58 and waited until 12:03. Then she began to walk.

There was a moment, when she was about a half-mile from the bench, when she wavered, and felt herself on the brink of collapse. It was not a failure of strength but a divided will—one to go on, one to stop and grieve.

She went on, driving herself forward with the grim promise that, if she kept walking, in time she would learn again to bear pain without hurting, and to see aloneness as a blessing.

Part Two

Part Two

CHAPTER 1

Her name was Roxanne Lark, she was twenty-six years old, and she waited alone in a parked car outside the doors of the school where she had once taught. Only one of the mothers parked in the same line along the curb noticed Roxanne, remembered seeing her there for the last two days, even recalled that then she had driven a different car. But she assumed that Roxanne was the parent of a transfer, and it did not strike her until later that transfers were unlikely so late in the term.

As the bells rang—audible from where Roxanne sat—and the children streamed out, Roxanne started the engine and pulled slowly around the corner, where the children who normally walked home would clear the buses, waiting cars, and the safety lady who wigwagged at the intersection. It was a warm spring afternoon. The children were laughing.

In the rearview mirror Roxanne saw the seven-year-old girl with the straight blond hair. When the girl had passed, Roxanne stepped from the car and said too loudly, "Dabny! Dabny Crawley!" The girl, one of those students who is never afraid to hear her name called, turned around, her face curious and open. "Dabny!" Roxanne said, walking up quickly. "Don't you remember me?"

"Miss Lark," Dabny said, and did not smile back. Roxanne had lost weight since Dabny had seen her last; her hair was cropped short, her smile forced.

"And who is this?" Roxanne said, looking at the dark-eyed girl beside Dabny. "Aren't you . . . Sondra?"

The dark-eyed girl shook her head and Dabny said, "No, that's Rebecca."

"Yes, Rebecca! Of course!" Roxanne said, having never seen the girl before. "Dabny, your mother called me and asked me to pick you up today and take you to your grandfather's house, so you can have a surprise party for him. My car's right over here."

Dabny Crawley had been told two dozen times never to get into a car with a stranger, and she remembered that advice, though the term was almost over and it was a beautiful spring day. But Roxanne Lark was not a stranger; she had been Dabny's kindergarten teacher.

They did drive to the home of Dabny's grandparents. Dabny knocked at the front door. The lady who opened the door (it was the maid's day off) smiled with surprise at seeing her granddaughter. Roxanne, smiling herself, stepped in after Dabny, pulled a heavy pistol from her purse, pointed it at the girl, and said to the woman, "Tell your husband to come here."

Dabny's grandfather, Harrison Crawley, had been, until his retirement three years before, one of the United States' most distinguished foreign ambassadors.

Because the Senators had come to the White House to discuss influence, more specifically the use of presidential status to influence senatorial elections, Baxter Stern was meeting them in the Oval Office. Stern sat stiffly upright behind the desk (he had not sat in the chair enough to make the leather comfortable) and fidgeted with the tobacco in his pipe while the Senators, Boaz Thornbull of Mississippi and Munson Osgood of Illinois, each rambled on in the lectures that everyone who came to the Oval Office these days seemed to want to deliver.

Reflecting on this phenomenon as she listened from her chair at the flank of the desk, beside John Livingstone, Ginny

Longstreet thought, *Maybe that's why Baxter Stern hates meeting people here.*

As if reading her thoughts Senator Thornbull said, "That's the trouble now, Mr. President. People are starting to think they aren't really dealing with a political power in this administration. We need more appearances from the White House, more public profile. It would make Senators up for reelection more important to their constituents because of a relationship with the White House." Thornbull was one of those Senators whose term was expiring.

"And it would make you seem more presidential as well, Mr. President," Senator Osgood said.

Stern, never looking up from his pipe, said, "The last Senator I invited here for a policy discussion took the opportunity to hold a press conference as he was leaving. Stood there facing the cameras with the White House right at his back and told everybody that this administration was impotent."

Osgood glanced at Livingstone as if surely *he* must see that the President had misunderstood them, and then said, "But he's not from our party, Mr. President. He's setting himself up to run against you."

"We're talking about loyal members of our own party who need your help for their own reelection," Thornbull said. "And if you need help later, sir, it's good to have the old friends still in office."

"Besides," Osgood added, "no one in our party would betray a privilege like that." Osgood even said this with a straight face.

Now Stern did look up. Thornbull had already started to add something else but Stern cut him off in midsentence by saying, "John, what steps will we have to take right away if, ah, our present legislative difficulties . . ."

Stern was finishing fewer and fewer sentences lately, so Livingstone took the cue from there. Looking at the Senators he said, "The polls show the public is concerned—probably because of all the attention this has received—with the difficulty we seem to have getting bills through Congress. I was thinking that we could even address this question directly in a statement made at the beginning of our next press conference."

"Ginny," the President said, "have you begun to work up anything . . ."

"Yes sir," Ginny said, folding her hands onto the note pad in her lap and lowering her eyes to the floor; and in the instant before she spoke, she wondered if Senator Osgood was looking at her legs, as he had done twice openly since they all sat down. "The lack of passage of the Administration's legislative proposals has created a lack of confidence, but not in the Administration alone. We might, in a short speech, simply state that the Administration has been making no backroom offers, no compromises which might directly benefit any so-called key Congressmen at the expense of the nation as a whole. We could then trust the public to decide for itself where the incompetence lies."

Ginny looked up, and saw that Osgood was no longer staring at her legs. And Boaz Thornbull, who had come into the room beaming at Ginny and telling her how happy he was to see a beautiful woman, a *Southern* woman, on President Stern's staff, now looked as if the buttermilk in his breakfast biscuits had just gone sour.

"Mr. President," Thornbull began, "I don't think—" But he was cut off as the door opened and a white-shirted aide hurried into the room.

Stern, with his narrow shoulders hunched tight and his head thrust forward, did not seem to be moving down the hallway as fast as he actually was. Two aides, murmuring in flat, rapid voices, flanked him, and the Senators followed breathlessly. The Senators had offered to leave but Stern had said, "Come with me, please, gentlemen. We'll see together how . . ." And they had followed, delighted.

Livingstone, behind the Senators, reflected that their presence was a stroke of luck. He did not know how bad the situation might be, but whatever it was, whatever the outcome, the presence of those two members of Congress made the President's actions safer from criticism. And then Livingstone realized, with shame, and fear for what he was becoming, that he was thinking of politics when the lives of innocent people were at stake.

Walking beside Livingstone, and there only because he had taken her by the arm and led her down the hallway with him, was Ginny Longstreet.

They got into an elevator whose floor fell away and then buckled their knees in a stop. The doors opened to a crowd. Ginny had always known there were marines in the sub-basement, but she had never suspected so many; they were spaced along the hallways and clustered into checkpoints, some in full battle dress.

The hall they hurried down split; on one side the marines stood so thickly at a checkpoint that even the Senators knew they must be guarding the War Room, the communications center linking the White House with the Pentagon. The President took the other fork, and they found themselves within a large room made crowded by consoles along the walls and a large table in the center. Four operators in headsets sat at the consoles; two more stood by as supervisors, monitoring communications channels. At the table, a wizened ferret of a man was referring to an aerial photograph and building a display. All wore civilian clothes.

Even the President froze for a moment in the hard bright light, as if they had stumbled into an operating room. The President tilted his head in the direction of the Senators and mumbled, "I had this room set up, part of . . . reorganization. Terrorism is just too . . . Jurisdictional problems—military? FBI? Civilian?" With that he walked away to one of the standing men, who pulled the headset from one ear only and began to speak softly and rapidly to him.

Livingstone turned to the Senators. "The President has set up a special group for combating terrorism. As the President was saying, we have enormous problems dealing with terrorism. The acts themselves are irrational and unpredictable, and once they happen it's always been difficult to coordinate the various enforcement agencies. Our new antiterrorist group is small. Besides the communications people here, we have twenty field operatives, drawn from our intelligence services but combined now in one unit."

"Twenty men?" Thornbull said. "How is that enough? Sometimes you need a small army!"

"You're absolutely right," Livingstone said. "The organization I'm speaking of is a brain trust. We can have one of these men on a hot spot within minutes anywhere in the country, within a few hours almost anywhere in the world. Then not only is the advice we get accurate and current, but the other forces we have available—commandos, S.W.A.T. teams, or even local sheriff's departments—can be coordinated by an expert."

"Brilliant," Thornbull said.

"If it works," Osgood said.

"That's right," Livingstone said. "This is our first test. The program is only a few months old, but we've done our best. But the logic is sound. Didn't you suggest such a special force last year?"

Both Osgood and Thornbull, whose suggestion had amounted to a public statement that the United States "just had to do something about terrorism," now glanced at each other. "The President took your recommendations quite seriously," Livingstone said, and turned away, leaving himself with one more sin to repent of.

Across the room Baxter Stern stood silent, tugging at his chin. He made a half-glance toward the Senators and the information coordinator walked over to them. He said, "They have Harrison Crawley, his wife, and his granddaughter. Possibly others. We don't know how many terrorists there actually are, and from what groups. They seem to be from different factions."

"Where are they?" Thornbull demanded.

"They're in the top of the Washington Monument," the coordinator said. Ginny Longstreet, looking to the display table, saw the ferretlike model-builder raise an eighteen-inch white spire above the plastic trees of a carpet park.

Livingstone broke the silence. "What do they want?"

"So far we've only received a single note. It demands that a twenty-thousand-watt public address system be set up before the monument and aimed toward the White House. Apparently they want to force Harrison Crawley to read a statement. Then they say the President will be required to make admissions on national television. That's all they've indicated so far."

"What can we do?" Osgood said quietly.

"We have an operative there," the coordinator said. "He is trained in minute observation, and . . ."

But John Livingstone ceased to hear the rest of the conversation from the moment he looked across the room and met Baxter Stern's lost, frightened eyes.

CHAPTER 2

Stern!

What you fear most has happened. The people you have oppressed have united. Now you must answer for your crimes and the crimes of the sham government you control. A public address system (20,000 watts) will be placed before this monument to monarchy and will be directed toward the White Palace. You must also make admissions to the entire country, over the airwaves you controlled to spread lies. We are willing to die, as our brothers and sisters have died—by your hand—before us. The difference now is that we are ready to kill.

C.O.R.
Coalition of Retribution

Beneath the carefully typewritten message, a quivering hand had written "For God's sake" three times, one below the other. The letters expanded and distorted with each repetition, but the vague shape of the characters matched a sample of the handwriting of Harrison Crawley.

He read the note a final time, folded it, and stuck it into his back pocket. "Wait. That's the original," Dooley said. "Shouldn't you leave that here?"

"No," Kidd said quietly, without turning from the monument.

The two had arrived at the police cordon at exactly the same time, and together they had questioned every witness—the tourists who had been expelled when the terrorists had taken charge and the monument guards, young, unarmed federal park rangers, who had been held, then released with the typed message. Taking the original note back into the scene was against procedures, and Dooley would have argued. But Kidd was entranced. Somehow Dooley feared breaking that trance more than he feared anything else.

"Good luck," Dooley said numbly, to deaf ears.

Kidd took off his jacket, exposing a white short-sleeve shirt, adorned with a too-thin polyester necktie. He reached into his side pants pockets and pulled out the inner lining, and as he started walking toward the entrance of the monument, the inverted linings stuck out and waved at his hips, small white flags of truce.

A hundred yards of pavement and grass lay between the barricades and the monument. He walked with his arms straight overhead, his fingers spoked out, like a man reaching for a ladder from heaven. His unnaturally stiff stride was not an affectation; Dooley, through his field glasses, could see the fingertips vibrating. "Mixload," Dooley said to the plainclothes agent standing at his shoulder, and the agent pumped four slugs and two cartridges of double-ought buck into the shotgun he held concealed at the barrier. The slugs, single lead projectiles, would be safest in the confines of the monument, especially with hostages present. And if after firing four of those there was still danger, then there was the buckshot.

Thirty feet from the entrance, which was sharply shadowed in the afternoon sunshine, Kidd heard a surprised male voice shout, "Somebody's coming!" A crunch of amplified static echoed from the concrete chamber, and then the voice shouted again, "A man is coming! A *man is coming!*" The barrel of a machine gun jerked around the edge of the doorway and the voice, harsh with fear, said, "Stop!"

He halted with his face five feet from the quivering muzzle hole. Behind the barrel he saw the face of a Black man, eyes wide and smeared in red behind rimless spectacles. Kidd, his bare arms still stiff over his head, said very slowly, "Do you understand English?"

The stunned gunman, who had grown up in Detroit, said, "What? Wh—Of course!" And then, thrusting the gun out farther so he could hold it with one hand, he fumbled at the walkie-talkie at his belt and said, "Hello! Hello!"

"I came to talk to your leaders."

"Hello?! What?" crackled over the walkie-talkie. It seemed to be a woman's voice.

"Wait! There is a man . . ." the sentry said, without remembering the talk button on his radio, and then pressed it to repeat himself, cutting off an incoming message. Abandoning the walkie-talkie, he shouted, "Who are you?"

"Browne. With an 'e.' Martin Thomas Browne. My identification is in my shirt pocket. Please check it. If you want." He stepped forward and the sentry jumped back; the automatic gun danced in the air. "Please," Kidd said, stopping dead still and keeping his arms stretched. "The safety is off on your weapon. Please. Don't shoot me by accident. Please. I came to talk about your demands."

The sentry, his attention called to the potency of his gun, grew less frantic. He seemed to focus on the man before him for the first time—the long bare arms, the too-big shirt collar that made the neck look weak, the liners poking from the pants pockets, the horn-rim glasses.

"Do you accept our conditions?" the Black sentry said coldly. He even smiled.

"Yes. Part of them."

The smile drained away like water below pond ice. The sentry raised his radio. This time he got it to work.

When the elevator door opened the sentry had Kidd facing the wall, his palms reached flat against the concrete, his feet spread. *He's been arrested before,* Kidd thought.

A woman's voice, forced and thin, said, "Tie him. Blindfold him!" There was a shuffle of guns changing hands and then the sentry seized Kidd's arms and strapped them with tape. He threw a bandana around Kidd's face and tied it tight, but when he spun Kidd around he saw the blindfold had caught on a corner of the glasses. "His glasses, Charlie!" the woman said, and the sentry snatched the horn-rims off, tossed them on the floor, and frantically retied the bandana.

But Kidd had glimpsed the face of the woman, standing with the sentry's machine pistol held on him.

Blind now, he felt a shove toward the elevator, and resisted. "My glasses," he said, and was frightened by the confidence which creeped so strangely into his voice. "I need them, I don't see properly without them," he said, and then feared he sounded too mousy.

There was a hesitation. Then he felt the glasses stuffed into his shirt pocket—by the woman, he thought. From a light push he staggered into the elevator, and heard the door close.

There was only one person breathing beside him on the way to the top, and that person, he knew, was Roxanne Lark.

Roxanne Lark. Twenty-six years old. *Summa cum laude* graduate of Oberlin. Daughter of an automobile executive and alcoholic mother. Married . . . somebody Uno . . . *Nate* Uno —gifted, Black, one of the founders of the Communist League of America. She was with Uno on the day he died, at a demonstration that turned into a gun battle between the C.L.A. and members of the Ku Klux Klan. Roxanne was later shunned by the Communist League for publicly advocating terrorism.

When he had seen her file, something about Roxanne Lark had reminded Kidd of Linda.

The elevator stopped, the door opened, feet shuffled. In the darkness behind his blindfold he heard the pounding of his own heart. He also thought he heard crying. Someone shoved him into a chair. Male fingers, clumsy with nerves, took off his blindfold.

The observation room of the monument was a square doughnut around the elevator shaft. He was seated in the center of one of the square's sides, the elevator door to his left, the auxiliary stairs in front and to his right. Several feet before him were two stools, one with a battery-operated television perched on it, the other supporting a knapsack. Just around the corner to his left he could see Harrison Crawley and his wife Margaret, sitting with their backs against the outer wall. Between them was Dabny. Mrs. Crawley pressed the girl's head to her bosom with one hand, and with the other gripped her granddaughter's fingers in a handkerchief. It was Mrs. Crawley, not Dabny, who was crying. The barrel of a machine gun pointed down toward Harrison Crawley's chest; whoever was holding it stood around the corner against the inner wall, out of Kidd's view. Roxanne Lark, pale, eyelids flickering around her blue irises, stood in front of the stools with a heavy pistol, a Magnum, in her right hand. The man who had taken off his blindfold remained behind him, silent.

"Well?" Roxanne Lark said.

Kidd sat motionless, pale.

"Free his hands," Roxanne ordered. When nothing happened she looked over Kidd's head. "He is an emissary! We will treat him like one!" She spoke with a forced stiffness, as if her authority depended on her righteousness, and Kidd thought, *Has Roxanne formed her "Coalition" with people from causes entirely different from her own?*

A knife glided through the tape around Kidd's wrists, and he heard a single step behind him, backing away again.

"Do you need food?" Kidd said, and the quake in his voice was real.

"We have our own," Roxanne Lark snapped.

"Do you need medical attention?"

"No!" she shouted, but then her eyes darted to her hostages against the far wall. "We need only to have our demands met! Are you ready to agree?"

Very slowly Kidd reached toward his pocket, but though his

hand moved as through water, Roxanne's pistol jerked toward his face. With her action the person guarding the Crawleys sprang halfway around the corner, then back again. It was a girl, dark-skinned. An Iranian, or an Arab; he got only a glimpse. Did she belong with the man behind him, the one with the knife? Was the guard at the monument entrance Roxanne's lover? "My glasses. My glasses," Kidd said.

"All right!" Roxanne yelled.

He put on his glasses and said, "Please. Bind my hands again."

"What?! Why?!"

"Please bind them," he said, holding his wrists together and pushing his trembling hands out toward her. "Please. I don't want to be shot. I think you are very nervous. Please. I don't want to be killed by accident. I did not come to harm you. I came to talk."

She lowered the pistol, posturing as if to show Kidd—or the others in the room—that she was fully in control of the situation and herself. "Will you meet our demands?"

When he hesitated she said, "We will kill them. Don't doubt that we will." Crawley's wife sobbed louder, and Crawley reached and squeezed her shoulder.

"I came to discuss your demands with you," Kidd said, and reached again to his pocket. Roxanne's palm squirmed on the butt of her pistol. Very slowly he withdrew the paper and unfolded it. He adjusted his glasses as if to read, just as Roxanne snatched the page from his hands.

She took a step back from Kidd and her eyes went wild.

He had been sure that showing them the original note would tell him something. Roxanne Lark had spent hours and days choosing each word, had typed the note with fastidious care, because she was an intellectual, she believed in rhetoric and took it seriously. The evidence now that her note, her words of liberation, had not gotten to the throne of power, had not gotten past even the police barricades, rocked her. She had a minutely organized plan and was not prepared to cope with the unexpected, such as the poor functioning of the walkie-talkies within the concrete and steel building, or with the idea that some bureaucrat would come as an intermediary, as if this was a petty crime instead of a revolutionary act.

The confirmation of one hunch of Kidd's somehow confirmed for him another: that Roxanne had enlisted the aid of comrades with whom she shared fanaticism alone. She depended upon the force of her intellect to control them. Kidd said, "I telephoned the police with your demands."

"The police?! This was for the President of the United States!"

"Yes. We can do that. But I thought we could already meet your first demand. Set up the P.A. system. But you must tell me what you plan to say."

"That is impossible!" Roxanne Lark said, and from the corner of his eye Kidd saw the young woman with the machine pistol again step around the corner, to glance over Kidd's shoulder at the man with the knife. What were they thinking, if Roxanne's plan was not working as she had promised it would?

Kidd said, "We need to know who will talk, and what they will say. Both on television and on the monument lawn."

Roxanne leaned her face to Kidd and shouted, "No! I will tell you nothing! I will give you the statement the President is to read over the networks! I have a television here to monitor, to see that he does it. Then we will speak from the lawn. Then we will have a plane fly us to . . . our destination, and then the hostages will be released. Otherwise they will die! All of them!"

In a very quiet voice Kidd began, "We only need to know—"

But Roxanne reached out, snatched his collar, and tugged; he stood, impotently. "Listen!" she screamed. "Listen! We don't have much time! These people will be dead people! Listen to me! Just look!" She snatched up from the stool holding the knapsack a folded piece of heavy paper, and crammed it into Kidd's hand. He stood motionless, then unfolded the paper.

At first he could not tell what it was; it looked like nothing he had ever seen. It was two inches long, white, a slender cylinder. Blood blossomed on the paper around the severed end. It was a finger.

When Kidd looked up, it was to the little girl who still refused to cry out. But her grandmother wailed.

And Roxanne Lark, who could have killed the girl, who could have killed them all by putting her pistol into their mouths, but who could have never sliced away the finger of a child, dead or alive, screamed, "You have to do exactly as I say!"

Kidd dropped the finger, sagged against the stool that held the knapsack, and put a hand to his mouth. Roxanne screamed something else at him that he did not hear. He staggered and bumped the other stool; the television broke on the floor. Roxanne jumped closer, shrieking, gaping down at the television. Everyone else in the room froze.

Maybe it was then, at the moment he instinctively bumped the television; maybe it was at the moment he saw the finger. Or maybe it was something in him, something that stretched from those moments to the past beyond his birth, which leaped from the depths and swept away all other identities, not only the recently assumed character of Martin Browne but the other, older, yet still false personae by which Jeff Kidd had always known himself, that knowledge tainted only by the faintest whisper of suspicion that he might be what he became at that moment.

He drove his knee into Roxanne Lark's stomach, twisted the Magnum from her cracking fingers, and whirled.

Against the consoles they had gathered, cold and sweating like melting drifts of snow. No one had spoken since the communications supervisor had pressed the headset against his ear and said, "All right. He's going in." Now the President, wearing a headset of his own, stood beside the supervisor, and behind them, tactically deaf, were the two Senators, Thornbull and Osgood. Behind the Senators stood John Livingstone and Virginia Longstreet. The only person who had not drawn up to the consoles was the Repliclerk, who stood over the silent table, jammed now with one-inch wooden police cars, ambulances, S.W.A.T. trucks, and pools of plastic markers and cardboard arrows showing the placement and proximity, in distance and time, of troops; and though he stood motionless, and his eyes behind their orange-tinted spectacles did not shift from the table, his hearing too seemed trained on the supervisor. The tips of his fingers were poised on the tabletop, as he waited for the words that would bring his model to life.

"Shots!"

Everyone looked at the supervisor. He said again, "Reporting . . . *shots!*"

The President gawked at the supervisor as if he had not heard the same report—"*Shots from the tower*"—shouted clearly into his own headphones.

They crowded closer then, feeling the heat from each other's bodies. The four without headphones froze in the murmur that poured in an unintelligible stream from the earpieces of the others, the deathly near-silence lasting so long that each of them felt the mad urge to scream.

Dooley, standing at the barrier beneath the trees, heard the first of the muffled pops that echoed from the spire, and jerked his face upward. The sound was smothered. The area surrounding the monument was quiet enough for him to hear the hiss of traffic from the nearby streets and Beltway, and Dooley wanted desperately to believe the noise was only a backfire. But in another instant the sound came down twice more.

Kneeling next to him were two Big Ears—technicians listening through hand-held audio dishes which they pointed toward the monument's mouth and summit. The dishes could pick up a quarterback's huddle instructions in the center of a stadium full of cheering people, could in fact hear a whisper at 300 yards, and when Dooley whirled to the Big Ears, they both looked up and said simultaneously, "Pistol shots!"

Because the observation windows at the top of the monument offered a 360-degree view of the knoll, they had scattered their S.W.A.T. teams about in plain clothes, and they were not yet prepared for a combined assault. Dooley, closer to the monument than anyone else, snatched the shotgun from the agent next to him and rushed the entrance.

Collier, stationed beside the communications truck, was appalled. His reflex was to order his men to hold, to be sure their attack was fully coordinated. But seeing Dooley sprinting to the monument door, he shouted to his squads, "Secure the entrance!"

Dooley broke from the fading daylight into the shadowed entrance, leveling the shotgun at nothing. He pressed his back against one wall, edged his way deeper into the entrance, then leaped, swinging the barrel from side to side but finding no target. The assaulting agents gathered at the door and fanned in behind him.

The base of the monument, like the summit, consisted of a corridor ringing the elevator shaft; Dooley made his way around the first corner and still found no guard. He inched his way along the inner wall, wildly reminding himself of the mixload. *Aim for the belly*, he thought.

When he had almost reached the corner, he heard a shuffle of steps, moving away. Knowing the S.W.A.T. agents would be converging from the other side, he sprang around the corner, leveling the shotgun.

Charlie, the muscular Black who had first accosted Kidd as he entered the monument, was just whirling, firing a burst toward the men coming from the other side. He swung back, toward Dooley. His eyes, impossibly wide already, bulged even further when he saw the shotgun, and as the machine pistol jerked upward Dooley caught him with two slugs. The second severed his spine.

Dooley dropped to one knee, aiming toward the top half of the body as one of the S.W.A.T. men jumped forward and kicked the machine pistol away.

Dooley and ten other agents climbed the stairs, not wanting to risk the elevator. When they were almost to the top, Dooley shouted, "Browne?!"

Kidd's voice came back, "It's clear."

When they reached the landing, they found the Crawleys huddled in a corner. Harrison Crawley held Margaret Crawley, and Margaret held Dabny. Of the three, only Mrs. Crawley was hysterical; her face was pressed against the wall, and still she kept shuffling her feet, as if to get farther away from the girl with the machine pistol crumpled on the floor beside them.

One of the agents stepped on the wrist of the young Arab who still held the knife. The precaution was reflexive; the Arab's sternum was shattered open.

Kidd was on his knees, throwing up.

Roxanne Lark was squatted beside the elevator. Were it not for the smear trailing down the wall, it would have seemed that she had simply sat down, in the attitude of a siesta. Dooley bent to look at the lowered face. He rose quickly.

The White House Crisis Room supervisor ducked his head, grabbing and pressing both earpiece bulbs, and said without breath, "Repeat . . . ?" He twisted around on the others and shouted, "Safe! All safe!"

At some point during the shouting celebration which followed, Ginny's gaze fell on the modelmaker's meticulous, stillborn city. Later Ginny would recall that moment as the first hint of a premonition that she was somehow more intimately involved with what was happening than she was able rationally to know. But in the moment itself, her impression was much more immediate than her later recollection would suggest, for as she stood there, glancing to the Repliclerk, still motionless as before but now lifeless as a switched-off lamp, and then back to his city, she saw the scene he had made and felt it garish. Without flesh. Without pain. Without blood.

CHAPTER 3

The ambulances sang through the falling twilight, their flashing red lights vivid against the graying sky. Collier held Kidd's arm, supporting him as they staggered toward the open rear door of the ambulance backed up to the monument entrance.

He sat Kidd down and stood in the back door, shielding Kidd from lights, noise, and telephoto lenses.

The front of Kidd's shirt was yellow and sticky with vomit, his once-shiny polyester tie now dull and wet. His eyes were lifeless, gray as the sky, gray like his skin. His face, his bare wrists, were spattered in blood, real blood, which to Collier, who had seen gouts of blood before, seemed somehow unreal.

"Is he hit?" the doctor said, thinking from Kidd's appearance that the original report might have been wrong.

"No," Collier said. "But take him to the hospital anyway." Pushing Kidd's legs within the compartment, he stared once more at Kidd's face, then turned and yelled, "Jacklin! Get in here. Ride with him. Stay with him."

Kidd rode toward the hospital. There was not a scratch on him, but he did not resist when they had him lie down. He did not speak, and to the doctor and agent riding with him, he seemed neither to see nor hear. Like a man exposed to some great light and noise, he was deadened to all else.

But the flash and boom were still with him, still vivid behind the opacity of his eyes.

He saw Roxanne Lark falling back as his knee hit her, saw the Arab with the knife leaping forward, saw the flash between himself and the Arab and saw the body go hurtling back. Roxanne had screamed, the Arab girl guarding the Crawleys had jumped once again toward the corner and then hesitated. Her head was twisted so she could see him, her torso angled toward the people she was ordered to guard. In panic she started to spin, as the shot caught her. Her body fell across Mrs. Crawley.

There was never any panic on Roxanne Lark's face. Blood ran from her mouth but her eyes were placid, either dumb from the blow or from acceptance of fate, Kidd would never know. But as he whirled back to her she was twisting at the detonator she had pulled from the knapsack.

Kidd's memory stopped there.

CHAPTER 4

Ginny's new office was the same size as her old one; space in the White House's lower floors was precious. But everything else was richer—the desk, chairs, lamps, carpet, and even the cream color of the walls. The stack of newspapers now came to her complete, all forty at once, and this morning every headline referred to what had happened the day before at the Washington Monument. Some read: "FOUR TERRORISTS DIE; CRAWLEYS SAFE." One of the more sensational ones screamed: "SHOOT-OUT!"

The writers of some of the stories, especially those which appeared in the later West Coast editions, had learned of the amputation of Dabny Crawley's finger, and the tone of these reports was more heated, bearing banners like: "DEATH SQUAD FINDS DEATH—THEIR OWN." And one headline said, "FINALLY WE FIGHT BACK."

Ginny had arrived at her office early and had almost gotten through the whole stack of papers when a messenger dropped off a folder. Inside was a thirty-page report, with a note clipped to it: "Ginny—Read your papers first. Then read this. Then come see me. J.L."

The report, compiled overnight, was crisp and careful. The first of its three sections was a rundown on the formation, organization, and procedures of Operation Counterstrike.

The second section was drawn from accounts of the Crawleys, mainly Harrison, on what had happened. The attempt of the document's authors to set out only the basic facts of such a heated incident made this section seem to Ginny especially cold. It began with Dabny's kidnapping and ended with the Crawleys' arrival at the hospital. With wide, accelerating eyes Ginny read the details that no one in the Counterstrike control room had known the night before. How Roxanne Lark

had been Dabny Crawley's kindergarten teacher. How the terrorists insisted that Harrison Crawley sign their demand note,
and when he had refused to cooperate in any way, how one of
them ("Arab Male," the report called him; "that awful Arab
boy" was what Mrs. Crawley said) had sliced off Dabny's right
index finger without threat or warning, not only to their horror
but also, as Harrison Crawley reflected later, to the shock of
"Caucasian Female—Lark." How the Negotiator had arrived,
how he had acted; how he had shot first Arab Male holding
the knife; and then all the Crawleys had ducked, closing their
eyes until, after two more shots, they would see both Arab Female and Caucasian Female—Lark lying dead.

Section Three contained information from the debriefing of
the officer who went in as the negotiator. Browne—the report
never identified him in any other way—unrolled a series of ob-
servations and intuitions, and Ginny, her mind already awash
in visions of the scene, began to feel the events as personal experience. The Coalition of Retribution was not listed in any
intelligence files, Browne reported, and therefore it was most
likely a group just formed. The group had a meticulous plan,
but they made amateurish blunders; their walkie-talkies, for example, did not operate well within the monument. The recognition of Roxanne Lark, whose file he knew, gave him "an indication of the disposition of the group." But the presence of
the Arabs suggested a complex arrangement, and Brown told
his debriefers of the spot hypothesis he had formed: that in a
sudden crisis, the terrorists, divided in their loyalties, might
hesitate.

The most chilling statement Ginny found in the whole report was the one from Browne that after he saw the severed
finger, he was "no longer thought-sorting."

"Browne reports no anticipation of disarming," the authors
of the brief went on to say; but when he had the gun he apparently thought clearly. Once he shot the Arab male, the
Arab female froze . . .

She reread the entire report. She read Section Three for a
third time. She stared at the wall for several minutes, her eyes

unfocused. Then she got up and walked upstairs to John Livingstone's office.

Livingstone's collar was open, the tie loosened and wrinkled. He was hunched over his elbows, staring intently at the walnut desk top, and he looked up only after Ginny had closed the door and sat down. He leaned back, feet on his desk, hands clasped behind his head, and said, "The President wants to make a speech announcing the success of his new program to fight terrorism while he hands out medals."

"Medals?"

"Yes. To that officer, Browne. And the head of Operation Counterstrike. He even wants to give one to Dabny Crawley."

After a pause Ginny said, "I think that's a terrible idea."

"So do I. But tell me your reasons. I need to hear them."

"There's so much wrong with it, I don't know where to start. This administration has been criticized as short on action. Now something has actually happened as a result of a program the President started. That speaks for itself. Doesn't it?"

Livingstone stared up at the ceiling. "Osgood and Thornbull are already claiming credit. They're talking about being at the O.C. control room when it happened, and letting the press *deduce* that their presence was more than chance."

Ginny sat very still, staring at Livingstone. Livingstone looked at her, looked away, and lowered his feet to the floor, sitting upright. He said, "Okay. He's been under enormous pressure. *Of course* he's under enormous pressure, that comes with being President, it's part of the definition of the job. But we do have to remember he's a man."

"Yes. Right," Ginny said slowly. "And the approval ratings are lower than they've ever been. But standing up and claiming credit is sort of . . ."

"Yes. It is cheap." Livingstone looked away again and said, "Give me some other reasons."

"Well, I'm not sure what the President wants to use a speech to say. If it's to declare some kind of victory over terrorism, I'd say that's a bit premature. Tomorrow, or next week, we could have another incident that could turn out just the other way around. And people died in this incident. They may have deserved it, but they died. Four young crazy people, and now they're dead and it's just not . . . I don't see the President making a celebration over it."

"Yes. That's what I told the President myself."

"And?"

"I don't know. He says he isn't sure. He may still want to make a speech."

Ginny watched Livingstone carefully. "I'll tell you something else, John," she finally said. "Those reasons I just gave you for not making this a media event may be the most obvious, but they're not the best."

"So what's the best reason?"

"The agent, Browne . . . By the way, the report says that's his code name. They want to keep him anonymous, right?"

"Right. For his own protection, I guess, and so he can remain active in the program. Which is another reason to stay away from a public display. But go on, tell me the best one."

"Browne was never supposed to take that gun and start shooting. The report refers to it as an 'improvisation.' It's easy to miss it, but the fact is, none of the procedures of Operation Counterstrike called for that."

As she said this, Livingstone had not taken his eyes off her. "You're right. Again," he said. "And that's the key. Did you notice, reading it, how Browne seemed shaken by what had happened? He was cool under the circumstances, very objective, and then he saw that finger and something just happened to him, and you can't tell me that a man who felt that way wouldn't also feel something about the fact that he killed a woman precisely because she hesitated. You're right. Whoever wrote that report didn't want to come out and say, 'Browne went beyond his orders,' but that's what happened."

Livingstone rose and began to pace in loping steps across the carpet. "A man disobeys orders at a moment when orders don't matter. And now, is the President going to stand up and take credit for the orders?"

After a moment when neither spoke, Ginny said, "A private

reception, at the White House. Stern can give Browne a deco-
ration. He can make a simple statement about how happy the
nation is to have its citizens safe this time."

"Can you write something?"

"Yes. Of course."

CHAPTER 5

Senator Thornbull stood beside his wife beneath a Persian
chandelier, whose thousands of dangling facets caught and
multiplied the brilliance of the polished ballroom floor and the
colors moving across it. Diplomats, Congressmen, media lu-
minaries, and assorted spouses swirled past, and Thornbull
greeted everyone by name if he knew it and with a loud
"Hello!" if he did not. His wife kept the same smile throughout, her only greeting a nod of the head.

Senator Osgood entered the ballroom with his wife, Dot.
"Munson!" Thornbull bellowed, and barreled across the room.
They greeted each other as long-lost friends. It had been forty-
eight hours since they stood on the steps of the White House
with the President, announcing the safety of the Crawleys.
Now they felt like hosts of the evening's party.

There were over a hundred people gathered in the White
House East Room, not including the waiters, mingling with
trays of hors d'oeuvres and drinks, the security men, and the
musicians who played softly on a corner stage. For the last day
and a half, Forbis had called Livingstone repeatedly with questions that always worked out the same: "The head of the
House Ways and Means Committee wants to know why he
hasn't gotten his invitation yet. What do I tell him?" A half-
hour later Forbis was on the line again. "Ambassadors from
fifteen countries have already called about the gala," Forbis
would say, as Livingstone thought, *Gala—it's already become
that.* "How can I refuse them?" UN representatives asked if

they could fly down, and heads of state, even from some nations known for their tolerance of terrorists, sent regards.

Livingstone had not been completely candid with Ginny during their meeting the day before. It was Forbis, not the President, who felt strongly that the ceremony should be a big event. Livingstone had swayed the President to his—and Ginny's—theory. But still Forbis, by manipulating the guest list and then the arrangements, had shaped the event to his own vision.

Along one wall stretched tables draped in linen, bearing hundreds of individual slices of cherry pie, deep crimson against the white cloths. Opposite the tables rose a blue-skirted dais, bedecked by flags surrounding a podium bearing the presidential seal. Beside the dais was a massive display of flowers, sent to the White House by a Texas businessman (and supporter of Stern's campaign); the central feature of the arrangement was a white-carnation replica of the Washington Monument, eight feet high.

Because the plans for the ceremony had kept changing, Ginny Longstreet had been busy all day long with various drafts for the President's address. At Livingstone's pleading, the President had rejected the idea of a major address, to Ginny's great relief; the efforts of the others to embellish the incident seemed as hollow as her own. At last the President had asked her to write "just a handful of sentences" for the gathering.

From her cubicle in the basement she called the Oval Office, and Mrs. Kerley told her the President had asked that she bring the draft to his study. Ginny hurried upstairs, threaded her way through the corridors, was admitted by a guard into another stairway, and felt the same hushed feeling, the need to tiptoe, that she always experienced when entering the presidential living quarters. She had been to the President's private study three times before, always for meetings which included Livingstone, and had noticed that even Livingstone fell quiet when within Stern's haunts.

She knocked on the door, entered when she heard, "Come

in!" and found Livingstone there with Stern. Both men wore tuxedoes and were smoking pipes. She handed the typewritten, all caps, double-spaced sheet to the President, who began immediately to read it.

Livingstone glanced at her, then said abruptly, "Why aren't you dressed?"

"This is perfect," Stern said, not looking up from the text.

Ginny nodded to the President, who still did not raise his eyes, and she said to Livingstone, "I haven't had time yet."

"Where's your dress?" the President said. "We can't have the most beautiful woman in Washington, and the *only* beautiful woman in this administration, not there tonight." He frowned at her. "I go on in fifteen minutes."

Ginny hurried back down to her office and grabbed the bag hanging behind the door. She had known she must attend the ceremony—in the last months she had become a fixture at White House functions—but all day she had occupied herself with other thoughts. Now, suddenly, she was rushing madly.

She dashed across the hall to the lounge, where there was a dressing area and shower. She pinned her hair back, showered and dried quickly, withdrew the clothes and accessories from her bag. She put on the beige blouse—long-sleeved, lace, pinched at the waist, square at the shoulders—and the matching skirt, with high heels. It was a simple outfit, but elegant enough for any occasion. Brushing out her hair, she pinned it back again loosely behind her neck. She snatched up the velvet choker, secured it around her throat, and stopped as she saw herself in the mirror. The choker was green, the color of her eyes; it was the first time she had ever worn it, the first vanity she had knowingly allowed herself.

Snapping back to action, she touched up her makeup, curled on lipstick, even daubed the back of her neck with perfume. Then, gathering everything back into the bag, she tossed it into her office and hurried upstairs, poking at the strands of hair which kept slipping from the clasp behind her neck.

She almost ran into Livingstone at the interior entrance to the East Room. "My," he said.

"What are you . . . why aren't you with the President?" she said.

"He and Mr. Forbis gathered the delegation in the Oval Office. I thought I'd come watch the show from the house seats." They looked down the hall, saw a pair of Secret Service agents at the head of a large procession, and went into the ballroom together.

Ginny and Livingstone had just taken a position in the center of the room, fifteen feet from the low platform, when a sonorous voice from somewhere boomed, "Ladies and gentlemen, the President of the United States!" Every eye turned toward the door and the orchestra struck up "Hail to the Chief." As President Stern marched in at the head of a string of men, Boaz Thornbull was the first to applaud, his huge hands flapping together like loose shutters in the wind.

The procession mounted and strung out across the dais, then faced the crowd and the applause. Ginny stood at John Livingstone's shoulder and filled her mind with wondering if what she had written would be right.

The President stepped to the podium. Looking smaller behind the big blue seal, he said, "Ladies and gentlemen. Before I make a statement I'd like to introduce to you Mr. Walter Collier, who is the director of Operation Counterstrike, our intelligence division responsible for the freeing of the hostages two days ago. Walter . . ."

Collier stepped up to the microphone and with great effort said, "Thank you, sir. Uh . . . the President has asked me to just explain briefly what uh . . . procedures were being followed during, uh, the incident . . ."

The incident. Ginny glanced up at Collier, whom she had never seen before. He looked so ill at ease, not dashing like a spy or even dumpy in the colorful spymaster way of novels; just plain normal, and yet a man in charge of an important job for the President of the United States. That was comfort to Ginny Longstreet, the firsthand experience of flesh-and-blood people being the participants in the melodramas of history; it was that experience that had always inspired her, she believed, had always sharpened her and shoved her to keep her speeches straightforward. *I've been out of touch,* she thought. *All day long I've been writing speeches about this big event, and I haven't even seen the man who . . .*

She pulled her eyes up and across the platform.

The recognition rushed up to her as the surface of the water comes at a cliff diver—a weightless, accelerating fall until the full shock hit her. She recoiled, physically jerking away.

Livingstone felt her convulsion and turned to look at her. She was so white he grabbed her hand, saying, "My God, are you all right?" The green eyes, hard, glistening, did not move. He followed their gaze to the man standing twenty feet away from them on the dais. Livingstone looked back at her and said, "Ginny?"

At the podium Collier was saying, ". . . was the very last contingency covered in our, uh, general training. We had made allowances that if opportunities should arise at the actual scene for the defusing of the situation, the agent could, at, uh, his discretion . . ." But Ginny heard none of it. She stood motionless as Collier stepped back to his place in line and the President stepped forward.

Her eyes were still fixed on Kidd when the President's voice, like a memory, sounded somewhere, saying the words she had written: "There are many times when I, as President, realize that courage is called for in the decisions of peace, in the millions of decisions made each day in this country when Americans affirm their essential faith in our government and in each other by living their lives as fully as possible while respecting the freedom and integrity of others to do the same. And yet there are times when individuals or groups arise who do not respect this ideal, this sense of decency and freedom, and who would, with raw force and terror, try to compel us on a path of their choosing, and not ours. And then we are reminded once again that to protect the liberty in which we put our common faith, we must risk not merely prestige, or even principle, but sometimes life itself. Today, we . . ."

As the President spoke, Jeff Kidd looked up at his back. He squinted, as if to focus the rush before him into something comprehensible, and he glanced back down. But in that glance he had caught something peripherally, the unnatural, white-faced stare he was getting from someone before the dais, and his eyes flicked up again, and back down.

And then his head came up, his eyes opening, narrowing, widening again. His lips parted; his jaw froze.

The President was saying, ". . . anonymity, for security reasons. But we believe that, though his name must go unrecognized, his courage must not." Applause swept the room.

Kidd saw the people on and around the dais clapping—all except Ginny Longstreet, who stood at John Livingstone's shoulder; and Livingstone himself had begun applauding and then had stopped, taking her arm again.

And to Livingstone, Kidd seemed not to realize that the applause was for him; he kept staring at Ginny Longstreet's eyes.

Kidd looked at last at the President, and moved slowly forward, walking like a man whose legs are asleep. The President shook his hand and grinned, used to dazed expressions upon people receiving presidential honors. Smothering the last of the applause, Stern said, without notes, "We're proud of you. Of course, more . . . we're grateful. The Congress, the Congress is voting on a special honor for you, but today, I'd like to give you this, this medal, as the highest honor that the Chief Executive can bestow. Thank you."

Kidd glanced down at the gleaming disk in the open box the President had put into his hand. The President stepped back from the podium and left him alone there, as the applause and even cheering built in the hall. Kidd stared dumbly at the crowd and turned around and walked back to his place in the line.

There was some confusion on the dais, as no one seemed to know what to do next. Then Forbis whispered in the President's ear, "Sir, I think they want to ask questions."

With that Stern stepped back up to the podium and said, "Uh . . . I know many of you would like to know the, uh, some of the, uh, details of the incident and of, uh, the agent. He . . . we won't have any more speeches tonight, but, uh, he will have a press conference tomorrow. Tonight is just for his honor, and, uh, for you to meet him."

Kidd was looking toward her again, but he was borne away, carried in a press of people who did not seem to want to hear anything from him, just to touch him, squeeze his hand, tell him, some with tears of emotion, how they had felt when they first heard the news of the captives' liberation, how their sense of self-identity was changed. Kidd drifted; at that moment he seemed without will.

Ginny stood still and stared at the floor. Livingstone watched the scene around Kidd, throughout the entire hall, and then turned to her and said, very gently, "Ginny, who is he? A friend?" He saw the question seep into her, he saw the confusion float across her face. "I see." He took her hand and walked with her to the edge of the room, out of the swirl.

Kidd stood in front of the flower arrangement of the Washington Monument, as the same surge of people who had borne him there like a log in water now flowed past. They grasped at his hand, which, to the surprise of all and the thrill of some, was noticeably cold; and they spoke in pronouncements. *"Très, très bien!"* the French ambassador said, actually clicking his heels and making a sharp half bow as he spoke, as his wife pinched Kidd's palm with her straight, tanned fingers and nodded her head slowly.

And, "The Prime Minister sends the congratulations of the people of Great Britain, and pledges our shared resolve against terrorism," the diplomat who followed her intoned.

Kidd's head would nod as they spoke, but was out of rhythm, and his eyes stared, seeing only another pair of eyes, green as stone.

She remained with Livingstone, across the room, where the President had joined them. At all functions involving the international community there was an unapproachability about the President, because of the significance attached to the smallest expression or gesture in the game of diplomacy. Therefore at public functions Livingstone served not only as a companion to the President but also as a buffer. Now Livingstone had his ear inclined to Stern, as the President whispered something about the French ambassador's wife. But Livingstone's mind was on Ginny. She was visibly trembling.

The orchestra began to play. Stern lifted his chin and smiled. To Livingstone he said, "Well, we'd better not let Thornbull and Osgood take all the credit." Thornbull and Osgood were at that moment standing in front of Kidd, and the White House photographer, the only one in the room allowed to have a camera, was discreetly snapping pictures from across the room, using a telephoto lens; Osgood had asked for the shots himself. Stern walked toward the group.

Livingstone turned, looked at Ginny for a moment, and then followed the President.

Ginny stood motionless in the center of the room, as couples began to dance around her. She glanced about, discovering she was alone. She followed Livingstone.

"Tell me something," Thornbull was saying to Kidd, in a low, conspiratorial voice. "That was a forty-five Magnum you used, wasn't it? Do you think it's as good as a nine-millimeter?" Kidd's eyes turned slowly toward him, and Thornbull went on, "See, the military is changing over, but I'm not sure the forty-five isn't the best damn thing for stopping power you can have. And when it gets down to the nut-cuttin', stopping power is . . ."

But the Senator did not finish. He heard Osgood say, "Hello, Mr. President!" and turned quickly from Kidd to smile at Stern. Then, in the choreography of protocol, the two Senators stepped back, leaving Stern squinting up at Kidd.

"I hope this hasn't turned into another trial for you, Jeff," Stern said. It was the first time all night anyone had used Kidd's name; Livingstone froze, then looked around to be sure that no one else had heard. "We didn't want this to get so big, but it had to. But, uh, it doesn't have to be all stiff. You're not on display. I wanted it to be a kind of . . ." Stern wanted to say "celebration," but Livingstone had warned him against that word. "Well, just more comfortable," Stern said.

At a loss for anything else to say, Stern looked around. "Uh, did you meet John Livingstone? My, uh, right arm!"

Livingstone shook Kidd's hand.

"And this," Stern said, "this is my voice. Virginia Long-street."

She had been standing not five feet away, but, unlike when they were a room apart, they had not looked at each other, had kept their faces turned away. Now, as Stern touched her elbow and pushed her forward, they were suddenly eye to eye.

And again, as it had been before, it was Ginny Longstreet who had a strength or a resolve or a new energy or whatever it was and moved first, holding out her slim white hand and saying, "Hello, Mr. Kidd. How are you?"

Stern, smiling uncomfortably, suddenly frowned and whispered quickly to Livingstone, "Did she say his name? How did she know that?"

Livingstone looked at the two of them standing there, the color gone from both their faces. Kidd was gripping her hand tightly, then suddenly let it go and shoved both hands into his pockets. Kidd's lips moved. Neither Stern nor Livingstone heard the sound, but the word was "hello."

The quietness of his voice unsettled her; his voice had always been soft, but there was something in the sound of it now that was distant and unfamiliar. There was a harshness in it now.

That harshness, which Kidd himself felt, surprised him as much as her. All night he had felt numb, had been numb for the last two days, had in fact been numb in a subtle but definite way for the last year of his life, except for the hidden meetings he had shared with a stranger on the dark streets of a Washington winter. And now here she was again, right before him, with the crystal light splashing through her hair and richly dressed, powerful people all around her, and nothing at all seeming real to him except her eyes and the feeling in his stomach which was not the strange hope and joy he had always felt with her but a kind of pain. He was shaken by that feeling; he clutched at it, tried to squeeze it away.

And she, seeing the frown come onto his face, felt drained of hope and strength. As lonely people always do, she had felt a secret urgency in her loneliness, a sense that it was growing and was going to overwhelm her and that she desperately needed to break through to someone else—to him—but that if she did the turmoil she carried would surely repel him. Now she heard, for the first time, the growing distance in his voice, and it confirmed for her what she was all too ready to believe —that all the hope and joy she had ever felt with him were a cruel joke told her by her own need.

In the desperation of his failing dreams Kidd said the first baldly honest thing he had said in months, since he had last seen her. "I've missed you."

She could not speak. She could not move her feet, or her hands.

"I didn't know!" Baxter Stern said, stepping between them and smiling. "You must know each other."

Looking at Stern, Ginny said, "We've met."

The orchestra had begun to play a new tune. Stern's eyes grew wider, he grinned and said, "Why don't you dance?"

"Mr. President," Livingstone said, "I don't think—"

"It's not inappropriate, Livver, come on. Everyone else is dancing, and this is a private gathering anyway."

"Yes," Kidd said, looking back at Ginny.

He put his right hand slowly to her waist, grasped her hand with his left, and they began to move. Their pace was slower than the music, it was out of time with everyone and everything around them, but as Stern and Livingstone stood watching they saw there was a world between Virginia Longstreet and Jeff Kidd separate from any other.

Ginny, her eyes startled, saw the jumbled reflections of chandelier points, flowers, and swirling gowns in the gray of his irises. And he, looking at her, saw the lock of hair falling beside one green eye, the hint of freckle still alive beneath the powder, the lipstick tossed on hurriedly and flecked onto the skin at one corner of her mouth, and she was impossibly beautiful to him, more beautiful than he could have remembered or imagined. And nothing else existed for him at that moment— not his past, or hers, not four dead people in a stone tower, not Jamie, wherever he was—only their movement along the polished floor, the hardness of her body behind and the softness in front, the awe on her face, the tremble in his stomach, and the sound of the violins.

They never moved out into the center of the room, but stayed at the same spot, swaying.

Everyone saw them; everyone looked away. They were in time now with the music, making small movements, more holding each other than dancing. To the surrounding people, people of politics and diplomacy, it was uncomfortable to look within that circle of intimacy.

But Baxter Stern stood by, watching unashamedly, in fact ostentatiously, beaming. Livingstone looked back and forth, from Ginny and Kidd to the President.

It was on Stern's face that Livingstone first saw a sign of trouble. Stern was peering toward the couple, squinting in question. As Livingstone looked back to Ginny and Kidd he saw the reason. They were arguing.

It was a slow, reluctant argument, completely quiet. She said something to him and looked down; his face became wooden, he said something brief, and her face came up again, her eyes sharp and alight. She stopped dancing and spoke again. He took his hand slowly from her waist, released his other hand from hers, shook his head, very slowly, and said something else.

Her chest began to rise and fall. Suddenly she lunged, knocking her hands against the points of Kidd's shoulders. He went backward, unresisting, like a man who wanted to be hit, who felt he deserved to be. He went back loosely, not reacting at all until he hit the table, and then he overreacted, grabbing at the edge he had backed into and jostling it more, then spinning, reaching up to catch the flower Washington Monument that came toppling over. When he grabbed at the arrangement, its balsa and chicken wire understructure collapsed.

As the dummy monument bent over Kidd's shoulder, showering him with carnations, Ginny Longstreet ran weeping past Livingstone and Stern, both struck dumb in astonishment.

CHAPTER 6

"Good Lord! Did you see that?" the President asked Livingstone.

"I think everybody in the place saw it, sir. I don't know, maybe one or two of the musicians missed it, but everybody else saw it."

"Maybe we should have them redo it. The house photographer seems to have missed it."

The President was able to say this to Livingstone without any outward expression, and as Jeff Kidd struggled among the flowers and shook the collapsed chicken wire framework, releasing a further shower of petals, the other guests stood by in a hush. The President gave them no sign: his normal, dour expression made him look neither offended nor amused. The crowd began to murmur in a limbo of nonreaction.

The President first nodded to the musicians and they began again to play, and then with a single motion of his index finger he pulled one of the Secret Service men to his side. As Livingstone went over and helped Kidd extract himself, Stern whispered to his aide, who turned quickly and disappeared.

When Livingstone pulled the chicken wire from Kidd, he saw that Kidd was flushed but did not look embarrassed; his blood was surging. And Kidd was no longer cloudy-looking; his features had taken on an edge, and his eyes were brilliant. He brushed off his shoulders and sleeves and said, "Oh. Mr. Livingstone."

Livingstone flicked away a couple of petals that were clinging to his own coat and said, "I take it you and Virginia Longstreet are old friends."

Kidd and Livingstone stood staring at each other. Then a voice said, "Did you say something rude to that young woman, Mr. Kidd?" They turned around to see the President standing beside them. "I can't imagine that," Stern said, "but I have to be sure."

Kidd hesitated and Livingstone said quietly, "I think they are old friends, sir."

"Oh. Yes I see."

The Secret Service man the President had sent away returned and whispered something into the President's ear. Stern looked up and said, "You will find her, I believe, in the Rose Garden."

As Kidd left the party the President turned and looked at Livingstone. Some of the visitors later swore that the President smiled; others said no, that it was just his normal grimace.

One of the faceless Secret Service men led Kidd to the edge of the Rose Garden and stopped. "I think you'll find . . . in the gazebo, sir," he said, and walked away.

The garden looked deserted. In the distance the dome of the Capitol glowed yellow against the blackness. The heavy air was rich with the smell of the roses, the muffled sound of music swam out from the ballroom.

He began walking toward the white crest of the gazebo that he could just see in the center of the garden. The paths were covered with grass; his steps made no sound.

As he reached the gazebo he saw her. She sat on the bench on the opposite perimeter, hunched over, motionless. He stopped at the stair and said, "Ginny."

She looked up, and was startled. She stood.

Kidd stepped up onto the circular floor of the gazebo. It was fifteen feet across, and he walked to the center before he stopped. She faced him, defiantly.

"I'm sorry," he said.

"I was there," she said. "I went back. I did not lie."

"I know, I know. I'm sorry. It's just that . . . the night after I came to your house, I waited on that bench for you. I waited."

Her hands quivered as she held them up; her voice shook. "What could I do? Don't you understand . . . ? There were times when I couldn't do everything I wanted!"

"I know," he whispered. "I know. It's just that you were . . . to me . . ." He knew that he could not walk across the floor and hold her. It was that knowledge that made him despair enough to say, clearly, "You tested me, Ginny. It was cruel for both of us. I don't blame you. And I don't blame myself for failing. I still love you. If I never see you again, if I can never do anything more than believe that the time I spent with you was what it seemed to be, then . . . I'll always love you." He looked away. "I didn't know that until just now. I'm glad I found it out with . . ."

She reached to his hand, and took it in a crushing grasp.

CHAPTER 7

She shifted hard, pounding the old Volkswagen Beetle along Constitution Avenue. Kidd sat beside her, watching the pumping of her legs as she shifted again, the grip of her fingers on the wheel and gear lever, the animation of her head as her eyes swept the road and the mirrors. He could not keep from staring; he saw something aggressive and masterful in her, something he had never seen in her before. When she said, in a rich, throaty voice, "Where are we going, anyway?" he suddenly started to laugh.

She glanced at him twice, then laughed too.

They drove along for several blocks without speaking. "Why don't we take a walk?" he said.

"Where?"

"Anywhere."

They were passing beside a long stretch of park. "Right here?" she said.

"Why not?"

She swung the car around a corner and darted into a parking space. Kidd got out and went to open her door, but she was already out, and as she locked the doors he walked around the car, looking at the dented yellow fenders and the University of Maryland decal flaky and fading on the back glass. He said, "You drive this car to the White House, huh?"

"Yeah," she laughed. "Livingstone—John Livingstone is my boss—he's been after me to get rid of it. He begs me to let him send me a black limo whenever I'm supposed to show up for anything official. But he really doesn't mind, it's a joke now. Even if I had the money for another car I think I'd keep this one. Just out of spite."

Kidd stood with his hands in the pockets of his tuxedo jacket and poked at a tire with the polished toe of his shoe. "It's . . . just so strange," he said. "You work for John Livingstone. Livingstone—you work for the President! Why didn't you ever tell me that?"

"I told you I wrote speeches," she said, smiling. "And that I worked on a presidential campaign."

"I know. There are a lot of people in this town who write speeches and work on campaigns. I should have known, I know. I just didn't put it together. That shows how much you can miss when you . . . have your mind on something else."

They stood there, four feet apart, looking at the car and down at the pavement as much as they looked at each other.

"I don't know," she said. "Maybe I did hold it back a little. I did want to—Oh my God! Jeff . . . Oh my God!" She snatched both hands to her mouth.

"What? What?"

"How could I?" she whispered. She squeezed her eyes shut, then opened them again to gaze into the park behind him.

He turned and looked. The Washington Monument rose golden above the cherry trees.

"Ginny . . . It's all right. Really. It's all right."

She wiped at her face. "I don't know how I could be so thoughtless."

"It wasn't thoughtless. And to tell you the truth, I'm glad we stopped here. See, I—you know I have this compulsion to face up to places."

She looked at him. He looked away.

"Tell me something," he said. "How's Jamie?"

"Jamie's in an asylum. He's been there since a week after I saw you last."

There was a long silence, during which they both stared at the trees. "Listen," she said. "Let's do take a walk. But not here. I know a better place than this."

CHAPTER 8

They paused in the entrance foyer. "I'll just be a minute," she said, starting up the stairs, then stopping. "Would you like some coffee or tea?" Without giving him time to answer, she stepped down again and headed for the kitchen. Kidd followed.

The house had the incongruous quality of neatness in a junkyard, or of a transient making a home in a condemned building. The walls were still indelibly smudged, the plaster gouged, and there was even less furniture than there had been before. But there were signs of order; a pad and a sharpened pencil lay beside the new telephone perched on a stand in the hallway; the kitchen smelled of scented cleanser, and there were no dishes in the sink. Ginny put a kettle on the stove, drew two cups from the cabinet, and opened a cannister on the counter top. From it she pulled two tea bags. "It's imported," she said. "My vice."

When the tea was ready she turned to the kitchen table, hesitated, and said, "Let's go into the living room."

She raised the windows all around. A breeze glided in, carrying the scent of grass. Beside the cold black fireplace was a single chair with an ottoman—where she reads, Kidd thought—and she motioned him to sit, settling onto the ottoman herself. Kidd perched on the edge of the chair, so that their heads were at the same level.

"Do you like the tea?" she said.

"Mmm. It tastes . . . red."

She smiled and sipped again.

"How did you decide to take Jamie to the asylum?" he said.

"His parents did it." She stared out the window. "The night, the night after you came, we . . . had an incident. He got burned, on his arm, and got a little violent. The woman I had staying here with him quit the next morning, and I took Jamie to his parents' house, and asked them to watch him just during the days until I could find someone else. While they had him they found his burns, got upset, and called the doctor. That was to check on me more than Jamie, I think. Anyway, I had trouble finding the right person to hire—it takes somebody special, I couldn't leave him with just anybody—and on the fifth day, when I drove to their place after work to pick Jamie up, they weren't there. Nobody was there. They hadn't left a note. I waited for them. When they got back they told me they had taken him to the home the doctor had been recommending."

Kidd said nothing.

"They weren't holding up very well, keeping him. But what they said was that they took the doctor's advice that Jamie would be better off there, at least until I could replace Mary. They paid for his first three days in the asylum," she said, and then hearing the bitterness in her own voice she looked up, and her face became as placid as the night outside the window.

Neither spoke. In the bushes the crickets rattled. Somewhere in the distance a dog barked at the moon.

When Kidd glanced up from his tea cup, she was looking at him. "I knew it would be you," she said. "Somehow I knew. When I first heard about an agent going in for the hostages, I knew you had to be involved. I don't know how, what connections I made, but I knew all along that it would be you."

"I wish we could have finished our dance," he said.

She smiled. It seemed a sad smile; he was no longer sure of anything. "We can finish it," she said. "I have the music they were playing."

"The exact tune?"

"Yes." She stood and walked to the bookshelves in the corner. There was a full row of albums, one end neater than the rest, and out of this ordered section she withdrew a record. She turned to the stereo system—something Jamie must have bought, Kidd thought—components stacked into a metal rack, with wires leading to massive speakers in either corner of the room. Suddenly the room came alive with violins and cellos.

She walked to him. He put down his cup, stood, and reached for her clumsily. They began to sway, slowly, and as he felt her within his arms he saw that he was wrong—that she was not relaxed and definite, that she was stiff with tension. He tried simply to move without stumbling, to keep time.

"What is that music?" he said.

"Vivaldi."

He could smell her hair as it swayed around her, he could feel the grip of her hand, tottering between limpness and squeezing. The music sang through the speakers, an orchestra playing unseen from the corners of the dark room; he could hear the bite of the bows against the strings.

He stopped moving, lifted her chin, and saw eyes more full of question than any eyes he had ever known.

She looked up at his face. It was not the calm, confident face that she had imagined in her dreams; it was a face shot full of life, sharp with fear and daring.

The only kiss she could remember, the only one she had ever really known, was Jamie's, and it seemed to her that Jamie's kiss had always been as it now was—lifelessness itself. But when Jeff Kidd leaned down and brushed his lips against hers, life was vibrant within them; and from that moment, for that one evening, all the questions within Virginia Longstreet ceased to exist.

CHAPTER 9

Morning came softly to Ginny Longstreet's house, the humid spring sky going from violet to deep rose; it was tinged with blue when the telephone rang. It jingled four times before Ginny's slow fingers picked it up and she said, "Hello?"

"Ginny. Good morning." It was Livingstone.

"Good morning."

"Ginny. I'm sorry to dis—to call so early."

"You always call early, Mr. Livingstone." That bright flirtiness was back in her voice, and she knew it.

Livingstone heard it too. "Uh, yeah. Listen. Ginny. I know there's no one there with you but I thought I should tell you that if there were someone there with you then it might be a good idea if he left discreetly. I mean this is all just speculation of course, but you know there was kind of a, well, there was some excitement last night at the party that maybe you heard about and the trouble is that stories tend to get out and reporters can be obnoxious and there might be some at your door and anybody who was going out might get his picture taken. That may not matter to some people and it wouldn't matter of course to you, but isn't it interesting?"

"Yes, John. It is."

"I just thought I'd call you to say that. Funny how we think of people when we first wake up."

"Yes."

"Well, I'll see you later. By the way, you don't have to come in today. I mean you can if you want to. I understand that Mr. Browne is having a blind press conference today but of course you could just hear that on the radio if you had any interest in it."

"Yes. Thank you."

"Okay, I'll see you—"

"John, wait a minute. Why would I have an interest in him?"

God, she is getting snappy, isn't she? Livingstone thought, and then said, "Oh, I don't know. Some of the Secret Service guys saw you leave last night. Said there was a man in your car who looked a lot like Mr. Browne. Of course it was dark. Probably a mistake. We'll have to replace them if they can't be more careful."

"Yes."

"Okay, Ginny, I'll—"

"John. One other thing. Ask the President if he wants to see me sometime today."

"Uh, okay. Sure. Any special reason?"

"Tell him I just thought that he must still have something important to tell me. After the, uh, excitement at the party last night, he sent a man to my office to tell me to meet him in the Rose Garden. He never showed up. The *President* never showed up. I thought he still must want to see me. Ask him, won't you?"

"You really are pushing, you know that, don't you?"

"Good-bye, John."

They stopped at the back door in the kitchen and held each other, hot in the shaft of sunlight coming through the glass. She opened the door, he kissed her again, and stepped out. But her touch on his arm stopped him. "Jeff. Last night, when we . . . I just want you to tell me before you go . . . Did I hurt you?"

For an instant, he paused.

Back upstairs in her bedroom, she stood at the window and watched as he entered the trees, on the path that she had told him would lead to a cross street, up to a certain bus stop bench, where the early shuttle would pick him up. As he disappeared into the shelter of the hickory leaves, luminous in the sun, he was still laughing.

CHAPTER 10

Livingstone fiddled with the volume and tuning dials. The White House trinket man who installed the receiver and the dual cabinet speakers that morning had already tuned in the right station and had experimented himself to set just the proper volume for Livingstone's office, so that Livingstone needed only to switch the unit on, but he was edgy.

Kurtz, sitting in one of the plush swivel chairs, watched Livingstone and pondered the incongruity: the man who had shaped every living American's concept of broadcast journalism was clumsy with the simple controls of a radio.

Sherwood watched Livingstone too, but his impressions were different. He looked at the expensive stereo unit, the calibrations on its dial glowing in blue and red, and thought of how Ginny Longstreet had told them when she took over the speechwriting unit that all those things they did to stay in touch with the American public actually created the wrong perspective. The average person doesn't read twenty newspapers, or compare network coverage, or scan magazines of various political philosophies, she had said. The average American reads part of one paper, or hears snatches of one broadcast, and does that with the kids fighting and his back hurting. *Where*, Sherwood asked himself, *was that populist spirit now, since she had been promoted, since her office was in the White House, one floor below Livingstone's? Why didn't they all go out and listen to the broadcast in a car, where most Americans would be if they heard it at all?*

Ginny sat in the middle of the office, flanked by Kurtz, Sherwood, and Livingstone's empty seat. She stared toward the wall space between the two radio speakers as if it were a movie screen, showing scenes the others could not see.

Livingstone turned up the volume, tuned the channel out, back in, back out, and back in again, and an announcer's resonant yet subdued voice said, ". . . from the State Department building, where the conference is expected to commence at any moment. There are at least forty journalists gathered here. There are no photographers and pictures will not be allowed. There is a small table at the front of the room, with a group of microphones, and—Here! We've just had the agent enter. Behind him are the Secretary of State, the director of the Central Intelligence Agency, and the director of the FBI."

Ginny, her eyes unfocused at the wall, saw the room five

blocks away, the tight crowd of reporters, the Cabinet officers standing dull and nervous at the door while Kidd settled uneasily into his seat.

There was a sound of chairs scraping, the reporters settling, distant coughing, and then, close to the microphone, a throat clearing. A voice, smothered and a bit fuzzy, said, "I am here today to answer, if I can, your questions regarding the events surrounding the kidnapping of former ambassador Harrison Crawley, his wife, and their granddaughter three days ago, and the rescue operation which followed. The President has directed me to be as candid as possible within the boundaries of our security obligations, and I will try to answer you as fully as I can."

A reporter, sounding distant at first and then closer as someone trained a microphone on him, said, "How soon after the kidnapping of the Crawleys were you first called into the situation?"

"The initial kidnapping of the child occurred about two fifty-two in the afternoon. The elder Crawleys were taken about three-twelve, and at that time the situation was unknown to any law enforcement agencies. The monument was occupied at four-forty and the note of demands was given to the monument rangers as the perpetrators expelled them. I was called at four forty-eight."

The same reporter's voice said, "So you were called in as soon as the monument was occupied. Does that mean Operation Counterstrike is a force that will be used immediately in any hostage situation?"

"Agents can be deployed immediately, but whether they are or not depends on jurisdiction. The response was so quick in this case because the Washington Monument is under immediate federal control."

Another voice said, "Does that mean the agents of Operation Counterstrike will not participate in hostage situations which are not within federal jurisdiction?"

"Good God!" Livingstone burst out, shocking Kurtz and Sherwood as well as Ginny. "They want to accuse us of being narrow and unresponsive?"

"No," Kidd's voice said from the radio. "In emergencies, various agencies routinely cooperate. Jurisdictions are established by law. Domestically O.C. operates within the charter of the FBI, internationally within that of the CIA."

Livingstone mumbled to Ginny, "I should have known he'd have been briefed to handle a question like that." Ginny, surprised not only by Livingstone's volatility but now by his openness, felt Kurtz and Sherwood, excluded from the exchange, stiffen.

Over the radio another reporter, female, asked, "What, then, is the actual number of agents involved in Operation Counterstrike?"

Without hesitation Kidd answered, "I cannot tell you that."

"Will you tell us how they are deployed?"

"No."

The female voice persisted. "Will you or can you give us any indication why you were selected for the program?"

Kidd hesitated. "All of the people in Operation Counterstrike have come from either the FBI or the CIA. Those agencies have their own criteria. I'd rather not say anything beyond that."

"Can you tell us then why you were selected for the first incident in which O.C. was involved?"

During a longer hesitation, Kidd deliberated. "I helped in the selection and training of the O.C. force. I believed that in this first incident, I should go."

There was a rumble of surprise among the reporters at this. "You were one of the founding officers?" two reporters asked at once.

"I was part of the original team, yes," Kidd said.

For several minutes the questions were polite; the queries about the terrorists' weapons, their past records of violence, and the danger to the hostages and their ultimate safety were open compliments. One reporter even dispensed with questioning altogether, making a statement about Kidd's bravery and the service he had done, and Livingstone wondered for a moment if they had been too careful with their screening of journalists for this conference.

His misgivings were short-lived. A voice with a whiskey rasp said, "If your purpose is to guarantee the safety of hostages, then why do you allow drastic acts that put them in much greater danger?"

Livingstone, leaning closer to the speakers, suddenly sat back and said, "That's Sam Emmett! How did he get in there?"

In the tone he used for answering questions he had been prepared for, Kidd said, "The safety of people being held hostage by terrorists is not ours to guarantee. We wanted to free the hostages from the danger they were in already, with as little increased risk as—"

But Sam Emmett's rasp broke in, "I don't want to argue semantics, I want to know if you don't think that what you did was extremely risky and only missed precipitating a disaster because of enormous good luck."

"I don't deny the good luck. Decisions . . . aren't objective. Based on the best judgment we can—"

"Are you trained to kill?"

"We are trained."

"To kill?"

"To save lives, as best we can." Kidd seemed to realize the words sounded empty.

"No!" Emmett yelled, and there were cries of disapproval from the other reporters, but Emmett shouted them down. "No! No! Excuse me for asking such unpleasant questions, but I feel someone has to! On whose authority did you decide to kill those four people? How did you make the judgment that they had to die?"

There was a pause as if the radio had gone dead, and Livingstone leaned forward and whispered, "Tell him they decided that themselves when they started cutting the fingers off seven-year-old girls. Tell him that!"

But Kidd's voice did not come back, and Emmett said, "I think it's very important to ask ourselves what this secret governmental force is, that can send trained killers into a situation, and these men can become judge, jury, and executioner!"

Very quietly, so quietly that Ginny Longstreet had to lean toward the speakers herself, Jeff Kidd said, "Ladies and gentlemen, I don't have anything else to say. The conference is over."

CHAPTER 11

"Jeff," she said as she opened the front door.

"I'm sorry I'm late," he said, stepping in. She shut the door and they hesitated to hug each other until they both felt too awkward to. "I didn't hear you drive up," she said.

"I parked on the next street," he said. "I don't know why."

"Come in! Let's sit . . . in the living room." He followed her in, and she waited for him to take the chair. But when he had, she only stood in front of the ottoman and said, "Have you eaten?"

"Uh. No, I haven't." His fingers drummed on the ends of the armrests.

"Let me fix you something. Really. Come on. Something simple."

They went into the kitchen. Watching her standing over the stove stirring a pan of soup he said, "Do you have a screwdriver?"

"Yes. Over there. In that drawer."

He opened the utility drawer, too tidy and uncluttered for a man to have used. There was a single screwdriver among the bottle openers and plastic soda caps. He tightened the screws which held the iron pot rack over the stove, stepped back neatly, and put the screwdriver away again.

"Hey. Thanks!" she said. "That thing's been crooked for months."

"It was loose. It could have come off."

She nodded and turned slowly back to the soup.

When they sat down at the table he tasted the broth and said, "That's great."

"I just heated it."

"You heated it very well." They did actually smile at each other then.

"Jeff. It was rough on you today, wasn't it?"

"At the press conference? Did I sound that bad?"

"No. No! I thought you came off really well. With . . . dignity. And I could never say a word if I were in front of reporters like that."

"Come on."

"Writing words isn't saying them. It's just so much pressure and some people are hostile."

"That's what you have to expect, I guess." He took several spoonfuls of soup, casually. "Okay. Yeah. It does bother me. But I don't know what to do about it."

"I know."

He stopped eating.

He put his hand over hers. "After the press conference, I had two hours to kill before I came over here. So I sat in my apartment and waited. The time just crawled by. I put off showering and shaving until the last minute, and then I was a half-hour late. I haven't done that since high school. I think I did it because I like having something I look forward to."

"I understand," she said.

"We've told each other about a lot of things, but we still have so much talking to do. I want to do that so much. But I don't think I can do it tonight. I can't be good company."

"You don't have to be good company."

"I want to be!" he said hotly. "That's the point! I want us to just sit, and get to know everything about each other, in a room with the lights on. And tonight I don't feel up to it. That makes me mad and frustrated with a lot of people. Not with you."

They kissed once, briefly, at the front door.

Kidd sat in his apartment. It was the first time in three days that he had been truly alone, without doctors, debriefers, politicians, reporters, strangers on the highway, without Ginny Longstreet or the immediate expectation of seeing her. Now he felt isolated. He also felt abandoned, but he told himself that was because of the sudden contrast.

But the machinery had dropped him: he thought that as he leaned back on the flimsy foam backing of his couch and stretched his legs straight out before him, his heels catching in the thin carpet. He saw himself as having been involved in a process, a game of work and crime and duty, in which he could struggle and influence the flow of events, but which he could not stop. The machinery of the process ground on, without his choice or anyone else's, and then it reached its limit and quit. The game ended and it was time for the man to start being a man again, but there was no blueprint anymore, no mechanical determination of sequence and situation. He was simply alone in an apartment that did not seem like his, with nothing of his own but his life, and that felt so diffused, so much without substance, that it seemed to mean nothing at all.

He thought things through in just that way. He felt utterly confused, and understood that confusion in terms of processes, machines, and a human life that was in shambles.

Only his feeling for Ginny Longstreet was beyond his conscious if labored analysis, but even so—or perhaps for that very reason—that too seemed a sheer power which overwhelmed him and carried him forward, without his knowledge or choice of the outcome. As he sat on the couch, bending over now, wrapping his fingers around his skull and pressing, he fought for understanding, doomed already by his resignation, believing the answers were beyond his reach when he did not know what the problems were.

It was his nature to analyze, but though he had confidence in his analysis of others, he had tried during the last year to avoid it in himself. Yet as he sat there he felt his agitation growing, and he struggled. He was, he told himself, a man of decisions, a man of outcomes. When faced with a choice, he could appraise the likely outcomes and the possibilities and limits of his ability to shape those outcomes. And then he would choose.

But two times in the last three days he had acted differently, committing himself fully in a way that ignored outcomes and existed only in a single moment without past or future. The first was when he snatched the pistol from Roxanne Lark and began killing people. The second was when he loved Ginny Longstreet.

He could even analyze that observation, finding ways in which his decisions had already been made by fate or genes or even by an accumulation of smaller choices. He knew, for example, that he had felt drawn to Ginny Longstreet from the first moment he saw her.

But in both cases there had been an instant; a moment of decision, like a leap.

As he sat there alone in his apartment, in that black confusion which was all the more overwhelming and incomprehensible because it followed so quickly the joy and peace of the night before, he did not understand if he had made leaps of faith, or of despair.

But he felt himself falling.

CHAPTER 12

From the moment Dooley had reached him at the top of the monument, other agents had been ordering Kidd's schedule for him. So when he went to work that morning, without anyone telling him to, he had the sense of showing up uninvited at a party.

He felt stranger still as he went to his desk and found it cleared of the stacks of dossiers and source material that had been on it the day the incident began. Dooley's desk, next to his, was a mess of notes and files. Kidd was just reassuring himself by checking for the personal belongings in a side desk drawer when Dooley walked in.

"Jeff!" Dooley said, surprised to see him. He dumped another stack of briefs onto his desk, and that seemed to remind him; he looked to Kidd and said, "Hey, don't panic. I'm the one who cleared your desk off. When we started the follow-ups we—"

Kidd held up a hand and said, "I know, Tenny. All the stuff was here, I knew somebody had to be all over it. So how's it going?"

Dooley sat down on the one uncovered edge of his desk, facing Kidd. "Okay. We had great reaction time on it. Collier had guys in here working even before I could get back from the scene. Your telling us it was Roxanne Lark was the key to the speed. None of the bodies had any I.D. on them, and the Crawleys couldn't tell us anything for hours. But Collie had Roxanne's name punched into the computer, right from the field post, and her dossier numbers lit up, just like you'd planned it. They found a cross-reference to welfare. She was drawing benefits after the death of her husband. That gave us her address, and we had men there within ten minutes of when you came out of the monument. We beat the public identification on her by a good two hours, so we had all the neighbors to ourselves. That was great because—"

"I know why you want to beat the media," Kidd said sharply. Then he smiled, too quickly. "Sorry, Tenny. Go on."

Dooley looked at Kidd.

"Yeah, well . . . it looks for sure that there was no conspiracy beyond the four we—you—got," Dooley said. "We got all over the Communist League of America, and they talked with us pretty freely. In fact they were happy for the chance to lay out some rhetoric. Lark planned her deal totally apart from them. They—the C.L.A., I mean—have been trying to deradicalize their image, because they're trying to recruit mill workers in the South, and somebody has explained to them that they won't get anywhere with the rednecks by blowing up national monuments."

"Yeah," Kidd said, and stared away from Dooley. After his edginess, he thought it wrong to say "Good job."

"By the way," Dooley said, "you've been getting mail."

"What?"

"Fan letters. Telegrams. 'The Agent of the Monument' they call you. And pies. Over a hundred pies."

"*Pies?*"

"Washington Monument. Cherry pies. Get it? Like yellow ribbons and the hostages from Iran. Everybody wants to participate. There've been human interest stories all over television about the people who are sending them in."

Kidd stared down. "What . . . what . . ." He could not seem to find the question he wanted to ask, and finished instead, "do you do with them?"

"We fluoroscope them, like we do everything else that comes here—check them out, cross-reference the return address, if there is one. There haven't been any bombs, and only about two dozen of the letters have asked how you enjoy being a killer and a pig."

"Yeah."

Dooley took another long look at him. "Glad to have the debriefs over?"

"Yeah. Say. How come I got it all?"

"Hey, don't think I escaped altogether. But with me it wasn't much more than a shooting report. All I did was cut a nigger in two with a shotgun. That's just a noise violation. They saved the wringer for you. This was a new program, remember. New programs get scrutiny, especially when they succeed."

They sat a few moments in silence. "Tenny. Tell me something. You think about the guy you shot?"

Dooley looked away. "I killed a man before. Another Black guy. I say 'man,' he was a damn kid. Bank robbery, interstate flight, we took him at a motel. I went in first, he reached for his bedside table, and I killed him. There was a gun in the table, and he was a killer. But I can't walk into a motel room without seeing his body spread across the bed. Real young, and frail-looking."

Both men looked out the window, which showed the other

windows on the opposite side of the courtyard. At last Kidd said, "I'm sorry you got stuck with all the work the last few days."

But Dooley was not ready to change the subject. "Don't be sorry. I wanted the work. Because I'll tell you something." He looked straight at Kidd. "Guys—our guys—want to hear about it, when you've blown somebody away. They're fascinated with it, and they ask about what happened, how it felt. It happened the first time, and it happens now. The more I work, the less it happens."

Kidd looked away.

"One·other thing I guess I ought to tell you, Jeff."

"Tell me."

"We found strychnine in four of the pies."

Kidd stopped off in Collier's office. Collier seemed surprised to see him, and encouraged him to take a few days off to rest.

Kidd went home.

CHAPTER 13

Sam Emmett's performance at the Operation Counterstrike news conference had churned up a torrent of verbal emotion. Debate over Emmett's behavior and the questions he raised took up as many column inches and broadcast minutes as did follow-up coverage of the actual terrorist event. But Emmett himself had kept silent on his own controversy, and the news services, politicians, gossips, pundits—everyone in Washington who exists because of public contention—searched each issue of the *Constellation* for Emmett's next stroke.

The *Constellation* had recently launched a late edition, which went out before lunch to newsstands in the city and as an afternoon paper for the suburbs. That edition contained this column:

DÉJA VU?
by Sam Emmett

Whenever a killing takes place during the activities of a conventional law enforcement agency, investigating teams determine if the shooting was "within policy." No such consideration can be made about the recent killings at the Washington Monument, because in the case of Operation Counterstrike, *no such guidelines existed.*

The agent who did most of the killing, who appeared at Operation Counterstrike's press conference (if such an anonymous performance can be called an "appearance" or a "press conference"), did not answer many questions. One answer he did give suggested that policies controlling the FBI and CIA apply to Operation Counterstrike.

Perhaps the agent believes that. But the Administration does not. Immediately after the killing, a paper circulating within the White House indicated that the agent *acted on his own.*

To us this raises disturbing questions. What kind of supervision is being applied to this new and secretive intelligence service? After the hard lessons we have learned in the past two decades of the need to reconcile the activities of the CIA and FBI with the Bill of Rights, has Operation Counterstrike been created to sidestep the sticky issue of protection of civil liberties?

The haunting questions are not merely theoretical. Four young people died on Tuesday. Granted they were sick—one has to be sick to cut the finger off a child—but it may be that very fact which indicates the complexity of their actions. Certainly there is a dark instinct in all of us which lusts for the blood of anyone who would abuse a child (although it might be remembered that in the minds of those who died, what they had done was not as bad as what they might had done: they killed no one, but Roxanne Lark's husband died in the streets of Greensboro).

The public wants to see terrorism defeated. Rattlesnakes and lightning kill more Americans each year than terrorists do, but there are no votes in conquering rattlesnakes. People are happy; they are baking cherry pies. The day after the terrorists were killed, the Stern administration threw a White House bash; rumors say the celebration included a drunken brawl, which involved the O.C. agent—from the monument.

I have been criticized for my attitude about Operation Counterstrike. Forgive me if I cannot take the deaths of four disturbed young people so lightly.

Certainly, many will say, "They got what they deserved." But how can we ever know that for sure?

When we discover among us a secret organization, with agents empowered to kill at their own discretion, we have many questions to ask. But the Administration pleads that, *for security reasons* . . .

Isn't it frightening when we recall the other times, recent times, when we have been put off by that phrase?

Stern was tight-lipped and pale with rage.

"A gestapo!" he screamed. "He's accusing me of forming some kind of gestapo!"

Livingstone and Forbis sat in the Oval Office, stilled by the rare fury.

"Operation Counterstrike is a completely controlled, brilliantly conceived, expertly supervised, thoroughly legal operation! An agent—the best one we have—takes initiative, he does something unexpected, he *saves people's lives!* You have to do the unexpected to save lives sometimes, you have to take initiative. That's why Collier picked men like that! And now they're some kind of executioners? And I've turned loose a gestapo?"

Stern raised both fists, quivering, and let them fall slowly upon the top of his desk. "No one can believe it, can they?"

Forbis said, "Senator Thornbull just called me. He was angry. He said that if the Administration could not uphold its intelligence responsibilities, then he personally would see to it that Congress takes greater control."

"That dirty—"

"After taking so much credit for O.C. in the first place, he thinks he'll be blamed if it's improperly supervised," Forbis said.

"Improperly supervised! I can't believe anyone thinks that! Not of this! And what is this paper he talks about, circulating the White House?"

"The 'after incident' paper we got from Collier, I think," Forbis said.

"That was a fact sheet, not a policy investigation," Stern said. "I wanted to see how O.C. had functioned its first time out. And the report showed it functioned magnificently! How can it be construed as showing killers turned loose?"

Livingstone spoke for the first time. "The public is often uncomfortable with spontaneity or evidence of emotion from people in power, Mr. President, from politicians or intelligence agents. It shows they're too human. And it worries people into thinking someone might raise himself above the law."

Neither Stern nor Forbis saw any relevance in the comment.

"Have you checked with Collier? And the intelligence directors?" Stern said to Forbis.

"Yes, Mr. President, and they all assure me that the leak could not have come from their departments."

"There are a lot of people in the CIA and the FBI," Livingstone said. "I don't see how the directors could be so certain, so quickly, that their agencies weren't involved."

"Counterstrike is a small and tight subset," Forbis said tartly, "and very few people had access to the paper Emmett refers to."

Livingstone knew Forbis was right, but resented his tone anyway, and surprised himself by arguing back so quickly. "There's the Congressional Intelligence Supervisory Committee. They've been apprised of all matters relating to Operation Counterstrike, including the follow-up report of the monument incident, and they could have leaked—"

"They didn't get that report," Forbis said.

"Wait. What?" Livingstone said.

"The brief circulated with our staff was a snap analysis, not an in-depth follow-up," Forbis said, as if that explained something.

Livingstone stared at Forbis and suddenly understood. Forbis was saying that he was screening information which went to the congressional committee responsible for evaluating intelligence activity. Livingstone was shocked. He understood the drawbacks of a congressional inclusion system, but it was a fact of life, and Livingstone not only disagreed in principle with subverting the procedure, but as a practical matter felt it best to establish friends on the committee rather than antagonize them with sleight of hand. But the part that really troubled him was that Forbis's statement was news to Livingstone only; Stern already knew and had approved Forbis's tactic of screening information.

"So we're in trouble with all of Congress over this, not just Thornbull."

No one answered.

"Well," Livingstone said, "I think we need to be forthcoming about O.C. I believe we can be perfectly candid with the public, and have their support, just admitting that Counterstrike is a new operation and maybe we should have had all policies spelled out. That was an oversight. But we have displayed effective action against terrorism. They appreciate that. As for the agent shooting out-of-policy, he clearly—"

"That's not the damn issue!" Stern hissed, and Livingstone stopped talking with his mouth still open.

"The issue," Stern said, his eyes narrowing as if he saw the word hanging in the air before him, "the *issue* is that someone within this administration is hurting us, intentionally. These aren't just leaks, they're selected bits of truth that add up to big lies. They're hard *not* to believe! We address the questions that arise from the press. We've done that all along, we did that with the Bortchers thing. But the continuing issue is that this administration seems incapable of controlling the flow of information. And that's not an effort to control the public's freedom to know!" Stern yelled, looking directly at Livingstone. "It is an effort to be efficient and credible. How can anyone expect us to negotiate a delicate foreign treaty, if everyone knows the stains on our underwear? I want these leaks stopped."

"How?" Livingstone said to Stern.

"Internal Security," said Forbis.

"They haven't been effective so far," Stern said.

"I haven't pushed them hard enough," Forbis said.

CHAPTER 14

"Is it us?" Livingstone said across the lunch table in the White House commissary.

"I don't know," Ginny said, looking down at her Gerry Ford Special and flaking off a chunk of cottage cheese with her fork. "Maybe."

On another day Livingstone might not have heard anything in that answer; today he pressed. "Maybe—it's possible? Or maybe—you're suspicious about someone?"

"No. No. Not suspicious about anyone. I mean I . . . You can suspect anybody of anything if you think about it enough. But yes. The problem may be in our department."

She told him about the copy of the policy guidelines missing from her desk just after the Bortchers speech.

"Good Lord! Why didn't you tell me that before?"

"I . . . didn't know what had happened to my copy. I thought maybe I'd lost it myself."

"Ginny."

"Well, I was going through a hard time then, I could have

been forgetful." She saw he did not believe that any more than she did. "But . . . I didn't take it that seriously. I mean . . ."

"What are you having so much trouble saying?"

She stared at him, then blurted, "I thought someone took it just out of petty jealousy. To shake me up. A prank."

Livingstone waited, expecting something more, and then realized he could answer his own questions. "All right. Kurtz and Sherwood. Kurtz *or* Sherwood might be capable of that. I assume you don't mean Thayer because he's retired now. But could it have been one of the secretaries?"

"I don't know. I hadn't thought of them at first, though I did later. That's what I mean about suspicion."

Livingstone twisted his glass of iced tea, spinning it in slick circles on the table. "Is that why you instituted the rule that every data paper handed out to the speech team will be registered by name, and each person must return his own copy?"

"Yes."

"Hmm. Did you let Kurtz or Sherwood read the incident report?"

"Not at first, no. But when the President was vacillating before the medal ceremony and wanted a full-blown speech, he sent down a copy as background. I passed it around, but I got it back."

"The office has a Xerox machine."

"Every office has a Xerox machine. And every administration has leaks. How serious could all this be?"

"Yeah. I don't know." Livingstone sat back in his chair, crossed his legs, and tried to look relaxed. But still he spun his tea glass. "Maybe I'm just naïve. You know, everybody always acts as if I was being humble not to want a major job within the Administration. That wasn't humility, that was common sense, I don't have expertise at all in the internal political workings of an administration, of Washington in general for that matter. And I do have a problem now, you see—" Livingstone stopped and smiled strangely. He uncrossed his legs and sat back upright. "I just realized something. I've just started doing what I've suspected others—okay, *Forbis*—of doing all along: conspiring with subordinates."

"We're not conspiring," she said, but in a tone too low for anyone else around them to hear.

"Not exactly, maybe. But I just caught myself wanting to look around, lean forward, and whisper in low tones."

"John, I have never found discretion to be ill-advised. In this place or any other."

"Okay," Livingstone said, smiling. Then he did look around and lean forward. "If the leak is in our department, it hurts me, whether I'm to blame or not. We haven't replaced Thayer yet. Part of the reason is that the President isn't making many speeches right now, but the other part is that Forbis resents not having control of more of the speechwriting process, and for me to choose another person forces the issue of his input. And I haven't wanted to force the issue. Maybe I'm too conciliatory an animal for Washington, but I don't like friction within an administration. But if we find the leaker is a speechwriter, one of *my* speechwriters, it suggests the scribes be put under tighter control."

"Forbis's control."

"Yes," Livingstone said, leaning back and looking away. He seemed very tired, and turned the conversation to a new broodmare that he hoped to buy for his farm in Virginia.

Just after the first ring, he answered: "Hello?"

"Jeff? This is—"

"Ginny."

"I called the office number you gave me, and they said you weren't available. I hoped that meant you were at home."

"It could mean anything, but you guessed right."

"Jeff, I have to see you."

There was a pause. "That's about the best news I could hear right now. When?"

"Well . . ."

"Now?"

"It doesn't have to be now, just . . . soon."

"What are you doing right now?"

"Nothing, I have some meetings later, but . . . We can talk tonight, I just . . ."

"I can be down there in fifteen minutes. Would you like to meet on the Mall?"

"Yes. Okay. I'll walk down from here."

"Say, at the parking lot?"

"Yes. I'll be there."

"Okay."

"Jeff? Thank you."

After a pause in which they each waited for the other to say something more, they hung up.

It was a ten-minute walk from the south gate of the White House to the parking lot of the Mall. Kidd was there waiting for her. He took her hand, and they skirted the knoll of the Washington Monument, reaching the Mall and walking toward the Capitol.

"It still surprises me that you would come here," she said. He did not answer.

The day was warm, the cherry trees fragrant in the sun. Tourists crisscrossed the Mall, stood on the walkways pointing and taking pictures, joggers trotted by on the grass. "Have you seen the papers?" Ginny said.

"No. What?"

"The *Constellation* just ran a column by Sam Emmett. He says Operation Counterstrike had no guidelines about shooting. That what happened at the monument was something . . . the agent did on his own."

"Yeah?" Kidd seemed merely puzzled.

"He says he got his information through a leak, and he interprets it all as meaning that O.C. isn't run properly. Over at the White House they're taking that as a big deal. You don't seem surprised."

"Well, no. I'm not, actually. I haven't seen the column, but it's not so different from the rest of the media attention, is it?"

"Well, no. I guess it isn't."

"I don't mean to be casual." He saw that she was still surprised by his non-response. "Do you remember when I told you I'd tell you some horror stories, about the way it's been for the intelligence services for the last few years? Well here's a story.

"Collier, the man who hired me for O.C., was the S.A.C., the Special Agent in Charge, of the FBI office in Jackson, Mississippi. This was ten years ago. At the time the Bureau was at war with an especially hostile faction of the Klan. Now. Collie got word, through an informant, that a member of Black September, the same Palestinian terrorist group that killed the Israeli athletes at the Munich Olympics, was in Mississippi, hobnobbing with members of the Klan. And the Bureau wondered, *What the hell is he doing here?* And so, like they'd been doing for two decades with agents of foreign governments, they did a clandestine entry into the Palestinian's hotel room. It wasn't a break-in, they didn't take a thing, it was strictly a covert operation for gathering intelligence. Through that, and the rest of their investigation, they established the plot. The terrorist was there to recruit white Americans, the Klansmen, and to take them to Libya. There they would be trained as assassins. They would come back to America. They would assassinate prominent Jews all over the country.

"They arrested the Palestinian. He didn't even deny the plan. But what he did deny was that he had done anything illegal, or that the FBI could prove what he'd done. A long legal battle began. The last of it—I suppose the last—was four months ago, right before you and I met. That was when a grand jury, after a ten-hour grilling of Walter Collier, decided not to indict him; not the terrorist, but Collier—for depriving the Palestinian of his civil rights, by breaking into his home.

"The terrorist, by the way, is still in this country, quite legally, though he isn't a citizen.

"Now. President Stern made Collie head of Operation Counterstrike. That was a gutsy move. And maybe it makes up some for what Collie felt, and still feels, every time he thinks of the whole thing.

"So all I'm saying now is, I knew there would be flak over anything that happened with O.C. Anything. And the public has a right to ask questions. That's . . . how it is."

Ginny walked, staring at the gravel.

"Is that what you wanted to see me about? To talk about the press thing?" Kidd said.

"No. It isn't." They stopped, and crossed the Mall toward the National Gallery.

"I didn't think it was," Kidd said.

She walked along, searching for words, frowning up at the sky, looking down at her skirt swaying with her steps. "Jeff. I'm worried about you."

"Why?"

"Last night, when you came to the house, and you didn't feel like talking . . ."

"I'm sorry, I know I was—"

"No! Don't be sorry. I don't want you to be sorry. I want you to talk if you need to, and not if you don't. But I'm afraid that . . ." She stopped and faced him. "Maybe you do need to talk. God, there must be so much you're feeling. I'm afraid you do, or you will. And I won't be a good listener."

"Are you saying this to me because of Jamie?"

Her eyes went stark wide. Then she said, "Yes. I think I am."

He took her hand again, and they walked. "I don't know how to say this to you. I don't know how to tell you so you'll know it. I can talk to you. I know I can. If Jamie didn't, then he didn't. For me, if I'm keeping anything from you, then I'm keeping it from myself. And maybe I am doing that, because I'm having dreams. Do you believe in dreams? That they tell us something?"

"Yes," she said, and thought of a dark night, on a winter street.

"I do too. And I've been dreaming. I see myself in a room. It's very small. People are coming at me. One is my ex-wife, but the dream's not about her, because I have a gun, and I'm shooting. It's like the gun is shooting, I'm just holding it, trying to turn it, but everywhere it goes it tears into something. It's not exactly people it hits, just parts of people, faces, chests, their insides. The bullets go right through people, right through the walls, and hit other people outside the room, people everywhere. I keep trying to turn the gun, but it keeps shooting. Until I wake up."

"My God, my God . . ." she whispered.

"I'll get over it. Maybe I wouldn't have dreamed it last night if I had told you about it before."

Ginny was aware of her heart thumping in an empty chest.

"Ginny, there's something else I ought to tell you."

"What?"

"You're crushing my hand." He raised his arm, and hers with it; his fingers were bunched together within her grip like asparagus, purple to the tips.

She released his hand and gasped. He laughed and hugged her.

"Look, you've got a meeting now, right?" he said as they walked back toward the parking lot. "Are you free later?"

"Yes."

"Then I'll pick you up. You and I are going on a date."

They parted in the parking lot. She walked back toward the White House. As she walked she felt the surge of spring in everything around her.

Kidd watched her until she was out of sight; she looked back once and waved. When she had disappeared, he walked back up the knoll to the entrance of the Washington Monument.

After the incident, President Stern had ordered everything repaired immediately, and though there were no more marks or stains, the crowds, three times their normal size, still looked for them. Kidd had to wait in line until he could ride the elevator to the top, where he went from viewport to viewport, and stared out over the city.

CHAPTER 15

"I loved it, Jeff. I really loved it," she said as they went up the walk to the front door.

"The movie was terrible!"

"But the Milk Duds and popcorn were so good!"

She opened the front door and went in. Then she stopped. "Aren't you . . . ?"

"No. It's a date. Right?" he said.

He kissed her quickly. "Good night, Ginny."

"Jeff?" she called as he started down the walk.

"What?" he said, turning but continuing to walk away, backward.

"Uh. Thanks!"

"Thank you!" At his car he did stop. "Good night, Ginny."

Peter Pugh lay smiling at the ceiling. Next to him, his girl friend was deeply asleep. They had shared three bottles of wine with their meal, and she would not awaken until almost noon. He had never told her what they were celebrating.

He could not believe the day he had had. After months of nothing, a call from Forbis.

And then that amazing stroke of—luck? Fate?

And that inspiration.

CHAPTER 16

Sam Emmett sat at a table in the corner of one of his favorite bars, part of the Saturday night circuit he made through Georgetown. He was twisted away toward the bar, laughing loudly at something a drunk legislative assistant was saying there; when he turned back he saw Peter Pugh sitting across the table from him.

"Sorry," Emmett said without missing a beat. "I've already given to the Boy Scouts." He laughed very loudly.

"Do you remember me?" Pugh said, smiling.

"The rich kid."

Pugh continued to smile. "Yeah."

Emmett was smiling too, suddenly, and then he was not smiling; his face was cycling through expressions. Emmett took a sip from his whiskey and said, "Whatever you want to say to me, hurry up with it. I've got a reputation to protect."

"Precisely." Pugh folded his forearms in front of him as he leaned on the table. He paused a moment, gave a shrug, and said, "I want to know who your source of information is. I've had several groups of people, in several different departments, under surveillance for a while. I haven't found out yet. Of course, I will sooner or later, but I want to know sooner. It would make my career."

"It would ruin mine."

"Oh no. Not if *I* were the one who found out. I've had taps on phones, I've followed people, I've got enough to *incriminate* even people who have never leaked anything, just by saying, 'Why were you an hour late from your lunch break on such-and-such a date?' "

"But why?"

"I told you. It would make my career."

"No, you ass! I understand completely your ambition. I'm talking about *my* ambition. Why should I help you?"

"I'll trade. I have information you'd love."

"How do you know I'll give you anything? Because I promise you, I'd never tell you anything. Even if you give me something first."

"I knew you'd say that, of course. So I thought I'd prove to you how good my information can be." Pugh leaned back in his chair and grinned, as if he saw Emmett dangling at the end of a spider's filament. "When I leave," Pugh said, "look under the napkin that your drink is sitting on. You'll find a thin envelope, with negatives in it. Have them developed. You'll be surprised."

Pugh stood. Emmett's fingers loosened around his glass, held it more delicately. Pugh was enormously satisfied that the bit of theater he had improvised as he sat down had been effective. Encouraged by this success he said, "You'll never doubt that I can deliver information, *insights* shall we say, worth more to you than what I'm asking you to give me."

Pugh walked out.

There was an envelope under Emmett's napkin, a white,

semi-transparent envelope, containing little squares of thirty-five-millimeter negative. Emmett slid the envelope quickly into his pocket, and glanced around to make sure no one else had seen. He was not sure what this Pugh's game was, but he was convinced he was not a mere kook; insane maybe, but the Washington kind of crazy, the young would-be Napoleon who has access to dynamite.

Emmett was wrong about Pugh. Pugh was inexperienced, and a bit carried away with the game, but he was totally rational. He was simply that most dangerous kind of man who inhabits the halls of power: he believed in his own plans.

Emmett spotted, in the opposite corner of the room, a young photographer who was just getting started with the *Constellation*. Calling the kid over, Emmett slipped him the negatives and told him to go back to the office and make prints. The photographer had a date with him, but he left her waiting and rushed off immediately.

Forty minutes later he came back and handed Emmett another envelope. The first print was of Jeff Kidd and Ginny Longstreet walking hand in hand along the Capitol Mall. Emmett did not know their names but he knew who they were.

But the other picture was even more intriguing. It showed Jeff Kidd, in the same clothes he was wearing in the picture with the woman, standing in line at the entrance to the Washington Monument.

CHAPTER 17

Ginny opened her eyes at six-thirty. She stared at the clock, thinking at first that she had overslept. She was a half-hour ahead of her normal schedule, but she was wide awake, and got up.

She had decided long ago that without a rigid schedule her spirit would become as limp as Jamie's disused flesh; so for the last few years she had lived by the same routine. She normally rose at seven and did thirty minutes of exercise and thirty of reading before work. Today was Saturday, when she increased her exercise and reading to an hour each, before cleaning the house and going to the market. But now she walked around her bedroom for a half-hour, barefoot on the wooden floor, and when seven o'clock did come she did not feel like starting her calisthenics. She finally showered, intending it to be a long, languorous soak. But once she got in she did not feel like lingering. She dressed and went downstairs.

She discovered that the boy who delivered morning papers to her neighbors did not do so until seven-twenty. She discovered that cartoons had gotten gaudier, less violent, and less intelligent than they were when she was growing up, though one station still showed Bugs Bunny.

At seven minutes before eight, she called Jeff Kidd.

"Hello," he said in a husky voice.

"Jeff. This is Ginny. I woke you, didn't I?"

"No! Of course not." She knew he would have said the same thing if she had called at 4 A.M.

"I know it's early," she said. "I was just thinking of taking a drive, and I wondered if you'd like to go."

"I'd love to! Where?"

"I'd thought about driving up to Baltimore. They're doing restorations in some of the old parts. I think they've got some interesting shops and restaurants."

She followed the directions he had given her, and when she reached the apartment, he was standing outside. "I'd have you in," he told her, "but the place has a contagious disease."

"Which is?"

"Gloom."

They drove into the Maryland morning, past suburban clusters of houses and shopping centers built in a mix of Colonial and Cape Cod, past more open country, where houses were surrounded by white running fences and horses stood in threes. She drove the Volkswagen as she had before, gripping the wheel with her elbows spread wide, grabbing the shift knob deep in a verticle palm, her thighs pumping up and down over the clutch and accelerator every time she blew past a truck on a grade. She noticed he was watching her, was even suppressing a smile, and she interrupted a sentence about the difference between Maryland and Virginia horse farms to say, "What! What is it?"

"Nothing!" he said, and the second time she glanced from the road to him he was smiling, and seemed about to laugh.

"What?!" she yelled, downshifting again as she gunned the car around a laboring Winnebago, and smiled herself, as if she knew.

"Nothing!" he said again, shaking his head. He thought of what it might be like to say, *I think the way you drive is . . . well,* sensual! But he could not. And yet the thought of it, and another half-angry, half-teasing glance from her, made him laugh.

And she laughed too, not fully knowing the reason.

In thirty minutes they were in the new heart of Old Baltimore, where heavy bricks 140 years old mounted into three-story shops and houses, facing each other over streets where trees grew from concrete boxes in the sidewalk. They drove and looked, without direction, until they turned a corner onto a street tightly packed with restaurants and shops sporting broad windows and narrow signs. At the first open parking space, Ginny hit the brakes and hammered the car in.

"Lock it?" Kidd said, getting out.

"Are you kidding?"

The Tidewater haze had burned off early, so that the leaves spread above the sidewalks were a sharp green against the blue sky showing above the building rows. They walked past a florist's shop where painted flower carts stood outside a broad doorway of oak set into brick; they stopped at the window of another shop and watched a candlemaker carve designs from multi-dipped forms of scented tallow. Further along, around corners, down alleys, were other shops: rare books, English wallpaper, German clocks; the feel of Moroccan leather, embossed vellum, the smell of oiled walnut, musty pages, and everywhere—the redolence of coffee.

"Do you think they blow it down the street?" Kidd said, inhaling and wetting his lips. "Do they do it on purpose?"

Ginny drew a long breath through her nose and sighed. She grinned and checked her watch. "Let's find a place for lunch. Don't let me get sidetracked."

They walked back out onto the main street and stood looking, sniffing for the coffee aroma to point them to a restaurant.

"I'm not sure," she said. "Maybe down that way." She pointed in a direction they had not been, but then followed his gaze to a storefront behind them, where a high-necked blouse with lace sleeves stood erect upon a headless blue velvet mannequin.

"That blouse is you," he said.

They took a few steps closer, but stopped still away from the window. Ginny took in the white triangular mold of the bodice, and the lace, spidery against the blue background. She chuckled. "Can you see me in that at work?"

"Why not?"

"Come on," she said, and drew him away.

They passed one coffee shop and then another, looking for one that was not overcrowded, overdecorated, or overcute. "Still too full," she said at a third. "Don't you think? Oh, look at that!" She pointed to the far side of the street, and pulled Kidd across the cobblestones to the front of a narrow store. In the window was a broad piece of upholstered furniture, with rounded, padded arms, an open, walnut frame base, and a beige background fabric that struck Kidd because the green of the pattern stitched on it was exactly the color of Ginny Longstreet's eyes.

"Let's go in," Kidd said.

"No. We need to eat."

"Come on." He led her inside.

The store made up for narrowness with length; it stretched like a cavern. Halfway back a delicate man in suspenders, a white shirt, and a Windsor-knot tie was polishing beeswax into a tabletop. He glanced up as they came in, but kept polishing.

Kidd was turning to the window when Ginny caught his arm in both hands and said, "Isn't this place beautiful? Look at all this!" She steered him farther into the room, where they saw brass lamps, oak-and-glass tables, rolltop desks. Kidd halted at one grouping where a carved mantel placed against the wall and bracketed by Colonial maps and hunt pictures suggested a masculine study; before the imaginary fireplace stood a leather chair that looked red on the side toward the window, deep brown in the lamplight around the mantel.

Kidd leaned his nose to the chair and breathed in. He put a hand on either side of the winged back and squeezed. Then he looked up at Ginny and grinned sheepishly. "Nice, isn't it?"

"Sit down," she said.

"No, no, come on," he said, and led her back toward the window.

She stopped at the couch, touched the fabric slowly, and pulled her fingertips away. "It is beautiful." She ran her palm down the curved back, onto the padded arm, and pressed down from her shoulder. Then she stepped away. "Come on, let's find a restaurant," she said.

"May I help you people with something?" the man in the suspenders said behind them.

"We were just browsing," Ginny said.

Kidd said, "This is a beautiful—sofa, is that what you call it?"

"A *stretched love seat*," the clerk said precisely. "It's our own design."

Kidd pursed his lips, trying not to feel stupid. "I love this color," he said, rubbing his hand over the fabric. "I'd call this background beige, I guess, but—"

"Putty," the clerk interrupted.

"Putty?"

The clerk, noticing Kidd's raised eyebrows, said, "That's what the designers call it."

"And what do they call this color?" Kidd said, pointing to the stitched design.

"Greenstone," the clerk said.

"Greenstone and putty . . ."

"Come on," Ginny said. "We've got to find a place for lunch."

Around a corner, in an upstairs restaurant the furniture store clerk had recommended as "tranquil," Ginny and Kidd ate hot crab sandwiches with iced tea, saving space for coffee and the Marylander's Chocolate Mousse advertised on a chalkboard by the doorway. The restaurant was decorated as a Colonial tavern; their conversation drifted to restorations.

"Between here and Richmond there are so many great old places," Kidd said. "Some of them have War significance— Civil War, that is."

"Was there some other?"

"Those old houses lack a lot, but I've seen places that had chapels in the cellar, where Confederates hid from Yankees."

"A restoration would be an endless investment, I think," Ginny said. "It could drain you. But it might pay in the long run."

"The only things that will pay are the things you care about, the things you'd want to do even if they didn't pay," Kidd said. "I . . . I have an uncle who's a farmer, and once on a visit I went with him to feed his cattle. I helped him toss a couple of bushels of corn into the pasture, and he stopped and leaned on the fence, so I leaned there with him, and after a few minutes he said, 'You know, a man that throws feed over the fence and then just walks away, he won't be worth a damn as a farmer. A good farmer will aways stand there for a few minutes, just watchin' 'em eat and get fat.'" Kidd grinned. He toasted her with his tea. "If you love it, do it. Advice I have seldom followed."

"Why don't you buy that chair? You loved it."

"I loved the way it smelled and felt. But I'd look ridiculous in it. It's an aristocrat's chair."

"Maybe a middle-class man is the only one who can sit in an aristocrat's chair and *not* look pompous."

The waitress brought the mousse, and after they had moaned over their first mouthfuls, Kidd said, "Why don't you buy that couch? Excuse me—that stretched love seat?"

She pulled a chocolate haze across the stark white saucer. "I can't." When the pause got uncomfortable she said quickly, "I have simple tastes. I mean, I admit I liked the couch—excuse me, the stretched love seat. But if I bought it, it would be for the name of the colors—*putty* and *greenstone*. I would stick it in my living room and put a sign on it for a year or so saying, 'KEEP OFF THE PUTTY AND GREENSTONE!'" A smile opened on her face, but before it bloomed it turned bitter. "Even if I could buy the sofa—screw the wimp in the furniture store, it's a sofa—I wouldn't take anything I really liked, and . . . It would just look bad by itself."

"Ginny, I don't want to pry . . ."

"You couldn't pry."

"Okay. Are you . . . okay for money?"

"The care for Jamie is expensive. It takes most of my salary. But, like I said, I have simple tastes. And the house is paid for."

Kidd seemed surprised.

"Jamie made a big down payment on the house, and the rest of his signing bonus he put into stocks. He lost a lot of that. A couple of weeks before he shot himself—when, it turns out, he'd had a big fight with his coach—he called his stockbroker and told him to sell what was left and pay off the rest of the house. He didn't leave me any note, but he had called his broker. I didn't know about it until . . . later, when the broker called and told me about it. He had seventy-five thousand dollars for me." She sipped her coffee and said, "So I paid off the house."

They sat in sober silence for several minutes, until Kidd said, "You know, I've never thought of Jamie as somebody who walked around, had normal things to say. Somebody who bought a house, talked to a stockbroker . . . talked to you. I've never really thought of him as a real person."

Her eyes defocused, staring toward the last smears of her mousse. "He was real." She looked up suddenly. "Is real."

"How often do you see him?"

"Every Sunday. I'm driving down tomorrow."

"May I go with you?"

"Yes. If you want to. Yes."

They spent the afternoon in Old Baltimore, shopping, buying nothing. They picked up a pizza on the way home, and ate it in front of the fireplace, where they had built a blaze from a crate they found in her garage. After the pizza she made a potful of popcorn. He talked for two hours about the numerous times the Army of Northern Virginia repulsed the Army of the Potomac in its drives on Richmond. He discovered that she, having studied Lincoln's presidency in detail, knew more about those campaigns than he did. So he described Stonewall Jackson's Valley Campaign, about which he knew everything.

Then he asked her to dance.

CHAPTER 18

They drove out through the rolling green hills where the oaks and hickories were a chartreuse and the stands of spruce a blue-green. The sky was light and hazy with the humidity of spring. Kidd's car had an air conditioner but they did not need it. Ginny wore a sundress, an off-white. Beneath the lace hem her calves were lean, brown, and moist.

They did not talk much. At first he chatted a lot, making conversation; he told her about odd teachers he had had in high school, embarrassing moments on blind dates in college—stories he had told often before and fell back on now, wanting to entertain her. But about twenty miles out of Washington she reached over, took his right hand from the wheel and held it quietly in hers. They did not talk much after that.

In an hour they turned off the interstate. Twenty minutes later they reached the long, circular drive that led up to the house, which had once been a widow's mansion. Wan white women and wiry Black men walked around the manicured front lawns or pushed blanket-covered forms in wheelchairs along paths bordered by pansies.

He stopped the car in the graveled parking area, shut off the motor, and started to get out. Her hand on his forearm stopped him. "Jeff. Thank you," she said. "It's enough that you brought me. I'll go in alone."

He waited in the car for an hour. He tried for some of that time to play the radio but all he got were two stations playing gospel music and one farm report.

When she came back to the car her cheeks were dry, but the bottom of her nose glistened and her eyes were rimmed in red. They drove out of the driveway, away from the Violet Ridge Country Home, and they were silent. Then, ten miles before the interstate, she leaned slowly over and put her head against his shoulder.

He reached up and cradled her head in his right arm.

After a while he spoke, the first time either of them had said anything after leaving the asylum. "Listen. Ginny. Would you like to go somewhere? Take a trip? You could get the time off, we could go . . . anywhere. Would you like to do that?"

She sniffed hard, thought for a moment, and with her cheek pressed against his shoulder said, "Not really."

He nodded, though she did not see it. After a few moments he said, "Is there anything you can think of right now that you would like to do?"

A minute later she lifted her head and looked at him. "Yes. There is," she said. "I'd like to go back to that big hollow house that I live in, and make it into a home."

CHAPTER 19

Everything is empty. Everyone is empty. He stands in the room. He has walked in somehow. There is a book open on a table. A yellowed light shows on the

*pages, there are names in the book. People, old peo-
ple, want him to write his name in the book. He does
not want to write his name in the book. They are
staring at him. He picks up the gun on the table. No,
it is not a gun, it is a pen. He writes his name in the
book. He steps back, and the old people squint from
across the room, trying to read his name.*

*There are no boys in the room, he is the only boy.
Where is it? Will someone take him there? He recognizes no one, what if his mother has brought him to
the wrong place? He walks around a corner, finds a
wide door, and sees the coffin. There it is! There are
more old people he does not know in the room. They
do not look at him. He is at the coffin. There is a
mannequin of a boy inside. Oh! This is the
showroom. This is where they bring people who want
to buy a coffin, they open one up and put a dummy
in it to—*

Kidd tore in terror from his sleep. His hands clutched at the
damp sheets. Panting, he relaxed his fingers, then squeezed
again at the bunched cloth.

It was not his dream of Roxanne Lark; that was a different
room, different faces.

But why, after all these years, should he have dreamed about
Calvin Herms?

CHAPTER 20

At the junction where the main outlet of Ginny's neighborhood met the road to the Beltway, there was a small shopping center, made up to look like an Alpine village. Between
the market and a yarn shop was a paint store. On her way to
work, Ginny stopped there, and on her way home that evening

she stopped again. She walked quickly up to the man behind the counter, who gave her a puzzled smile. Pulling from her purse the color card, she handed it to him and said, "This is the one I want."

He frowned at the card. "What's the matter?" Ginny said quickly. "You do have it, don't you?"

"Oh, sure, we have it. It's a blend, we make it up special." Finally looking up from the card he said, "How much do you want?"

"Uh, enough for a living room?" The man stood still, staring at her from beneath bushy brown brows. "Medium-sized. Well, fairly large."

He nodded slowly and stepped over to a wooden table spattered with a thousand dried pigments. "What color is it now?" he said.

"The living room? Ah, a sort of beige."

Pulling cans from beneath his mixing table and setting them on the spattered surface, the man said, "This should cover pretty good, then. I expect you'll need about five gallons." He began to pry the lids off the cans; Ginny was surprised that the paint inside was white. Before he opened the last can the man stopped and said, "On special mixes there's no refunds. But I can mix an exact match later. If you want to wait and just get four . . ."

"No. Thank you. I'll take all five right now."

Using a baffling-looking machine studded with dials, tubes, and levers, he began to pump out the pigments in some mysterious ratio; Ginny watched, fascinated, as squirts of black, blue, and even a drop of shocking yellow plopped into the paint. "I didn't expect to see you back so soon," the man said as he repeated the process for each can. "Most of the ladies in this neighborhood'll fuss with color chips for weeks before they want anything, and then it's just a pint to slap on the wall and change their minds."

"Yes. Yes, I suppose that's true." Ginny knew she had been rushing, and even now she did not want to slow down.

"You got brushes, rollers? Drop cloths? Masking tape?"

"No, I'll need all that."

While the paint was shaking violently in the mixer, he took her around the store and gathered all the supplies she would need. When she did not know what spackling compound was, he explained to her about patching nail holes and chips in plaster with the white paste, a putty knife, and sandpaper. Then he went into the storeroom and came out with a big can, crushed at one end. "Good as new," he said. "But I can't sell it. You can have it."

When she paid him he said, "You might get stuck, but you can do it. Call me if you have a problem. Advice is free." And as she was leaving he called to her, stopping her at the door. "And lady? If you change your mind about the color, you just bring it back. I'll say I mixed it wrong."

When Kidd called her that night, she said she couldn't go out to eat because she was painting. "Painting? Painting what?" he said.

"The living room. At least to start."

When he got there with the sack of hamburgers, she already had the drapes down, the furniture, books, and stereo dragged out into the hallway, the drop cloths and newspapers spread out on the floor, and spackling dust in her hair. He walked into the living room wide-eyed. "When did you spackle that wall?" he asked, stunned.

"Tonight. Just now."

"You're, uh . . ." Touching the smooth white blotches with his fingertips he said, "You need to wait till it's dry before you sand . . ."

"Yeah. I mean I just sanded it. I put the spackle on this wall before I moved the furniture. I just had to try it."

"Well . . . Give me a putty knife. And for crying out loud, tie a cloth or something over your hair."

Together they masked the floor and ceiling moldings, and he rigged up some unshaded lamps to give them more light. He told her they should spackle and smooth all the walls before they started painting, but she said she couldn't wait to see the color, so while he repaired cracks and the holes from picture nails, she broke out a new roller and went to work on the wall she had done first.

When she stepped back to look he came and stood behind her, but he did not squeeze her. He feared to intrude. But together they stared at the new wall, alive with a fresh coat, slate gray.

Several hours later she was crouched in the middle of the newspaper-strewn floor, furiously stirring a fourth full can. Kidd grabbed and held her hands, sticky with damp paint, and when she looked up at him in surprise he said, "Ginny. It's past one. I'll be glad to stay as long as you want to work, but this is no one-night job. You've got to let that first coat dry completely to make the second coat really smooth. Why don't we stop for tonight? I'll come early tomorrow to help you."

Drawn from a distance, she seemed to see him for the first time all evening. She lowered the stirring rod back into the paint can, slowly scraped the excess off the rod, and then put the cap on.

Looking away from Kidd she said, "I'm afraid if I stop, I might not ever finish."

"You'll finish," he said. "I swear you will."

In the kitchen they ate the reheated hamburgers. They did not talk much; she sat close to him at the kitchen table, and seemed to appreciate his being there, but she still had that distance in her stare, and when he held her hand she squeezed it hard, as if to tell him that she wanted him close, but could not feel him now.

He left to go back to his apartment, promising to come directly from work the next afternoon to get the painting started again. He urged her to get a good night's sleep.

But she woke herself at five-thirty the next morning, painting another hour and spackling a wall of her bedroom before she showered and went to her office.

That day she would make plans for the refurbishing of every room in her house, except one.

CHAPTER 21

The parking lot was gravel spread over grass; bright spring shoots popped up all around the stones and bent against the tires of the parked cars. The house itself was wooden, white, rambling, completely surrounded by screened-in verandas. Kidd stood beside his car and felt the evening air float by, carrying alternately the cool scent of blossoming dogwoods and the hot pepper smell of frying chicken.

As Ginny pulled up the sound of her tires crunching in the gravel reminded Kidd of country reunions and tent revivals. She got out smiling and he kissed her lightly on the cheek. "What a beautiful, beautiful place," she said, her eyes soaked with the wet green of the grass.

"You didn't have any trouble finding it?"

"No, no, your directions were good. I just can't believe there's anything like this so close by."

He walked her along the path, across a busy veranda and into the house. They passed through noisy dining rooms where portraits of Presidents hung on every wall. Nixon was still prominent over the fireplace in the central banquet room. A teenage waitress in a floor-length Colonial skirt led them to a table on one of the side verandas. "Iced tea for both of us," Kidd told the waitress, who smiled and hurried away.

"What else?" Ginny said.

"You know, I don't know if I ever told you how refreshing it is to be with someone who's well-cultured."

"Oh?" Ginny said, smiling in a way that was more sly than she intended. "Your Yankee wife didn't drink tea?"

"Hot coffee in the middle of July."

"Whereas you had iced tea for Christmas dinner, right?"

He laughed very loudly. "That's right! It is right!" And even in his laughter Kidd realized that the only other time he had spoken of his wife to Ginny was in a dead sober calm, alone at midnight. He wondered, in that instant, if Ginny would ever feel free enough to speak of Jamie—if not with a smile, at least without a chill.

He leaned forward quickly and said, "This place is owned by the Noseworthy sisters. That's right, the Noseworthy sisters, that's their real name. They're twins, in their sixties. My brother-in-law met them when one had appendicitis and the other insisted she had to have hers removed at the same time, because if Thelma's appendix was bad, then Elma's must be too. I'm not joking, what's so funny? He assisted in the anesthesia—he's a resident—and afterward, when they woke up side by side in the recovery room, Thelma turns to Elma and says, 'Sister, let's take that house Brother left us and open us up a restaurant.'"

"What?!" Ginny giggled.

"First thing out of her mouth. Elma says, 'Good idea.' A month later they sent my brother-in-law an invitation for the whole family. Of course, he had to come see it, wouldn't you? They didn't have any trouble with the zoning because they've got a cousin on the zoning board. Besides they own a thousand acres in the county. They call the place 'T & E's All-You-Can-Eat.'"

Kidd led her to the main food tables, where ten different vegetables lay in steaming silver trays beside platters of fried chicken, baked fish, and a molten beef stew. Over the serving table was a hand-lettered sign reading, "Take All You Want Eat All You Take." They were still smiling when they sat down again at the table on the veranda.

She said, "Can I ask you how work is? I don't want to get into something you can't tell me, but I just wonder how you are."

"Yes, sure, it's not, uh, there's no reason for you to be afraid to ask, and there's nothing for me to worry about keeping from you. Work is . . ." He found himself unable to say anything about his work, and he felt self-conscious about the time it was taking to answer. "I can't really tell you how work is. Not because there's anything you shouldn't know, it's just . . . I don't know what I'm doing now. I don't know what they're doing with me. I go to work and I sit at a desk." Collier had told Kidd that morning that he wanted him to write a manual on the selection and training of O.C. agents. Kidd did not know what to make of it: he was on his way up, or out altogether. Or it meant nothing, except that he was out of the action. "Uh, thank you for asking, Ginny."

"I'm just not sure how much you can talk about. Even if you want to," she said.

He nodded. He poked his fork into the buttered yams on his plate but did not eat. "Tell me something. What about your work? Do you find—is there meaning in it for you? *Meaning*, that sounds so . . ."

"California?"

"Yeah! I just mean that . . . speechwriting isn't something that occurs to most people as a career. You've told me about how you got into it through Livingstone and all that, but I mean . . . People seem to find what's important to them either inside their career or outside it. I just . . ."

Kidd trailed off, uncomfortable and unsure what he was trying to say.

"I think I know what you mean," she said. "I think, I think you're asking if my work sustains me, and what it is about it that matters."

"Precisely! I think."

"Yeah," Ginny said, her eyes defocused and wandering. "That's a good question. In my case, actually, I did have an idea of being a speechwriter when I was younger. I didn't think of it in that way, but that's what it was. It came to me in church."

"Oh boy. I can't wait to hear this!"

"Well, you know, I told you about my father. He was very popular with the congregation. His sermons were scholarly, which pleased everybody because that meant a service was never unsettling. His voice was deep and powerful. And his delivery was grandiose, not even so much in the way he chose his words, though he was verbally elegant, but in the way he pronounced them: *'Our Most Ho-ly Heavenly Fahh-ther!'* He would pray like that, too, and his prayers, his prayers weren't—

they didn't seem so much petitions to God as they were lectures to the congregation: *'We know that we have failed in our faith, that we have pretended to perceive Almighty Gawd in abstractions while ignoring the manfestations of His Being within our neighbor . . .'* Do you know what I mean?"

"Yes," Kidd said. "I know what you mean."

"I don't mean to be making fun of him."

"You aren't. Go on. Please."

"When I was about fifteen the church hired a new assistant pastor, right out of the seminary. He had been a football star at U.Va. He had this thick hair and strong jaw, and broad shoulders," she said, smiling, even blushing a little, "and I had an enormous crush on him." In her embarrassment, she drew out the word "enormous," quickly adding, "He had a little bottle-blond wife who always smiled and had this dippy little laugh." Ginny pressed her lips together in a caricature simper, and then laughed at the viciousness of the female jealousy that could survive when the rivalry itself was only a memory.

"My father didn't let him preach much at first; he'd just get to make announcements during the service, or quote a verse. He had this big, happy grin full of even teeth, and he'd always flash it and say, 'Make a Joyful noise unto the Lorrrd!' just before the choir would sing. That was the first time I'd ever really been aware of what my father was doing. 'The Lorrrd Gawd!' My father was so steeped in it, that manner seemed, well, primordial. But Mr. Fields hadn't really gotten it down yet. Still, that was just something I noticed, I wasn't put off.

"When he got to preach, I would listen enraptured, and think of all the emotion that must be behind everything he said; I would imagine his private thoughts. But he never really said anything personal. Maybe that's why I did make up my own ideas about him.

"It got really plain to me when I went away to college. You know how everybody thinks of college as a carefree time—sometimes I even think of it that way myself. But of course it isn't that way at all, it can be bleak really, when you're not sure if you know everything, or nothing, when there's so much to worry about, when—when you first start to worry about the things, things like love and life and death, that you learn later not to worry about, in order to survive. Well when I would come home to visit, I'd go to church and then I'd think, *He doesn't say a thing, really, he doesn't give a thing. If only he'd step up into the pulpit and say, 'There are times when I don't know where God is, or what He wants. There are times when I don't feel like making a joyful noise.'* That, by the way, is part of the theology I keep now—that God Almighty did not intend for human beings to always be certain, or to always smile.

"Anyway. I didn't have any idea of being a speechwriter then, of course, but I think that's when I first discovered the disposition to write words for other people to say. And as far as whether I get meaning out of it, whether it matters—that *was* the original question, wasn't it?—I guess that all depends on what it is I say. *They* say. Freudian slip."

They laughed again. Then she said, "What are you thinking?"

Caught off guard, he realized he had been staring. "I'm sorry, I just . . . I just found the key to something about you, something—or a lot of things—that had never quite fit together and just fell into place."

"What? What is it?"

He shook his head and waved his hand, as if to deny that anything he said, or thought, should be taken seriously. "I'm sorry, Ginny, I don't mean to be analyzing you!" He saw that she was not satisfied, but went on. "Do you go to church at all now?"

"No."

"Why not?"

"I guess for one thing, because of the way I grew up, I never developed the feeling that I had to be in touch with a clergyman or in a church to encounter God. And for another thing, when Jamie . . . when he shot himself, Mr. Fields called me, and he said, 'The Lord works in mysterious ways.' That's what he said. 'The Lord works in mysterious ways.'"

She turned to look out through the screen, toward the night falling on the Manassas fields.

"You know something, Jeff?" she said, with her face still

turned from him. "Every time we talk, it's a revelation for me. Even when I'm talking, I find out things I never realized about myself."

She looked back to him, and he was grinning. "How do you like the beans?" he said.

Looking down at her plate, poking at the beans with her fork, she said, "They're delicious. They have honey in them, don't they?"

"Beats me. But they are good."

When the waitress came and cleared the plates, Ginny opened her purse, withdrew the five color cards she had gotten that morning at the paint store, and asked him which one he thought would look best for her bedroom.

"You're not painting tonight, are you?" he said.

"Of course! The night is young."

The waitress returned, bearing saucers. "What's this?" Ginny said.

"Dessert!" the waitress said, smiling.

Ginny groaned. "I don't have room for another bite!"

"Eat what you can and take the rest home," the waitress said, setting the saucers before them. "It's our complimentary dessert, all month!"

It was cherry pie.

CHAPTER 22

They had just started for the evening when the doorbell rang. Ginny looked up from the strip of floor molding she was painting and said, "Who could that be?" She set her narrow brush carefully atop her can of paint, stood from her knees with a groan, and answered the door. "John!" she said in complete surprise. "Come in!"

Livingstone walked into the foyer. "Hi, Ginny. Sorry to just

—Oh, hello!" he said, looking through to the living room and spotting Kidd on a ladder in the far corner.

Kidd stepped down, walking quickly over. "Mr. Livingstone," he said respectfully. Livingstone did not seem at all surprised to see him.

As Livingstone shook Kidd's hand, Ginny said, "John, this is—"

"I know! Mr. Browne!" Livingstone smiled slyly at them both. Then he took a step back to view Ginny in her work clothes. "I always knew you could get grubby, but I never thought I'd see it!"

"We're painting," Ginny said, wiping a big smear on the back of her hand off on the leg of her jeans.

"Well I hope you got some on the wall." Looking through the wide entranceway of the living room, then slowly walking in, Livingstone said, "Oh, yeah. You sure did. Wow. This is really beautiful!"

The walls were now satin with gray, the ceiling a lightened shade of the same color. The crown and floor moldings were a pure gloss white, as were the window frames and sash, and the mantel. "Gosh," Livingstone said. "You've really been working." Kidd noticed, or thought he did, that Livingstone's eyes held on Ginny for just a moment then, in a look of appraisal, or indecision.

"Yes," she said, not hiding her excitement with his approval. "We're almost finished with the second coat on the moldings, and Jeff—Mr. Browne—is starting the bookshelves right now."

"It's beautiful. It really is."

She began to walk around, talking about all the deliberations she had gone through in choosing the color, how the room had a different feeling during the day, maybe because the various pigments came through in different lights, how she wondered if the gray would match the floor, how she worried if she had chosen too dark a shade. She was immensely pleased with her choice, and Livingstone saw that.

"Oh, I'm rattling!" she said, catching herself. "Did you come by for business? Is there anything wrong?"

"No," Livingstone said. "You've just had color chips on your desk the last two times I've been to your office, and since I was . . . out here to see some friends tonight, I wanted to drop by and see what you were up to."

"That's great!" Ginny said. "Let me make some tea."

"No, no I have to go."

At the door Ginny said, "John. Thanks for coming." Livingstone stopped and hugged her. She was surprised by that, and pleased. And when Livingstone shook hands with Kidd he also reached up and gripped him on the shoulder, in a way that to Kidd seemed fatherly. "Nice to see you again," Livingstone said.

They started to paint again. Ginny was saying that Livingstone's visit was the first time in a year that he had been by the house, when the phone rang. She went into the hallway to answer it. "Hello," Kidd heard her say, and then there was nothing. She hung up the receiver, stood for a moment, and walked back into the living room. Kidd watched her. "It was an obscene phone call," she said slowly. "I never got one of those before."

"What did he say?"

"It wasn't a he, it was . . . a woman."

"A woman? It wasn't a joke?"

"No. It was no joke."

"Well what did she say?"

"Just one word. 'Whore.'"

She picked up her brush and went back to painting before he could walk over to her. But she stopped when he said, "You didn't recognize the voice, did you? It was nobody you know?"

"I just heard one word," she said lightly. "But no, nobody I know would . . . It's nothing, just some kook."

Yet in that strained and vicious voice there had been something strangely familiar. But she went back to the floor molding, and in her work forgot the call.

Kidd wondered, as he painted the bookshelves, if Ginny had noticed that Livingstone was carrying a newspaper folded in his side coat pocket. If she had, she was not troubled by it, or by the call. She worked and chatted happily about what colors might look good in other rooms.

But that night, when they were finished with the living room and he was ready to leave, she asked him to stay.

And even when she had fallen asleep in his arms, she held him absolutely close, as if dark fate were a cat, thin as shadow, perched on the foot of the bed and waiting to slide between them if she gave it the slightest space.

CHAPTER 23

Kidd was at his apartment, getting ready for work. He was about to step into the shower when the phone rang.

"Jeff!" Dooley said. "Where have you been?"

"Do we have an alert?"

"No," Dooley said, after a hesitation.

"I was . . . where I told you I would be if I wasn't somewhere else," Kidd said. "Did you use the number I gave you?"

"Yeah, it was off the hook!"

He had not known. So the phone call had troubled her that much. "I'm sorry, Tenny, that was an accident. How serious is this? You could have sent a car."

"It's not that serious, but I wanted to talk with you first. There's been an article. Last night's *Continent*. It ran again this morning, in the *Constellation* . . ."

Pugh truly admired the article that Emmett had written. He sat at his desk with the paper open, comparing the display in the morning edition with what was in the sister edition the night before, and he thought, *That Emmett really is a master.*

Emmett had taken on just the right tone—matter-of-fact and mocking, all at the same time. The government had a new intelligence service, highly efficient, extremely discreet. The confidentiality of its agents was carefully protected. Journalists were not supposed to ask troubling questions of Operation Counterstrike's hero.

But here he was, parading publicly, "within sight of the White House," with a presidential speechwriter "notorious for her stunning looks." Without Pugh's stroke of fortune to have put Virginia Longstreet under surveillance just at the time she went out to visit Kidd, that meeting would have been completely incognito, lost in a tourist crowd where no one could recognize them, but Emmett had portrayed them as flagrantly displaying themselves. He did not give their names; he did not have Kidd's name, though he certainly had gotten Ginny Longstreet's. Still, Emmett left the publication of her name to the other news agencies which that morning had picked up the story. One of the television networks had already discovered Kidd's name and broadcast it, with Ginny Longstreet's.

Emmett simply ran their pictures: the one of them talking and the one of Kidd waiting to enter the monument.

Emmett mentioned that the woman was the one "rumored to have been involved with the agent in some drunken stumbling at the closed White House celebration of the Operation Counterstrike activities," but he said nothing further about the nature of their meeting in the Mall. In the picture they were only talking; Emmett left it to the public to infer what they were talking about.

But he did ask openly why any man would be so fascinated with the place where he had brought a group of people to their deaths that he would stand in a line to visit it.

When Ginny walked through the White House gate, the guard looked at her strangely; not suspiciously, but knowingly. And when she walked into her office, Maggie hesitated, and then said good morning with excess enthusiasm.

Ginny passed through Maggie's space to her office, sat down, stretched both arms wide, and grabbed the corners of her desk. The surface was tidy, with the newspapers piled on the floor in a corner. "Maggie! Come in here!"

"Just—just a minute!" Maggie called, and spoke once

quickly into the phone, finishing the call she had just started. Then she walked in, a green steno pad pressed between her palms, her fingers crawling along the last page.

Ginny leaned back in her chair and said, "What's been happening?" Maggie seemed not to understand the question. Her fingers still crawled along the pad. She tucked in her chin to peer out beneath her brows. "This morning, Maggie. What's going on? Have Kurtz and Sherwood turned in their three-pointers for that labor union speech?"

"Oh! Well," Maggie said. "Uh, yes! Mr. Sherwood and Mr. Kurtz both dropped three-pointers off last night. In fact, Mr. Sherwood called and asked me to type his rough draft. His secretary's sick."

"Sherwood's written a draft, before the three-pointer's been approved?"

"Yes. Mr. Kurtz, too."

"Hmm! They're sure working hard."

"Yes."

"But the President hasn't said anything?"

Again Maggie stared at her as if maybe they were conversing in two different languages. "About what?" Maggie said.

"About the three-pointers. He hasn't sent down any notes?"

"Not lately," Maggie said, and turned abruptly and walked from the room.

Ginny sat for a moment and then walked out to Maggie's desk. Maggie put the phone down when she saw her there. "Okay," Ginny said. "I want you to tell me what it is right now. Is it newspaper? Or radio and television?"

"Newspaper," Maggie whispered.

"So what are they saying?"

"Just that you . . . that you and . . . Oh! Mr. Livingstone!" Maggie did not add, "Thank God!" but it was there in her tone as Livingstone appeared at the door.

"If Maggie called you, it's trouble," Ginny said.

Back inside Ginny's office, Livingstone showed her the Emmett articles, and the coverage that was appearing in other papers. The *Constellation*, true to form, had not given its story to the wire services, so the other papers had to quote Emmett directly. But unlike Emmett, they had identified her by name. And Kidd's name, Livingstone told her, was sure to appear in evening editions everywhere.

Ginny said nothing. Livingstone tried to get her to sit but she kept pacing. Then she stopped in the corner of the office, her eyes unfocused toward the wall. Livingstone looked down. A long time went by before he spoke. "You know, all my life I've thought about, in one form or another, the question of a free press and what power there is in the media, what influence in the written and spoken word. You see something like this and you think, *People shouldn't be allowed to write trash like that*. But really they *should* be allowed, they *must* be allowed. There's no question about that to me.

"So I start thinking, *Okay, the journalist that trades on that sort of thing is slime, and he must have a slimy audience to get away with it*. But you know that's not true either. People—everyday, good people—are concerned about the other people who influence their lives, who wield power in one form or another, who make decisions, and it's only natural that they should be interested in information. And only right that they should get it. Except that they don't get the whole story. A journalist—if you can use that term for Sam Emmett—has the power to tell just enough of a story to create a public judgment, without ever lying and yet creating an absolute falsehood, surrounding something that is beautiful, profound—in short, *human*—with a layer of nonhumanity, the abstractions of 'he does this, she does that,' which no one in the world would judge the same way if they lived the life of the person written about. I hate that. I really hate it. I have to remember what Jefferson said, that if he had to choose between a world without government and a world without newspapers, he would—"

It was the sudden focusing of her eyes that stopped him.

She walked over and sat down behind her desk. "John, could you just leave me by myself for a while?"

CHAPTER 24

Kidd stood on the street beside a cart from which a vendor sold Nutty Buddies. The street was busy with traffic but most of the pedestrians had already caught their buses or reached their favorite bars.

"Jeff . . . is that you? Hell, yes! How the hell are you doing?!" The giant Black man who had appeared beside him, and was pumping his hand so enthusiastically, wore a tremendous smile.

"Peaks?" Kidd said.

"Come on, man, it hasn't been that long! The last time I saw you was when Dooley and I were in Munich! How is he, anyway? You know my oldest boy calls that redneck bastard 'Uncle Tennyson'? Hey, what do I care, huh? As long as he doesn't call him 'Daddy'!"

Kidd was distracted, his smile forced. On his shoulder Peaks placed a massive hand that was powerful in its gentleness. "Hey man," Peaks said, "I can't tell you how proud I was of you. All of us were, and still are."

"Yeah. Good. Thanks," Kidd said.

"Hey, can I buy you a drink?"

"Thanks, no, Wesley. Some other time."

"Aw hell, don't tell me you're too busy! They gave you time off, I know they did because our section tried to get you down to talk to us about that hit you made. Listen, you gotta have a drink with me! I'm just dying to hear some details, just what you can tell that will stay in the family, you know? But all the guys—"

"Hold it, Wesley. Hold it." Peaks stopped but kept the friendly, surprised look on his face until it faded under Kidd's stare and his words. "Cut the 'old buddy' crap. I like you and you know it but this accidental meeting isn't gonna get me off

the street. You can go back and tell Collie you tried real hard.
I'll even tell him for you. But you're not tough enough to take
me—not right this minute—and unless you're willing to shoot
me you better back—" Kidd looked over Peaks's shoulder and
broke off; his eyes got very still. Sam Emmett had just walked
out of the *Constellation* Building.

Emmett hurried along with that uneven bounce of his. He
was going to the Yorktown Bar, where he always went, and
was rushing only because the juices of controversy were flowing
through him. He swung his left arm wildly; his right arm hung
almost still.

He was making a noise that was not a whistle but was high-
pitched and rhythmic. It was unconscious; it came from the
center of his chest like a coo, like a baby's feeding sigh. The
sound suddenly cut off with an intake, a half-hiccup, when a
man stepped from the street onto the sidewalk, not five feet
from him. They were face to face before Emmett saw him
coming. It was Jeff Kidd.

Emmett lurched to a stop. Kidd did not touch him but he
looked so alert, anticipating any movement before it happened,
that Emmett felt held. "Mr. Emmett. I want to talk with
you." Kidd's voice was flat, toneless.

"All right!" Emmett said. "Talk." He grinned.

Kidd had thought of endless versions of what he wanted to
say to Sam Emmett, and had settled first on none of them—
then on all of them. Now he was certain only that he was
going to talk to Emmett, but he could not find the words. "I
didn't like your . . . When you bring me up, it's one thing,
but when you . . ."

"So?" Emmett said, taking advantage of Kidd's stumbling.
"So?! Lots of people don't like what I write! So? Are you trying
to threaten me?" he yelled. "Get out of my—"

The palm hit the base of his throat with such force that his
knees buckled, but it was the fingers snapping around his
throat that most jolted him. He went back against the brick
wall of the building behind him but his head did not dash on
it. An index finger penetrated around and behind his trachea;
the other fingers clamped his carotid artery, and the thumb on

the opposite side pressed both artery and windpipe. Emmett could make no noise, he could barely breathe, and there was just enough blood going to his brain for him to hear. With both hands he clutched without strength at the wrist before him, and he gawked at the wild gray eyes at the other end of the arm.

"Now you listen to me!" came a whisper full of hiss and heat. "I'm not here to kill you, I'm here so I won't kill you, I think maybe if I tell you just how I feel then the temptation to tear you into pieces won't get too great. So I have this to say to you." Kidd raised his free left hand and pointed the index finger between Emmett's eyes. (Even furious, Kidd had his instincts; he was reminding Emmett that he held him with but one hand.) "You're the most despicable little coward I know. And I may be a coward too, I may be scum, no better than you. You're welcome to come after me all you want, to try to prove whatever you think I am. You fight me with words, I'll never fight you except with words. But if you bring people I love into it, innocent people, then I'll kill you."

Kidd had put Emmett against the wall too quickly to attract a crowd. The two were barely conspicuous, motionless as they were, and from a distance Kidd seemed to be simply holding Emmett upright. A few people, seeing the flush in Emmett's face and the fury in Kidd's, had stopped, but at a safe distance. They could hear nothing being said. Peaks stood across the street at the outer fringe of the group stopping to peer at the two men—secretaries going home late from work, street kids on bicycles. Peaks watched them all. He saw the tall, slim teenager coming down the street, saw him from the time he stepped out of the *Constellation* Building to the time he jerked to a halt, snatched the lens cap off the camera that was dangling around his neck, and went running forward.

The other spectators made a rough semicircle on the street and sidewalk but the photographer pierced this barrier, jostling a woman who turned angrily at having her own view disturbed. He stepped up close enough to hear Kidd's voice say, "Do you understand me?" and began snapping pictures.

Kidd was just releasing Emmett—he sagged limp against the

wall—when someone rushed up and collided with the photographer. The camera popped from his hands and bounced at the end of the safety strap as a voice bellowed, "What is this! What's going on?" The man, Peaks, stretched his arms wide and screamed, "This is what happens when a city turns away from God!" Peaks pointed a huge finger into each spectator's face. "Such iniquity will befall you and you and *you* if you do not repent!"

As the photographer snatched up his camera again he saw the back release was snapped open, all the film exposed. He swore and began to tear the film away to reload. When he looked up again Kidd was gone.

"Drunk again?!" Peaks bellowed at Emmett, struggling to his knees. "Ah, iniquity!" Peaks walked away, shaking his head. No one would look at his face.

"Who was it?" the rookie photographer said, grabbing the bar table with both hands. "I know you know who it was."

"I told you, a bookie," Emmett said.

"You just said a jealous boyfriend!" the photographer pleaded.

"He's jealous of his money, not his woman," Emmett said and tried to laugh; but that made his throat hurt. He tossed down his scotch. His eyes darted around the room.

"I almost got his picture," the photographer said.

"You got nothing. Just get out, huh. I don't drink with rookies. Besides it may be dangerous around me." He laughed, and this time it hurt less.

CHAPTER 25

When he had zigzagged his way five blocks from the *Constellation* Building, Kidd went into a restaurant lobby and pretended to be waiting for someone, to let any last random witness clear before he used his car. It was at the restaurant that he at last felt he could call Ginny.

In order to get the operator at the White House switchboard to put him through to her, Kidd had to identify himself as Martin Browne. Still Ginny said hello hesitantly.

"Ginny."

"Jeff."

"Ginny. I'm so sorry."

"No. No. Don't."

"Have you . . . ?" He forgot what he had started to ask.

"How are you? Are you okay?" she said.

"Me? Oh, I'm fine, I told you I expected this sort of thing. For me, not for you." Remembering the question he had lost he said, "Have you been in trouble there? Have they gotten down on you?"

"Oh, no! The President is furious, but not with me. He apologized that I'm caught up in it. Everyone's apologizing to me," she added, with some bitterness.

"Well, you—"

"Listen, Je—Listen. I don't really feel like talking on the phone. Why don't we talk later?"

"Yes. All right. I'll . . . call you later."

"Yes. All right."

He was hesitating, just about to hang up, when she said, "Jeff?"

"Yes?"

"I know who the woman was who called me last night. The obscene one."

Suddenly ready to do to a woman what he had just done to Sam Emmett, Kidd said, "Who?"

"Mrs. Whittaker," Ginny said. "Jamie's mother."

Later he called her from his apartment. "Ginny, I . . . want to tell you how sorry I am."

"You don't have to apologize to me. You didn't do anything."

"I just . . . I hate it so badly that I've brought all this on you. I wish there were something I could say or do . . ." He had not told her about his confrontation on the street with Emmett.

"Why should you say or do anything?"

"Because it bothers you."

"No it doesn't."

"Yes it does. It does."

"No. It doesn't. I don't *like* it, I don't particularly *like* being called a whore. But it doesn't bother me."

"Wait. Please. I don't remember anybody else calling you a whore. Even the tabloids, the ones with the headlines that say, 'Actress Pregnant by Elvis Presley's Ghost,' they won't call you a whore. Even as cheap and shallow as they are, they wouldn't . . ." He stopped.

"Besides Jamie's mother, Ginny, who else calls you a whore, for what you've done with me?"

"No one. I guess . . . no one."

"Yes. Somebody does. You do. Somewhere in you, it's what you call yourself."

"Jeff, we're both tired. Why don't we talk later."

"Later? Okay. Fine. We'll talk later."

CHAPTER 26

Sam Emmett sat in his office and he fidgeted. He always fidgeted, but this was different, because he felt something big was up, that he was close to something. The feeling came from no precognition, it was really a reflection of the impact he had already made, because with his last story he had embarrassed and angered the Administration, and that provided him a real sense of achievement. John Livingstone had, in his last press briefing, even lectured the gathering of journalists on press responsibility.

Emmett smelled blood and tasted glory. The power to unmake a king was as great, or greater, a power to him as the power to make or even be one. And he still felt the power of potential; so far he had written nothing about Kidd's attack upon him.

The telephone rang, Emmett picked it up, and the secretary said, "He says you know him and you'll want to talk to him but he won't give his name."

"Screw him," Emmett said and hung up.

But the secretary rang back and said, "He says it has to do with a deal."

Emmett thought for a minute and said, "Put him on."

"Six o'clock, at the bench in the park where French Drive turns into Independence," Pugh said. "Know it?"

Emmett hung up.

That spring day in Washington belonged in August—hot, amazingly humid. Shirts clung to chests, skirts stuck to legs. Pugh and Emmett sat four feet apart on a park bench and watched the heat-dazed tourists drift by.

"Aren't you taking a risk calling me to set up an appointment?" Emmett said, one side of his mouth smiling.

"If your phone were tapped, I'd know it," Pugh said.

Emmett, suddenly impatient, snapped, "What do you want?"

"I'm ready to make a deal," Pugh said. "I want to know who your source in the White House is. Your other source, besides me. For that I'll give you some information."

"You're a fool, Pugh," Emmett said. "Why should I tell you anything?"

"The information is worth it, even better than what I gave you before. You'll be delighted with it. And it's something you can use. I can't."

"Why can I use it when you can't?"

"I got it with a wiretap. An illegal one. I wanted to do some tracing just to find out where to look, and then prove things later."

"I don't want trouble."

"Oh, spare me."

"You know what I mean, you ass! I don't like to get tied up in allegations."

"The information I can give you will not be denied."

Emmett thought for a long time and then said, "How can we make the trade? All I have from you is your opinion that what you've got is hot. For all I know it's shit. I'm not going to pass you a name before I know what your information is worth. But if it's like you say, that just the information alone is of value, then why are you going to tell me before you know the name? I may decide not to give it to you."

With the same smug calm that Pugh had shown Emmett when they met before in the bar, Pugh withdrew two small, folded pieces of white paper from his pocket. Pugh said, "You tell me the department, the executive department that your leaker is in and I'll give you number one. That's no risk for you because I already know the department anyway and it will just show me you're acting in good faith. After you read what's on the first paper then you tell me who your man is, and I give you the last half of my information."

"No. You start."

Pugh smiled. "I knew you'd say that. You wouldn't feel good unless you bargained. I'll be glad to start. My information is useful only when combined."

"What's on the first paper?" Emmett said.

"On one paper is a name."

"And on the other?"

"I told you. The rest of the information."

"But if it's complete, why are you willing to give it to me before I tell you the name of the informant?"

"When you see what I have you'll know its importance. Besides, I can add details. But only if I'm satisfied with what you give me."

Pugh handed Emmett one of the papers. Emmett unfolded it quickly. Typed in the center of the white square was the word "homosexual."

Emmett stared at the paper and then said, "The person who gives me my information works as a speechwriter."

Pugh handed over the second paper. Emmett looked at it still folded in his palm and said, smiling, "You're *sure* I'll tell you, after I've read it?"

Pugh's face turned grim. "The information will please you. It is complete, but there are other details I can add. But you will be pleased and you will tell me what I want to know."

Emmett unfolded the tight square. Written in the center of the white page was "John Livingstone."

CHAPTER 27

Ginny was sitting at the desk in her old cubicle in the speechwriters' suite of the Executive Office Building. Kurtz and Sherwood were with her. Because she felt ridiculous using a conference room for just the three of them, and because she did not like to summon them across the street to her office in the White House, she would come back here whenever they needed to have a discussion. It was not a strictly unselfish choice; Ginny felt at home in the dull bare cubicle.

They had just started discussing possible speeches for a union conference the President had been invited to attend when the phone on the desk rang, then the intercom buzzed. Kurtz's secretary always took charge of the phones during these meetings, and would only signal her for an important call; Ginny answered. The secretary said, "It's Mr. Livingstone."

"Of course I'll talk to him," Ginny said. Kurtz and Sherwood openly watched her. "Yes," she said. "Yes . . . all right."

She hung up the phone and looked at Kurtz. "Adam, Mr. Livingstone wants to see you in his office."

"Oh! Sure. Of course," Kurtz said, standing up. "I'm sorry to interrupt the meeting. You go ahead. I'll catch up. Maybe I can borrow your notes, Malcolm."

"Sure," Sherwood said.

They heard him, on his way out, stop and say to Maggie

that he had to go to Mr. Livingstone's office and that was where he would be if any calls came, but he would be back shortly. It was as if he had just made a promise never again to do anything that was the least bit impolite.

Sherwood and Ginny looked at each other. "I think we can put off this meeting for a while," Ginny said.

"Yeah. Sure," Sherwood said. He stopped at the door, decided not to try to say something, and went back to his own cubicle.

As much as Kurtz had tried to be steady as he walked into the office, he faltered to a stop when he saw Forbis and Pugh sitting there. Livingstone sat at his desk and looked exhausted.

Kurtz moved to a chair against the wall to Livingstone's left and sat down.

Livingstone spoke right away. "Adam, you know Mr. Forbis, and that is Mr. Pugh. Mr. Pugh is a member of the Internal Security department, which has been investigating the leaking of confidential material from the executive branch."

Kurtz put both hands onto the arms of his chair and tried to stand up, to walk out then. But he could not.

". . . has been going on for some time," Livingstone was saying. "They have allegations—I don't call it evidence, just allegations—that suggest, strongly, in their opinion, that the person within this department who is responsible for the . . . intentional . . ."—Livingstone seemed to have trouble saying that word—"dissemination of that information is you. This is no trial, Adam, and I give you my word that nothing you say is being recorded in any fashion. I may be doing you a great disservice even to ask what I have to ask you now, and if I am, I want you to forgive me. Tell me the suggestions are false and these gentlemen will have to go on with their responsibilities as they see fit. But I must ask you now, Adam: Are you the person responsible for intentionally leaking clearly confidential executive information to the press?"

Kurtz's head dangled between his shoulders. A sound came from somewhere within his chest.

"Adam . . ." Livingstone's voice was deep and clear. "What did you say, Adam?"

"I'm so . . . so sorry."

Livingstone sat back in his chair. He looked at Forbis, and then back to Kurtz. "I am too, Adam," he said.

Kurtz looked up. His eyes had grown more clear, sober. "What do you want me to do?" he said.

"Yes. Well," Livingstone said. "I'm not sure what Mr. Forbis and Mr. Pugh want. But I wanted the truth and you have told us that. And I believe what the President wants, all he really wants, is for the leaks to stop. But I'm afraid you're going to have to leave your job."

"There could be a hearing . . ." Pugh said.

"There does not need to be a hearing," Livingstone said sharply, "and I don't see any reason, as I understand the circumstances at the moment, for any further pursuit of the particulars of this case. If you would like to resign, then you may leave."

Kurtz stood, and walked steadily to the door. But he stopped there and turned. He seemed unable to push himself the last few feet out of the room. "What . . . am I going to do?" he asked no one.

"Don't put me down as a reference, Adam. But don't look over your shoulder, either. We will not follow you."

When Kurtz was gone Forbis smiled at Pugh, who grinned and slapped his hands together. "Got him!" Pugh said.

"Yep. You really did," Forbis droned. "I've got to say it, I wasn't sure, not on what you had. But you got him."

Livingstone stared at the top of his desk and did not speak. Forbis said, "It must be a relief to get that problem out of the department finally, John."

Livingstone looked up. "Congratulations, gentlemen. I think we should tell the President together. Both of you should come with me."

"I think that maybe you should tell the President privately, sir," Pugh said. "You and Mr. Forbis. I'm glad we got lucky and found the right man. And I appreciate your willingness to give me credit. But I honestly wouldn't want to enjoy too much the catching of Mr. Kurtz. It is, after all, the destruction of a career."

"Yes," Livingstone said. "All right. We'll tell the President this afternoon."

"Good," Forbis said, and stood with Pugh to go.

"I never asked him why," Livingstone said.

Forbis and Pugh looked at each other. "Why?" Pugh said to Livingstone. "He wouldn't have told you. He would have said something about disagreeing with the President's policies, or about the public's right to know. He would have dressed it up as a matter of principle. But the truth is, he did it for the obvious reasons: jealousy, the excitement you get from being a conspirator, and the sense of power that comes from being with a more powerful man, and knowing secretly that you can destroy him. But he would have never admitted that."

"Yes. I suppose not," Livingstone said.

Next door Sherwood had begun to pace. He knew it was over for Kurtz. As Ginny sat there at her desk she realized Sherwood must have known for some time, suspecting, as all of them had, that the leaks came from their department, and knowing that he was not himself the culprit. Emmett's smearing of Ginny early in the week must have eliminated any thought that she could have been passing information, leaving Kurtz the only real possibility in Sherwood's mind. Ginny could scarcely imagine what Sherwood must be thinking now.

And what about Kurtz? That day when he had come into the office she sat in now, and asked for her protection—he had been so distraught! He must have panicked because Emmett had printed all the figures so close to the exact ones he had leaked. When he was not caught, and the panic subsided, Kurtz must have felt more secure than ever, even encouraged. But that day in the office, he had fooled her.

Men could fool her.

Everyone could fool her.

She could fool herself.

Why had she not been able to talk warmly, intimately, honestly with Jeff Kidd since the article about them came out in the papers? Jeff was trying desperately. So was she. But something was wrong. Or gone.

When Kurtz came back in to gather up his personal belongings, Ginny and Sherwood remained in their cubicles. They had each decided that if Kurtz did not want to see them, they would not shame him, and if he did want to see them, he could knock. No knocks came.

CHAPTER 28

"Do you want to stop for a while?" he said as a burst of lightning exploded in the woods not fifty yards from the road.

"No. No. I feel safer in the car."

So Kidd drove slowly through the summer storm. The clouds had gathered black and threatening over the bluish western mountains and then boomed across the hot valleys on their sweep to the Atlantic. Rain surged against the windshield; the batting wipers gave intervals of visibility. Ginny sat beside him stiffly, her right arm straight before her, holding the dashboard with her fingers and willing the car toward safety.

Kidd tried to keep his mind on his driving; that should not have been hard in such a storm, but was. His mood was as turbulent as the sky, but had nothing to do with the clouds and the rain. He had felt the same way leaving McLean, when the sun had been shining.

Another burst of lightning cracked somewhere around them, turning the purple air a pale yellow. He glanced at her. She sat motionless, even as another thunderboom sizzled and rattled beside the car. He had hoped they could talk on the trip down, have a private, intimate, even easy conversation. But he knew now that in her mind, as in his own, they had already arrived.

The clouds had broken into a glowing indigo, dropping random wads of rain as they turned into the drive. They parked, and she said, "Jeff. You really don't have to do this."

"I know."

When he had said that he was coming with her, all the way this time, he had thought he understood it—that he had to share even this darkest part of her life with her, that he had to face for himself the reality of their relationship. But the closer they drew to the mountainous wet house the more hollow he felt, as those reasons dissolved within him into the fragments of empty words. Now his urges were physical and definite. He mounted the white stairs against the desire to turn and run back to the car; and as he followed her through the wide chestnut and leaded-glass door and smelled the thick outdoor aroma of wet Virginia boxwoods blend with the warm smell of people shut up all day, he felt the first faint promise of nausea.

But he bore on with the strength of his unwillingness—he was unwilling to succumb to or even to admit his urges, unwilling not to go forward. He walked stiff beside her through the orange lamplight of the entrance hall, even managed a smile to the pale nurse who sat at the reception desk as Ginny bent to sign the guest register. Reading what she had written, the reception nurse said, "Oh, Mrs. Whittaker. It's so nice to see you again." Ginny did not meet his glance as they followed the reception nurse down a gray hallway.

They came to a large parlor where a dozen dazed people sat, all staring in the same direction. *The sound on the television is turned off*, Kidd thought, and then noticed with a chill that the picture was turned off, too, the antenna lead disconnected because of the proximity of the storm. He hurried to stay up with the nurse and Ginny.

At some point the receptionist must have rung a summoning buzzer because as they reached the long conservatory, Jamie was being led in at the other end by a second nurse. They met about midway, the receptionist saying brightly, "Hello, Jamie, how are you today!" as the other nurse, with an almost somnambulistic forcefulness, guided him down onto a wicker love seat. The receptionist moved away with the nurse to the far end of the conservatory where they began to talk and laugh in whispers, sharing cigarettes from the nurse's pack. Ginny and Kidd sat down opposite the love seat, Ginny pulling up her chair until her knees were almost touching Jamie's.

Jamie was dressed in pressed slacks and a bright long-sleeved sport shirt. His hair was neat and clean, brushed down over the temples so that the scars did not show. His skin was red; he had been getting a lot of sun. But the color looked unnatural, like a rosy haze over gray, and Kidd felt the nausea still seeping in his guts. He looked away, to the only other group in the room, a young family clustered around a cadaverous grandfather who, like Jamie, sat in a wicker seat with his back to the windows. Kidd wondered if it was a standard arrangement on visiting days at the Violet Ridge Country Home that patients were always faced away from the windows, so that the paying patrons were spared a well-lit glimpse of death.

". . . and you're getting good food?" Ginny was saying. "You look good, Jamie. It's good to see you. I've brought Jeff down to see you. Do you remember Jeff? He wanted to visit you too."

"He doesn't know me," she said, without looking to Kidd. "Every time I come, I'm more of a stranger."

She half stood and shifted over beside Jamie on the seat. Hesitantly, delicately, she placed a hand on his shoulder, and kept the other lightly on the cap of his knee. "Have you been in the pool? The doctor says you like swimming."

Ginny kept talking in that one-way conversation, too much like a prayer. Jamie's face was placid, unmoved. Kidd wanted to look away, but could not, something held him, locked him, to those blue eyes, doll-like, that flesh coated with a tan that might as well have been makeup, that face familiar, a dream, a memory . . . *Herms!*

Calvin Herms. A boyhood friend who had crashed a big brother's motorcycle into a tree. He had died in the hospital, and since he was Kidd's age and a member of the same Sunday school class, Kidd was taken by his mother to the funeral home. Kidd wore a blue seersucker sport coat; he had never been able to forget it. He walked into the sickly-sweet smelling, flower-cluttered atrium, signed the visitor's register, and looked around for what to do next, his bewilderment unheeded by the drowsy undertakers and distant family members who stood by in official mourning. Then, spotting the corner of a coffin in an adjoining room, he began to walk toward it, soundlessly moving across the padded carpet, as in a dream. Jeff had seen one other corpse in his tender years, a great-grandmother of ninety-three, laid out in one of the bedrooms of a farmhouse, looking not much different in death than she had in life. But what lay before the thirteen-year-old Jeff Kidd as he approached this second coffin was nothing like what he understood of death, or remembered of his friend. There was orange, artificial hair sprouting from an obviously plastic forehead, the wooden-looking cheekbones were deeply rouged, even the eyelashes were stuck on and painted. *This is their sales office,* the boy Kidd thought quite plainly. *They display their caskets here. They've just got a dummy laid out in this one to . . ."* In total calm, without the slightest reverence, he had walked to the very edge of the coffin, had even shot a look toward the undertakers with the thought that they might mistake him for a browsing customer, and was glancing back again when the awful truth hit him, maybe at the same instant that his eyes fell to the coat the body in the coffin was wearing, the same blue seersucker that so many boys had bought that spring from the town's one big department store. He lost his balance, but did not stumble, and did not rush, until he reached the outside and the stairs down to his mother's car. After one glance at his face she took him home, where he kept himself awake until the next dawn, afraid of what he might dream.

And suddenly now Jeff Kidd understood his nausea, and one of his nightmares. The face of Jamie Whittaker was a reminder of the mockery of life he had seen in that open coffin.

Jamie was rocking now, faster and faster, and Ginny was talking to him rapidly, pleading. Kidd leaned forward, trying to focus on what she was saying. It was, "No, Jamie . . . No. No!" She had begun to cry, and Kidd gawked, uncomprehending, even as he saw that Jamie had seized Ginny's hand and as he rocked was rubbing it across his swollen groin.

Kidd lurched to his feet, but hesitated; in that protracted instant it seemed to him that Ginny was not struggling. But when she staggered to her feet, sobbing, Kidd leaped toward Jamie and clutched his thick shoulders. "No!" Ginny screamed, and in that crazy moment, in the ambiguity Kidd had felt in Jamie's presence from the first, he did not know if she meant Jamie, or him. He let go.

Ginny snatched at her hand, but Jamie still held it clamped at the wrist, pressing and moving it up and down. She sobbed again, cried out, and with a kick and a twist tore herself away. The visiting family at the other end of the conservatory was gasping in horror, the attendants were tearing toward them, and Ginny, refusing Kidd's embrace, was now screaming hysterically and turning away from—and then gaping back to—Jamie as he continued alone to masturbate.

"Ginny . . ." he said. No answer. "Ginny," he said again, but still she did not look at him.

He had gotten her to the car, through the cold and now steady rain that left her face spattered so that he could not tell if the drops were rain or tears. Just out the gate she had stopped sobbing, and had not uttered a sound in the ten miles since then. Now she sat still and silent in the dampness of the stuffy car.

He offered her his handkerchief. She took it and wiped away the beads on her face. She handed the handkerchief back with a definiteness that said she would not be needing it again, and stared at the misty windows.

Finally she said, "I thought he was going to get better. With time and professional help."

"It's impossible to predict," Kidd said. "In a brain injury, if the involuntary centers in the brain stem aren't damaged then there's usually improvement with time. But in the case of trauma to the frontal lobes, especially if there's loss of actual matter, like . . . then nobody can give an accurate prognosis."

She turned very slowly, and stared at him, and to her unspoken question he said, "I looked it up."

"Yes," she said, turning back to face her clouded window. "I just bet you did."

Her voice was as cold as the rain.

CHAPTER 29

It was not easy for Kidd to pace in his apartment. He had placed the sofa Collier had sent him perpendicular to the bare wall of the living room area, and had set the two mismatched chairs in the center of the floor across from it, so that there was no straight path through the apartment's middle. *My conversation nook*, he thought in self-derision as he stepped around one of the fat, faded chairs. Some inner voice tried to whisper that he could easily rearrange things, that though the apartment would still look bleak at least it would be different and he would have room to pace, but he drowned that voice out, saying aloud, "What? And ruin my *conversation nook?*" He chuckled blackly, and remembered, remembered without consciously thinking, that as long as he had been in this apartment, there had never been anyone there for him to sit down across from.

For an uninterrupted though curving path, he paced back and forth between the far side of the living room and the adjoining square space that the apartment manager had called a dining area. The only furniture there was a card table and two chairs his sister had pressed on him, along with a tablecloth and some dishes, when he moved out. He kept the blue cloth on the table, though it clashed with the chartreuse shag carpet. As Kidd moved back and forth, the carpet took on a dull shine.

He thought he was trying to think. But he could not hold a thought, realized that, and then thought, *Maybe I'm trying not to think.* He pivoted and walked back toward the sofa and chairs.

Trying *not* to think was anathema to Jeff Kidd. He believed, at least consciously, in facing everything, and throughout his life if anything caused him fear or trouble he would hammer away at it, mentally or physically, until he could break it down. But now he was agitated and confused, and trying to think, or trying not to, kept him in the same state.

He pivoted again, slowly, almost lethargically, and then rammed a fist into the open palm of the other hand. Just as quickly he dropped his hands limply. On the way back across the floor he thought of all sorts of actions he might take to shake himself from what he thought of as his malaise. He could take a trip, if he knew where to go and could afford it. He could take up a new sport or write a book or study a language. He should find a better place to live. He felt like doing none of those things, he saw himself as flawed for being unwilling or unable. He hated himself.

Still pacing, his gaze caught on the light fixture hanging over the card table in the dining area; it was gold-colored tubing, bent into five capital Js which supported glass bulb flames. The whole mess hung from a chain intertwined with the electrical cord. As Kidd stepped closer he reached up, and from the slightest touch the fixture, weightless, bounced and swung.

Something about that made him furious. His eyes snapped wide, and in his thoughts he saw himself jerking that cheap, hollow, flimsy liar of a chandelier, ripping it from the thin warped ceiling in a spray of broken plaster and frayed wire.

He stilled his hand, steadied the fixture, turned and walked quickly to one of the chairs, where he sat down.

All right, he thought. *All right. I've got to get at this, some way. I've got to figure out what's wrong with me. Physician, heal thyself.*

He asked himself if he was angry. He answered that he was

not. In pain? No. Lonely? Yes, well maybe so. But what made him want to rip light fixtures from the ceiling?

And what made him unable to communicate now with Ginny Longstreet?

Now that was a good question.

If the problem was from her side, there was nothing more he could do. In the last days he had tried everything—leaving her to herself and trying to talk things through, going over to help her paint and staying home. He had even tried taking her back to T & E's All-You-Can-Eat, to draw from a pleasant memory in their brief history. But the result was always the same: they were tense, they always seemed ready to argue, though that had not happened; it was something neither of them would allow. Besides, if they were angry, it was about nothing except this impenetrable distance.

That left the blockage on his side. Was there anything he was holding back? She had asked him that day on the Mall if he was smothering the turmoil over his experiences within the monument. Maybe that was it.

Sitting now alone in his apartment, Kidd looked across at the sofa, and imagined Ginny sitting there. "What did you see that day, when you turned toward Roxanne Lark?" his vision asked him.

"I saw . . . I saw the gun come up, my pistol, between her and me," he said.

"And what did you do?" his visionary Virginia Longstreet said in her silent alto.

"I pulled the trigger," Kidd answered, his voice shaking.

"And what did you see?" she said to him.

"I saw . . . I saw . . . I saw the bullet . . ." He stopped, sighed; his breath grew still. He stared at the empty couch before him and said, "I saw half her face torn off."

His chest shook with his breath, and the empty couch before him blurred. "I just couldn't tell which half."

He squeezed his eyes shut, pressed his fingers to the inner corners of his lids, then opened his eyes wide. He no longer tried to see her there.

"Okay. Maybe I could tell her that. But what good would it do?" he said aloud.

And as he got up to pace again, he thought, *And how could I tell her that the only person I'd like to see dead is Jamie?*

CHAPTER 30

Collier only once asked Kidd, "How's it going?" Kidd immediately started spouting about notes he was making, when Collier said, "I meant how is life going, not the manual! Just tell me about the manual whenever it's ready."

Kidd had not even started the project, he would sit at his desk each morning, write down words such as "goals" or "needs" or "purpose," which were supposed to develop into key sentences but never did, and then he would go talk with Dooley. Dooley was evaluating the deployment of O.C. agents in Europe and South America, which interested Kidd. But the project was Dooley's, and after a couple of hours of questioning, listening, and meddling, Kidd would go back to the Bureau's library.

It was after another day of this same routine that he went back to his apartment and called Ginny. She was not home, but called him fifteen minutes later to say she had to stay late at work, evaluating some prospective presidential speechwriters, so she could not make dinner. He asked if he could come to her house later. She said that would be okay.

He got there about nine. She had just gotten home, and as she went upstairs to change he walked around in the living room, idly surveying the paint job.

He had started to the kitchen, thinking he would see if there was anything in the refrigerator he could use to make a sandwich for her, when he stopped at the den. "Ginny?" he called.

"What?" she said, coming down the stairs.

"All the paint cans are gone in here. Are you doing some other room first?"

"No," she said, walking in beside him. "I'm not painting anymore. For now."

He wanted to ask her why, but she walked back out, toward the kitchen. "I was just going to make you a sandwich," he said, following her. "Are you hungry?"

"Not really. What about some tea?"

"No thanks." As she started to fill the kettle he said, "Ginny, why don't we take a walk? We haven't done that for a long time."

New leaves blotted out the stars; tender, they did not rustle. A heavy rain had fallen that afternoon, and the pavement was now drained and damp.

They walked slowly. He hesitated to take her hand, but when he did she held it tightly.

"Let's go down this way," she said. "There's a place here we never got to." They took a turn descending to a stone bridge spanning a swollen creek. They stopped and looked upstream.

"Ginny, are you mad at me?"

Still watching the water she said, "I keep telling you. No."

He reached to touch her and stopped his hand. "I don't know what you want from me, Ginny. I don't know."

"I don't either," she whispered.

Kidd felt himself without strength. He had, for some time, felt himself without will, with only destiny, and that now bleak and cold. Now he was powerless, and in that impotence he floundered, looking to her as if she might know a direction. "Have I failed you?" he said.

"No. No. No."

"I must have!" he said loudly. "I've either done something I shouldn't have, or not done something I should've. What is it?" When she still stared away from him he lowered his voice and said, "I'm sorry. I just keep having this feeling that I've let you down. And if there's something I've done wrong, I want you to say it. I can't stand this."

Her head rose, then her eyes. She looked at him, but looked down again before she said, "You hate him." After a long pause she looked back up and said, "You hate the sight of Jamie. He makes you sick."

Kidd had to stare at her for a very long time. "No," he said finally, "I'm not sure that's right. I have a reaction, yes. But I don't blame him for it. Something in me gets sick when I see him. Is that his fault? Is it my fault? I don't know." He pushed the tip of a finger along the mortar between two stones. "But yes. It is true that I don't feel good when I see him."

She kept her face down.

"Ginny," Kidd said, his voice steady but faint. "What are you feeling? What are you doing? Who do you blame?"

"Blame?" she said. "Why do you say that?"

"I don't know. I feel like you're blaming somebody. It must be me."

"I don't blame you, Jeff. Not for anything. I . . . The only thing I blame you for is that you didn't find me before."

"Before what?"

"Before Jamie."

Somewhere a night bird flew, on muffled, frantic wings.

"I called the asylum today," she said. "I'm going down to-morrow, to pick him up."

"What are you going to do with him?" Kidd's voice was barely audible.

"Bring him home."

"Ginny. No."

"I have to."

"No. No."

"I *have* to!"

He turned from her, back to face the stream. "Is that why you stopped painting?"

The question broke her momentum, and her voice. "Yes . . ."

"Ginny. Ginny." He reached and took her shoulders. That was all—an embrace at arm's length.

Unyielding, she said, "It has to be this way, Jeff. You see that! You have to!"